Backpacking and Outdoor Guide

Richard Dunlop

RAND McNALLY & COMPANY
Chicago • New York • San Francisco

PHOTO CREDITS

Boyd Norton i; Joan Dunlop v, 7, 23, 29, 30, 31, 35, 43, 50, 51a & b, 56; *Beautiful British Columbia* 1; Ontario Ministry of Industry & Tourism 2, 45, 49, 155, 156; Florida Department of Natural Resources 4, 66; Arkansas Department of Parks and Tourism 10; Wyoming Travel Commission 14, 168, 177, 179; Wisconsin Department of Natural Resources 17, 153; Washington Department of Commerce & Economic Development 20, 58; Vermont Development Department 22; National Park Service/Richard Frear 24, 28, 126; USDA, Forest Service 34; Oregon State Highway Division 36, 40, 190; Maryland Division of Tourism 38; Warren Asa of AYH 46, 47; Washington State Travel Development Division 48; West Virginia Department of Commerce 54, 60, 121; Florida Department of Commerce 59, 71b; *Call of Kentucky* 63; Canadian Government Travel Bureau 65, 181; Ohio Department of Development 70, 72, 75; Hawaii Visitors Bureau 71a, 187; Utah Travel Council 74; Tennessee Valley Authority 76, 118; Robert Wenkam 81; State of New Hampshire 86; National Park Service 88; Massachusetts Department of Commerce 91; State of Maine 92; Nova Scotia Communications and Information Centre 95; Department of Tourism, Fish and Game, Government of Quebec 97; Milt and Joan Mann/Van Cleve 98; New York State Department of Development 103a; Pennsylvania Travel Development Bureau 103b; New York State Department of Commerce 105; Okefenokee Swamp 107; Kentucky Department of Public Information 112, 126; Florida News Bureau 114; State of Tennessee 123; South Carolina Department of Parks, Recreation & Tourism 128; Nebraska Game Commission 139, 146; Michigan Tourist Council 141; Missouri Tourism Commission 144; South Dakota Tourism 149; Oklahoma Tourism Department 163; Texas Highway Commission 165; Colorado Department of Public Relations 172; Southern California Visitors Council 185

formerly titled *Outdoor Recreation Guide*

Copyright © 1979, 1978, 1977, 1974 by Rand McNally & Company
All rights reserved
Library of Congress Catalog Card Number: 78-59608
Printed in U.S.A.

Contents

List of Maps   iv

Introduction   v

RECREATIONAL ACTIVITIES

Camping	1
Backpacking & Trail Riding	14
Wilderness Survival	28
Wilderness Cooking	32
Hiking	36
Orienteering	43
Bike Hiking & Camping	45
Rockhounding	51
Canoeing & Rafting	54
Boating & Boat Camping	63
Sport Diving	68
Conservation & Wildlife	72

REGIONAL DIRECTORY

THE NORTHEAST	80
THE MID-ATLANTIC STATES	98
THE SOUTH	106
THE MIDWEST	132
THE SOUTHWEST	158
THE ROCKIES	167
THE PACIFIC COAST	181

Index   192

About the Author   194

List of Maps

UNITED STATES 78–79

THE NORTHEAST 83

THE MID-ATLANTIC STATES 101

THE SOUTH 109

THE MIDWEST 135

THE SOUTHWEST 161

THE ROCKIES 171

THE PACIFIC COAST 183

Richard Dunlop

It is not in the cards for Americans to waste energy.

"The joyride of under-priced energy is over," says John H. Gibbons, director of the U.S. Office of Energy Conservation. "The issue now is rational and nonwasteful use of energy."

This does not mean giving up the great North American outdoors with its manifold opportunities for healthful recreation. Camping, backpacking, hiking, biking, canoeing, rafting, rockhounding, orienteering, sport diving, and other outdoor pursuits do not require fossil fuels. They call only on muscle power.

While we Americans are reexamining our lifestyles in the light of the limited energy resources at our disposal, we should examine our lifestyles in the outdoors as well. We will discover greater pleasure and deeper meaning in depending on ourselves and our own skills instead of on unnecessary gadgets.

It is clearly a waste of energy to use machines when no machines are necessary, but it is scarcely wasteful to drive to a beautiful place to hike or to camp. It is rational to explore opportunities for outdoor recreation close at home to avoid long auto drives, and it is even more rational to use planes, trains, and buses to travel to recreational areas whenever possible. Trains and buses can take you to Yellowstone National Park, and once you are in the park, buses can transport you to the most fascinating places and the best trails.

In a more energetic America the healthiest and happiest way to go will be on your own two feet, or with a bike's wheels thrumming beneath you, or dipping a paddle into a brawling stream.

Introduction

Stars crinkling overhead at night on the High Plains of Texas, the piney breath of mountain air in British Columbia's Coast Mountains, the sound of a loon laughing across a lake on Michigan's Upper Peninsula, the good ache of tired muscles after a day's hard hike on the Appalachian Trail, the aroma of bacon frying over a campfire in the Ozarks—all these can be part of a vacation in the great North American outdoors.

Camping, backpacking and trail riding, hiking, orienteering, bike hiking and camping, rockhounding, canoeing and rafting, boating and boat camping, sport diving, and conservation and wildlife are the most popular outdoor activities that will take you back to nature. Camp beside the sea at Acadia National Park in Maine; sleep underneath the stars on the Padre Island National Seashore of Texas; backpack down the rugged backbone of Isle Royale, the Midwest's only national park, in Lake Superior; ride a rubber raft through the churning current of the Colorado River; go orienteering in the rolling hills of old Virginia; or scuba dive to a coral reef in the Virgin Islands. Varied as outdoor vacations may be, all have one thing in common: an outdoor vacation relates a

v

human being to his living environment, renews his perceptions, deepens his understanding, and rekindles his zest for life. It is paradoxical, but often a person becomes much more fond of his fellowman when he can get away from crowds and in the serenity of the wilderness sort himself out and resolve his own conflicts.

In this time of environmental and energy crisis, an outdoor vacation takes on new significance. Each kind of vacation described in this book requires particular preparation and training, special skills and equipment, and usually physical conditioning as well. Each offers particular satisfactions, pleasures, and rewards. Each calls upon a person to be a good citizen of the outdoors.

Where can a family, an individual, or a group of friends backpack along a mountain trail, canoe down a whitewater stream, or enjoy any other outdoor vacation? In each chapter of this book there are suggestions about places—close to home or in other parts of the United States or Canada—a person can go to for a certain vacation activity. The last half of the book is an extraordinary directory to each region of the United States and Canada, indicating the outstanding outdoor vacation possibilities that this author, his staff, and colleagues throughout the United States and Canada can recommend. You'll find a brief account of each place and what it has to offer, so that you can judge for yourself whether it interests you.

President Lyndon Johnson once commented that "beyond the limits of the city lies another America." This is the America of the open country and the wilderness. The vast public lands managed by the Bureau of Land Management alone afford the American people room to roam. Ride across a tawny sand dune in a beach buggy, rappel up a rock cliff or climb a glacier, hike, boat, or camp—the public lands administered by the B.L.M. offer enormous potential for recreation and for the study of wildlife. The national and state parks and forests are even more splendid for outdoor vacations, and across the border in Canada other vast areas await the camper, backpacker, or canoeist.

The last three decades of the 20th century in North America are bound to be known to future historians for many things that would have seemed incredible only a decade ago. There have been great strides in technology, a vastly increasing metropolitan population, and all the problems inherent in a high-energy civilization. It is true that we have more leisure time than ever, more mobility, higher standards of living, and higher personal income. At the same time there is a new awareness of our natural environment, our relation to it, and the necessity of conserving our resources and our sources of energy.

The need for human fitness has become evident to most people too. Every year more and more citizens, young and old, are looking to life in the outdoors, not only for better health, but for an inspiration to moral fitness as well. While many people are seeking in the outdoors a better approach to living, others simply seek escape from the pressures and the commonplaces of the busy cities and the grids of high-speed interstate highways or the jet planes that tie them together. In this modern world where conformity, given half a chance, stifles individuality, Henry David Thoreau's advice has greater meaning than ever.

"If a man does not keep pace with his companions, perhaps it is because he hears a different drummer," wrote Thoreau. "Let him step to the music which he hears, however measured or far away."

Thoreau in his life at Walden and the modern backpacker exploring the far side of the High Sierras are brothers in spirit. To travel under your own steam, to enjoy with your senses the smell of a mountain meadow after a rainstorm or the coolness of a mountain stream at the end of a hard climb are good for any human being.

All things have a special savor in the outdoors. It is a truism that coffee smells better perking over a wood fire and a person sleeps better in the open, but incidents can seem funnier and friendships run deeper out-of-doors too. At Camp Kulik in the Katmai National Monument of Alaska, a huge brown bear named Fletcher is as much a resident as any of the campers. Fletcher is fed at the back door of the cookshack and occasionally sleeps on the front porch of a camp cottage. "Which created a Camp Kulik rule," says Alaska outdoorsman Rick Kiefer, "about leaving your porch light on at night in case you had to make use of the plumbing facilities next door. It would tend to spoil a whole night's sleep were a groggy fisherman to step out his darkened door and onto a wall-to-wall live bearskin rug!" Fletcher and his exploits are definitely bigger than bear size when the fishermen of Camp Kulik start yarning about him.

As for friendship, a group of strangers brought together to share a demanding outdoor experience get to know one another very well and form friendships that go way beyond the casual acquaintanceships of the city. A couple that takes their honeymoon in the wilderness, away from the trappings and clutter of civilization, truly return to their home as man and wife. Marriage puts down deeper roots in the out-of-doors, and parents' rapport with their children is enhanced.

An outdoor vacation can be a hike around the incredibly deep and blue waters of Crater Lake in Oregon or a watery slide down Sliding Rock Falls in the Pisgah National Forest of North Carolina. Hells Canyon, the deepest gorge on the North American continent, is an exciting place to be, but so is Grasshopper Glacier in the Custer National Forest of Montana, where thousands of grasshoppers were frozen into the ice about 200 years ago. The rare trumpeter swan can be found in the Copper River delta of the Chugach National Forest in Alaska; the California condor, the largest bird in North America, is in the Sespe Wildlife Area of Los Padres National Forest.

In short, an outdoor vacation is whatever a vacationer wants it to be. Each chapter in this book details an adventurous way to enjoy the great outdoors that is your natural heritage.

Camping

"Be plain in the woods," urged Horace Kephart, who several generations ago popularized camping through his book, *Camping and Woodcraft*. "We seek the woods to escape civilization for a time and all that suggests it. It is one of the blessings of wilderness life that it shows us how few things we need to be perfectly happy."

When Kephart, a St. Louis librarian, was camping by himself in the Missouri Ozarks, most of his fellow Americans were still bent on escaping from a surfeit of outdoor living brought about by life on the frontier. It was only yesterday that families in covered wagons were camping their way westward across the continent in search of new homes. The naturalist Ernest Thompson Seton had yet to found the Woodcraft League of America, and the Boy Scouts were still an obscure English youth movement. Outdoor living was something that most Americans, the memory of the frontier still fresh in their minds, put up with if they couldn't get indoors. Only a few fanatics such as Kephart, true descendants of Daniel Boone or Jim Bridger, preferred to roam the forest and sleep on a bed of pine needles when any sensible man knew four solid walls made a cozy house and a feather bed guaranteed a good night's rest.

In today's urbanized America the pleasures of the indoor life are too much with us, and every year more than 5 million American families go camping. They camp in almost 17,000 campgrounds in the United States and Canada with more than 1,150,000 campsites and make use of 5 million tents and 5 million recreational vehicles. According to a survey made in 1975 by the Kampgrounds of America, 80 percent of the campers travel with recreational vehicles (RVs); the remainder prefer to camp in tents. Although tent sales have gone up annually about 8 percent for the last eight years, it appears that most Americans still prefer to ignore the admonishments of Kephart, Seton, the Scouts, and such adult groups as the Sierra Club, and seek to keep the blessings of wilderness life at arm's length when they set out to escape civilization for a time. Camping in an RV with refrigerator, gas stove, heater, air conditioner, and the other knickknacks of an affluent America, they find the wilderness is at its best when seen through a picture window. It doesn't matter to them that the tent camper, slapping mosquitoes about his cooking fire, looks upon them and their elaborate rigs as the very embodiment of the gadget-ridden society that he seeks to escape. The tent camper may trace his lineage to the American frontiersman, but the RV camper gives his fealty to Jules Verne and the marvelous machines that carry people on an adventure in utmost luxury. Both have a place in our recreational life providing they don't threaten the remainder of North American open lands and wilderness or place a further strain on the nation's energy supply.

One thing that tent and RV campers have in common is a desire to get away from it all. They seek to escape the pressures of home, school, or the job. They're looking for fresh air, sunshine, and a more natural life. They want to find a new family closeness and to teach their children a healthier and happier way to live.

RV and tent campers also share a sociability that is rare among people who stay in motels and hotels. An RV pulls into a numbered site in a private campground in Florida,

and almost before the driver has the motor switched off the woman in the RV at the neighboring site invites the newcomers over for cake, freshly baked in her oven, and a cup of coffee. A tent camper sets up in an Ontario provincial park, and his neighbors quickly strike up a friendly conversation and soon ask his family to go along on a night hike to listen to timber wolves howl. Both RV and tent campers are gregarious, but the tent camper is more likely to be distracted by the pleasures of the outdoors from the amiable pleasures of sociability. He is more likely to camp away from the crowds.

Camping bridges all kinds of social gaps. Some years ago my son Rick, then aged 13, and I parked our truck camper beneath some trees at a Forest Service camp on the flanks of Oregon's Mount Hood. Next to us, migrant field workers, worn out from picking pears in the Hood River valley orchards, put up their tents. Their barefoot kids ran into the woods in search of firewood. Men and women hurried to set up for the night, shouted at the kids, cuffed one, joked with another. Children with cane poles and worms on their hooks ran to a tumultuous stream and soon came back with trout. Rick and I hiked along the stream with some of the migrant kids.

"Got to look lively," said Billy, a 12-year-old from the Missouri Ozarks. "Last year the water rushed a man over the falls."

We saw signs of grizzly and hurried back to camp.

"Got to build a fire to keep away the bears," said Billy's father when he heard about the signs.

We dragged fallen limbs out of the forest and chopped them to fire size. Our new friends and Rick and I cooked together, ate together, and then sat around the roaring fire. It might not have been needed to keep off the bears, but it was protection against the cold that came sliding down the mountain slopes from the glacier fields. Rick got his guitar out of the truck and played and sang songs, mostly for the ears of two girls, one blonde and one chestnut. Earlier in the evening I had seen the girls watching the boy with the big grin who chopped wood and kindled the fire for their mother. They had washed away the dust from their faces and bare legs in the stream, and now they listened with shining eyes and asked shyly for Rick to sing the same songs over and over. Their father took Rick's guitar and struck up the old songs of the frontier. The flames died down. The bright-eyed children and the mother nodding in her weariness were right out of the pioneer past. Soon we went off to our sleeping bags and blankets. I've camped with such diverse people as the Sioux in South Dakota, the Apache in Arizona, and the Basque sheepherders in the Idaho mountains. And always a shared meal, friendly talk, and firelight have drawn all of us around the campfire into a circle of friends.

Admittedly, many tent and trailer campers camp mainly to save money while they are traveling. Motels and restaurants become more expensive every year, and an average family of four can save up to $20 a day by camping. They can cut costs of meals as much as two-thirds. While en route to scenic and historic landmarks and other travel destinations, they make one-night stands in private and public campgrounds that have sprung up handy to the interstates and other well-traveled roads. They start early in the morning and quit the road by mid-afternoon to find a place in the jam-packed grounds. They take advantage of the reservation systems offered by the big camp chains to be assured of a place to park their camper or set up their tent at the end of the day. They put up with a lot to save money, but they often return home with the realization that the happiest and most profitable experiences of the trip weren't the things they went to see and do but the fun and conviviality they had while camping. The Golden Gate Bridge was certainly a sight for the kids to see, but the youngsters will longer remember the ranger-naturalist in a state park in the Sierras who took them on a brief hike through the high forest and showed them a ground squirrel's nest.

Camping Begins at Home

A successful camping trip doesn't begin in a Minnesota woods where the pines sough in the wind or on Padre Island where the Gulf's waters lave over the seashells on the beach. It begins at home. Spread out maps, brochures, and books about the places to camp on a big table, and let the family contemplate the different possibilities. There is fine camping in national parks and monuments, national forests, in Army Corps of Engineers recreation areas, in public lands administered by the Bureau of Land Management, in state and county parks and forests, and in private parks as well. The Tennessee Valley Authority sites in the Middle South are outstanding. The Land Between the Lakes, administered by the TVA in western Kentucky and Tennessee, is a particularly appealing area. Canadian national, provincial, and local parks are every bit as fascinating to consider. So are Canadian crown lands.

There are also Indian reservations for a camping vacation that will fascinate your own tribe of "Indians" at home. The Apache welcome campers to their 1,664,827 acres of ponderosa forests, high country lakes, and rangeland in Arizona. The Navajo reservation of 16 million acres sprawls across large parts of Arizona, New Mexico, and Utah and is the largest Indian land in the nation. There are camping sites in Navajo tribal parks at Monument Valley, Lake Powell, and Little Colorado River gorge. The Sioux of South Dakota show visitors to camping sites on the Little Cheyenne River and near the town of Pine Ridge, and the Alabama-Coushatta tribe of Texas also has campgrounds in the mysterious Big Thicket country. The Crow offer camping in the Bighorn Canyon recreation area in Montana; the Blackfeet have campsites at Chewing Blackbone, Duck Lake, and Two Medicine, close to Glacier National Park. The Flathead reservation near the small town of Dixon, Montana, also contains campsites that are open to visitors.

Indians like kids. The Apache showed our youngsters how to fish Indian style, and the Sioux showed them how to do the Omaha dance, a social dance of friendship that Hollywood movies usually portray as a war dance. Most of the Indian campsites are primitive. They offer campers not only a chance to get back to nature but also to get acquainted with the first Americans.

Take into account the differences in the kinds of campgrounds provided by different government agencies. Corps of Engineers sites are usually related to water sports, and there is almost always a boat-launching ramp handy. They are often in parklike areas with central rest rooms. Forest Service and state forest camps are more woodsy, with more separation of campsites by belts of shrubbery and trees. These campsites are often created around a geographic point of interest, and they blend well into the location. Sometimes they have the washroom amenities desired by many campers, but in many camps the old-fashioned privy is still in vogue. In some of the Forest Service camps it is even necessary to bring in your own water or at least to be prepared to treat the water with tablets or by boiling.

National parks and monuments and state parks are apt to be part of a scenic or historic attraction. So are Canadian national and provincial parks. They all offer modern conveniences as a rule, with washroom facilities including hot-water showers.

Why the differences? The reasons are fundamental. The Forest Service, under the Department of Agriculture, manages the forests for the multiple use of resources, so that water, timber, forage, wildlife, minerals, outdoor recreation, natural beauty, wilderness and clean air, hunting and fishing are all enhanced. Congress established the national parks and monuments to preserve outstanding recreational, scenic, inspirational, geological, and historical values and to make them available permanently for public use and enjoyment. These areas are managed by the National Park Service, under the Department of the Interior.

Where to camp? The Department of Agriculture's Forest Service administers 186 million acres of national forests and national grasslands, of which some 14 million acres are set aside as wilderness and primitive areas. The 154 national forests contain an almost incredible diversity of ecosystems and geologic formations. A family can camp among the temperate rain forests of the Olympic Peninsula of Washington or in a tropical rain forest in the Caribbean National Forest on the island of Puerto Rico. The national forests are spread out over the nation so that a camp-out in sylvan surroundings is only a day's drive away from almost any city, town, or farm in the land. The campsite may be on the shore of a blue lake in the Upper Peninsula of Michigan or beside an irrigation reservoir in Arizona. It may be on an ocean beach in Georgia or on an alpine meadow in the Colorado Rockies. On February 23, 1973, Owen T. Jamison, assistant director, Division of Recreation, U.S. Forest Service, told the Third Annual American Camping Congress at Nettles Island, Florida, something of the Forest Service's philosophy.

"Although we do provide for a wide range of experience levels, we feel that the primary need of the American public, to be met by National Forest System camping, is for the family camping experience which provides a maximum opportunity to know and to experience nature and to experience a contrast to urbanization in a leisure-time atmosphere," he said.

"We all know that life seems to become more complex every day—by 1980 it is only reasonable to assume that the complexities and pressures of modern living will again have increased manyfold. We do not feel that it necessarily follows that our future campgrounds should have a similar increase in complexity and development standards. Within the National Forest System, we will strive to provide camping experiences to meet the social and psychological needs of the camper of the future and campgrounds which will protect the natural and national resources that exist within our National Forests."

National Forest recreational areas have been established in locations that are easily accessible by major highways. They are intended for public use and enjoyment while conserving scenic, historic, scientific, and natural history landmarks. Spruce Knob-Seneca Rocks in eastern West Virginia, Mount Rogers in southwestern Virginia, Shasta-Trinity in northern California, and Flaming Gorge in Wyoming-Utah are among these areas. Some RV campers may be a bit dismayed at the lack of facilities, but the national forests, we are promised, will not develop campgrounds that will significantly alter the forest environment.

Today the National Park Service, under the Department of the Interior, faithful to its charge to "conserve the scenery and ... wildlife ... and leave them unimpaired," is restricting the number of campsites in the national parks and monuments so that camping in the parks will not destroy the very thing the campers seek to enjoy. Still, there are 92 areas in the National Park System with campgrounds, with a total of 30,000 individual campsites. Camping in such overcrowded national parks as Yellowstone and Yosemite has become a dubious thing in the height of the summer season, but there are other, less-popular national parks that may be considered for satisfying camping experiences. The Department of the Interior points out that there is excellent camping in under-used Cumberland Gap National Historical Park, only 80 miles north of overly popular Great Smoky Mountains National Park. The Bighorn Canyon National Recreation Area often has empty camping sites and is only 130 miles east of crowded Yellowstone. Other National Park Service areas that could easily take more campers are: Grand Canyon National Monument, east of Lake Mead; the North Rim of Grand Canyon National Park; Bryce Canyon and Canyonlands national parks in southern Utah, close to popular Zion National Park; and Big Bend National Park on the Mexican border in Texas. Still another possibility for spring and fall camping is Organ Pipe Cactus National Monument, a 514-square mile piece of Arizona desert where the campground has been set down in a natural garden, filled with organ-pipe cactus, saguaro, cholla, and ocotillo.

Canada's national park system also suffers from some overcrowding, but since there are 28 parks with a combined area of more than 50,000 square miles, a camping family can find elbowroom in most of them. The most under-used parks in the system are: Prince Albert in Saskatchewan, Riding Mountain in Manitoba, Kejimkujik in Nova Scotia, Fundy in New Brunswick, Terra Nova in Newfoundland, and Kluane in the Yukon. Kluane is one of Canada's newer parks, and its 8,500 square miles include the awesome St. Elias Mountains.

Today campers are beginning to bypass crowded campgrounds in national parks for magnificent camping sites in national forests that offer in beauty what they lack in conveniences. On a July day in Rocky Mountain National Park, the campsites were crowded with tents and RVs. Radios blared, kids darted about, and the atmosphere was about as much wilderness as is a suburban subdivision on a Saturday afternoon. Yet only a few dozen miles over Trail Ridge Road and down some easily passable wooded roads into the Arapaho National Forest, some of the most beautiful natural campsites in North America were completely empty.

"We tell the campers about the unused campsites," a ranger explained, "but they're hooked on being close to stores, laundromats, and people they can talk to. Many so-called campers just feel scared if they get into the real woods, and yet there's nothing at all for them to be scared about."

In planning your camping vacation, consider camping in national forests instead of national parks, and state forests instead of state parks. The camping area in Fayette State Park in Michigan's Upper Peninsula is filled night after night all summer, and rangers have to turn people away. Yet only some 10 miles away down gravel roads lies a splendid state forest camping area beside Portage Bay. There are water pumps and privies, a sandy swimming beach, pine-shaded campsites, and the virtual certainty that deer will come browsing about your camp in the dusk. Only a handful of families take the rangers' advice and camp there.

Another suggestion is to strike out for parts of the country that are not overrun by tourists. Follow your own interests and hobbies. Our family tent camped along the 648 miles of the old Mullan Military Road from Fort Benton in Montana to the ruins of Fort Walla Walla in Washington. We not only traced the old road but explored Montana's abandoned gold camps. We found splendid campsites in national forests and once on the grounds of old Fort Shaw. For five consecutive nights, we camped without any neighbors at all. Yet some 40 miles north of us and some 40 miles south of us along major tourist arteries, every campground was jammed. Another summer when we camped along the route of the Oregon Trail, we discovered that long sections of the now-deserted trail can be followed, and they run through areas that are wilder today than in covered-wagon days. There are enormous stretches of unspoiled North America waiting for you to explore, providing you don't mind roughing it and are trained in outdoor skills and good manners.

Crown lands in Canada and public lands in the United States do not have organized campgrounds, but people who are well trained in wilderness camping and who live by the outdoorsman's law can camp in them. Most of these lands are not accessible by road, but parts of the American and Canadian West and the northern reaches of Ontario have some camping sites that an auto tent camper can reach. An admonition: Be sure you are not on private land. Most people will prove hospitable, but a few have a "trespassers-will-be-prosecuted-to-the-full-extent-of-one-shotgun-and-a-hound-dog-with-big-teeth" mentality. And another admonition: Public authorities and outdoorsmen in both the United States and Canada are becoming increasingly annoyed and disturbed by campers who leave trash behind them and who have little inkling of conservation.

As your family is sitting around your table loaded with maps and brochures, think of all the possibilities. If you're a rockhound, your wife is a bird-watcher, your daughter wants to ride horseback, and your son wants to swim, you could try and find a place to camp where you can all do the things you like the most. Or perhaps you might want to pick a place where some of your family's interests are served on this trip, with the promise that on the next one the interests of the other members of the family might be pursued.

When you've made your decision, start making a list of all the things you should take along. This is particularly important in tent camping. A big RV can resemble Fibber McGee's proverbial closet, but no tent camper can afford to squander space. Take into account the kind of weather, terrain, and activities at the campsites you have picked. Even your youngest children should join in and at least make a list of the things that they personally plan to bring with them. They'll start learning at home the fun of taking their share of the responsibility for a good camp. Don't feel too superior to take a lesson from the Boy Scouts. In a good troop's camp, the boys do almost everything, and the scoutmaster staff do practically nothing but teach, counsel, and share the outdoor experience for better or worse. In a typical family camp, the boys and girls do practically nothing and the parents do almost everything. Boys in a Scout camp usually have a rare good time, and the kids in a family camp are often bored and restless. From the start, count your children in on the planning and all the chores.

Your Individual Camping Gear

What should you bring along? The list will vary, but there are some things that will stand you in good stead everywhere. For most camping, each person should bring: a canteen, jackknife, flashlight, personal toiletries, two towels and a washcloth, raincoat or poncho, hat, handkerchiefs, at least three changes of underwear, six pairs of hiking socks, hiking shoes or boots and sneakers or moccasins to serve as camp shoes, two extra changes of clothing, a warm jacket, sweater, swimsuit, lip salve, and insect repellent. You might put everything in a pack, duffel bag or, if you are auto camping, even a small suitcase. Your sleeping bag, ground cover, and air mattress and air pillow if you want them, can be packed separately in an accessible spot.

It is easy to pack if you put all your personal equipment out on a bed. Place your underwear, socks, and handkerchiefs in separate plastic bags. When you want them, they'll be easier to find. They'll also stay cleaner and, in case your pack gets caught in a sudden downpour, they'll remain dry. Naturally you'll put the things that you won't need right away or will rarely need at the bottom of your pack. Such things as your flashlight and poncho belong at the top of the pack where they'll be handy. Other things that you may want in a hurry can be put in the side pockets of a pack, and such things as a jackknife can go in the pockets of your clothing. If an individual needs things for his hobby—a camera or a rockhound's hammer, for example—he should be responsible for them, and if possible he should fit them into his pack.

For a Good Night's Rest

What kind of sleeping bag is best? It depends upon the climate where you are planning to camp. Goose-down bags are ideal for cold weather, but when camping in the dog days of an Arkansas July, they can be far too warm for sleeping comfort. Yet if you unzip your goose-down bag all the way or lie on top of it, you are too chilly. You perspire or freeze. The amount and kind of fill in the bag determine whether the bag will be warm enough only on a night when the temperature remains over 50 degrees, whether it can keep you toasty on a cool night when the temperature may drop to 20 degrees or whether you will be comfortable on a bitter-cold winter night when the temperature may fall to way below zero.

Some manufacturers fill their sleeping bags with carpet clippings or the leavings from the production of insulated underwear. The material in these bags lumps up, and cold spots develop. Goose-down bags are the warmest, but they are expensive, costing somewhere around $80, and resin-treated polyester fiber bags have been greatly improved in recent years and should be fine for camping from late spring through fall. While you are looking over bags in the store, inspect the zippers to make sure they are strong and durable and that there is an insulated fabric seal on both sides of the zipper. A cold zipper against your back on a chilly night can wake you out of a sound sleep.

If you are going to be camping in established campgrounds where there is little possibility of creating a soft bed for the night with the assistance of natural duff, you'll also want an air mattress. Be sure you buy one that is big enough. A six-footer balances uneasily on top of an air mattress intended for a child. If the outer edges are higher than the center of the mattress, this will help keep you from rolling off. Rubberized nylon is strong and durable. On the other hand, some campers find that foam pads thrust under the hips are all that they need for comfort, particularly if they can put an air pillow under their head. Still others prefer to bring along a folding cot. Aluminum frames support canvas or duck covers. Double-decker cots are available for those who require them for saving space.

Today's Versatile Tents

Although today's campers may head for the woods in a luxury motor home or trailer, a converted truck, pickup truck with camper body, or a tent trailer, it is the tent camper who gets closest to nature. If you haven't looked over the tents available today, you're going to be happily surprised. The heavy canvas tents that you remember from your days in the army or in yesterday's Boy Scouts have given way to such things as pop-tents with no guy ropes, stakes, or center poles. The fiberglass rods sewn into sidewall pockets can be raised quickly into position. Some new tents have self-supporting frames that are inserted inside the corners. The most popular tents have exterior frames of lightweight, anodized tubular aluminum, and they are made of a poplin drill, which is a closely woven, lightweight variety of canvas that resists mildew. These tents usually have sewn-in, vinyl-coated nylon floors that do not tear easily and can be cleaned with soap and water. Heavy-duty zippers that will not catch, lap-felled seams, reinforced double seams at stress points, net-covered windows, and inside storm flaps on the windows are all things to look for in buying a tent. A family of four needs at least an 8′ x 10′ tent, and a family of six should have a 10′ x 14′ size. Some families prefer to buy two tents instead of one large one so that the parents can have one tent and the kids another. This allows for greater privacy and differences in bedtimes.

There are other things to think about in buying a tent. A light-colored tent roof will reflect the sun's hot rays and also make the interior seem brighter on dull days. A canopy over the door and a hood over a window not only deflect sunshine but also allow for ventilation on close, rainy days when everything in the camp seems about to change into mushrooms. Some of the tents pack into a duffel bag that is scarcely larger than a sleeping bag and weigh less than 25 pounds. A bag for tent stakes is essential if you are to keep from losing some of your stakes every time you take down your tent.

You may also decide to buy a dining fly. A tarpaulin made of canvas or heavy builders' plastic can be stretched between trees and poles in your camp to make an outdoor kitchen or lounging area for use in case of rain. You may also stretch the tarp between the doors of two tents to make a covered breezeway similar to the dogtrots of a pioneer cabin.

Be Plain in the Woods

Keeping in mind Kephart's admonishment to "Be plain in the woods," campers should leave at home all the unnecessary gear that abounds in sporting goods shops and mail order catalogs. Your family camping checklist should include: a compass, food chest, cooler, cooking equipment with nesting utensils, a frying pan, measuring cups and serving plates, a large spoon and fork, a spatula, roll-type can opener, potato peeler, carving knife, paring knife, ladle, sugar, salt and pepper containers, waterproof matches, cooking gloves and tongs for taking a hot pot off the fire. You will find that a grate with folding legs to place over your fire will also come in handy at many campsites.

Camping gear should also include: a brush saw, three-quarter ax, a mill file for sharpening the ax, a sharpening stone, extra rope, collapsible spade, a sewing kit, complete first-aid kit, toilet paper in a plastic bag, and two plastic 2½-gallon water containers or a 5-gallon container. For doing the dishes you'll want: a rubber scraper; scouring pads; dishcloths; detergent in a plastic container; two washtubs, one for wash water and the other for hot rinse water; a roll of paper towels in a plastic bag; and a litterbag.

If you cannot cook on a wood fire where you are going, you may be able to use charcoal. Otherwise you will want to bring along a portable camp stove. This may range from a simple spirit burner to a propane stove using disposable cylinders or one fueled by white gas. The lantern needed to light your camp at night may be powered by electric batteries or it may be a propane or gas lantern. Extra wicks are valuable to have along.

Camp Provisions

During pioneer days the Stewart party trekking over the Oregon Trail ate as a rule two meals a day of "oatmeal mush, bacon sides with pilot bread, fried in the fat, and coffee." Today's camping family should have no trouble surpassing these victuals. If you plan to move your camp often by car or are camped near stores, you'll be able to buy fresh supplies every day. Otherwise you'll want to purchase canned and freeze-dried foods, which are available in sporting goods stores and in many grocery stores. By shopping in grocery stores for such things as dehydrated chicken tetrazzini and shrimp de Jonghe, you save a substantial sum over what such foods cost in sporting goods stores. The canned beans, spaghetti, and hamburger routine may satisfy many camping families, but you need not go that route.

Before you leave home is the time to plan out the menus for every meal you intend to eat in camp. Later on you can change around if you wish, but this will allow you to develop a shopping list that will insure that you have the ingredients you need in your camp when you start cooking. Keep things simple, and remember that even the pickiest eaters at home may develop gargantuan appetites in the outdoors.

In our base camps we tend toward quick-and-easy breakfasts of bacon and eggs, instant hot cereals, cold cereals, pancakes made from mixes, and fruit juices from powders. Because lunch comes at the height of the day's activities, it is best to resort to make-it-yourself sandwiches and soup. Cookies and candy are good luncheon desserts.

Evening is the time to splurge. A one-pot stew, steaks, chops, or chicken fried or grilled, vegetables either fresh or from the can, instant rice or potatoes—all are popular. Often edible wild plants can be worked judiciously into the meal. Dry soups are quick and easy to prepare, and they make a fine before-bedtime snack or appetizer. A balanced diet is necessary if a family is going to keep energy levels high and stay healthy, particularly if they will be camping for any length of time.

Many campers who are heading for campgrounds that are close to stores nevertheless stock up on everything before they leave home. It is usually better, for economy's sake, to buy staples such as salt, pepper, cooking oil, sugar, and powdered milk at home but to purchase such things as eggs, meats, bread, fruits, and vegetables closer to your campsite. Perishables go in the ice chest, which can be kept chilled better by block ice than by ice cubes. Some weekend campers freeze lemonade or homemade soup in cardboard milk containers at home and use them instead of ice for keeping food cool. This can be a space saver, and the liquids can be used when they thaw out. Instead of packing staples in glass jars, which can break, experienced campers use covered plastic containers for packing.

Probably you won't have any trouble getting all the individual and family equipment and supplies into the trunk of your car or into the back of your station wagon. If sports or hobby gear makes this impossible, then you should buy or rent a lightweight car-top carrier. If you do put a carrier on your car, put your tent into it since the tent should be the first thing off the car when you set up camp.

Most people think that packing the car is one of the most unpleasant chores in preparing for a happy auto camping trip. This is usually because one person takes too much of the chore upon himself under the mistaken supposition that he alone knows just where everything should go. The whole family should help. It's not a difficult thing at all. Simply pack together things that are used together: sleeping bags and air mattresses; water containers, ice chest, and cooking gear where you can get at them easily if you want to stop along the way for a snack or want to start preparing a meal as soon as you reach your campsite. Lanterns and flashlights should be kept handy in case you arrive at your site after dark. You'll find that if every member of the party has his own bag or suitcase, there'll be a lot less muss in finding personal things quickly. Things that you don't use often should be packed out of the way so they don't have to be unloaded every time you set up a camp or stop by the road.

A family that is just taking up camping may find it useful to enroll in a family camping course given by the YMCA or some other service organization. The Red Cross also offers courses in first aid that are well worth your while, not just because you'll be more effective in an emergency but because your training will give you greater self-confidence and peace of mind when going into the wilderness.

At least a family would be well advised to set up their new tent in their backyard and get the hang of their cooking equipment before leaving home. A weekend camping trip or two in a nearby woods would be useful in showing the family's readiness for more adventurous camping. Equipment could be tested, and skills practiced. Everybody could learn to work together to make a camp successful. You may even want to rent or borrow equipment to go camping for a weekend just to see if you enjoy the experience. Chances are that you will, but why invest in a lot of gear if you really aren't sure?

Setting Up Camp

In a crowded campground you usually have little choice as to where you should set up your tent, but if you venture off the beaten path, you can take your pick of places. Once I listened to Lydo Harvey, an Apache Indian, telling our visiting children where to pitch a tent.

"Kids want to pitch their tent beneath a big tree so it will be safe from the storms, but it won't be safe!" he said. "Lightning strike the tree, and somebody's nice kids get cooked right where they are. A wind comes up in the night, and a dry limb breaks off and falls down right on top of you. Make your camp where little trees or bushes block off the wind, but don't be scared of rain and hail; they won't hurt you the way the lightning will."

Lydo Harvey might have added that if you pitch your tent beneath a tree, you may also listen to the water dripping off the leaves long after a storm has ended. Birds roosting on the limbs may try out a little bombardiering at your expense; sap falling down on your canvas may be even harder to clean. Because the breeze can't get at you, you'll not only be hot on a torrid night, but you'll also be more likely to have a host of hungry mosquitoes buzzing about you. Tree roots can complicate things when you're trying to drive your stakes in. It is also a good idea to stay away from an overhanging cliff, for rockslides, loosened by a storm, may drop on you.

A good spot to put your tent on a summer day would be where the friendly morning sun can shine upon you but where shade from nearby trees will keep off the hot sun of the afternoon. During the fall or spring, you'll probably want sun on your tent all day long. A knowledgeable camper checks over the terrain to see where water will run in case of a storm. He never sets up in a gully, a wash, or at the foot of a hill, where water collects. In any part of the country, a wash can be a wet and unpleasant place to put a tent, but in the desert Southwest it can be very dangerous. A flash flood from a downpour in the mountains can strike without warning. In most marshy areas, mosquitoes and heavy dew can also be problems. A knoll is a good place for a tent, unless you pick the highest point around, where the wind can get at it. Since ditching is prohibited in most camping areas today, it might even be helpful to pitch your tent on a slight slope instead of a level spot. This will enable water to drain off your site more readily, and you will discover that sleeping with your head higher than your feet is pretty comfortable.

Place your tent with its back to the wind, which in North America usually blows from the west. Put the tent upwind from your fireplace so that you won't be smoked out, and be sure it is a safe distance away from the fire so that sparks can't reach it.

Sticks and stones can be mighty uncomfortable for sleeping on. Before setting up your tent, pick the area clean of any hard objects. Make certain that there are no roots that will jab you in the ribs. You may also want to put some leaves or other duff beneath where you are going to bed down for the night. Never cut evergreen boughs or gather living plants as cushioning. How carefully you prepare your bed depends in great part on whether or not you happen to be a devotee of the air mattress.

You may wish to put down a plastic ground cover to protect the floor of your tent. Some veteran campers say this is the thing to do, because the cover will keep the moisture that sweats out of the ground from wetting your tent and causing the canvas to mildew. Other campers argue just as strenuously that a ground cover beneath your tent causes moisture to condense on the canvas floor. In my own experience, moisture can form from either cause, depending on the variables of temperature and humidity. A ground cover at least will protect your tent from mud and dampness when you pitch it after a storm. Some campers also put a small rug inside their tent door so that people entering the tent do not track mud onto the floor. The rug can be taken out and shaken a lot more readily than can the tent floor.

A good campsite should have drinking water handy. If it is a developed site, there'll doubtless be a pump or a tap nearby; otherwise you'll have to take your water from a stream or a lake. Don't just assume that a limpid stream that looks pure is safe to drink, and don't take the word of another group of campers. Chances are, they don't know any more about the water than you do. Ask a ranger or someone who really knows, and if there is any doubt at all, use water-purification tablets. If you prefer, you can also boil water to make it safe to drink. In some places, you must boil the water. On Isle Royale in Lake Superior, for one place, the moose have contaminated the water close to shore with liver flukes. The water looks clear, and it would be potable except for the flukes. These can be killed only by boiling.

Most developed campsites also have sanitary facilities, and a few tent campers carry along either fold-up toilets that use disposable bags, or hassock or pump types that employ chemicals and are self-contained. Digging your own latrine poses no problem. Carefully stack the sod to one side. The latrine should be located so that it will not contaminate your water supply and can be screened for privacy. It can be filled in as used and completely filled in when you break camp. Carefully replace the sod so that you do not leave a scar in the forest.

Campfires

Once you've set up your tent and stowed away your gear, some of the party should start getting the food ready for cooking while others get the fire ready. If you are camping on the plains you are in what was once buffalo-chip country. Since even in frontier days little wood was to be found, pioneers cooked over fires built with the chips. Francis Parkman wrote of his party following the Oregon Trail that "Many of the ladies can be seen roaming over the prairie with sacks in hand, searching for a few buffalo chips to cook their evening meal. Some of the ladies are seen wearing gloves, but most of them have discarded their gloves and are gathering the buffalo chips with their bare hands."

Pioneers claimed that the chips burned like peat and that a steak cooked over a buffalo-chip fire was particularly flavorful and required no pepper.

Today you may be cooking on a stove or with charcoal. Otherwise, the fire builders should collect enough tinder, kindling, and fuel wood to cook the entire meal before building the fire and lighting it. There are few things more aggravating than to have a fire start dying

out and to discover that there is no supply of wood just when the cook needs the heat to finish his meal.

Wood gatherers shouldn't be satisfied with enough wood for the cooking fire. They should collect enough wood for a possible evening warming fire and a breakfast fire too. Put the wood under cover so that a night rain won't upset the morning cooking plans.

Unless the area has been well picked over by other campers, you'll probably find enough deadwood on the ground and hanging from trees. Break the branches with your hands and feet if you can. You may use a brush saw to cut the wood to size. An ax should not be used unless it alone will do the job, for it is the most dangerous tool in camp. Be sure that any children in the camp are well trained in how to use the ax safely before you trust them to cut wood with it. If there are more than a couple of people in the camp, set up an ax yard too. Rope off an area where all the wood is to be chopped, and be sure only the person wielding the ax is in the yard.

An Australian was asked what kind of eucalyptus sprig he puts into his billycan to help flavor a good cup of tea.

"I only use one kind of eucalyptus," he replied. "The kind that grows nearest to my back fence."

Similarly a camper uses only one kind of wood for his fire—the kind that is handy to his camp. He prefers the woods of such broadleaf trees as the oak, maple, beech, hickory, birch, gum, and even such faster burning broadleaf woods as cottonwood and buckeye; but if all he can find is conifer woods he'll be satisfied with cedar, spruce, fir, hemlock, or other trees with needles. Conifers may burn faster and smoke up his cooking utensils more, but a camper has to make do with what he has.

If there is a designated place for a fire in your camping site, use it. Otherwise use an existing fire scar. Under most circumstances, a fire should not be built under overhanging limbs or against a log or tree. All flammable leaves, pine needles, and duff should be scraped from the firesite until you have a space from six to ten feet in diameter that is free of burnable material. The width depends upon the weather conditions. Be sure also that there are no exposed roots in the area.

Place all your materials in order. First comes the tinder, then the kindling, and then the fuel—all within easy reach of the fire builder. Employing either a tepee or a crisscross lay, light your fire from the windward side. Your match lights a handful of tinder, and this catches the kindling. If you feed the lee side of your fire with first kindling and then larger stuff, you'll soon have a healthy fire going. Be patient until a bed of coals forms, and you'll have a good cooking fire.

Few campers give any serious thought to mastering the art of starting a fire by flint and steel, by friction, or with the aid of a burning glass, but most will at least bring along some kitchen matches that have been waterproofed by dipping them in nail polish or melted paraffin. Experienced campers know that wet matches have resulted in many a fireless camp. It is dangerous to use a liquid fuel to start a fire, but there are solid fuels such as Sterno that may be used in wet weather. Candle stumps also make excellent fire starters and are especially handy on rainy days.

As tinder you may use such things as paper, cedar bark or the outer bark of white birch, pine cones, pine that is full of pitch, fine shavings of dry wood, dry grass, such weedtops as goldenrod and aster, dry leaves taken right from the tree, fine dead twigs from a standing tree, and even such oddments as last year's birds' nests or a mouse nest. For kindling you may employ deadwood from a standing tree, heavy weed stems, or split wood. If the weather is wet, you'll find that deadwood still on a tree dries out faster than wood on the ground. The heartwood of a limb or a log will also prove to be dry. Your fuel wood should be of any practical size, but if the log is more than three inches in diameter or so, it will burn better if you split it. Whether you build a hunter's fire between a pair of small logs or two rows of rocks, or kindle a trench fire, you will have a good cooking fire. You can build a fire against a rock to provide warmth, and you can build a big bonfire for fun and sociability. Perhaps a bit of advice from that wise Apache Lydo Harvey would be in order. Build the right fire for the job you want it to do.

"Indian makes little fire and sits close," he explained to our camping family. "White man makes big fire and sits back far."

Whatever kind of fire you build, be sure that you put it dead out before you go to bed or before you leave your camp. Douse water on the fire and stir it until you can put your hand in it safely. When there is no smoke or steam, feel each stick to be sure that none of them are hot. If you have no water in camp, moist dirt and sand can be stirred into the coals until you are certain that they are all dead out. Just covering the fire won't do. A wind can strip off the dirt you put on top, and the fire can spring up, a menace to the woods and all it contains.

Since wood fires blacken cooking pots and pans, you may want to daub the bottoms of your utensils with soap or detergent before putting them over the fire. When you are through cooking, you can then easily wipe off the soot. As soon as the cook finishes preparing the meal, he should put water on to heat for washing dishes. Then everybody can sit down together for a convivial meal. The water will be hot when the meal is over, and the fire builders, now turned dishwashers, can fall to at washing the dishes. It is critical that they get all the food and grease off the dishes and cooking utensils so that nobody gets camp stomach. If there is a handy place to set out the dishes, they should be air dried. If not, they can be dried with paper towels.

At a developed campground it is a simple matter to put garbage and trash into the cans provided for that purpose. While you are at it, pick up any litter that previous campers may have left at your campsite and dispose of that too, for this is the mark of a seasoned camper who has an appreciation for the outdoors. If you are in a primitive camping site, you must burn as much of your garbage as possible. Even wet garbage can be dried out in the fire and burned. You can clean out cans, remove both ends, and squash them. Carry them and other unburnable trash with you in a litterbag until you come to the first trash can. Once it was considered all right to bury trash or garbage, but now with so many campers using even primitive sites, this is no longer acceptable. Nobody wants to dig up somebody else's garbage when he thinks he's gotten away from it all. Wild animals also will dig up your garbage as soon as you've gone and scatter it around.

Although wild animals are not a serious problem even in areas where family campers have spoiled the wildlife with snacks, they can be a nuisance. A clean camp is the best protection against such midnight visitors as raccoons, porcupines, skunks, and bears. At Clifty Falls State Park in Indiana, where our family camped overlooking the Ohio River, a skunk made off with both a loaf of white bread and a loaf of rye from a neighboring campsite. He dragged them a short distance from the camp, took one bite of the white and spit it out. He ate an amazing portion of the rye, thereby proving that skunks also turn down the spongy white bread common in our land in favor of a more palatable bread.

A bear can smell dirty dishes a mile away and will come to investigate. Bruin will be frustrated if you store your foodstuffs in sturdy, preferably airtight, containers suspended by ropes between trees or keep your supplies securely locked up in the trunk of your car. At least never keep your food supply, snacks, or candy in your tent when bears are around. They'll slash right through the canvas to get at the goodies, and you unfortunately might be in the way.

If you find yourself in grizzly country, additional precautions should be taken. There is considerable evidence that grizzlies are irritated by the odor of both cosmetics and women who are menstruating. But these are scarcely good reasons for a woman to be afraid of going camping. After all, there is not much grizzly country handy to auto tent camping, and ordinarily family campers are not going to be anywhere near these fierce bears. Still, if a woman is indeed going into grizzly country, she ought to cultivate the natural look and leave her cosmetics behind. She also should use internal tampons when necessary, which can be burned after use.

Most snakes in North America are harmless, but there are such unfriendly fellows as copperheads, rattlesnakes, and coral snakes in some areas. You should carry a snakebite kit with you and be prepared to give appropriate first aid. The most important thing is to get a snakebite victim to a doctor, so that antivenom serum can be given as soon as possible. If it is going to take some time to get the victim there, you should use the small blade in your kit to slash the bite perhaps an eighth of an inch deep, cutting with the muscle, and then use a rubber cup to suction up the blood and poison. If you have no rubber cup in your first-aid kit, you may suck the venom out of the wound with your mouth without chancing complications for yourself. Simply spit it out. Keep the wounded area lower than the rest of the body if possible. A cloth or cord tied around the limb between the wound and the heart will also help impede the spread of the poison. Don't tie it so tight that you stop the flow of the blood. Don't let the victim become chilled, and don't give him any alcohol to drink.

The best first aid for snakebite is to keep away from the snake. None of the poisonous snakes are truculent, and they will not attack you unless they think you are attacking them. The difficulty is that they aren't very bright. If you're stumbling along a path and they can't get out of the way, they may think you plan to stomp on them and decide to get in a nip in self-defense. In snake country, never step over a log or rock so that your foot comes down on the unseen side, where a snake may be lurking. Go around the obstacle or step on top of it so that your next step is safely clear of any snake that may be there. At night don't set up a camp in a wooded or rocky area, for even with the aid of a flashlight, you are not likely to be able to make out the frightened reptile until he bites you. It is a far sounder practice to set up your camp in a clearing in any case.

In all truth insects and poisonous plants cause more problems for campers than do bears, snakes, or any other wild animals. Insect repellents will help keep away mosquitoes, ticks, and chiggers, but don't spray them near your tent. They will destroy the waterproofing and deteriorate nylon. Poison ivy and oak are not hard to recognize, and the most carefree child can be taught to stay away from them. Fortunately poison oak and poison ivy bear their leaflets in patterns of three, and they have white berries. The old adage "Leaflets three— let it be. Berries white—poisonous sight" is easy to remember and well worth following.

A safe camping trip begins at home. If parents have close rapport with their children, the kids will be safer in the woods. From the start, parents should make clear, commonsense safety rules. Rangers can scarcely be expected to undertake the supervision of children or teenagers if parents are not concerned with their welfare or safety. The National Park Service booklet on camping warns, "Watch your children. Your knowledge, experience, and wisdom can't help a child who is beyond your protective reach and warning voice."

Perhaps a good Scout troop has well trained your son or daughter in outdoor living. Perhaps you or some other person has trained your youngster. Then you can allow him far more independence since you know he has enough knowledge and experience to be safe. But I have rarely camped in a family camping area where I have not encountered a gaggle of kids who are undisciplined, heedless, and courting disaster. Their parents are either preoccupied with camp chores, having a good friendly gossip with other campers, or bent on their own amusement. They bring the careless patterns of their city or suburban family life at home into the woods, and the wonder is that more youngsters are not injured or lost.

Of course, campers should keep their distance from wild animals. All wildlife can be dangerous. Even a chipmunk can carry rabies. Those cuddly little bear cubs have a big and not so cuddly mother somewhere near. Campers should also let the rangers know if they are going to take a hike or horseback ride into the backcountry. They should not undertake adventurous explorations of caves or lake bottoms without talking it over with the rangers. The rangers know of hazards that they can warn about. They also will be on the lookout for an adventurer's return and will be able to organize a search and rescue if he doesn't come back in a reasonable time.

A cardinal rule for all campers, young and old alike, is never to go off on a solitary hike into the deep woods. If you have even a minor accident, without a companion you may have trouble getting back to camp. The "buddy system" also counts on the old adage that "two heads are better than one." At least you'll have companionship in trouble if something goes awry.

Many beginning campers fear getting lost in the woods. The best way to keep from getting lost is to make plans to keep from getting lost. At home, study a map of the area where you plan to camp so that you know something about it. When you arrive at your campsite, look over the map with a ranger. If you know the trail, roads, railroads, pipelines, or power lines that act as boundaries for the wilderness into which you are going, you will have a better chance of keeping tabs on where you are. Study the natural features—the hills and valleys, mountain ridges, swamps, lakes, and streams. These too can help you, and if you are in a real wilderness, they'll be all that you'll have to go on.

A compass in your pocket is indispensable in the woods. You may have a remarkably accurate sense of direction, but if the sky grows overcast, it is going to be hard for you to know the direction in which you're traveling without a compass. As you hike along a stream, fishing rod in hand, it is important to notice what is around you. Observe odd trees, the direction of a stream's current, a stump, a distinctive rock formation, anything that may offer you a point of reference later on. Keep yourself oriented with the terrain and the direction of the sun as you hike through the woods. Just as important, you should always plan on getting back to camp long before it gets dark.

But what if you do get lost? If you keep cool, you'll find your way again. If you get rattled, you are your own worst enemy. Sit down on a log or a rock and get your mind under control. The best thing to do if you cannot remember anything about how you came to be in your predicament is to walk uphill. A stream is apt to get you tangled up in heavy brush in a valley and may lead you into a swamp long before it will bring you to a lake, a larger stream, or civilization. At the top of a hill or mountain you can see farther. You may locate a landmark, man-made or natural, from your vantage point. Since prehistoric times, trails have followed the tops of ridges, and you may come upon such a trail. Moreover, atop a hill where timber is sparse, you will be easier to spot from the air. If you decide on a smoky fire as a signal, it will be easier for a rescue party to see if you've built it atop a hill. Firing three shots is a signal of distress, but unless you wait until after dark, your signal may well be taken for a hunter who can't shoot straight. Three shouts, three blasts on a whistle, or three flashes of light from a mirror are also signals of distress.

Don't be afraid of wild animals. Next to yourself, the elements pose your greatest threat. If you are lost in the hot desert, concentrate on keeping down the loss of body moisture. Keep your head covered and your clothes on even if you are burning up with the heat. Find some shade and get into it. Don't travel unless you absolutely have to and then only in the relatively cool morning or late afternoon.

Cold can be an equally dangerous enemy when you are lost. When you set out on a woods hike, carry along some waterproof matches and a couple of candle stubs so that you'll have no difficulty in making a fire even in the wet. A fire will keep off the cold, serve as a signal, and be a friendly companion in the dark. If you build a fire not far from a ledge or the roots of an uprooted tree, they will act as a reflector. Sit between the reflector and your fire, and you'll be toasty. If you cannot find a reflector of any sort, then build two fires and lie between them. The coals will keep you warm even after the fire has died down. If it's a question of survival, you're justified in keeping a fire going all night.

A camper should know his own limits. Just as he should not try to swim across a lake that is beyond his strength or skill, he should not try to climb a mountain or cross a snowfield that is beyond his training or physical condition. He should learn how to do things correctly and safely and get into sufficiently good shape to do them without difficulty. Even then he should take into account the effects of altitude, temperature, and extremes of aridity or humidity before he starts out on a strenuous activity. Even the hardiest of youngsters from the low country have to be given time to adjust to the demands on their hearts and lungs imposed by the thin air of high altitudes.

Campground etiquette is scarcely burdensome, but it is important if people of dissimilar backgrounds and interests are to camp happily near one another. If you arrive after the camp office is closed, don't bother the ranger or park manager. Find a campsite and set up your tent quietly. People who arrive late at night and shout instructions back and forth or drop tent hardware with a clatter are more than likely to draw glares from their neighbors in the morning.

Wherever you camp, you'll find some neighborly rules in force. It is a good idea to read and obey the signs and posters posted by camp managers or the rangers. Observe the state and federal laws protecting game and fish, and do not do any damage to trees, shrubs, and flowers. Fish, clothes, and dishes should not be cleaned in lakes or streams, and you will virtually be drummed out of a camping area if you do your dishes at the camp pump. As for firearms or fireworks, they are prohibited in or near camping or recreation areas.

Lively and happy kids having a good time camping are a pleasure not only for you but for most of your camping neighbors. But if your children are constantly screaming, crying, or getting into mischief, you can rest assured that everybody else will heave a sigh of relief when you move on. Both you and your kids should respect the privacy of another person's camp and cut through it only with permission and as unobtrusively as possible.

Dogs are more of a problem, and they are forbidden in many camping areas. If you check in advance and know that your dog is welcome, this still doesn't give him license to spend the night barking at the shadows or elusive woodland creatures or baying at the moon. Most places require that dogs be kept on leashes.

Howling kids and barking dogs won't put your family in nearly as bad repute as will a boisterous card game at night, a late hour's campfire replete with old-fashioned song favorites, or a loud portable radio or TV. Many campers doubt that you really belong in the woods if you have to have radio or TV to keep you amused, especially when radio and TV are two of the things that they've come to the woods to try and escape. It is easy to understand the disappointment and disgust felt by the ranger staff at Cumberland Gap National Park. Superintendent Amos Hawkins explained to us that one night they put on a real square dance with honest-to-goodness mountain fiddlers.

"None of the RV campers came," said the superintendent. "A ranger went over to see why, and they were all busy watching TV."

Finally the golden rule: seasoned campers always try to leave their site cleaner than when they found it.

Backpacking & Trail Riding

BACKPACKING

We scrabbled up the last precipitous stretch of rolling stones, called scree, to the summit of Chilkoot Pass. Snowcaps shouldered about us, and clouds of mist began to swirl in. Five junior-high-school-age boys, another man, and I were backpacking over the Chilkoot Trail, which gold rushers in 1898 had broken through the wilderness of Alaska and British Columbia, toward the land of the midnight sun. All day we had been crossing snowfields, as much as 100 feet thick, climbing over jumbled rocks called talus, and picking our way through the scree. We were weary.

It was July, and the summer sun, penetrating the fogs

that whirl through the pass, had melted the snow so that we could put our sleeping bags down on a patch of soft lichen within a quadrangle of huge rocks that formed a natural shelter against the wind. We fastened aluminized space blankets over us to break the wind further and to keep in body heat, and we snuggled down for a night's rest. Before one boy went to sleep he said to me, "I know after today that I could have survived in caveman days. I wish that we'd see Big Foot!"

Big Foot, the huge half-human creature thought by some to live in the mountain wilderness of the Pacific Northwest, British Columbia, and Alaska, did not put in an appearance during the night, but in the morning as we were cooking over our spirit stove, a black bear sauntered across a nearby snowfield and looked us over. He waddled into some talus, only to come out in a few moments for a second look at the strange creatures who had invaded his mountain domain.

Psychologists say that today's kids, not only in the city, suburbs, and small towns, but also on farms, because of the mechanization of agricultural life, need to relate themselves more to nature. Children find new strength in learning how to live simply in the open in harmony with the forests and streams. Adults, who can become denatured by the artificialities of modern existence, also require more outdoor life. This is one reason why people of all ages are backpacking over the more than 100,000 miles of trails that crisscross our wilderness and semi-wilderness areas from Maine to California, and over equally fascinating trails in Canada, Hawaii, and Alaska. They are taking pack trips on horseback over the many wilderness trails as well.

The boys with whom I hiked the Chilkoot Trail were well-trained Scouts, accustomed to living out of the packs on their backs in the wilds, but backpacking for kids is by no means limited to such rugged youngsters. If family beginners observe the commonsense rules of wilderness living, they can backpack without fear. They too can carry their camp on their back, cook their own meals, wash their dishes, and clean up their campsite just as do any other backpackers worthy of the name. Certainly it helps to have an experienced backpacker in the party, but it is not essential.

Plan Your Backpack

At the same time, a backpack cannot be as spur of the moment as some people think it should be. Backpacking is advanced camping, and it takes even more preparation at home than does a camping trip. If a family or a group of friends plan a backpack, the first thing to do is to pick an area and then get the best trail maps and booklets that can be obtained. National Park Service and Forest Service maps are available, and so are topographical maps published by the U.S. Coast and Geodetic Survey. Trail associations and hiking clubs also will send maps of such trails as the Appalachian Trail in the East, the Pacific Crest Trail in the West, and the Bruce Trail in Ontario.

Where to try out the possibilities of what Abraham Lincoln called "shanks' mare"? Here are a few places to whet your interest. Guadalupe Mountains National Park in Texas was opened in 1970, but it is still primitive in character and lacks developed public-use facilities. This makes it ideal for backpackers and trail riders, providing they bring in their own water. There is very little water and what there is has to be purified. More than 55 miles of trails are available, leading to such places as McKittrick Canyon, Pine Springs Canyon, and Dog Canyon. An arduous trail that is a test of anyone's horsemanship or hiking prowess leads to the summit of Guadalupe Peak, the highest point in Texas, and another leads to the top of Bush Mountain. From the mountain heights a hiker or rider can look out across the vast plains and salt basins to the south and west. He had better not be carried away by the views because the weather atop the mountains can be very treacherous. There are sudden high winds, and temperatures can fall below freezing.

This is the country through which the 19th century Butterfield Overland Stage ran, and a stage stop known as "The Pinery" is a horseback ride into historic Guadalupe Pass. The onetime headquarters of the Guadalupe Mountains Ranch is at Frijole Spring, and to ride up to the ranch buildings is to ride up to a West Texas ranch as it was in the 1870s.

Old logging roads provide fine backpacking in Minnesota's Arrowhead country, in the snowy Coast Mountains of British Columbia's Sunshine Coast, and in the Ouachita Mountains of Arkansas. The Forest Service has set aside the Caney Creek Wilderness in the Ouachita National Forest for wildlife management and backpacking. Jesse James used the Ouachitas of southwestern Arkansas as a hideaway, and moonshiners still operate their stills in hidden valleys. There are white-water creeks, foaming and leaping over boulders, the largest stands of shortleaf pine in North America, blue mountain ridges, bear and deer, and wild hogs. The country is wilder now than it was a hundred years ago, because many mountaineers have left their farms for low-country jobs. Those that remain are friendly and colorful, and the area is a great place for a backpack. All of Arkansas is indeed an ideal country for backpackers. Nearly 18 million acres of forest, some 60 percent of the state, spread over two mountain ranges. There are few developed trails in the state, but fire trails, abandoned railroad rights-of-way, and logging roads lead into the backcountry.

Other places to go? There is the Big Bend National Park of Texas, where hikers who are looking for solitude can find it on a jaunt along a trail leading into the Deadhorse Mountains. The only sound is likely to be the wind whistling over the limestone cliffs. The Marufa Vega Trail crosses an arroyo and descends to the edge of the Rio Grande at Boquillas Canyon, where there is a fine campsite. Somehow burros packed ore down this descent, but it is very dangerous for a shod horse. Hikers have no difficulty.

At the other end of the continent the Florida Wilderness Trail will prove to any doubting backpacker that Florida is far more than tinseled resorts and real estate developments. In time the trail will go all the way from Panama City to the Tamiami Trail, the highway that runs through the Everglades from Miami to the west coast of the state. The Wilderness Trail passes through Apalachicola National Forest, Osceola National Forest, and the Ocala National Forest. Not all of the trail has been marked, but backpackers wishing to pioneer can find their way.

A popular section that has already been blazed is in the Ocala National Forest. This area is called the Big Scrub because there is a dense understory of dwarf live oak and palmetto. The trail passes between two sinkholes that were caused when sections of the limestone that underlies this part of Florida dissolved and caused the earth to cave in. There are attractive primitive campsites on the south shore of Buck Lake and at the Farles Prairie Recreation Area.

The Midwest also has some extraordinary backpacking country. The Ozark-Shawnee Trail leads 115 miles from Grand Tower, Illinois, on the Mississippi River, through the ridges of the Shawnee Hills to the Ohio River. Towering hills, secluded hollows, caves, petroglyphs and pictographs left by the Indians all are in the Shawnee National Forest. A side trail leads to Cave in Rock in the bluffs on the Ohio River. This cave was once used as a den by river pirates, who preyed on flatboaters descending the river in pioneer days.

Isle Royale in Lake Superior is the Midwest's wilderness island. On a night when the moon is full, backpackers wait for the wolves to begin howling. A National Park Service ranger who visited our camp at McCargoe's Cove assured us that there were 26 adult wolves living on the island and that in the spring they had fine litters of pups. We thought it only right that the grown-up wolves should give their kids howling lessons, but it wasn't until the last night of our hike that it happened. We had returned to Rock Harbor to camp close to where the ferryboat from the mainland of Michigan's Upper Peninsula docks. The camp grew quiet. Up on the ridge a lone wolf howled, and from a distant ridge the whole pack howled back. Solo and chorus repeated several times. The sound chilled the marrow of our bones. It was demonic and timeless. Clouds scudded across the face of the moon, and the wind soughed through the balsams. This is what backpacking is all about.

Probably the best-known footpath in the United States is the Appalachian Trail. It wanders through 14 states from Maine to Georgia. Running along the mountain crests and through the wild lands of the Appalachians, its 2,000 miles make it the longest continuous marked trail in the world. Beginning at Mount Katahdin, a granite monolith in central Maine, it ends at Springer Mountain in northern Georgia. The trail is only a little above sea level where it crosses the Hudson River at Bear Mountain Bridge, but it reaches an elevation of 6,641 feet at Clingmans Dome in the Great Smokies. Benton MacKaye of Shirley Center, Massachusetts, a hiker and philosopher of the outdoors, dreamed up this trail along the backbone of the East. It incorporates such previous trails as Vermont's Long Trail and represents a constantly changing book of nature. In Benton MacKaye's words, "Remote for detachment, narrow for chosen company, winding for leisure, lonely for contemplation, the trail leads not merely north and south but upward to the body, mind and soul of man." This is the beauty of the trail and the essence of the wilderness experience.

An equally famous and more demanding trail, the Pacific Crest Trail, is now being opened along the rugged rooftop of the West Coast for 2,150 miles from Canada to Mexico. It runs through 25 national forests and five national parks. Every year more hikers are taking this trail, which is one of the New World's outstanding backpacking adventures. The John Muir Trail, now part of the Pacific Crest Trail, loops through the High Sierras for 200 miles from Happy Isles in the Yosemite National Park to Mount Whitney, the highest peak in the conterminous United States.

The Gila Wilderness in the Gila National Forest of New Mexico is the first wilderness area designated by the Forest Service. In 1968 Congress established the National Trails System to provide hikers and horseback riders with trails that are both challenging and significant. The Appalachian and Pacific Crest trails were made the first components of the system, but plans are being made for Continental Divide and Potomac Heritage scenic trails. Cross-country trails joining the East and the West are being studied along the routes of the Lewis and Clark Trail, the Oregon Trail, the Santa Fe Trail, and the North Country Trail. Backpackers and riders don't have to wait for these trails to be opened. The national forests contain such fine trails as the switchback trail to Lake Katherine high on the top of 12,500-foot Pecos Baldy Peak in the Pecos Wilderness of the Santa Fe forest. The national parks and monuments also contain splendid opportunities for backpacking and trail riding.

The National Forest wildernesses and primitive areas now cover 14½ million acres, in which there are no roads, no mass recreational developments, and no timber cutting permitted. These areas range from the 5,000-acre Great Gulf in the White Mountain National Forest in New Hampshire to the 988,655-acre Selway-Bitterroot Wilderness in Idaho and Montana. The glaciers of Glacier Peak in Washington, the jagged Minarets of California, the rushing torrent of the Salmon River in Idaho, and the mysterious Superstition Mountains of Arizona are all included in protected areas. The wilderness country of the United States has declined to about 2 percent of its original size, but it remains a sanctuary, not only for wildlife and scientific studies of the interplay of natural forces, but also for the human spirit.

Canada has larger wilderness areas, and these too offer

backpackers' trails. Canada's newest national parks are among the most fascinating possibilities. Kluane National Park, Nahanni National Park, and Baffin Island National Park together total 18,630 square miles, an area larger than the states of Massachusetts, Connecticut, and Rhode Island put together. Kluane National Park, located in the Yukon Territory about 100 miles west of Whitehorse, encompasses high tundra regions, rain forests, great glaciers, lofty Mount Logan, Canada's highest mountain, and the St. Elias Mountains, Canada's highest mountain range. The Alaska Highway skirts the edge of the new park, but there are no roads and no marked trails.

Nahanni National Park is in the southwest corner of the Northwest Territories. In its confines backpackers encounter the rare Dall sheep and such scenic wonders as Rabbitkettle Hotspring, which is similar to the springs of Yellowstone; Virginia Falls, twice the height of Niagara Falls; Third Canyon, which is almost as deep as Arizona's Grand Canyon; as well as Second Canyon; and First Canyon, which has 3,500-foot walls hollowed by caves. The only way into this spectacular wilderness is to walk in from the Fort Simpson road.

Baffin Island National Park, northeast of Hudson Bay, is even more remote. I flew over it recently on a TWA flight from Paris to Chicago that followed a northern route between France and the American Midwest. From the air huge Baffin Island is a shocking wilderness of mountains and glaciers, into which fjords knife for up to 30 miles. The Penny Ice Cap is as much as 6,000 feet in depth and covers 2,200 square miles. The park contains the site of several ruined villages of the Thule Eskimo culture, which flourished thousands of years ago, but the nearest Eskimo settlements now are at Pangnirtung Fjord and on Broughton Island. Baffin Island undoubtedly represents one of the most challenging areas in the world for backpacking adventure, and it should not be trifled with. Nahanni and Kluane both must be treated with respect too. Together with other remote wilderness areas in North America, they remain as distant goals for the backpacker, who is well advised to begin his experiences much closer to home under much more easygoing circumstances.

When should a backpacker take to the trails? It is a good idea to time your trip to optimum conditions. Only a gold-mad Klondiker would attempt to go over the Chilkoot Trail in December, but it presents no serious dangers in July. In the desert Southwest it is best to avoid the summer heat, for it can be deadly. Late winter and early spring bring out the desert blooms. In the southwestern mountains, conditions are favorable from June 15 to October 1. In the northern Rockies or the High Sierras, however, there is a much shorter hiking season, so that you should not go into the high country until July 15, and you should be out by September 15. If you arrive too early or stay too late, you're apt to find high waters to ford, meadows and trails soft and muddy, and the threat of a blizzard hanging over you. We hiked in

Arkansas in July and regretted it on four days when the temperature cleared 100. Hiking in Florida is best from December through March or possibly April; the temperatures are cooler and since this is the dry season, you'll not be bedeviled by rain and bugs.

A beginning backpacker or trail rider may prefer to have his first wilderness experiences with one of the organized parties of the American Forestry Association, the Wilderness Society, or the Sierra Club. However, if he does his homework well, obtains the necessary equipment, and gets into reasonably good physical condition, he will be capable of venturing forth on his own.

The Pack on Your Back

Naturally enough, the first thing a backpacker needs is a pack that is properly fitted and balances well on his hips. Whether you prefer a packboard, framework, or rucksack, you'll carry your load with more grace and less strain if it saddles a good share of the weight on your hips. The Kelty is a lightweight aluminum version of the packboard. It is angled at the shoulder and waist to follow the shape of the body. Only its nylon bands actually fit against the back, and since the pack comes in different sizes, it can fit different heights and weights. Waist straps from the lower part of the frame are fastened just below the waist so that the pack will not swing and flop about when you are stepping from rock to rock or hiking up a precipitous trail. The pack attaches to the frame.

Packs contain outside pockets and at least one inside compartment. The outside pockets are handy for things that you may need during the day. Items that are not going to be used very often may be put at the bottom of an inside compartment unless they are heavy. Heavy weights should be placed high on the back and as close to the body as you can get them. Just as in preparing for any other kind of camping trip, things that go together may be packed together in plastic bags both to protect them from moisture and to keep them accessible.

A sleeping bag for backpacking puts the premium on weight. A water-repellent, down-filled bag is best. One that is part down and part feathers is preferable to a

Dacron bag. Probably a 2½-pound bag will be warm enough. A bag also must be large enough to be comfortable and yet small enough to roll up into a compact bundle to be packed. The mummy-type bag is probably best for backpacking, but some people prefer a rectangular bag, mainly because they feel cramped in a mummy. If you think of a mummy bag as a warm suit of clothing that moves with the body when you move at night, it no longer seems so cramping. Some people accustomed to sleeping in beds beneath sheets and blankets carry their sleeping habits into the woods, and they attempt to move around within their mummy bags and soon feel as if they're in a straitjacket. In any case, when you unpack your bag for use, fluff it up so as to get the maximum use out of the insulation.

Being cold at night is usually avoidable. An added lightweight blanket will give warmth. Because you cannot be certain of finding any duff at your campsite to make your bed soft and warm, you may want to bring along an air mattress, probably an abbreviated one that reaches only to the hips, or a pad made out of foam rubber or ensolite. Ensolite is a material that has closed air pockets and will not absorb water as does foam rubber, which acts like a sponge. A moistureproof ground cloth is also a necessity for a good sleep.

If your head is cold at night, your feet will soon become cold. A mummy bag usually has a built-in hood for warmth. Other bags have a flap that will help shield your head from drafts. In addition many hikers wear a wool cap at night. Long-handled underwear and wool socks may be needed too. However, if you overdress for the night so that you perspire, you are very likely going to feel the full impact of the chill when it settles down on your camp later in the night. Moisture in your bag will soon have your teeth chattering. The only thing colder than cold is damp and cold together. For the same reason, a backpacker facing a cold night never wears clothing to bed that has become wet with perspiration during the day.

Another approach to keeping warm, to be considered only with a high-quality down bag, is based on the idea that the bag works with the body heat. Putting on long underwear stops the interaction between body heat and the bag and, in effect, insulates you from the warmth the down should provide. One girl we know claims that she sleeps more cozily and comfortably when wearing only minimal underwear inside her down bag. Some sleeping-bag manufacturers agree with this theory, but it may not work for everyone.

The right clothing for a backpack depends on the weather conditions you're likely to encounter and the kind of terrain over which you plan to hike. Tough pants without cuffs (which only pick up sticks, burrs, and pebbles), a visored cap, and a long-sleeved shirt are best. Pants should not be so tight that they bind when the hiker really gets into his stride. A hiker should also avoid wearing faddish trousers with such an exaggerated flare that they are apt to catch on bushes or rocks or so long that they drag on the ground, picking up dirt and trash and threatening to tangle the feet. Stylish clothing is all right for town wear, but practical clothing is what a backpacker requires for the outdoors.

In warm climates shorts may be worn providing your legs are tanned enough not to burn in the sun and you are not going through brush or over sharp rocks that may scratch or tear. Similarly, under benign circumstances when it is not too cold or, on the other hand, a blistering sun is not burning down on your shoulders, you may want to wear a T-shirt instead of a long-sleeved shirt. You should wear two pairs of socks so that one slides within the other and protects your feet from friction. The outer pair of socks should be heavy, hiking weight, and the inner pair should be light. This will help prevent blisters from forming. We keep a wind-breaking jacket or sweater and a poncho handy in case it gets chilly or rain begins to fall. Backpackers may start out a hike on a chilly morning wearing both a jacket and a sweater. As the day gets warmer, they peel off a layer or two of clothing.

It is hard to get backpackers to agree on what kind of shoes to wear. A hiker's feet are the most important part of his body, and how to keep them happy and blister-free becomes a matter of almost morbid preoccupation. A good pair of hiking boots is designed to take up shocks, to support ankles and arches under the weight of the pack, and to give good traction. In wet weather, rubber boots may be good, but leather shoes, ankle-high with eyelets and lacing, are favored by most hikers. These hiking boots are comfortable on rocks, scree, and steep climbs. We prefer lug soles because they grip the surface. There are special shoes made for hiking on snow or ice, but we don't bother with them. On most hikes snow and ice are only incidental to the bare rocks and earth of the trail. We carry sneakers, moccasins, or down slippers along for wear in camp.

You'll also need a change of clothing, spare socks, extra shoelaces, underwear, handkerchiefs, and such oddments as a towel, toilet kit, canteen, mess kit, knife-and-fork set, toilet paper in a plastic wrap, flashlight with spare batteries and an extra bulb, notebook and pencil, compass, jackknife, needle and thread, safety pins, and some 40 feet of nylon cord. A supply of waterproof matches and a few candle stubs for starting fires are also needed. If you do not use a tent, you may also want to bring along a mosquito net that will cover your head and shoulders. This is particularly valuable for children, who may go to bed in the shank of the evening when the mosquitoes are still at their worst.

You'll want a first-aid kit. Your first-aid kit might contain Band-Aids, compresses, four-inch Ace bandage, a triangular bandage, antiseptic, aspirin, eye wash, and adhesive tape. You should be prepared for such first-aid emergencies as burns, sprains, abrasions, and headaches. If you're going into snake country, you should carry a snakebite kit. Bring along a pair of toenail clippers on your backpacking trip too, and cut your toenails square. This will help to keep you from developing various nail and toe problems. Some hikers also powder their feet, and you may want to do this. All hikers make sure that their socks are the correct size and that they have neither holes nor wrinkles in them. It is hard for most children to understand that it is also important to keep your feet clean. Dirty feet blister easily.

For years we backpacked with only a tarp or space blanket to keep off the rain or dew, but with the development of lightweight tents we've switched to nylon two-man tents that weigh only 4¾ pounds including pegs and aluminum supports. A nylon tent may be light in weight, but it has its disadvantages. Breath condenses within it, and unless there is adequate ventilation, you may have a misty rain of your very own right inside your tent. We also have some nylon tents that come with nylon flies, which make it unnecessary to close up the inner tent when it rains. This heads off the condensation problem, but adds to the weight problem—the combination weighs 7½ pounds. In any case, a backpack tent should be lightweight and compact for easy carrying. A few sheets of plastic can also come in handy to cover equipment during a rain.

If you stick to one-pot meals on your backpack, you need only bring along a number 10 tin can and a small aluminum kettle. We carry a pair of lightweight, nesting cooking pots. We don't bother with a frying pan and not many other backpackers do either. Utensils, a collapsible canvas bucket or collapsible plastic water container are also needed. A small garden trowel will come in handy to dig a latrine in camp or a small "cat" hole on the trail. If you are going to be hiking in an area where there will not be sufficient wood for cooking fires or in one of the places where wood fires are prohibited, you'll want to carry along a lightweight, one-burner gasoline or spirit stove. Some backpackers pack a hand ax, but we far prefer a folding brush saw. It is lighter in weight and is more efficient in gathering wood for a cooking fire. Axes are the single greatest cause of accidents in any camp, and they represent an unnecessary source of danger, particularly if you have kids along when you head into the wilderness.

As you round up your gear, weight is the thing to keep in mind. The pack carried by an adult or teenage male should not weigh more than 25 pounds before he adds his share of the provisions and group equipment. The pack carried by an adult or teenage female should weigh less. Even the smallest child in your group should carry something, perhaps a load up to one-fifth of his or her weight. The strongest hikers in the group should be ready to carry more of the group equipment and provisions than the weaker ones, since no group is able to go farther than its weakest members can go. Even so, an adult male should not try to lug around a total weight of more than 50 pounds, and he ought to try to keep it down to something closer to 40 pounds.

Buffalo Bill, one of the preeminent backpackers and trail riders of his day, lived on bacon, hardtack, and black coffee when he was on the trail, but he knew how to entertain Eastern nabobs and European royalty on the range when he had a mind to. At one of his high country al fresco banquets he served: Soup—buffalo tail. Fish—cisco broiled, fried dace. Entrees—salmi of prairie dog; stewed rabbit; fillet of buffalo aux champignons; roast elk, antelope, black-tailed deer, wild turkey; broiled teal, mallard, antelope chops, buffalo calf steaks, and young wild turkey. Vegetables—sweet potatoes, mashed potatoes, green peas. Dessert—tapioca pudding.

Not many of your trail dinners served complete with purple mountain majesties or an awesome gorge are likely to come up to this repast whomped up by the old scout's cooks, but you are capable of some mighty satisfying trail dinners. Freeze-dried and dehydrated foods enable a hiker to get along very well on from one to one and a half pounds of food per day. Foods should be selected for their high nutritional value per pound. Almost all kinds of food are available now in instant form for backpackers. They range from cheese omelets and hash brown potatoes to chicken paprika or a Swiss steak dinner. Most of these foods have been put up in handy packages to serve four. On a recent two-week backpack in Arkansas, our party of 12 bought all our freeze-dried and dehydrated foods at neighborhood supermarkets and saved some $75 over what camping supply stores would have charged for similar products. We bought in larger packages and repackaged in plastic bags for our hike. If anything you have bought is packaged in glass, repackage it into anodized aluminum or plastic containers.

A good backpacking trip depends upon physical conditioning, equipment, and training. You don't have to be tough-muscled to start, but if you are rather soft this will limit the amount of distance you should try to cover and the type of terrain you should challenge. If you have turned to flab, it would be a good idea to begin with some easy hikes in your neighborhood or in a nearby woods or park to get back into condition. In case you have a health problem, you should check with your physician before undertaking a backpack. Heart, bronchial, or other trouble might be worsened either by strenuous activity or high altitudes, and you should get your doctor's advice before deciding on a trip. It also would be wise to have your tetanus boosters brought up to date before going into the wilderness.

Training is nothing to boggle the mind. All you have to do is learn to put up your tent in your own backyard instead of doing it for the first time on the trail, and practice building a fire and cooking over it. The rest of your family or group should learn how to do everything too, so that all can join in on the chores and the fun. Any kid that needs wet-nursing shouldn't be on a backpacking trip.

A backpacking family or group should also be mentally

prepared. If the backpacking represents any challenge at all, it is likely to bring about changes in the personalities of the individuals involved, hopefully for the better. A backpacker should be prepared to accept change in himself and in his companions. The wilderness is not a suitable place for a person who thinks he loses face if he decides to turn back when conditions require it, and it is no place for backbiting or hurt feelings over small slights. It is no place for people who don't want to do their share of the camp and trail chores. A lot of the fun a person has on a backpack depends upon his mental attitude. A backpack is no place to escape from yourself; it's a place to fulfill yourself.

In the comfort of your home take a good look at your experience and knowledge, your equipment, and your physical condition. Then plan a hike that will be within the limits of your capabilities. Backpacking is a sport that the elderly can follow, and it is equally open to young children. Hiking along a trail on Isle Royale, we came upon a young mother and father with a sturdy little boy of about four. The boy had a minibackpack of his own, but since his mother was carrying him at the time, it wasn't doing the family's weight-toting capacity much good. Such a hiking family with a small boy or girl can do very well, but it should confine itself to suitable distances and trail conditions.

Joe Wampler, one of the West Coast's veteran trailers, annually takes parties over the John Muir Trail.

"The age range of hikers is from 8½ to 72 years," he says. "One hiker of 70 did the entire Muir Trail."

On Wilderness Society hikes and trail rides, family participation is encouraged, but the society cautions in its booklet *A Way to the Wilderness,* "We have observed that parents with children under seven years of age on a trip often spend so much time concerning themselves with the youngsters that they do not fully enjoy the outing themselves." This is doubtless so, for we've encountered families on the trail in which mothers and fathers hover over much older kids in such a foolish fashion that neither adults nor children have a good time. They might as well have stayed at home.

The size of a group is also a rather elastic thing. The Wilderness Society limits its horseback trips to groups of no more than 16 and its hiking trips to no more than 18. Some parks and wilderness areas limit groups to as few as 10 in order to protect the environment. Your group should not be any larger than its leadership can handle without strain or tension. It should never be smaller than two, for even a seasoned backpacker ought to have company in case of trouble. Also, there ought to be a congenial soul around to share both the pleasures and troubles ahead.

On the Trail

At last you are heading for your jump-off point for your first backpack. If you are hiking in high altitudes and are not accustomed to them, you should not start over the trail until you've had a couple of days to get acclimatized. Give your heart and lungs a chance to adjust to thinner air at elevations over 6,000 feet, and your group will perform with more vigor and comfort on the trail. You'll minimize the chances of becoming ill with high altitude sickness.

Before you start over the trail, it is a good thing to make your final hiking plans. At home you have presumably roughed out your route over the trails shown on your map. You've set your sights on daily hikes of perhaps 10 miles and have counted into this total an extra mile for each 1,000 feet your topographical maps show that your trail climbs. An extra mile should also be figured for each 1,500 feet that the trail descends. You've figured in time for a swim in a mountain stream, berrying along the way, watching wildlife, or just stretching out on a grassy bank and watching the clouds drift by. Now as you get set for the first day's hike, keep in mind that you also need daylight hours for setting up camp, cooking dinner, and cleaning up.

Before you begin your hike, it is important to check in with a Forest Service or national park or state park ranger. (If there is no official available, find a local person who knows the area well and who can alert rescue parties if you do not return on schedule.) Let the ranger know the number of people in your party, their names, your proposed route and destination, your estimated time of return, and where you have parked your car. You'll also pick up your fire permit at this time and obtain any last-minute advice concerning fire conditions, the shape the trail is in, good places to camp, the availability and safety of water, and what the weather is likely to be. Even if the weather forecast is good, be prepared for bad weather. The ranger can tell you about what hazards may exist in the area you plan to enter and what particular attractions it may have. This is also the time to go over your maps with the ranger so you can be certain that you are reading them correctly.

Vic Gaines is a lean Forest Service ranger who is stationed at Mena, Arkansas. He directed us to a camping site at the head of our trail through the Ouachita Mountains, and he studied our map of old logging roads to let us know which ones would serve our purposes. Then he talked to our group about the pleasures and pitfalls of the mountains. He spoke not only about the wildlife and scenery ahead but also about ticks, chiggers, and poison ivy. After he told us that the water was befouled by wild hogs that romp in the streams, we were certain to pop halazone tablets into every canteen we filled. We made arrangements to touch base at another ranger station on the far side of the forest. A backpacker should either come out where he goes in so that a ranger knows he's finished his trip safely or make it certain as to where and when he will come out of the woods. Finally, it is important to let people at home know he's started into the wilderness and when he should return.

The trail may begin innocently enough in a picnic area and then meander through a pine forest mixed with stands of oak, shagbark hickory, and ironwood. Birds warble as you stride along at a brisk pace. Rocks stick up through the forest floor. Only a mile or so into the woods you come upon your first wildlife. A magnificent buck raises his antlered head and stares at you from only a few hundred yards away. Then he springs off with the arrow-flight grace that a deer alone can manage. You come to a jumble of talus blocks and have to work around them and finally up onto them. The going gets tough. You've started on your backpack.

Things are going to go well for you because you have prepared for the hike. The leader will put into practice the things that he's learned at home and on your trial hikes. He should set a pace that is easy for the member of the party with the shortest legs. It's not going to be much fun if a leader tires everyone out on the first day.

A steady and rhythmic pace will get a backpacker to his goal for the day with far less effort that the hurry-up-and-slow-down gait that characterizes some neophyte hikers. The pace should be an easy one that even the weakest hiker in the party can keep up for 45 minutes to an hour. At first it may be necessary for the leader to make a conscious effort to hike more slowly. But this technique will pay off, for later in the day the party will hike with less fatigue because they conserved their energy in the beginning. It seems to be particularly hard for young leaders to conserve their energy in the morning so that they have pep left for the afternoon. Two and a half miles per hour is a good hiking speed on an easy trail. Regular rest periods are desirable even if the hikers aren't tired. Then the hikers don't remove their packs, but

simply sit down, loosen their waistbands, and lean back. If the going has been rugged, this can feel far more comfortable and luxurious than any armchair at home. During a break on the trail, a hiker who feels that he may be developing a blister pulls off his shoes and socks to give his feet a glance. If a blister is threatening, he can head it off by covering the tender spot with a Band-Aid or some moleskin, which will reduce friction.

After we are on the trail for about half an hour in the morning, we pause to adjust our packs. Sometimes a pack will cut into a hiker's shoulders and make it necessary to readjust the straps. They may be either too tight or too loose. Perhaps his waistband needs tightening to keep the pack snug against his body. Some hikers like the waistband at about the height of their waist, but as a rule we keep the bands riding just above the hips.

The hardest place to hike on a backpack is at the rear. The leader assigns a strong and experienced hiker as the rearguard. The rearguard serves as an inspiration to the laggards and may also pick up pieces of equipment that sometimes fall off even experienced backpackers. The weakest hikers, far from being allowed to straggle behind, are placed up close to the front of the party where they will find they do very much better. If the party is made up of adults and kids, it is important for a responsible adult to stick to the rear. The one exception is in dangerous country, where he should either be in the lead or immediately behind a young leader so as to give him quick advice or take action himself in the event of an emergency.

You'll find hiking a lot easier if you swing your hips to lengthen your stride. Once I came upon a party of hikers in the French Alps, and my companion and I could not help but laugh. Their buttocks were swishing back and forth as they hurried along the road, and it was a comical sight. We quit laughing when we saw the speed their long strides were making. Since most North Americans are likely to put appearance before efficiency, a compromise stride might be employed. It is also important to toe in a little. This gives better balance, particularly beneath a pack's weight, and makes hiking easier. When you are climbing a hill, do not push with your toes. It may not injure an adult hiker, but pack-toting boys and girls, who are still growing, can pull their heel tendons in this way. Nobody likes to see a brave kid cry. A pulled tendon is very painful. Nobody likes to carry him or his pack, either.

As you climb a hill, zigzag if the pitch is steep. Just as a truck driver will gear his machine down to climb a grade, gear yourself down by taking shorter steps at approximately the same pace you've been using on level terrain. If you still get out of breath, stop and pause for a moment at every two or three steps. On steep downhill grades, a locked-knee rest stop will enable you to pause from time to time as long as you find it necessary. Then when you start down again, flex your knees, lean back a little, and cushion your steps. If you relax your body at the same time, you can rest while letting gravity help take you down the hill. The main thing is to keep your descent under careful control so that you don't take a header, which beneath a pack can be more than upsetting.

A hiking party should never hike to exhaustion. A reasonable daily limit for most hikers would be 8 or 10 miles, although there are hardy teams that easily make 25 or 35 miles a day. In the mountains of North Burma the Kachin people, with whom I served in the American Kachin Rangers during World War II, made an almost impossible 50 miles a day, starting early and going late at a pace that was as much a run as it was a walk.

Some rugged individualists will insist on hiking alone or splitting off from a group for forays of their own. This often leads to confusion and serious trouble. A party should stay together. If there are good maps and the country is familiar, however, it might be all right to have one part of the group forge ahead to establish a camp while the others come along at a slower pace, taking photos, viewing the wildlife, or simply nursing some aching muscles. No advance or rear group should ever be made up entirely of inexperienced backpackers who are not prepared to hike safely by themselves. In dangerous country there is real safety in numbers. One person alone runs a lot more risk than do two, and three or even four are safer than two.

On a typical day's hike our hikers eat a light, high-carbohydrate breakfast and then about 10 o'clock snack on beef jerky, pemmican, or chocolate. As a rule, we eat an uncooked lunch that is heavy with both carbohydrates and proteins, but no fats. Fats make a hiker sick to his stomach just as they do a person who eats a heavy meal and goes out and plays a strenuous game of football. A midafternoon snack is similar to that of the morning. We count on a big, well-cooked meal in the evening with plenty of liquids to make up for the loss of moisture from our bodies through perspiration while on the trail. Sitting around the campfire after dinner we sip hot chocolate or bouillon for the nourishment, the liquid, the warmth, and the sociability. It's also a good time to roast marshmallows. A chocolate bar just before turning in will stoke up the body's fires and keep a hiker warmer as he's falling asleep.

Not many years ago hikers were urged to practice what was called water discipline. It was argued that drinking too much water on the trail would cause a person to become nauseated and faint. This myth has been exploded, and now hikers are urged to drink water throughout the day. Perspiration on a summer hike will add up to a gallon daily. To keep up with this water loss, a hiker should drink at least a cup an hour. Since more water is actually needed than a person's thirst indicates, it is sometimes desirable to put extra salt on food just to stimulate thirst. Heat exhaustion will come quickly if water intake is not sufficient.

A party of hikers should stick to the trail. Blazed trail markers and other indicators show where the trail goes. If you come to a switchback, don't cut across to the next leg of the trail. It not only squanders the energy that you may need later, but it also cuts a track through vegetation that may not heal for a long time to come. It can open up the hillside to erosion.

Even if you are following a trail, keep oriented. Match your map to the terrain around you as you hike so that you know where you are and how far you have to go to your proposed campsite. Take mental notes on natural and man-made features of importance around you so that you'll be able to retrace your steps if you somehow get off the trail and become lost. It is important to keep oriented as to the direction you are hiking. Occasional compass readings will prove helpful.

It is also important to keep an alert eye out for possible dangers on the trail. Poor footing on a rocky ledge, rotten logs, or falling rocks are a few things to be on the lookout for. In climbing among talus, a loose boulder may roll from beneath the feet of a hiker and plunge down on a hiker coming up the trail below him. For this reason hikers avoid following closely after or beneath a companion when they are climbing among rocks. Sheer cliffs, steep grades, and hard-packed snowfields are also dangers of the trail that require care. The leader should pick a safe route across a snowfield. He avoids the edges of a field or rocks sticking out through the snow, because the crust will be soft in such spots. It may break beneath a hiker's weight and drop him through the field to rocks below. A hiker can also lose his footing on a slippery and steep field and go shooting down the slope to possible injury or death.

Every trail has its particular dangers. At the end of a day's hike in Arkansas, we had to check one another for seed ticks. After a night's sleep on a trail in the Big Bend of Texas, we had to look over our clothing and bedding for scorpions. They may not be deadly, but they can give a person a nasty sting. Poisonous snakes are also a problem in some areas. The same concern that a camper should show them must be shown by a backpacker. Timid as most snakes may be, a hiker, particularly in rocky country, has to be on the watch for them.

Wildlife usually represents little real danger on the trail. But on Isle Royale we talked to a backpacker who had been chased up a tree by an angered moose, and we heard of a doctor who was treed by the island's wolf pack. We were luckier on Isle Royale. We met only one moose cow and her calf on the trail, and she didn't wait long enough for our amateur photographers to unlimber their cameras before she set off with powerful strides and vanished over a forested ridge. Wherever you are hiking, though, you may find yourself confronted by an outraged mother if you come between a moose or buffalo cow and her calf.

Bears are another matter. We've never had any trouble with them either in camp or on the trail, but some hikers have had grim encounters with grizzlies. The same advice that campers in general should follow also applies with equal force to backpackers in particular. Cleanliness in camp is the best defense. Never sleep close to where you did your cooking, and don't sleep with food. Since backpackers are more apt to penetrate remote areas where grizzly, Kodiak, or even polar bears may be in residence, they are more likely to encounter these sometimes ferocious animals. The most dangerous bear of all is a sow who is fearful that a hiker means to harm her cubs. Bears become dangerous when they are approached too closely, are taken by surprise, and when they have lost their fear of men because tourists have spoiled them.

Sensible backpackers never hike alone in bear country, and they never bring along dogs, for they are bound to infuriate Bruin. If fresh tracks, excrement, or recent claw scrapings on a tree indicate that a bear is close ahead, make a detour. Spook him on purpose by keeping upwind so that he can scent you and follow his natural aversion to the odor of man and keep away. For the most part, an overly talkative companion on the trail is a nuisance, for he distracts his fellow hikers from enjoying the outdoors around them. But in bear country the babble of his voice, even if he is retelling a boring series of barstool jokes, can be a lifesaver. Hikers can also sing, rattle a cooking pot, or wear bells to warn bears that they are coming down the trail.

Bears were the most dangerous opponents that mountain men met in the wilderness West. Dr. William Fraser Tolmie, a British ship's surgeon and naturalist, made an early 19th century reconnaissance of the Pacific Northwest. He looked for herbs and made the first ascent of Mount Rainier. He also met a trapper named Mackay and jotted down in his journals that "Mackay has had many encounters with the bear, and the best way he says when a wounded bear rushes at you is to stand and reload and when he comes near if your gun is unloaded look at him steadily and he will not attack but raise on his hind legs, will continue to return your gaze until tired of his position when he betakes himself quietly off."

This sounds like a dubious method of dealing with an aroused bear. In the first place, a bear usually will not harm you if you don't harm him. It is true at least that when confronted with a bear, you must remain calm. You can't beat a bear in a run, so there is nothing to gain by trying to flee. Obviously you don't walk toward the bear; you either remain motionless or back slowly away from it. If the bear rises to his hind feet, you know that he is contemplating an attack. Sweet-talk him. He may understand from the tone of your voice that you wish him no harm, but while you're chatting with him, look for the nearest tree to climb. Sometimes you may drop a canteen or a cap to distract him from you as you slip away.

In dangerous bear country set up your camp where there are trees handy. But if there are no trees within reach when a bear attacks, the best thing to do is fall to the ground on your stomach or side with your legs pulled up to your chest. Clasp your hands over the back of your head and play dead. The bear may only sniff at you or give you a few not-so-affectionate slaps. It takes a great deal of nerve to take the opossum's way out of trouble, but it is the best thing to do.

A thunderstorm is another serious danger on the trail. If the sky lowers and it looks as if a storm is brewing, do not continue to ascend a trail. It is a good idea to stay off high ground and ridges in a storm because your chances of being struck by lightning there are all too good. A shallow cave, a cliff edge, a lone tree, or a tower are also treacherous to be near in a storm. A hiker who is caught in the open without a chance of getting into the protection of brush or trees should remove any metal gear from his person and crouch with only the soles of his shoes touching the ground.

A snowstorm in the high country can be even more hazardous. When snow begins to fall, stop or fall back to the nearest safe point. Set up a survival camp. It is sensible to continue on to your original destination only if it is at a reasonable distance and you are clearly oriented as to where you are and have good visibility. A backpacker should not sit or lie down in the snow to rest, nor should he exercise so much that he works up a sweat. Overexposure and freezing can result. A seasoned backpacker learns to roll with nature's punches and does not fret if he has to alter or abort a plan. At the very least, a storm is a good test of his equipment, his training, and his willpower.

To cross a stream a backpacker first looks for rocks or a log that may allow him to cross dry-shod. He is care-

ful of his footing and never leaps from stone to stone, because a slip and a tumble into a swift current can be a serious thing when he is wearing a pack. If he has to wade the stream, he removes his shoes and socks. When the bottom cannot be seen or has sharp rocks or debris on it, he puts his shoes back on. In case the current is swift enough that it may sweep him off his feet, he uses a rope belay and may set up downstream rescue posts. It is important to keep socks dry, for wet socks make blisters almost inevitable. A cautionary word: It is far better to hike scores of miles out of the way looking for a bridge or a safe crossing or to return over a trail than to attempt to cross a stream in flood.

Backpackers with experience stop early enough to set up their camp before dusk. It is particularly dangerous to travel in the mountains after dark unless somebody in the party has expert knowledge of the trail. There is no need for a party to continue on along a trail, come what may, in order to reach a certain campsite. Backpackers carry on their backs everything they need for a safe and comfortable night, and they are usually far better off if they stop before dark overtakes them.

Off-trail backpacking should not be done by beginner backpackers, but once a group of hikers has mastered the craft, they will find even greater pleasure and satisfaction in going where their spirit leads them. A thorough knowledge of map and compass work and skill in orienteering are essential if an off-trail backpack is to be successful. But the ability to get around in the wilds is not restricted to a select few. Our ancestors, employing far less equipment, did it with impunity.

A backpacker who gets lost is in much the same fix as is any other camper, and he should follow the advice given to campers who have wandered away from camp. Because of the nature of backpacking, he may be in a more remote area than other campers are likely to reach. Ordinarily he should just set up a survival camp where he has water handy, build a fire, and make himself comfortable. If he stays put, he's more likely to be found, since presumably he's told other people approximately where he was going. He may have to wait only a few hours or perhaps a few days. Perhaps he can reconstruct his route. If he checks recognizable landmarks against a map, establishes his directions, and uses his head, chances are he'll discover that he isn't lost after all. If he decides to leave the spot, he should leave a note telling what direction he is going and then mark the trail that he makes so that a search party can follow him.

Unless your group has had considerable experience in backpacking, it is best to use established campsites. In some areas the rules require you to use an established site, or there may be shelters provided. If there is a shelter, live by the regulations established for its use.

A good campsite should have drinking water, firewood, level ground, and shelter from the wind. Winds blow mainly from the west, but they also will blow from a lake and down a canyon at night. A view or a babbling stream to lull you to sleep are fine things too, but make certain that the stream isn't likely to flood you out. Follow the same rules of good camping that any other camper follows. Face your tent away from the wind and toward the morning sun so that your equipment will have as much chance as possible to dry out before you pack it for the next day's journey.

When your party arrives at a campsite, pick a place for your fire. Existing fire scars should be used. Find a place for your beds. Gather all the tinder, kindling, and firewood that you need before you start your cooking fire. Make certain that you've followed safe fire-building procedures so that you will not endanger the camp and the woods around you. A backpacker protects the purity of the water supply as does any other practiced camper. He never washes his pans and dishes in a stream. Detergents and soaps can endanger aquatic life as well as make the water impure to drink, so he disposes of his wash water where it will not drain into a stream and where it will not injure nearby plants. Backpackers take turns with cooking, fire building, dishwashing, getting water, cleaning up the campsite, and burning trash. Everybody helps with such chores as digging the latrine or simmering the dried fruit for the next morning's compote. Before it gets dark, pick the rocks, sticks, and pinecones from your sleeping area. If possible, spread out pine needles, dried grass, or leaves. Erect your tents or simply put down your ground cover, air mattress or pad, and sleeping bags, and sleep beneath the stars.

Above all, be a fanatic about keeping a clean camp. In bear country, your life may depend on it; anywhere that you backpack, your reputation depends on it. If the last party of hikers who camped at your site left tin cans and other trash, give them the cussing out they justly deserve, but then clean up the mess. No backpacker wants to camp in a slum, and the trash can be as dangerous as it is unsightly. Backpackers burn all their burnable trash and garbage and then pack out all such refuse as flattened cans, bottles, and aluminum foil. They bury nothing, for they can rest assured that wild animals will only dig it up again.

When a backpacking group breaks camp in the morning, they make absolutely certain that every spark of the fire is out. In remote areas it is vital to avoid any risk of a forest fire. A backpacker also avoids smoking on the trail, not only because smoking cuts down the wind that he desperately needs on a strenuous climb, but also because it is a danger to the woods around him. If he is the sort who goes berserk if he can't have a cigarette, he finds a safe place, sits down, and buries any ashes in mineral soil or crushes them out on a rock. He has to carry the filter out with him, as he would any other trash. He may want to make a pocket ashtray out of a tinfoil lined, freeze-dried dinner packet. Otherwise he does his smoking around the campfire at night and explains to his fellow backpackers that he would like to give up the habit but just hasn't got the willpower.

TRAIL RIDING

If a backpacker meets saddle horses or horses, burros, or mules carrying packs on the trail, he moves to the side and remains quiet as they pass. A friendly "hello" doesn't hurt any, but he should avoid spooking the animals.

A horseback trip has its special pleasures. There's a feeling of camaraderie that has always linked riders together, whether they were knights, cowboys, or Tartar nomads. Sit around the campfire at night and listen to the horses grazing nearby, and you'll have some very primitive but deeply contented feelings.

You'll also get to know some fascinating guys who are outfitters or guides. We rode with Buck Newsome, a one-time border patrol ranger, into the Chisos Mountains of Big Bend National Park in Texas. The trail wound down into a canyon where high cliffs rose about us and a red hawk wheeled overhead. We came upon a waterfall that dashed out of a cleft in a mountain and tumbled hundreds of feet to the canyon floor. I'll never forget my half-mad horse, Pawnee, for he sneezed in the cold shadows and became a virtual equine hypochondriac. In the bright sun, he was full of exuberance and sniffed flowers almost as a Frenchman sniffs a good brandy.

When the day's ride was done, we sat and talked with Buck about the old days on the border. After our ride into the mountains, I understood why western historian Walter Prescott Webb once remarked, "Big Bend fever is called being homesick for a place you can never call home." The Big Bend is far too fierce a country to make home, but it will always have a deep claim on anybody who has camped, hiked, or ridden in it.

On most organized horseback trips, the horses are gentle professionals who know the trails and don't mind teaching you about them. The horses can be suited to your own riding skill. Pack stock carry the loads so that a trail rider doesn't have to worry about lugging his own gear. This doesn't mean that you can bring along the most elaborate outdoor equipment and clothing, because outfitters strictly limit the amount of dunnage they will carry for you on the pack stock. It is not only more expensive to bring along additional pack animals, but it also increases the impact of your group on the environment of the very wilderness that you've set out to enjoy. With some once-exciting pack trip areas already closed to horses because of overgrazing at camping sites, it is critical for trail riders to protect the remaining places.

Today there are still fascinating areas open to pack trips. Riders can explore the saguaro cactus lands of the Superstition Mountains of Arizona and look for the Lost Dutchman Mine. They can ride into the high mountain valleys of the Pecos Wilderness of New Mexico. The Bob Marshall Wilderness near Missoula, Montana, is one of the last strongholds of the grizzly. In Canada the Banff National Park wilderness is a glory of flower-strewn alpine meadows, high passes, and lakes with the unforgettable names of Ogg and Magog. Even Yellowstone National Park, with its torrent of auto visitors, has wilderness areas that are a haven for elk, moose, and bear. You'll find a lonely, unspoiled geyser much as it was when the region was known as "Colter's Hell." A pack trip will take you far from the haunts of RV and auto tent campers, but horses cannot begin to take you into the rough terrain that a man traveling on his own two feet can go.

There are fine horseback trip areas in the Black Hills of South Dakota and in the East as well, and a rider doesn't have to set out into the wilderness to find riding pleasure. Wisconsin has miles of trails in the Kettle

Moraine State Forest and at Wildcat Mountain State Park. The New Prospect Horseman's Campground is at the Northern Unit of the Kettle Moraines, and the Horseman's Recreation Area is in the Southern Unit. A fenced corral, parking space for horse-hauling rigs, and water for your mounts are all available; but the real enjoyment comes from the trails and, after a day's vigorous ride, from the pleasure of sitting around a campfire with your convivial riding companions. Minnesota is also opening up the 70-mile-long Minnesota Valley Trail, which loops along the Minnesota River from Fort Snelling State Park near St. Paul south to Le Sueur. Ohio has developed a horseman's camp with hitching rail at Bear Lake, in the magnificent wooded hills along the Ohio River.

Most people who go packing travel with a pack trip outfitter, who usually provides everything but a sleeping bag and air mattress. A rider may prefer going with an outfitter such as Joe Wampler, who offers horseback trips over the John Muir Trail in California, to the bottom of Havasu Canyon in Grand Canyon National Park, or into the Chiricahua Mountains of Arizona. Or the trail rider may instead decide to go with the American Forestry Association's Trail Riders of the Wilderness. The Trail Riders make 22 annual rides into the western high country from Arizona to Montana and into the Canadian Rockies for periods of from one week to 12 days. There are also five eastern rides: two in the Cacapon Mountains of West Virginia, and three in the beautiful Great Smokies of North Carolina.

The Wilderness Society also offers outstanding horseback trips into such places as the Weminuche Wilderness of Colorado, the Selway-Bitterroot Wilderness of Montana, and the North Cascades Wilderness of Washington. The society also operates hiking trips with pack stock into the wilderness in much the same way as early-day explorers traveled. Some of the finest of these trips are into the remote Kenai National Moose Range from Kasilof, Alaska, and into the Washakie Wilderness from Jackson, Wyoming.

The Sierra Club also offers burro trips to such places as Miter Basin in the Sierra Nevada and other horseback trips into the high country of California. Saddle trips into the Teton Wilderness Area just south of Yellowstone National Park and east of the Grand Teton National Park are also possibilities.

Another popular thing to do is to go along on one of the annual trail rides that have grown up across the country since the Rancheros Visitadores (Visiting Ranchers) first rode out of Santa Barbara, California, in 1930 to commemorate the early days of the Golden State. In the pioneering days, ranchers rode from ranch to ranch to join in on the fiestas. The six-day Black Hills Trail Ride in South Dakota is open to all riding members of the family and begins in Custer State Park. Many other rides are stag, and the ride conducted by Las Damas (The Ladies) out of Wickenburg, Arizona, is for women only.

Some trail rides are small local affairs that may be gotten up at the drop of a ten-gallon hat, but others may be well organized and have an enormous number of riders. Fourteen hundred riders take the Maywood Trail Ride in southwestern Nebraska. Since the town of Maywood has a population of only 300, it is not surprising that the people riding out onto the western plains have come from all over the country. The Badlands Trail Ride in North Dakota; the 100-mile ride from Victoria, Illinois, sponsored by the Illinois State Stock Horse Association; and the Chief Joseph Trail Ride in the Northwest are all outstanding. The Chief Joseph Ride appeals to history buffs, and every year it follows another path of the celebrated chief. The cost is low, but a participant must ride an Appaloosa horse, a breed perfected by the chief's Nez Percé Indians.

Whether you provide your own animals or rent them, you must know how to handle them correctly and load them properly. A burro may carry about 75 pounds in weight, and a mule or horse will bear up to 200 pounds, depending upon its strength. When you camp, your stock should be kept out of the campground area. You should not tie your stock to trees, for the animals will paw and trample the soil over the trees' root systems. In a busy summer, after a number of parties have passed on a horse trail, the trees can be in a very sorry condition. String ropes together or locate a hitchrack away from the trees. Hobbles will keep your stock from wandering off at night. It is also desirable to bring along pellets or grain to supplement the stock's forage, so that they don't overgraze the areas where you camp.

On a pack trip you'll find you are happiest if you wear sturdy blue jeans that have been softened to keep them from chafing, long-sleeved shirts, and a broad-brimmed felt hat. Some riders also wear long-handled underwear to keep the chafing at the minimum. The backpacker goes to great lengths to keep his feet from blistering, but the rider gives just as affectionate care to what is for him a more important part of his anatomy.

A trail rider usually takes along more than a backpacker does because he has less stringent weight restrictions. The trail rider will want not only a sleeping bag and air mattress but also probably a lightweight extra blanket. Certainly a slicker or raincoat that he can wear either when riding or walking, tent, cooking utensils and other camp gear, food, riding boots or high shoes, and moccasins or sneakers for camp. He will need to pack his personal belongings in a stout duffel or side-zipper bag much as he would pack for a backpack. His fishing rod should be in a metal case. The total weight of his personal gear should not be more than 50 pounds.

They say in the Black Hills that "the outside of a horse is the best medicine for the inside of a man." This well may be. At least a citizen who hikes or rides soon forgets his workaday job and discovers that life on the trail is both easygoing and friendly.

Wilderness Survival

Four 12-year-old boys, bent on testing their wilderness survival skills, left our outdoors training camp at Portage Bay on the Upper Peninsula of Michigan and hiked to the tip of a wooded peninsula. They wore long pants, long-sleeved shirts, and hiking shoes. They had chosen to carry a poncho and a jackknife, and they each had a piece of flint. Just before leaving camp each also had reluctantly accepted a canteen of water.

It was mid-July, but anticipating a cool night, they immediately fell to work cutting poles from dead trees and lashing them together with plant fibers to build a snug shelter out of their poncho. This makeshift "tent" was set back against the protective roots of a fallen tree. Nearby, one of the boys then scraped his flint with a knife until a spark caught a handful of fluff from cattails and dandelions with tiny slivers of pine worked in. Birch bark and pine twigs made the tinder, and soon the boys were putting on kindling and fuel wood and had a fire for warmth and cooking.

What to cook? One boy tended the fire and the others, using their newly acquired knowledge of edible plants, went out to look for food. They pulled up burdock and arrowroot to boil the roots for vegetables. They picked thimbleberries, raspberries, and tiny wild strawberries. They made strawberry-leaf tea for a hot drink. They set snares for rabbits, but no rabbit obliged them. They waded in the shallow waters of the bay and discovered crayfish sheltering beneath the rocks. In no time at all they had a flavorful soup made of crayfish tails.

That night they stretched out on their still-hungry bellies in the sand around the fire and talked. They were determined to be better providers in the morning. The dark around them grew scary. One boy kept thinking of a bobcat that he'd surprised an hour or two before as the beautiful animal lapped a drink of water from the bay. Another boy kept wishing that they'd cooked the crayfish farther from their shelter. Perhaps the cooking smells might attract a bear, and who needed a bear at a time like this? Shooting stars flashed and streaked. The wind soughed mysteriously in the pines. A loon cackled out on the bay. Then in an ensuing silence they heard heavy footsteps approaching.

"I looked at Ed," said one boy later on, "and his eyes were big as apples."

Dazzled by the fire, they could not see what it was in the dark. There was a blurred something there, big and hulking. Then it turned and went crashing off into the forest. They slept fitfully, scrunched together in their shelter to stay warm, each wanting to be one of the boys in the middle. Finally the sun came up out of the bay, spangling the new morning with light.

"I watched the sun rising out of the water," one boy recalled. "It was life."

In the early morning light, the boys stared at the bear tracks that led to within ten feet of their campfire. Back at the training camp that night they talked about what their brief experience in wilderness survival had meant to them.

"We learned a few things that it would be good to know in a real emergency," said one.

"It was a challenge," said another.

They agreed it gave them more confidence in themselves and felt that it would help them not only in the woods, but also carry over to home and school. They also said they had a deeper respect for the wilderness and were more eager than ever to learn how to do things right in the out-of-doors.

"I'll remember it all my life," summed up one boy.

Some people think that wilderness survival experiences are perhaps all right for boys, but that they are not appropriate for girls. This is patent nonsense. A 12-year-old girl, as her survival test, left her training camp and trekked alone into the Alaska wilderness north of Fairbanks for a similar experience. Unknown to her, a silent observer from her camp watched as she built a trap and snared a ptarmigan, broiled it over a fire she had started with flint, and built a shelter against the cold. Did she think the experience was worthwhile?

"I'll remember it all my life," she said, sharing word by word the reaction of the boy at Portage Bay.

Of course, men and women who are training boys and girls in the outdoors way of life should never put them in a position where they may jeopardize their health and safety. They should be certain that the area in which the youngsters are practicing their skills is secure from either wilderness dangers or from the sick outreach of mankind's disturbed society.

Training and experience in wilderness survival provide a person, young or old, with psychological and spiritual values, but at the same time the practical knowledge learned may save lives. Major Tom Stover, Chief of the Survival Training Division, Headquarters, Air Transport Command, is in charge of the Air Force's training in water survival, Arctic survival, and wilderness survival. It is his job to direct the 36th Combat Crew Training Wing at Fairchild Air Force Base, 12 miles from Spokane, Washington. This is the famous wilderness survival school to which all pilots and navigators and other members of flight crews, men and now women too, must go before they can take up their crew duties. Before the Air Force required crew members to attend the school, scores of flyers lost in jungles and forests after their planes were forced down either due to accident or enemy action could have survived had they known how to deal with wilderness conditions. Rescue teams found that they often had been uninjured or only slightly injured, but that they had panicked and had done everything wrong.

"Many crew members are from big cities," Major Stover explains. "They get scared of a tree that isn't surrounded by pavement. They get rattled and start blundering around. Once a person is in a survival situation,

it is too late to instill the knowledge necessary to survive."

Major Stover, as well as most other wilderness survival experts, doesn't believe that it is necessary to learn more than the basic skills that provide fire, shelter, food, and potable water, and first aid if necessary.

"Know these skills and you'll have self-confidence, which will keep you cool in an emergency," he believes. "Then the ingenious mind of the Yankee can go to work and make life supportable if not comfortable in any wilderness."

Every backpacker or wilderness camper should carry along a survival kit. Air Force personnel, for instance, are issued kits which contain such things as waterproof matches, flint and steel, signal mirrors, even flares to attract searching parties. They are also issued the Air Force Manual 64-3, which is available to the public from the U.S. Printing Office, a handy and compact book to carry into the field.

Grandma Gatewood, the legendary hiker who first traveled the entire Appalachian Trail from Georgia to Maine at the age of 69 and went on to hike trails all over the nation until her death in 1973 at the age of 85, carried a "possible" bag, just in case she got into trouble. She favored needle and thread, a Swiss Army knife, first-aid supplies, and a spoon. The mountain men of the western frontier carried such things as a bow drill, flint rock and charred cloth, a stretch of fishing line, feathers for fletching arrows, and sinew. They knew, as a modern hiker should know, that a "flint" may be any hard stone, such as agate, quartz, or jasper, as well as flint itself. A pocketknife makes the most likely piece of steel to carry.

Today's backpackers and canoeists should put together their own survival kit instead of buying one ready-made at a sporting goods store, and they should practice survival techniques employing the items in it at home so that they won't waste what might be precious time in field conditions.

A fire can be a life and death matter. It provides warmth, heat for cooking, and perhaps attracts rescue parties. On a regular outdoor expedition, waterproofed matches are the best answer. You can dip wooden matches in paraffin and put them in a small, closed container.

If you don't have matches, whether through choice as a wilderness test or through unforeseen circumstances, there are several other ways to start a fire.

To light a fire with a magnifying glass, eyeglasses, the lens from a field glass or a flashlight, or the bottom of a pop bottle, focus the sun's rays onto a tinder bundle. Even a piece of ice shaped like a lens can concentrate the sun's rays enough to light a fire.

Flint and steel is the most popular way to start a wilderness survival fire. The main thing to keep in mind is to be sure the tinder is very fine. The pith from a dry cattail, from a plant stem, or a piece of charred cotton cloth makes good tinder. Strike the steel downward against the flint in order to spray the hot spark into the tinder bundle, which should be located directly below. When there is a wisp of smoke, blow on the spark, and be sure the breath is gentle and long. As the spark glows red, cradle the tinder bundle in your hands and pick it up. Blow some more. When the spark spreads and glows redder still, blow a little harder until it bursts into flame. Putting the bundle back down on the ground, you can add kindling, the smallest stuff first, then fuel wood until at last there is a bright and warming blaze.

The Indians also made fire by friction. They rubbed sticks together with the aid of a bow drill and fire board. According to Ernest Thompson Seton, their trick was in picking a wood for the fire board that was soft enough to wear away and produce punk and yet hard enough to wear slowly. Otherwise there would not be enough heat to light the punk. For this purpose they preferred such woods as balsam fir, cottonwood roots, tamarack, red cedar, white cedar, and white pine. The eastern Indians often used cedar; the northern Indians, cedar or balsam fir; and the western Indians, cottonwood or sagebrush roots.

In cold areas, a shelter is also critical. One quick way is to girdle a conifer with a knife or ax, grab its lower branches, and pull it over. Slash branches from the lower trunk and pile them over the end that you are going to use as a shelter. If you are only practicing wilderness survival, a living tree should not be destroyed in this fashion, but the method provides a good way to obtain shelter in a hurry in a real emergency.

Another quick way is to make a pile of leaves and tunnel into it. There should be more leaves beneath you than over you. A poncho or tarp may also be rigged up as a shelter, and it may be possible to get out of the weather in a cave or beneath a rock overhang.

One thing is certain. It is not a good idea to place a camp on a windy high point or in a gully, where it may be struck by a flash flood. Take advantage of natural windbreaks and locate on dry, level ground.

A cliff or rock overhang and the roots of an uprooted tree can make fine reflectors. You should build your fire so that you can sit between the fire and the reflector. If there is no reflector to be found, you may be able to build one out of either logs or stones, or you can build two fires and sit between them. Even after the flames die down, the coals will keep you warm.

The body can't stand extremes of heat any better than it can extremes of cold or wet. Survival in the desert requires that a person slow down the evaporation of body moisture. Jedediah Smith, the mountain man, often "buried" himself in the desert sand, with his head sheltered by shady bushes to keep alive during the murderous heat of the day. If you're marooned in the desert, you should at least keep your clothes on even if you're sweltering. Above all, you should keep your head covered. You should find shade if it is at all possible and conserve your energy and moisture content. You should travel only in the early morning and late afternoon when the heat is less severe.

Water is essential to survival. If it is taken from brooks and rivers, ponds and lakes, it may be necessary to purify it either by boiling for five minutes or by using water purification tablets. It may be necessary to dig for water. Look for damp ground as a place to dig. Low ground, particularly where cattails, willows, or other water-seeking plants grow, is also a good place to dig. So is the foot of rocks where dense vegetation grows. The concave, shady banks of dry riverbeds can also be a good place to dig.

Looking for water in the desert is both more difficult and more critical. Australian aborigines can divine where water is located by merely concentrating on it, but for most people it is better to look along ridges, where water from the rare storms collects in potholes. Desert animals stay alive because they know how to find these treasure troves of water. Scout along narrow cracks in the rock and in canyons for them.

A survival still is another way to obtain water. A clear piece of plastic about six feet square; a pot, or a piece of aluminum foil or other waterproof material; and a drinking tube are needed. Excavate a bowl-shaped pit in the desert, in beach sands, or in a dry streambed. It should be about three feet across and two feet deep. Fix a container of foil or other material in the middle of the pit. Then spread pieces of cactus or other plants around the container. Put the large plastic piece over the top, and pile rocks or soil around the edge of it to hold it down. Put a rock as big as a hand immediately over the container and push it down about a foot. The sun beaming on the plastic causes waterdrops to form on the bottom side within 45 minutes. They eventually run down to the point and drip into the container. Then the water can be sipped up through a drinking tube. In a day's time two pints of liquid are produced by such a still. A pint will be distilled in a night. Since an average person needs about a gallon of water to live a day in the desert, it would take two such stills to keep him alive.

To return in good health from a wilderness survival training activity or from an emergency situation, you should know something about first aid and medicinal plants. You should keep your body and clothing clean. If you don't have soap with you, you can use peeled yucca root or the inner bulb of the soap plant. The bulb of the soap plant also will help keep infection from sores and cuts. In the Southwest, green mesquite beans can be boiled for a soup that cures dysentery, and the sap of the mesquite is used on sores as a salve. In the north, the pitch of the lodgepole pine and the roots of the curled dock make good disinfectants.

Whether for the challenge of it, as an experience to remember, or as a means of saving lives, wilderness survival experiences have become very popular with both young and old. They bring a person closer to nature than almost any other activity. A veteran of wilderness survival experiences understands how the Sierra Club's first executive director, David Brower, could say, "When you get out of the city and into the wilds, you hear the planet speak."

Wilderness Cooking

In the heyday of the fur trade, a mountain man in the high Rockies had his own way with a venison steak. He cut a green shoot about three feet long and a half-inch thick. Instead of sticking the steak on the stick, he split the stick with his knife and inserted the meat into the slit. The green wood sprang back together and firmly held the steak. Sharpening one end of the stick, he thrust it at an angle into the ground next to the fire so that the meat was suspended over the coals.

A mountain man could also notch the end of a green stick to suspend a kettle over a fire or use a stick to lift a hot pot. A hunting knife might make up one essential part of his eating irons. He could cut a shoot from a sapling, peel off its bark, and sharpen its point to make a serviceable fork. He knew how to make a flat piece of bark into a plate or twist the bark around to form a conical drinking cup. He could even cook in a birch-bark pot. Birch bark is highly flammable, but a mountain man could put a birch-bark pot directly on the coals, providing it was completely filled with water. The water kept the thin bottom and sides of the pot cool enough so that they would not catch fire. A mountain man learned these tricks of the wild from his friend and enemy, the Indian.

Today in the wilderness, you can do much the same sort of thing, but there is one increasingly important consideration. Are you really in the wilds, where only a few people go every year, or are you in an area where, even though it may be the backcountry, the sheer number of people backpacking and camping is beginning to be an ecological burden? The explosion of enthusiasm for the outdoors way of life is paying America dividends in health and recreation, but at the same time it is making it almost indecent in overburdened areas to cut a single growing shoot or strip a piece of birch bark from a tree, or for that matter to trap or hunt game, or relentlessly pursue edible wild plants unless they are in considerable supply. The rash of books telling Americans how to live off the land do no damage providing they are read with due consideration of the responsibility of outdoors people to protect the wilderness against exploitation.

In most backcountry today, edible plants, game, and fish should not be expected to provide the means to live off the land, but only as extra provisions for a camp, canoe trip, or backpack.

Backpacking and canoeing take a lot of energy, and you will find that you'll use upwards of 3,500 calories every day. This means eating some two-and-a-quarter pounds of packed-in food, providing it has little water content and a high caloric value. No wonder that many people on wilderness trips do their best to add wild foods to their larder. Still, in most places these wild plants should be used sparingly so that everybody can enjoy at least a taste of natural provender and so that there will be plenty left for future generations.

Besides relying on wilderness plants, game, and fish to give accent to meals of freeze-dried backpack foods, it is a good idea to cultivate a few tricks of your own concerning what to bring from home. One Illinois backpacker carries along a few cans of sardines, because when the going gets tough, she finds that even the oil in which they are packed tastes good and provides warmth and energy. Another backpacker favors spun honey, which is both light in weight and solid, to take the place of the lumps of maple sugar carried by the French voyageurs on northern canoe trails. One woman likes a thickish cup of goop to get herself and her party out of sleeping bags in the morning. It consists of a teaspoon of brewer's yeast, a teaspoon of Tang, and high protein meal, all mixed in hot water. It can provide the energy needed for a stiff mountain trail. The same woman sometimes sips a hot nightcap compounded of instant chocolate and coffee with a dollop of brandy just before retiring.

Drought conditions, recurring particularly in the West over the last few years, make it necessary to be very careful in fire building. Alarmed by disastrous fires caused by careless people camping in tinder-dry forests, brush country, and grasslands, certain state legislatures have enacted strict laws forbidding fires on the ground. The list of states banning campfires is growing, and it would be a good idea for you to find out in advance whether the area that you wish to visit has such a ban. If wood campfires are no longer permitted, you must carry along a butane or propane cartridge stove or a stove fueled with white gas. Such a fire may not have the friendliness and good cheer of a wood fire, but it is an efficient way to cook. It also frees you from setting up your camp close to a supply of wood. With your stove in your pack you are equally at home in the mountains above timberline and in an area where a whole season of backpackers before you may have exhausted the fuel wood.

Still, it is a wood fire that provides most outdoors people with heat for cooking. A pot placed over its flames is used to boil the dehydrated meals of the backpacker, on one hand, and, on the other hand, to simmer a soup made of watercress, burdock, wild onions, and chopped bacon. When the flames have burned down to coals, meat can be roasted over them either on a skewer, on a mountain man's green stick, or directly on the embers.

If a camper has no pan or grill, he can always cook his fish, meat, or pancakes on a flat rock heated in the fire. He should be sure to avoid rocks that may have water in them or they may explode when they are heated. Flying fragments can cause injuries. Sandstone is the best stone for the purpose since it does not hold water. Glassy rocks of volcanic origin are the worst, since moisture often is trapped in them. The main thing is to select rocks that to the naked eye have coarse grains and crystals, for the porosity of these rocks allows water to escape. A dense rock, principally of igneous origin, cannot be trusted.

A camper may make pancakes out of flour that he has brought with him from home or he may grind up the starch roots of the cattail or biscuit-root and mix it with water to make a cake, which he can cook in the ashes. He can twist his dough around a green stick and hold it over the embers. He simply unwinds the twisted bread from the stick when it is ready to eat. In Australia, I've seen outbackers make a traditional down under bread called damper. They wrap the dough in green leaves and put it into hot ashes. When a knife stuck into the packet comes out clean, the bread is ready to eat.

One of the most practical ways to cook in the wilds without benefit of equipment brought from home is the steam pit. It can be dug with a flat rock to the size that fits the amount of food to be cooked. The next thing to do is to line the bottom and the sides of the pit with flat stones. Then you build a wood fire on the stones. After it has burned for an hour or more, scoop out the coals. Next, spread wet green grass or green leaves on the hot rocks. On top of the grass, place your roots, greens, and meats. Then spread a second thick layer of wet leaves or grass and cap the pit with a large flat rock. Over this, pile dirt to seal the pit. In two or three hours, depending upon the heat stored in the rocks, you are ready to take out a tasty and nutritious meal cooked by the steam from the wet grass or leaves.

Tomatoes, potatoes, and corn are a few of the native North American vegetables that were domesticated by the Indians and which found their way into the settlers' larders. There are many wild edible plants to be found in the forests and meadows of the land that equal or even surpass these popular plants in flavor and nutrition.

Many of the most nutritious plants grow in wet places. The arrowhead, sometimes called the swamp potato, is one of these. With its dark green leaves, shaped like arrowheads, and its characteristic white flowers, the swamp potato is easy to spot near water and marshes. Its roots extend deep into the damp soil. When autumn comes, tubers form along the roots. You can dig these up and bake or roast them over the coals.

Another plant that enjoys damp places is the tall bulrush. The spring is a good time to gather young bulrush shoots and eat them either raw or boiled. Later on, when the plant flowers, the pollen can be mixed with meal for baking. The seeds, which form still later in the season, may be ground and mixed with meal also. The rootstalks when peeled, can be eaten, either raw or boiled.

Since they can be dug up even in the winter, they are an important food in wilderness survival. Bulrush roots also make a good flour. Clean them thoroughly to remove the mud and then boil them. When they have cooled and dried, they can be ground up as the principal ingredient or to augment wheat flour in pancakes.

The cattail is still another common North American plant that grows close to streams and swamps. Its narrow knifelike leaves reach as high as six feet tall. It is one of the most useful of all wild plants. The head, when still green, can be boiled or roasted in the same way as can an ear of corn. Its roots can be eaten raw or cooked, and the young shoots can be snacked upon raw or cooked, as if they were asparagus. The pollen also can be used as a flour to make wild bread or griddle cakes.

Nobody can claim that the dandelion and the burdock are in short supply. Most homeowners wish that they were indeed endangered species. Yet both are valuable plants when encountered in the wild, where they have not been sprayed by herbicide. Young leaves of both plants can be eaten in a salad or boiled as greens, although it is necessary to change the water at least twice in cooking dandelion or it will have a rank flavor. Dandelion roots may also be roasted or fried, and the yellow blossoms can be dipped in a batter and fried. Burdock roots, once their outer layer has been stripped away, can be boiled and eaten too.

There are several thousands of edible plants in North America. They run the gamut from yellow dock and milkweed to wild grape, stinging nettle, and sunflowers. Sunflower seeds are eaten raw or roasted, not only in the wilderness but at city cocktail parties, and they can even be ground up and immersed in hot water as a substitute for coffee.

Most of the edible plants known to today's outdoors enthusiasts were known to the Indians and the frontiersmen who learned their ways with food from them. It seems only appropriate that in cooking wilderness foods known to the Indians, Indian methods of cooking should be used. A unique method was employed by the Assiniboine, who dug a hole, which they lined with a buffalo hide. Putting the meat to be cooked in the hide, they added such greens as dandelion or burdock. They covered the hide's contents with water and then dropped piping hot stones into it until the water boiled and cooked the meal. A modern-day camper isn't likely to have a buffalo or even a cow hide handy, but he can always line a hole with plastic if he wants to try hot-rock cooking. A cook must not drop the hot stones onto the plastic or they will burn a hole in it. A basket or a bucket placed within the cooking pit should receive the hot stones.

I've seen both the Hunkpapa Sioux in South Dakota and the aborigines camped in a river bottom near Alice Springs in the Australian outback bake fish and birds in clay. They pat out a clay blanket from about a half inch to an inch in thickness. Wrapping the blanket around the meat and any savory herbs that may lend additional flavor, the cook makes certain that it is watertight, so that no juices can escape. The meal wrapped up in clay is placed in the coals. This is one of the most agreeable of primitive wilderness-cooking methods, because in the sealed compartment of clay, the meat and herb flavors mix together.

Nor does a wilderness camper have to go thirsty for a refreshing beverage. Roasted and powdered seeds make a presentable coffee, and so will the root of the chicory plant or the root of the dandelion. The roots of the dandelion should be well cleaned and then dried in the sun or before a campfire. The camper pares them into slivers when they are well dried. He grinds the slivers between two stones, Indian-style, to create a powder that will make a cup of wilderness coffee that isn't likely to be forgotten. It is a bitter brew, and some sweetening would be in order.

Prejudices about food do not belong in the wilds. One young man on a wilderness survival exercise on Wisconsin's Rock Island claimed that on one hand he was starving and on the other hand he couldn't bring himself to eat the crayfish tails simmering in his pot. The hunger pangs grew too sharp, and he took a first tentative bite. The tails proved delicious. Since his return to civilization, he now goes about claiming that he detests all fish except for shrimp and crayfish. A woman on a Minnesota canoe trip refused to taste the mess of dandelion greens, prepared by a fellow canoeist.

"It looks just like spinach," she complained.

Carbohydrates are found in the main in plants. Sugar, starches, cereals, and fruits are the best things to live on in the wilds. Although proteins found in meat, fish, and eggs are important in repairing body tissues, you can get along for a considerable period of time without them. For this reason, wilderness cooking experts recommend that you put the emphasis on plants for your table in the wilds. This is particularly important if you are short of water, since the body needs more water to utilize proteins.

Before you go to a wilderness, you should learn about the edible plants it contains. Find out what they look like from a book and go to an area near your home where they grow to study them so that you will be able to recognize them when you are in the field. Learn what kind of terrain they prefer so that you'll know where to look for them. Learn what poisonous plants may lurk in the area too. Learn how to recognize them so that you can avoid them. You would scarcely want to mistake the deadly water hemlock for nourishing wild parsnips.

Unless you recognize for sure the plant that you have decided to eat, take a test taste of it. It may be possible to remove an unpleasant taste, as in the case of dandelion greens, by boiling the food more than once or it may be only necessary to chop it up or crush it and then pour hot or cold water over it.

A sour or bitter taste does not mean that a plant is poisonous. After all, a lemon is sour, and a radish can be bitter, but yet neither is poisonous. To test an unknown plant, you can hold a small quantity of it—either raw, boiled, or baked—in your mouth for some five minutes. If there is no burning sensation, it is usually safe to swallow it. If within eight hours, there are no ill effects, such as nausea, cramps, or diarrhea, you should then try about a handful of the plant. If within another eight hours, you suffer no ill effects, you can be reasonably certain that the plant is a safe food.

Tubers and roots, bulbs and stems, grains, and fruits all are worthy of your attention as edible wild provender. They all supply starch, which is very nourishing. Since raw starch is hard for the stomach to digest, it is necessary to cook the food before it can be eaten. Vegetables in the wild may be succulent leaves, pods, seeds, stems, and roots. They also are best cooked. Many ferns can be eaten, and nuts, such as hickory, hazel, and beech, are found throughout much of the United States and Canada.

The wilderness can also provide presentable teas. Sassafras roots and stems cut into pieces and boiled make a tea. So do dried strawberry leaves and rose hips. Sumac will furnish a camper with a bracing sour drink that will quench the thirst as thoroughly as will lemonade, which it resembles in taste.

Eat and drink found in the wilds can, in a time of need, furnish a person with the means to stay alive. They can at least augment the supplies carried by a backpacker, canoeist, or primitive camper. To know how to use primitive cooking methods which require no pots and pans can be insurance against going hungry in the wilds. They also provide a happy change of pace from the usual run of camp cooking.

Hiking

Summer never comes to the tundra above the tree line in Rocky Mountain National Park, and the miniscule plants with their tiny flowers grow slowly. The old trail beaten into the lichen by the moccasins of Ute Indians still can be seen. In some places in the Rockies the very tracks of a dinosaur can be followed along an escarpment to where his fossil bones perhaps lie buried. Harry C. James, a conservationist and outdoorsman in the Southwest, put down his sleeping bag on the desert floor of Monument Valley one dark night. All night long the unyielding rock beneath him robbed him of sleep. When in the morning he took up his sleeping bag, he looked to see what sort of monstrosity he had been lying upon. It was a fossil dinosaur track. Nearby there was another, and not far behind still another. The ages-old trail led into the antediluvian past of the continent. A hiker who starts out on a trail should know that he is following in the footsteps of prehistoric man and perhaps even of the giant beasts of long ago. The land is ancient, and many mysteries lie just beneath the surface or are exposed for the observant eye to see.

It isn't necessary to be a backpacker to enjoy a hike down a trail. All you have to do is park your car where the trail begins and start. Of course, you should wear sturdy hiking shoes and, to head off blisters, socks that won't bunch or wrinkle. You should put on jeans or twill to keep brambles and brush from scratching your legs and to keep mosquitoes and other bugs from getting in their nips. You'll want a hat to keep off the sun and usually a canteen full of water. A lunch and some other things in a day pack, possibly a walking stick in your hand, and you're ready. Some trails require special preparations, and there is know-how in hiking too, but it is an outdoor activity that not only appeals to almost everyone, but also can be done by almost everyone.

The National Forest Service even provides trails for the handicapped, so that people with physical or visual disabilities may also enjoy the outdoors. The Roaring Fork Braille Trail in the White River National Forest near Aspen, Colorado, and the similar trail in the San Bernardino National Forest of California were the first two to be built. Now there are nine national forests with trails that handicapped people can follow. On these trails blind people can listen, feel, and smell the forest around them as they go along the path.

There are splendid trails all over North America that are ideal for day hikes. A hiker can sight a moose across a Wyoming lake, glimpse the brilliant blue of a glacier through the lush foliage of a rain forest in Alaska, watch an alligator slide into the ooze of the Okefenokee Swamp of Georgia, or take a deep lungful of mountain air on a nature trail on the flanks of Washington's Mount Rainier.

Exploring on Foot

There are some extraordinary places to explore on foot. The Great Sand Dunes National Monument in Colorado features a trail that begins in a verdant forest, ascends tumbling streams through leafy glens, and emerges on a parched desert, where sand dunes reach a height of nearly 1,000 feet. In Idaho's Craters of the Moon National Monument, the Devil's Orchard Trail leads through an eerie region of cinder fields and crater walls. In the monument too is the Great Owl Cavern, a lava tube that is some 500 feet long, 40 feet high, and 50 feet wide. In the Cave Area, another trail goes to still other tubes, one of which, the Indian Tunnel, is over 830 feet long. Here on this landscape so similar to the face of the moon, hikers come upon old Indian trails. The Indians followed the Great Rift and used the lava tubes as shelters from storms and winter winds, as hideouts from their enemies, and as fortresses that defied attack.

Hawaii also has its moonscape. Haleakala Crater on the island of Maui is in Haleakala National Park. It is a world of old splatter vents, lava flows, and ash that resembles the moon's face to such a degree that some of the astronauts hiked through it to get accustomed to the sort of surface that they'd find on the moon itself. This huge crater, 21 miles in circumference at the rim and 3,000 feet deep, has 30 miles of trail. Mark Twain, that indefatigable hiker, walked down into the crater and spoke for all the other hikers who have ever ventured into it. In *Roughing It,* he said: "I felt like the Last Man, neglected of the judgment, and left pinnacled in mid-heaven, a forgotten relic of a vanished world."

Hike the Logger's Trail through the Sinnissippi Forest near Oregon, Illinois. There you will become acquainted with Illinois' first tree farm, where the earliest plantings of white pine were made in 1910 by Frank O. Lowden, governor of Illinois from 1915 to 1919. Follow the hiking trails at Bandelier National Monument in New Mexico, trails that should be undertaken with appropriate preparations, for they can take a whole day's time. One of the most unusual trails in the country is at Key Biscayne, just across Biscayne Bay from Miami. To follow the trail you actually go to sea. The Bear Cut Nature Trail starts at the Bear Cut Bridge. Hikers slip on sneakers to protect their feet as they wade along the beach of this lush island. They explore a forest of mangrove trees, look for conch shells, baby moray eels, horseshoe crabs, and all the other creatures that live along the beach. The trail leads to the world's only fossilized black mangrove reef. At low tide, when naturalists lead hikers to the reef, it is possible to make out the root structure of the mangroves that grew there up to 2,000 years ago.

Breaking an Auto Trip

On a lengthy motor trip, a family will find the days are far more agreeable if they stop from time to time to enjoy a hike along a trail. Even in view of the slower speeds required by the energy crunch, motoring on vacation can still be the best way for a family to travel. A more leisurely approach to a trip can lead to a more enjoyable time; and Sundays, when gasoline may be difficult to buy, would be ideal for a long hike or a canoe trip. The children in particular will appreciate the chance to unlimber from the car, but everybody will benefit.

Driving to Florida? Stop at the Ocala National Forest near Ocala, Florida, and hike the Big Scrub Trail. Television viewers who have watched the boy Jody and his pet deer in the late-hour movie *The Yearling* will soon recognize the sand pine forest as the Big Scrub. The trail runs for 4.4 miles through dwarf live oak and palmetto, crowding beneath tall trees. Eight miles north of Umatilla the trail crosses Florida 19. The Big Scrub Trail winds through piney hills in a primeval country that still remembers the padded footfalls of the Seminole.

On the way to Florida you might also stop at Cheaha

State Park in Alabama to hike the Odum Trail. It starts on top of the highest point in Alabama, Cheaha Mountain, and runs southward along a mountain crest to High Falls. There are beautiful views of the Coosa River far below in its green valley. There are wild flowers, deer, foxes, wild turkeys, and wild pigs. Bird-watchers spy hawks, owls, crows, doves, quail, and redheaded woodpeckers. Rockhounds can study the spectacular and varied rock formations.

To begin the hike a family drives east of Talladega on Alabama 96 to the park and goes to the foot of the microwave tower. Since the trail is nine miles long, you'll probably want to bring a lunch. Make sure your canteens are filled too, because there isn't any drinking water until you reach the end. Along the way, you'll probably meet troops of Boy Scouts, for the Scouts of the area opened up the trail to help encourage people to hike.

Neighboring Mississippi also has a fine trail for a Florida-bound family to try. Some 20 miles north of Gulfport the Tuxachanie Trail leaves Mississippi 49 and follows the route of an old logging railroad that carried timber to the sawmills at Howison. It was built by workmen from Ireland who employed hand tools and scoops hauled by mules. The railroad has now vanished, but you'll find some reminders of it as you hike.

There's a pond where the fishing is good along the trail, and at one place dooryard flowers planted by a pioneer housewife still bloom on a deserted farm. A footbridge takes the trail over West Creek to a stand of mountain laurel. In the spring the laurel bursts into spectacular bloom. In the fall red flowers grow in the sandhills, and hundreds of migrating yellow butterflies dance among them.

The Tuxachanie Trail leads among timber grown tall since the virgin forest was cut about 40 years ago. You'll cross cattle ranges and the Harrison Experimental Forest to the site of a moonshiner's still put out of business by a revenuer raid. Copeland Spring along the way was named for a juvenile delinquent of the early 19th century. James Copeland was a thief by the age of 12. When he was 15, he burned down the Jackson County Courthouse in order to get rid of an indictment that had been entered against him. He escaped into the forest and buried his loot. Poor Jim ended up at the end of a noose in 1857 in Old Augusta on the edge of the forest. If you are delayed on the trail until dusk and a youth in rough, old-fashioned clothes comes up to you and wants to borrow your flashlight, don't let him have it. It might be Jim Copeland trying to get a light so he can continue to look for his treasure.

Hiking to meet a ghost is scarcely the most popular reason for following a trail, but Texas has a haunted trail too. The Texas Forestry Association maintains the 10-mile Oil Springs Trail that begins about 20 miles southeast of Nacogdoches from Farm-to-Market Road 226 between Woden and Etoile. It follows the route of the Nacogdoches and Southeastern Railroad, long since defunct, and cuts through the East Texas Piney Woods where you'll find 67 species of trees and shrubs as well as gorgeous but delicate wild orchids.

The trail passes Oil Springs, where in 1866 L. T. Barret sank the first oil well west of the Mississippi River. Oil gushed from the earth when he reached 106 feet in depth. Although Indians drank the oil that bubbles from the streams nearby to cure illness, you'll do better to drink the water from your canteen.

As for the ghost, the trail is said to be haunted by the spirit of a railroad brakeman who wanders along what was once the right-of-way swinging his lantern. Unlike Jim Copeland, he's not searching for his treasure. He's looking for his head, which was sliced off in a train accident long ago.

Tips for Hiking

Wherever you drive, there are trails worth a few hours or a day of your time. They require a modicum of preparation, but a few suggestions might be in order. Clothing should be suitable for the weather and the trail. If the day is hot and the sun direct, a hiker who does not have a deep suntan would do well to wear a long-sleeved shirt or at least a cotton-knit shirt to keep from getting a sunburn. A cotton kerchief tied around the back of the neck will keep his neck from burning. On a well-marked trail, some girls may prefer to wear culottes or an A-line skirt, which give them charm while allowing for a good stride. But jeans will protect a girl's legs from brambles, poison ivy, or bugs more effectively.

A covering for the head is essential. Some women like a kerchief, but a peaked fisherman's cap or a straw hat will serve as well. In any case, a hat should be well ventilated for summer hiking and have a broad brim to shelter the face from the sun and the eyes from the glare.

The day hiker keeps in mind the backpacker's trick of wearing several layers of light clothing instead of one big heavy coat. This allows him to be warm in the morning chill, to remove first a jacket, then a sweater, to leave only a T-shirt when the heat of the day is upon him. The same principle holds true for keeping warm on a winter hike, but heavier clothing must be used.

Good pockets in clothing are important. A bush jacket can hold a plethora of things: lunch, a book on birds or rocks, perhaps some waterproof matches, a jackknife, a map, a compass and, for some areas, a snakebite kit. A musette, or pouch bag, slung across the shoulder will replace such a jacket in warm weather. The main thing is to keep your hands free so that you can walk with an arm-swinging natural stride. Some hikers claim that a walking stick gives them an easier swing and a more rhythmic gait. They find a stick useful in balancing on a log spanning a stream or as a prop in climbing up a slippery hill. Other hikers say that a walking stick would only be in their way and never carry one.

Shoes are almost as important to a day hiker as they are to a backpacker. If you're doing more than 10 miles on your hike, you should wear hiking shoes or ankle-high boots with nonskid soles. Sneakers or sturdy Hush Puppies will be all right for easy hikes. Socks too are important. If the hike is a long one they should be hiking socks, and two pairs. Outer heavyweight ones and inner lightweight ones should be worn.

If you are hiking in the desert, a few other things should be taken into account. No matter how short the distance you plan to go, it is critical that you carry at least a quart of water. If you're going to be out for a good part of a day, two quarts will not be too much. The more water you can tote, the happier and the safer you'll be, for in the desert's heat and dryness, the body uses up moisture at a prodigious rate.

A desert hiker is doubly concerned about sunburn, because even on overcast days, the sun can burn him. The same general suggestions for hot-weather hiking in general obtain to desert hiking in particular, but they should be followed without fail. Clothes should not be kept tight; they should be loose to allow for circulation. Sneakers absorb the heat from the sand and rocks, and your feet will be cooler and happier in hiking shoes or boots. Your first-aid kit may have a few extra things in it too: not only bandages and gauze squares, but water purification tablets and tweezers to pull out thorns and cactus pricklers that you may unfortunately encounter along the way.

On easy well-marked trails you may not need a map, but a map is always valuable to have along. Check your course as you go to be sure you're on the right track. If your trail is difficult, keep in mind the same skills that a backpacker uses, and follow his procedures in case you become lost. A tip about hiking in the arid Southwest: Unless you are accustomed to the effects of the clear air on distances, you may think that a mountain is much closer to you than it actually is. A ridge that seems some 5 or perhaps 10 miles away, and therefore within reasonable hiking range, may actually be 20 miles away.

Mountain trails also should be undertaken with due attention to the effects of altitude on the heart and lungs. It is so easy to drive from near sea level into the mountains that the body scarcely has a chance to adjust. Even healthy and active kids and adults can be felled by mountain sickness, so it is wise to take it easy in the high country until you've become acclimated.

Most trails do not require any special physical conditioning on your part, but a hiker refrains from overexerting himself. If he doesn't continue hiking until he feels tired, the exercise does little to strengthen his muscles. Of course, it isn't sensible for a sedentary city dweller to go out and suddenly start rushing up the trail to the top of Georgia's Stone Mountain. He should first improve his muscle tone by walking or jogging about his neighborhood if he has in mind a vigorous hiking trail. However, most nature trails in state and national parks and forests can be followed by a human jelly roll.

A Special Kind of Walker

A hiker is a special kind of walker who looks for interesting things to see and do along the trail and for the challenge of distance, a rough terrain, or a hard climb. As a Wisconsin naturalist, George Knudsen, explains, "The act of using legs in everyday work is called walking. And if they are used to take longer journeys through the woods and fields, this is called hiking."

A hiker maintains a steady pace that is easy for him. He covers anywhere from two to two and a half miles an hour and judges the amount of time he believes it will take him to hike a trail accordingly. He equips himself for a trail, considers the altitude, weather, and terrain, and feels at home with nature. He carries a flashlight if there is any possibility that he will still be on the trail at nightfall. In case he is going into a wild area or is going to undertake dangerous activity, he is just as certain as is a backpacker to consult with a ranger. Even if a motorist stops his car by the road and sets out on a hike down a wild trail, he can leave a note in his car telling where he has gone and when he left.

In many state and national parks it is required that a hiker stay on the marked trail, for his own safety and also to protect the environment. Hiking cross-country has its pleasures too. In many places a hiker can strike out for himself. Nor are hike-where-you-will opportunities limited to the West or the North Woods of Maine, Minnesota, or Canada. In Wisconsin, hikers on state lands are not restricted to trails, and it is a happy experience to roam the deep woods of Wyalusing State Park, at the juncture of the Wisconsin and Mississippi rivers, or to tramp over the rolling grasslands of Governor Dodge State Park to the cliffs and buttes that are reminiscent of western Nebraska.

An off-the-trail hike need not be far from a main road. Once at the ruins of Casa Grande, Arizona, I set out for a dawn stroll among the gnarled trees and mesquite that stretch beyond the ancient outer walls of the prehistoric dwelling. I walked away from the empty windows and doors from which the people of another time looked out on the same desert and mountains that I looked upon. Birds sang; the streaks of salmon light illuminated the eastern sky over the mountains. A coyote yelped a last comment on the night. The sands became tawny in the rising sun, and the desert awakened. The sun washed the still, silent stones of the dwelling and the desert, and I felt very much part of this place and its past.

Are these thoughts banal? Perhaps to a party of people, brittle and sophisticated, chattering in a city apartment, competing stridently with one another for attention, such thoughts would scarcely pass muster; but out on the floor of the desert, these thoughts represented reality. A Gila monster crept along a slight rise ahead of me and lifted its miniature dragon's head to peer out at a lightening world. A roadrunner sprinted past. Probably the party in the city apartment for brittle and sophisticated people represents the true banality. At least to a hiker in the desert at dawn it seems that way.

Some hikers prefer hiking alone or with only a friend or two; some prefer hiking in groups. Groups should stay together if there is any possibility at all that some hikers might take the wrong trail. Young people, in particular, tend to wander off the track and get lost unless they've been trained. If the trail is demanding, there should be an experienced adult with them. Some people prefer hiking with a hiking club or such groups as the Sierra Club or the American Youth Hostels.

Some hikers enjoy going on annual hikes. Over 1,200 participants show up at the base camp of the Phoenix Dons Club in Arizona's Superstition Mountains for the yearly Lost Gold Trek, a search for the Lost Dutchman Mine. The Dons, who ride out to their camp, show parties of about 50 people over the seven-mile trail that passes by points mentioned in the tale of Jacob Walz, the "Lost Dutchman," who lost his life prospecting for a fortune in gold in the mountains. When the hikers return from the trail, they sit down to a miner's lunch and barbecue with all the trimmings. Another annual hike has its main appeal to Civil War buffs. Hikers proceed from the Perryville Battlefield State Park at Perryville, Kentucky, over either the Dug Road March or the Dry Canteen Trail, each covering 15 miles. Another well-known annual hike takes place on the last weekend of August at Boulder, Colorado, when hikers set out from town to walk to a live glacier. It's a day-long hike that ends with a hearty mountain meal.

Hiking for Health and Pleasure

An eminent heart specialist, Dr. Paul Dudley White, claimed that walking is the best exercise for strengthening the heart. The legs, he said, are a person's "second heart," and as they work they help the heart pump the blood about and keep a person healthy. Certainly hiking helps to take off weight too, but the main thing is that it makes people feel good.

There's always something to see over the next hill or around the next bend, and hiking doesn't have the monotony of stationary conditioning exercise or even jogging. It occupies the mind as well as the legs, is inexpensive, and can even get a person into places that he can't reach in any other way. So hiking makes it possible for a hobbyist to follow his particular bent in the field. A hiker is often also a photographer, a bird-watcher, rockhound, mushroom-gatherer, berry picker, or a person who revels in the whisper of leaves on a fall day or the sound of a stream babbling beside the path.

To me a hike gains extra savor when there is a historical reason for taking it. Some of my happiest hiking hours have been spent following the routes of old Roman roads through the west of England, in France, Germany, and in Lebanon. To explore the past while exploring the present is a special pleasure for me, and I've hiked on all the continents of the world for this, to me, exciting purpose.

In this country too, a hiker with a historical turn of mind can hike over Daniel Boone's route on a section of the Wilderness Trail that still remains in the Cumberland Gap National Historic Park, or trace the Santa Fe Trail across Kansas, or follow the Oregon Trail to the Pacific Northwest. Other hikers prefer to trek along the old canal towpaths that exist in the East and Midwest. There's not only the celebrated towpath along the Chesapeake and Ohio Canal from Washington, D.C., to western Maryland, but in Illinois the towpath along the Illinois and Michigan Canal. Along the latter trail, Wild Bill Hickok, then a quiet youth aged 17, drove a horse pulling a flatboat on the canal. One day young Bill ran into a strapping bully who ordered him off the path. When Bill didn't move, the other grappled with him. Both tumbled into the canal, where the bully drowned. Bill panicked and headed for the West and a life as the frontier's fastest draw.

A trail to a ghost town in Montana, a path leading to an old apple orchard atop a Vermont mountain, and a hike among the ponderosa of the Fort Apache Indian Reservation in Arizona, all are fascinating. Some of the best hikes are taken in search of a romantic yarn. Hikers set out through the Shepherd of the Hills Country in the Missouri Ozarks because of the popular book of that name, and last summer my wife, who is incurably romantic, and I set out to follow the Leigh Lake Trail in Grand Teton National Park because it leads to the island on which Owen Wister's "Virginian" honeymooned with his pretty schoolteacher bride. It was a good hike in the late September sun with a piney smell all around us, the air brisk, and the Grand Tetons standing out sharp and clear. We came out on the east shore of Leigh Lake, and having made out the island, hiked to a narrow crossing point. We enjoyed a romantic tryst of our own on a small island just right for two.

Today old trails of the past are being reopened for modern hikers, and new trails are being created. Old aqueducts, abandoned railroad rights-of-way, logging trails, beaches, and national seashores are all ideal for rambling. All of the national parks and monuments have trails that are intended for day hikes. The Shenandoah National Park in Virginia, for one, has 200 miles of footpaths. As in most national parks, the nature trails are for easy hiking, but the circuit hikes are for those who are ready for long walks. Longer hikes of up to 10 miles are for people in good physical condition.

Set out on any of the Shenandoah hikes, and it'll be a pleasure. Herbert Hoover was an avid fisherman, and he had a summer fishing lodge high on a hill overlooking the Rapidan River. One of the most interesting hikes in the Shenandoah leads to the lodge and a caretaker's cabin. It begins at the parking lot at the Visitor Center just past milepost 51 on the Skyline Drive, and it is a good trail for a motorist and his family to take. You walk along the Rapidan Fire Road through the Big Meadows, where sometimes you'll come upon grazing deer. You hike through thin woods, which grow denser as you go. Just below a locked gate, you fork right along the fire road and climb up a hill. The Rapidan is on your left. You cross it on a footbridge and find yourself at Hoover's Camp. Sit down on the veranda and rest up from your hike at the place where, in the late 1920s, an American president used to find escape from the cares of office.

A hiker has many reasons to hike. Perhaps you'd rather get a closeup look at the world's oldest living things. The Ancient Bristlecone Pine Recreation Area is in the Inyo National Forest high on the rocky sides of California's White Mountains. In this high country, the Schulman Grove Picnic Area is at 10,100 feet, and a hiker should be acclimated before he starts out over the two trails that lead from the grove into the forest. Methuselah Walk winds through the twisted trees to the 4,300-year-old Methuselah tree. Another shorter trail leads to Pine Alpha, the first tree to be dated over 4,000 years. Sand, ice crystals, and wind have buffeted these ancient trees for centuries upon centuries, but still they survive.

There are trails in the East as well as in the West. A hiker can walk where the Pilgrim Fathers first rambled when they came ashore in the New World on Cape Cod. In the Cape Cod National Seashore, Massachusetts, start at a parking lot just off US 6 near Truro, and walk among pitch pine and thickets of bearberry to the sandy beaches. You'll find the place where the Pilgrims discovered a corn cache buried by the Indians. You'll pass a glacial kettle left from the last ice age, explore a blueberry swamp where azaleas bloom, and climb over the bearberry heath to a high hill. You'll find the bearberries seedy and not very juicy, but there'll be blueberries along the way too. At last your trail leads down through pines into a bushy valley where the Pilgrims found a spring. This is where they had their first drink of New World water. Later you may also want to hike over the nearby Small's Swamp Nature Trail, an hour's easy stroll through an unspoiled natural area.

Each trail you hike is unique. Deer feed among the wild orange groves and alligators bask on logs as you hike over the catwalk through the cypress swamp of the Highlands Hammock State Park near Sebring, Florida. Sometimes the 'gators come up on the walk, but more often they stay on a muddy bank, looking like a log—10 feet or so of sunning monster.

Hike up the trail to the top of Sugar Loaf Mountain at Greers Ferry Lake, Arkansas. You have to start your hike with a boat ride, for the mountain is entirely surrounded by the man-made lake. When you get to the top of the mountain and look out on the panorama of blue lake, mountains, and valleys, you'll know you're in one of the most beautiful places in the Middle South.

The Avalanche Lake Trail in Glacier National Park, Montana, an easy walk, is unsurpassed in beauty. It starts at the Avalanche Campground just off the Going-to-the-Sun Road. You follow a stream boiling down out of the mountains. Glacial waters, milky in appearance, from Sperry Glacier, roll stones downstream to carve out potholes in the streambed. At Avalanche Basin you come upon half a dozen waterfalls tumbling down the 2,000-foot cliffs. Although this trail doesn't go into the backcountry and there's not much of a chance that you'll confront a grizzly, it would be a good idea to jiggle some rocks in a can or sing a song as you go, in case there are any wandering bears. You're more likely to see hawks and eagles wheeling overhead or to catch a glimpse of bighorn sheep on the slopes above you.

The Olympic National Park in Washington is renowned for its Rain Forest Nature Trail. It begins at the end of the Hoh River Road on the ocean side of the park. Hike up the river through a luxuriant forest where over 140 inches of precipitation fall every year. Sitka spruce tower over you. The largest of all has a 41-foot-1-inch circumference, and the tree is just off the trail. You'll see 70 kinds of mosses, some on rocks, some draped over trees. You may even come upon a Roosevelt elk. It'll shake its mighty head and antlers and walk away with royal tread. It's at times like this a hiker knows his life in the outdoors has a wonder and beauty to it that cannot be surpassed.

Orienteering

Orienteering has much of the appeal of a road rally to its growing number of enthusiasts, but it doesn't burn up fossil fuel since it calls on a participant's own two legs to get him around. It uses map and compass to find the way through the fields and forests of a gentle countryside or the most rugged mountain terrain to a goal. A person skilled in the art of orienteering is a modern-day pathfinder.

For a beginner it can be tricky. On a recent orienteering problem in the Bay de Noc State Forest of Michigan's Upper Peninsula one of our training teams ended up mired in a swamp, another got lost and came out on a large pond that wasn't even on the map, and a third got chased off an enclave of private land by a dog with incredibly big teeth. All of the team members had a great afternoon in the woods and were ready for a more successful try the next day.

Orienteering for the sport of it is one thing, and orienteering as an essential tool of the hiker and backpacker is another. Both purposes call for the same training and skills. In orienteering, a person may work alone or in a group. He learns to travel by map and compass, by using only a map or only a compass. He can find his bearings in a strange countryside.

In an orienteering meet each team is handed a topographical map of the area on which checkpoints are indicated within small circles. Each team has to set a compass course. Out there in the terrain itself, flags or markers have been located at precisely the points indicated on the map by the small circles. The object is to find the markers.

In orienteering you have to know how to read a topographical map so that you can recognize at a glance the roads, rivers, fields, buildings, towns, all the man-made and natural features of the landscapes. Blue shows water. Brown lines indicate the contours of hills and valleys.

You also must know how to use a compass so that you can take a bearing, and how to use a compass to orient a map so that it is lined up exactly with the features of the landscape where you are standing.

There are other techniques to learn. If it is, for example, a 50-degree course from checkpoint A to checkpoint B on a riverbank, a veteran knows that he should aim either to the left of the control point or to the right. He realizes that nobody is perfect and that if he aims right at the marker, he may miss it by a few hundred feet and not know whether it is upstream or downstream. In a timed contest he can lose precious minutes searching in the wrong direction. If he deliberately aims downstream from the marker, he knows that it can only be upstream and will be able to find it more readily. The offset technique can be used when a road as well as a stream crosses the direction of travel.

It is also necessary for you to know how much distance your pace covers. A pace is every two steps. Each individual has a different stride. If you know how long your pace is and can judge your speed, you can calculate distances covered with surprising accuracy. You'll want to study the map to learn how many feet you must climb and how steep the climb is going to be. Every time you climb 100 feet, it's comparable to walking a quarter of a mile.

The first thing you do when tackling an orienteering field problem is to find your exact location on the map. You then locate the point on the map to which you are going. You use your compass to check the correct direction from the place where you are standing to the goal. You draw a beeline on the map from the place where you are to where you want to end up.

The beeline may be the best route to take, but usually it is not. Checking the map you may discover that the beeline crosses a lake, a steep cliff, and a swamp. There also may be no natural or man-made features for you to follow. The trick is to alter your course to take advantage of such things as a stream course or a road that will help you reach your destination without getting lost. At the same time you will avoid swimming the lake, climbing the cliff, and wading the marsh.

You begin by setting a compass course from where you are to the road which you've decided to follow to where it intersects a stream that in turn flows to a railroad bridge, which your map shows you is a mere 1,000 yards from your target. The things shown on the map, man-made and natural, that guide you along the route you follow are called the collecting features.

It is valuable to note the time when you set out from your starting point to the road. Make a note of the time you reach the place where the road reaches the stream and again where the stream reaches the railroad bridge. You can tell from the map the distance you have traveled, and since you also have an accurate measure of the time that has elapsed, you can tell how fast you are going and judge how long it will take you to reach the next major collecting feature.

The bridge or any other spot on the map from which you will take a compass reading to determine what your bearing is to your final destination is called the attack point. Once you've come that far it is a snap to reach the goal.

If a road or trail can be used on the way to your final checkpoint, by all means use it. Sometimes there is no man-made route to help you. Then you have to use your knowledge of map reading to decide how to cross the terrain ahead of you with a minimum of difficulty. A more roundabout route is often the best way to go cross country.

Wilderness orienteering represents a fascinating experience, which is not for beginners. Once your skills have been well tested in cross-country orienteering, you will be ready to challenge a wilderness area. First you should become well versed in hiking, camping, canoeing, first aid, and other skills that are essential for success and safety under more demanding outdoor circumstances.

There are several different kinds of competition. Score, cross-country, line, relay, and route orienteering are all popular. They all represent a test of your ability to interpret instructions accurately, use a map and compass with skill, and plan a route to be followed with good judgment.

The time you take in covering an orienteering course is also a critical point. A fast runner may have a competitive advantage in an orienteering race, but not if he can't handle his map and compass work with precision and use his head to find the most efficient way to cover the terrain.

For more information on sport orienteering, write to the U.S. Orienteering Federation, Box 1081, Athens, Ohio 45701.

Bike Hiking & Camping

"Bike riders are unusual in many ways, I found. They would rather swallow a gum wrapper than litter up a highway; they're as nimble with a wrench as is a copy editor with a pencil, and they record days by such recollections as 'the rainy day,' 'the hilly one,' or the 'sunny one with the wind at our backs.'"

So it appeared to *Chicago Tribune* reporter Joy Darrow Baim, who rode with a parcel of bike hikers for 332 miles over the Wisconsin Bikeway, from La Crosse to Kenosha. The cyclists cruised through nine counties at an average 40 miles a day, spotted 21 deer, nibbled cheese at the Swiss settlement of New Glarus, and admired cranberry bogs along the way.

Bike hikers are a hardy breed of cyclists who set out on

tours of the open country. They are likely to be the sort of people who at home ride their bikes to work or school, understand the fine art of bike maintenance, and prefer 10-speed machines of lightweight construction. Sometimes they sleep in motels at night, but more often they camp or find a place to rest in one of the American Youth Hostels, which are spotted here and there across the nation.

They include such people as a blind man and his wife who rode a tandem bike on a 1,500-mile jaunt. She gave a point-by-point commentary on what they were passing as they pumped along back roads, country lanes, and bike paths. Pat Kenney, a 16-year-old from San Carlos, California, pedaled 6,800 miles one summer from California to Florida to New York to Chicago. Pat averaged speeds of 40 miles per hour on the straightaways and reached better than 60 miles per hour on downhill runs in the mountains. He managed to get a speeding ticket in Florida for doing 50 in a 35-mile-per-hour zone. An Alaskan youth, Bob Layman, also 16, rode from Anchorage to Detroit, some 4,100 miles. Since an oldster, Lyman Frain of Philadelphia at the age of 80, biked from New York to California, it is apparent that bike hiking is a pursuit of both the young and the old. Frain didn't even take up bike riding until he was 72.

There is no doubt that the nation is going through a bicycle explosion. Paul Dudley White, the eminent cardiovascular specialist, spoke for the bike riders, of which he was one:

"Their numbers have been growing by leaps and bounds in the last two decades. Their ages range from 4 to 84. They are riding tandems, unicycles, middleweights, touring bikes, adult three-wheelers, racers, and novelty bicycles of all kinds (and this doesn't include several millions more who ride tricycles!). They ride for fun, health, sport, and transportation."

Bob Cleckner, national field director of the Bicycle Manufacturers Association of America, estimates that there are over 100 million American bike riders. They include kids and grown-ups. They ride as individuals, with friends, or with such groups as the Scouts, the League of American Wheelmen, American Youth Hostels, or the International Bicycle Touring Society.

Bicycling is a way to fitness and health, according to Dr. White.

"Let us bequeath our children more than the gadgets that surround us," he said. "If bicycling can be fully restored to the daily life of all Americans, it can become a vital step toward rebuilding health and vigor in all of us."

Dr. White claimed further that "Bicycles are an answer for both brain and body. If more of us rode them, we would have a sharp reduction in the use of tranquilizers and sleeping pills."

A California physician, James Fallows, puts the matter more colorfully.

"Pedaling not only tightens the legs and the gut, but improves circulation and expands lung capacity. And a biker builds a set of back muscles that can withstand any exertion short of Merlin's rack."

A bicycle is ideal for a family vacation. A biker can cover far more miles than a hiker can. A bike costs relatively little to own and requires no fuel. If properly maintained, it can stand hard use. Biking bridges the generation gap too, and there is freewheeling fun for a family that bikes together. It requires no special skills nor physical strength, and tall or short, rich or poor can enjoy it. On a bike hike, as Warren Asa, western regional director of the American Youth Hostels, explains, "you travel slowly enough to really see your surroundings, but fast enough to know you are on a trip.... You become part of the trip and the trip becomes part of you."

In this mechanized age, a bike hiker finds himself riding in harmony with his environment. He has an ecologically "clean" vehicle, and he can smell, see, and hear everything about him. His ride can be a very soothing experience.

Certainly there are problems involved with bike riding in the age of the automobile.

"Obviously, we need many more bicycle paths," said Dr. White. "When my father was a young man, he and his friends once rode from Boston to Albany to New York and back to Boston, completing a triangular journey of hundreds of miles. It is impossible to conceive of such a trip today...."

Planning a Bike Hike

The tyranny of the automobile, according to the National Safety Council, makes it hazardous for bikers on most of the nation's highways. Vincent Tofany, president of the Safety Council, says, "The recent bicycle boom has resulted in nearly 100 million bikes taking to the roads with little or no provision for their inclusion in the traffic mix. The 1,100 bike-related deaths reported in 1975 are intolerable."

A family starting out on a biking vacation must first lay out a route that will take them down the back roads where there is a minimum of auto and truck traffic. Good maps are critical when making plans. By writing to the highway departments in the state or provincial capitals, it should be possible to get state or provincial road maps. The county engineer at the courthouse in the county seat of the counties you are thinking of visiting should have more detailed maps, which will show you the roads that will be safer and more agreeable for you to use. Some states, such as New Hampshire and Wisconsin, offer maps that show bike paths and suggested roads for bike use. The American Youth Hostels has published a *North America Bicycle Atlas,* by Warren Asa, which is by far the best compendium of possible bike trips for you to consult.

Where to go? In the Middle Atlantic states, the old Chesapeake and Ohio Canal Tow Path is a favorite for cyclists. If you don't bring your own bike, rental bicycles are available at both the south and north ends of the path. Canal banks elsewhere make excellent biking paths. The Illinois and Michigan Canal near Chicago offers such possibilities, and so do the paths along the irrigation canals near Phoenix, Arizona.

Cape Cod National Seashore in Massachusetts features a scenic bikeway that takes bike hikers to lighthouses and swimming beaches. There are youth hostels handy. Ohio is justly proud of a self-guided bike tour through the Amish country. Bicyclists stop at a harness shop and roll over covered bridges and a trestle bridge. The Buckeye State's Old Mill Bikeway begins in Rising Park at Lancaster, Ohio, and runs for 35 miles through the country. Padre Island National Seashore in Texas gives cyclists a chance to ride the hard-packed beach sands and to sleep in the open. Florida's Hillsborough River, Highlands Hammock, and Myakka River state parks all have bike trails and bicycle rentals.

The first bikeway in the United States to cross an entire state, and probably still the most notable, is the Wisconsin Bikeway. It uses lightly traveled county highways and township roads for most of its length. It winds among rich dairy farms to such varied attractions as Blue Mounds State Park, Baraboo's Circus World Museum, and Grand Dad Bluff near La Crosse.

Thirty miles of an abandoned railroad right-of-way between Elroy and Sparta make up an unusual segment of the bikeway. Bikers find the grades no steeper than 3 percent, because this was an appropriate grade for the old Chicago and Northwestern Railroad locomotives. Forested hillsides where trilliums and bloodroots flourish and songbirds sing give way to fertile rolling meadowlands.

There are three tunnels bored through the solid sandstone of the hills. The northernmost tunnel is an engineering marvel of the 1870s. To carve it, workmen cut two shafts downward to the tunnel level. Then two crews dug outward to meet crews digging in horizontally from the outside.

Today a fine rock screening covers the right-of-way so that a bike's wheels can whir over the miles with no trouble. There are campsites along the trail, and if you want to sleep beneath the stars, nobody has any objections. A youth hostel is located four miles off the trail near Wilton. Bikes can be rented at Sparta, Elroy, Wilton,

Norwalk, and Kendall on the Elroy-Sparta section of the bikeway.

In picking a route for biking, a family should look for areas with little vehicular traffic, interesting things to see and do, and overnight accommodations. They might think of circling the island of Kauai in Hawaii to take a first-hand look at volcanic geology and Polynesian cultural patterns. Or they might follow the route of the Butterfield Overland Stage from Calexico, on the Mexican border, to Hemet, in California. The cactus, ocotillo, and rare elephant trees of the Anza-Borrego Desert State Park and a palm grove are all on the trip. A tour of the Texas hill country, a journey along the Great River Route that shadows the Mississippi, a ramble along the historic Natchez Trace, or a bike tour of Nova Scotia are all fascinating.

Picking Your Equipment

First of all, you need a bike. High-rise bikes are meant only for kids to lark around on close to home, and the middleweight, although strong and durable, is too hard to pump for bike hiking. The lightweight is designed for riders who need speed, easy handling, and endurance. With its narrow, high-pressure tires and touring-style handlebars, it is ideal for open country use. Most lightweights are equipped with derailleur gears that make hill climbing easier and allow for more speed on level ground. There are 5-, 10-, and even 15-speed bikes available, but the 10-speed is by far the most popular for bike hiking.

Some bike hikers enjoy riding tandem, and tandems are indeed pleasurable for couples who want to take a spin down a country lane or around a park. Going downhill on a bikeway, they are faster than a single bike is likely to be, but they are more unsteady. Going uphill they are a drag. The person who rides ahead has to pump a great deal harder than his companion. Because a tandem cannot carry enough camping equipment for two people, it isn't suitable for bike camping.

Some bike riders who have only recently been graduated from the old balloon-tired single-speeder find it hard to get accustomed to the drooping handlebars of a lightweight bike. But these handlebars make long-distance riding easier on the back. Also, because a person leans forward when grasping the low handlebars, they allow for better breathing and offer less wind resistance. At speeds above 14 miles per hour, wind resistance accounts for half of a biker's energy output, and his position on the bike can become critical. What's more, a fair amount of the body's weight is supported by the arms on the bars. The arms act as cushions for a lot of the road shock. This means that there is less weight on the saddle, and therefore a rider is less likely to develop saddle sores.

When riding a bike, the comfort of your saddle is as important as it would be if you were riding a horse. The saddle should be high enough so that your leg is just about straight when the pedal is in the lowest position. If you ride with your saddle too low, your legs fatigue more quickly and may cramp. The saddle should be kept at the same level as the top of the handlebars and should itself be horizontal to the ground. As any biker will tell you, you and the saddle of your bike have a very intimate relationship, and you want this to be a congenial one. The saddle should be of good leather, and you should condition it well with neat's-foot oil rubbed into the underside. Some bikers pound the top of the saddle with a stick to make it more pliable. "Break your saddle before it breaks you," is their motto. Some bikers also rub themselves, not with neat's-foot oil, but with a cream that will help take up the friction of the saddle. A suggestion: Don't get a saddle so wide that your legs rub on it when you are pumping the bike. A woman can take a somewhat wider saddle than a man.

For every pound of weight you add to the pack you carry on your bike you vastly multiply the demands on your energy when you start pumping up a hill. There is no reason why a bike hiker can't keep the weight of his gear down to that of a well-trained backpacker. How a biker distributes his weight is also important. I've seen riders with their packs on their backs. This is all wrong. It is far better to put the weight on the bike. A pair of rear-mounted saddlebags is ideal. Some are made of canvas, some of a tough waterproof nylon; they have zippered compartments to help you distribute the weight evenly. There are even packs that come with a strap so that you can take them off your bike and use them as a backpack if you wish. The bags fasten to a rear carrier.

Smaller bags of the same type may also be carried over the front wheel or mounted between the seat and the handlebars, but this is undesirable. You'd be better off to do without some of the things you think you need if you can't fit them into the twin saddlebags strapped to the rear carrier. One trick that will help: the lower down on your bike that you place the heavier weights, the better for your balance and the less tiring it is for you to pump up a hill.

A sleeping bag, a tent, and a mattress or ground cover, such as you'd take on a backpack, will pack atop your carrier or inside your bags. Most of the other gear that you'll need is similar to what a backpacker requires. The weight you save by dropping out the things that won't be needed by a bike rider is more than taken up by the bike tools and equipment that you ought to pack along in case of need. Your tool kit should include such things as small adjustable wrenches; pliers; screwdrivers, both blade and Phillips; a tire-repair kit; a small can of cycle oil; and a pair of work gloves for handling the chain. A pair of tire irons, spare tire or tube, extra spokes and brake blocks, a rear brake cable, gear cable, and a tire pump and gauge may all come in handy. How many spare parts you take along depends upon whether you're going through a well-settled area or not.

Because of the cupidity of your fellowman you will also have to take along a really strong bike lock and a redoubtable case-hardened steel chain or heavy steel cable. When you leave your bike unattended you should run the chain through both wheels and the frame. Tie the chain around a tree, a bike rack, or anything else that will be formidable enough to frustrate a bike-napper. A bike hiker carries less dehydrated food than a backpacker, mainly because he does not, as a rule, reach true wilderness country and finds it much easier to replenish his supplies as he goes.

Clothing will vary depending upon the season in which you are going to tour and where you are going. A bike hiker is apt to dress in a more civilized way than does a backpacker, because the biker is likely to be in and out of towns and may be staying at motels or doing things that require a fairly decent appearance. A boy or man may want a pair of shirts, one short-sleeved and the other long-sleeved; a pair of slacks and a pair of shorts; shoes, one pair for cycling and one for walking; a raincoat or a poncho; a Windbreaker and a sweater; two changes of underwear; socks; a hat; bathing trunks; and handkerchiefs. Girls find wrinkle-proof clothes best. Some like skirts and blouses; others prefer slacks. Scarves can be substituted for a hat. Toilet kits, towel and washcloth, toilet paper, a money bag or small wallet are all needed.

Veteran bike hikers, who are all too familiar with the apparent near blindness of many motorists, wear brightly colored clothing as protection. The clothes should have enough white in them to show up well in the dusk. Many riders also strap six-foot-high fiberglass wands to the rear of their bikes. A red flag that will glow in a car's headlights at night flutters from the top and can be seen by a motorist as he surmounts a hill behind a rider.

Ride Safely

Bikers not only wear brightly colored clothing, but they also follow safe riding practices. Riding in a straight line with the traffic on the right-hand side of the road, they obey all traffic signals and stop signs. The traffic laws cover a bike rider just as strictly as they do a motorist. When riders are in a group, they should keep at least three bike lengths apart. They should not ride more than two abreast and should form a single line when auto traffic is present. They use the appropriate hand signals to advise other bikers and motorists of their intentions, but they don't trust their life to the signals. They know that in the United States—unlike Europe, where bicyclists on the roads are expected—many motorists don't see anything but other autos or possibly an elephant if it strolls onto the highway. A safe biker rides defensively at all times and thinks both for himself and the motorist who is bearing down on him.

A biker always maintains control of his bike and adjusts his speed to traffic and road conditions. If he stops for a rest, he gets his bike completely off the road. He looks ahead as he pedals. Certainly he glances about at the countryside, moves his head from side to side, and checks over his shoulder from time to time, but he keeps his eyes on the road ahead most of the time. Both hands belong on the handlebars. "Look ma, no hands," is for a stunting boy on a safe street at home. A biker never hooks onto a moving vehicle, for although it may not be tantamount to suicide, it comes too close for comfort.

There are other road hazards that a bike hiker must take into account. If there is sand or gravel on a curve in the road, a biker makes the turn at a slow speed so that he doesn't risk a wipeout. A chuckhole hit at a high speed can blow a tire, dent a rim, and toss a rider head over teakettle. A rider who is moving at such a speed that he cannot avoid the gravel or hole should ride right through it instead of slamming on the brakes or swerving desperately, for such last-minute maneuvers will only make his wipeout more serious.

A biker crosses railroad tracks, streetcar tracks, and storm-sewer gratings at a right angle. The iron surfaces of a bridge can be slippery when wet, so that a biker must ride straight, without swerving or braking. For that matter, when riding in the rain, a biker must keep in mind that it takes twice as long for his rim brakes to catch hold and that his rubber tires will skid as well. Steep hills that have a rough, dirt, or gravel surface also can throw a rider. He is better off if he takes the time to dismount and walk his bike down the hill.

Walk your bike across busy intersections, and watch out for parked cars. Motorists often throw their doors open without checking for an approaching bike. If as you cruise down the road bringing up the rear of a group, presumably in single file, a car comes up from the rear, shout the word "car," so that the other riders can hear. Whenever you pass another biker, you should shout out, "Coming on your left."

Dogs are an even bigger problem to bike hikers than are motorists. Attracted by the sight of a turning wheel and an unprotected calf, farm and town dogs alike decide that a biker is the next best thing to a mailman. Some bikers sweet-talk a dog, toss him a dog biscuit or a stick to chase; others rage at him so that even a brave dog quails. Some bikers get their pants ripped or their shins nipped, but the biggest danger from a dog is that he may lunge into your front wheel and throw you for a header. A dog, in any case, is quite definitely not a bike hiker's best friend.

Bike hikers avoid riding in the dusk or at night, but there are times when they have no choice. Then luminescent or white clothing comes in handy. A light in front and a big red reflector or light in the back are essential. Some riders tie a small flashlight or a white handkerchief to their left ankle to help alert drivers that they are on the road ahead.

Fighting Fatigue

Even a hardy bike hiker who has toughened his muscles with cycling at home and who is accustomed to "making a century," that is, doing 100 miles in a day, has to fight fatigue. As does a backpacker, the bike hiker keeps his supply of energy steady by snacking on energy-producing carbohydrates as he goes. He keeps his tires well inflated. The lower the tire pressure, the more energy the wheel consumes as it rolls along the road. A rider pedals at the same speed, but he shifts gears so as to climb a hill with more ease. Even so, climbing a hill requires the most energy. The rider must lift his bike, his clothes, his pack and all it contains, and himself up the grade.

"If the grade is very slight, say an imperceptible one percent," says Fred De Long, the Chicago biking expert, "in a mile this weight is carried to the height of a five-story building. But if the grade is very steep—say one in four, the entire weight must be lifted the height of a flight of stairs about every 13 feet of travel. So it is apparent that a lightweight, uncluttered bicycle is a great advantage—as well as is lightweight clothing."

Energy is needed to accelerate. Energy is turned into heat and lost whenever you apply the brakes. This is why a steady and not too rapid pace is the least fatiguing way to cruise across the countryside.

Since many bike hikers live in metropolitan areas where it is dangerous or disagreeable to ride, they have to find a way to transport themselves and their bikes to a more serene and beguiling place to start their hike. A Chicago biking club begins its excursions into the country in the middle of the night to escape the heavy city traffic during the day. Bike clubs or the American Youth Hostels may arrange transportation on buses or trains. A St. Louis club takes its bikes to the country from a downtown levee on a chartered riverboat. Some airlines will fly the bike as baggage when a biker flies to another part of the country, but they levy a sports equipment express baggage charge. For example, TWA charges an extra ten dollars to carry a passenger's bike anywhere in the continental United States. Containers for the bike are supplied free of charge at the baggage service office at the airport, but it is best to put in a request for the container in advance. Amtrak will load your bike on a railroad baggage car, in lieu of an allowable piece of baggage, with the payment of a handling charge of three dollars for a journey up to 500 miles, and five dollars for over 500 miles. No articles may be attached to the bike. If you use a cardboard carton for your bike, you will have to remove the pedals and lower the handlebars. Greyhound buses will carry a bike as a passenger's baggage at no extra charge, but the bike must be boxed, its handlebars turned sideways, and pedals removed.

More and more you will see bikes—jammed in an auto's trunk or in the rear of a station wagon, or loaded on a car-top, trunk-lid, or bumper-mounted bike carrier—riding over the traffic-ridden highways to the freedom of the countryside, where a bike hiker or camper can renew his zest for living as he spins on two smoothly gliding wheels under his own natural power.

Rockhounding

A Pine Bluff, Arkansas, electrician and his family were scrounging for diamonds at the Crater of Diamonds near Murfreesboro. His infant daughter spotted a shiny stone and popped it in her mouth. Fearful that she would choke, he pried open her jaws and plucked out a $5,000 gem. Either because they are built closer to the ground or have keener eyesight, rockhounding kids at this extraordinary state park almost always spot more diamonds than do their folks.

Most visitors to the Crater of Diamonds believe that diamonds are a rockhound's best friend. A few years ago a Dallas, Texas, woman found a 15-carat stone, which when cut brought $75,000. The largest stone discovered at the 78-acre diamond-bearing volcanic pipe, the only

51

diamond mine on the North American continent, is the Uncle Sam Diamond, which weighed 40.23 carats in the rough, 14.42 carats when cut. The Star of Murfreesboro weighed 34.25 carats in the rough, and the Star of Arkansas weighed 15.31 carats in the rough. All together, some 60,000 stones have been found in the mine. Rockhounds, who find about 200 stones a year, may keep what they find, but they are advised to have their stones examined and certified as genuine by an official of the park.

Glaciers brought a thin scattering of diamonds to the kettle moraines of Wisconsin and to the fields of Indiana. In Indiana, diamonds have been found in Brown and Morgan counties. The largest of them weighed 4.87 carats. Some have well-shaped crystals, but most of them have been fractured by the grinding glaciers.

Some rockhounds prefer to look for sapphires at Montana's Eldorado Bar Sapphire Mine. Here they attend educational seminars, offered through the Continuing Education Department of Rocky Mountain College at Billings, and dig for sapphires. One man found an exquisite blue crystal tipping the scale at 28 carats. The miners lug their gravels to the shores of Hauser Lake and wash them in search of the stones. If gem hunting palls, they turn to gold panning.

North Carolina's Cowee Valley supplies not only sapphires but rubies too. Rockhounding families work along the Caler Fork of Cowee Creek. Their screening boxes turn up precious rubies and sapphires, garnets and amethysts. There are eight major ruby mines where Cowee Creek babbles around Situ Hill. These mines are the source of the notable Cowee pigeon-blood ruby. Nearby is Mason Mountain, equally renowned as a source of rhodolite garnet, a stone of rose and lavender, which is found at only one other place—in Africa. Rose Creek is the source of the ruby-red pyrope garnet.

Five miles east of Franklin, North Carolina, is Corundum Hill. Once the hill supplied corundum for industry, but with the development of synthetic abrasives, corundum was no longer needed and the mines closed down. Miners excavating for corundum had been delighted at finding pretty little rocks of deep red and cornflower blue. After the mine closed down, rockhounds discovered that the pretty little rocks that they had so often admired were rubies and sapphires. For a set fee of three dollars per day, rockhounds can dig around for stones to their heart's content. Standard operating procedure is, finders keepers.

North Carolina on the whole has over 300 varieties of gemstones and minerals of interest to rockhounds. They range from agate and amber to tourmaline and zircon. But the state scarcely can outdo Idaho, which appropriately calls itself the Gem State. North Carolina's gem areas have been explored and explored again, but many of Idaho's areas are so remote that they haven't been given more than an occasional cursory search. Agate, jasper, opal, and agatized and opalized wood are found with the lava flows of the southern part of the state. The northern part of the state has all of these plus garnet, emerald, sillimanite, and fossil flora. The central part has aquamarine, ruby, garnet, and some diamonds. Search Succor Creek in western Owyhee County for red and green agates and thunder eggs, which are geodes with the center filled with fluids or hollow and lined with quartz crystals. Fire opal is found in the lava beds of Squaw Butte near Emmett in Gem County. Rubies and pink garnets are found at Rock Flat near New Meadows in Adams County. These are only a few of Idaho's scores of collecting areas, and a rockhound can wander happily throughout the state.

The Rocky Mountains as a whole are incomparable collecting areas. Colorado's Rockies are a paradise for mineral collectors and fossil hunters alike. Arizona, the copper state, has far more than copper to interest a rockhound. Lynx Creek, not far from Prescott, offers gold panners the chance to find small nuggets. Azurite of a bright blue; green dioptase, which is a complex copper silicate; and the prismatic crystals of yellow-brown vanadinite are all to be found.

South Dakota is also an extraordinary state for rockhounds, who discover millions of pieces of petrified wood in the Dakota Formation at the foot of the Black Hills. There are more than 250 different minerals worth collecting in the Black Hills. The enormous pegmatite dikes near Keystone, Hill City, and Custer are famous for the magnificent feldspar, spodumene, and beryl crystals, some of which weigh many thousands of pounds. These same dikes also contain mica, apatite, lepidolite, and fool's gold.

Canada also has magnificent geological sites. Labradorite is found on an island off the shore of Labrador and is hard to get at; but sodalite, which is used in making jewelry, is found in the Bancroft area of Ontario. Jade in British Columbia, peristerite and amazonite in Ontario and Quebec, chalcedony and jasper in British Columbia, Ontario, Nova Scotia, and Newfoundland all appeal to rockhounds. Red jasper can be retrieved from gravel pits along the Trans-Canada Highway near Corner Brook in Newfoundland.

A Rockhound's Life

What makes a rockhound? Floyd R. Getsinger, Arizona rockhound, was scouting a field trip for a rockhound club when a housewife from Prescott drove up. Taking out a shovel, a prospector's pick, and a gold pan, she went to work. Her first pan produced several colors and a nugget about as big as a grain of wheat. It wasn't a bad find, and he was surprised when she ignored the nugget.

"That one is too small," she explained. "I need only three or four more large nuggets to complete a necklace; that is what I am working for."

The increased value of gold has caused many rockhounds to take a serious interest in the precious metal.

Placer mining has the greatest appeal. Some rockhounds try their luck in residual placers where gold is accumulated in a spot by the disintegration of the rock that contained it, in hillside placers which once were in a stream bed or in gulch placers, once at the bottom of creeks, but by far the largest number of rockhounds explore creek placers. They may find gold in bedrock, in clay overlying the bedrock, or in joints and crevices where the rock has been broken. Rockhounds should explore the entire width of the stream because the pay streaks are rarely regular. The streaks usually are parallel to the water's flow.

Not all rockhounds are so picky as the Prescott housewife. Some study rocks as a scientific pursuit. Others collect them to see how complete an exhibit they can form or look for stones that they can polish, cut, and engrave as jewelry. Rockhounds may specialize in gems, fossils, or gold nuggets. Women are just as avid collectors as men, and children become especially enthusiastic, since rockhounding fever seems to run in families.

A rockhound's tools are simple. He requires a prospector's pick, hammers, rock points and wedges, crowbars, shovels, spades, and a sifting screen. If he follows his enthusiasms into the backcountry or into the wilderness, he will have to learn the techniques of camping and backpacking and outfit himself accordingly. At least he is wise to bring along a compass, maps, waterproof matches, sheath knife, a whistle in case he gets so ensorcelled with rocks that he gets lost, a canteen, sturdy boots, a hard hat, safety glasses, work gloves, and a pocket first-aid kit.

He joins and corresponds with his fellow rockhounds in different parts of the country. He visits museums, such as the Lizzadro Museum of Lapidary Art in Elmhurst, Illinois, the Royal Ontario Museum in Toronto, or the Museum of the South Dakota School of Mines in Rapid City, that have notable rock collections. When he travels he stops in the schools of mines and geology in the states and provinces he visits to learn more about prime collecting areas.

When a rockhound goes into wilderness areas, he lets someone know where he is going and how long he'll be gone. He takes someone with him. He respects private mine rights and land rights and arranges well in advance for permission to visit a mine or quarry. Quarries, mine workings, and dumps, landslide areas in the mountains, beaches of seas and lakes, and streambeds are all places that he knows are worthy of his interest. There are few restrictions on rockhounds in most places, but he may not remove any rocks from the national parks or monuments in either the United States or Canada or from most state or provincial parks.

Canoeing & Rafting

CANOEING

Canoeing has its own jargon. If a paddler shouts "Right forward ferry," his partner knows that the canoe is to cut diagonally across a rapids, making use of the current to push it back upstream. A canoeist calls it "surfing" when a canoe is propelled into the "hole" formed in the water by currents dashing around a rock so that the canoe hangs there, balanced by the force of gravity and the rush of the current.

Canoeing has its skills too, and if you have any intention of challenging white waters, they must be mastered. A pair of skilled canoeists is a pretty sight. They are a well-balanced team that knows when power will get them through and when they must resort to finesse. They have expert judgment of the speed and direction of currents; the effects of rocks, snags, or downed timber in the stream; and what their canoe must do in response. They are past masters of the various paddle strokes. As a publication of the Colorado White Water Association puts it, "White water mastery means beating the stream you're challenging out of its hydraulic secrets. It means playing each eddy, riffle, and suckhole like a skier running a mogul-filled slope. Surely no sport offers more outdoor beauty combined with always pleasant, sometimes demanding physical and mental exercise."

Fortunately for the beginning canoeist, whose tribe abounds, flat stream and lake canoeing are not nearly so demanding. They are practical and safe for almost anyone if the canoeist observes water safety rules as well as the same basic rules required by any other trip into the wilderness or backcountry. A veteran camper or backpacker finds that his basic equipment and outdoor experience will stand him in good stead if he decides to follow a water trail.

Canoeing is increasing yearly in popularity. In the Boundary Waters Canoe Area of the Superior National Forest in Minnesota, the nation's prime canoeing wilderness, more than 160,000 people a year are setting off along the trails that run through streams and lakes for hundreds of miles. In contrast, during the halcyon days of the fur trade in the canoe country that stretches from Rainy Lake to Lake Superior, only about 350 French voyageurs paddled their canoes loaded with pelts and portaged the heavy loads over the rock ledges and down the trails, often knee-deep in mud in the rainy season.

Despite the use of lightweight canoes and equipment, portaging still can mean hard work and hardship, but this doesn't seem to detract a bit from the enthusiasm of a canoeist. Climb into a canoe and set it to skimming over the waters with the strokes of a paddle, and you feel clean and free. Your partner and you are in harmony not only with each other but also with the current and the woods around you.

Not long ago I canoed down Village Creek in the Texas Big Thicket with Neal Wright, a woodsman who has lived in the Big Thicket since boyhood. In any other part of the country, Village Creek would be called a river, and we found plenty of sometimes lazy and sometimes turbulent water to help us on our way. A pair of otters sported on a mudbank. Alligators sunned close to where we paddled. The virgin forest around us, a fascinating remnant of the wilderness that once spread across much of East Texas, is home to 7 of the 8 North American carnivorous plants, 33 wild orchids, and 42 different ferns. We could easily make out exotic plants along the banks as we glided by.

The Big Thicket is alive with birds. We kept an eye open for the ivory-billed woodpecker, thought to be extinct by most ornithologists but believed by many people to survive in the Big Thicket. There are Mexican spotted cats in the woods, bears, and a pack of rare red wolves. As dusk approached, we dallied on the creek, mesmerized by the birds settling down in the trees, the serenity of life in the wild. Then a fearful howl erupted out of the gloom only a few hundred yards from the banks of the stream. There's nothing like a red wolf howling in the dusk to set a canoeist paddling for a safe lift-out place well downstream and on the opposite bank. It's a trifle scary, but it certainly makes you feel part of the wilderness through which you're paddling.

Canoe Trails

In 1973, despite the record floods that swept down the Mississippi River, Reid Lewis, a French teacher at a suburban Chicago high school, and the Reverend Charles McEnery, a former navy ensign who became a Jesuit priest, portrayed Louis Joliet and Father Marquette in a reenactment of the 1673 canoe exploration of the heart of America. The eight crew members of the 1973 expedition included Jeff LeClerc, a 13-year-old Boy Scout, who was fortunate to be picked to represent the boy who was on the original trip. Dressed in clothing and moccasins handcrafted by one of the crew members, paddling replica canoes, eating from pewter dishes, and sleeping on the riverbank, the modern expedition traced the route of the first French explorers as part of the Mississippi River Tricentennial.

The continent today has many polluted streams that would have dismayed Joliet and Marquette, but fortunately there remain many waterways that canoeists can enjoy without holding their noses or running too much risk of becoming contaminated. There are even some remote places where they can drink the water.

A canoeist picks water to canoe that matches his skill and inclinations. The Arkansas River beneath Granite in Colorado ranks among the most prodigious white-water challenges in the United States. It surges through Pine Creek Canyon with a fury that strikes terror into even veteran white-water enthusiasts. Below Buena Vista there's a relaxing eight-mile run along lofty mountains, the Collegiate Peaks, before the river roars through Brown's Canyon.

"After this," notes the Colorado White Water Association, "the famous 25-mile race course from Salida to Cotopaxi offers few terrors except Bear Creek, Tin Cup and Cottonwood Rapids. These have been sworn at in at least ten languages. The Royal Gorge is boatable only by experts. Below it, this great river calms down as it passes quietly into the plains."

The streams of the Pacific Northwest and British Columbia are formidable too. They are mountain streams that in a twinkling become rushing rivers that calm down only for a short distance before they reach the sea. The Cariboo River in British Columbia's Bowron Lake Provincial Park appeals, as the British Columbia writer Harry P. McKeever says, to "humans who revere the wolf and his cousins, and my colleagues go when the city has become too much and the inner person pleas for release." A canoeist on the Cariboo neighbors with not only the wolf but also with the grizzly, mountain caribou, beaver, and such birds as grebes, herons, geese, ducks, grouse, and waxwings. He carries in supplies for 7 to 10 days and then a few days more in case he is stormbound, because this eventuality is all too common.

The canoeist makes the circuit of the lakes—Bowron, Indianpoint, Isaac, Lanezi, Sandy, and Spectacle—and goes shooting down the silt-laden Cariboo River in defiance of tree trunks protruding from the banks. He is careful not to run beyond Unna Lake, for fear that he will be swept over 80-foot Cariboo Falls. The threatening winds of Lanezi Lake are just as formidable a challenge, and canoeists hug the shores, ready to land before they are swamped.

On the opposite extreme is canoeing in Georgia's Okefenokee Swamp. My wife and some Georgia friends and I set out along the watery trails that wind through the "land of the trembling earth." Once the Seminoles followed these trails in dugout cypress canoes. There are no chances of white water whatsoever, only a maze of channels dyed coffee color by the tannic acid from the cypress bark. Egrets waded near the canoe, Spanish moss drooped from the trees, and the fragrance of the hurrah bush permeated the air. Here and there we came upon holes dug into the ooze by wallowing alligators.

"There's good fishing in the wallowing holes," claimed Jimmy Walker, a swamper and director of the Okefenokee Swamp Park, who was with us.

A 13-foot 'gator sloshed down a muddy bank and into a deep pool. We poked a pole into the pool to try and get her to surface for a picture, but she refused to put in another appearance. A 'gator never attacks unless a canoeist bothers the young or hunts them.

"But," said Jimmy, "they'll eat a dog any chance they can, so you shouldn't bring your pet into the swamp."

Canoeists follow the Okefenokee Canoeing Trails from the Folkston side of the swamp. They enter the wilderness either at Kingfisher Landing, Duck Island, or the Suwannee Canal, and are limited to one party on each canoe trail daily. Outfitters point out, "There is no fast water and very little dry land. Your paddle will be used every inch of the way as you wind through cypress forests or cross open 'prairies' exposed to the sun and wind."

At night canoeists put up backpacking-type tents on 14' x 20' platforms erected in the swamp for their convenience. Since they may not build a wood fire on the platforms, they must bring along gasoline, bottled gas, or spirit stoves. Many canoeists become so intrigued by this mysterious swamp, which has a compelling beauty of its own, that they return time and again. They obtain guides and cross the swamp to the Florida side. From there they can take the Suwannee River Canoe Trail, camping on the riverbanks, as far as the Gulf of Mexico, 270 miles away. There is only one stretch of white water just above White Springs, Florida, and inexperienced canoeists portage around it.

There are many canoeing opportunities in between the raging torrent of Colorado's Arkansas River and the still waters of the Okefenokee. For instance, there is Georgia's Satilla River, which gained infamy as the river portrayed in the motion picture *Deliverance*.

"Why almost anybody can canoe that river," Carolyn Carter, a Georgia outdoors woman, told us. "It's the last of Georgia's wild and scenic rivers. Its sandbars of pure white sand are located around every bend and are ideal for picnicking and swimming while on your trip."

Carolyn might have added that there also aren't any kooky backcountry folk lurking around its rapids. White water stretches are not dangerous, but they must be handled with skill.

Most of the eastern states have good canoeing. Canoeists start from Hancock, New York, and descend the Delaware River for a weekend. They spend Saturday night at Callicoon's Upper Delaware Campground and shoot the white water down to Narrowsburg. The Chicklacamoose Canoe Trip was pioneered by the Boy Scouts of Clearfield, Pennsylvania, and runs for 80 miles down the West Branch of the Susquehanna River from Clearfield to North Bend. The West Branch was once an important Indian canoe trail, and it remains an outstanding river for intermediate canoeists.

The New England states and the Great Lakes states have fine canoe streams too. There is also canoeing in South Dakota where the Lewis and Clark Historical Canoe Trail was pioneered by another group of Scouts, some 200 strong. This trail runs from Pickstown to Springfield on a section of the Missouri River that is almost unchanged since 1804, when Lewis and Clark passed along it. Canoes dodge sandbars and tree-studded islands. The 53-mile trip makes a good weekend jaunt, since there is a primitive camping area at the Curt Snodon Ranch, on the Nebraska side of the river, west of Niobrara.

The Arkansas and Missouri Ozarks are famed for their canoe streams, and so are the states of Minnesota, Michigan, and Wisconsin. The Brule River in Michigan's Upper Peninsula rushes through challenging rapids into Green Bay. Minnesota, the land of 15,291 lakes and 25,000 miles of rivers and streams, has scores of canoe trails ranging from the St. Croix and the Minnesota rivers to the Boundary Waters streams and lakes.

In picking a place to put your canoe into water, you might think of eastern Canada as well. Algonquin and Quetico provincial parks in Ontario offer splendid streams, but so does La Verendrye Provincial Park in Quebec. Canoe trails have been explored and mapped from park headquarters at Le Domaine, where there are also outfitters. The Tobique is a river tucked away in the northeast corner of New Brunswick. Its 85 miles of wilderness-canoeing waters run from tranquillity to foaming adventure. It averages a drop of some seven feet per mile. Probably the most exciting stretch is between Nictau Lake and the historic village of Nictau—30 miles of wilderness; fast, shallow water; rapids where tight turns are necessary; and splendid scenery. There may be a few logs left over from previous years, but the log drives on the river have been discontinued by New Brunswick timber companies.

Getting Ready to Canoe

"The more you carry in your head, the less you have to carry in your packsack," says Don Beland, a canoeman, who with his partner won the tough 200-mile, 38-portage Canada-U.S.A. International Canoe Derby, in the Quetico Provincial Park and the Superior National Forest, with a time of 33 hours and 38 minutes. Every ounce that a canoeist loads into his canoe ends up on his back when he has to portage from one stream to another. A canoeist's personal gear, clothing, and footwear are similar to those a backpacker carries, but the canoeist is more likely to bring along fishing tackle because he is often in a fine position to augment his supplies with a bit of judicious casting. If he is going into the wilderness, he carries freeze-dried and dehydrated food with him, but on many canoe routes he may be able to supplement his rations by buying food from farms and towns that he passes. Berries are plentiful along many canoeing streams as well.

With today's equipment, the modern canoeist is a far cry from the voyageur with his stocking cap and buckskins. A canoeist is certain to pack all his personal gear in waterproof bags, and these in turn are placed in packsacks for storing aboard the canoe. If he is going to defy rocky rapids with the possibility of icy spills in near-freezing water, he may also wear a wet suit. And many white-water canoeists wear crash helmets as protection against the rocks. In most states and provinces canoeists are required to wear life jackets, and most canoeists wear them whenever they climb into a canoe.

Canoeists have long since given up the birchbark and hollowed log canoes of the Indians for canvas covered, fiberglass, or aluminum models. Each type has its adherents. A 16-foot fiberglass canoe is rugged and will take rough water, but it weighs almost 80 pounds and is heavy for a long portage. An aluminum 15-footer weighs a little over 50 pounds, which makes it ideal for portage, but an unhappy encounter with a rocky rapids can play havoc with it.

Regardless of what kind of canoe a person uses, he carries good spare paddles. A boat should be decked with at least a third of it sealed off or contain the equivalent in secured air tanks. There should be secure handgrips at each end of the canoe. At least 25 feet of floatable safety line with an easily seen softball-sized float threaded on the end should be carried by the veteran paddlers in the party, in particular by those in the tail boat. A canoeist makes certain that there are no loose ropes to ensnarl the paddler.

Millions of canoeists own their own canoes, but others rely on outfitters at the shove-off points to supply them with canoes. An outfitter may also provide complete camping equipment, including sleeping bags and food, or he may supply only a partial outfitting, assuming that his customers will bring their own personal equipment and food. Most outfitters also can provide a guide if one is needed. At least they'll talk over your maps and routing with you and give you good advice on the streams and lakes you plan to cover.

Many canoeists join the American Canoe Association, which offers a variety of services. The association sponsors canoe cruising; flat-water, slalom, and marathon racing; and canoe sailing; as well as instruction in safety and canoe handling. Its guided cruises are among the safest ways to canoe in otherwise dangerous waters. The American Canoe Association and its divisions also maintain camp areas along canoeing streams for its members.

The Wilderness Society also organizes group canoe trips, as does the Sierra Club. Sierra Club canoeists are noted for their hardiness and love of adventure. Some 55 members of the Miami group of the Ohio chapter on a winter's day canoed down Kentucky's wild Red River from Koomer Ridge Campground in the Daniel Boone National Forest. They fought wind, snow, and swift water, because as their leader, Ray McLain of Cincinnati, said,

"There was plenty of opportunity for learning." At one time the canoeists had to turn their crafts about and back paddle in order to shield their faces and hands from the stinging wind and snow. Such canoeing is not for everybody, but it certainly offers a change of pace for a dull winter's weekend. Many other Sierra Club canoe trips are intended for family groups with teenagers and offer varied paddling down such streams as northern California's Eel and Klamath rivers.

The American Youth Hostels also provides canoeing in different parts of the country. Families canoe on streams that are appropriate to canoeists of limited skills and experience. The American Forestry Association's Trail Riders of the Wilderness program also includes canoeing. The Trail Riders along watery trails tour the Allagash River in northern Maine, a stream with just enough white water to afford necessary excitement, and the tranquil lakes of Minnesota's Boundary Waters Canoe Area.

Meeting the Challenge

The challenge of canoeing is far more than white water. It can be a wind over a broad expanse of lake. A canoe can be easily maneuvered in shallow water or within shelter of land, but the wind can whip up big waves on a wide lake, and a canoe, particularly if it is heavily loaded, can be swamped. Some lakes, such as

Lake Winnipesaukee in New Hampshire, are counted unsafe for canoeing because they are subject to sudden high winds and high waves. All large lakes should be treated with respect. A canoeist should plan to cross open waters in the morning or late evening, when they are usually calm. During the afternoon the canoeist stays in sheltered waters. If strong headwinds threaten, he paddles for shore and waits out the storm. Sometimes a squall hits without warning. If there is no time to reach the shore, it is a good idea to lie down flat in the canoe. This procedure will lower the center of gravity, thus stabilizing the canoe, and will help keep it from upsetting.

Rain also can soak a canoeist. He covers his gear in the canoe with a waterproof groundsheet and puts on a rainproof jacket. Insects are another affliction. North-woods canoe trails sometimes are bedeviled by black flies and mosquitoes. Repellent for face and hands, cover-up clothing, a backpacking-type tent, and a breezy island campsite are the best defenses against an uneasy night. The worst of the insects can be avoided by canoeing either in the spring or the fall.

Safety on a canoe trip depends on organization and planning at home, the right equipment, training and physical conditioning, and on common sense. If you aren't sure you're equal to a stretch of white water, portage. A canoeist should study maps, ask questions, and perhaps go and take a look at a river before he decides to run it. Particularly if the river is a small one, he should find out when the best water flow would be available. Spring high waters can make Alaskan, Canadian, and New England waterways dangerous. In the fall in some dryer parts of the continent, many streams are too shallow to be passable. The temperature of the water is critical too. Let a person be upset in water under 60 degrees, and he'll soon be chilled to the bone. He must get ashore as soon as possible. Most white-water canoeists wear a wet suit to protect them in upsets if the water is under 60 degrees. The buddy system is just as important in canoeing as it is in hiking, and for the same reasons.

A group that sets out to canoe a river should designate lead and tail boats so that there are skilled canoeists both showing the way and bringing up the rear. A canoeist keeps firmly in mind one of the basic tenets of the American Canoe Association: "The safety of the paddlers always comes before the safety of the boat, particularly in cold water." In an upset, a canoeist should not fight the currents and should stay on the upstream end of the boat if he can.

The Sierra Club's Ray McLain is an advocate of defensive canoeing.

"Rather than go as fast as possible—faster than the current," he explains, "we go slower than the current by backwatering. This allows us to have more time to make decisions, to choose the right angle from which to approach a rock. It's especially good for beginners."

Although Ray McLain is right, it should also be pointed out that some equally veteran canoeists paddle faster than the current as they enter a rapids. It may give them less time for decisions, but it gives them better control over the canoe.

A canoeist worthy of his paddle shows all the qualities of other good outdoorsmen. Campsites on some of the most popular routes in the Boundary Waters Canoe Area are deteriorating because of overuse and poor outdoor manners on the part of some canoeists. A canoeist back from Quebec's La Verendrye notes that "Garbage... the bane of mankind is already in evidence in the most remote regions of this huge land." Some canoeists in remote areas still believe it is all right to bury edible garbage or even to spread it around the campsite for wild animals to devour once the party has pushed off. This is wrong. A canoeist should follow exactly the same code as a backpacker follows.

Canoeists find public campsites along many streams. If they are camping for the night on private land, they are expected in most cases to obtain the owner's permission. In many places they must obtain fire permits as do other campers, and canoeists should obey all the sound wilderness practices concerning fires.

RAFTING

Ever since Mike Fink and other self-styled half-alligator, half-man flatboaters drifted down the Ohio and the Mississippi rivers to the New Orleans market, float trips have been the easy way to get there. Huck Finn and Jim, a runaway slave, climbed aboard a raft and let the current take them to adventure. Today's floaters emulate Huck and Jim far more than they do Mike Fink as they float such streams as are found in the Missouri and Arkansas Ozarks, drift slowly down the Black Creek in Mississippi, or tackle the Rogue River of Oregon and the mighty Colorado. It's adventure they're seeking.

A floating party may glide down a lazy stream or shoot down a rapids. They use johnboats, dories, neoprene boats, and several other kinds of current-borne rigs as the floaters let gravity and the water do most of the work. We used rubber rafts on the Rio Grande where it rushes through Mariscal Canyon in the Big Bend National Park of Texas. There were four of us in the raft, three men and an 18-year-old youth. Long before we came to the Slot we had been drenched many times by flying white-water spray.

Now the Slot was right ahead. The river foamed through a narrow gate in the rocks. We caught hold of a ledge and held tight against the current until a park ranger, who knew the way through the treacherous rapids, swept by in his raft.

"Keep to the right!" he shouted above the roar of the waters and plunged into the foam.

We cut loose. Paddling furiously we drove into the Slot. We kept to the right but still smashed head-on into a jagged rock. Water boiled into the raft, but then we were through and racing down a swift current into a lazy eddy. We were all wearing life jackets, as rafters should, and our food was wrapped in waterproof plastic bags and securely tied to our raft so that it couldn't drop into the current if we upset. We had plenty of excitement, but there was no real danger.

By lunchtime we had floated and paddled down the canyon to Smugglers' Crossing, where Mexican *contrabandistas* ford the river under cover of night. We went ashore on the Mexican side and ate our picnic lunches. There were other rapids ahead and stretches of river so serene that we could see the brilliant colors of the canyon walls reflected in them. Some streams are easier than the Rio Grande for floaters, and some are much more difficult. For instance, a 310-mile run down the Colorado includes 70 rapids. All in all, floating is a carefree way to travel, with succeeding episodes of adventure and interludes of calm.

A floater keeps his baggage to a minimum, and he makes certain that he has a waterproof duffel bag for his bedroll and a ground cloth. If he is going to bring along a camera, binoculars, or other valuables, he puts them in a waterproof can for protection. A floater goes easy on clothing. Blue jeans or slacks, a sweat shirt, sweater and lightweight Windbreaker, poncho, sneakers for the raft and hiking shoes for exploring the shore, heavy socks, swim clothes, sunglasses, and a broad-brimmed hat that ties down are on his list.

Some floaters have rubber rafts of their own and organize parties for a weekend or a few weeks of floating. Most floaters descend the rivers with outfitters, who can be found on most of the popular streams. Even United Air Lines offers float trips, two through Canyonlands National Park and one through the Grand Canyon. The National Wildlife Federation sponsors conservation safaris down the Colorado River. The Sierra Club offers river trips that allow floaters to explore hard-to-get-to regions, to enjoy off-river activities, and to share in the rough-water excitement. The American Forestry Association also takes floaters on such trips as the Missouri River Pioneer Adventure that offers both magnificent scenery and historic landmarks. The association's rigid rivercraft floats through canyons of gleaming white cliffs and stops to allow the floaters time for brief hikes to points of interest. The descent starts at old Fort Benton in Montana, once headwaters of navigation for steamboats, and drops downstream for 160 miles to James Kipp State Park. Just for a change, the floaters spend the last night sleeping in log cabins at the ghost town of Zortman.

Arkansas and Missouri are renowned for the limestone canyons of the Current, Jacks Fork, Eleven Point, White, Kings, and Buffalo rivers. The trout fishing is superb as floaters laze downstream in flat-bottomed craft called johnboats. Now and then the travelers help the boat along with a few pushes from a pole, for the streams are shallow. In the East, West Virginia has float trips through the tumbling rapids of the New River, and New York offers trips by lazy johnboat down the Delaware from Callicoon.

Pacific Coast float trips are entirely different. Exciting mountain streams tumble down to meet the sea. The Tuolumne of California comes thrashing out of the mountains to provide a spectacular floating stream. Not only Oregon's Rogue River but the McKenzie as well open up a world of rocky narrows and deep forests. The John Day and the Owyhee rivers take floaters through the volcanic tablelands east of the Cascade Range. Across the border in British Columbia there are equally exciting trips down the Chilcotin and Fraser rivers, through the boiling rapids of Moran Canyon.

In the mountain West, there are exciting trips on the Snake, which runs through Hells Canyon, and its tributary the Salmon. The Salmon is known as the "River of No Return," because nobody is likely to make his way upstream against its raging torrents.

The explorers who first floated the rivers of the West discovered deep canyons of forbidding beauty. The Grand Canyon of the Snake River in Wyoming is such a canyon. In 1876 Lieutenant Doane and his party took seven days to run through this precipitous, timbered canyon. Looking up at the towering walls of twisted limestone, they wondered if they would ever make it through the fearful rapids to safety. Since then the chasm has been called the Mad River Canyon, because the Snake goes mad during its passage through it.

Today in a neoprene raft and with professional river runners at the sweeps, a vacationer can race through this exciting canyon in from three and a half to four hours. Joan and I joined a party of 18—nine women, eight men, and one 12-year-old boy—who were planning to run the canyon in two rafts as part of a five-day trip down the Snake, organized by Denny Becker's Parklands Expeditions based in Jackson Hole. Becker first floated the canyon 11 years ago in a kayak and claims he did so right side up most of the time.

It was mid-September and this was to be the last trip of the season. Already there had been snow in the Grand Tetons, which look down on the river, and Jack Frost had colored the aspens in the foothills. Denny allows a personal gear list of 30 pounds maximum and suggests such things as a warm sweater and jacket, a pair of trousers and shorts, shirts, underwear, two pairs of heavy socks, sneakers, hiking boots or heavy tennis shoes, bathing suit, a hat that can be tied on, gloves, flashlight, sunglasses, insect repellent, suntan lotion, lip salve, bar of (biodegradable) soap, washcloth, towel, toothbrush and toothpaste, white toilet paper, and a small day pack. All the gear was to be packed in a duffel bag that could be put inside one of the rafts' waterproof compartments.

Parklands Expeditions would supply a sleeping bag, ground cover, a tarp for each family, life jackets, rain gear, and all the provisions. Cameras when not in use were to be stored in waterproof boxes.

We joined the party at their first camp on the shores of Jackson Lake in Grand Teton National Park. Harvey Norris and Dick Murphy, a pair of Snake River rats, were the guides; and Jean Sedar and Maureen Schmitt, muscular, attractive maidens, were the swampers who got wetter than almost anybody in trying to help the rafts off rocks and bars.

A boat took us across Jackson Lake to the camp, where the ladies immediately fell to comparing their flowered long johns. Joan won because she had butterflies on hers. We used outboard motors to run down the lake to the river. We stopped to lunch on the lakeshore. A mule deer sauntered out onto the beach and observed us unafraid. Some of us hiked up a canyon to a pair of tumbling waterfalls, while others fished. We gathered at the raft. Across a small inlet the 12-year-old boy, Rick, was casting from a gravel bar when a moose with an enormous rack strode out of the woods only 50 feet or so from him. The moose gave the boy an appraising look, decided he represented no trouble, and having studied us for a moment began to drink great greedy slurps of water and rummage about for plants. It was the rutting season, and a bull moose can be dangerous, so we called to the boy to remain quiet.

"Can someone come over here?" Rick quavered.

When assured that it would be better if everybody stood still until the moose had drunk its fill, the boy became a statue. Finally the moose shook a shower of water over himself and, giving the boy one last glance, withdrew with great dignity into the forest. Rick sped back to his parents as fast as he could run. A float trip is a lot more than running rapids.

Every day had its special interest. It might be a hike up Moran Creek or a particularly bruising bout with a sandbar. We discovered at the first camp that our fellow floaters fitted into two categories: selfish people who as soon as the rafts touched shore, seized the best tarps and scampered off to set up their own camps, and the public-spirited ones who helped to unload the raft and do other chores and invariably ended up with the skimpier coverings. By the end of the trip the selfish people were beginning to realize that their look-out-for-number-one mentality was not in keeping with life on the river.

One of the girls, whose legs were brawny enough to be those of a boy, still played a recorder like a wood nymph as we relaxed by the shore. She gave a lecture on how to operate the field potty with something of the air of an airline hostess giving flight information. Once we were on the river, we left the motor ashore, for it would no longer be needed. The current would now do the work. Osprey wheeled overhead, mergansers and Canada geese floated on the stream, and from time to time we saw a great bald-headed eagle soaring high in the sky or looking down from an eyrie atop a tall tree. The great bird appeared motionless, but his eyes kept us ever in his view as we passed through his domain.

From time to time we raced through white water—a taste of the Mad River Canyon yet to come—but most of the time the current sped us along smoothly and silently through a mountain world of unspoiled beauty. One night as we were sleeping, Joan and I were awakened by a pair of horsemen who rode down out of the mountains. It was a hunter and his guide, and they had a haunch of elk venison tied to one of the horses. They lit a fire and then in the light from the flames saw our shelter on the riverbank.

"Has anybody got a light in there?" the guide asked.

Because they had no shelter, they wanted to ford the Snake but could not do so safely in the dark. I got up and aimed a flashlight over the rushing flood of the river so that they could pick their way through the ford.

Our last day took us into the Mad River Canyon. We put everything into watertight compartments in preparation for the rapids ahead. Our first rapids were exciting, with spray sweeping over the raft. The next were even more of a challenge.

"Luckily the rapids are more or less regular," explained Harvey. "There are limestone reefs that reach across the river, causing the water to get wilder than the devil, but then there are always deep pools afterwards. That gives rafters a chance to collect themselves. Then come the next rapids."

We took turns at being at the front of the raft, for that's where the thrills are. We bore down on a cataract that we could tell from Harvey's face was bound to be the granddaddy of them all. Joan and I were up front. We hit it right in the middle of a colossal swirl of water. We plunged down into the maw, and a huge, eight-foot-tall wave broke over us. The raft snapped up and down like a giant rubber band, and Joan and I did magnificent backward somersaults and ended up in the river. The current sped us ahead of the raft downstream, but we held on. It was a little too chilly to enjoy the dunking, but getting tossed into the river is part of the fun of rafting.

The Colorado and its tributaries offer the most demanding and exciting trips of all. The Green and the Yampa rivers cut through the mountains of Dinosaur National Monument to create a dramatic float trip. In Canyonlands National Park, another portion of the Green River on its way to its union with the Colorado offers an outstanding float trip, but it is the Colorado itself that never fails to thrill adventurous floaters.

"It's a living magnificent thing, this Colorado River," sums up Joe Monroe, Colorado River rat, guide, and one of the outstanding river photographers. "It's wild and untamed, and down on its brown torrent looking up at those great canyon walls, a man feels miniscule and yet proudly a part of the creation around him. This is a good mood for man to be in."

Boating & Boat Camping

On a street in Winona, Minnesota, eight neighbors put down eight identical hulls in their backyards. The hammering and sawing started at one end of the block and moved right down the street as the men and boys worked together in the spirit of an old-fashioned barn raising to shape first one hull and then another. When the brouhaha of boat building was over, eight families each had a homemade houseboat that they could furnish to their individual tastes and interests.

Winona is a town in the Hiawatha Valley of the upper Mississippi River, and as has the rest of the nation, it has discovered the pleasures of water living. Some Winonans take to houseboat living with such vim that they spend the whole summer on the river. (On weekday mornings

Dad jumps in the family runabout and commutes to work in town.) Other families are equally dedicated to riverboating in a more resplendent cruiser.

Better than 43 million people in the United States enjoy some sort of boating activity, and there are some 3,500 different kinds of boats available, ranging from the most plebeian little runabout to the most patrician yacht. The entire population of cities such as Seattle, situated on magnificent boating waters, seems to take to a boat on a weekend. Not only the coastal waters of the United States and Canada but also the rivers and lakes are busy with boats of every type. Every year more than 100,000 people enjoy the pleasures of houseboating in Minnesota alone.

Marinas are everywhere, ranging from a homespun dock used by fishermen on a bayou south of New Orleans to the world's largest marina, the Marina Del Rey at Los Angeles. Marina Del Rey will berth at least 6,000 craft. Being a brightly hued fragment of Los Angeles, it is a bit freaky. A boater is apt to come upon Bill Burrud, of television's "Animal World," putting out to sea in his sloop, with a tiger apparently at the tiller. When another boat gets in the way, the tiger lets out a warning roar. He usually gets the right-of-way.

Many boaters are discovering that they can putter up a stream to a campsite that would be hard to reach in any other way, and spend a relaxing holiday. Others prefer to live aboard a houseboat that will take them to a quiet place away from it all.

Both houseboat and cruiser people have an easygoing friendliness. If a new boat pushes into a cove on a lake, its crew is bound to be invited over to a boat already there, for a beer or a cup of coffee. Still, houseboaters are different from cruiser families. They don't go in for boating garb, and they ignore the traditions of saluting flags and saying port, starboard, head, and galley.

"You don't care if the kids track sand all over your boat," one houseboating wife told us on the Mississippi. "Believe me, you just try that on a fancy cruiser and hear the captain scream!"

Some families start out with a cruiser and switch to a houseboat because they cost less to buy and operate. Other families start with a houseboat and switch to a cruiser because they have more style and speed and can navigate more challenging waters. Owning a houseboat is like having a floating cottage. It will sleep a lot of people for its size and provide substantial cooking and eating space. It is ideal for landing on a sandbar, because all a man has to do is beach the front end and then toss a hook ashore.

A decade ago there were only a few places where a family could rent a houseboat for a weekend or a few weeks. Today there are places to rent houseboats on good boating rivers and lakes from Florida to British Columbia. There are fleet operators in 42 states plus the Virgin Islands. Houseboaters putter through the forest-rimmed waters of immense Rainy Lake on the Minnesota-Ontario border or go cruising through the Everglades of Florida. There are houseboat rentals on boating waters in New England, the Middle Atlantic states, the West Coast, in Georgia, and in such unlikely places as Nebraska and North and South Dakota. The dams on the Missouri River have created lakes with close to 2,500 miles of shoreline for houseboaters to explore. Man-made lakes in Georgia, Kentucky, Tennessee, Arkansas, Missouri, and Texas are all popular with houseboaters and boat campers.

Houseboating appeals to quite the same people who enjoy traveling in a trailer or truck camper, for there is the same comfort and the same mobility. We tied our rented houseboat up to a lonely island in Minnesota's Rainy Lake where we could explore, fish and, in the evening, listen to a loon cackling deliriously to its mate out on the mysterious waters. When I came out on deck the next morning, I could see a doe spying on us from a thicket close to where we'd wrapped a line around a tree.

It is one thing to houseboat on an idyllic northern lake or a man-made lake in the Middle South and another to houseboat on the Mississippi River. We toted our gear aboard a houseboat docked at a marina on the Mississippi near Alma, Wisconsin. Frenchy, the marina boss, explained the boat well.

"It drives like a car," he said. "Backs up just like one."

Brad Krause, a youth from nearby Buffalo, was delegated to steer us out on the river and give us a few pointers about how to operate a boat. He revved up the 55-horsepower outboard that propelled the boat and backed up into Pomme de Terre Slough. It was indeed much as if he were driving a car. He explained the workings of the Kayot boat, its throttle, and how to start the motor as he wound among some stakes that Frenchy had thrust into the mud bottom so that boaters could tell where the slough was too shallow even for a houseboat. Houseboats have a shallow draft in comparison with cruisers and can pass over rocks that would dent the bottom of other boats. Houseboats also have watertight compartments that make it very unlikely that even a novice skipper will sink one.

Once we were in the main channel, Brad turned the wheel over to me and left by means of a runabout that came alongside. We bravely thrust our boat out into the main current.

The Mississippi is a maze of sloughs, backwaters, runs, and lakes that stretch from bluff to bluff to create a watery world dividing Minnesota and Wisconsin. Going upstream we kept the red buoys on our right and the black ones on our left. Soon we headed in for a sandbar because the warm sun on the deck suggested that the swimming might be great. We ran our twin pontoons ashore at the correct right angle, tied our ropes to trees, and settled down for an afternoon of idling on an island where monarch butterflies flittered about, waves rippled, and sand tickled our toes.

We watched a giant tugboat push 12 enormous barges up the river.

"What'll we do if we meet one of those guys in the channel?" one son asked.

"We try to go around it instead of under it," I replied.

Tows resemble a football field being shoved through the water, and they are the bane of both houseboats and cruisers on the Mississippi.

We backed out neatly and headed for Alma and Lock Number Four of the Corps of Engineers. The great gates swung open, and the light turned green. A trim launch entered the lock and tied up near us. The Corps extends free lockage to all boats, great and small. Soon we were on our way upstream.

One son at the wheel had developed a fine knack of swatting flies with a swatter while keeping the boat on true course. A wind arose, and choppy waves broke over our front deck whenever the channel twisted in such a way as to bring us into them. People waved from boats as they passed, and the living was easy.

That night we went ashore on another sandbar. We tied up to the trees, and soon Joan, my wife, had a fine meal cooking on the stove. The swimming was splendid. Later, when it grew dark, we sat up on the top deck and watched the moon shimmering on the water. A tow passed in the dark, its great Cyclopean searchlight scanning the water for navigational markers. We slept that night between clean sheets and under warm blankets. An otter splashed beside our boat, and our noses told us that a skunk passed close by on the bank. In the morning we were wakened by church bells from a town on the Minnesota shore and found fresh bear tracks about 10 feet away.

A houseboating or cruising vacation can turn out just about any way that you want it. You can swim or scuba dive, fish, just lounge in the sun, or enjoy the company of other boaters who tie up in your vicinity. Sightseeing is a pleasure for boaters too. On our Rainy Lake trip we stopped to see the entrance to a gold mine that was worked long ago, and on the Mississippi we paused in several river towns. The Intracoastal Waterway is a fabled route for Atlantic and Gulf coast boaters who want to include sightseeing with cruising, and the New York State canal system links up with Canadian canals so that a boater can cruise up to 2,000 miles.

Rental houseboats are equipped with a compass and a complete set of navigational maps for the area in which you are boating. The engine presents no problem. If it overheats, a red light flashes on the dash in front of the skipper and a horn blows.

Even if a houseboater has had little boating experience, he soon develops the knack of detecting a sandbar, a rock, or a snag from the ripples breaking around it. He learns to use landmarks, buoys, lights, and charts and to understand the navigational truism that "good pilots don't shortcut." A boater allows leeway for the wind and the current. A cruiser, sitting low in the water, is more moved by the current than the wind; a houseboat, riding high, is more affected by the wind than by the current. In a river a boat handles best when pushing up against the current. On the way downstream, it must go faster than the current or it cannot be steered. A boater never lets his boat drift in strong currents. Such navigational fine points become second nature to a boater, whatever his stripe.

A boater always heads into high waves and keeps his speed down. He also crosses the wake of another boat in the same fashion and avoids sharp, fast turns. Remembering that a boat does not have brakes, he puts his motor in reverse to bring it quickly to a stop. If a propeller gets entangled in weeds, he puts the motor into reverse and accelerates briefly.

Most rental houseboats are of the twin-pontoon hull variety and are capable of speeds up to 10 miles per hour. Some have a V-style hull and an inboard engine and can reach 25 miles per hour or more. The faster inboard boat is more difficult to handle, and at many marinas houseboat operators are not too happy about renting this to a family that doesn't have boating experience.

A houseboat does not have either the beauty or the speed of a cruiser, but it is roomy and can sleep anywhere from four to eight people. It has its own head, a compact galley with stove, oven, refrigerator, sink, storage cabinets, and a dining area with a table and benches that make up into a double bed at night. A rental boat comes equipped with dishes, cooking utensils, pots and pans, blankets, pillows, and towels. Operators provide everything from the broom to sweep off the deck and deck chairs to life jackets, life cushions, and other gear required by the Coast Guard to be aboard the boat. You bring along your personal gear, remembering such indispensable things as swim clothes, beach towels, and jackets and sweaters for the cool breezes that often blow out on the water even on warm summer days. Most of the supplies that a family needs can be purchased at the marina or nearby stores and at towns along the route of the cruise.

Comfort and Safety

Many of the amenities of "civilization" have been added that appeal to those who would not enjoy the more rugged, primitive, boating adventure. Boats are now equipped with push-button gearshifts and electric starters. Convenient galleys have electric ranges and refrigerators. There are even electric flush toilets, showers, and indoor-outdoor carpeting. Runabouts have been made so easy to operate that even the children can handle them.

Some boaters talk a good game. They can use nautical terminology with impressive skill and usually succeed in convincing the beginner that there's more to safe boating than there actually is. Whether a person is a sailor or a powerboater, he doesn't become a better boater by learning mere words but by applying common sense and the results of his own observation and experience.

The basics of boating are best learned by taking a course, many of which are provided free in the interests of safe boating. Public schools, the U.S. Power Squadrons, the U.S. Coast Guard Auxiliary, and boat dealers all may offer instruction. In Vancouver, British Columbia, the Maritime Museum gives a popular course for small-boat handlers. At the museum, Capt. Cyril Andrews, Master Mariner, welcomes all boaters to his classes on the International Rules of the Road at Sea.

"If you plan to put out into busy Vancouver Harbour, even in a bathtub, you should know the rules of the road," he advises.

Whether you put out into the harbor of a busy port city such as Vancouver; mosey about Lake Sidney Lanier, a popular houseboating lake near Atlanta; or venture up the Mississippi's channel, you'll find water-going police enforcing the "rules of the road" that have been established to protect the safety and rights of boaters and other people using the waters. Power-happy water cowboys are loathed by everybody from swimmers and scuba divers to fishermen, canoeists, and other motorboaters with a sense of responsibility. They are also ticketed by the police. A courteous and safe boater watches his wake.

The rules of the road on the water have been called courtesy afloat, but they're more than that. They are meant to prevent accidents. If a boater is to avoid a collision, he has to know what the skipper of the next boat is going to do under any circumstances. A powerboat skipper realizes that a sailboat has the right-of-way except when a sailboat is overtaking and passing a powerboat, but the sailboat skipper is also foolish if he insists on his right-of-way over clumsy and less maneuverable, large powerboats.

Just as an auto driver does not insist on his right-of-way if to do so would cause a collision, a boater avoids a collision at all costs. Nobody wants to sink carrying to the bottom the knowledge that the law was on his side. Four or more short blasts of the horn or whistle from the skipper means that he sees danger and is in doubt about what the other boat is going to do. He slows down, stops, or reverses his motor. He doesn't go ahead until he has exchanged the correct passing signals with the other boat.

When boats cross, the boat to starboard, that is, the right side, has the right-of-way and is expected to hold its established course and speed. A boat passes an approaching boat port-to-port whenever possible. A blast from the whistle of each boat indicates that this is what they intend to do. When the boats are so far from one another that there is no real possibility that they can meet head-on, they may pass starboard-to-starboard. The boats exchange signals of two blasts on their whistles so that the skippers understand what each is going to do.

A boat overtaking another must give way to the boat ahead. Two short blasts on a whistle indicate that the boat will pass to port; one short whistle blast indicates that it will pass to starboard. It doesn't pass until the boat being overtaken replies with a similar signal. Four whistle blasts mean danger. Both boats then wait until it is safe to pass.

No boat should ever leave shore without an anchor; whistle or horn that can be heard for at least half a mile; a white light for emergency signaling; and a life jacket, vest, or cushion that has been Coast Guard approved for each person aboard. Small children or nonswimmers who are on the water should wear a life jacket at all times.

Other equipment that a wise sailor brings aboard includes: a portable radio for weather reports; flashlights; spare spark plugs; oil and grease; extra line; a spare anchor; a tool packet that contains an adjustable wrench, screwdriver, hammer, spark-plug wrench, pliers, cotter pins, wire, assorted nuts and bolts, friction tape, string; and a length of strong manila, dacron, or nylon rope that can be used for towing. When we were houseboating on the Mississippi, the operators who rented us the boat did not put a tool kit aboard. Backing off a sandbar one afternoon, we were carried by the brisk current against one of the old wing dams that extend just beneath the surface. We pulled the motor to save it from hitting the dam, and in so doing, disconnected the rod that turns it when the steering wheel is turned. To our dismay there was no hammer aboard so we had to beach as best we could and scout the shore for a rock to knock the pin that holds the rod back into place. Some boat operators are not as careful as they should be about what they put aboard a houseboat for the safety of their guests. They take care of such details as fresh linen that are noticed immediately by the family, but they tend to skimp on far more important things that in the excitement of departure are apt to be overlooked, particularly by trusting landlubbers.

The kind of anchor used on a boat varies with the size and weight of the boat and the waters in which it cruises. The anchor line must be strong and long enough to anchor the boat safely. Veteran skippers say that the line should be at least six times as long as the depth over which you will possibly anchor, but if you encounter strong winds and heavy wave action even this may not be enough rope. The knots on your anchor rope are critical, and they should be checked from time to time to be certain that they will hold.

The anchor should not be tossed into the water. After checking to see that the line is coiled properly and will flow smoothly as the anchor descends and that neither your feet nor gear are in the way, you slip the anchor into the water and lower it slowly and carefully. When you raise it, coil the line as you bring it into the boat. Sometimes an anchor may get wedged between rocks or debris on the bottom or dig into the mud. Circle the fouled anchor with your boat under power to break it free. Then stop the boat, for it is both dangerous and illegal to run with your anchor dragging.

Emergencies do not happen very often, but they can occur. Even beginner crews should know that if a flag flies upside down it means distress. So do flares, a white flag, torches, bells, whistles and horns, or any other way of getting the attention of rescuers. If you are in a small boat and it overturns, try to get hold of a life preserver. In any case, swim to the boat and hold onto it. It is foolhardy to try to swim to shore, for it usually is much farther than it looks. If somebody falls overboard, throw him a life preserver or cushion and circle around quickly. As you come alongside of the person, shut off your motor. Then hold a paddle or line to him and lead him to the stern before you help him aboard. You should not dive for an unconscious person unless you're a good swimmer. Learn the lifesaving skill of mouth-to-mouth resuscitation.

A note to boat campers: Backpackers can always tell when they are approaching highways, and canoeists can tell when they are approaching waterways that powerboaters use. There is a sickening increase in the amount of litter, and campers can be blamed for only a small part of it. The same code that governs the right conduct in the outdoors on the land, governs conduct on the water. Any bottles, cardboard containers, cans, food leftovers, and other waste should be carried back to your home dock or launching area. Any camp or picnic site that a boating family uses should be left in better shape than they found it, for the outdoorsman wars on the slovenly habits of some of his fellow citizens with determination whether he canoes into the wilds or comes to it in a houseboat or cruiser.

Sport Diving

Diving with self-contained underwater-breathing apparatus in the Florida Keys opens up an exciting watery world of soft coral the color of a good rosé wine, blue and green or purple plants waving above yellow sand, and fluttering fish of fantastic shapes and hues. Such exotic beauty lures scuba divers into the labyrinthine reefs and the depths of the sea.

Other divers explore the continental shelves or the waters of the Great Lakes for sunken ships or look for extraordinary rocks or shells. Lloyd Enright, a Vancouver scuba teacher, dives in the waters surrounding British Columbia's Gulf Islands because he likes to play with the friendly octopus.

"They won't hurt you," he says. "A little one will nestle

on your arm as if it is a kitten. A big one's tentacles spread to 15 feet, but they also are harmless. An octopus is the nicest creature in the sea."

It was Benjamin Franklin who invented the original swim fins, and Japanese pearl divers long have worn goggles with bamboo frames. American Indians used the snorkel principle to hide from their enemies beneath the surface of ponds overgrown with water plants. None of this would have amounted to much except for Jacques Cousteau, the French naval officer, who in 1943 invented a sophisticated system for diving using high-pressure, compressed-air cylinders and a demand regulator. Cousteau's adventurous underseas explorations, his writing, and his arresting motion pictures popularized sport diving.

Sport diving appeals to people who love the water, and these for the most part are good swimmers. A scuba diver has to be in good physical condition too, and he should have a physical examination to see that he is not suffering from such problems as asthma, heart ailment, sinus blockage, or a perforated eardrum. He takes his instruction in a class sponsored by a diving shop, at the YMCA, or in an Explorer Scout program. He must learn from a qualified instructor at an accredited diving school if he is to become a certified diver. In most diving areas, only certified divers may refill their tanks with compressed air for diving or rent equipment.

Scuba diving begins with snorkeling. A snorkeler swims with his head underwater while breathing through the snorkel tube. Swimming becomes a thing of real ease when the swimmer does not have to lift his face out of the water from time to time to breathe. Of course, a beginner often takes water in his tube. He appreciates being in shallow water where he can put his feet down on the bottom if he gets a surprise mouthful of water when he expects another breath of air.

A proficient snorkeler learns to dive after taking a deep breath. He can study the bottom and as he comes to the top, blow hard into his tube to clear it of water. Then he continues the swim.

Snorkeling doesn't necessarily require a teacher, but scuba diving definitely does. A scuba diver's equipment consists of a tank, holding the compressed air that he will breathe, and a regulator that balances the air flow with the water pressure as he changes depths. Under ordinary circumstances his tank has about an hour's supply of air, and this gives him considerable range in exploring the floor of a river, lake, or sea. A harness straps the tank to the diver's back. At its top there is an air shutoff valve to which the regulator is connected by a fitting. It is the regulator that brings the air through a flexible hose to the mouthpiece. Cousteau's ingenious invention lets the air go at the exact pressure of the surrounding water so that when the diver plunges deep, his breathing is as easy and normal as it is at the surface.

Scuba divers drill ceaselessly on ways to meet emergencies. They learn the way to share a single air tank with another diver, how to get in and out of their gear under-water, and how to regain and clear the water from a mask that falls off during a dive. They learn that the buddy system in sport diving is even more important than in other outdoor activities: It is absolutely mandatory that no one dive alone.

There are dangers lurking in the deep waters. The wolf eel of the British Columbia coast is heavy jawed and evil. One diver stuck his arm into the lair of a six-foot eel, and his limb was broken with a crunch. Moray eels are a danger too in Florida waters, but they won't attack if a diver doesn't bother them. Barracuda and sharks rarely bother divers either. Coral and barnacle shells can be sharp enough to slice a diver open, but by far the biggest danger beneath the surface is man himself. A person who loses his head when trouble arises should never go scuba diving.

A rectangular red flag with a white diagonal bar is the international dive symbol. When it is flying, it means a diver is down. A diver should not descend without the flag being clearly visible to boats. Having familiarized himself with the waters where he intends to dive so that he knows what tides and currents to expect, the diver then learns what sea life is likely to be encountered. If there are scorpion fish, stinging coral, or sea urchins in the vicinity, he wants to be forewarned.

A diver needs an operation base, preferably a boat, where he can rest. He stays reasonably close to it so that if his strength or air supply fails, he can return to base with safety. He does not continue to dive when he is tired. He always makes certain that his air supply is pure and that he knows what to do in case either he or a member of his group develops the bends. Finally, if he is using a spear gun, he never points it at anything that he does not intend to kill. He never fires a spear gun if there are other divers in the area or if the water is so murky he cannot see exactly where the projectile is likely to go.

Where to Dive

John Pennekamp was a Miami newspaper editor with a lasting interest in conservation. More than anybody else, he was responsible for the Everglades National Park. Today the John Pennekamp Coral Reef State Park on and around Key Largo, Florida, protects 100 square miles, containing living coral formations. This is the largest underwater public recreation area in the United States. As many as 500,000 vacationers visit the park every year, but only a quarter of these snorkel or scuba dive. The majority of the visitors content themselves with viewing the underwater world through glass-bottomed excursion boats or bicycle-pedaled pontoon-type rafts. The park contains 40 of the 52 different kinds of coral found in the Caribbean and the Atlantic, and there are over 600 varieties of fish and some 1,200 kinds of marine plants.

There is good diving in lakes throughout the country and in the Great Lakes. On the Bruce Peninsula of Ontario, divers base at Sublimnos, a mini-underwater habitat headed by Dr. Joe Mac Innis of Toronto's Ocean

Systems, Inc. Mac Innis, who has dived with Jacques Cousteau and the American astronaut Scott Carpenter, points out that 48 percent of Canada is under water and that research into lake and ocean floor food and natural resources is critical. The group at Sublimnos has undertaken the "study of physical, chemical, meteorological and biological conditions in fresh water" in the pellucid waters of Georgian Bay. Students at Sublimnos may share the facilities with scientists. As a starter, 50 high school youngsters from all over Ontario, each an accredited scuba diver, came to stay at the habitat for one three-day exploration.

Minnesota's fabled lakes are a mecca for divers, according to William Matthies, a scuba diver from Brainerd, Minnesota. Matthies dives to recover such things as wedding rings, snowmobiles, and once, a flintlock rifle. He located five snowmobiles that fell through the ice in one week. He also finds rare coins.

"Most of the coins came out of slot-machines that apparently were discarded during Prohibition days," he says. "Usually people would drive to the middle of a bridge, park, then pitch the stuff out of trucks into the river. That's why divers often swim beneath bridges when they're looking for artifacts."

California vies with Florida in diving areas. There are at least 500,000 skin divers in the Golden State. Two of the coastal state parks have underwater extensions. San Diego city buses take divers to Torrey Pines State Reserve. Forty-two miles south of Monterey is the Pfeiffer-Big Sur State Park. The mountains shoulder down to the sea, and divers wearing wet suits against the chilly waters explore secluded coves. There are sea lions and sea otters, kelp beds, and better than 50 varieties of fish. Sometimes divers can get an underwater look at a whale scratching barnacles from his back on a rocky chimney thrust up from the sea floor.

Southern California divers also find that La Jolla Cove is a spectacular place. Small kids play on the beach and swim in the shallows, but the cove is also the beginning of a submarine canyon that reaches for 17 miles. At the mouth of the canyon is an underwater archeological site. Some 6,000 years ago an Indian village flourished on the spot and then sank into the ocean. It is illegal to collect pottery from the site as souvenirs, but park authorities welcome the aid of well-trained divers in solving the riddle of these long-vanished people.

Hawaii is another skin divers' mecca. Kealakekua Bay, close to where Capt. James Cook landed on the island of Hawaii, is a new state park. An underwater trail is being marked through shallow and deep waters. Trunk Bay on St. John Island in the Virgin Islands appeals to snorkelers as well as to scuba divers. The bay is in the Virgin Islands National Park, and national park service ranger-naturalists lead underwater tours for beginners. In 1961 Buck Island Reef, off the island of St. Croix, was made into a national monument to protect its extraordinary marine life. Buck Island Reef is an exciting adventure for advanced scuba divers, who can visit the intriguing grottoes.

Shipwrecks and Bottom Snappers

A bottom snapper is not a variety of fish. It is a variety of diver, who devotes much of his time on the bottom to taking photos. A bottom snapper looks for water of the utmost clarity as well as colorful formations of coral and sea fauna and flora.

Bottom snappers and other divers as well also look for shipwrecks. The waters of Nova Scotia alone hide some 3,000 wrecks, many dating back several hundred years. Only a few of them have been located. The search goes on in both winter and summer, since in 1965 divers located the 18th-century French naval ship *Le Chameau* off Louisbourg and found that it still contained a treasure of gold and silver coins and other valuables. Finds must be reported to the local Receiver of Wrecks. If the Receiver of Wrecks and the Director of the Nova Scotia Museum in Halifax consider the objects to be of historical significance, a reasonable sum is paid to the finder and the artifacts then become the property of the Nova Scotia Museum and a valuable addition to Nova Scotia's knowledge of its past.

Florida's wrecks range from old Spanish galleons sunk in a hurricane off Cocoa Beach to such ships as the Russian freighter *San Pablo* torpedoed by a German submarine during World War II, 10 miles southeast of Pensacola Pass. Scuba divers know that a telephone pole on the beach at St. Andrews State Park marks a spot 200 yards offshore where there is the wreck of a schooner. Not all wrecks carry treasure, but this doesn't matter to divers. They dive off Key West to inspect an old steel-hull freighter that sank in the 1920s while carrying a shipment of nails to help repair the railroad to Key West. Nor are all the wrecks of the nautical sort; a favorite wreck, a mile west of the Destin Bridge, is that of a B-25 plane.

Some divers who dive for treasure have brought sport diving into disrepute with archeologists and historians because of their ignorant and wanton behavior if they make a find. Similarly spearfishers, who bang away at almost everything that swims by, are in disrepute with conservationists. Rangers arrest and fine them in state and national underwater parks, and on British Columbia's Sunshine Coast, spearfishers are run out of the area without ceremony.

"They fire at anything that moves," a diver at Earl's Cove reef in British Columbia told me. "A mother lin cod is so tame you can pet her, and I can't imagine what sport these idiots find in shooting her, but they do. One party left 500 pounds of fish to rot on the dock when they went home. There's no place in sport diving for people like that."

Conservation & Wildlife

"It is a wonderful thing to be a naturalist," a naturalist at a British Columbia provincial park says, "even a bit of a one. Naturalists are seldom bored. Their lives are constant explorations of discovery."

In this time of environmental crisis a vacation devoted to wildlife and conservation can be both pleasurable and significant. An environmental camping trip could take a family to the renewed forest lands of Ohio that the Central Ohio Coal Company and the Hanna Coal Company stripped for coal, but then, beginning in 1944, reforested to create a constant source of timber and a recreational area open to the public. A family could visit the Dismal Swamp of Virginia where coal formations may be studied much as they existed in the Pennsylvania period.

A wildlife vacation can be an action vacation. In Utah the Ute Indians have established a resort at Bottle Hollow. Guests may take part in a wild-horse roundup on the *Nu Tuveep*, which is Ute for "Indian Land." On a hike into the forests of Quebec's Laurentides Provincial Park, a person who is at least a bit of a naturalist will see woodland caribou, which now roam the park after being flown from the far-north Ungava region by biologists of the Quebec Department of Tourism, Fish and Game.

A wildlife vacation can mean collecting leaves, birdwatching, stargazing, or searching for edible or medicinal plants. It might mean a trip to Isle Royale to learn about the relationships between the moose and the wolf pack that live in this island wilderness national park or a trip to Ontario's Algonquin Provincial Park where rangers call the timber wolf pack with recorded howls, and on cue the wolves howl back.

For families or youth groups who want to see how education and the outdoors go hand in hand, a camping visit to the Land Between the Lakes, developed by the Tennessee Valley Authority in Kentucky, would be in order. At the Conservation Education Center, classroom groups live and study in the outdoors. An interpretive building, nature trails, a "see and touch" educational farm, and wildlife in abundance teach the lessons that man must learn if our society is to remain viable. A youth station provides housing and dining for youth groups.

Everywhere there are fascinating things to see and do. In Louisiana's Kisatchie National Forest there are some 250 species of birds, including the rare red cockaded woodpecker and Bachman's sparrow. The bald eagle also can be seen in areas around Corney and Saline lakes. Campers in Maine's Acadia National Park can climb to the top of 1,530-foot Cadillac Mountain and look out over green forest, sparkling blue sea, and hazy-blue islands. On the eastern shore of Mount Desert Island, waves have tunneled 82 feet into the shore to form Anemone Cave. At ebb tide, pools on the cave floor are a microcosm of life—delicate sea anemones; tough, hard-shelled barnacles; plants and animals all living together in a natural community.

"Man is whole when he is in tune with the winds, the stars, and the hills as well as with his neighbor," former Supreme Court Justice William O. Douglas says. "Being in tune with the apartment or the community is part of the secret. Being in tune with the universe is the entire secret. Man's greatest mission is to preserve life, not to destroy it. When the land becomes the symbol of sterility and poverty, when the wonders of creation have been destroyed, youth has no place to go but the alleys, and a blight lies across the land."

The new outdoorsman is far more interested in the ecological scene and the wonders of creation than he is in gunning about a lake in a powerboat or even in hunting and fishing. If he goes hunting, it is with a camera. He will go on a whale hunt off the Pacific coast with a camera instead of a harpoon. Dr. Ray Gilmore, a noted marine biologist at Scripps Institute of Oceanography, takes vacationers armed with cameras whaling out of San Diego. Each year the California gray whales migrate from the Bering Sea to the warm lagoons in Baja California to mate. After the cows have foaled, the whales return in family groups over the same watery course to Alaska. Gilmore brings his boat within 50 feet of the surfacing whales and on occasion even as close as 10 feet so that the photographers have a real chance for pictures. How intelligent are whales? Dr. Gilmore claims that they are most likely as intelligent as porpoises, and it is no small feat to get close to them since they are understandably wary of man and his noisy boat. Probably because of their intelligence and ability to avoid capture, the gray whale herd is increasing today at a rate of about 11 percent each year.

An ecological vacation need not take a person to sea. He can stop off on an auto trip to Florida and hike the Canal Diggers Trail at the Okefenokee National Wildlife Refuge in Georgia. The woods around him have one of the most extraordinary populations of woodpeckers in the nation. This is the place to see downy and hairy woodpeckers and yellow-bellied sapsuckers, to say nothing of pileated woodpeckers and redheaded woodpeckers. To survive, woodpeckers need aged trees, and the vacationer who hikes along the Canal Diggers Trail will see the aged timbers riddled with woodpecker holes.

The western mountains of Georgia also have places of ecological fascination. Where only a few decades ago worn-out cotton fields stretched up and down foothills of the mountains, Callaway Gardens has been created not only as a place of beauty where native stands of azalea and laurel exist close to exotic trees and flowering shrubs from all over the world, but as a demonstration of how splendid forests can be made to grow on an impoverished land that never should have been used for agriculture. The nature lover who hikes back into the hills will find that nature has resumed her sway and that only a grove of white oaks remains atop some of the hills to show where once a farmer dwelled and tried to scrape a meager living out of the highland soil.

Presque Isle, the most popular state park in Pennsylvania, is also of surprising ecological interest. This peninsula, thrust into Lake Erie, is only a few miles from the city of Erie, but it has escaped the destruction of the lakeshore and remains much as the pioneers knew it. For thousands of years the lake has washed at the narrow neck to the mainland. Mike Warga, the park superintendent, told our visiting family that a violent storm could make an island out of the peninsula overnight. The polluted waters from the western reaches of the lake eddy closer and closer to the beaches and inlets of the peninsula every year, but with efforts being made to rescue Lake Erie, there is renewed hope that the peninsula will be spared.

A trail takes hikers to the foot of the Perry Monument on Misery Bay. Here in the lagoon Oliver Hazard Perry built the ships that won control of the Great Lakes from the British in the Battle of Lake Erie during the War of 1812. When his men finished their construction, they moved the boats on rollers over a sandy spit to the open waters of the lake. Today the spit has thickened and lifted due to the natural land-building activities of the lake, and the sandspit supports a forest. Perry's feat is now impossible. Out in the lake we could make out colonies of sea gulls whirling about the sandspits that are still forming.

Pennsylvania is also the state of Turk Jones. Jones, a Philadelphia advertising man, retired into the mountains in 1945 and began to replant the unsightly slashes in the earth left by strip miners near Clearfield. Experts said he couldn't plant for ten years, but he planted anyway. The trees grew luxuriantly, and his 1,200 acres are magnificent proof that nature can heal. Walk with Jones as, swinging his crooked stick, his dog sniffing at his heels, he talks with soft-voiced reverence and love about the superb stands of Scotch and red pine and white birch, and you'll learn something of wisdom.

A naturalist's vacation can take a family to the huge Wood Buffalo National Park on the border of northern Alberta and the Northwest Territories to see the rare ice age bison described by the Canadian Wildlife Service as "a towering beast that stands more than six feet, weighs over 2,000 pounds, is better than 12 feet from nose to tail, with a dark, shaggy coat." The animal is about 20 percent larger than the ordinary plains buffalo.

A naturalist's vacation can be in southern Michigan. Go for a stroll in the Allegan State Game Area near Allegan. In the 1890s the saws buzzed and screamed through tens of thousands of board feet until only a few white pine, Michigan's state tree, remained. As we hiked along the trail just east of Swan Creek Pond, once the millpond for Smith's sawmill, we could see how the pines are again spreading out into the forest of mixed white oak, red oak, sassafras, and elm. The trail is only eight miles long, but it led us to muskrats slipping into a stream, a hog snake slumbering peacefully, blue-winged teal, little green heron, and some spooky wild turkeys. Along the trail are Indian marker trees. Ottawa Indians bent saplings to show the way the trail ran, and now more than a century and a quarter later these trees showed the way for our family to walk where the Indians' moccasined feet had gone.

Wildlife Habitats

In deciding on where to go for a wildlife and conservation vacation, a family might consider the basic habitats that the continent provides. There is the desert, with its wildlife in sharp competition for the limited food and water supplies. The Great Basin is the largest desert on the continent and reaches from the Rocky Mountains to the Sierra Nevada. The low deserts such as the Mojave and the Sonora are fascinating too because of their giant saguaro and creosote bushes. Coyote and gila monster are just two denizens of those southwestern dry lands.

America's prairies stretch between the Rockies and the forests of the East. Prairie wildlife is mostly to be found on the western ranges, although there are a few surviving prairie enclaves such as Goose Lake Prairie in Illinois, near the place where the Kankakee and Des Plaines rivers meet to form the Illinois. There are the forests of the East and the North, the tundra of the high mountains, Alaska, and northern Canada, and the lakes and streams. Each has its own wildlife whereby man may learn the lessons of adjustment to the environment and survival.

Many ecological vacationers find that conservation goes hand in hand with recreation. They take their vacations with groups fielded by the Boy Scouts and Girl Scouts, the Sierra Club, the National Audubon Society, the Friends of the Earth, the Wilderness Society, and the National Wildlife Federation. The vacationers explore wilderness areas threatened with destruction by developmental interests to better defend them. They increase their understanding of life cycles and man's natural relationship to his environment and wildlife. Many of the trips are led by noted scientists and conservationists, and the ventures range from float trips down the Colorado through the Grand Canyon to backpacks through Alaska's Romanzof Mountains.

The Wilderness Society offers 76 trips of all kinds on horseback, on foot, in a canoe, or by float. Most of the trips are in the West, but there are some in the Adirondacks, the Great Smokies, the Everglades, the Okefenokee Swamp, and in the Minnesota North Woods. The National Wildlife Federation's Conservation Travel Safaris concentrate on areas where there are problems such as highways, dams, or jetports that promise to destroy more of the open country.

The National Audubon Society operates camps for adults. Nature education camps are located at sanctuaries near Greenwich, Connecticut; on Hog Island, in Maine's Muscongus Bay; at Devils Lake, in Wisconsin's Baraboo Range; and at Trail Lake Ranch, in Wyoming's Wind River Range. Some courses carry university credits; all are interesting and germane to the central issues of today's environmental crisis.

The Sierra Club, a pioneer in ecological understanding, also offers a score or more of special wilderness trips that are devoted to cleanup, roadhead cleanup, and trail maintenance. Because these are working trips, they are subsidized by the club's Outings Committee and the Sierra Club Foundation. They cost as little as $25 to $50, which makes them among the least expensive of all outdoor vacations.

A cleanup trip is typically a 10-day hike by up to 25 people into the wilderness to bring out trash left by litterbugs. The hikers restore campsites, burn whatever litter they can, and pack out what remains. A roadhead cleanup takes a party of 10 and a leader to where the road ends and the trail begins. Here they camp. They clean up the accumulated mess, hand litterbags to campers, and fan out into the backcountry to carry out trash. A trail maintenance trip takes hardy backpackers into the wilderness, where they mark or reroute trails to protect areas from overuse or erosion.

The Web of Life

Some wildlife vacationers seek to get a glimpse of rare or endangered species. They journey to a prairie dog village in South Dakota or Wyoming, not only to watch the intriguing prairie dogs but perhaps to spot the black-footed ferret, now one of the world's rarest animals. The black-footed ferret cannot survive without prairie dogs. The ferret takes up residence in their burrows, and when he gets hungry he eats one of his plump neighbors.

A vacationer may seek out a grizzly bear, for only some 850 remain today south of the Canadian border, or journey to Alaska to see the great white polar bear, which savage and unthinking hunters have brought close to extinction. In Hawaii such a vacationer may find the mother green turtle still lumbering up onto remote beaches to lay her eggs. Many of the once-safe, turtle-nesting beaches have been usurped for subdivisions, hotels, and tourist attractions, and the turtle also is in grave trouble.

The effects of DDT and other kinds of man-made pollution have brought many once-numerous species of fish to near extinction too. Even the proud North Atlantic salmon is becoming rare.

"Man is a part of the vast web of life and cannot escape the natural consequences of his actions," observed former Secretary of the Interior Stewart Udall.

Some wildlife vacationers go into the woods out of their concern for endangered species. They try to see rare wildlife in much the same spirit that people collect rare coins or postage stamps. However, under some circumstances, their visit can be a threat to the animals that they want to see.

In 1935 the Red Rock Lakes National Wildlife Refuge was established in Montana to protect the trumpeter swan, the world's largest waterfowl. Only something like 70 birds were known to survive. Today these big white swans are so numerous that they are being reintroduced into habitats where they have not lived for generations.

Success with the trumpeter swan led to the establishment of the Aransas National Wildlife Refuge near Corpus Christi, Texas. During the summer the whooping cranes live in the northern Canadian wilderness, but in the winter they come to the refuge in Texas. They are gradually increasing their numbers, but tourist traffic to their reserve has to be carefully regulated so that sightseers don't lessen the birds' chances for survival. To be a threat to wildlife, you don't have to be as miserable a human as the Wyoming rancher who hunted bald eagles on his ranch from a helicopter. All you have to do is be a thoughtless or lazy tourist who insists upon visiting wild animals from the comfort of his car, a powerboat, or a low-flying plane.

Ecological Wonderland

North America is full of surprising ecological wonderlands. Not far from Chicago, the Indiana Dunes State Park and the Indiana Dunes National Lakeshore contain some of the most magnificent of all living dunes. Take a trail through the shifting sands and you'll discover prickly-pear cactus that would do credit to the Arizona desert. Georgia's Skidaway Island contains a marsh of rare beauty. Ecologists study the sloughs through both wet and dry cycles. At the Ocean Science Laboratory on the island, visitors can learn about the marine life of the area and the effects of contaminants on the environment.

Huge mountain ranges shaggy with forests in Idaho's Panhandle are a wilderness preserve unchanged since the days when the Nez Percé and the Shoshoni lived in them. A family can study this wilderness or take a boat along the St. Joe, a stream that flows right between Round Lake and Chatcolet Lake. It is among the world's highest navigable streams. White-flowered syringas line the banks, and camas plants lift their blue blossoms up for photographers. It is a river of beauty, but a vacationer who looks beneath the surface will have much more to think about than beauty alone. Perhaps he'll learn that the Indians used the stems of the syringa to make bows and arrows and crushed the leaves for soap. In the autumn they dug up the bulbs of the camas and baked or roasted them for a meal. If they were too hungry to wait for the bulbs to cook, they ate them raw.

The natural community of a marsh on Skidaway Island, the beautiful flowering plants of the St. Joe River that the Indians made part of their way of life, the prickly-pear cactus of the Indiana Dunes, all are parts of the North American outdoors waiting to be discovered.

Regional Directory

THE NORTHEAST 80

    Connecticut 82
    Maine 84
    Massachusetts 87
    New Hampshire 87
    Rhode Island 90
    Vermont 90
    New Brunswick 92
    Newfoundland & Labrador 94
    Nova Scotia 95
    Prince Edward Island 96
    Quebec 96

THE MID-ATLANTIC STATES 99

    New Jersey 100
    New York 100
    Pennsylvania 103

THE SOUTH 106

    Alabama 108
    Arkansas 110
    Delaware 112
    Florida 113
    Georgia 115
    Kentucky 117
    Louisiana 120
    Maryland 122
    Mississippi 123
    North Carolina 124
    South Carolina 126
    Tennessee 127
    Virginia 128
    West Virginia 130
    Puerto Rico 131
    Virgin Islands 131

THE MIDWEST 133

    Illinois 134
    Indiana 137
    Iowa 138
    Kansas 139
    Michigan 139
    Minnesota 142
    Missouri 144
    Nebraska 146
    North Dakota 147
    Ohio 147
    South Dakota 149
    Wisconsin 151
    Manitoba 154
    Ontario 155

THE SOUTHWEST 158

    Arizona 160
    New Mexico 162
    Oklahoma 164
    Texas 165

THE ROCKIES 167

    Colorado 169
    Idaho 170
    Montana 173
    Nevada 175
    Utah 176
    Wyoming 177
    Alberta 179
    Saskatchewan 180

THE PACIFIC COAST 182

    Alaska 184
    California 185
    Hawaii 187
    Oregon 188
    Washington 189
    British Columbia 190

Pacific Ocean
VANCOUVER ISLAND
Str. of Juan de Fuca
C. FLATTERY
OLYMPIC NAT'L PARK
Vancouver
Calgary
Saskatoon
Diefenbaker Lake
S. Saskatchewan R.
CANADA
L. Winnipegosis
L. Manitoba
Regina
WASHINGTON
Puget Sound
Seattle
Olympia
Spokane
MT. BAKER 10,778 FT.
ROSS LAKE N.R.A.
LAKE CHELAN N.R.A.
ARROW DAM
WATERTON-GLACIER INTERNATIONAL PEACE PARK
MT. RAINIER NAT'L PARK
Portland
Columbia R.
Salem
MT. HOOD 11,235 FT.
Lake Wallula
Pendleton
WALLOWA MTS.
Snake R.
OREGON
C. BLANCO
CRATER LAKE N.P.
Missouri R.
Great Falls
Ft. Peck Reservoir
MONTANA
Helena
Lake Sakakawea
NORTH DAKO
Bismarck
GREAT PLAINS
Yellowstone R.
Billings
GRANITE PK 12,799 FT.
YELLOWSTONE NAT'L PARK
Yellowtail Res.
Bowman-Haley F.C. Res.
Lake Oahe
SALMON RIVER MTS.
BORAH PK. 12,662 FT.
IDAHO
Boise
GRAND TETON N.P.
CRATERS OF THE MOON NAT'L MON.
Pocatello
Snake R.
WYOMING
GANNETT PK. 13,785 FT.
BLACK HILLS
HARNEY PK. 7,242 FT.
Rapid City
SOUTH DAKO
Pierre
BADLANDS N.M.
Eureka
Klamath R.
MT. SHASTA 14,162 FT.
LAVA BEDS N.M.
LASSEN VOLCANIC N.P.
Humboldt R.
Elko
Casper
N. Platte R.
Scottsbluff
NEBRASK
Great Salt Lake
Salt Lake City
WASATCH RA.
UINTA MTS.
Cheyenne
Reno
NEVADA
GREAT BASIN
L. Tahoe
Carson City
Sacramento R.
Sacramento
CALIFORNIA
San Francisco
Monterey Bay
San Joaquin R.
YOSEMITE N.P.
Walker L.
WHEELER PK. 13,061 FT.
Sevier L.
UTAH
ROCKY MTN. N.P.
S. Platte R.
Platte R.
Republican R.
Grand Junction
MT. ELBERT 14,431 FT.
Denver
COLORADO
CANYONLANDS N.P.
Green R.
Cedar City
Sevier R.
Fresno
KINGS CANYON N.P.
SEQUOIA N.P.
MT. WHITNEY 14,494 FT.
DEATH VALLEY N.M.
LOWEST PT. IN U.S. -282 FT.
ZION N.P.
BRYCE CANYON N.P.
Colorado R.
Lake Powell
Blue Mesa Res.
PIKES PK. 14,110 FT.
Pueblo
Hays
KANS
Arkansas R.
Dodge City
Las Vegas
L. Mead
GRAND CANYON N.P.
GLEN CANYON DAM
MESA VERDE N.P.
SANGRE DE CRISTO RA.
PT. CONCEPTION
STA. CRUZ I.
STA. ROSA I.
MOJAVE DESERT
Los Angeles
JOSHUA TREE N.M.
STA. CATALINA I.
SAN CLEMENTE I.
San Diego
Salton Sea
COLORADO PLATEAU
PAINTED DESERT
CANYON DE CHELLY N.M.
Navajo Res.
Santa Fe
PETRIFIED FOREST NAT'L PARK
Albuquerque
ARIZONA
Phoenix
BALDY PK. 11,590 FT.
Gila R.
Yuma
NEW MEXICO
Pecos R.
LLANO ESTACADO
Canadian R.
Lake Meredith
Amarillo
Oklahoma
OKLA
Red R.
Lubbock
Tucson
ORGAN PIPE CACTUS N.M.
SAGURO N.M.
WHITE SANDS N.M.
SIERRA BLANCA 12,003 FT.
CONTINENTAL DIVIDE
SACRAMENTO MTS.
STA. CATALINA 10,135 FT.
El Paso
CARLSBAD CAVERNS N.P.
Odessa
Rio Grande
TEX
EDWARDS PLATEAU
Amistad F.C. Res.
Austin
Del Rio
San Ant
BIG BEND NAT'L PARK
MEXICO
Ft. Wo
Wich
50°
45°
40°
35°
30°
125°
120°
115°
110°
105°
100°
RUSSIA (U.S.S.R.)
Anadyr
BIG DIOMEDE
LITTLE DIOMEDE
Bering Str.
PT. HOPE
Barrow
BROOKS RANGE
Arctic Circle
Fort Yukon
ALASKA
Yukon R.
Nome
ST. LAWRENCE I.
HIGHEST PT. IN U.S. MT. MC KINLEY 20,320 FT.
MT. MC KINLEY NATL. PARK
Fairbanks
ALASKA RANGE
C. ROMANZOF
ST. MATTHEW I.
NUNIVAK I.
Bethel
Bering Sea
Anchorage
MT. KENNEDY 13,905 FT.
Seward
PRIBILOF IS.
KATMAI NATL. MON.
Bristol Bay
ALASKA PEN.
Gulf of Alaska
GLACIER BAY NAT'L MON.
Juneau
Sitka
ALEXANDER ARCHIPELAGO
KODIAK I.
Pacific Ocean
UNIMAK I.
ALEUTIAN ISLANDS
ATTU I.
KISKA I.
RAT IS.
ANDREANOF IS.
Dutch Harbor
CANADA
Miles 0 50 100 200
HAWAIIAN ISLANDS
KAUAI
NIIHAU
OAHU
Honolulu
MOLOKAI
LANAI
KAHOOLAWE
MAUI
HALEAKALA N.P.
CRATER OF HALEAKALA 10,023 FT.
MAUNA KEA (VOL.) 13,796 FT.
HAWAII
Hilo
HAWAII VOLCANOES NAT'L. PARK
Miles 0 25 50 75
©RMCN.

UNITED STATES
Barren Areas Above Timber
Evergreen Trees
Deciduous Trees
Shrub
Medium Grass
Short Grass
Tundra
Barren Arid Areas
Below Sea Level No Vegetation Shown
National Capitals
State Capitals
Cities and Towns
State Boundaries
1 inch = 220 Statute Miles
Miles 0 25 50 100 150 200
Lambert Conformal Conic Projection
95° 90° 85° 80° 75° 70° 50°
45° 40° 35° 30° 25°
Lake of the Woods
Rainy L.
L. Seul
Red L.
Leech L.
Duluth
Lake Superior
ISLE ROYALE NAT'L PARK
Marquette
Sault Ste. Marie
MINNESOTA
Minneapolis
St. Paul
Minnesota R.
WISCONSIN
Green Bay
Wisconsin R.
Mississippi R.
Milwaukee
Madison
Lake Michigan
MICHIGAN
Traverse City
Lansing
MANITOULIN I.
Georgian Bay
Lake Huron
Detroit
Toronto
L. Ontario
Lake Erie
Toledo
Cleveland
Buffalo
NEW YORK
Syracuse
Albany
L. Nippissing
Ottawa
Ottawa R.
Montreal
MT. TREMBLANT 3,150 FT.
St. Lawrence R.
Campbellton
MACTAQUAC DAM
MT. KATAHDIN 5,268 FT.
MAINE
Augusta
ACADIA N.P.
Portland
Montpelier
VT.
N.H.
MT. WASHINGTON 6,288 FT.
MT. MARCY 5,344 FT.
ADIRONDACK MTS.
Concord
MASS.
Boston
C. COD
Providence
R.I.
Hartford
CONN.
LONG ISLAND
New York
N.J.
Trenton
Philadelphia
Allegheny F.C. Res.
PENNSYLVANIA
Pittsburgh
Harrisburg
Dover
DEL.
Delaware Bay
C. MAY
Baltimore
M.D.
Annapolis
WASHINGTON (D.C.)
Potomac R.
Chesapeake Bay
SHENANDOAH N.P.
W. VIRGINIA
VIRGINIA
Richmond
C. CHARLES
Norfolk
Smith Mtn. Res.
Roanoke
Roanoke R.
OHIO
Columbus
Cincinnati
Ohio R.
Charleston
Frankfort
Louisville
KENTUCKY
MAMMOTH CAVE N.P.
BARKLEY DAM
Lake Barkley
Kentucky Lake
IOWA
Des Moines R.
Des Moines
Davenport
Omaha
Lincoln
ILLINOIS
Peoria
Chicago
South Bend
INDIANA
Indianapolis
Springfield
Illinois R.
Wabash R.
Carlyle F.C. Res.
Evansville
CENTRAL PLAINS
MISSOURI
Kansas City
St. Louis
Jefferson City
OZARK PLATEAU
Table Rock Res.
Lake Hudson
Tulsa
Beaver Res.
BOSTON MTS.
Ozark Res.
ARKANSAS
Dardanelle Res.
Robert S. Kerr Lake
Little Rock
OUACHITA MTS.
Millwood F.C. Res.
Memphis
TENNESSEE
Nashville
Knoxville
GREAT SMOKY MTS. N.P.
Chattanooga
Tennessee R.
APPALACHIAN MTS.
BLUE RIDGE
MT. MITCHELL 6,684 FT.
NORTH CAROLINA
Raleigh
Charlotte
C. HATTERAS
C. LOOKOUT
C. FEAR
SOUTH CAROLINA
Columbia
Savannah R.
C. ROMAIN
Atlanta
GEORGIA
Birmingham
ALABAMA
Alabama R.
Montgomery
Chattahoochee R.
Walter F. George Lake
Savannah
CUMBERLAND I.
Jacksonville
Tallahassee
FLORIDA
Apalachee Bay
Mobile
Mobile Bay
MISSISSIPPI
Jackson
Pearl R.
Mississippi R.
Shreveport
Red R.
Sabine R.
Toledo Bend Res.
Sam Rayburn F.C. Res.
LOUISIANA
Baton Rouge
New Orleans
MARSH I.
Atchafalaya Bay
CHANDELEUR IS.
C. SAN BLAS
Mississippi Delta
Houston
Omaha
Kansas City
Tampa
Tampa Bay
CAPE KENNEDY
L. Okeechobee
The Everglades
Miami
C. ROMANO
EVERGLADES NAT'L PARK
C. SABLE
Florida Bay
FLORIDA KEYS
Key West
Straits of Florida
Great Bahama Bank
BAHAMA ISLANDS
GRAND BAHAMA I.
GREAT ABACO I.
BIMINI IS.
NEW PROVIDENCE
ELEUTHERA I.
ANDROS ISLAND
CAT I.
GREAT EXUMA I.
Tropic of Cancer
Havana
CUBA
Atlantic Ocean
Gulf of Mexico
Longitude West of Greenwich

THE NORTHEAST

Thoreau was fond of taking the train in Concord, Massachusetts, and riding to Troy, New Hampshire, where he would get off and climb Monadnock Mountain, that rugged peak capped with stone that speaks of New England's out-of-doors. The mountains of New England and of Atlantic Canada have been worn by centuries of snow and ice and buffeted by wind and rain, but they still offer a challenge to any outdoors vacationer. They are a respite from the town and the frets of daily life.

This region, which extends from the meadows of Connecticut down east to the rocky coast of Maine and beyond into the Atlantic provinces of Canada, is as varied as a moose striding through the forests of Maine and a sport diver exploring a reef off the coast of Nova Scotia for a sunken wreck. It is the land where sap drips from the metal spile thrust into the maple tree when the snows still lie deep around the trunk. A sugaring-off is a celebration to welcome the coming warmth, a time when a countryman boils sap to make syrup and delicious candy hardened in the snow. Vacationers stop by a sugaring-off and join in this northern rite of spring.

Connecticut, Maine, Massachusetts, New Hampshire, Rhode Island, and Vermont make up the New England states. New Brunswick, Newfoundland and Labrador, Nova Scotia, Prince Edward Island, and Quebec are the provinces of Atlantic Canada. They are as renowned for cobalt blue lakes, rushing streams, placid ponds, and broad rivers as they are for mountains, bold coasts, sheltering harbors, and sandy beaches. Those who live in the region or visit there often have their own favorite places. One man may hike and hike again over the abandoned narrow-gauge railroad that runs from Wiscasset to Rangeley in Maine. Another man, believing with Thoreau that "the bluebird carries the sky on its back," goes bird-watching on summer mornings in the Berkshires of Massachusetts.

Hike out to the tongue of rock on the coast of Maine and look out over the darkening Atlantic. Behind you spread the ocean-girt cliffs and beaches. At the same time sailors, their practiced hands at the tiller, scud across the bays and sheltered inlets among the peninsulas and islands of the ragged coast. They can never agree on where it is best to sail. Some opt for the historic waters off Newfoundland or the Gulf of St. Lawrence, while others argue in favor of the waters around Nantucket and Martha's Vineyard. Some say that the changeable winds off the coast of Maine make this the most exciting place of all to hoist a sail.

Rockhounds find the region fascinating. Each has his preferred places depending upon the nature of his geological bent. Nathaniel S. Shaler, a famous Harvard geologist in the 19th century, spoke for a magnificent headland on Martha's Vineyard. "Gay Head presents by far the most striking geological feature on our eastern shore," he said. "These beds contain a greater variety of fossils than can be obtained in any other part of the coast region of New England.... A series of great cliffs leading down to the sea; these are of sands and clays having an amazing variety of colors, giving to the whole a brilliancy unexampled except at Alum Bay, Isle of Wight. Red, black, yellow, green and white, with many intermediate tints, are blended in bands which stand nearly vertical on the cliff. Some of the sands abound in sharks' teeth and bones of whales, and in other monuments of another time. Far out to sea we may perceive by the lines of breakers where lie the remnants of the cliffs which have been eaten back for miles. The sands and clays melt in the ravenous waves; the boulders are harder to grind, and remain after the rest has gone."

New England and the Canadian Atlantic provinces are studded with places to camp, to boat and canoe, with state and provincial parks and forests, and with national parks. Cape Cod National Seashore preserves some 40 miles of wide beaches, towering sand dunes and, when the winds are right, a rolling surf that is a thrill to encounter. Families with children are particularly fond of the seashore, a place of wonder.

Atlantic Canada has a Gallic accent to much of it and a Scottish flavor to much of the rest. Hikers head into the fastness of the Chic-Choc mountains in the heart of Quebec's Gaspé Peninsula in search of the wood caribou. Boaters trace the Saguenay, a river of extraordinary beauty.

This is also a land where the Appalachian Trail begins. Hike up the trail along the Hunt Spur of the West Branch of the Penobscot River in Maine. You cross the Tableland and reach Baxter Peak. On the way you come to Katahdin Falls, a tumult of water splashing down among rocks. In this vast domain this is only one spot of rare beauty. In Kent Falls State Park, in Connecticut, if a vacationer is partial to cataracts, there is a waterfall of rare beauty. Arched by hemlocks, the falls leaps over two drops.

To some the beauty of the region is best exemplified in the blue asters and stretches of a slope carpeted with mayflowers and checkerberries; to others it is Mount Katahdin, the highest peak in Maine, where the first light of the new day strikes the United States.

Acadia National Park, Maine

CONNECTICUT

Camping

BLACK ROCK STATE PARK, near Watertown. There is year-round camping in a wooded setting.

DEVILS HOPYARD STATE PARK, near East Haddam. Year-round camping in wooded setting overlooking Chapman Falls.

HAMMONASSETT BEACH STATE PARK, near Madison. Connecticut's most popular state park fronts for 2 miles on Long Island Sound. Campsites for short-term camping only are situated in open fields, but the saltwater bathing is outstanding. This and certain other state parks participate in Connecticut's Emergency Stopover Program for out-of-state travelers. During the camping season and after dark only, properly equipped campers may set up for the night in overflow areas. They must vacate the site by eight o'clock the next morning.

HOPEVILLE POND STATE PARK, near Voluntown. There is fine camping in woods close to the pond.

HOUSATONIC MEADOWS STATE PARK, near Cornwall Bridge. The camps are in wooded settings along the headwaters of the Housatonic River. They are open year round.

HURD STATE PARK, near East Hampton. Camping sites are in the woods near the Connecticut River.

KETTLETOWN STATE PARK, near Southbury, offers year-round camping on sites in fields and woods.

LAKE WARAMAUG STATE PARK, near Kent. There is year-round camping in the woods overlooking the lake.

MACEDONIA BROOK STATE PARK, New Preston. There are year-round camping sites in both fields and woods.

MASHAMOQUET BROOK STATE PARK, near Pomfret. Camping is in a wooded setting. Nearby Wolf Den campground is open all year for group camping.

PACHAUG STATE FOREST, near Canterbury. Campers set up their tents in the primitive sites.

PUTNAM MEMORIAL STATE PARK, near Redding. Nonprofit youth groups camp year round on the site of the Continental Army's 1779 winter encampment under Brig. Gen. Israel Putnam's command.

ROCKY NECK STATE PARK, near East Lyme. Short-term campsites in open fields and semiwooded settings are close to splendid beaches along Long Island Sound.

TAYLOR BROOK CAMPGROUND, near Torrington. The campground is in a wooded environment.

WHITE MEMORIAL FOUNDATION AND MUSEUM, at Litchfield, offers a tent camping area.

Backpacking

APPALACHIAN TRAIL. The celebrated trail enters the northwestern part of the state north of Salisbury and passes close to the highest point in Connecticut. It winds through the worn-down remnants of a once higher range that provide scenic hiking. Cream Hill, Red Mountain, and Mohawk Mountain are on or near the trail, which crosses into New York southwest of Kent.

Hiking

AMERICAN LEGION STATE FOREST, near Riverton, offers fine hiking trails.

BLACK ROCK STATE PARK, near Watertown. A wooded trail leads to a scenic overlook. This park is particularly interesting in the autumn, for the foliage is colorful.

COCKAPONSET STATE FOREST, near Killingworth. There are extensive hiking trails.

FLANDERS NATURE CENTER, Woodbury. The trail runs past bogs, marshlands, a beaver pond, and through the fields and woods.

FORT SHANTOK STATE PARK, near Montville. Hikers head out through the open fields where a Mohegan Indian village once stood.

GILLETTE CASTLE STATE PARK, near East Haddam. Hiking trails lead through the woods.

HAYSTACK MOUNTAIN STATE PARK, near Norfolk. The park is popular with hikers in the fall when the leaves have turned. The view from the tower at the top of the mountain reaches into Massachusetts.

HURD STATE PARK, near East Hampton. The woods are laced with interesting hiking trails.

JAMES L. GOODWIN STATE FOREST, near Brooklyn, contains fine trails for hikers.

KENT FALLS STATE PARK, near Kent. Hikers take to the trails that run along the stream.

LARSEN SANCTUARY, Fairfield. Five miles of trails lead through this preserve to reveal wildlife in varied habitats.

MACEDONIA BROOK STATE PARK, near Kent. Hiking over wooded trails is excellent.

MASHAMOQUET BROOK STATE PARK, near Pomfret. Hiking over forest trails is splendid.

MESHOMASIC STATE FOREST, near Hebron. There is extensive hiking.

MOHAWK MOUNTAIN STATE PARK, near Cornwall. Trails lead to the peak of the mountain.

MOUNT TOM STATE PARK, near Bantam. Hikers take the trails into the mountains.

PACHAUG STATE FOREST, near Canterbury. Hikers set out over trails that lead to a magnificent rhododendron sanctuary that is in full bloom early in July, to a mysterious castlelike stone house that was left unfinished by its builder, and to the summit of Mount Misery.

PENWOOD STATE PARK, near Simsbury. A hiking trail runs through natural woodlands to a high rise overlooking the Simsbury Valley.

POOTATUCK STATE FOREST, near Fairfield. There are extensive hiking trails.

ROCKY NECK STATE PARK, near East Lyme. Hiking along the crescent-shaped beach on Long Island Sound has its appeal.

SLEEPING GIANT STATE PARK, near Hamden. Scenic hiking trails lead to the peak of Mount Carmel.

SOUTHFORD FALLS STATE PARK, near Oxford. A scenic hiking trail follows Eight Mile Branch to Southford Falls.

WADSWORTH FALLS STATE PARK, near Rockfall. Trails follow the stream through the woods.

WHITE MEMORIAL FOUNDATION AND MUSEUM, Litchfield. Excellent self-guiding trails lead through the state's largest nature preserve. One trail is intended for the blind.

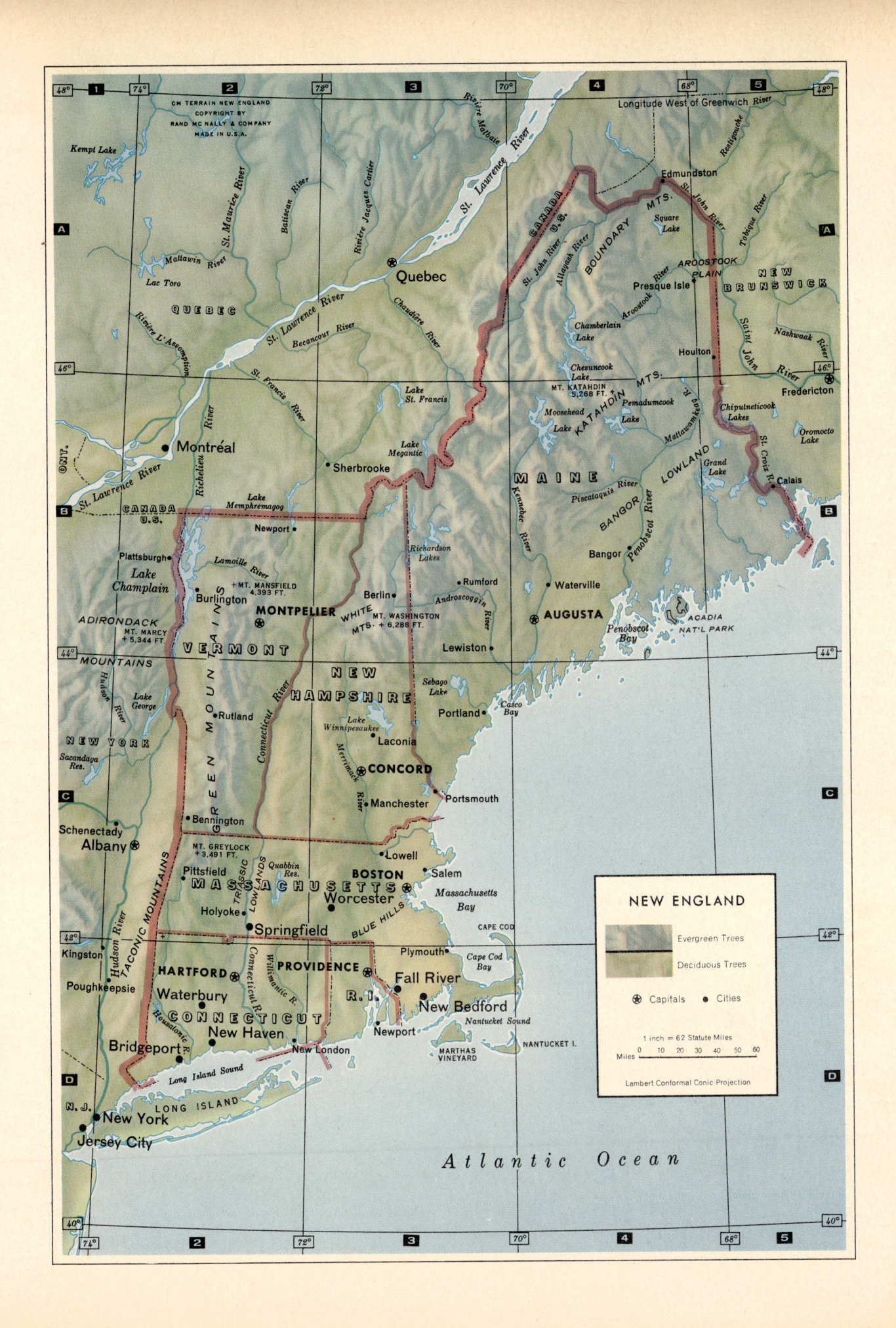

NEW ENGLAND

Evergreen Trees
Deciduous Trees
✪ Capitals   • Cities

1 inch = 62 Statute Miles
Miles 0 10 20 30 40 50 60

Lambert Conformal Conic Projection

Canoeing

FARMINGTON RIVER, from the Massachusetts line to the Connecticut River at Windsor. The 80 miles of white water and smooth canoeing are for experienced canoeists. Scenery is outstanding. Precaution: The water level is subject to fluctuations from the opening and closing of sluice gates and rain. Colebrook Dam and Rainbow Dam are among the impoundments.

HOUSATONIC RIVER, from Fall River to New Milford. Smooth and white-water canoeing challenges an expert. The river passes Housatonic State Forest and Housatonic Meadows State Park, where overnight camping is permitted. Precaution: Check with Hartford Electric Light Company at Fall River Power House for word of possible sudden river-flow fluctuation. Several dams are on the river.

LITTLE NARRAGANSETT BAY, Stonington. Napatree Point and Sandy Point Island protect the bay to make saltwater canoeing safe. Access area is at Barn Island. Precautions: Powerboat traffic can be heavy, and the winds can be brisk.

Boating

CONNECTICUT RIVER. Boaters in the Connecticut River should know the Federal Rules of the Road, because boaters are sharing the river with commercial vessels. The river mouth presents hazards. Among the access points are: Enfield, just south of the old bridge in Thompsonville; Farmington River at Windsor and just south of the Windsor-South Windsor Bridge in the village of Wilson; Riverside Park, 400 feet north of Bulkeley Bridge in Hartford; Wethersfield; Rocky Hill; south of the Portland-Middletown Bridge in Middletown; Haddam Meadows State Park; mouth of the Salmon River at East Haddam; under the Baldwin Bridge at Old Saybrook.

LONG ISLAND SOUND. The sound is the heart of one of the East Coast's most renowned boating areas. It is the most protected body of salt water in the region, and the Connecticut shore has many harbors, coves, islands, and inlets. The boater has a choice of open water, scenic rivers, estuaries, and wooded inlets. There are busy marinas and secluded anchorages. The sound is big enough so there is plenty of room for boaters despite its popularity, but on a summer weekend the vicinity of City Island and the mouth of the Connecticut River are apt to become overcrowded. Precautions: Weather in the sailing season is usually good, but thunder squalls may blow up in July and August. A boater keeps a weather eye on the northwest over the shore where the storms build up. He takes refuge in the lee of the land or in a harbor or cove. Because of the prevailing winds and the tides it is best to make an early start so that the day's run is completed by midafternoon.

Conservation & Wildlife

AUDUBON CENTER, at Sharon. There are self-guiding trails through this 520-acre sanctuary as well as an interpretive building.

CONNECTICUT ARBORETUM, on the Connecticut College campus at New London, is one of New England's finest small nature preserves and nature study areas. Part of the preserve is a cultivated arboretum, and part is kept as nature created it so that hikers can see unspoiled open land. The Thames Science Center at the arboretum has interpretive exhibits depicting environmental studies.

DINOSAUR STATE PARK, Rocky Hill. Naturalists with an interest in the early days of life on earth will find the recently discovered tracks of *Eubrontes* and *Anchisauripus* dinosaurs from the Triassic period fascinating. Excavations are in progress at the site.

FLANDERS NATURE CENTER, at Woodbury, has an extensive environmental center and workshop. Self-guided nature walks lead through bogs, marshlands, woods, and open fields and past a beaver pond.

HIDDEN VALLEY NATURE CENTER, near New Fairfield. The sanctuary contains an observation platform, self-guiding trails, and a bird blind for photographers. Nature programs are presented in the amphitheater.

JAMES L. GOODWIN STATE FOREST, near Brooklyn, has an extensive arboretum and conservation center.

LARSEN SANCTUARY, at Fairfield. The nature center displays the local wildlife at the headquarters of the Connecticut Audubon Society. There are over five miles of trails devoted to the study of varied habitats.

MACEDONIA BROOK STATE PARK, near Kent. This is considered one of the state's finest areas for studying nature.

MCLEAN SANCTUARY, south of Granby. This 3,400-acre wildlife refuge offers a varied terrain and a variety of birds. Naturalists explore the refuge on foot.

NATIONAL AUDUBON SOCIETY CAMP, near Greenwich. An adult nature education camp is operated at the sanctuary. Courses qualify for university credits. A one-week ecology workshop is offered.

PACHAUG STATE FOREST, near Canterbury, is a 24,000-acre nature preserve that is almost entirely undeveloped.

PEQUOT-SEPOS WILDLIFE SANCTUARY, across from the Denison Homestead in Mystic, is a small but choice nature study area. A trailside museum is devoted to conservation exhibits.

WHITE MEMORIAL FOUNDATION AND MUSEUM, at Litchfield. The state's largest nature center offers opportunities for bird-watching. Among the self-guiding trails is one for the blind. The museum has a fine natural history collection, including 3,000 colorful butterflies.

WILLINGTON GAME FARM, at Willington, is devoted to the preservation of endangered species. Among them are South American llamas, a Tibetan yak, West Indian sheep, and miniature deer.

MAINE

Camping

ACADIA NATIONAL PARK. A forest fire swept Mount Desert Island in 1947 but left a towering spruce forest called the Black Woods, which gives its name to one of two campgrounds in the park. Seawall is the other campground. Both campgrounds are excellent but apt to be overcrowded in July and August.

BAXTER STATE PARK, northwest of Millinocket. Camping in this wilderness preserve of 200,000 acres is memorable. Abol Stream campground is a secluded woodland camping area, and Katahdin Stream campground offers a splendid view of Mount Katahdin. Nesowadnehunk campground is a good base from which to explore the western mountains of the park, and South Branch Pond campground is at the foot of The Traveler. Russell Pond and Chimney Pond campgrounds can be reached only by trail.

COBSCOOK BAY STATE PARK, south of Dennysville. "Cobscook" is derived from an Indian term meaning "boiling tide," and the campground is near the restless waters.

84 THE NORTHEAST

HURRICANE ISLAND in Penobscot Bay, is the site of an Outward Bound camp. Professionally trained men instruct youths in an approach to wilderness living that amounts to a way of life.

LILY BAY STATE PARK, north of Greenville. Campers enjoy the magnificent mountains and evergreen forests. Fishing is excellent.

MAINE FORESTRY DEPARTMENT AUTHORIZED CAMPSITES are situated within the Maine Forestry District, which encompasses 10½ million acres, primarily in unorganized townships. Camping in these primitive sites brings a camper close to his environment. Development is kept at a minimum. A camper need not obtain a permit to kindle a fire at an authorized campsite, but if he is camping elsewhere in the forests he must obtain a permit from a Maine state forest ranger. The sites usually are equipped with a fireplace, picnic table, and a pit toilet. Drinking water is available at almost all of the sites, but campers are urged to boil or chemically treat the water.

SEBAGO LAKE STATE PARK, Naples. The camping area is close to Naples and offers splendid beaches.

Backpacking

APPALACHIAN TRAIL begins in Baxter State Park at Mount Katahdin, a granite monolith in the Maine wilderness, and runs past lakes and streams and along the crests of mountain ranges to cross into New Hampshire.

BAXTER STATE PARK. Campsites at Russell Pond in the center of the park can be reached only over trails. One trail leads from the Roaring Brook campground, and another leaves from South Branch Pond campground. Backpackers enjoy hiking into this site, setting up their camp, and then exploring the many trails that fan out in the vicinity. The Chimney Pond campground is also popular with backpackers. Trails lead to Baxter Peak. There are lean-tos, tent sites, and two bunkhouses that hold 12 persons each.

Hiking

ACADIA NATIONAL PARK. A trail leads among the evergreens to the shore at Otter Point. Lobstermen haul in their "pots" offshore. There are 150 miles of trails in the park, leading to the summits of mountains and along the rocky shores where the surf splashes.

BAXTER STATE PARK, northwest of Millinocket. Splendid trails reach into this park that contains Maine's highest peak, Mount Katahdin, as well as 46 other mountains. The Abol Trail leads from Abol Stream campground to the top of Mount Katahdin. Numerous trails also run from Katahdin Stream campground. A trail leads to the top of Doubletop from Nesowadnehunk campground. Russell Pond campground is handy to such fine trails as Lookout Trail, the Wassataquoik Road, and the Old Pogy Road. For hikers who want to find their own way up a mountain, The Traveler is the finest trailless mountain in the park.

BRADBURY MOUNTAIN STATE PARK, near Freeport. An easy trail leads to the top of the mountain. There is a sweeping view of Casco Bay and the White Mountains.

CAMDEN HILLS STATE PARK, north of Camden. A foot trail reaches to the top of Mount Megunticook, the highest peak of the Camden Hills.

GRAFTON NOTCH STATE PARK, west of Rumford, has interesting trails in the Mahoosuc Range southwest of Old Speck. The Appalachian Trail is popular with day hikers in this vicinity.

MOUNT BLUE STATE PARK, near Weld, affords fine trail and climbing country, topped by Mount Blue itself.

Bike Hiking & Camping

COAST OF MAINE. Bikers begin at York Harbor, close to the New Hampshire line, and ride "Down East" along one of the most magnificent coasts in the world. They avoid US 1 because of its heavy auto traffic and follow secondary roads that hug the shore. Bikers find campgrounds at the end of a comfortable day's journey. It is also congenial to take gravel roads and old logging roads that head inland into the wilderness for a day of off-the-beaten-track enjoyment. Local chambers of commerce can advise on interesting routes to take. Most bikers end up at Acadia National Park.

Rockhounding

ACTON VICINITY is a good place to look for galena, a steely gray, metallic colored mineral, which always comes in perfect cubes. Galena is found also in eastern Washington County.

BENNETT QUARRY, near Buckfield. Rockhounds find a variety of gemstones of high quality, including apatite, amblygonite, gem beryl, topaz, and tourmaline.

BLACK MOUNTAIN, some 10 miles northwest of Rumford on Maine 120 and left on a dirt road at Roxbury Notch. A rockhound finds old pits and quarries along the top of the mountain. Lepidolite, pink tourmaline, spodumene, and exquisite white beryl are to be found. Just after crossing the Rumford line on the road to the mountain ridge, additional beryl deposits are situated to the left.

GOODHALL QUARRY NO. 10, at Sanford, is a fine place to find vesuvianite, a silica mineral that ranges from brown to very dark green. Well-developed rectangular or block-shaped crystals are usually found near limestone beds.

JASPER BEACH, near Bucks Harbor. The red beaches in the area contain red rhyolite, which makes outstanding polished specimens.

MOUNT MICA, north of South Paris, is a popular place to find tourmaline, gem beryl, lepidolite, and a variety of other minerals. Pegmatite from this vicinity has found its way into thousands of rockhound collections.

NEWRY VICINITY. Mines near this town are excellent for collecting tourmaline, apatite, beryl, and rose quartz.

PARIS-HEBRON LOCALITIES, northwest of Hebron, include the Foster and Mount Marie mines and the Mills and Haverinen quarries. The dumps and quarry walls contain gem beryl, garnet, tourmaline, and quartz crystals. Occasionally rockhounds find the rare minerals: columbite, tantalite, and pollucite.

RUBELLITE MINE, on Maine 26 northwest of South Paris, is a fine place to find gem beryl, rutile, pollucite, varicolored tourmaline and, above all, fluorescent pegmatites.

SWIFT RIVER TRIBUTARIES yield flakes of gold. Rockhounds pan for gold.

TAMMINEN QUARRY AND HARVARD QUARRY, northwest of South Paris, were worked commercially for feldspar, but they are now inactive. Among the stones found in the mines are gemstock tourmaline, apatite, beryl, and rose quartz.

TOPSHAM AREA, situated about 4 miles north of Topsham on Maine 24, include quarries where rockhounds may turn up red garnets, green tourmaline, and smoky quartz crystals. Some gem topaz has been discovered over the years.

Saco River, New Hampshire

Canoeing

ALLAGASH WILDERNESS WATERWAY. Canoeists put in at Chamberlain Lake and paddle on to Donley's Point and Eagle, High Bank, Churchill, and Long lakes. In this wilderness area, close to the Canadian border, a modern-day voyageur may see white-tailed deer, moose, beaver, muskrat, and bald eagle. Downstream from Green Point, the route passes through Musquacook to Five Finger Brook and Ramsey Ledges to Allagash Falls. It continues on down the St. John River to Rankin Rapids and St. Francis. There are a pair of portages, and both white-water and flat-water stretches. There is an American Forestry Association Trail Riders of the Wilderness program on the Allagash.

BELGRADE LAKES CIRCLE TRIP begins near Oakland and runs through North Pond, Great Pond, Long Pond, Messalonskee Lake, and back to Oakland. It is an enjoyable two-day trip.

KENNEBEC RIVER, in the vicinity of Waterville. From Carry Brook Eddy to the Forks, there are 9 miles of difficult rapids, with water levels fluctuating from shallow to dangerous. Check at the Harris Generating Station for information on flows. The state of Maine realizes that some expert canoeists are going to insist on running the East Outlet of Moosehead Lake or the rapids below the dam at Indian Point. The Outlet may be run only after checking the stream carefully from the shore and checking as well about pulp logs and flow rate at the Kennebec Water Power Company in Waterville. Below Indian Point, canoeists, no matter how expert, should stay out. The river roars into a gorge and becomes impassable with no return.

LITTLE ANDROSCOGGIN, from above West Paris to South Paris, is broken by a tumultuous rapids at Snow's Falls.

LITTLE OSSIPEE RIVER to the Saco River provides some of southern Maine's most redoubtable canoeing. Some stretches are for strong, experienced groups only.

RANGELEY LAKES afford an interesting canoe trip through such lakes as Mooselookmeguntic, Capsoptie, and Richardson.

SACO RIVER from Swan's Falls to Hiram offers 33 miles of safe water, including only one easy rip. There are no portages. Below Hiram another 44-mile stretch runs to the ocean, but there are 8 to 10 portages around dams, rips, and gorges.

ST. CROIX RIVER, from Vanceboro to Kellyland. There are 33 miles of rough rapids that will test the most experienced canoeist. The river rates as very difficult according to the A.M.C. Canoeing Guide.

ST. CROIX VOYAGERS, at Auburn, offers extraordinary camping-canoeing trips organized by Linwood Dwelley, one of the state's best-known guides. The trips follow wilderness rivers.

SHEEPSCOT RIVER. From Montville to West Branch there are sharp drops requiring a line or carry and one to three portages. Below Sheepscot Pond the river is for experts.

Boating & Boat Camping

COAST OF MAINE is one of the New World's outstanding boating areas. Boaters sail the briny deeps from scores of splendid and hospitable harbors. Among these are York Harbor, York Beach, Kennebunkport, Portland Harbor, Bar Harbor, Boothbay Harbor, Camden, Monhegan Island, Popham Beach, and Islesboro. Casco Bay off Portland Harbor has hundreds of islands that help make this one of the most popular of all the coastal boating areas.

MAINE SAILING SCHOOL, at Northport, offers coeducational training to sailors.

WARREN ISLAND STATE PARK, Penobscot Bay, can be reached by boat only and provides docking and mooring facilities on the lee side. Boaters may either sleep aboard their boat or moor it and camp in a park shelter or their own tent.

Conservation & Wildlife

ACADIA NATIONAL PARK. On the eastern shore of Mount Desert Island is Anemone Cave, where waves have tunneled 82 feet into the shore. At ebb tide delicate sea anemones, hard-shelled barnacles, and many other plants and animals can be seen in the pools on the cave floor.

BAXTER STATE PARK, northwest of Millinocket, is a gift to the state of Maine by a former governor, Percival Baxter, and is "to be kept in its natural wild state and as a sanctuary for wild beasts and birds." Among the park's animals are: moose, white-tailed deer, black bear, mink, weasels, snowshoe hare, and both the fisher and pine marten. The birds include not only such northern Maine favorites as the Canada jay and pipit but the much more rare spruce grouse, which are common here. The forests range from northern hardwood to northern coniferous, and there are also alpine zones with arctic plants.

86 THE NORTHEAST

HOG ISLAND, on Muscongus Bay, is a National Audubon Society camp where courses are offered in nature education. The camp's certificate is recognized by many school systems for in-service credits for teachers.

HOLBROOK ISLAND SANCTUARY, on Penobscot Bay, south of Bucksport, protects a natural area for ecological study purposes.

JACKSON LABORATORY, Bar Harbor, is the leading center for research into mammalian genetics. During the summer there are visitor programs.

MASSACHUSETTS

Camping

BEARTOWN STATE FOREST, at Monterey. Camping sites are primitive and appealing to those who like to rough it.

GREYLOCK MOUNTAIN STATE RESERVATION, Adams, has fine camping sites. Campers set up their tents on the shoulders of Mount Greylock, highest point in the state.

HORSENECK BEACH STATE RESERVATION, at Westport, has 100 camping sites.

PITTSFIELD STATE FOREST, at Pittsfield, offers camping sites with improved sanitary facilities.

ROLAND C. NICKERSON STATE PARK, at Brewster, offers splendid camping in a pine forest. There are 400 sites.

SALISBURY BEACH STATE RESERVATION, at Salisbury Beach, offers camping close to the sea.

Backpacking

APPALACHIAN TRAIL enters the state northeast of Williamstown and twists along the summits of the Berkshires. It crosses into Connecticut southwest of Great Barrington.

Hiking

BASH BISH FALLS STATE FOREST, at Mount Washington, contains fine hiking trails.

CAPE COD NATIONAL SEASHORE. The Pilgrim Springs Trail starts at the interpretive shelter near Truro and runs among pitch pine and thickets of bearberry to the long sandy beaches. The Pilgrims went this way when they first landed in the New World, and modern-day hikers come to the place where the Pilgrims found a corn cache left by the Indians. There are other fine trails in the seashore area, and a hiker can ramble down the beaches to suit himself.

J. A. SKINNER STATE PARK, north of Holyoke. Hikers ascend Mount Holyoke for a 70-mile view of the Connecticut Valley.

PURGATORY CHASM STATE RESERVATION, south of Worcester. A trail follows the chasm, which is ¼ mile long and up to 70 feet deep.

Bike Hiking & Camping

CAPE COD NATIONAL SEASHORE. A network of bikeways leads to beaches, cranberry bogs, and historic lighthouses. The Province Lands Trail is an 8-mile loop and takes a biker to sand dunes. The Eastham Bikeway goes to the Nauset Lighthouse. The Little America Youth Hostel at Truro is handy to the trail.

NANTUCKET ISLAND. Bikers take a ferry from Hyannis on Cape Cod to the island. Sand dunes, seafarers' villages, and beaches all appeal.

Boating

CAPE COD. The waters surrounding Cape Cod are popular with boaters. Inlets and islands abound, and friendly harbors are always within easy reach.

Conservation & Wildlife

CAPE COD NATIONAL SEASHORE. There are many nature walks that explain the ecology of the cape. In the summer, guided walks through the Nauset Marsh begin at Coast Guard Beach. Guided walks through the Province Lands at Provincetown run through the dunes and beech forests past ponds to the sea. There are other trails in the Pilgrim Heights area. The Pilgrim Springs Trail and Small's Swamp Nature Trail run through the salt meadows. Ducks and other waterfowl inhabit the marshes. There are also pitch pine forests and bearberry heaths around kettles formed long ago by melting glacial ice. In the Marconi Station Area, at Wellfleet, nature lovers follow the White Cedar Swamp Trail.

NAUSET BEACH. Bottle-nosed whales are sometimes seen from the beach.

ROCK HARBOR. Harbor seals often sport in the harbor of this Cape Cod town.

WELLFLEET BAY SANCTUARY, near Wellfleet on Cape Cod, is owned by the Massachusetts Audubon Society. There are summer jeep tours along the beach, a September nature camp-out, and a Christmas bird count.

YARMOUTH HISTORICAL SOCIETY TRAILS begin at the Yarmouth Historical Society center in Yarmouth Port and run through lovely woodlands and meadows. Wild cranberry, copper beeches, and Cape Cod pine are on the trails.

NEW HAMPSHIRE

Camping

CRAWFORD NOTCH STATE PARK. North of Bartlett is the Dry River campground. It is ideal for campers who want to hike mountain trails.

FRANCONIA NOTCH STATE PARK, north of North Woodstock. Lafayette campground is ideal for family camping.

JIGGER JOHNSON, west of Conway on the scenic Kancamagus Highway in the White Mountain National Forest, offers easy access to Swift River and its trout.

MOOSE BROOK STATE PARK, just west of Gorham. The campground is an excellent base for mountain climbing.

OLIVERIAN, southeast of Haverhill. Campers enjoy the majestic trees and hike the trail to Mount Moosilauke and other peaks in the White Mountain National Forest.

TUCKERMAN RAVINE, south of Gorham. The campgrounds can be reached only over the Tuckerman Ravine hiking trail. No wood fires are allowed.

WATERVILLE, northeast of Campton on Mad River Road. There is wading for kids in Mad River.

Backpacking

APPALACHIAN TRAIL. The trail enters the state east of Gorham and traverses the White Mountain National Forest to cross into Vermont near Hanover. This section of the trail represents some of

THE NORTHEAST 87

Allagash River, Maine

88 THE NORTHEAST

the northeast's finest backpacking. Moreover, it is tied in to hundreds of miles of excellent trails in the national forest, a splendid wilderness area. The Appalachian Mountain Club maintains nine huts high in the mountains from Center Notch in the east to Lonesome Lake in the west.

WHITE MOUNTAIN NATIONAL FOREST. Backpackers follow the trails to the Sawyer Ponds Scenic Area and Greeley Ponds Scenic Area, where there are open-front shelters for overnight camping. The trails can be counted on for agreeable half-day hikes. There are a number of more demanding trails in the national forest's 1,100-mile network. They are good for short backpacks or for jaunts of several days' duration. There are shelters in the high country along many of the trails for the use of hikers who remain out overnight. Campfire permits are required for all fires, including portable stoves, built at other than improved roadside campgrounds and picnic areas. The Appalachian Mountain Club, 5 Joy Street, Boston, Massachusetts, one of the oldest of all outdoor clubs, can provide detailed trail maps. The maps also may be obtained locally.

The White Mountain National Forest is one of the remaining wilderness areas in New England. Stretching 724,000 acres in New Hampshire and the western part of Maine, the forest contains the northeast's highest peaks and the finest network of hiking trails. The Appalachian Mountain Club maintains about 350 miles of trails and 18 shelters. The nine huts are operated for hikers at the distance of a day's hike from one another. College boys and high-school-age boys pack supplies to the huts, cook meals, and do basic caretaking. Both boys and girls apply for the conservation jobs in the outdoors.

Lakes of the Clouds Hut is at 5,000 feet above tree line in the rugged Washington-Monroe Col, 1½ miles from the summit of Mount Washington via the Crawford Path. Mizpah Spring Hut is at 3,800 feet on the side of Mount Clinton beside the Webster Cliff Trail, some 2½ miles from Crawford Notch. Zealand Falls Hut is at 2,700 feet beside the scenic falls at Whitewall Brook, 5½ miles from Crawford House via the Mount Avalon and A-Z trails. Galehead Hut is at 3,800 feet on the ridge connecting Mount Garfield and Twin Mountains. Greenleaf Hut is at 4,200 feet above tree line, 2½ miles from Profile Clearing. Lonesome Lake Hut has a central building and two bunkhouses and is on the shore of a mountain pond, 1 1/3 miles from Lafayette Place. Pinkham Notch Camp is at 2,032 feet and is the headquarters for the North Country System. It is open all year around. Carter Notch Hut, at 3,450 feet, is located in one of the roughest notches in the mountains near Carter Lake. Madison Spring Hut is above tree line in the Madison-Adams Col. Huts provide bunks, mattresses, pillows, and blankets in dormitories for men and women. Meals are served family style between 7 A.M. and 6 P.M. by hut men.

Hiking

BEAR BROOK STATE PARK, northeast of Suncook. There are 20 miles of interesting hiking trails.

CRAWFORD NOTCH STATE PARK, north of Bartlett. The park's extensive trails are tied into the Appalachian Trail system.

MONADNOCK MOUNTAIN, near Dublin and Jaffrey, has been called the "most climbed mountain in America" and is ideal for a comfortable summer day hike.

MOUNT CARDIGAN, in Alexandria and Orange counties, is a popular place for hikers. Hikers familiar with the area know that the weather can change in a twinkling. Whether strolling on an old logging road or fire road or heading into the wilds, it is important to be prepared, with warm clothing, extra socks, and sturdy hiking shoes.

PILLSBURY STATE PARK, northwest of Hillsborough. Hikers enjoy 3,000 acres of rough terrain.

WELLINGTON STATE PARK, near Bristol. Hikers follow trails that reach around the peninsula.

WHITE MOUNTAIN NATIONAL FOREST. There are hundreds of miles of trails ideal for hikes of any length. Among the fine hiking trails are the Boulder Loop Trail; the Champney Falls Trail to Mount Chocorua; the Bolles Trail to Paugus; the Sawyer Pond Trail; the Brunel Trail to Owl's Cliff; the Sabbaday Brook Trail, which reaches to scenic Sabbaday Falls; and the trails leading to Church Pond.

Bike Hiking & Camping

AMERICAN YOUTH HOSTELS CYCLE TRIPS. The AYH has mapped out four-, seven-, and ten-day trips and two-week bike hikes in the state, where there are hostels at strategic places. The Office of Community Recreation Service, Department of Resources and Economic Development, Box 856, Concord, New Hampshire 03301, will send details.

Rockhounding

BAKER RIVER VALLEY, near Benton. Prospectors pan for gold nuggets in the streams and occasionally find them.

PALERMO MINE, Groton. Once the mine was famous for its mica, but it is now known for its feldspar and beryl.

Canoeing

ANDROSCOGGIN RIVER, from Errol to Berlin, offers flat-water and white-water canoeing. The water level is constant so there is reliable white water all year.

CONNECTICUT RIVER, Pittsburg from the covered bridge. Call the New England Power Company at Pittsburg to learn what the water discharge on the river is. Easy rapids stretch for 9 miles. Below Colebrook there are 16 miles of varied rapids and current. Only the rapids around the breeched Lyman Falls Dam in Columbia are hazardous. If the water is high, keep to the west bank; in medium water use the old canal on the east side. There are several other good Connecticut River trips. There are 14 campgrounds along the river, as well as other camping areas close to the river, which are used by canoeists.

SACO RIVER, below Redstone covered bridge in Conway, offers flat-water canoeing in the summer.

UPPER AMMONOOSUC RIVER, from West Milan to Stark, is good flat-water canoeing in the summer. Between Stark and Groveton are three or four rapids that require intermediate-level water for canoeing, but they may be waded down in low water.

Boating

LAKE WINNIPESAUKEE, Gilford. On this lake, largest in the state's lakes region, there is excellent boating from many launching sites. Other lakes are: Squam, Winnisquam, Newfound, Ossipee, and Wentworth.

NEWFOUND LAKE, near Bristol, provides 8 miles of breezy waters to challenge Sunfish and day sailer skippers.

NEW HAMPSHIRE SEACOAST REGION is popular with boaters. The Piscataqua River and the Great Bay offer sheltered boating. There are important harbors on the coast at Seabrook, Hampton, Rye, Portsmouth, and New Castle. Along this coast, beaches alternate with rugged promontories and rocky areas.

Conservation & Wildlife

BEAR BROOK STATE PARK, northeast of Suncook. The heavily forested park is rich in wildlife. There is an Audubon Society nature center.

MOUNT WASHINGTON, highest peak in the northeast, is reached by a cog railway, an auto road, or by trail. The wind atop the mountain has reached a record 231 miles per hour. In this alpine zone are found plants and insects usually found only in the Arctic.

RHODODENDRON STATE PARK, at Fitzwilliam, preserves more than 16 acres of spectacular wild rhododendron maximum. A well-marked walking trail leads around the glen that contains the beautiful stands of shrubs from which the park takes its name.

WHITE MOUNTAIN NATIONAL FOREST is home to deer, bear, moose, grouse, and hare as well as such furbearers as beaver, mink, raccoon, marten, fisher, wildcat, and lynx. Self-guided nature trails lead from the Kancamagus Highway. Labels on numbered stakes and booklets explain the lessons of nature, landforms, and the multiple uses of the national forests. The Rail 'N River Trail has an easy grade and takes about 30 minutes, but the Boulder Loop Trail is good for a half-day hike.

RHODE ISLAND

Camping

ARCADIA STATE PARK, Arcadia. There are 25 tent and trailer campsites close to a section of the Appalachian Trail.

BURLINGAME STATE PARK, Charlestown, 755 tent and trailer campsites are located in a wooded area on the shores of Watchaug Pond.

FISHERMEN'S MEMORIAL STATE PARK, Narragansett. The camp is in a shore meadow overlooking Block Island and Rhode Island sounds. Reservation only.

FROSTY HOLLOW AREA, Exeter, has two Adirondack shelters reserved for adults and supervised groups.

GEORGE WASHINGTON CAMPING AREA, Glocester. The campsites are in a wooded area overlooking the Bowdish Reservoir.

NINIGRET CONSERVATION AREA has 50 sites at two primitive areas, with access by a sand trail that requires four-wheel drive.

Hiking

ARCADIA STATE PARK, Arcadia. Hiking trails lead in all directions of the compass.

GEORGE WASHINGTON CAMPING AREA, Glocester. While waiting for their ship, the H.M.A.S. *Perth*, to be commissioned, Australian sailors made an 8.2-mile-long trail. They called it the "Walk-about Trail" after the habit of aborigines in their own country of going on a nomadic "walkabout."

Biking

BLOCK ISLAND is ideal for bicycling.

Rockhounding

DIAMOND HILL, at Cumberland, is a mile-long mass of veined quartz left by mineral water flowing along a fracture in the earth's crust eons ago. It fascinates geologists.

LIMEROCK, a quarry near Lincoln, welcomes visitors. The quarry was first opened in 1643 by Thomas Harris and is probably the nation's oldest operating quarry.

Canoeing

PAWCATUCK RIVER. Canoeists on the river stay at Canoe Camp Sites in the Burlingame Management Area along the river at Charlestown. Open year round, there are two overnight sites. Another two sites are at the Carolina Management Area along the river at Richmond.

Boating

BLOCK ISLAND. Boats are numerous in the waters around the island.

BRISTOL. Sailing and shipbuilding have always been part of the way of life in Bristol County. Seven America's Cup defenders were built in Herreshoff Boatyard in Bristol.

NEWPORT. The celebrated Newport-Bermuda races begin here. The classic America's Cup races have been held in Rhode Island waters for more than 40 years.

RHODE ISLAND SOUND. The waters of Rhode Island Sound, of Block Island Sound, and of Narragansett Bay are among the fine sheltered boating waters in the East. Newport is one of the region's outstanding boating centers. Greenwich Bay is a sheltered and commodious harbor for boatmen.

Conservation & Wildlife

BLOCK ISLAND. Almost every bird species using the Northeast Flyway, including the peregrine falcon, can be seen during Block Island Bird Week each fall.

NORMAN BIRD SANCTUARY, Middletown. Marked trails lead through the wildlife preserve.

VERMONT

Camping

ALLIS STATE PARK, at Brookfield, has 21 campsites including three lean-tos.

ASCUTNEY STATE PARK, 3 miles northeast of Ascutney village, has 49 campsites including 10 lean-tos.

BOMOSEEN STATE PARK, 21 miles northwest of Rutland, is on the west shore of Lake Bomoseen. There are fine campsites. At Half Moon Pond camping area there are also campsites and lean-tos.

BRANBURY STATE PARK, 10 miles southeast of Middlebury, is on the east shore of Lake Dunmore. There are 39 campsites.

BRIGHTON STATE PARK, southeast of Island Pond village, has 84 campsites including 21 lean-tos.

BUTTON BAY STATE PARK is 7 miles west of Vergennes on Lake Champlain, south of Basin Harbor. There are 70 sites.

CALVIN COOLIDGE STATE FOREST is 14 miles southeast of Rutland. There are 60 campsites with 35 lean-tos. There is primitive camping also.

D.A.R. STATE PARK is 11 miles southwest of Vergennes on Lake Champlain. The 71 campsites include 20 lean-tos.

ELMORE STATE PARK, at the north end of Lake Elmore, 5 miles southeast of Morrisville, has 64 campsites including five lean-tos.

EMERALD LAKE STATE PARK, 22 miles south of Rutland at Lake Dorset. The 105 campsites include 36 lean-tos.

GIFFORD WOODS STATE PARK, 11 miles northeast of Rutland. There are 47 campsites including 21 lean-tos.

GRAND ISLE STATE PARK, 20 miles northwest of Burlington on Lake Champlain, has 154 campsites including 30 lean-tos.

GROTON STATE FOREST, between Montpelier and St. Johnsbury. There are nine separate recreation areas in this extraordinary forest. Areas reached only by foot trail are designated for primitive camping.

KETTLE POND, located on Kettle Pond, some 25 miles east of Montpelier, is restricted to youth groups. There are three groups of five lean-tos and two groups of six lean-tos.

MAIDSTONE STATE FOREST, 27 miles southeast of Island Pond on Maidstone Lake, has 83 campsites including 37 lean-tos. Roads to the campsites are steep, and heavy vehicles should not be on them.

MOUNT MANSFIELD STATE FOREST, northwest of Waterbury. Outdoor recreation is varied in this largest of the Vermont state forests. Camping is at Little River, Smugglers Notch, and Underhill.

Backpacking

APPALACHIAN TRAIL. Crossing into the state at Norwich, the trail runs west to the vicinity of Rutland and then turns south along the crest of the rugged Green Mountains. A section of the Long Trail is part of the route. South of Bennington the trail crosses into Massachusetts. There are five Adirondack shelters on the Long Trail section. Vermont has over 700 miles of trails; many shorter trails connect to the Appalachian Trail.

DARTMOUTH OUTING CLUB, Robinson Hall, Hanover, New Hampshire, maintains trails in Vermont. The club will send maps and a description of the trails.

Hiking

ASCUTNEY MOUNTAIN, near Windsor, has splendid trails. The Ascutney Trail Association, Windsor, Vermont 05089, publishes a "Guide to the Trails of Ascutney Mountain."

BOMOSEEN STATE PARK, 21 miles northwest of Rutland. Hiking trails start at Half Moon Pond.

CAMELS HUMP STATE PARK, southwest of Waterbury. There is a day hiking trail to the top of Camels Hump.

ESSEX COUNTY FIRE TOWER TRAILS provide excellent hiking.

GIFFORD WOODS STATE PARK, 11 miles northeast of Rutland. Day hikers enjoy the park's trails, which include a section of the Appalachian Trail.

GREEN MOUNTAIN NATIONAL FOREST. There are fine mountain trails here.

GROTON STATE FOREST, between Montpelier and St. Johnsbury. Fine hiking trails lace the forest.

MAIDSTONE STATE FOREST, 27 miles southeast of Island Pond. There are fine hiking trails.

MOUNT MANSFIELD STATE FOREST, northwest of Waterbury. This magnificent state forest contains many outstanding trails. Trails begin at Little River, Smugglers Notch, and Underhill.

Biking

VERMONT BICYCLE TOURING, Bristol, offers many tours over the entire state,

Gay Head, Massachusetts

ranging from weekends to 28 days, for all levels of expertise.

VERMONT HOSTEL TOUR, begins at Guilford, near the Massachusetts line, and runs north to Richford, near the Canadian border. This rugged 200-mile trip has been planned by the American Youth Hostels, and cyclists stop at the hostels along the way.

Rockhounding

BRISTOL AREA. There are deposits of gravel, sand, cobbles, and silt brought down from the north by the glaciers. Rockhounds find quartz, jasper, basalt, and olivine among the assorted rocks.

BROAD BROOK, near Plymouth, yields placer gold in small quantities. The gold was discovered long ago, but local farmers also discovered that they could earn more money farming with less labor than if they panned for the elusive gold.

BUTTON BAY STATE PARK, 7 miles west of Vergennes. Button Bay "buttons" are concretions found along the beaches of Lake Champlain. They weathered out of the clay banks of the shore.

CHIMNEY POINT BRIDGE, on Vermont 125 west from US 7 near Bridport. The rocks on the Champlain lakeshore are rich in such fossils as Ordovician trilobites and brachiopods bryozoans.

HUNTLEY QUARRY, Leicester Junction. Crossing Otter Creek and the railroad tracks near Leicester, a rockhound comes

Mount Katahdin, Maine

on a quarry with excellent examples of hydrothermally deposited calcite crystals.

PARROT JASPER MINE, Colchester. There are copper minerals such as bornite and chalcopyrite as well as cutting-quality jasper, banded with hematite.

ROCK OF AGES QUARRY AND EXHIBIT, south of Barre on Vermont 14. There are tours of the quarry from 8:30 A.M. to 5:00 P.M., May 1 to October 31. The Craftsman's Center is open daily from 8:30 A.M. to 4:00 P.M. Free samples of granite are usually given to visitors. Other granite quarry tours are offered at the Jones Brothers Company and the Wells-Lamson Quarry.

VERMONT MARBLE COMPANY EXHIBIT, Proctor. Interesting exhibits show the origins and types of Vermont marble, its mining, processing, and uses. Free samples are usually given to visitors.

Canoeing

CONNECTICUT RIVER. Canoeing on this most majestic of New England rivers is varied. Although its lower waters are polluted, it is scenically magnificent throughout its length. The river can be swift and dangerous in the spring and placid in the summer. There are 13 dams between the Canadian border and the Massachusetts line, and the New England Power Company can furnish information through its Lebanon, New Hampshire, office. It maintains canoe campsites at Wilder, Bellows Falls, and Vernon Ponds.

OTTER CREEK, from Wallingford or Rutland to Lake Champlain, is popular with canoeists.

WINOOSKI RIVER, from Middlesex to Lake Champlain, attracts canoeists.

Boating & Boat Camping

LAKE CHAMPLAIN. Boating on this historic and beautiful lake is excellent, but boaters have to be wary of strong winds blowing north and south, for these can turn the lake into a whitecapped menace. There are two special anchorage places, in Malletts Bay and St. Albans Bay, and there are numerous marinas. Champlain Islands, north of Burlington, has a campground as well as a marina. Burton Island State Park has campgrounds that can be reached by boat only. There are campsites and lean-tos.

Conservation & Wildlife

GREEN MOUNTAIN NATIONAL FOREST. This vast upland wilderness is home to bear, deer, and ruffed grouse.

NEW BRUNSWICK

Camping

ANCHORAGE PROVINCIAL PARK, on Grand Manan Island overlooking the Bay of Fundy, has 50 campsites.

CAMPOBELLO PROVINCIAL PARK, on Campobello Island, near the Roosevelt International Bridge from Maine. There are a 9-hole golf course and camping in this seacoast park above a pebbled, crescent-shaped beach.

FUNDY NATIONAL PARK. There are fine campgrounds at Chignecto, Point Wolfe, and park headquarters. The Micmac Group campground is available for organized groups.

GRAND LAKE PROVINCIAL PARK, east of Fredericton, has 139 campsites on the shores of New Brunswick's largest freshwater lake.

JARDINE PROVINCIAL PARK is located at Richibucto. There are 41 campsites right on the ocean, and a fine sand beach.

KOUCHIBOUGUAC NATIONAL PARK, on the shore of Northumberland Strait, has a campground at Kouchibouguac Sud and group camping at Fontaine.

LAKE GEORGE PROVINCIAL PARK, north of Harvey, is a small park with 28 campsites located on a 3-square-mile lake with a sandy beach.

LAKESIDE PROVINCIAL PARK, east of Jemseg. There are 132 campsites on Grand Lake.

MACTAQUAC PROVINCIAL PARK, 15 miles west of Fredericton, offers splendid camping both summer and winter. Winter campsites have electrical outlets, dry toilets, well water, and kitchen shelters with stoves and firewood.

MOUNT CARLETON PROVINCIAL PARK, 33 miles east of Saint Quentin, offers primitive camping in a wilderness setting. Mount Carleton, at about 2,690 feet, is the highest mountain peak in New Brunswick.

MURRAY BEACH PARK, north of Cape Tormentine, has 110 campsites.

NEW RIVER BEACH PROVINCIAL PARK, west of Saint John. Camping is near a ½-mile-long beach, with picturesque rocky offshore islands.

OAK POINT PROVINCIAL PARK, north of Saint John, on the St. John River, where swimming in the brackish water may be enjoyed.

PARLEE BEACH PROVINCIAL PARK, east of Shediac, with 101 campsites, is noted for warm, saltwater swimming and for a lobster festival in August.

SUNBURY - OROMOCTO PROVINCIAL RECREATION PARK, 18 miles southwest of Fredericton on French Lake, is ideal for camping families.

THE ENCLOSURE PROVINCIAL PARK, west of Newcastle, with 100 campsites, is near the Miramichi River and its 600-foot beach.

VAL COMEAU PROVINCIAL PARK, south of Tracadie, offers campsites on a low cape dotted with spruce. There are saltwater or brackish water beaches on either hand.

Backpacking

FUNDY NATIONAL PARK. Within the park 50 miles of hiking trails connect to the Fundy Hiking Trail, which links Riverview village, near Moncton, to the park.

MACTAQUAC PROVINCIAL PARK, 15 miles west of Fredericton, has a new wilderness trail.

Hiking

FUNDY NATIONAL PARK. The park is crisscrossed by hiking trails.

GRAND MANAN ISLAND. The Red Trail leads to a rock formation called the "Hole in the Wall." Another hike crosses tidal flats at low tide to Ross Island, where early foundations from the first settlement may be seen. Access to Ross Island may be made dry-shod only during the four hours of low tide.

KOUCHIBOUGUAC NATIONAL PARK. Hike the long stretches of coastal dunes or one of the trails through remote parts of the park.

MACTAQUAC PROVINCIAL PARK, 15 miles west of Fredericton, offers hiking trails. Cross-country skiing is popular on the trails in the winter.

Biking

GRAND MANAN ISLAND, reached by ferry from Black's Harbor, between St. Stephen and Saint John on Route 1, is in the Bay of Fundy. Biking on the island is carefree.

Rockhounding

ALBERT COUNTY. Gypsum, anhydrite, and selenite may be found at the large gypsum quarries at the Canadian Gypsum Company, near Hillsborough. South of Hillsborough is a locality famous for the rare mineral albertite.

GRAND MANAN ISLAND, reached by ferry from Black's Harbor, between St. Stephen and Saint John, has crystal aggregates lying as pebbles on the shoreline. Dark Harbor, Northern Head, and Red Point are excellent for collecting amethystine quartz crystals, red hematite, and greenish brown chlorite at low tide only. Rockhounds should check with islanders before scouting along the base of cliffs so as not to be caught by high tide.

Geologists find the Red Point area of interest. They walk down to the beach from the Red Point gravel pit and turn right for about 100 yards to where volcanic new rock on the left meets sedimentary old rock on the right. There is magnetic sand on the beach.

SAINT'S REST BEACH, near West Saint John. Placer gold may be found at high tide level. Epodite suitable for polishing may be found also. Collecting should be done at low tide.

ST. STEPHEN NICKEL PROSPECT, just north of the border town of St. Stephen. The nickel prospect yields massive pyrrhotite and chalcopyrite.

TETAGOUCHE FALLS MANGANESE PROSPECT, near South Tetagouche. Excellent crystals of manganite and pryolusite may be found in pits. Small nodules of pinkish rhodochrosite may be found in the red slate below the falls. Large trenches on the north bank of the river contain manganese.

Canoeing

Detailed canoe trail maps are available from the Department of Natural Resources, Lands Branch, Room 575, Centennial Building, Fredericton, N.B., Canada.

KENNEBECASIS RIVER, from Penobsquis to Hampton or the city of Saint John. The river alternates between swift and shallow, and deep and meandering, and flows mainly through farmland.

MIRAMICHI RIVER, from Boiestown to The Enclosure Provincial Park. Canoeists of intermediate skill can enjoy paddling their craft as the river passes through forest and farmland.

NEPISIGUIT RIVER, from Nepisiguit (Bathurst) Lakes to Bathurst Power Dam. The Micmac Indian name means "angry river." It has a swift current and passes through scenic country. There are camping areas at Moose Brook, Popple Depot, and Indian Falls Depot.

OROMOCTO RIVER, from Mill Settlement to the St. John River at Oromocto, is a scenic, good traveling river, not usually requiring any portages.

PORTOBELLO CREEK, from Church Road, Maugerville, to Lakeville Corner. A deep, meandering stream with very little current, the Portobello offers excellent canoeing requiring intermediate skill.

RESTIGOUCHE RIVER, from Cedar Brook to Christopher Brook, Campbellton, offers 93 miles of swift, scenic canoeing. Restigouche, a Micmac Indian name, means "river with branches like the fingers of a hand."

ST. CROIX RIVER, from St. Croix to Grand Falls. Experienced paddlers canoe the 41 miles of this scenic river.

ST. JOHN RIVER. The upriver canoe trip starts at the mouth of the St. Francis River, and the takeout point is at Edmundston. The river is swift and both shallow and deep. There are river islands and gravel bars for camping. The middle section of the river also provides good canoeing from Beechwood to takeout point at Mactaquac and at Woolastook Provincial Park as well. The lower St. John trip begins at Mactaquac Dam and ends at the city of Saint John.

TOBIQUE RIVER, from Nictau Lake for 30 miles to Nictau Village, is virgin wilderness with fast, shallow water. Challenging rapids and tight turns lend excitement. Below the village, tributaries widen the stream, but there are still two more miles of rapids before the still waters of the Tobique Reservoir. It is easy paddling to the Narrows, over 50 miles away.

UPSALQUITCH RIVER, from an upriver point at Twenty-five Mile Brook to Robinsonville. The swift and shallow stream courses for 52 interesting miles. There is camping at Twenty-five Mile Brook and at the Forks.

Boating

BAY OF FUNDY. Boating among the islands of the bay is outstanding. Grand Manan Island has popular harbors.

MACTAQUAC PROVINCIAL PARK. A sailboat marina has 40 individual moorings, and there is a launching ramp and storage area for the use of visitors. There also is a powerboat marina with 40 moorings.

ST. JOHN RIVER. Boating on the largest river system on the Atlantic coast south of the St. Lawrence is popular, but before entering the river from the Bay of Fundy, yachtsmen should consult the Municipal Tourist Office in Saint John. The office can furnish information on the Bay of Fundy tides, the highest in the world, and the Reversing Falls and will even give complimentary pilotage through the falls.

Sport Diving

GRAND MANAN ISLAND. Divers explore the Bay of Fundy waters near the island.

Conservation & Wildlife

FUNDY NATIONAL PARK. The park is a wildlife sanctuary, and the animals are accustomed to people. The wildlife includes black bear, bobcat, Virginia deer, and moose. There are nature trails, both self-guided and guided. Between Herring Cove and Alma and at river mouths, rocky or sandy flats are bared at low tide. Tidal pools contain such marine life as periwinkles and sand hoppers. The park has two forest zones. Along the summer-cool coast are yellow and white birch scattered among red spruce and balsam fir. On the higher ground of the warmer plateau are stands of sugar maple, beech, and yellow birch; the low, swampy areas support red spruce, balsam fir, and red maple. The forests are recovering from a century of logging, which took place before the national park was established.

GRAND MANAN ISLAND. There is a gull nesting area at the Bowdoin Scientific Station. Eider ducks nest in the area from mid-May to the end of June.

KOUCHIBOUGUAC NATIONAL PARK is on a north-south bird flyway.

MACTAQUAC PROVINCIAL PARK, 15 miles west of Fredericton. There are fine nature trails. One leads for 6 miles through the evergreens to a pond where beavers are busy both summer and winter.

WOOLASTOOK WILDLIFE PARK is located a few miles up the St. John River from Mactaquac on the Trans-Canada Highway. The park displays native New Brunswick animals and birds in their natural surroundings.

NEWFOUNDLAND & LABRADOR

Camping

BARACHOIS POND PROVINCIAL PARK, near Stephenville. There are splendid campsites in this and other provincial parks.

GROS MORNE NATIONAL PARK. Five campgrounds in a park of mountains, lakes, bays, and ocean.

TERRA NOVA NATIONAL PARK, one of the underused parks in the Canadian system. Newman Sound and Alexander Bay campgrounds accept tents and recreational vehicles. There are three primitive campgrounds and a group campground in the park.

Backpacking & Trail Riding

TERRA NOVA NATIONAL PARK. On overnight hikes visitors may camp outside the established campgrounds, but they must register with the park warden before and after each trip and obtain a fire permit. There is a riding trail in the northern part of the park.

Hiking

GROS MORNE NATIONAL PARK. James Callaghan Trail climbs up rough shale and rock to the base of Gros Morne mountain and a view of the park, and out to the Gulf of St. Lawrence.

TERRA NOVA NATIONAL PARK. Fine fire roads and hiking trails tempt hikers.

Biking

TERRA NOVA NATIONAL PARK. Cycling is a fine way to see the park.

Rockhounding

NAIN. In the vicinity of this northern Labrador town, rockhounds find rare and much-prized labradorite, first discovered in 1770 on a nearby island.

RED JASPER PITS, near Corner Brook, on the Trans-Canada Highway. These gravel pits yield fine jasper.

Canoeing

TERRA NOVA NATIONAL PARK. Canoeing is permitted on all the freshwater lakes except Rocky Pond.

Boating & Boat Camping

TERRA NOVA NATIONAL PARK. Launching facilities are on Newman Sound. Once the park could be reached only by boat. There are still primitive campgrounds accessible only by boat.

Conservation & Wildlife

TERRA NOVA NATIONAL PARK. This rocky, forested park on Bonavista Bay is a living outdoor museum. The bogs and muskegs include members of the heath family such as bog laurel, Canada azalea, and bog rosemary. Mosses and lichens cover the bog floors. Land animals include moose, black bear, beaver, lynx, and snowshoe hare. In the bay are harbor seal, blackfish, and pilot whale.

NOVA SCOTIA

Camping

BATTERY PROVINCIAL PARK, east of St. Peters. Camping is on Bras d'Or Lake.

CAPE BRETON HIGHLANDS NATIONAL PARK. There is no camping outside of the 7 campgrounds except by permission of the park warden. During high fire hazard periods no permission is granted.

ELLENWOOD PROVINCIAL PARK, near Deerfield, is a natural campground on a lake.

GRAVES ISLAND PROVINCIAL PARK, located east of Chester, offers camping on the ocean.

KEJIMKUJIK NATIONAL PARK. Camping is outstanding in this wilderness park. Another of the underused parks in the Canadian system.

MIRA RIVER PROVINCIAL PARK, east of Sydney. Camping is excellent on the river. Nearby is the Fortress of Louisbourg National Historic Park, an old French stronghold, which is now under reconstruction.

THE ISLANDS PROVINCIAL PARK, west of Shelburne, offers camping on the ocean, on a long, sheltered harbor.

VALLEYVIEW PROVINCIAL PARK, north of Bridgetown. Campsites are on a mountain overlooking the beautiful Annapolis Valley.

WENTWORTH PROVINCIAL PARK, 50 miles east of Amherst, provides camping in a mountain valley.

Diving—Nova Scotia

WHYCOCOMAGH PROVINCIAL PARK, on Bras d'Or Lake, gives campers a view of the lake from the mountain.

Backpacking

ACADIAN TRAIL. This hiking trail will run along the coasts of Nova Scotia and New Brunswick to join the Appalachian Trail in Maine. Sections of it have already been marked. From Cheticamp to Inverness, the trail winds over beaches, grassland, along highways and unpaved roads, and through wilderness. Most of the trail is near small brooks with water that is safe to drink, but the section from Inverness to Terre Noire has only the ocean's salt water handy. There is a log cabin on the trail at Petit Etang and a lean-to 6 miles south of Petit Etang. Another lean-to is 8 miles north of Inverness. Campgrounds are situated at handy intervals along the trail.

CABOT TRAIL. The Cabot Trail is a scenic motor road encircling Cape Breton, also followed by many backpackers.

Hiking

CAPE BRETON HIGHLANDS NATIONAL PARK. The park has 20 hiking trails that lead along the seacoast, around lakes, and into the barren interior. Day hikes are in the Black Brook, Warren Lake, and Cheticamp areas.

CAPE SPLIT, in the Annapolis Valley district, has a rugged countryside, partly traversed by good trail. Keep to the high point of the hardwood ridge and avoid logging trails, which go nowhere.

DIGBY NECK. Brier Island offers the hiker some excellent shore trails, as does Sandy Cove in the middle of the neck.

PEGGY'S COVE, in the Halifax area, has a popular 12-mile hike through a wooded area that includes several lakes. The trail stretches from the Prospect Road near Goodwood to the Peggy's Cove Road at Glen Margaret.

UISGE BHAN FALLS WALKING TRAIL, 10 miles north of Baddeck. The trail runs from Forks Road to the falls.

WHYCOCOMAGH PROVINCIAL PARK, on Bras d'Or lake, has fine trails.

Bike Hiking & Camping

CABOT TRAIL. Bikers follow the scenic motor highway around Cape Breton. There are camping sites along the way.

Rockhounding

COBEQUID BAY AREA, at Five Islands. Zeolites may be found on the offshore islands. Calcite, heulandite, and pyrite can be found along the shoreline at McKay Head, Wasson Bluff, and from Swan Creek to Clarke Head.

JOGGINS, in Cumberland County, is famous for 235,000,000-year-old fossils of the Upper Carboniferous period, exposed in the cliffs along the shore.

MINAS CHANNEL, from Cape Split to Cape Blomidon, is one of the top rockhounding areas of the province. Amethyst Cove, about midway between the capes, produces fine amethyst. Exceptional geodes are discovered at Cape Split.

PARTRIDGE ISLAND, near Parrsboro. Amethysts, agates, chalcedony, and trap rock minerals are found on shore.

Canoeing

ALMA LAKE, near Squirreltown Station. Canoeists put in at the Shannon River Bridge and paddle through Alma Lake, Ponhook Lake, and Medway River to Medway, a 60-mile trip. A similar trip branches off first at Ponhook Lake and goes through Lake Rossignol and the Mersey River to Liverpool for an 82-mile trip.

THE NORTHEAST 95

BRAS D'OR LAKES. Canoeists put in at St. Peter's and canoe the lakes to Strathlorne, then to Baddeck through St. Patrick's Channel, to Lake Ainslie, and back to Strathlorne, a distance of 105 miles.

HALIFAX TO TRURO. Canoeists go through Dartmouth locks, Banook Lake, Micmac Lake, the two locks at Port Wallace, and Porta Bella locks. They take Lake Williams and Lake Thomas, the Wellington River, and Shubenacadie Lake to Maitlant. They then follow the eastern shore of Cobequid Bay and the Salmon River to Truro. The trip runs for a total of 74 miles.

KEJIMKUJIK NATIONAL PARK. Four canoe route systems traverse 16 lakes, with 23 portages.

Boating

BAY OF FUNDY. Boating is exceptional in this bay. There are fine harbors on the bay and on the long Atlantic coast.

Sport Diving

SEVERAL THOUSAND MILES OF COASTLINE and clean, clear water make Nova Scotia a sport diver's mecca. Harbors, bays, and inlets are readily accessible. Thousands of islands provide beaches for rest sites. Since the time of the first European explorers to the present, the turbulent seas have foundered ships on the coast so that there are at least 3,000 known wrecks. Underwater photography is a growing pursuit in the area. Air stations and dive shops are located in the larger cities. Divers prefer the ¼-inch-thick wet suit and use similar gear to that used in northeastern United States. Precaution: Divers not accustomed to tidal currents should take them into account. The Cape Breton and Yarmouth-Digby areas can be treacherous. Bay of Fundy tides can make diving hazardous, and nonresident divers should dive only with local skippers or divers. Diving is limited mostly to slack tides. Also, the collecting of lobsters is forbidden, and spear fishing is legal in salt water only. Salvage laws dictate that any portion of a shipwreck must be declared to the local receiver of wrecks. Artifacts found underwater must be turned over to the director of the Nova Scotia Museum for examination as to their historic value.

Conservation & Wildlife

BIRD ISLANDS, accessible during the summer months by cruise boat from the Sydney Mines area of Cape Breton Island, are home to large colonies of puffins, cormorants, razorbill mures, and a variety of gulls.

CAPE BRETON HIGHLANDS NATIONAL PARK. There are some 21 species of mammals in the park, including the lynx, Keen's bat, snowshoe hare, black bear, red fox, short-tailed weasel, white-tailed deer, otter, flying squirrel, and pine marten. There are moose, and in 1968–69 woodland caribou were flown into the park to reestablish themselves. The national park is home to a number of birds, of which over 150 species have been recorded.

PROVINCIAL WILDLIFE PARK, Shubenacadie. Naturalists honor the park for its work in wildlife conservation and propagation. There are woodland walks leading to such park residents as Canada and Brant geese and trumpeter swans. Mammals in the park include bear, caribou, otter, fox, raccoon, moufflin sheep, cougar, deer, and moose.

PRINCE EDWARD ISLAND

Camping

PRINCE EDWARD ISLAND NATIONAL PARK. The three campgrounds at Stanhope, Cavendish, and Rustico Island are especially suited to both tent and trailer camping. The camping area at Brackley is reserved for Scouts and other well-trained groups.

PROVINCIAL PARKS. There are 15 provincial parks, with most providing trailer and tent sites.

Hiking

BONSHAW TRAIL. A 15-mile hiking trail runs from South Melville to St. Catherines.

PRINCE EDWARD ISLAND NATIONAL PARK. Hiking the beach is enjoyable, but there are also other, regular trails, which lead to Bubbling Spring and Balsam Hollow.

Rockhounding

GEORGE ISLAND. The north shore has celadonite, an emerald-green mineral.

ORWELL BAY, near Charlottetown, has hematite beds up to six inches thick.

Boating

PRINCE EDWARD ISLAND NATIONAL PARK. Saltwater boating facilities are at Covehead Bay.

Conservation & Wildlife

MILLTOWN CROSS not only has a bird sanctuary frequented by Canada geese, blue geese, and black ducks, but also has a herd of buffalo.

PRINCE EDWARD ISLAND NATIONAL PARK. Water and wind have created sand dunes and spits along the 15 miles of seacoast in the park. Freshwater ponds, swampy hollows, saltwater and freshwater marshes, and woodlands are all natural life habitats of exceptional beauty and meaning. A varied plant life and animal life give the park lasting appeal. In this park are over 185 species of birds, the largest and most conspicuous of which is the great blue heron. On Rustico Island is a rookery for these birds.

QUEBEC

Camping

FORILLON NATIONAL PARK. Cap Bon-Ami and Petit Gaspé campgrounds accept tents and trailers.

PARC NATIONAL DE LA MAURICIE (La Maurice National Park). Camping is at Rivière à La Pêche, Mistagance, and Wapizagonke sites.

PARC PROVINCIAL DU MONT-TREMBLANT (Mount Tremblant Provincial Park), 90 miles north of Montreal. Montrealers and other visitors alike enjoy camping here.

Backpacking

PARC NATIONAL DE LA MAURICIE (La Mauricie National Park). Backpacking the trails brings hikers into intimate contact with the Laurentian wilderness. Although no camping is allowed outside designated campsites as a rule, a backpacker may camp overnight providing he has advised a park warden and obtained a permit.

Hiking

PARC NATIONAL DE LA MAURICIE (La Mauricie National Park). Nature and hiking trails are south of Lake Wapizagonke.

PARC PROVINCIAL DE LA GASPESIE (Gaspesian Provincial Park), on the Gaspé Peninsula, has trails that ascend Mount Albert, Mount Logan, and Mount Jacques-Cartier, with its summit of 4,300 feet. There are splendid views of the St. Lawrence River and the Chic-Choc mountains.

PARC PROVINCIAL DU MONT-ORFORD (Mount Orford Provincial Park), in the Eastern Townships 65 miles from Montreal, has a trail to the mountaintop.

Biking

PARC NATIONAL DE LA MAURICIE (La Mauricie National Park). Bikers may use the hiking trails.

Rockhounding

HULL-WAKEFIELD AREA. In the vicinity of Hull and Wakefield are mines yielding mauve-colored wilsonite and dark red, mauve, and yellow jasper.

THETFORD MINES AREA, in the Eastern Townships, has several good chipping locations for soapstone (suitable for ornamental objects), rose-colored garnet crystals, serpentine, and antimony.

Canoeing

PARC NATIONAL DE LA MAURICIE (La Mauricie National Park). Canoe routes lead through the national park. Many of these routes have basic camping facilities and lead to places inaccessible by roads.

PARC PROVINCIAL DE LA VERENDRYE (La Verendrye Provincial Park), 150 miles north of Ottawa, is a wilderness over 115 miles wide at one point. Canoe routes have been mapped out, and canoe rental services established. Map and route information can be obtained at park headquarters at Le Domaine. Trips range from two- or three-day weekend circuits to seven-day expeditions covering 100 miles. The trips run mainly through lakes connected by flat-water rivers or portages. There are a few white-water stretches.

PARC PROVINCIAL DES LAURENTIDES (Laurentides Provincial Park), 30 miles north of Quebec City, is renowned for canoeing on the Montmorency River.

Boating

FLEUVE ST. LAURENT (St. Lawrence River). Boating is popular on this greatest of Canada's rivers. Lac des Deux-Montagnes (Lake of Two Mountains), formed where the Ottawa River meets the St. Lawrence, is particularly thronged with craft.

PARC NATIONAL DE LA MAURICIE (La Mauricie National Park). Only crafts of 10 horsepower or under are allowed on Lake Wapizagonke.

RIVIERE DES OUTAOUAIS (Ottawa River). A boatman passes many historic sites as he sails up this river. There are fine campgrounds and marinas.

RIVIERE RICHELIEU (Richelieu River) flows north out of Lake Champlain and provides a fine route for boaters. A boater may ascend the Hudson from New York City, cross to Lake Champlain by canals, and finish his trip by a journey down the Richelieu to the St. Lawrence.

RIVIERE SAGUENAY (Saguenay River). Flowing down from Lac St.-Jean in the remote north woods, this historic river, once the route of fur traders, is a route for pleasure craft. Lac St.-Jean itself is a splendid lake for sailing.

Conservation & Wildlife

ILE DE BONAVENTURE (Bonaventure Island), reached by tour boat from Percé

La Verendrye Provincial Park, Quebec

on the Gaspé Peninsula, is one of six gannetries in North America. More than 50,000 gannets live in this large colony. To watch the gannet with its six-foot wingspan in flight is to appreciate the beauty of motion.

PARC NATIONAL DE LA MAURICIE (La Mauricie National Park). The park is in a transition zone between the boreal forest and the deciduous forest of the St. Lawrence lowlands. Moose, beaver, otter, and mink are abundant. Lynx, eastern timber wolf, and red fox are the predators.

PARC DU PAUL-SAUVE (Paul the Savior Park), at Oka. There is a nature appreciation course for young people.

PARC PROVINCIAL DES LAURENTIDES (Laurentides Provincial Park), 30 miles north of Quebec City, is the home of a herd of woodland caribou. They were flown to the area from the far north Ungava region by the Department of Tourism, Fish and Game biologists.

PARC PROVINCIAL DE MONT-TREMBLANT (Mount Tremblant Provincial Park), 90 miles north of Montreal. There are nature interpretation hikes and wild game and flora studies atop a 600-foot hill, at La Corniche.

THE NORTHEAST 97

Catskills, New York

THE MID-ATLANTIC STATES

This is the region of supercities surrounded by suburbs and satellite cities, but it is also a country of forests and lakes, of dashing streams and quiet meadows. It is only a brief journey from the towers of Manhattan to the untouched water meadows of New Jersey where muskrats live, and the hiking trails of the Poconos and the Catskills are only an easy bus ride from the center of Philadelphia or New York.

The mountain glens of Pennsylvania are unspoiled, national forests sweep through the valleys and up over the ridges, and camping is a pleasurable pursuit. Backpackers not only can follow the Appalachian Trail across New York, New Jersey, and Pennsylvania, but they can strike out over the oil lease roads of the once-flourishing western Pennsylvania oil fields and discover that the highlands were bypassed by the tide of industrial life, which kept mainly to the valleys. By keeping to the ridges, a hiker finds not only easy going but all the pleasure of being away from things, with the certainty that when he wishes he can always descend into a valley to find a handy town store where he can replenish his supplies.

Stretching from New England to the Great Lakes, from the outdoor vacationland of the St. Lawrence Valley to the Mason-Dixon Line that delineates the Old South, the Mid-Atlantic States encompass New York, New Jersey, and Pennsylvania. New York possesses not only the Catskills but the Adirondacks, wooded mountains to stir the imagination. New York State boaters not only have the magnificent waters around the Thousand Islands in the St. Lawrence but the splendid sheltered waters of Long Island Sound, the majestic Hudson, and the fjordlike Finger Lakes. Long Island has 1,000 miles of shoreline with bays, inlets, and marinas. Boaters vacationing on Long Island water discover coves and anchorages galore, plus the Shinnecock Canal, which provides a sea-level passage from Shinnecock Bay to the Great Peconic Bay.

Populous as New Jersey may be, it has tracts of timbered mountains reaching up to 1,803-foot High Point, the loftiest peak in the Kittatinny Mountains. There are highland lakes set in the forests, and streams and rivers that appeal to boaters and canoeists. The New Jersey shore is justly renowned for its sandy beaches, its inlets suitable for boats, its salt marshes where life goes on as in primordial times.

Pennsylvania's variety of terrain gives it a savor of its own. There are the rolling piedmont plateau and rugged mountains and narrow valleys. It even has a Grand Canyon of its own in the 1,000-foot deep Pine Creek Gorge in Tioga County. Pennsylvania can even claim a lake where the fish are so thick that the ducks walk on their backs. This is the Pymatuning Reservoir in the northwestern part of the state. Pennsylvanians say that when vacationers throw bread into the lake, the fish swarm to get the bread. The lake's ducks also want their share of the bread, but when they try to swim to it, they find the fish so thick that they must waddle along on top of them. They are forced to walk on a carpet of fish to get their share, or so it is said.

Pennsylvania has its natural wonders. At Hawk Mountain air currents attract migrating hawks. The fierce birds wheel and turn in the currents with all the pleasure of human glider enthusiasts. Unthinking hunters were in turn attracted to the mountain by the birds and began the slaughter of the hawks until nature lovers bought the mountain to protect them.

Where do prairie flowers still grow naturally in the Mid-Atlantic states? They can be found in Jennings Blazing Star Prairie on Pennsylvania 528 in Butler County. Owned by the Western Pennsylvania Conservancy, the prairie is open to the public, providing visitors do not disturb the beautiful blooms.

Where on the Hudson can white-water canoeists test their skill? At North Creek in the annual White Water Derby, canoeists compete in a challenging run through frothing waters. For the first 100 miles of its course, the Hudson is an Adirondack stream with stretches of flat water and rapids.

Where in New Jersey does one of the nation's oldest conservation groups operate a Conservation Education Center? It's at North New Brunswick. At the Boy Scouts of America's national headquarters, a half-mile nature trail is a school of the outdoors with displays and observation stations "showing how nature sustains life on our planet." There are deer in the brush, and visitors discover the tracks and sign of raccoons, skunks, and field mice along the trail.

Take a quarter-mile boat trip on an underground river and receive an object lesson in geology at the Natural Bridge Caverns on New York 3 in Natural Bridge in the St. Lawrence area of New York, or hike the lonely trails of the Abram S. Hewitt Forest of New Jersey's Passaic County. The 1,890-acre forest is undeveloped except for hiking. Go to Pennsylvania's Presque Isle to study an internationally famed geological situation. Starting at the tip of the peninsula on Lake Erie and working inland, you'll see all the stages of land formation from fresh beach sand to the climax forest. Each cycle takes 600 years, but a vacationer can see it in 20 minutes.

NEW JERSEY

Camping

ALLAIRE STATE PARK, 12 miles southeast of Freehold. Fine camping close to the historic Howell Works.

BULL'S ISLAND RECREATION AREA, 7 miles north of Lambertville. Campsites are between the Delaware River and the Delaware and Raritan Canal.

HIGH POINT STATE PARK, northwest of Sussex, offers camping along the Kittatinny Mountains. The park contains the highest point in New Jersey.

JENNY JUMP STATE FOREST, high up on Jenny Jump Mountain, in Warren County, offers camping amid lovely views of the Delaware Water Gap.

LEBANON STATE FOREST, 17 miles southwest of Lakehurst. The campsites are in a 27,103-acre pine forest.

PARVIN STATE PARK, west of Vineland, provides camping near Parvin Lake.

STEPHENS-SAXTON FALLS PARK, northeast of Hackettstown, has camping near the Musconetcong River.

STOKES STATE FOREST, 3 miles northwest of Branchville. Campers enjoy sites in this beautiful, forested mountain country.

SWARTSWOOD PARK, northwest of Newton. Camping is near beautiful Swartswood Lake.

VOORHEES PARK, north of High Bridge. There is camping in the hills of Hunterdon County.

WHARTON STATE FOREST, Atsion. The campsites are in this largest of the state's forests, which contains over 99,638 acres of pine.

WORTHINGTON STATE FOREST, east of Delaware Water Gap, provides camping near the Appalachian Trail and the Delaware River.

Backpacking

APPALACHIAN TRAIL crosses from New York north of Upper Greenwood Lake and continues in a westerly direction to High Point, which at 1,803 feet is the highest ground in the state. From there the trail runs mainly south along the ridge of the Kittatinny Mountains to cross the Delaware into Pennsylvania at the Delaware Water Gap.

Hiking

ABRAM S. HEWITT FOREST, in Passaic County, contains 1,890 acres and is undeveloped except for hiking.

HACKLEBARNEY PARK, southwest of Chester. Hikers enjoy the beautiful gorge along the Black River.

HIGH POINT STATE PARK, northwest of Sussex, offers hiking along the Kittatinny Mountains.

NORVIN GREEN STATE FOREST, northwest of Pompton Lakes, is undeveloped except for hiking trails.

PALISADES INTERSTATE PARK. There is hiking in the 13-mile tract along the Hudson River Palisades from Fort Lee, in Bergen County, to the New York line.

PARVIN STATE PARK, west of Vineland. Trails lead through the woods in this fine state park.

STOKES STATE FOREST, 3 miles northwest of Branchville, is popular with hikers.

WORTHINGTON STATE FOREST, near the Delaware Water Gap, has hiking trails, including 6 miles of the Appalachian Trail.

Canoeing

WHARTON STATE FOREST, at Atsion, contains winding streams that attract canoeists.

Boating

INTRACOASTAL WATERWAY. Boaters follow these sheltered waters to Delaware Bay. There are private and state marinas to provide facilities.

SPRUCE RUN RESERVOIR, north of Clinton. Small boats may be launched at specific locations in the reservoir.

Conservation & Wildlife

BASS RIVER STATE FOREST, in Burlington and Ocean counties, is the oldest state forest in New Jersey. Its long-established forest plantations of several species of trees are of interest.

BULL'S ISLAND RECREATION AREA, 7 miles north of Lambertville, offers nature study opportunities because of its luxuriant plant growth and many varieties of birds and mammals.

CHEESEQUAKE PARK, northwest of Matawan, has an abundance and variety of flora amid a heavily industrialized area.

ISLAND BEACH STATE PARK, southeast of Toms River, is a 10-mile strip of sand dunes bounded by the Atlantic Ocean on the east and Barnegat Bay on the west.

PARVIN STATE PARK, west of Vineland, has a great abundance of flora and birdlife.

PENN STATE FOREST, west of Manahawkin, preserves an unbroken forest, which can be seen from Bear Swamp Hill.

RANCOCAS PARK, west of Vineland, is undeveloped and gives opportunity for nature study.

SANDY HOOK PARK, reaches northward into New York Harbor. Spermaceti Cove area and the holly forest close by are natural areas.

STOKES STATE FOREST, 3 miles northwest of Branchville, contains Tillman Ravine, a natural gorge of rare beauty. It is being kept undisturbed as a laboratory of the rocks, soil, and climate.

WHARTON STATE FOREST, at Atsion, has guided tours through the Batsto nature area and the Batsto Village restoration.

NEW YORK

Camping

ADIRONDACK PARK, more than twice the size of Yellowstone National Park, has public campsites, operated by the New York State Department of Environmental Conservation.

CHENANGO VALLEY STATE PARK, northeast of Binghamton, has secluded tent and trailer sites in a park with two lovely lakes.

FAIR HAVEN BEACH STATE PARK, north of Fair Haven, offers a fine wooded camping area on the southern shore of Lake Ontario.

GILBERT LAKE STATE PARK, northwest of Oneonta, provides camping in wooded, hilly land. There are also cabins.

MIDDLE ATLANTIC STATES
Evergreen Trees
Deciduous Trees
Grass
Capitals
Cities
1 inch = 73 Statute Miles
Lambert Conformal Conic Projection
CM TERRAIN MIDDLE ATLANTIC STATES COPYRIGHT BY RAND MC NALLY & COMPANY MADE IN U.S.A.
Longitude West of Greenwich
QUEBEC
ONTARIO
NEW YORK
PENNSYLVANIA
NEW JERSEY
MARYLAND
DEL.
WEST VIRGINIA
VIRGINIA
OHIO
CONNECTICUT
MASS.
VT.
N. H.
ADIRONDACK MOUNTAINS
CATSKILL MOUNTAINS
ALLEGHENY PLATEAU
ALLEGHENY MOUNTAINS
APPALACHIAN MOUNTAINS
GREAT VALLEY
GREEN MOUNTAINS
TACONIC MOUNTAINS
BLUE RIDGE MTS.
SHENANDOAH NAT'L PARK
Atlantic Ocean
Lake Ontario
Lake Erie
Georgian Bay
Long Island
Chesapeake Bay
Delaware Bay
Ottawa
Montréal
Toronto
Hamilton
Niagara Falls
Buffalo
Rochester
Syracuse
Utica
ALBANY
Troy
Schenectady
Binghamton
Elmira
Jamestown
Erie
Watertown
Plattsburgh
Burlington
Montpelier
Rutland
Bennington
Pittsfield
Worcester
Holyoke
Springfield
Hartford
Waterbury
New Haven
New London
Bridgeport
Kingston
Poughkeepsie
New York
Newark
Jersey City
TRENTON
Scranton
Wilkes-Barre
Bethlehem
Allentown
Reading
Philadelphia
Camden
Wilmington
Penn's Grove
Lancaster
York
HARRISBURG
Altoona
Johnstown
Pittsburgh
Youngstown
Cumberland
Clarksburg
Baltimore
Annapolis
Washington D.C.
Dover
Atlantic City
CAPE MAY
CAPE CHARLES
CAPE HENRY
Norfolk
Richmond
Lynchburg
Roanoke
Sherbrooke
Newport
North Bay
MT. MARCY 5,344 FT.
MT. DAVIS 3,213 FT.
SPRUCE KNOB 4,860 FT.

GREEN LAKES STATE PARK, 11 miles east of Syracuse. Campers enjoy the two green lakes that once were the plunge basins of a great glacial waterfall.

HARRIMAN STATE PARK, west of Haverstraw. There is camping in this immense area near the palisades of the Hudson.

HITHER HILLS STATE PARK, west of Montauk. Camping area is not far from Montauk Point, the eastern tip of Long Island.

LETCHWORTH STATE PARK, near Castile, has both tent sites and camping cabins.

ROBERT H. TREMAN STATE PARK, south of Ithaca. Campsites are in a woodland near the lower entrance.

SELKIRK SHORES STATE PARK, 3 miles west of Pulaski. Tent sites and camping cabins overlook the mile-long shoreline of the park.

TAUGHANNOCK FALLS STATE PARK, north of Jacksonville. The camping area overlooks beautiful Cayuga Lake.

THOUSAND ISLANDS, St. Lawrence River. State parks in this region provide excellent camping.

WATKINS GLEN STATE PARK, Watkins Glen. Campsites are at the southern end of Seneca Lake.

WILDWOOD STATE PARK, east of Wading River, provides camping on Long Island Sound.

Backpacking & Trail Riding

ADIRONDACK-CATSKILL REGION. Trails lead through this magnificent mountainland to provide some of the best backpacking in the East. Over 600 miles of trails pass such points as Mount Marcy in the north and South Mountain in the Catskills. Horse trails have been established through wilderness areas. Each rider must provide his own mount and equipment and use good judgment in planning for and throughout the trip. Administered by the Division of Lands and Forests, Bureau of Forest Recreation, these facilities provide basic shelter for horsemen and horses. For a booklet of information on the trails, write to Department of Environmental Conservation, Division of Lands and Forests, Albany, New York 12201.

APPALACHIAN TRAIL enters New York northwest of Wingdale and crosses the Hudson on the Bear Mountain Bridge. The trail traverses Bear Mountain State Park and crosses into New Jersey south of Warwick.

Hiking

ADIRONDACK PARK. Hiking trails lead to scenic overlooks and favorite fishing spots. The Blue Mountain Trail is a favorite of many hikers.

ALLEGANY STATE PARK, west of Olean, has a fine network of trails.

CATSKILL PARK. Hiking is outstanding on a host of trails.

CHITTENANGO FALLS STATE PARK, north of Cazenovia. Scenic trails trace a diagonal course through the gorge below the falls.

CLARK RESERVATION, at Jamesville, has a great stone crescent gouged in the limestone wall of Butternut Valley by an Ice Age cataract the size of Niagara.

FINGER LAKES TRAIL. A wilderness trail crosses Schuyler, Seneca, and Tompkins counties. Maps may be purchased from FLTC, P.O. Box 18048, 12 Corners Branch, Rochester, NY 14618.

LETCHWORTH STATE PARK. Trails lead to scenic overlooks on the spectacular Genesee River Gorge.

ROBERT H. TREMAN STATE PARK, south of Ithaca. Trails in the glen lead to 12 waterfalls and "Devil's Kitchen," a recess on one side of the glen.

WATKINS GLEN STATE PARK, at Watkins Glen. Hikers follow trails at the foot of sheer shale walls to waterfalls. The deep rock gorge encloses 19 waterfalls.

Biking

FIRE ISLAND NATIONAL SEASHORE. Bike trails lead through the largest remaining barrier beach on the south shore of Long Island.

SHELTER ISLAND, by ferry from Greenport on Long Island, has no traffic to make a biker's life miserable and is a pleasure to explore. By taking another ferry, a hiker can go from South Ferry, on the island, to the Long Island mainland at Sag Harbor.

Canoeing & Rafting

ADIRONDACK PARK affords white-water canoeing on the Upper Hudson River. There are 180 miles of canoe routes. The Adirondack Canoe Trail starts at Old Forge and runs through the Fulton Chain Lakes and Raquette, Saranac, and Loon lakes.

DELAWARE RIVER canoeists put in at Hancock, stop the first night at campgrounds at Callicoon and shoot the white water to Narrowsburg for a trip of 25 miles. Float trips are also made from campgrounds at Callicoon using aluminum johnboats.

GREEN LAKES STATE PARK, 11 miles east of Syracuse, offers canoeing on lakes of a cool green color.

Boating

ERIE CANAL. Houseboats and launches alike find the canal to be a waterway into the state's history.

FINGER LAKES of central New York are popular boating lakes. They include Canandaigua, Keuka, Seneca, Cayuga, Owasco, and Skaneateles, ranging from 12 to 50 miles long, fjordlike, and blue in their settings of high hills.

LONG ISLAND SOUND. Westchester County and Long Island ports look out on this remarkable boating area. (See Connecticut).

THOUSAND ISLANDS of the St. Lawrence River. Actually, there are at least 1,800 islands, and each of them seems to have a boathouse and a dock. Boaters put about among the channels and through the locks.

Sport Diving

ADIRONDACK PARK. Scuba diving is popular in many of the park's lakes.

Conservation & Wildlife

ADIRONDACK PARK. The "Forever Wild Amendment" to the state constitution of 1895 keeps this enormous forest preserve safe from encroachment. For nature lovers this vast private and public domain is one of the glories of the East.

BEAR MOUNTAIN STATE PARK, west of Haverstraw. There are five museum buildings filled with collections of flora and fauna of the region and a nature trail at Bear Mountain.

CATSKILL PARK. Protected from encroachment by civilization, the park is

Whiteface Mountain, New York

Pine Creek, Pennsylvania

noted for its wildlife and the beauty of its forested mountains.

FIRE ISLAND NATIONAL SEASHORE, although only 60 miles from Manhattan, protects waterfowl of many species and has nature walks to such fascinating spots as the Sunken Forest and Sailor's Haven, a woodland with American holly and black gum.

MONTEZUMA NATIONAL WILDLIFE REFUGE, west of Auburn, protects waterfowl. Some 250 species of birds have been recorded here. The largest concentrations of waterfowl are during the months of April and October. There were as many as 100,000 ducks in the marshes during one October. Since public use cannot be allowed to threaten the nesting of the birds and their enjoyment of the crops, visitors view the wildlife from refuge dikes. Motorists usually are allowed to drive along the Main Pool Dike road starting at headquarters, but only hikers are allowed on the Storage Pool Dike.

SAPSUCKER WOODS AND THE LABORATORY OF ORNITHOLOGY, Cornell University, Ithaca. Four miles of trails lead through the woods overlooking a pond about 2 miles northeast of the Cornell campus. There is a bird observatory.

PENNSYLVANIA

Camping

ALLEGHENY NATIONAL FOREST, in the vicinity of Warren, has many fine campgrounds. The 11 national forest campgrounds are: Allegheny, 7 miles east of Warren; Beaver Meadows, 30 miles south of Warren; Buckaloons, 6 miles west of Warren; Dewdrop, Kiasutha, and Willow Bay, on the Allegheny Reservoir; Hearts Content, 18 miles southwest of Warren; Kelly Pines, 14 miles east of Marienville; Loleta, 10 miles southeast of Marienville; Minister Creek, 20 miles south of Warren; and Twin Lakes, 5 miles northwest of Wilcox.

BLACK MOSHANNON STATE PARK, near Philipsburg, provides family camping as well as youth group camping.

BLUE KNOB STATE PARK, near Bedford, offers camping with a view of the Allegheny Mountains.

CHAPMAN DAM STATE PARK, west of Clarion. There is camping near a fine beach.

THE MID-ATLANTIC STATES 103

COLTON POINT STATE PARK, southwest of Wellsboro. Camping is close to Pennsylvania's Grand Canyon.

COOK FOREST STATE PARK, northeast of Clarion. Camping is in a virgin forest.

COWAN'S GAP STATE PARK, northeast of McConnellsburg, has camping near a lake.

CROOKED CREEK STATE PARK, 4 miles south of Ford City, offers camping close to a reservoir.

FRENCH CREEK STATE PARK, 14 miles southeast of Reading, offers camping in 6,022 acres of woodland.

GREENWOOD FURNACE STATE PARK, west of Lewistown, offers camping with a view of the mountains.

HICKORY RUN STATE PARK, north of Jim Thorpe, has campsites near the famed Boulder Field.

KEYSTONE STATE PARK, 7 miles north of Latrobe, provides excellent camping.

LAUREL HILL STATE PARK, west of Somerset, has camping in a rustic setting.

LYMAN RUN STATE PARK, southwest of Galeton, provides camping in a wooded setting.

OLE BULL STATE PARK, south of Galeton, has camping on the grounds that once belonged to Ole Bull, the noted Norwegian violinist.

PARKER DAM STATE PARK, north of Clearfield. Camping is in a woodland setting.

RICKETTS GLEN STATE PARK, west of Wilkes-Barre. Campers enjoy three lakes, a profusion of waterfalls, and deep swirling rapids in narrow gorges.

WORLDS END STATE PARK, just east of Forksville, has camping sites close to the S-shaped gorge that is among the most beautiful in this area of narrow stream valleys and steep mountains.

Backpacking

APPALACHIAN TRAIL crosses into Pennsylvania at Delaware Water Gap and follows the ridge of Blue Mountain, the front range of the Alleghenies. Eight miles beyond the Susquehanna River, the trail descends to cross the Cumberland Valley by secondary roads to the northern flank of the Blue Ridge, known in Pennsylvania as South Mountain. The trail follows the crest of the Blue Ridge to the south past Pine Grove Furnace, Caledonia, Mont Alto, and Old Forge parks to cross into Maryland close to Beartown.

HORSE SHOE TRAIL branches from the Appalachian Trail north of Harrisburg and meanders to the east past Hopewell Village National Historic Site to Valley Forge.

LAUREL HIGHLANDS TRAIL starts at Ohiopyle State Park and runs through state forests and game lands for over 50 miles to the Conemaugh River, near Johnstown.

NORTH COUNTRY TRAIL in Allegheny National Forest winds from the forest's southern boundary for 95 miles to the Willow Bay Recreation Area on the eastern shore of Allegheny Reservoir, one mile south of the New York border.

Hiking

CATAWISSA OUTLOOK, near Berwick. From a point a few hundred yards after crossing Catawissa Creek on the Second Street bridge in Berwick, hike up the old lumber road to the bluff. The summit provides a splendid view of the river.

GREENWOOD FURNACE STATE PARK, west of Lewistown, has trails that lead to the sites of the historic furnaces.

LEONARD HARRISON STATE PARK, 10 miles southwest of Wellsboro. Trails lead to Pennsylvania's Grand Canyon, one of the deepest canyons in the eastern part of the United States.

MOSHANNON STATE FOREST, north of Clearfield, has the 160-mile Quehanna Trail System, beginning at Parker Dam State Park.

RICKETTS GLEN STATE PARK, west of Wilkes-Barre. A trail leads from Watersmeet over the mountain range to the far side. The deep ravines, 33 waterfalls, and rock formations make the 7-mile hike rewarding if strenuous.

Bike Hiking & Camping

PENNSYLVANIA DUTCH CIRCLE begins in Lancaster at the heart of the Pennsylvania Dutch country. It is a 75-mile American Youth Hostels trail that takes advantage of the fact that motorists on the beautiful roads drive more cautiously because the Plain Folks also use them for their black buggies. Heading north through Neffsville to Lititz, the trail twists through Rothsville, Leola, New Holland, East Earl, and south to Ledge. It runs west to Bird-in-Hand and loops to the south to touch Strasburg before returning to Lancaster. The AYH recommends the trail for families with small children, because it is not strenuous and there are many points of interest.

Canoeing & Rafting

ALLEGHENY NATIONAL FOREST. The Allegheny River is excellent for fast-water canoeing. During the spring the upper waters of Tionesta Creek, a tributary of the river, provide exciting canoeing, but during the summer the creek is usually too shallow. Both canoes and rubber rafts are used on the Clarion River despite discoloration from industrial discharges. The river's deep gorges are sufficiently beautiful that some vacationers are willing to forgive it its pollution.

DELAWARE RIVER, from Dingmans Ferry, where there are canoe rentals, offers fine canoeing. There are a few rapids to negotiate and flat-water canoeing. Camping is along the stream bank.

SUSQUEHANNA WATER TRAILS, in the vicinity of Tunkhannock. For 100 miles the Susquehanna winds through the Endless Mountains. There is a meandering series of pools and rifts. Uninhabited islands are frequent. The Great Bend Trail reaches for 19 miles from the Pennsylvania Fish Commission access above Lanesboro to the Kirkwood-Conklin Bridge at Kirkwood, New York. The 88-mile Bradford-Wyoming Trail starts at the Pennsylvania Fish Commission access near Sayre, in Bradford County, and runs to Falls, in Wyoming County. It is a five- to seven-day trip, with camping on the river at such places as Hornbrook County Park, Echo Beach, LaBeur's, Dickenson's Locust Grove, Grace Calvert, and Onawandah. The 90 miles of white-water trails on tributaries are exciting in March and April and in wet years through May. These include: Sugar Creek, Schrader Creek, Towanda Creek, Wyalusing Creek, Tunkhannock Creek, Tunkhannock Creek's South Branch, Bowman Creek, and Loyalsock Creek. They range in difficulty from Sugar Creek, which is easy to moderately difficult, to the South Branch of the Tunkhannock and the Loyalsock, which both have extremely difficult passages.

WEST BRANCH OF THE SUSQUEHANNA RIVER, from Clearfield to North Bend. The Chicklamoose Canoe Trip is an intermediate canoe trail that runs for 80

North Lake, Catskill Forest Preserve, New York

miles. The trail was once an important Indian route.

YOUGHIOGHENY RIVER, Ohiopyle. Float tours on the river start at Ohiopyle and last from one hour to five days. The most impressive rapids are known as the "double hydraulic," a curling wave thrown up in a narrow, swift rapid between two huge rocks. There are both smooth-water and white-water sections of this run through the Allegheny Mountains of southwestern Pennsylvania. Outfitters are in Ohiopyle.

Boating & Boat Camping

ALLEGHENY NATIONAL FOREST. Boating is excellent on the 12,000-acre Allegheny Reservoir. Campsites at Handsome Lake, Pine Grove, Morrison Run, Hopewell, and Hooks Brook, all in the national forest, are reached only by boat. Precautions: Water levels in the reservoir fluctuate. They are at their lowest ebb in December and highest in March or April. Speed limits are strictly enforced.

PYMATUNING LAKE, west of Meadville, on the Ohio border, has 17 miles of water, excellent for sailing.

SHENANGO RIVER LAKE, north of Sharon, on the Ohio border. Boaters enjoy these waters.

Conservation & Wildlife

COOK FOREST STATE PARK, northeast of Clarion. There are 29 miles of well-marked trails, which take hikers through forests filled with 90 varieties of birds.

HEARTS CONTENT SCENIC AREA, near Warren, in the Allegheny National Forest, preserves a virgin forest of mixed white pine and hardwoods as a living museum.

MILL GROVE, west of Norristown. This museum and wildlife sanctuary was the home of young John James Audubon, where he gained his first impressions of American birds and wildlife on trips into the forests surrounding the estate. Nearly 6 miles of trails wind past feeding stations, nesting boxes, shrubs, and trees which attract numerous species of birds.

PRESQUE ISLE STATE PARK, at Erie. This peninsula thrust into Lake Erie has escaped the destruction of the lakeshore and remains much as the pioneers knew it. The natural land-building activities of the lake have thickened the spit, which now supports a forest. There is a wealth of plant life and small wildlife to be found in the park.

TURK JONES TREE FARM, near Clearfield. Here are 1,200 magnificent acres, proving that nature can heal the ugly scars created by man with his strip mining. In 1945 a Philadelphia advertising man planted trees on this barren eyesore when everyone said it couldn't be done. The trees flourished.

THE MID-ATLANTIC STATES

THE SOUTH

The natural heritage of the South is as varied as the sandy dunes of Cape Hatteras National Seashore, on the North Carolina coast; the leafy bayous of Louisiana's Cajun country; and the mysterious Reelfoot Lake left in western Tennessee by a cataclysmic earthquake of the early 19th century, which tossed out of its bed the mighty Mississippi River, writhing and splashing its vast torrent across the countryside. Of course, in planning outdoor recreation in the South, it is impossible to forget the mighty ramparts of Appalachia, the sunny coasts and interior lakes and streams of Florida, or the man-made strand along Mississippi's Gulf Coast.

Just because it is different, Louisiana's Cajun country has an irresistible appeal.

"If you were to step into my boat, m'sieu," says a Cajun guide to a visitor from up north, "I should desire that you part your hair in the middle so that there would be no upset, n'est-ce pas?"

Cajuns claim they can float their pirogues on the dew. They call all English-speaking visitors "Yankees," whether they come from New England, New York, or from another part of Louisiana. This is a country that is half land and half water, and it is the land of the alligators, the opossum, the muskrat, and the coypu.

A hiker can follow in Daniel Boone's steps on a remnant of the Wilderness Trail that still can be traced through the Cumberland Gap, or he can camp along the Natchez Trace, once the pioneer artery of commerce between Nashville at the end of one branch of the Wilderness Trail and Natchez, graceful city on the Mississippi.

The very sound of the states of the South is musical: Alabama, Arkansas, Delaware, Florida, Georgia, Kentucky, Louisiana, Maryland, Mississippi, North Carolina, South Carolina, Tennessee, Virginia, and West Virginia. In the sunny Caribbean are Puerto Rico and the Virgin Islands, two added American outdoor recreation areas of extraordinary beauty.

Throughout the South and on American soil in the Caribbean are outdoor wonders. Arkansas is not called the "Wonder State" for nothing. One state park near Murfreesboro contains the only diamond mine in the United States. Arkansas also has remarkable underground rivers, caverns of real beauty and grandeur, and medicinal springs that gush piping hot out of the earth at Hot Springs National Park.

The very mountains of Arkansas run at right angles to most United States ranges. The Ozark, Boston, and Ouachita mountains reach east to west instead of north to south. A backpacker in the Boston or Ouachita mountains finds tumbling waterfalls, forested cliffs, and—even on the hottest days—refreshing streams in which to take a dip. Hiking the backcountry roads through the hills, a backpacker almost expects to meet the "Arkansas Traveler" himself, because the rail fences and razorback hogs and the smell of wood smoke rising over a mountain clearing are unchanged from a century ago. If anything, Arkansas and also the mountains of the east, stretching from Virginia south to the last nub in Georgia, are wilder today than they were a century ago.

Delaware is next to the smallest state in size, but this doesn't keep it from offering marvelous ponds full of wildlife, dunes for sunning, and beaches for swimming, clamming, and crabbing all the way from Smyrna to Lewes. Its neighbor, Maryland, is equally fascinating, ranging in appeal from Chesapeake Bay marshes, home of the grouse, to mountain pools reflecting flowering laurel in the west of the state.

"Mountaineers are always free," is cut into the pedestal of a statue of a mountaineer on the grounds of the West Virginia capitol at Charleston, and life for a vacationer in the mountains of West Virginia and Virginia too is free and untrammeled. The Appalachians reach mountain high and valley low. Camping sites have been cut into the forests, and trails wind along the mountain ridges so that vacationers can enjoy the high country. A hike along the cool slopes, mantled by rhododendron and basswood, is always memorable. North Carolina, South Carolina, Georgia, Kentucky, Tennessee, and northeast Alabama also have their share of the Appalachian vacationland.

Georgia possesses the golden sea islands and the trackless Okefenokee Swamp, where canoeists must not take a dog along for fear that he will make a tasty lunch for the omnipresent alligators. Florida also has its labyrinthine wilderness, the Everglades, a weird land of saw grass and cypress swamps, where Seminole guides alone can find their way among the hammocks. Then there are the Keys, stepping-stone islands leading into the subtropical seas.

To some vacationers the out-of-doors South is the TVA's Land Between the Lakes, ranging from northern Kentucky across the western part of the state into Tennessee. To others it is the Great Smokies or the pinewoods and bluffs along the Mississippi River in Tennessee. But everywhere in the South there are fascinating natural things to see.

Okefenokee Swamp, Georgia

ALABAMA

Camping

CONECUH NATIONAL FOREST, near Andalusia, has a fine camping area.

DESOTO STATE PARK, 7 miles out of Mentone. The campgrounds are close to the Little River Canyon, known as the Grand Canyon of the South.

HORSE PENS PARK, near Oneonta, contains bizarre stone sculptures where Indian ponies once were kept in a natural stone corral. There are camping areas and sometimes hootenannies to keep the campers entertained.

JOE WHEELER STATE PARK, near Town Creek and the Wheeler Dam, provides camping areas.

LITTLE MOUNTAIN STATE PARK, near Guntersville, caters to the increasing tribe of tent campers. A wooded camping area is beside Guntersville Lake.

MONTE SANO STATE PARK, 4 miles from Huntsville, has camping sites.

ROCK BRIDGE CANYON, near Hodges. There is camping in rustic serenity. A huge sandstone arch spans the canyon.

TALLADEGA NATIONAL FOREST. There are four camping areas divided equally between the two divisions of the forest: the Oakmulgee, located in west central Alabama, and the Talladega division in northeastern Alabama.

TUSKEGEE NATIONAL FOREST, near Auburn and Tuskegee, has a camping area.

WILLIAM B. BANKHEAD NATIONAL FOREST. There are three camping areas in this 181,000-acre forest, noted for its limestone gorges, the Lewis Smith Reservoir, and two natural bridges.

Backpacking

CUMBERLAND MOUNTAINS of northern Alabama are green-cloaked hills that have been cut by wind and water to provide a rich scenic backdrop for a backpack. The backpacker with a keen eye for geological features will find the mountains of particular interest.

Hiking

CHEAHA STATE PARK, 25 miles northeast of Talladega. The Odum Trail starts atop Cheaha Mountain and winds southward along a mountain ridge to High Falls. There are splendid views of the Coosa River winding through its lush valley far below. The 9-mile trail was opened by Scouts to encourage interest in the southern out-of-doors. Hikers should carry a canteen; there is no water until the end of the trail.

CHEWACLA STATE PARK, 3 miles south of Auburn, offers hiking trails along the fall line that separates the piedmont plateau from the coastal plain.

DAUPHIN ISLAND. Hikers can stroll along the packed sand of the beach or idle along tree-shaded lanes.

DISMALS WONDER GARDENS, near Phil Campbell. A trail leads through a narrow slit in a boulder cracked by an earthquake and continues up a narrow canyon. There are grottoes, waterfalls, six natural bridges, and dismalites, tiny phosphorescent worms that glow in the dark.

HURRICANE CREEK PARK, east of Cullman. A trail winds up a natural spiral staircase where waterfalls splash. A pool with a white sand bottom lies at the bottom of a deep gorge.

JOE WHEELER STATE PARK, near Red Bank. Trails lead through the scenic park.

MONTE SANO STATE PARK, 4 miles from Huntsville, has 15 miles of trails.

OAK MOUNTAIN STATE PARK, 16 miles south of Birmingham, has several miles of hiking trails to such places as Peavine Falls and Gorge.

WHEELER NATIONAL WILDLIFE REFUGE, near Decatur. Nature trails lead through the 35,000-acre refuge.

Biking

AZALEA TRAIL, Mobile. For 35 miles the trail leads through the residential districts of the city famous for its azaleas. The chamber of commerce will advise bikers when the blooms will be at their best, but the trail is worth following at any time of the year.

POINT MALLARD PARK, at Decatur. A 3-mile scenic trail, suitable for biking, leads along the banks of the Tennessee River.

Canoeing

LITTLE RIVER CANYON, south of Fort Payne. Daring canoeists and rafters take their craft through the 3-mile canyon. When the flow is great, they run the risk of being swamped; when it is too little, the rapids are too rocky to pass. Nobody should try the Little River without understanding the water conditions.

TVA LAKES AND RIVERS. Canoeists are exploring the TVA impoundments and the rivers of the TVA system. (See TVA Lakes under Boating and Boat Camping for additional information.)

Boating & Boat Camping

GULF COAST. The sheltered waters of Mobile Bay and the Intracoastal Waterway afford fine saltwater boating. There are handy marinas, and boat repairs are located in major ports. Bayou La Batre and other bayous lead a boater to idyllic shrimp-fishing villages. Cypress and live oak trees line the 500,000 acres of brackish waters in the bayous, where tides mix salt and fresh water. Among the most attractive ports of call for boaters is Dauphin Island, where seafood dining on the famed Bon Secours oysters, scampies, and tender crabmeat can only be excelled in the restaurants of Mobile.

LAKE MARTIN, near Alexander City, offers fine boating in a man-made lake with 760 miles of shoreline.

TVA LAKES. TVA reservoirs have made Middle South states such as Alabama into a boater's paradise. There are hundreds of public-access areas along the 10,000 miles of shoreline. Alabama alone has 400,000 water acres in the impounded lakes. Access roads, parking areas, and boat-launching ramps make it easy to get started on a water holiday. Slips are located on the lakes at Muscle Shoals, Decatur, and Guntersville, and repair services are available at several of the larger towns and communities.

Not only outboards, but yachts and sailboats furrow the waters, for there are over 50,000 recreation boats kept on the waters. From Scottsboro to the Tri-Cities, interest in sailing is growing yearly, and there are yacht clubs at Turtle Point and Muscle Shoals on Wilson Lake and at Guntersville and Brown's Creek on Guntersville Lake. The North American Yacht Racing Union sponsors races. Sailing doesn't stop for everybody in the winter months, and frostbite races are held.

Recreation boats may pass through the locks at the great dams on the rivers. A short distance downstream of the lower gate there are bell ropes suspended from the wall. A boater pulls this rope to signal the lock operator that he wishes to lock through. Boat events every year in-

SOUTHERN STATES

clude speedboat races and sailboat regattas. The National Outboard Association sanctions the outboard racing in the Tennessee Valley lakes. Overnight camping is allowed on many miles of public shorelines, and there are a few improved campsites at boat docks and at state parks. Organized group camp areas on TVA lakeshores are used by the Scouts, YMCA, and other youth groups. A safety note: The TVA advises that "peculiar hazards to safety exist at TVA dams where waters rush over spillways and through sluice gates and turbines. Many of these operations are automatic and occur without warning." Maps of the TVA lakes and rivers may be obtained by writing to the TVA Map Library, Chattanooga, Tennessee, or TVA Maps and Engineering Records Section, Knoxville, Tennessee. Chambers of commerce and tourist organizations in the TVA lakes region also keep supplies of these maps for sale. Houseboats are available in the Pickwick Lake area and in the towns of Huntsville and Florence either by the week, weekend, or midweek.

Sport Diving

GULF COAST. Clear coastal waters create an underwater playground for scuba divers. Spearfishing for rough fish is permitted.

TVA LAKES. Lake waters are becoming popular with scuba and skin divers.

Conservation & Wildlife

BELLINGRATH GARDENS, near Theodore, are among the Middle South's most beautiful gardens and include atmospheric nature walks where swans cruise on pools overhung with Spanish moss.

DESOTO STATE PARK, Fort Payne. The falls leap a spectacular 110 feet into a rock basin. The cliffs overlooking the dramatic scene are draped with mountain laurel, rhododendron, and wild azalea. The Little River Canyon is the deepest gorge east of the Rockies, and the Little River is the only river in the country that forms and flows on a mountaintop. The scarlet and bronze canyon walls are a beautiful complement to the wild flowers that blossom in the spring.

DISMALS WONDER GARDENS, west of Phil Campbell on Alabama 43, is an unspoiled beauty spot in private hands, open to the public at a fee. The hidden canyon was named by Scotch-Irish settlers because of the supernatural atmosphere. Tiny, turned-on phosphorescent worms light up at night to create an eerie glow. The worms come out at sunset in the summer after a warm and rainy day and climb up the rocks to as high as 50 feet. Their winking and blinking light make a night visit to the park fascinating. A narrow trail traces the stream known as the Dismal Branch to sandstone grottoes, two waterfalls, and six natural bridges. The Sunken Forest is one of the oldest wild forest areas in the eastern United States. The natural arboretum includes 27 species of native trees and more than 300 different plants.

HURRICANE CREEK PARK, near Cullman. A mile-and-a-half nature trail crosses a swinging bridge and mounts a spiral staircase past silvery waterfalls. Mexican burros and a cable car take less hardy visitors to the top of the craggy gap.

NATCHEZ TRACE PARKWAY. Along the old highway that winds for 450 miles from Nashville, Tennessee, to Natchez, Mississippi, are a number of interesting nature areas. A modern highway follows the pioneer trace, and a motorist can cruise along its course enjoying both historic and natural spots.

NATURAL BRIDGE PARK, near Haleyville. The longest natural bridge in the southeast is made up of two sandstone arches vaulting 158 feet across the ravine. The lacey ferns, wild flowers, and a giant magnolia with 14-inch blossoms are worth seeing.

NOCCALULA FALLS, Gadsden. The park not only contains a sparkling waterfall that drops 100 feet from a limestone ledge but a fine botanical garden.

WHEELER NATIONAL WILDLIFE REFUGE, east of Decatur. From October to March, huge flocks of wild geese and ducks make their home in this refuge. The 50,000 geese make up the only large concentration of wild geese in the state. Guns, however, may not be brought into the refuge even in autos except during public hunts and with a permit. Dogs must be left at home. Overnight camping is prohibited except by well-trained Scouts or equivalent youth groups.

ARKANSAS

Camping

BUFFALO POINT, 20 miles southeast of Yellville. Campsites are close to the swiftly running Buffalo National River in the Ozark mountains.

BULL SHOALS STATE PARK, 11 miles west of Mountain Home, offers camping on the White River. There is fishing on both Bull Shoals Lake and the river.

CROWLEY'S RIDGE STATE PARK, 15 miles north of Jonesboro. Dogwood blooms in spring in the 265 acres of this rolling ridge running down the fertile delta of eastern Arkansas. Campers enjoy a freshwater swimming lake and an eight-acre fishing lake.

DAISY STATE PARK. Daisy, on the northern shore of Lake Greeson, has a number of self-maintained campsites.

DAVIDSON STATE PARK, on the Black River, 8 miles southwest of Pocahontas, offers camping in wooded seclusion. Old Davidsonville is the site of Arkansas's first post office and land office.

DEVILS DEN STATE PARK, 18 miles south of West Fork. Nestled in a picturesque valley of the Boston Mountains of the Ozark National Forest are 4,885 acres of wilderness, sandstone bluffs, and clean, natural streams. There is also a small lake for fishing.

HOT SPRINGS NATIONAL PARK. Gulpha Gorge Campground is located in a rustic gorge. Thermal springs provide government-controlled baths along nearby Bath House Row. There is a 14-day limit from April 1 through October 15, and a 30-day limit the rest of the year.

LAKE CATHERINE STATE PARK, 12 miles west of Malvern, on the smallest of three lakes that surround the resort city of Hot Springs. The heavily wooded shoreline provides good campsites.

LAKE CHARLES STATE PARK, 14 miles west of Hoxie. Individual campsites are separated by belts of native trees and shrubs in this rolling and wooded park.

LAKE CHICOT STATE PARK, 8 miles north of Lake Village. Camping is on Arkansas's largest natural lake. The lake is an oxbow, an abandoned channel of the Mississippi, separated from the river by high levees. Old cypress trees inhabit the lake, providing good fishing spots.

LAKE DARDANELLE STATE PARK. The park includes three areas on the lake's shoreline, all with campsites. The Russellville and the Ouita areas are near Russellville; the Dardanelle area is across the lake, near Dardanelle.

LAKE OUACHITA STATE PARK, 6 miles northwest of Mountain Valley. Campsites are on the lake. Three Sisters Springs is in the park.

MORO BAY STATE PARK, 19 miles northeast of El Dorado, is at the junction of Moro Bayou and the Ouachita River.

MOUNT NEBO STATE PARK, 7 miles west of Dardanelle, atop an 1,800-foot mountain overlooking the Arkansas River valley. Campers enjoy coolness in midsummer.

NATIONAL FORESTS. Arkansas boasts of three national forests, which together contain more than three million acres of timberland. The Forest Service has developed 42 campgrounds at scenic points, most of them located in rugged, beautiful, mountainous terrain, designed to blend into the forest atmosphere. Most of the major camping areas are closed from November 1 through May 1. For information on Ouachita National Forest, write Forest Supervisor, Ouachita National Forest, USFS Box 1270, Hot Springs, Arkansas. For information on both the Ozark and the St. Francis national forests, write Forest Supervisor, Ozark National Forest, P.O. Box 1008, Russellville, Arkansas 72801.

PETIT JEAN STATE PARK, 21 miles southwest of Morrilton, 800 feet above the Arkansas River valley. The mountaintop park contains Cedar Falls, one of the highest waterfalls in the South; caves; and a deep canyon.

WITHROW SPRING STATE PARK, 5 miles north of Huntsville, offers camping in a forested valley setting. The park's giant spring never goes dry and feeds War Eagle Creek, which meanders through the park.

Backpacking

NATIONAL FORESTS. The wilderness terrain of all three of Arkansas's national forests—Ouachita, Ozark, and St. Francis—lends itself to backpacking. Old logging roads, firebreaks, and deserted railroad rights-of-way abound, making excellent paths into remote areas. The Forest Service has marked a new backpacking trail through the Ouachitas, which will in time extend for 200 miles. The trail pioneered by our Troop 333 backpackers opens up a country of brawling mountain streams, waterfalls, and rocky overhangs. For further information on this area, see National Forests under Camping.

Hiking

BUFFALO POINT, 20 miles southeast of Yellville. Trails lead to hidden springs and caves.

DEVILS DEN STATE PARK, 18 miles south of West Fork. Paths lead hikers through weird rock formations with gaping cracks and crevices. The newly completed Butterfield Trail is the only overnight trail in the state park system.

GREERS FERRY LAKE. South of the dam, hikers climb Mossy Bluff Trail up a hillside for a panoramic view of the lake and the dam.

HAW CREEK FALLS RECREATION AREA, Ozark National Forest, 12 miles southwest of Pelsor. Intrepid hikers follow an old logging road, last used around 1910, to within sight of the gorge that is the entrance to "The Shut-Ins," the headwaters of Hurricane Creek, a remote and beautiful spot.

HOT SPRINGS NATIONAL PARK, Gulpha Gorge Campground. Trails go through lush mountain forests and to thermal springs.

LAKE CHARLES STATE PARK, 14 miles west of Hoxie. A blacktop trail winds its way around the lake.

MOUNT NEBO STATE PARK, 7 miles west of Dardanelle, has mountain trails for hikers.

PETIT JEAN STATE PARK, 21 miles southwest of Morrilton. Numerous trails crisscross the park.

Rockhounding

COLEMAN'S CRYSTAL MINE, north of Hot Springs. Amateurs unearth valuable quartz crystals for a small daily fee.

CRATER OF DIAMONDS STATE PARK, 2 miles south of Murfreesboro, only known diamond crater on the North American continent. Rockhounds find over 350 stones a year and may keep their finds, but are advised to have them certified as genuine by a park official. Gems found at the crater range from 1 to 40 carats. The only black diamonds ever found in a pipe mine have been discovered here.

HOG SCALD HOLLOW, 10 miles south of Eureka Springs. A winding dirt road off Arkansas 23 leads to an unusual rock basin with large kettle holes formed ages ago by churning waters. A rock path and natural steps lead to the foot of Auger Falls. From time to time the creek bed will be dry in spots, becoming a rockhounder's paradise for fossils.

Canoeing & Rafting

BUFFALO RIVER, from Boxley to Buffalo City, a distance of 133½ miles. This fine free-flowing river has been declared a national river, which will forever preserve its wilderness character. Except during extreme dry periods, the lower half of the river can be floated anytime. Normally after May 1, unless following local rains, the upper portion, from Ponca to Pruitt, is too low to canoe. Canoe rentals are available at Ponca, Pruitt, St. Joe, Yellville, and Buffalo River State Park. There are also johnboat trips of the Current, Jack Fork, Eleven Point, White, and Kings rivers, as well as the Buffalo.

Boating & Boat Camping

BULL SHOALS LAKE, on Missouri border, massive impoundment of the White River, home of the "lunker bass." Over 1,000 miles of shoreline provide hidden coves and inlets.

GREERS FERRY LAKE, in the rugged Ozark foothills of north central Arkansas. Many camping facilities surround the lake. Boaters dock at the island in the upper part of the lake to take Sugar Loaf Mountain Trail to the 1,000-foot summit for a 360-degree view of the slopes and blue waters.

LAKE CHARLES STATE PARK, 8 miles northwest of Hoxie, has good boating.

LAKE CHICOT STATE PARK, 8 miles north of Lake Village, offers boating and fine fishing on this largest of oxbow lakes in the state. Oxbow lakes formed in the old Mississippi River bed when the great river changed its course.

LAKE DARDANELLE, near Russellville, an impoundment of the Arkansas River. Boats can negotiate the locks at either end of the reservoir, as well as explore Illinois Bayou, the Big Piney, and Shoal Bay. Docks and launching ramps are dotted strategically around the lake.

LAKE GREESON, an impoundment of the Little Missouri located in southwest Arkansas. This medium-sized lake has many coves and inlets that make excellent hideaways.

LAKE OUACHITA, near Hot Springs, a

backup of the Ouachita River, has unsurpassed scenic beauty, excellent fishing, and water sports of all kinds.

Sport Diving

GREERS FERRY LAKE, in north central Arkansas on the Little Red River. Divers find the water clear even to depths of 150 feet.

LAKE GREESON, southwestern Arkansas, has crystal clear waters for diving.

NORFOLK LAKE, backed up on the North Fork River in the Ozark highlands of north central Arkansas and southern Missouri. Its clear waters are a favorite of sport divers.

Conservation & Wildlife

DEVILS DEN STATE PARK, 18 miles south of West Fork, has a naturalist program in season.

HOG SCALD HOLLOW, 10 miles south of Eureka Springs. A winding dirt road off Arkansas 23 leads to the hollow, where hikers can observe an abundance of wildlife, which is attracted to the wild berries and grapes in summer and persimmons in the fall.

HOT SPRINGS NATIONAL PARK, Gulpha Gorge Campgrounds. There are summer interpretive programs.

DELAWARE

Camping

CAPE HENLOPEN STATE PARK, Lewes. A primitive camping site is located in an area of big pitch pines and open dunes close to where coastal guns were placed during World War II. Only advanced Scouts or others experienced in outdoor living may use the area; other groups camp in the Youth Camp area near the Visitor Center. There also is a family camping ground.

DELAWARE SEASHORE STATE PARK, south of Rehoboth Beach. There is year-round family camping close to the beach.

ELLENDALE STATE FOREST, just south of Ellendale, permits camping, but no facilities are provided.

OWENS STATE FOREST, east of Greenwood, allows camping but does not provide facilities.

REDDEN STATE FOREST, north of Georgetown, permits camping but does not provide facilities.

TRAP POND STATE PARK, Laurel. There is an excellent camping area.

Hiking

DELAWARE SEASHORE STATE PARK, south of Rehoboth Beach. The many miles of ocean beach lure hikers as well as swimmers.

TRAP POND STATE PARK, Laurel. There are unmarked trails leading through the park, which includes 800 acres of pines surrounding the pond.

Boating

DELAWARE SEASHORE STATE PARK, south of Rehoboth Beach. There is boating in the ocean and in the sheltered waters of Indian River Inlet.

HOLTS LANDING STATE PARK, west of Bethany Beach on the south shore of Indian River Inlet. Boating in the inlet is outstanding.

INTRACOASTAL WATERWAY. Boaters follow the sheltered waterway for the length of the state.

General Butler State Park, Kentucky

Conservation & Wildlife

BRANDYWINE CREEK STATE PARK, northwest of Wilmington. A nature program is offered in conjunction with the Delaware Nature Education Center located in the park. Meadows and woodlands roll to the brink of the Brandywine.

CAPE HENLOPEN STATE PARK, Lewes. The Pinelands Nature Trail reveals moving dunes, the end of a bog, the results of a violent wind and rainstorm and of a recent fire. The plants, the fallen trees, the dramatic effects of a firelane that worked, all can be studied. The trail is maintained by the Sussex Gardeners and Lewes Boy Scout Troop 1. Only a half-mile south of the park there is a fine section of bogs and high dunes. The park naturalist leads tours through this town-owned area from time to time. The Seaside Nature Trail and a Seabird Nesting Area are also in the park.

KILLENS POND STATE PARK, southeast of Felton. The pond and the surrounding lands have been left undisturbed.

PETERSBURG WILDLIFE AREA, southwest of Dover. The Delaware Department of Natural Resources and Environmental Control and Boy Scout Troop 338 of Marydel have developed the Woodlands Nature Trail, and the Scouts maintain it. Numbered posts tell the story as you go, from the beds of turkeyfoot to the greenbrier thicket and a stand of cedar, holly, and sassafras. The trail is of equal interest in all four of the seasons.

TRAP POND STATE PARK, Laurel. Island Trail takes a hiker past the largest variety of trees in any Delaware state park. Birds are of particular interest in the nesting season. The first dam was built in 1790 to create Trap Pond, and the present dam dates to the CCC period of the 1930s. The pond is home to ducks and geese, herons, frogs, turtles, and otters.

FLORIDA

Camping

BLACKWATER RIVER STATE FOREST, in extreme western panhandle. Camping sites are at Bear Lake, Munson Recreation Area, Karick Lake, and Red Rock, though camping is not limited to these areas. Rivers, with their white sandbar beaches, invite swimming.

EVERGLADES NATIONAL PARK, at southern tip of Florida. Campgrounds are found at Long Pine Key and Flamingo, with a limit of 14 days from Nov. 15 to April 15, and 30 days the rest of the year.

FLORIDA CAVERNS STATE PARK, 3 miles north of Marianna, in panhandle, features camping amid a disappearing river, a large spring, and many caverns. Swimming is in "Blue Hole."

JOHN PENNEKAMP CORAL REEF STATE PARK, on Key Largo, offers camping for water enthusiasts. The first undersea park in the continental United States, most of its 75,130 acres lie in the Atlantic Ocean. The park contains the only living reef formation on the North American coast.

JONATHAN DICKINSON STATE PARK, 13 miles south of Stuart, offers camping where Jonathan Dickinson, of shipwreck fame, landed in 1696. Jupiter Inlet is good for fishing, and the Loxahatchee for swimming.

MIKE ROESS GOLD HEAD BRANCH STATE PARK, 6 miles northeast of Keystone Heights. Campsites are near Gold Head Branch, a stream that meanders through a lovely ravine. There is swimming in Lake Johnson.

MYAKKA RIVER STATE PARK, 17 miles east of Sarasota, offers two camping areas in the state's oldest and largest (in land area) park. The Myakka River is noted for fishing, boating, and wildlife.

OCALA NATIONAL FOREST, east of Ocala. Campgrounds are at Juniper Springs Recreation Area and Alexander Springs. This is the Big Scrub, the largest stand of sand pine in the world.

SANIBEL ISLAND, off the coast near Fort Myers Beach, offers camping on the best shelling beach of the Western Hemisphere.

Backpacking

FLORIDA WILDERNESS TRAIL. Many sections of the planned 650-mile north-to-south trail are open. The trail passes through three national forests—the Apalachicola, Osceola, and Ocala. The route through the Big Scrub in Ocala National Forest has been blazed and contains primitive campsites on the south shore of Buck Lake and at the Farles Prairie Recreation Area.

MYAKKA RIVER STATE PARK, 17 miles east of Sarasota, has a 3-mile trail through oak and palm hammocks to a camping area on Bee Island. The trail is limited to 12 persons at any given time, ensuring privacy. Hikers are asked to register with the park attendants.

TORREYA STATE PARK, 12 miles north of Bristol. The trail starts at the antebellum Gregory House and ends 2 miles down the Apalachicola River at a campground atop a high bluff that commands a sweeping view of the river. Hikers should register with park attendants. The trail is limited to 12 persons at a time.

Hiking

BEAR CUT NATURE TRAIL, Key Biscayne. At low tide hikers don foot-protecting sneakers to follow a naturalist to the world's only fossilized black mangrove reef.

JACKSON RED GROUND TRAIL, Blackwater River State Forest, follows an Indian trail once used by Andrew Jackson. From the southwestern point at Red Rock, the trail continues northeasterly to Karick Lake.

EVERGLADES NATIONAL PARK, southern tip of Florida. There are several self-guiding nature trails between the main visitor center at Royal Palm and the Flamingo Visitor Center.

HIGHLANDS HAMMOCK STATE PARK, 6 miles west of Sebring, has 10 miles of foot trails, including an elevated catwalk through a cypress swamp.

Bike Hiking & Camping

HIGHLANDS HAMMOCK STATE PARK, 6 miles west of Sebring, has a 2-mile loop road through junglelike swamps and a wild orange grove. Bicycle rentals available.

HILLSBOROUGH RIVER STATE PARK, 6 miles southwest of Zephyrhills. The trail makes a 2-mile loop, affording views of ancient cypress trees, old oaks, and wildlife. Rentals available.

MIKE ROESS GOLD HEAD BRANCH STATE PARK, 6 miles northeast of Keystone Heights. The 5-mile trail along park roads passes a lovely ravine on its way to Lake Johnson. Rentals available.

MYAKKA RIVER STATE PARK, 17 miles east of Sarasota. Bikers follow 13 miles of park roads to spot deer, alligators, and other wildlife. Rentals available.

NORTH FLORIDA SPIN. The American Youth Hostels has mapped out a bike tour from St. Augustine to Cypress Gardens, a flat, easy 180-mile ride, which stays primarily on lightly traveled roads. The trip can be made any time of year. There are some campsites along the route, but it is mainly a motel trip.

SANIBEL ISLAND, off coast of Fort Myers. The island is only 12 miles long and 3 miles wide, and biking is popular. There are rentals.

Canoeing & Rafting

BLACKWATER RIVER CANOE TRAIL flows for 40 miles through the western highlands of Florida. Its tea-colored waters contrast with white sandbars at every bend in the twisting stream. The trail begins west of Laurel Hill, at Florida 180, 2 miles south of the Alabama-Florida state line, and ends in the Blackwater River State Park, near Harold.

ECONLOCKHATCHEE RIVER, 28 miles of wilderness from 9 miles east of Orlando on Florida 50 to the St. Johns River. About a nine-hour trip, it has many broad sandbars for camping.

EVERGLADES NATIONAL PARK. In the Flamingo area are three marked canoe trails of 14 to 22 miles, round trip. Primitive campsites are widely spaced along the trails. The required camping permits and mimeographed maps of the trails may be obtained at the ranger station at either Flamingo or Everglades City.

ICHETUCKNEE RIVER, 3 miles of shallow, clear water, entirely within Ichetucknee Springs State Park, 4 miles northwest of Fort White. Equally popular with tubists, the canoe trail begins at Ichetucknee Springs and ends at Florida 238.

OCALA NATIONAL FOREST. Juniper Springs pours out 8,300,000 gallons a day, giving birth to a "run," which twists through an unspoiled wilderness. A canoeist can drift down to the bridge 7 miles below, to be met and brought back to the springs.

OCHLOCKONEE RIVER, from Florida 20, about 23 miles west of Tallahassee. Part of the canoe trail goes through the Apalachicola National Forest with its campsites. The trail takes 18 to 20 hours.

PEACE RIVER, from US 98, just east of Fort Meade, to Florida 70, west of Arcadia. Hardly a house is visible along the way, and there is plenty of wildlife.

SHOAL RIVER, from Florida 285, about 4 miles north of Mossy Head, to Florida 85, 4 miles south of Crestview. Few signs of civilization show in the 24 miles.

SOPCHOPPY RIVER. The trail starts on forest road 346, 5 miles north of Sopchoppy, and winds for 15 miles through Apalachicola National Forest. Check gauge under bridge at start—the best canoeing level is 10.0–12.0.

SUWANNEE RIVER CANOE TRAIL, beginning at Lem Griffis Hunting and Fishing Camp, 18 miles north of Fargo, Georgia. You can stop at Suwannee River State Park in Florida or continue all the way to the Gulf of Mexico. The Suwannee rises deep within the Okefenokee Swamp in Georgia, and its dark, cypress-stained waters flow quietly. The water lightens farther south as many springs feed it. Above White Springs there is white water that should be portaged or canoed with caution. Much wildlife will be seen in the woods skirting the river. There are six camping areas between the beginning of the trail and the Suwannee River State Park.

WACISSA RIVER, a 14-mile route beginning at Wacissa Springs, a few miles east of Tallahassee, to twist and turn through the Aucilla Game Management

Alligators—Everglades, Florida

Area before entering the Aucilla River near US 98 between Perry and Newport. This is one of the more primitive of Florida rivers.

WEKIVA RIVER. An eight- to twelve-hour cruise of 15 miles starts at Wekiva Springs in Orange County and ends at Emanuel Landing at the St. Johns River.

WITHLACOOCHEE RIVER, 82 miles between Silver Lake in the Croom Game Management Area of the Withlacoochee State Forest, 9 miles south of Bushnell on US 301, and Inglis on US 19-98. Although a lot of the riverfront is posted, there are large portions where overnight camping is permitted.

YELLOW RIVER has 50 miles of canoeing waters for a two- or three-day trip, starting about 15 miles south of Crestview on Florida 2 in the panhandle.

Boating

INTRACOASTAL WATERWAY. Over 8,000 miles of tidal shoreline plus thousands of navigable lakes and rivers offer unlimited opportunities for cruising in sheltered waters. For instance, a boat can be launched in Lake Tohopekaliga at Kissimmee, in the center of the peninsula, and reach either the Atlantic Ocean or the Gulf of Mexico without ever leaving the water.

WILDERNESS WATERWAY, winding for 99 miles between Flamingo in Everglades National Park and Everglades City through rivers, creeks, and inside bays of mangrove wilderness on the Gulf Coast. The waterway is marked, and there are several primitive campsites. Boaters must file a "float plan" at the ranger station before embarking. The Park Service recommends that only craft less than 20 feet long make the trip, because of narrow creeks and many shallow places.

Sport Diving

The state of Florida publishes an excellent booklet which lists the innumerable diving possibilities in the state, ranging from saltwater diving to inland and cave diving. The best months for diving along the coastline are May through September, when the waters are warmer and the visibility greater. Inland, most divers prefer the winter months. The cold weather destroys the algae which means the water is noticeably clearer, and the lower rainfall in winter means a lower watertable. The water in springs, caves, and sinkholes remains at a constant temperature of 70 degrees, with higher temperatures at greater depths, and visibility well over 100 feet. For the booklet write: Department of Commerce, Collins Building, Tallahassee, Florida 32304.

Conservation & Wildlife

CORKSCREW SWAMP SANCTUARY, on Florida 846, southwest of Immokalee, is a major nesting ground for the dwindling flocks of wood ibis, the only North American stork. The white ibis and the snowy egret also call this home. Giant bald cypress trees, the oldest living things in eastern North America, shelter alligators, otters, raccoons, fox squirrels, bobcats, and other animals.

EVERGLADES NATIONAL PARK. Exhibits at the Royal Palm interpretive station and Flamingo Visitor Center tell the story of man's struggle to prevent the extinction of the Everglades' rare and endangered bird species.

FLOATING ISLANDS begin from small clumps of roots or matted grass that have sunk to a lake's bed. During high water or hot weather, the clumps are forced to the surface by formation of gas. Gradually vegetation takes hold, and trees and plants start growing. These islands are common where heavy rainfall and hot, humid weather prevail. The largest and most interesting of these are to be seen on the lakes near two state parks, Lake Griffin and Marjorie Kinnan Rawlings. Both parks have boat ramps from which the lakes can be reached and the islands seen.

HIGHLANDS HAMMOCK STATE PARK, near Sebring. The 10 miles of foot trails make it possible to see turtles, alligators, and a variety of herons and egrets. A sightseeing trailer also takes visitors on tours of the flora and fauna.

SANIBEL ISLAND, off the coast near Fort Myers Beach, has a wildlife refuge and is a rewarding place for bird-watchers. The roseate spoonbill and species of ibis, egret, and heron may be seen.

GEORGIA

Camping

AMICALOLA FALLS STATE PARK, 16 miles northwest of Dawsonville. There is camping in the park famed for 729-foot Amicalola Falls, the highest waterfall in Georgia.

BLACKBURN STATE PARK, 7 miles southwest of Dahlonega, provides camping grounds in the heart of the gold-panning country.

BLACK ROCK MOUNTAIN STATE PARK, north of Clayton. The park, named for the cliffs of dark granite, is a favorite among campers.

CLOUDLAND CANYON STATE PARK, north of La Fayette. Camping is fine in what was once Cherokee land.

DEEP HOLE RECREATION AREA, 18 miles southeast of Blue Ridge on Georgia 60. The Forest Service campgrounds are open May 1 through October 31.

DESOTO FALLS CAMPING AREA, northwest of Cleveland, is open from May 1 until October 31 for tent and trailer camping. It is operated by the Forest Service.

FORT MOUNTAIN STATE PARK, 5 miles east of Chatsworth. Campers pitch their tents close to the mysterious ancient fortifications atop the mountain.

HART STATE PARK, north of Hartwell. The campsites are close to Lake Hartwell, favored by fishermen.

HIDDEN CREEK CAMPING AREA, west of Calhoun. There are tent and trailer campsites in a Forest Service campground.

JOHN TANNER STATE PARK, between Carrollton and Mount Zion, is a new park open to campers.

LAKE BLUE RIDGE CAMPING AREA, southeast of Blue Ridge. Camping in grounds operated by the Forest Service.

LAKE CONASAUGA CAMPING AREA, east of Chatsworth. The Forest Service campground offers both tent and trailer camping.

LAKE RUSSELL CAMPING AREA, east of Cornelia, is a Forest Service camp for tent and trailer campers open from May 1 until October 31.

LAKE SINCLAIR CAMPING AREA, south of Eatonton, is a Forest Service campground.

LAKE WINFIELD SCOTT CAMPING AREA, south of Blairsville in the Chattahoochee National Forest, offers both tent and trailer camping.

MORGANTON POINT CAMPING AREA, east of Blue Ridge, is a camping area

THE SOUTH 115

operated by the Forest Service. Open May 1 through October 31.

MOCCASIN CREEK STATE PARK, 25 miles north of Clarkesville, is ideal for campers who want to fish in Lake Burton.

RABUN BEACH AND CAMPING AREA, south of Clayton, is a Forest Service camp offering both tent and trailer camping. It is open from May 15 to September 15.

RED TOP MOUNTAIN STATE PARK, 6 miles southeast of Cartersville, on the shore of Lake Allatoona, has camping grounds. A Civil War battle raged on the site.

SANDY CREEK PUBLIC USE AREA, north of Fort Gaines, is a Corps of Engineers camping site. It is on the Walter F. George Reservoir as are the Cotton Hill Public Use Area, the Sandy Branch Public Use Area, and the Pataula Creek Park.

STONE MOUNTAIN has 500 campsites beside the lake, where the music of the carillon may be heard while the camper cooks his meals.

SWEETWATER CREEK CAMPING AREA, west of Canton, is operated by the Corps of Engineers and is open all year. Located on Lake Allatoona.

TALLULAH RIVER CAMPING AREA, southwest of Clayton. The Forest Service camp is open to tent and trailer camping from May 15 to November 15.

TATE BRANCH CAMPING AREA, northwest of Clayton, is operated by the Forest Service for both tent and trailer campers and is open year round.

TUGALOO STATE PARK, 8 miles north of Lavonia. The park juts out into Lake Hartwell, and the campsites are outstanding.

UNICOI RECREATION EXPERIMENT STATION, 3 miles northeast of Helen, operated by Northeast Georgia Mountains Authority, in the Chattahoochee National Forest. The experiment station is expanding, and when completed will provide comprehensive programs, teaching, and research for the recreation industry, the only facility of its type in the world. There is tent and trailer camping.

UPPER STAMP CREEK CAMPING AREA, east of Cartersville, is a Corps of Engineers camp located on Lake Allatoona.

VICTORIA BRYANT STATE PARK, 4 miles west of Royston. There is a developed campground.

VOGEL STATE PARK, 11 miles south of Blairsville, offers excellent camping.

YOUNG DEER CAMPING AREA, northeast of Cumming on Lake Sidney Lanier, is operated by the Corps of Engineers for tent and trailer campers. At nearby Two Mile Creek Public Use Area there are additional campsites on the lake. Campsites are also at Shady Grove and Sawnee public use areas on the lake.

Backpacking

APPALACHIAN TRAIL crosses into Georgia northwest of Clayton and runs through the Chattahoochee National Forest to Springer Mountain.

Hiking

BLACKBURN STATE PARK, 7 miles southwest of Dahlonega. The Pioneer Trail follows a road formerly used by gold miners along tree-shaded slopes and a streambank rich in ferns and flowers.

JEKYLL ISLAND STATE PARK. Hiking the tawny beaches of the island is a carefree pursuit.

RABUN BALD TRAIL, near Clayton, leads to the top of 4,663-foot Rabun Bald Mountain, where there is a splendid view of the surrounding Chattahoochee National Forest.

STONE MOUNTAIN. The Cherokee Trail's first mile is tough, for it climbs to the windswept top of Stone Mountain. The trail begins at Confederate Hall, and on the way up a hiker has a fascinating view of the giant memorial carvings. The trail encircles the mountain for another 7 miles and returns to the hall.

Biking

CALLAWAY GARDENS, Pine Mountain. Bicyclists rent cycles to go riding through the gardens.

DE SOTO'S SORTIE. This American Youth Hostels trail begins at Macon and runs to Augusta, where it crosses into South Carolina to terminate at Edgefield. The trail runs from Macon to Milledgeville, Sandersville, Louisville, and Waynesboro on its way to Augusta, and takes a biker to such Georgia landmarks as the Sidney Lanier cottage in Macon; the fine old homes of Milledgeville, once capital of the state; the Old Market House of Louisville; a pioneer home in Waynesboro; and the White House built in 1750 in Augusta, a city founded by James Oglethorpe.

JEKYLL ISLAND STATE PARK. Bikers ride around the island's paved roads, over which auto traffic moves with appropriate care and slowness. Bikes may be rented at the nine-hole golf course.

Rockhounding

BLACKBURN STATE PARK, 7 miles southwest of Dahlonega. Visitors to the park may see a gold mine and try their hand at panning for gold.

GOLD HILLS OF DAHLONEGA, at Dahlonega, contains the famous Crown Mountain goldfield, where the 1829 Georgia gold rush took place. Hydraulic mining washed Preacher Cut into the side of the mountain as miners sluiced the gold-rich dirt and rocks into the valley for panning. Today panning is strictly a do-it-yourself proposition for rockhounds.

Canoeing & Rafting

CHATTOOGA RIVER. Southeastern Expeditions, 7 miles east of Clayton on US 76, features day-long and overnight raft trips on the white-water river of the movie "Deliverance."

OKEFENOKEE CANOEING TRAILS, Okefenokee National Wildlife Refuge, near Waycross. One of the nation's greatest water wildernesses affords one of the most unique canoe systems. There is no fast water and very little dry land. The Okefenokee "Long Paddler" must use his paddle every inch of the way through cypress forest or open, wet "prairies" exposed to the sun and wind. There are seven designated canoe trips ranging from one to three days in duration. Kingfisher Landing, Davis Landing, and the Suwannee Canal are entrances to the trails. Note: In order to make a trip over these trails a quality experience and to protect the wilderness, each canoe trail is limited to one party a day and each party is limited to a maximum of 10 canoes and 20 persons. Mosquitoes are no problem except after dark from April through October. Deerflies are a nuisance in the summer, and insect repellent and mosquito netting are musts. If canoeists do not molest either the snakes or the alligators, they should have no trouble with them. There should be no swimming allowed, and pets may not be taken into the swamp because they are likely to end up as a snack for alligators. Drinking water must be brought along. Lightning is the most dangerous thing about an Okefenokee Canoe Trail trip.

Camping on the trips is limited to designated overnight stops. Because firm land is not available at every stop, canoeists must be prepared to sleep in their canoes or to suspend hammocks between the trees. There are some platforms raised out of the mire for the comfort of canoeists. Since open fires are not permitted, it is necessary to bring along a spirit stove. Canoeists may camp only one night at a stop.

Guided johnboat trips also take visitors into the Okefenokee. Professional guides take the 14- to 16-foot shallow-draft boats across the "land of the trembling earth" from Okefenokee Swamp Park near Waycross on the northeast side to Stephen C. Foster State Park near Fargo. On the two-day trip boats follow trails known to the Seminoles to such places as Billys Lake and Dinner Pond.

SATILLA RIVER CANOE TRAIL. For 149 miles below Waycross the Satilla is one of the state's most exciting wild and scenic rivers. Sandbars of pure white sand are ideal for picnicking and swimming. The trail ends at Woodbine.

SUWANNEE RIVER CANOE TRAIL begins at the Lem Griffis Hunting and Fishing Camp, 18 miles north of Fargo. The river snakes through a wide flood plain, which reaches into Florida. The upper portion of the river passes through dark swamps, but farther south the waters lighten as the river goes through limestone banks. There are campsites along the way. Canoe liveries are in Folkston.

WITHLACOOCHEE CANOE TRAIL. I-75 parallels the Withlacoochee and is rarely more than a few miles away, but from 2 miles west of Valdosta downstream the river is an outstanding canoeing stream. It rushes southward over limestone rocks. Banks are sandy, which makes it easy to launch the canoes at any number of points where highways intersect. The 56-mile trip makes an easygoing three-day trip, and there is free camping at designated primitive campsites. American White Water Affiliation standards rate the river class 3. This means it is a good river for a family float, but that it presents a few modest white-water stretches. There are sandbars and islands to land on where camping is a get-away-from-it-all pleasure.

Boating

JEKYLL ISLAND STATE PARK. The Intracoastal Waterway passes between the island and the mainland. The marina on the island has both freshwater and saltwater slips, and there are facilities for both fuel and supplies.

Conservation & Wildlife

CALLAWAY GARDENS, Pine Mountain. The beautiful Beaver Creek Wilderness shows how a forest can be restored from what was once run-down cotton land. The garden collections of rare flowering shrubs from all over the world are of exceptional beauty as well. The azaleas are of special interest. Opened in 1952 as a 2,500-acre sanctuary for wild flowers, native plants, and wildlife of the southern highlands, Callaway Gardens have become a southeastern beauty spot.

OKEFENOKEE NATIONAL WILDLIFE REFUGE, 7 miles southwest of Folkston, preserves nine-tenths of this vast domain of water, woods, and wildlife. From wood ducks and herons and egrets to alligators, the Okefenokee is an extraordinary world. Cypress, bay and gum trees streaming with Spanish moss, a water stained the color of tea by the tannic acid from swamp vegetation, are aspects of the swamp. There are walking trails, a wildlife drive, and a 4,000-foot boardwalk that leads over the swamp to an observation tower. Note: Travel on the refuge is limited to areas designated by the officer in charge. Boat visitors must register with the concessionaire before leaving the boat dock. When going into the more remote parts of the swamp, a visitor must be accompanied by a registered guide. No firearms are allowed, and swimming is not permitted.

The peat bog, filling a huge saucer-shaped depression, once part of the ocean floor, is one of the best places on the continent to view alligators.

OKEFENOKEE SWAMP PARK, Waycross. The nonprofit park is a significant example of what conservation-minded private citizens can accomplish. A visit to the swamp begins at a notable museum, which includes a room with one-way-vision glass for viewing deer and other animals feeding in the adjacent swamp at dusk. A 2-mile boat trip takes visitors to the boardwalk in the swamp. School groups of all ages from grammar school to university find this area to be a splendid center of natural studies.

SKIDAWAY ISLAND, near Savannah, is the home of the fascinating Skidaway Institute of Oceanography and the University of Georgia Marine Institute. Visitors learn about the environmental quality programs concerned with the geochemistry of heavy metals, the effects and fate of these metals in marsh ecosystems, and mechanical alterations due to dredging. Geology programs are concerned with continental shelf geophysics and sediment transport. Aquaculture research relates to the culture of shrimp and flounder. There is a colorful aquarium, and staff members will talk to conservation groups and others with a serious concern in the coastal waters. The marsh is of exceptional interest to naturalists.

STONE MOUNTAIN STATE PARK. The Nature Trail is of considerable interest. It meanders close by a winding stream. The Azalea Trail is planted with azaleas of every hue.

KENTUCKY

Camping

BARREN RIVER LAKE STATE RESORT PARK is close to Mammoth Cave and contains 101 campsites for recreational vehicles and tents.

BIG BONE LICK STATE PARK, near Walton, south of the Ohio River on Kentucky 338, just off I-75, has camping sites.

CARTER CAVES STATE RESORT PARK, Olive Hill, has tent and trailer campsites.

DANIEL BOONE NATIONAL FOREST. There are campsites situated throughout the forest, which has its headquarters at Winchester.

GREENBO LAKE STATE RESORT PARK, near Greenup, also has camping sites.

JENNY WILEY STATE RESORT PARK, Prestonburg, provides campsites.

KENLAKE STATE RESORT PARK, Hardin, has camping.

KENTUCKY DAM VILLAGE STATE RESORT PARK, near Calvert City, has both tent and trailer camping.

KINCAID LAKE STATE PARK, Falmouth, has the largest recreational complex of all the state parks. There are 80 full-service campsites.

LAKE BARKLEY STATE RESORT PARK, near Cadiz, has 80 campsites.

LAKE CUMBERLAND STATE RESORT PARK, on one of the world's largest man-made lakes, Lake Cumberland, has docks near the campground.

LAND BETWEEN THE LAKES. This TVA-developed outdoor recreation area is a 170,000-acre playground in Kentucky and Tennessee. There are three major campgrounds, and two more in the offing. Rushing Creek was the first campground and is located on the Rushing Creek embayment near the Kentucky-Tennessee line. Hillman Ferry Campground is about 4 miles south of Barkley Canal on Pisgah Bay. Both tent and trailer sites are situated along the lakeshore. Camp Energy is a year-round group camp by reservation. At lake access areas there are additional camping facilities.

MAMMOTH CAVE NATIONAL PARK. There are campsites in a 145-site area. Campers must bring their own fuel.

NATURAL BRIDGE STATE RESORT PARK, Slade. There are tent and trailer sites.

PENNYRILE FOREST STATE PARK, Dawson Springs. Campsites are available.

Backpacking

KENTUCKY LINCOLN TRAIL, Hodgenville. The trail leads for 34 miles and takes two days to hike. There is camping at Knob Creek Farm and at the Elizabethtown Ball Park. Arrangements should be made through the Old Kentucky Home Council, Boy Scouts of America, P.O. Box 21068, Louisville, Kentucky 40221.

LAND BETWEEN THE LAKES. This 170,000-acre peninsula separating Kentucky Lake from Lake Barkley has trails that follow old wagon roads and pioneer paths. They lead to remains of moonshine stills and old iron furnaces and to grazing buffalo. Camping with running water and showers may be had at Rushing Creek and Hillman Ferry, but primitive camping is to be had throughout the TVA area.

RED RIVER GORGE, east of Clay City, offers a backpacker the chance to hike trails along the floor of the gorge where even on a hot summer's day, all is cool. The gorge is cut deep into the western slope of the Appalachians. Daniel Boone wintered in a cave in the gorge. Backpackers can park their cars at Daniel Boone National Forest campground parking lots and start their hikes over access trails. Among the outstanding trails are: Rock Bridge Nature Trail, which begins at the Koomer Ridge Campground; the Swift Camp Creek Trail; Buck Trail; and Pinch-

Hematite Lake, Land Between the Lakes

118 THE SOUTH

em Tight Trail, a veritable catwalk between two precipices. Backpackers may camp where they like in the forest except along the paved roads, within close proximity to trails, at picnic grounds, or at scenic overlooks.

Hiking

BEAVER TRAIL, Lake Malone, is 11½ miles long and leads to Copperhead Gulch and Glacier Shelf.

BIG BONE LICK STATE PARK, near Walton. The Old Bison Trail leads to 120-year-old Big Bone Baptist Church. There is camping in the park.

BLUE LICKS BATTLEFIELD STATE PARK, Mount Olivet. The Buffalo Trace is 27 miles long and leads to points on the scene of the last battlefield of the Revolutionary War.

BREAKS INTERSTATE PARK, on the border of Kentucky and Virginia, has trails that trace the rim of the largest canyon east of the Mississippi.

CARTER CAVES STATE RESORT PARK, near Olive Hill, offers surface hiking trails.

CUMBERLAND FALLS STATE RESORT PARK, Corbin, has hiking trails that go to majestic Cumberland Falls, the "Niagara of the South."

CUMBERLAND GAP NATIONAL HISTORICAL PARK. Hikers can follow the original Wilderness Road, first pioneered by Thomas Walker, a doctor, who discovered this gap through the Cumberland Mountains in 1769. Daniel Boone took the Wilderness Road into Kentucky. Another trail leads along the high ridge separating Kentucky from Virginia to mountain villages that cannot be reached in any other way.

DANIEL BOONE NATIONAL FOREST trails lead through the Red River Gorge. The Long Hunters Trek extends for 13 miles. In the southern part of the forest a trail leads to Yahoo Falls, a 113-foot falls on the South Fork of the Cumberland River near Whitley City.

KINGDOM COME STATE PARK, near Cumberland, has fine hiking trails.

LAKE MALONE STATE PARK, near Dunmor. Hiking trails ring the lake, which is popular with fishermen.

LAND BETWEEN THE LAKES. Excellent hiking trails run throughout this 170,000-acre peninsula between Kentucky Lake and Lake Barkley.

MAMMOTH CAVE NATIONAL PARK. Caveland Trail runs for 10 miles.

MASSACRE TRAIL, Middletown. The trail runs for 12 miles to the sites of Chenoweth Massacre and Floyd's Defeat. There is an 8-mile optional extension to the 12-mile trail, and camping can be arranged in Long Run Park, Middletown.

NATURAL BRIDGE STATE RESORT PARK contains a trail through the Red River Gorge.

OHIO RIVER TRAIL, Brandenburg. The trail starts at Otter Creek Park and runs to such points as Morgan's Cage and Indian hunting grounds. There is camping in Otter Creek Park.

OX CART TRAIL, Fairdale. The 18½-mile trail starts at Fairdale.

PENNYRILE FOREST STATE RESORT PARK, south of Dawson Springs, has hiking trails that lead through the 15,000-acre forest.

PERRYVILLE BATTLEFIELD STATE SHRINE, at Perryville. Hikers follow the Dug Road March or the Dry Canteen Trail along routes taken by Civil War soldiers. Each hike is about 15 miles long.

PINE MOUNTAIN STATE RESORT PARK, Cumberland Gap. The Mischa Mokwa Adventure Trail is 21 miles long.

SHAKER TRAIL, Auburn. The trail begins and ends at the Shaker Museum in Shakertown. The trail circles through the hilly, wooded country for about 15 miles.

TRIPLE ARCH TREK, Pine Ridge. This trail, sponsored by the Kentucky Mountain Hikers of Middletown, runs to Rock Bridge, Turtle Back Arch, and Swift Creek Camp. There are campsites in the Natural Bridge State Resort Park and the Daniel Boone National Forest.

WILDERNESS ROAD TRAIL, Pineville. The Boy Scouts have opened a trail along the historic Wilderness Road through Cumberland Gap.

Biking

BLUE GRASS, Lexington. The Lexington Wheelmen have arranged a number of scenic and historical bike tours through the Blue Grass Country. Contact: Bluegrass Wheelmen, Inc., P.O. Box 1397, Lexington, Kentucky 40501.

Canoeing

CUMBERLAND RIVER. Put in at Kentucky 204 bridge, Redbird, for a light whitewater run along rocky bluff and forested shores. At Cumberland Falls the white water becomes rougher, and scouting is needed in the longer rapids of the river where the end cannot be seen. Take out is at Noe's Boat Dock at the end of Kentucky 1277.

LAND BETWEEN THE LAKES. Canoeing on Kentucky Lake and Lake Barkley is restricted to the quiet coves and inlets. Sudden storms create rough waters, and high winds make canoeing risky on the broad expanse of waters.

RED RIVER, in the Daniel Boone National Forest, is wild and scenic. Canoeists put in at Koomer Ridge Campground and head downstream. Other canoeists are exploring the South Fork of the Cumberland River and the upper waters of the Licking and Kentucky rivers in eastern Kentucky. The Green and Barren rivers in central Kentucky also offer canoeists opportunity for adventure.

Boating

LAKE CUMBERLAND STATE RESORT PARK. Houseboat rentals are available on this vast man-made lake.

LAND BETWEEN THE LAKES. There are 20 access areas on Kentucky Lake and Lake Barkley with boat-launching ramps. Mooring areas for boats are located at campgrounds. Limited camping facilities are at all access points. One of the most popular trips is the "Ride around the Rivers," cruising not only Kentucky Lake and Lake Barkley but the Cumberland, Tennessee, and Ohio rivers. Along the route are docks for picking up supplies and quiet coves for fishing.

OHIO RIVER. Marinas on the river and public and private launching ramps help make boating on the beautiful Ohio popular.

ROUGH RIVER DAM STATE RESORT PARK, near Short Creek. Houseboats slip over the lake's surface in this 35-mile-long watery playground.

Conservation & Wildlife

BERNHEIM FOREST, 25 miles south of Louisville, is a private preserve with 10,000 acres. It is an arboretum, and its rare trees, shrubs, and flowers are identified with tags. The park is an animal refuge, and there is a live wildlife exhibit and a nature museum.

JOHN JAMES AUDUBON STATE PARK, near Henderson, is a bird sanctuary and nature center worthy of the great naturalist himself.

LAND BETWEEN THE LAKES. At the Conservation Education Center, classroom groups live and study in the out-of-doors. There are nature trails, including one for the physically handicapped; a "see and touch" educational farm; an interpretive building; wildlife in abundance; and a Youth Station that provides housing and dining for student groups.

"Through this experience we hope each visitor will gain a greater awareness and understanding of his natural environment," explains the Tennessee Valley Authority's John S. Lyon.

LILLEY CORNETT WOODS, near Whitesburg, has hiking trails leading through virgin timber. The Kentucky Division of Forestry conducts tours every day. Some of the trees in this mixed mesophytic forest are 400 years old.

MAMMOTH CAVE NATIONAL PARK. The above-ground portion of the park encompasses 51,000 acres of forested knobs and valleys. It is a nature preserve with white-tailed deer and small game. Professional naturalists lead interesting nature hikes through the park during the summer months.

NATURAL BRIDGE STATE RESORT PARK, Slade. The rugged, high stone cliffs and arches of the park are of exceptional interest. The effects of millions of years of erosion by wind and water can be studied. The surrounding Daniel Boone National Forest contains another dozen major natural arches as well as many smaller ones.

LOUISIANA

Camping

BAYOU BODCAU RESERVOIR, at Bellevue, offers campsites for tent and trailer campers, operated by the Corps of Engineers.

CHICOT STATE PARK, near Ville Platte, offers camping in the northern reaches of Acadiana.

FONTAINEBLEAU STATE PARK, on the north shore of Lake Pontchartrain, has a large tent and trailer camping area.

GRAND ISLE EAST STATE PARK, on the southeast Gulf Coast of the state, is ideal for campers who want to be close to the sea for the crabbing and seafood, for which Grand Isle is unsurpassed in the South. Primitive campgrounds are along the beach.

INDIAN CREEK RECREATIONAL AREA is in the Alexander State Forest near Woodworth. There are campsites.

KISATCHIE NATIONAL FOREST, in central Louisiana, reaches from Natchitoches to Alexandria. All of the 12 recreation areas in the forest have camping sites. Corney Lake Recreation Area, northeast of Homer; Cloud Crossing Recreation Area, west of Dodson; Gum Springs Recreation Area, west of Winnfield; Stuart Lake Recreation Area, west of Pollock; Dogwood Recreation Area, south of Bellwood; Long Leaf Vista Recreation Area, southwest of Derry; Magnolia Recreation Area, west of Alexandria; Valentine Lake Recreation Area, southeast of Gardner; and Fullerton Lake Recreation Area, north of Cravens, are all good places to camp.

LAKE BRUIN STATE PARK, 4 miles north of St. Joseph, has fine camping facilities.

LONGFELLOW-EVANGELINE STATE PARK, St. Martinville, offers tent sites and trailer spaces shaded by moss-draped oaks.

SAM HOUSTON STATE PARK, on the west fork of the Calcasieu River, north of Lake Charles, has a modern campground.

TOLEDO BEND RESERVOIR, on the Louisiana-Texas border, has campgrounds along its 1,200-mile shoreline.

Hiking

CHICOT STATE PARK, near Ville Platte, has winding trails among the huge trees. A trail descends a high knoll and winds through sylvan ravines among giant cucumber trees and the southern magnolia.

FONTAINEBLEAU STATE PARK, north shore of Lake Pontchartrain near Mandeville, has hiking trails over the onetime summer estate of Bernard Xavier Philippe de Marigny de Mandeville, a Creole leader of the 19th century.

KISATCHIE NATIONAL FOREST offers a variety of trails, but the Long Leaf Vista Trail starting near Natchitoches is outstanding. Hikers come upon the yaupon, the shrub which produces red berries, which the Indians used as an emetic; longleaf and loblolly pines; bluejack oak; dogwood; and sassafras, from which pioneers made soap and tea. At Fullerton Lake there is a trail that leads to the ruins of what was once one of the largest sawmills in the South.

Biking

BAYOU TOUR. The American Youth Hostels laid out this semicircular tour of Acadian country from Lafayette to Lake Charles, with an optional side trip to Avery Island. If the trip is begun in Lafayette, the biker takes Louisiana 94 east to Breaux Bridge, crawfish capital, Louisiana 31 south through St. Martinville and New Iberia, Louisiana 14 west of Delcambre, Louisiana 82 south and west through the sparsely populated coastal area, Louisiana 27 west and then north to Sulphur, and Louisiana 90 east to Lake Charles. The 210-mile route is designed as a motel trip for any time of the year. Carry rain gear and insect repellent.

Canoeing

AMITE RIVER. Canoeists put in where Louisiana 10 crosses the Amite, southwest of Chipola. Takeout is at Louisiana 37 crossing, southwest of Grangeville. It is an idyllic river, with large sandbars for camping. There are a few pull-over points to avoid low water.

ATCHAFALAYA RIVER BASIN is a tangle of lakes and sloughs cut by cross bayous in the flood plain of the vast river. Boy Scout Troop 21 of Plaquemine has pioneered a trip that begins on Bayou Plaquemine in downtown Plaquemine and runs across the eastern tip of the basin to Lake Fausse Pointe, from there into the Charenton Drainage and Navigation Canal to Charenton, and then into the Bayou Teche to St. Martinville. The route was followed by the Acadians to reach southwestern Louisiana. Louisiana officials warn that this trip is to be taken with extreme caution unless the canoeist has guides or is personally familiar with the confusing labyrinth of streams. The basin is a genuine wilderness, and this 111-mile trip is not for a novice. There are wide expanses of water to cross, which can become dangerous in a sudden high wind, and much of the paddling is against the current. Good physical condition is an absolute prerequisite.

BAYOU LAFOURCHE. Canoeists are discovering that the watery main street of the Cajun country is a canoe trail that leads past Acadian farms and villages. Acadians claim that they can float their pirogues on the dew. There is plenty of water to float a conventional canoe.

New River, West Virginia

BAYOU TECHE, from south of Breaux Bridge to St. Martinville, provides scenic canoeing. The canoeists come ashore close to where Longfellow's Evangeline supposedly landed in the Acadian country. Camping is in Longfellow-Evangeline State Park in St. Martinville.

TANGIPAHOA RIVER. Put-in point is near Kentwood where Louisiana 38 crosses the river. There are overnight campsites on the river. There are a number of takeout points. The Louisiana 442 bridge crossing is the last convenient one.

WHISKEY CHITTO CREEK-CALCASIEU RIVER. The headwaters of Whiskey Chitto Creek, designated as a Louisiana Scenic River, are in the Kisatchie National Forest. The trip begins at Mittie and ends at Indian Village on the Calcasieu River. The waters are swift and clear, and there are numerous white sandbars for camping and resting. The park at the Indian Village provides a good takeout place. There is a bar that makes ideal camping close to Carpenter's Bridge, and there is primitive camping available at the put-in place at the Louisiana 26 bridge over the Whiskey Chitto, 1 mile southeast of Mittie. The canoe trip has been pioneered by the girl members of Sea Explorer Ship 648.

Boating

GRAND ISLE. Boats put out from the coastal island's marinas to explore Bayou Lafourche, the Barataria Waterway, and other bayous and lakes.

TOLEDO BEND RESERVOIR. Boaters can roam for days over this vast man-made lake with its 1,200 miles of shoreline. There is wilderness camping.

Sport Diving

GRAND ISLE. Scuba diving in the vicinity of offshore drilling platforms is popular. Divers hold a fishing rodeo out of Grand Isle and spearfish near the platforms.

Conservation & Wildlife

AVERY ISLAND, near New Iberia, is a wildlife preserve of rare beauty. Because of the foresight of Edward Avery McIlhenny, the island is home to a large colony of snowy egrets. During the summer nesting season some 100,000 birds live in Bird City. Blue herons, black ibises, ducks, gallinules, and other water birds find the island a sanctuary. Alligators, mink, muskrat, raccoons, and opossums abound in the marshes.

CHICOT STATE PARK, near Ville Platte. The Louisiana State Arboretum Trail has seven sections. Trails wind through sylvan ravines.

KISATCHIE NATIONAL FOREST. The forest preserves areas of scenic and ecological interest. The Kisatchie Hills are a botanical garden, with over 150 varieties of woody plants and vines. Some 250 species of birds can be seen, including the rare red cockaded woodpecker and Bachman's sparrow. The Magnolia Forest Walk, west of Alexandria, is adjacent to the Magnolia Recreation Area. Huckleberry, beech, blackjack oak, persimmon, red cedar, sycamore, and black cherry grow along the trail. Tiny footbridges cross ravines.

ROCKEFELLER WILDLIFE REFUGE, situated in the coastal marshes of southwestern Louisiana, has its headquarters at Grand Chenier. Hundreds of thousands of ducks, geese, coots, and wading birds come there each year, and it is a resting area for birds making the long flight to winter in Central and South America. Coypu, muskrat, raccoon, otter, and alligator make the refuge a year-round home. The refuge is open to visitors from March 1 through September 30, but permits must be obtained from the headquarters. There are few roads, and travel on the refuge is mostly by boat. There are no guided tours. The display area is open year round, and no permits are required to visit it.

MARYLAND

Camping

CATOCTIN MOUNTAIN PARK, 3 miles west of Thurmont, offers camping in the Owens Creek Campground from mid-April through October. There also is a primitive tent-camping area for Boy Scouts and Girl Scouts available on a reservation basis.

CHESAPEAKE AND OHIO CANAL NATIONAL HISTORICAL PARK. There are drive-in tent and trailer sites at McCoys Ferry.

MARYLAND STATE FORESTS. Several of the forests allow camping, but a permit must be secured from the forest superintendent. There are 30 improved campsites and 50 unimproved campsites with drinking water and sanitary facilities.

MARYLAND STATE PARKS. Maryland state parks have both improved and unimproved campgrounds, and campers should check with the Maryland Department of Forests and Parks, State Office Building, Annapolis, Maryland 21404, for information on what each park offers. At Assateague Island, Deep Creek Lake, Elk Neck, Point Lookout, and Shad Landing state parks, sites have been set aside for use by family groups on a reserved basis. A limited number of reservations are also accepted on a daily basis at Patapsco and Cedarville state parks and at Cedarville Natural Resources Management Area. New Germany State Park, near Grantsville, provides fine camping in the heart of the Savage River State Forest. Assateague State Park on Assateague Island, 6 miles south of the Ocean City inlet, has sites among the dunes. There is also a youth camping area.

Backpacking & Trail Riding

APPALACHIAN TRAIL. The wilderness foot trail passes through the mountains of western Maryland on its way from Maine to Georgia. From Pen Mar the trail hugs a narrow ridge along South Mountain. It then passes by the Washington Monument near Boonsboro and Gathland State Park. There are shelters with fireplaces, bunk platforms, and latrines situated along the trails. The shelters include Devil's Racecourse, north of Raven Rock; Pine Knob, north of Maryland 40; Rocky Run, south of Reno Monument Road, 10 miles north of the Potomac River; and Crampton's Gap, north of Crampton's Gap.

CHESAPEAKE AND OHIO CANAL NATIONAL HISTORICAL PARK offers a 184-mile backpacking trail of historic interest. Hikers follow the towpath from Georgetown in Washington, D.C., to Cumberland in western Maryland. The trail, developed by five Boy Scout councils in cooperation with the park superintendent and rangers, leads past old locks, aqueducts, and tunnels. There are campgrounds for hikers and bikers some 10 miles apart most of the length of the trail. These campsites are available only by walking or biking in and are used on a first-come, first-served basis. There is also walk-in tent camping at Antietam Creek and Mountain Lock campgrounds. From below Swains Lock to Cumberland horseback riding is permitted, but large riding groups must make arrangements with private landowners for camping accommodations.

Hiking

ANTIETAM BATTLEFIELD HISTORIC TRAIL begins at the battlefield Visitor Center, north of Sharpsburg.

CATOCTIN MOUNTAIN PARK, 3 miles west of Thurmont, has a number of fine hiking trails.

GAMBRILL STATE PARK, 6 miles northwest of Frederick, has extensive trails for hiking.

SAVAGE RIVER STATE FOREST offers a number of fine hiking trails into the backwoods near Grantsville.

WASHINGTON MONUMENT STATE PARK, 4 miles east of Boonsboro. There are hiking trails.

Biking

ANTIETAM NATIONAL BATTLEFIELD SITE. The National Park Service has designed a bike tour over 8 miles of paved roads that wind through the park.

CHESAPEAKE AND OHIO CANAL NATIONAL HISTORICAL PARK allows cyclists to ride the canal towpath, an elevated trail averaging 8 feet wide. Bikers are advised to push their bikes across aqueducts and culverts, for some of them are in poor condition. Rangers advise against night travel and urge caution after heavy rainstorms in the mountains, because portions of the towpath may be washed out or flooded. Bikers may camp in the designated spots along the canal.

Canoeing

CHESAPEAKE AND OHIO CANAL NATIONAL HISTORICAL PARK. There is splendid canoeing from Lock 4 at Georgetown, in the District of Columbia, to Violets Lock, Lock 23, near Seneca. Portages are necessary around each lock. Upstream from Lock 23 only a few stretches of the canal are deep enough for canoeing. They include: Big Pool, Little Pool, and Town Creek to Oldtown. Rangers warn that canoeing on the Potomac River is dangerous and should only be done by experienced canoeists. Portages must be made at Dams 2, 3, 4, and 5, the Williamsport power plant dam, and the PPG dam at North Branch. Between Dam 3 and the US 340 bridge downstream from Harpers Ferry or from Great Falls to the Chain Bridge, it is too dangerous for canoeing.

CHESTER RIVER. The Tourism Council of the Upper Chesapeake sponsors charter canoe trips of this 16-mile trail. The guide for the trip is an expert on the natural history of the Chesapeake rivers.

Boating

CHESAPEAKE BAY is exceeded only by Long Island Sound in boating popularity. There are nearly 134,000 pleasure craft registered in Maryland, and the bay is a busy place on weekends. Sailing schools in Annapolis and Baltimore and Arnold give a vacationing landlubber first-rate training on sailing boats.

POTOMAC RIVER above Washington provides boating in slack-water areas behind canal dams. National Park Service and state boat ramps provide public access to the river.

Conservation & Wildlife

ASSATEAGUE ISLAND STATE PARK on Assateague, 6 miles south of Ocean City inlet, is a barrier reef. Migrating waterfowl and the primary and secondary dunes are of interest. Visitors to the park are urged to stay off the dunes.

BATTLE CREEK CYPRESS SWAMP, near Port Republic, is a certified natural landmark preserving the northernmost stand of the bald cypress. The pinewoods tree frog breeds in the swamp, owned by the Nature Conservancy.

BLACKWATER NATIONAL WILDLIFE REFUGE, 10 miles south of Cambridge. Waterfowl taking the Atlantic Flyway from Canada to the Florida Keys stop off here. As many as 100,000 geese and 150,000 ducks have been on the refuge during the peak of fall migration. The principal species are mallards, black ducks, pintails, green-winged teal, blue-winged teal, American widgeon, and wood ducks. Foxes, raccoons, opossums, and skunks live in the preserve, and white-tailed deer are plentiful in the wooded areas. Also protected here is the rare Delmarva Peninsula fox squirrel, on the endangered species list.

CATOCTIN MOUNTAIN PARK, 3 miles west of Thurmont, is developing toward an eastern hardwood climax forest. Mountain valleys are now rich with black locust, wild cherry, sassafras, and yellow poplar. The white-tailed deer, raccoon, woodchuck, gray squirrel, chipmunk, opossum, and red and gray fox live in the park together with ruffed grouse, barred owls, and turkey vultures. The Hog Rock and Deerfield trails are nature trails. The Charcoal Trail has signs explaining the coal-making process.

CEDARVILLE NATURAL RESOURCES MANAGEMENT AREA, northeast of Waldorf, is a forestry demonstration and research area, a unique joint effort by Fisheries, Forestry, Parks, and Wildlife.

White-tailed Deer—Tennessee

EASTERN NECK NATIONAL WILDLIFE REFUGE, at the mouth of the Chester River, eastern side of Chesapeake Bay. The 2,285-acre island refuge is a major feeding and resting place for migrating and wintering waterfowl.

ELK NECK STATE FOREST, between North East and Elkton, abounds in wildlife. Wildlife food plots are maintained through the forest.

FORT FREDERICK STATE PARK, near Indian Springs, has an interesting forest demonstration area.

GREEN RIDGE STATE FOREST, east of Cumberland, contains 28,000 acres of forest land, the habitat of wild turkey, grouse, squirrel, and deer.

NEW GERMANY STATE PARK, 5 miles south of Grantsville, has self-guiding and guided nature walks.

SANDY POINT STATE PARK, at the western end of the William Preston Lane, Jr., Memorial Bridge, off US 50. The Atlantic Flyway brings migrating birds to the park.

SAVAGE RIVER STATE FOREST, near Grantsville, is the state's largest woodland devoted to watershed protection, research and demonstration, and the preservation of natural scenic areas. It is a fine northern hardwood forest.

SETH STATE FOREST, southeast of Easton, is for demonstration and research of lob-

lolly pine and hardwoods. No camping is permitted.

SWALLOW FALLS STATE PARK, northwest of Oakland, in Swallow Falls State Forest, preserves some virgin hemlock stands. There are self-guiding nature trails. The red pine plantations are among the best on the Atlantic Coast.

WASHINGTON MONUMENT STATE PARK, 4 miles east of Boonsboro, appeals to bird-watchers since it is in the Cumberland Valley, a flyway for migrating birds. Ornithologists make an annual count of migrating hawks and eagles at the park.

MISSISSIPPI

Camping

BIENVILLE NATIONAL FOREST. There is camping at Marathon Lake, east of Jackson.

DE SOTO NATIONAL FOREST. Campsites are at Airey Lake, north of Biloxi, and on the banks of the Biloxi River, north of Gulfport. There is also camping along the banks of Thompson Creek, east of Ovett.

HOLLY SPRINGS NATIONAL FOREST offers camping at Chewalla Lake, northwest of New Albany, and at Puskus Lake, east of Abbeville. There is also camping at Tillatoba Lake, east of Tillatoba.

HOMOCHITTO NATIONAL FOREST has camping at Clear Springs, southeast of Meadville.

J. P. COLEMAN STATE PARK, northeast of Iuka, has facilities for tent and trailer camping.

LEROY PERCY STATE PARK, near Hollandale, has campsites beneath moss-draped cypress.

MAGNOLIA STATE PARK, 6 miles east of Biloxi, has camping facilities.

NATCHEZ TRACE PARKWAY. The Jeff Busby Campground is located on the historic trail, 73 miles southwest of Tupelo. The camp is atop Little Mountain. There is another campground on the trace at Rocky Springs, 25 miles southwest of Raymond. There are several historical sites—an old church, a cemetery, and a deserted village of the early 1800s —on the grounds.

SHELBY STATE PARK, near Hattiesburg, has a camping area for tent and trailer campers.

TISHOMINGO STATE PARK, east of Booneville, provides sites for trailers and tent camping.

TOMBIGBEE STATE PARK, 5 miles east of Tupelo, has secluded sites for tent and trailer camping. Good places are Choctaw Lake, south of Ackerman, and Davis Lake, close to the place where the explorer Hernando de Soto once established his winter camp, east of Old Houlka.

Hiking

BIENVILLE NATIONAL FOREST. There are hiking trails at Marathon Lake, an old millpond. The area is east of Jackson. Hiking trails also lead along the lake at Shongelo, north of Raleigh.

DESOTO NATIONAL FOREST contains the Tuxachanie Trail, which begins some 20 miles north of Gulfport. The trail follows an old logging railroad that once carried timber to the sawmill at Howison. Hikers pass a good fishing pond and a deserted farm where dooryard flowers planted by a pioneer housewife still bloom. A footbridge crosses West Creek. The trail passes through the Harrison Experimental Forest to the site of an illegal whiskey still that was put out of business by revenuers.

HOMOCHITTO NATIONAL FOREST. A forest walk leads along the lakeshore. The site is southwest of Meadville.

TISHOMINGO STATE PARK, east of Booneville, has fine hiking trails.

Biking

NATCHEZ TRACE PARKWAY. Bikers can ride in comparative safety along the national parkway that follows the historic trace, since motorists are supposed to keep to slower speeds. There are camping sites at Jeff Busby and Rocky Springs campgrounds.

Canoeing & Rafting

DESOTO NATIONAL FOREST. The Black Creek-Beaver Dam Float trip runs for 50 miles down two of the most scenic streams in the state. Camping on white sandbars and swimming or relaxing in the sun are part of such a float trip. Floaters drift downstream at about a mile an hour and fish the quiet pools along the way. Only a few portages are required, but floaters should be on guard for underwater snags and shallow water. There are access points at Brooklyn, Moody's Landing, Janice Recreation Area, Cypress Creek Recreation Area, Fairley Bridge, and Big Creek. In the town of Wiggins, merchants have boats for rent.

Boating

FOUR LAKES. The Corps of Engineers created the Four Lakes of northwest Mississippi in a chain along I-55, between Memphis and Grenada. Arkabutla Lake, near Coldwater; Sardis Lake, between Sardis and Batesville; Enid Lake, north of Oakland; and Grenada Lake, northeast of Grenada all have boat ramps.

GULF COAST. From Pascagoula to Bay St. Louis, boating is paramount. There are launching ramps and marinas in most of the Gulf Coast towns, with facilities for all types of craft. Sailors and powerboaters alike find the gulf and the many rivers and bayous that lead into it excellent boating country.

MISSISSIPPI RIVER. There are small-craft harbors at Greenville and Vicksburg on the Mississippi.

OXBOW LAKES, formed when the Mississippi went on one of its periodical rampages, are popular with houseboaters. Lakes Ferguson and Washington are in Washington County.

Conservation & Wildlife

BIENVILLE NATIONAL FOREST. The Bienville Pine Scenic Area, south of Forest, contains virgin pine about 175 years old. There is a forest walk.

DELTA NATIONAL FOREST, west of Holly Bluff, is one of the nation's finest hardwood forests. The black Delta fox squirrel is found only in this forest.

MISSISSIPPI PETRIFIED FOREST, at Flora, preserves 36 million years of geological history in the form of giant petrified logs.

NATCHEZ TRACE PARKWAY. At Beaver Dam, 12 miles south of Kosciusko, a trail leads over beaver dams and canals.

TOMBIGBEE NATIONAL FOREST. On the Natchez Trace, 31 miles south of Tupelo, there is a fossil exhibit showing the remains of prehistoric marine animals that lived in the sea that once covered the lower Mississippi Valley.

NORTH CAROLINA

Camping

BLUE RIDGE PARKWAY. Along this mountaintop drive are several fine camping areas. Doughton Park has a 124-unit campground and trailer parking area close to the historic Brinegar Cabin, and at Julian Price Memorial Park there are another 196 units with trailer parking. Linville Falls also has a campground as does Crabtree Meadows.

CAPE HATTERAS NATIONAL SEASHORE has camping opportunities. Camping is permitted year round at three campgrounds and at another three as well during the summer. In order to anchor tents in the sandy sites, tent stakes of at least 12 inches are suggested. Although there are no utility connections, trailers are permitted at the campgrounds. The campgrounds are at: Oregon Inlet on the south shore of Bodie Island, near the bridge to Hatteras Island; Salvo, on Hatteras Island, 32 miles south of Nags Head; Cape Point, near the Hatteras Lighthouse at Cape Hatteras; Frisco, 5 miles northeast of Hatteras Village; Ocracoke, beside the ocean on Ocracoke Island; and another camp on the sound side of the island near Ocracoke Village.

CLIFFS OF THE NEUSE STATE PARK, near Seven Springs, has 377 acres along the Neuse River and offers both tent and trailer camping.

CROATAN NATIONAL FOREST, on the coastal plain, contains camping sites. There is one area at Cedar Point and another at Neuse River Recreation Area at Croatan.

GREAT SMOKY MOUNTAINS NATIONAL PARK. Campgrounds in this magnificent but over-visited national park are available on a first-come, first-served basis, and no reservations are taken except for group campgrounds. Smokemont, 6 miles north of Cherokee, is open all year. Other camping areas are at Deep Creek, 2 miles north of Bryson City; Balsam Mountain, 4 miles west of the Blue Ridge Parkway near Heintooga Overlook; and Clingmans Dome (in Tennessee), at the highest point in the park. Permits are required for camping in undesignated areas in the park, but there are primitive camping areas where no permits are necessary.

HAGAN-STONE PARK, Greensboro. The park 10 miles south of town contains campsites and is operated by the city of Greensboro.

JONES LAKE STATE PARK, near Dublin, offers both tent and trailer camping near the lake.

KERR RECREATION AREAS, developed by the Corps of Engineers around the Kerr Reservoir, with its shoreline of 800 miles, contain campsites at Satterwhite Point, 7 miles north of Henderson; Nutbush Bridge, 4 miles north of Henderson; Bullocksville Park, 8 miles north of Henderson; Kimball Point, 19 miles north of Henderson; County Line, 18 miles northeast of Henderson; and Henderson Point, 20 miles north of Henderson.

MORROW MOUNTAIN STATE PARK, near Albemarle, provides camping for tents and trailers.

MOUNT MITCHELL STATE PARK, near Micaville, offers camping atop the highest mountain in eastern America.

NANTAHALA NATIONAL FOREST, south and west of Asheville, provides facilities for up to 400 tent campers at Appletree Group Camp near Nantahala Lake, between Aquone and Andrews. There are other campsites at Cable Cove; Cheoah Point, on Lake Santeetlah; Hiwassee Lake, near Murphy; Horse Cove, on Lake Santeetlah; Jackrabbit Mountain, on Lake Chatuge near Hayesville; Standing Indian, west of Franklin; Tsali, on Mouse Branch near Fontana Lake; and Vanhook Glade and Cliffside, west of Highlands.

PISGAH NATIONAL FOREST, with 479,232 acres in the western mountains of the state, has a number of campgrounds. Bald Mountain campground is near the Tennessee border at the top of Unaka Mountains. Other sites worthy of a camper's tent are at Carolina Hemlock, Cove Creek (designated for group camping only), Mortimer, North Mills River, Powhatan, Rocky Bluff, Sunburst, and White Pines.

Backpacking

APPALACHIAN TRAIL. Some 200 miles of the trail follow the topmost mountain ridges through the Great Smoky Mountains National Park and the Pisgah and Nantahala national forests. The trail reaches the highest point of its entire length at Clingmans Dome in the Great Smokies of Tennessee. There are two overnight lean-to shelters available at 12-mile intervals in the Pisgah National Forest and eight trail camps with lean-to shelters in the Nantahala National Forest. In the national park there are other shelters and campsites. Camping is permitted along the trail in the park only at campsites, and a camping permit is required for each trip. Permits may be obtained either from a park ranger or warden or by writing to the office of the park superintendent, Great Smoky Mountains National Park, Gatlinburg, Tennessee.

GREAT SMOKY MOUNTAINS. Trail Riders of the Wilderness, operated by the American Forestry Association, offers an exciting annual trail ride into the backcountry.

PISGAH NATIONAL FOREST. Near Wagon Road Gap, the Shining Rock Wilderness has been set aside by the Forest Service to provide a primitive, natural environment. The area is accessible by trails. There are many springs to provide water for a backpacker, and camping is permitted. Hikers are required to take all necessary precautions against fire. The Linville Gorge Wild Area is an equally fascinating challenge to first-rate backpackers. Trails pass through virgin forest. Camping is permitted, but precautions against fire are absolutely essential. Hikers must inform a National Forest ranger or Blue Ridge Parkway ranger about hiking plans because of the element of danger in this adventurous area. Other trails in the Pisgah National Forest total 600 miles in length.

Hiking

BLUE RIDGE PARKWAY. There are fine hiking trails at Cumberland Knob and at Doughton Park, where 20 miles of paths lead through profuse laurel, azalea, and rhododendron. At E. B. Jeffree Park, a trail leads along a mountain stream to a cascade, and there is another hiking trail at Julian Price Memorial Park. The trail at Linville Falls leads to a spectacular view of the falls and Linville Gorge. Craggy Gardens also has trails.

GREAT SMOKY MOUNTAINS NATIONAL PARK. Trails originate at campgrounds and at Clingmans Dome (in Tennessee). Some 700 miles of foot and horse trails in the park lead to such places as Balsam Mountain and Smokemont. The Andrews Bald Trail is a 4-mile hike that starts from the parking area at Clingmans Dome. The trail is steep and stony and leads through a part of the forest that was burned over in the mid-1920s. The trail finally emerges onto grassy Andrews Bald Mountain, 5,680 feet above sea level.

PISGAH NATIONAL FOREST. Some 600 miles of hiking trails lead through the forest, which lies in the western part of the state near the southern end of the Appalachian Mountains. Among the notable trails are the Craggy Mountain Trail, 18 miles from Craggy Gardens to Little Cane River Gap; Higgins Bald Trail, from Busick to Mount Mitchell; Camprock Trail, from Loftis Cabin to Mount Mitchell; Mount Pisgah Trail, from Pisgah Parking Area to Mount Pisgah; Balsam Ridge Trail, from Tennessee Bald Mountain to Richland Balsam; and Lookingglass Trail, from US 276 to the top of Lookingglass Rock.

Rockhounding

COTTON PATCH MINES, at New London, is a source of gold. The North Carolina goldfield is the oldest in the nation and was opened in 1799 with the discovery of a 17-pound nugget by 12-year-old Conrad Reed.

COWEE VALLEY, near Franklin. There are 13 gem and mineral mines in Macon County, and amateur miners regularly find rubies, sapphires, garnets, and amethysts. Around Situ Hill are found the Cowee pigeon-blood rubies. Rhodolite crystals, radiant with rose and lavender, are found on Mason Mountain. At nearby Rose Creek rockhounds discover the ruby-red type pyrope garnet. When the corundum mine at Corundum Hill, 5 miles east of Franklin, closed down because of the competition from carborundum, miners turned to "pretty rocks" found in the corundum. These baubles turned out to be rubies and sapphires.

EMERALD VALLEY, near Hiddenite, provides emeralds as well as hiddenite.

WISEMAN MINE, at Spruce Pine, is favored by rockhounds searching for aquamarine.

Boating

CAPE HATTERAS NATIONAL SEASHORE has a marina on the north shore of Oregon Inlet. There are limited public boat slips at Ocracoke Village.

LAKE GASTON, at Henrico, is a man-made lake popular with boaters.

LAKE NORMAN, the largest inland body of water in the state, is an impoundment of the Duke Power Company. Sailing and boating are popular. There are boat docks, piers, launching ramps, and campgrounds.

PIMLICO SOUND, second in size only to Chesapeake Bay in the eastern U.S., has ample boating opportunities for both sail and power boats. The Intracoastal Waterway runs throughout.

Conservation & Wildlife

GREAT SMOKY MOUNTAINS NATIONAL PARK contains 1,300 flowering plants, 130 species of trees, and 52 species of fur-bearing animals. Nature tours are available from spring through October.

NANTAHALA NATIONAL FOREST. The Joyce Kilmer Memorial Forest is a virgin wilderness dedicated to the poet who celebrated "Trees." Maintained in its primitive and natural state, the forest is ever-changing but never-changing at the same time.

PEA ISLAND NATIONAL WILDLIFE REFUGE, situated within the Cape Hatteras National Seashore, is the winter home of greater snow geese and other species. The public may use the beaches, but permission to walk through the fenced areas on the sound side of Hatteras Island must be obtained from Refuge Headquarters on the Hatteras Highway.

PISGAH NATIONAL FOREST is a varied forest cover that includes flowering rhododendron, laurel, and azalea. The Shining Rock Wilderness preserves scenic mountains, waterfalls, flowering trees, and populations of deer, bear, rabbit, and grouse. The wilderness is one of the southernmost projections of the Canadian Zone. Linville Gorge Wild Area preserves the deep gorges cut by the Linville River's scouring action. The plant life on the riverbanks and in the gorge is varied and extraordinary, and the wildlife is abundant. Roan Mountain Gardens contain dense thickets of rhododendron of rare beauty when combined with stands of fir and spruce. Naturalists have studied this mountain since the 18th century. There are trails.

SOUTH CAROLINA

Camping

FRANCIS MARION NATIONAL FOREST, on the coastal plain north of Charleston, is the land of the "Swamp Fox" of Revolutionary War fame. A campground on the edge of the Guilliard Lake Scenic Area is outstanding.

HUNTING ISLAND STATE PARK, southeast of Beaufort. There is camping on this large barrier island.

OCONEE STATE PARK, 12 miles northwest of Walhalla, provides some of the state's best camping sites.

SANTEE STATE PARK, at Santee, has well-shaded and commodious campsites.

SOUTH CAROLINA BEACHES. Four beach state parks offer camping. Myrtle Beach and Huntington Beach state parks are on the Grand Strand; Edisto Beach State Park is near Charleston; and Hunting Island State Park is close to Beaufort. The campsites in various private campgrounds and in these state parks total approximately 8,000.

SUMTER NATIONAL FOREST provides camping at Cherry Hill, in the Andrew Pickens Ranger District.

Hiking

SUMTER NATIONAL FOREST has 15 miles of hiking trails in the Andrew Pickens Ranger District.

TABLE ROCK STATE PARK, situated 16 miles north of Pickens, offers a marked hiking trail leading to the top of the mountain.

WHITEWATER FALLS, on South Carolina 171 north of Tamassee. A hiking trail leads to the foot of the falls, the highest in the East.

Canoeing

CHATTOOGA RIVER in Sumter National Forest, from Earl's Ford to US 76, contains rapids of Class 1 and Class 2 difficulty. Below Earl's Ford the river drops over boulders and down ledges, and the rapids should not be undertaken except by experts. There is a Class 4 rapid at Dicks Creek Falls that most canoeists should portage. Note: South Carolina canoeists say that the flume of the rapid is an S-shaped course that is best traversed half-standing in the canoe so that the body as well as the paddle can be used to control the canoe. Below Sandy Ford the river falls over some easy rapids and enters the Narrows, a long and treacherous rapids. The trials by white water in this river reach their climax at Bull Sluice, which is hidden by large boulders. Bull Sluice is a Class 6 rapid to be run only by experts with decked equipment, and then only with rescue personnel and equipment standing by. The portage is over rocks on the west side. Below the US 76 bridge the river is almost impassable, and only experts using decked equipment should try it at all. There are many other rivers suitable for canoeing. An excellent booklet, "South Carolina River Trails," lists the rivers and gives details. Write: South Carolina Parks, Recreation & Tourism, Suite 113, Edgar A. Brown Building, 1205 Pendleton Street, Columbia, South Carolina 29201.

Boating

BEAUFORT. Miles of uncrowded waterways in the vicinity are ideal for boating and sailing.

CLARK HILL LAKE, on the Savannah River in Georgia and South Carolina, is well marked with navigation aids for boaters. Detailed navigation charts are available at the Resource Manager's Office near the dam. The lake is administered by the Corps of Engineers.

HARTWELL LAKE, on the border of Georgia and South Carolina, provides fine boating waters well marked with navigation aids. Maps are available at the Resource Manager's office south of the dam on US 29. There are four marinas.

LAKE KEOWEE is an impoundment in the piedmont area. Be sure to get a map of the lake before boating on it, since the lake level during the recreation season sometimes fluctuates as much as 25 feet as drawdowns are made by the Duke Power Company.

Conservation & Wildlife

CAPE ROMAIN NATIONAL WILDLIFE REFUGE is a sanctuary for migratory birds adjacent to the Francis Marion National Forest. Herons, gulls, plovers, terns, ducks, and the big white and American egrets live in the swamps and marshes. Nature enthusiasts may visit Bull Island only by boat.

FRANCIS MARION NATIONAL FOREST contains nature walks. There are more than 250 species of birds. Along Wambaw Creek, which flows into the Santee River, are forests of gums and cypress. Turkey, deer, waterfowl, and alligators can be seen in the creek. The eastern swallow-tailed kite nests in the banks of the creek in the lower reaches near the Echaw Road. The Guilliard Lake Scenic Area preserves a strip of terrace between the Santee River and the lake. Cypress and cypress knees up to eight feet tall are common. The forest is situated on the Atlantic Flyway, and there are many migratory birds to be seen.

TENNESSEE

Camping

BIG RIDGE STATE PARK, Maynardville, offers camping beside Norris Lake. There is a primitive Scout camping area as well as a group camp and 50 individual camping sites.

CEDARS OF LEBANON STATE PARK, near Lebanon, has camping sites for both tents and trailers.

CHICKASAW STATE PARK, Henderson. The largest of Tennessee's parks has an extensive camping area.

CUMBERLAND MOUNTAIN STATE PARK, Crossville, contains a spacious campground.

DAVID CROCKETT STATE PARK, Lawrenceburg, has one of the finest camping grounds in the state, and there is also a primitive Scout area.

GREAT SMOKY MOUNTAINS NATIONAL PARK. There are many campsites in this park that spreads across the Tennessee-North Carolina border.

HARRISON BAY STATE PARK, Harrison, provides 260 sites for tents and trailers.

LAND BETWEEN THE LAKES. The Tennessee portion of this vast TVA recreational area contains some excellent campgrounds as well as opportunities for primitive camping.

MEEMAN-SHELBY FOREST STATE PARK, at Millington, on the Mississippi River, has camping sites.

NATCHEZ TRACE STATE PARK, Wildersville, provides camping along the historic trace.

OLD STONE FORT STATE HISTORICAL PARK, Manchester. Campers put up their tents in the park protecting the mysterious pre-Columbian fort.

REELFOOT LAKE STATE PARK, Tiptonville. There is camping in the park beside the lake formed by the earthquakes of 1811.

Backpacking

APPALACHIAN TRAIL. The trail enters the state north of Mountain City and runs through the Kettlefoot Wildlife Management Area. It keeps to the high country of the Cherokee National Forest and the Great Smoky Mountains National Park and crosses into North Carolina on its way to the south.

Hiking

CUMBERLAND MOUNTAIN STATE PARK, Crossville. Here and elsewhere in the Cumberlands are beautiful, secluded trails.

GREAT SMOKY MOUNTAINS NATIONAL PARK. There are fine trails for both hiking and riding.

PICKETT STATE PARK, near Jamestown. A scenic trail leads to the home of World War I hero Sgt. Alvin York.

Canoeing

TENNESSEE'S WILD RIVERS are tributaries of the state's main streams, and canoeists are discovering that they are a real challenge. Among the streams that are attracting intrepid canoeists are Spring Creek, Blackburn Fork, the Roaring River, and the Conasauga. Floaters are enjoying the Duck River, the Buffalo, the Harpeth, and the Hiwassee.

Boating

GREAT LAKES OF TENNESSEE. The Tennessee Valley Authority has dammed the Tennessee River at a number of places to give the state 17 major lakes. There are another seven lakes developed by the Corps of Engineers on the Cumberland River. With more than 10,000 miles of shoreline, these lakes provide excellent boating. A boater can start at Old Hickory Lake near Nashville and, using canals and locks, go from one TVA lake to another on a cruise of more than 800 miles.

Sport Diving

GREAT LAKES OF TENNESSEE. Sport diving is gaining in popularity in these TVA lakes.

Conservation & Wildlife

CEDARS OF LEBANON STATE PARK, near Lebanon. The U.S. Department of Agri-

THE SOUTH 127

Blue Ridge Mountains, South Carolina

culture began a reforestation program here a number of years ago. The park protects the largest remaining stand of red cedar in the United States.

CUMBERLAND MOUNTAIN STATE PARK, Crossville, is located on the largest timberland plateau in the United States.

GREAT SMOKY MOUNTAINS NATIONAL PARK. A hiker in this beautiful mountain area encounters anything from a rabbit to a bear.

PICKETT STATE PARK, near Jamestown on Tennessee 154. There are natural bridges and wildlife.

REELFOOT LAKE STATE PARK, Tiptonville. The lake, created by earthquakes in 1811, has a partially submerged forest that makes an extraordinary natural fish hatchery.

ROAN MOUNTAIN STATE PARK, Roan Mountain. Rhododendron blaze with red on the mountaintop during the summer

VIRGINIA

Camping

BULL RUN REGIONAL PARK, south of Arlington, contains secluded campsites.

GEORGE WASHINGTON NATIONAL FOREST provides a number of camping areas. Information may be obtained from the district rangers or from the forest supervisor in Harrisonburg.

JEFFERSON NATIONAL FOREST provides a number of campsites in the Blue Ridge and Allegheny mountains. Campers may stay anywhere in the forest except where posted.

PHILPOTT DAM AND RESERVOIR, near Bassett, has campsites at Bowens Creek Public Use Area, Fairy Stone State Park, Goose Point, Ryans Branch Public Use Area, Salthouse Branch Public Use Area, Twin Ridge Marina, and Horseshoe Point Public Use Area.

SHENANDOAH NATIONAL PARK. There are four campgrounds. Big Meadows Campground is open all year. There are also 21 trailside shelters, each accommodating six hikers, and 21 primitive backcountry camping areas for which permits are necessary.

VIRGINIA STATE PARKS all have camping grounds. Vacationers may reserve sites at any Virginia state park by mailing their requests to the Virginia State Parks Reservation Center, Box 62284, Virginia Beach, Virginia 23462. Unreserved campsites are assigned on a first-come, first-served basis.

Backpacking

APPALACHIAN TRAIL. The trail passes through the Shenandoah National Park and a portion of the George Washington National Forest. There are trailside shelters, and the Potomac Appalachian Trail Club maintains five trail cabins for hikers. Advance reservations and keys must be obtained by mail from the club at 1718 N Street, N.W., Washington, D.C. 20036. Farther south in the Jefferson National Forest, there are also trail shelters designed for six persons or less. Larger groups may camp in designated areas. These are level spots with no facilities. Hikers are urged to carry a snakebite kit with suction cup because both rattlesnakes and copperheads may be encountered. Bring insect repellent, for ticks and biting gnats can be a nuisance too on this trail.

MASSANUTTEN MOUNTAIN TRAIL, near Luray. The trail climbs the mountains for views of the Shenandoah River below. An outfitter at Bealers Ferry Recreation Area will provide everything required. There are trail shelters.

Hiking

GEORGE WASHINGTON NATIONAL FOREST. The Pig Iron Trail is an old wagon road that leads past a charcoal hut to the remnants of Elizabeth Furnace. Other outstanding trails in the forest are Ramsey's Draft, which leads into a primeval forest; Woodstock Tower, for one of the nation's most panoramic views; Elkhorn Lake Dam, which follows a service road along the shore of a mountain lake; and Crabtree Falls, which is a spur road off Virginia 56 leading to the base of a waterfall.

GRAYSON HIGHLANDS STATE PARK, west of Grant, offers trails that lead up rugged Mount Rogers, which, at 5,729 feet, is the highest peak in Virginia. There are magnificent views of the lesser mountains that surround Mount Rogers as well as interesting subalpine terrain to study.

JEFFERSON NATIONAL FOREST contains many hiking trails and areas in which veteran hikers can venture cross-country on their own.

SEASHORE STATE PARK, Cape Henry in Virginia Beach. There are some 40 miles of hiking trails through this beautiful dune region.

SHENANDOAH NATIONAL PARK. Trails lead through the land of the corn squeezers, where corn is distilled into mountain moonshine, a land of vistas and tumbling waters, of serpentine paths rising and falling over Blue Ridge Mountain shoulders. Among the circuit hikes in the Shenandoah National Park are the Bluff Trail, Big Devil Stairs, Piney Branch, Jeremys Run, Hazel Country, Stony Man Mountain, Old Rag Mountain, South River Falls, and the Hoover Camp Trail. Herbert Hoover was an avid fisherman, and he kept a summer fishing lodge high in the mountains overlooking the Rapidan River. The lodge is accessible only by a trail that starts at the parking lot at the Visitor Center just past milepost 51 on the Skyline Drive.

Biking

BLUE RIDGE PARKWAY. Bikers in good condition can ride the parkway, but only in single file. A bike must have a light in front and a reflector in back to enter a tunnel. Bikes may only use hiking trails that are so designated by posted signs.

SHENANDOAH VALLEY. A two-day trip begins at New Market Gap Visitors Information Center atop Massanutten Mountain and takes a biker along Passage Creek and on over Lion's Tail Trail to Camp Roosevelt, the site of the first Civilian Conservation Camp, where a biker can camp for the night. After a long hill ascent, the biker winds his way down into the Shenandoah Valley; from here he returns to base camp at Bealers Ferry. An outfitter at Bealers Ferry Recreation Area will provide the necessary equipment.

Canoeing & Rafting

JAMES RIVER. Above Richmond the James is a fine floating stream, with narrow channels, large boulders, and intermittent shallow waters to add zest. Most floating on the James requires some portaging over rocky stretches, so johnboats and canoes are used. From Columbia to Cartersville and from Cartersville to West View are one-day float trips.

SHENANDOAH RIVER. River outfitters at Bealers Ferry Recreation Area near Luray put canoeists into the river for an excursion of from 30 to 40 miles. Guides lead carefree float trips. Floaters camp along the river. In May, June, and July canoeing is combined with wild-food excursions with a guide who is adept at living off the land. Most access points on the Shenandoah are on the popular South Fork, but there are others on the main stream and on the North Fork.

Boating

BUGGS ISLAND LAKE provides 48,000 acres of fresh water. The Corps of Engineers impoundment has boat ramps and camping areas.

EASTERN SHORE. The outstanding boating on Chesapeake Bay is facilitated by easy water access from landings along the eastern shore.

PHILPOTT DAM AND RESERVOIR, near Bassett, has fine boating. There are campgrounds at Mize Point, Beech Point, and Deer Island which are accessible by water only.

Conservation & Wildlife

CHINCOTEAGUE NATIONAL WILDLIFE REFUGE. A visitor center and extensive trails enable visitors to bird watch and glimpse the wild ponies.

DISMAL SWAMP, south of Virginia Beach. Coal-forming formations may be studied much as they existed in the Pennsylvania period of earth's history.

GOSHEN PASS NATURAL AREA, on the southwest face of Little North Mountain, northwest of Lexington, protects a rugged terrain. Grains of ancient sandstone fused by great pressure and heat from the tough quartzite rocks of the pass.

LICK CREEK NATURAL AREA is 20 miles northeast of Marion. Visitors hike into this lovely area, typical of mountain slopes and valleys of western Virginia.

PARKERS MARSH NATURAL AREA, in the Onancock area of the eastern shore, is a projection of land that can only be reached by boat or by wading the water of the "Thorofare," a canal connecting Back and Onancock creeks. No camping is allowed except as may be required for scientific purposes, and special permission must be obtained from the Division of Parks.

SEASHORE NATURAL AREA in Seashore State Park at Cape Henry near Virginia Beach. The natural area covers 2,700 acres, and there is a nature trail.

SHENANDOAH NATIONAL PARK. Famed for its wild gardens, its streams and falls, and its overlooks, this national park has many fine nature trails. One of these, the Swamp Nature Trail, begins at the Big Meadows Amphitheater and loops for 2 miles along a winding game trail, an intermittent swamp, and a meadow.

WRECK ISLAND NATURAL AREA, 7 miles east of Oyster. The island is a barrier island separating the eastern shore from the Atlantic. Salt marshes interlaced with guts and creeks are a haven for wildlife such as otter, mink, and coon. There is a variety of beach grasses and stunted wax myrtle, offering a refuge to birds of many species as well. The island is accessible only by boat. The sand dunes are 12 feet high.

WEST VIRGINIA

Camping

AUDRA STATE PARK, near Buckhannon. There are both tent and trailer sites in the park.

BABCOCK STATE PARK, near Clifftop, is a fine place to camp.

BLACKWATER FALLS STATE PARK, near Davis, offers camping close to the falls, a popular outdoor attraction.

CONAWAY RUN LAKE, Alma. There are primitive camping sites.

COOPERS ROCK STATE FOREST, 13 miles east of Morgantown, provides tent and trailer sites.

FORK CREEK PUBLIC HUNTING AREA, Nellis. Campsites are rustic.

GREENBRIER STATE FOREST, near Caldwell, is noted for its camping.

KUMBRABOW STATE PARK, southeast of Huttonsville, provides fine camping in the deep forest.

MONONGAHELA NATIONAL FOREST. The Forest Service provides campgrounds at Lake Sherwood, Pocahontas, Summit Lake, Big Rock, Laurel Fork, Stuart Recreation Area, Smoke Hole, Horseshoe, Bear Heaven, Red Creek, Spruce Knob Lake, Locust Springs, Bird Run, Blue Bend Recreation Area, and Cranberry.

NORTH BEND STATE PARK, Cairo. Campsites are available for tents and trailers

TETER CREEK LAKE, Belington, is a good place to camp.

TOMLINSON RUN STATE PARK, south of Chester, offers fine camping.

TYGART LAKE STATE PARK, south of Grafton, has fine camping.

WEST VIRGINIA FAMILY PARKS. Camping in these popular state parks is particularly attractive. The parks are Babcock, in the New River Gorge region at Clifftop; Bluestone, on Bluestone Lake; Lost River, on land once the property of the Lee family of Virginia, in the highlands east of Elkins; Tygart Lake on a Corps of Engineers lake near Grafton; Holly River, secluded sites in a profusion of hemlock and rhododendron, on the Laurel Fork; and at Watoga, on Watoga Lake, south of Marlinton.

WEST VIRGINIA STATE FORESTS. Camp Creek, Coopers Rock, Greenbrier, Kanawha, Kumbrabow, Panther, Cabwaylingo, and Seneca forests have camping.

Backpacking & Trail Riding

CACAPON MOUNTAINS. The trail ride sponsored by the American Forestry Association's Trail Riders of the Wilderness begins at the Coolfont Recreation stables at Berkeley Springs. Riders go out onto the mountain and along its rim to Bear Wallows, then south to Seldom Seen Valley. For variety's sake a one-day float trip on the Cacapon River breaks up the trip. The riders return to their horses to follow the historic Chesapeake and Ohio Canal to the upper Potomac, to Balance Rock, and then back home.

MONONGAHELA NATIONAL FOREST. Forest Service trails hug the ridges, and there are very few trail connections to the valleys. Logging roads and fire trails link ridges and valleys and can serve as connecting trails for backpackers.

Hiking

CABWAYLINGO STATE FOREST, near Dunlow, features the Sleepy Hollow Trail and views from Tick Ridge, where there is an observation tower.

GREENBRIER STATE FOREST, near Caldwell, has hiking trails.

HARPERS FERRY NATIONAL HISTORICAL PARK. Trails include the Maryland Heights Trail; the Loudon Heights Trail, which connects with the Appalachian Trail; and the Jefferson Rock Trail.

MONONGAHELA NATIONAL FOREST. The Forest Service trails include: Little Allegheny, Meadow-Creek Mountain, Middle Mountain, Beaverkick Mountain, Slab Camp-Civil War, Peach Orchard Ridge, Greenbrier River, Blue Line, and Brushy Mountain. Trails are blazed except where they are so easy to follow that blazes are not needed. The old logging railroad that once followed Seneca Creek from Spruce Knob Mountain northeast to where the creek flows into the North Fork at Seneca Rocks is only an abandoned right-of-way now. Its grades are a backcountry trail for hikers.

TOMLINSON RUN STATE PARK, south of Chester, has outstanding hiking.

Canoeing & Rafting

CANYON OF THE CHEAT RIVER. Mountain Streams and Trails provides a trip down the Cheat on an inflatable raft constructed especially for this wild river. There are no dams or impoundments on the river. The rally point for the Cheat River trip is at the Community Park in Albright. The 12-mile run of almost continuous rapids ranges from mostly Class 3, some Class 4, and a few Class 5.

GAULEY RIVER. The Wildwater Expeditions Unlimited also offers extremely rugged white-water trips down this turbulent stream, but only advanced white-water rafters are accepted. The rafters must have made at least two trips down the New River's lower section before they may try this adventurous descent.

GREAT GORGE OF THE YOUGHIOGHENY is a mecca for paddle boaters. Neophyte kayakers start the descent at Railroad Rapids at the end of the Loop, but seasoned kayakers paddle through the white-water rapids of the Loop. Inflatable kayaks and rubber rafts are used in the gorge. Ralph McCarty's Mountain Streams and Trails, outfitters for the descent, are at Ohiopyle, Pennsylvania.

NEW RIVER CANYON. Wildwater Expeditions Unlimited of Thurmond runs one-day and two-day raft float trips down this white-water river. Put-in point is at McCreery Beach near Prince, but the outfitter provides round-trip transportation from Thurmond to the put-in place and from takeout point at Fayette Station back to Thurmond. The New River roars through a canyon known to West Virginians as the "Grand Canyon of the East." Using 8' x 8' rubber rafts, the floaters run 15 miles the first day and 15 the second. Shore lunches and a night of tent camping are part of the river fun.

Conservation & Wildlife

CATHEDRAL STATE PARK preserves a virgin forest of extraordinary beauty, which was made a registered national natural landmark because it possesses "exceptional value in illustrating the natural history of the United States."

CRANESVILLE SWAMP, near Cranesville. Formed more than 25,000 years ago, the swamp contains plant and animal life characteristic of the Arctic Circle.

DOLLY SODS, near Davis, has strange rock formations and flora shaped by the mountain winds.

MONONGAHELA NATIONAL FOREST. The Cranberry Mountain Visitor Center, 23 miles east of Richwood on West Virginia 39, is an introduction to the Cranberry Glades. Reindeer moss and other arctic plants live in this high-country bog. A boardwalk trail leads over the layers of peat, where naturalists have discovered pollen deposited before the last ice age over 10,000 years ago. There are conducted nature hikes over the trail to Cranberry Glades and over the Timberlore Trail. At Spruce Knob there is an interesting foot trail that circles the rim of the knob. The red spruce are fascinating, for they have been sculpted by the prevailing west wind. A huckleberry plain is nearby. Because fires have prevented the development of humus, the area is dominated by heath shrubs instead of trees. Careful game management in the national forest has restored the wildlife here.

*PUERTO RICO

Hiking

CARIBBEAN NATIONAL FOREST. La Mina Recreation Area is the jumping-off spot for hikers taking the trail to the top of El Yunque peak, highest point on the island. From the top of the mountain, you can look down on both the Atlantic and the Caribbean. One of the trails leads to the Pinnacles and a sentry tower that dates back to early Spanish colonial days.

Boating

COASTLINE OF PUERTO RICO. The coastline is protected in many places by coral reefs and cays. The most accessible are off Fajardo on the northeast coast and at La Parguera in the southwest,

*Not mapped.

where small islands of mangrove clumps dot the waters. There are sloops that may be rented at Fajardo. Some have auxiliary power. U-Drive-It boats are available by day or half-day on the bayfront at La Parguera. There are marinas at Fajardo, on Isleta Marina about a mile off Fajardo's coast, at Playa Sardinera, and at San Juan.

Sport Diving

COASTLINE OF PUERTO RICO. Boats from Fajardo take snorkelers to the coral reefs off Fajardo and off La Parguera, in the southwest, where the waters are dotted with mangrove clumps. The Caribbean School of Aquatics at the Hyatt Hotel operates a 36-foot, dive-charter boat and dive shop. The school has air compressor and dive platform. Sloops at Las Croabas, Fajardo, can be rented with crew for sailing and snorkeling. Carlos Florez offers rentals, airfills, and scuba instruction on the beachfront. Other rentals can be arranged at La Parguera, on the south coast, and at Boqueron Beach, on the southwest coast. Major hotels offer snorkeling services. Divers are warned not to pick the coral, since it is home and food for mollusks and fish and a protection for the island shoreline. Major hotels and outfitters offer snorkeling services.

ICACOS KEY. Snorkelers favor the pellucid waters off the shore.

Conservation & Wildlife

BOTANICAL GARDEN OF THE UNIVERSITY OF PUERTO RICO at San Juan is on the grounds of the Agricultural Experiment Station. Paths take hikers through a jungle of strange lianas, a bamboo promenade, lotus lagoon, and orchid garden. Exotic palms and trees are identified by signs.

CARIBBEAN NATIONAL FOREST. About 25 miles east of San Juan, this is the only tropical forest in the Forest Service system. The Luquillo Experimental Forest contains 28,000 acres and some 240 different tree species, only 6 of which grow in the continental United States. More than 100 billion gallons of rain fall on this rain forest every year. Some of the exotic trees are the graceful Sierra palm; tree ferns; colorado trees, which often have a short, crooked and even hollow trunk; and bromeliads growing on tree trunks and producing bright red spikes. Fragrant white ginger grows in the forest as do the sultana impaciente. Parrots flit about, and through all the forest sounds the two-note call of the coqui, the little Puerto Rican tree frog.

FEDERAL EXPERIMENT STATION at Mayagüez, has the largest collection of tropical plants in the Western Hemisphere.

PHOSPHORESCENT BAY, near Parguera fishing village on the western section of the south coast. On a moonless night the ripples of a boat's wake scintillate with light. A large population of luminescent dinoflagellates in the water are responsible for this phenomenon. A launch sails from the pier at Villa Parguera for nightly visits to the bay.

RIO ABAJO STATE FOREST, south of Arecibo. Teak trees predominate in this forest beside Dos Bocas Lake.

*VIRGIN ISLANDS

Camping

VIRGIN ISLANDS NATIONAL PARK on St. John Island has idyllic camping in a tropical setting on Cinnamon Bay. Reservations should be made well in advance since there is a great demand for the beautiful sites. Tents and equipment can be rented.

Boating

CRUZ BAY, on St. John, is a popular sheltered harbor. The waters surrounding the Virgin Islands offer sunlit boating. There are other fine harbors and sheltered beaches on St. John.

Sport Diving

BUCK ISLAND REEF is absolute beauty. Snorkelers explore this Caribbean reefscape, located off the northeast coast of St. Croix. Boats take snorkelers from the wharf at Christiansted. Snorkeling equipment can be rented.

GREAT LAMESHUR BAY, at St. John, was used for the study of "Inner Space" carried out by four aquanauts in a sea lab.

MAGENS BAY BEACH, on St. Thomas, called one of the world's most beautiful beaches, is as popular with snorkelers as it is with swimmers and sunbathers.

VIRGIN ISLANDS NATIONAL PARK, St. John Island. Trunk Bay has an underwater trail on its reef. Naturalists have marked the coral and other marine life.

Isle Royale, Michigan

THE MIDWEST

The heartland of America remembers the voyageurs, who first paddled river and lake trails through the deep northern forests, and the boatmen, self-styled half alligator and half horse, who first poled their flatboats along the river highways of the Ohio and the Mississippi. Canoeing and boating are still popular pursuits, and there are times in the north of Minnesota or the Upper Peninsula of Michigan that a canoeist is a brother in spirit to the hardy voyageurs who went before him. Things are changed very little in all that really matters, and the pine forests still crowd around the northern lakes to bring peace at the end of a strenuous day.

The Midwest is a region of great cities and prosperous farms, but the land has an enduring continuity so that there are unspoiled pockets of natural beauty everywhere. The Turkey River valley in northeastern Iowa is such a beauty spot, and so is the Kettle Moraine State Forest of Wisconsin. In the Kettle Moraines a backpacker, only a score or so miles from Milwaukee, hikes through an up-and-down countryside that seems to be hundreds of miles into the wilderness. Glacial boulders, terminal moraines, drumlins, and deep kettles left by the retreating glaciers prove as intriguing as they are challenging.

The prairies of the Midwest reach ever higher as they sweep west until they culminate in the rocky hulks of the Nebraska buttes and the Black Hills, where bison still wander across their ancestral range. The Black Hills have splendid trails for horsemen to follow. Rougher trails offer backpackers and hikers a terrain as beautiful as it is varied. The climb to the top of Harney Peak in the Black Hills, highest mountain east of the Rockies, takes a hiker to a rocky outcropping from where it seems that all the world is spread out below. There are canyons to explore and placer streams to be panned for gold. There are also two magnificent caverns—Jewel Cave and Wind Cave, both protected by the National Park Service—to wander in.

Somebody once called the Badlands of South Dakota "hell with the fires out," and a rancher described them to a visitor from the East as "a hell of a place to lose a cow." They are a phantasmagoria of colors and weird shapes that fascinate any geologist.

The Midwest has the broad plains of Kansas and Nebraska, but it also has hills. Brown County, Indiana, is a vest-pocket Appalachia, with tarns and waterfalls, a good place to camp and to hike. The Missouri Ozarks, the hill country of northwestern Illinois or the Shawnee Hills of southern Illinois, the Nebraska Sand Hills, and the Porcupine Mountains of the Upper Peninsula of Michigan all make appealing vacation country. There also is Isle Royale, a wilderness island in the icy waters of Lake Superior, preserved as a national park. Moose live on the island, and so do wolves. To lie awake in camp at night and listen to the wolves howling is to know that the Midwest still has its wild side.

The heartland of America is made up of Illinois, Indiana, Iowa, Kansas, Michigan, Minnesota, Missouri, Nebraska, North Dakota, Ohio, South Dakota, and Wisconsin. Added to this broad land are Manitoba and Ontario, Canadian provinces containing some of the most magnificent outdoor recreation areas on the continent. Since the days when fur trappers and early settlers got around the Canadian wilderness in birchbark canoes and York boats in the summer and dogsleds in the winter, this has been a country that strikes fire to the imagination. Many of the old trails are marked so that canoeists or hikers can explore the past as they vacation in the present. Ontario's south contains one out of every three Canadians, but the province also contains vast wilderness areas including 250,000 lakes, give or take a few thousand.

The Midwest also has wonders close to population centers. The high bluffs of the Mississippi River near Savanna, Illinois, are home to the eagle, and houseboaters on the river often see the noble birds circling high overhead or perched on the topmost branch of an old tree, surveying their domain with what can only be called an eagle's eye. On the Mississippi there are sandbars on which to beach a boat and picnic or just idle in the sun, and there are lazy backwaters and side channels that demand to be explored. A blue heron rises from a copse of sycamore, or a giant catfish noses up to a baited hook.

There are coyotes, bobcats, fox, and deer in the forest preserves that encircle the city of Chicago. It isn't necessary to travel for days to reach the out-of-doors. The Midwest is that sort of place.

ILLINOIS

Camping

APPLE RIVER CANYON STATE PARK, northwest of Stockton, has fine campsites in rugged woodlands.

BIG SLOUGH AND THOMSON CAUSEWAY, at Thomson. There are plenty of campsites and good fishing.

CHAIN O' LAKES STATE PARK, near Fox Lake, has six campgrounds. Oak Point campground is on the Fox River, 5 miles west of Antioch; Turner Lake campground is close to Fox Lake off US 12.

CRAB ORCHARD NATIONAL WILDLIFE REFUGE. Campsites are on Crab Orchard Lake.

DIXON SPRINGS STATE PARK, near Golconda, is located on a giant rock formation in the Illinois Ozarks. There are camping sites and fine picnic areas.

FERNE CLYFFE STATE PARK, near Goreville, has splendid campgrounds.

GIANT CITY STATE PARK, at Makanda, provides campgrounds near a site where prehistoric Indians built a buffalo trap.

KANKAKEE RIVER STATE PARK, near Kankakee, has two campgrounds, one at the east end and the other at the west end of the park. There also is a camping area for youth groups.

MASON STATE FOREST, northwest of Forest City, has camping areas.

MISSISSIPPI PALISADES STATE PARK, near Savanna, offers camping in a valley sheltered by the magnificent bluffs along the Mississippi River.

SHAWNEE NATIONAL FOREST, in the Illinois Ozarks of southern Illinois, has some fine camping at Pounds Hollow, near Karbers Ridge; Tower Rock, near Elizabethtown; Lake Glendale, 25 miles south of Harrisburg; and Lake Egypt, south of Marion.

STARVED ROCK STATE PARK, near Ottawa. Campers pitch their tents beside the Illinois River close to the huge rock on which legend says a trapped Illinois Indian party starved rather than surrender to the Iroquois.

WHITE PINES FOREST STATE PARK, north of Dixon. Campers enjoy the serenity of the state's last remaining stand of virgin white pine.

Backpacking & Trail Riding

MISSISSIPPI PALISADES STATE PARK. The Aspen Backpack Trail leads into the primitive area. Primitive camping is in the backpack area. There are horse trails and camping for riders at Sorrel Campground.

OZARK-SHAWNEE TRAIL. For 115 miles from Grand Tower on the Mississippi River to Battery Rock on the Ohio, backpackers follow the Ozark-Shawnee Trail through the Shawnee Hills. Much of the trail runs through the Shawnee National Forest following country roads and forest paths. There are supply points at village general stores along the way and camping sites at comfortable distances apart.

Hiking

BUFFALO ROCK STATE PARK, near Ottawa. Trails lead to the top of the rock.

CAVE-IN-ROCK STATE PARK. Trails lead to the historic cave where the bloody bandits who preyed on Ohio River flatboaters once made their headquarters.

CHANNAHON PARKWAY STATE PARK, near Channahon. Hikers start at the old canal locks built in 1840 and hike along the towpaths of the canal. Once Wild Bill Hickok drove mules pulling a barge on this path.

COOK COUNTY FOREST PRESERVES, in the vicinity of Chicago, offer several hundred miles of trails through forests miraculously preserved so near the city.

GIANT CITY STATE PARK, Makanda, offers excellent hiking past interesting rock formations over marked trails.

ILLINOIS PRAIRIE PATH. Hikers follow this trail through the western suburbs of Chicago along the abandoned right-of-way of the former Chicago Aurora and Elgin Railway. One branch of the trail begins at Pratt Wayne Woods near Wayne and at Wheaton meets the other branch originating to the southwest at Molitar Road near Aurora. The main trail runs east of Wheaton to a point beyond Elmhurst. Camping in Du Page County forest preserves may be arranged, but permission must be granted in advance. Riders also follow the path.

JACKSON HOLLOW, south of Zion Church, reached over Forest Service Road 124, is at the heart of a small wilderness of hollows. The area can be dangerous and should be entered by experienced hikers only.

KANKAKEE RIVER STATE PARK, near Kankakee. Foot trails follow the brink of Rock Creek Canyon. Side trails run to the canyon floor.

LOWDEN STATE PARK, Oregon. Trails overlook the beautiful Rock River.

MATTHIESSEN STATE PARK, southwest of Ottawa. Canyon trails are worth exploring. A trail leads to a beautiful falls on the Vermilion River.

MISSISSIPPI PALISADES STATE PARK, Savanna, offers fine hiking on the bluffs overlooking the river.

SHAWNEE NATIONAL FOREST contains a network of trails.

STARVED ROCK STATE PARK, near Ottawa. Rugged trails lead to the top of the precipitous rock and up the rough ravines.

Biking

COOK COUNTY FOREST PRESERVES. The Salt Creek Trail begins at Bemis Woods South, west of La Grange, and runs through the woods to the Brookfield Zoo, at Brookfield.

ILLINOIS PRAIRIE PATH begins at Pratt Wayne Woods near Wayne and runs to a point east of Elmhurst along the abandoned right-of-way of the former Chicago Aurora and Elgin Railway. Designated a national trail, the path has become a favorite route for bikers. A branch at Wheaton extends southwest to Molitar Road northeast of Aurora. There are camping facilities in the Du Page County forest preserves along the way, but permission to camp must be obtained in advance.

Rockhounding

BOSS ISLAND, southwest of Vienna, once was deep within an ancient cypress swamp that covered much of the Cache River bottoms. Ancient fossils are common here.

DUBUQUE DAM. From the vicinity of the dam on the Mississippi to as far south as Cordova and Port Byron, beautiful banded agates are found.

GEODE PARK, Warsaw. A stream flowing down to the Mississippi River has cut into shale and clay to reveal geodes, formed ages ago when this area was at the bottom of the Gulf of Mexico. Inside each geode is a crystalline world.

MIDWESTERN STATES

HUNTING BRANCH, Bell Smith Springs, contains fossil seashells in the limestone deposits along the Ohio. Some favorite searching spots are limestone outcrops, rocky streambeds, and quarry pits.

JO DAVIESS COUNTY. Around the one-time lead capital of Galena is the state's richest mineral-collecting area. Rockhounds find specimens of galena, sphalerite, and pyrite as well as some anglesite, calcite, cerussite, chalcopyrite, limonite, marcasite, and smithsonite.

MISSISSIPPI RIVER GRAVELS, near Grand Tower, are good spots to look for agate.

WILL COUNTY. Near Wilmington is a good place to look for Pennsylvania plant fossils in the spoil banks from strip mines. Permission to enter quarry areas must be obtained from the owners.

Canoeing

BIG MUDDY RIVER is a challenging canoeing stream from access point at the city park in Murphysboro for 41 miles to its mouth at the Mississippi. Much of the bottom is muddy, but there are also areas of sand and gravel. There is a campsite in the Little Grand Canyon. Canoeists are warned against migrating copperheads and cottonmouths. Takeout point should be at the Illinois 3 bridge, unless a canoeist wishes to paddle up the Mississippi to Grand Tower or downstream a good distance to Cape Girardeau on the Missouri shore.

BIG VERMILION RIVER. Put in at Kangley Bridge for a 2-day trip to Starved Rock State Park off Route 80. Five-foot whitewater near Route 178 can be dangerous for nonexperts. Also beware of the broken dam chute between Routes 178 and 71. The best paddling is in high water periods.

EMBARRAS RIVER has 130 miles of canoeable water with a fall of three to four feet per mile. Fluctuations of water can be drastic and rapid. Canoeists put in the Embarras at the bridge on Illinois 130 about 1½ miles south of Villa Grove. Canoeists use the southwest corner of the bridge. On the way canoeists may stop to see the Lincoln Log Cabin State Park. Some canoeists go all the way to the mouth of the river in the Wabash and take out from the Wabash at St. Francisville.

LOWER FOX RIVER from west of Norway to Wedron. Canoeists pass beneath cliffs hung with cedars and Canadian yew. Canoeists also paddle the upper Fox, but the numerous dams require more portages than many are willing to make.

ILLINOIS-MICHIGAN CANAL is a good canoeing stream from 20 miles northeast of Morris to 5 miles west of the town. There are public launching areas at the Dresden Island Lock and Dam and at Gebhard Woods State Park. Campsites are at Channahon Parkway State Park and at Gebhard Woods State Park, but permits for camping at these parks are required. A popular one-day canoe trip begins at the Channahon Parkway State Park and ends at the Aux Sable Creek aqueduct.

ROCK RIVER is an excellent canoeing stream, but it is scarcely a wilderness river. Put-in point can be at the state line near Beloit, Wisconsin. Portages will be necessary at dams at Rockton and Rockford. The most scenic section is downstream from where the Kishwaukee River flows into the Rock. There are limestone bluffs overlooking the waters. The portage at the Oregon dam is easy. From Oregon to Dixon the river offers 20 miles of scenic canoeing. The takeout point for canoeists is at city park in Dixon, some 2 miles above the Dixon dam.

SANGAMON RIVER. Canoeists put in at the Lincoln Trail Homestead State Park near Decatur and canoe downstream to Lincoln's New Salem. The river bottom is mostly sand and gravel upriver of Springfield, but downriver of the city, it is muddy a good part of the way. Depth ranges from a foot over riffles to 12 feet in some pools. Carpenters Park at the edge of Springfield has a camping area, however no drinking water is available. Canoeists portage around the dam in Springfield. Some canoeists decide to continue on to Beardstown. Camping sites are near Oakford on the north side of the river under the bridge on Illinois 97.

Boating

LAKE MICHIGAN. Boating is popular on all of the Great Lakes, and there are excellent harbors along the Illinois shore of Lake Michigan. Lovely wooded shoreline with sand beaches offer pretty views. Both Chicago and Waukegan, in particular, have notable harbors.

MISSISSIPPI RIVER. Houseboating on the Mississippi has become almost a way of life, and Illinois river ports are all popular home ports for houseboaters. Other boaters use the excellent river marinas as well.

Conservation & Wildlife

BEALL WOODS, near Mount Carmel, contains trees as tall as 160 feet. This 636-acre forest is the largest untouched timber area in the Midwest. It contains both bottomland and upland forests.

COOK COUNTY FOREST PRESERVES. Busse Forest near Elk Grove Village is a rich forest of oak, sugar maple, and basswood on upland sites and swamp white oak and ash in marshy areas.

CRAB ORCHARD NATIONAL WILDLIFE REFUGE, west of Marion, successfully blends conservation with outdoor recreation. There are three lakes.

GOOSE LAKE PRAIRIE NATURE PRESERVE, in Grundy County, is the largest remnant of virgin prairie in the state, supporting an abundance of waterfowl and rare birds.

ILLINOIS BEACH STATE PARK, Zion, contains a nature walk through a natural dunes area.

MORTON ARBORETUM, Lisle, near Downers Grove. Miles of trails lead through this 1,425-acre arboretum of woodland plants. Founded in 1922, the arboretum has one of the nation's most impressive collections of trees and shrubs.

PINE HILLS ECOLOGICAL AREA AND LARUE SWAMP, south of Grand Tower. Botanists find the swamp by the Mississippi River to be fascinating. The view from Pine Hills over the river is outstanding.

SHAWNEE NATIONAL FOREST contains such exceptional conservation areas as the Oakwood Bottoms Greentree Reservoir. Waterfowl and upland animals find food and shelter in this remarkable oak forest.

SINNISSIPPI FOREST at Oregon. This pioneer tree farm is a lesson in ecology. It was started in 1910 by Frank O. Lowden, governor of Illinois from 1915 to 1919, when he put in the first plantings of white pine. A logger's trail starts at the forest office and runs through the forest. Hikers can study timber types and soil conditions along the trail. Many of the hardwoods native to Illinois, as well as pines, can be found. There are also interesting sand slopes, swamps and bogs, and rock outcrops with appropriate vegetation.

UNION COUNTY CONSERVATION AREA, south of Anna, is the wintering ground for flocks of Canada geese.

INDIANA

Camping

BROWN COUNTY STATE PARK, Nashville. There are campgrounds for both horsemen and families.

CHAIN O'LAKES STATE PARK, 5 miles southeast of Albion. There is a modern campground.

CLIFTY FALLS STATE PARK, near Madison. Campgrounds overlook the Ohio River.

HARRISON-CRAWFORD STATE FOREST, near New Albany, has outstanding camping close to the Ohio River. Campsites on the riverbank and on the high bluffs are available.

HOOSIER NATIONAL FOREST. There are many fine campsites in the forest, particularly in the Hardin Ridge area.

LINCOLN STATE PARK, at Lincoln City. The campground is near where Abraham Lincoln spent part of his boyhood.

MC CORMICK'S CREEK STATE PARK, near Spencer, has modern campgrounds nestled among the pines. There also is a beautiful primitive campground beneath spreading beech trees.

RACCOON LAKE STATE RECREATION AREA, near Rockville. Camping is permitted only in the campground area.

SPRING MILL STATE PARK, near Mitchell, has camping with modern facilities.

TURKEY RUN STATE PARK, north of Marshall. There is a public campground as well as two group camps for youth.

WHITEWATER STATE PARK, near Liberty, provides modern camping. Some sites will accommodate trailers.

Hiking

BROWN COUNTY STATE PARK, Nashville, not only has hiking trails but also has trails for horses. The superintendent can give details to riders who bring their own horses.

CHAIN O'LAKES STATE PARK, near Albion. A trail from the campground runs through the woods along a hillside and drops down into a valley along the channel around Finster Lake. It ends at the schoolhouse. There also is a loop trail through locust trails, fields, and a hardwood forest around Dock Lake.

CLIFTY FALLS STATE PARK, Madison, overlooking the Ohio River, has interesting hiking trails along canyon walls, creek beds, and cliff tops.

LINCOLN STATE PARK, Lincoln City. There are several trails. A circle trail begins at the boat dock and runs around the south shore of the lake to the fire tower and back to the dock. Abraham Lincoln, whose Indiana boyhood home was nearby, often hiked some of the trails in the park.

MC CORMICK'S CREEK STATE PARK, Spencer. Foot trails run along the creek as it flows through a limestone canyon. There are also bridle paths. Trails lead through pine and beech forests to ravines, deep stone gullies, and an abandoned quarry from which stone was taken to build the Indiana State Capitol.

MOUNDS STATE PARK, near Anderson, has several hiking trails along the White River. One trail begins at the pavilion and leads through a ravine and oaks to the Great Mound, constructed during a transition period from the prehistoric Adena to the Hopewell culture. The Great Mound, the largest of the nine well-preserved earth formations in the park, is 9 feet high and almost ¼ mile in circumference. There are also bridal paths through the wooded park.

POKAGON STATE PARK, near Angola, includes a trail through the primitive areas of the park, which include a swamp.

SHADES STATE PARK, near Waveland, has a trail past interesting sandstone formations with scenic views of Sugar Creek and Silver Cascade. Another trail runs through Pearl Ravine.

SHAKAMAK STATE PARK, Jasonville, has fine trails including one that follows the shoreline of Lake Shakamak.

SPRING MILL STATE PARK, near Mitchell. An interesting trail loops past Donaldson Cave gorge, through dense woods with sinkholes, Donaldson Woods, and past Bronson Cave and Twin Caves.

TURKEY RUN STATE PARK, north of Marshall. The hiking trails are of exceptional interest. They lead to a covered bridge, along cliff edges, and to abandoned quarries.

VERSAILLES STATE PARK, Versailles. A trail runs to Bat Cave, past limestone outcroppings, to a pioneer graveyard. The park has over 5,800 acres, and hiking is good through wooded hills.

Biking

CALUMET TRAIL, adjacent to Dunes State Park, runs for 9.2 miles through dunes and blowouts. The trail passes through the Dunes National Lakeshore.

COVERED BRIDGE TOURS, around Rockville. There are two self-guided bike tours of Parke County beginning in Rockville. They stick to back roads and bring a biker to many of the county's colorful covered bridges. The tours begin at the Rockville tourist center.

HOOSIER HILLS ROUTE runs for 27 miles from Liberty Park in Batesville to Versailles State Park. There is camping in the state park.

MOUNDS STATE PARK, Anderson, has a bike trail that leads to prehistoric sites.

Rockhounding

DEVILS BACKBONE, Madison. The area was bulldozed away to build a power plant, and trilobite fossils have been revealed.

GLACIAL DEPOSITS. Left by the melting glaciers, gold nuggets are discovered by rockhounds in the rocky debris. In Owen, Brown, Morgan, and Jackson counties, gold is panned from streambeds in Lick Creek, Salt Creek, Beanblossom Creek, Sycamore Creek, and Gold Creek. Rockhounds panning for gold also come upon small bright red garnets, sapphires, and diamonds. Diamonds found in Indiana are few and far between, but there have been about 60 worthwhile finds, including a four-and-seven-eighths-carat stone. Amethyst and agate may also be found in the diggings.

MARTIN COUNTY HEMATITE RANGE, near Shoals, provides Indiana's highest quality iron ore. A blast furnace built in the 1870s used this ore until late in the 1890s.

Canoeing

SUGAR CREEK. Magnificent scenery awaits canoeists between Shades and Turkey Run state parks.

WABASH RIVER, from Bluffton to the Ohio River, is a canoeing stream 360 miles long, with three portages.

WHITE RIVER. The East Fork from Columbus to Mount Carmel, Illinois, has 175 miles of canoeing, with four portages. The other fork, from the west

THE MIDWEST 137

edge of Anderson to Mount Carmel, Illinois, has 210 miles with six portages.

WHITEWATER RIVER. Canoe trips cover some 40 miles between Laurel and I-74, 20 miles below Brookeville.

Conservation & Wildlife

INDIANA DUNES NATIONAL LAKESHORE. The bluffs, the lake and the dunes, the black oak forest, and ponds and swamp make this a remarkable ecological area. In Indiana Dunes State Park, there are fine trails through the dunes covered with black oak, a climax forest, spring flowers, and ferns, and the fascinating Furnessville Blowout. The variation in vegetation makes a fine refuge for birds of many species.

MC CORMICK'S CREEK STATE PARK, Spencer. The Environmental Educational Center shows steps being taken to halt the deterioration of the environment.

IOWA

Camping

AMBROSE A. CALL STATE PARK, near Algona, has an undeveloped campground.

LACEY-KEOSAUQUA STATE PARK, near Keosauqua, has camping in the state's largest park.

LEDGES STATE PARK, near Madrid, has fine campsites.

STEPHENS STATE FOREST, northeast of Chariton, offers primitive camping.

WILD CAT DEN STATE PARK, on the Mississippi River near Muscatine, is a favorite camping ground.

YELLOW RIVER STATE FOREST, near McGregor, has primitive camping sites.

Backpacking

YELLOW RIVER STATE FOREST, near McGregor, offers ideal terrain for a three-day backpacking hike along the limestone bluffs and through the hilly woods.

Hiking

BACKBONE STATE PARK, near Dundee, has interesting hiking trails.

138 THE MIDWEST

HERBERT HOOVER TRAIL, West Branch. The trail runs for 23 miles from West Branch, Herbert Hoover's birthplace.

LAKE AHQUABI STATE PARK, near Indianola, offers trails for hikers.

NINE EAGLES STATE PARK, Davis City. There are fine hiking trails.

SHO-QUO-QUON GEODE TRAIL, Burlington. The trail runs for 21 miles from Crapo Park in the city to Geode State Park.

Biking

IOWA HILLS AND VALLEYS TOUR begins and ends at Davenport. Sponsored by the American Youth Hostels, the trail loops along part of the Great River Road beside the Mississippi. It explores Iowa's pretty hills, deep valleys, and forests.

Rockhounding

AGATE PIT, 2¼ miles northeast of Harpers Ferry on the east side of the railroad tracks, is a gravel pit where agates are found.

CORALVILLE RESERVOIR. During low-water stage at the reservoir, coral may be collected from the Cedar Valley limestone.

COUNTY BLACKTOP ROAD CUT, 3½ miles southwest of Rockford Brick and Tile Company pit on the south side of the road. Lime Creek shale fossils are abundant here.

GEODE STATE PARK, southwest of Danville, offers rockhounds the chance to look for geodes, rocks whose hollow interiors contain beautiful crystal formations. The muddy-looking rocks are dug out of creek beds.

GITCHIE MANITOU STATE PRESERVE, north of Sioux City, contains quartzite.

LEE COUNTY QUARRY, northeast of Sandusky, contains an abundant supply of small geodes.

QUARRY, 2¾ miles northwest of Harpers Ferry. Brachiopods and bryozoans are found in the Decorah-Platteville formations.

ROCKFORD BRICK AND TILE COMPANY CLAY PIT, a half mile west of Rockford. Brachiopods are collected from the Lime Creek shale in the stripped surface and dump piles at this world-famous location.

Canoeing

BOONE RIVER, from Webster City to the Des Moines River, is a challenge because of its varying currents. There are entertaining rapids. Put in on the south bank just below Millards' Bridge across the Boone, 2 miles south of Webster City, and take out in the Des Moines a mile or so below the confluence. Just beyond Belleville Bridge, on the right, is a good takeout place.

DES MOINES RIVER, from Kalo to Lehigh. Canoeists put in 4 miles south from US 20 on US 169. Just below the highway bridge, the left bank provides an easy put-in place. On the way, there is camping at Dolliver Memorial State Park. Takeout point is on the left downstream side of the river, just above the Lehigh bridge.

TURKEY RIVER from Elgin to Garber. Canoeists follow the largest river in Iowa's "Little Switzerland." The upper river is calm, but the middle section has a strong current over a rocky bottom. The lower section, from the vicinity of Elkport to the Mississippi, has a bottom of silt and sand, and the current is once again slow. From Elgin to Garber the valley is narrow and bounded by rugged bluffs. The rate of fall is seldom less than four feet per mile and reaches six for long stretches. There are no dangerous rapids or obstructions except for a dam at Elkader. However, canoeists may encounter a few fallen trees. Put in at the bridge abutment on the upstream side at Elgin. Shortly after the Volga River enters the Turkey from the right, the river enters open farmlands and is no longer a challenging stream. At Garber there is a good takeout place on the right bank below the bridge.

WAPSIPINICON RIVER, from Independence to Stone City, provides one of the state's top canoeing experiences. A two- or three-day trip of about 50 river miles begins at the put-in point at Independence on the right bank upstream from the Iowa 150 bridge. There are portages around the dams at Quasqueton and at Troy Mills bridge and dam. There are other portages around dams farther down the river.

Boating

MISSISSIPPI RIVER, around Lansing. Houseboats may be rented here for vacation cruising along the 320 miles of Iowa's Mississippi River shoreline. There are sandbars for camping or for tying up for a picnic.

Prairie Chickens—Nebraska

Conservation & Wildlife

BLUFFTON FIR STAND, just across the Iowa River from Bluffton, this forest contains a rare balsam fir stand.

CAYLER PRAIRIE, southwest of Spirit Lake, contains at least 219 species of plants in a virgin prairie.

GITCHIE MANITOU, northwest of Larchwood, preserves prairie and brushland along the Big Sioux River. The pink stone outcrops of Sioux quartzite contain a beautiful pool.

PILOT KNOB, southeast of Forest City, preserves a sphagnum bog with rare plants. There is an example of "old field" succession.

WHITE PINE HOLLOW, Luxemburg, has the largest remaining stand of native white pine in Iowa.

WOODMAN HOLLOW, northwest of Lehigh. A deep ravine contains rare plants.

KANSAS

Camping

COUNCIL GROVE DAM AND RESERVOIR, just north of Council Grove. Campgrounds are at Canning Creek Cove, Dam Site, Neosho Park, Richey Cove North, and Richey Cove South.

JOHN REDMOND DAM AND RESERVOIR, near Burlington, offers camping in Corps of Engineer campgrounds at the Dam Site, north and south; Hartford Ramp; Hickory Creek, East and West; Otter Creek; Redmond Cove, north and south; and Strawn Ramp.

KANAPOLIS DAM AND RESERVOIR, near Ellsworth, has camping at the Tunnel Outlet, Venango, East Shore State Park, and Langley Point.

MARION DAM AND RESERVOIR, near Marion, has year-round camping at Hillsboro Cove, French Creek Cove (West), Durham Cove, Cottonwood Point, and Marion Cove.

Trail Riding

WAGONS HO covered-wagon trips begin at Quinter and follow the old Smoky Hill Trail. Vacationers ride either in the wagons or on horseback. The trail riders sleep in the wagons, in tents, or under the stars.

Biking

OLD PRAIRIE TRAILS, from Kansas City to Washington, over blacktop roads. This AYH trail takes bikers along the route of the Santa Fe Trail as far as Council Grove and then north into the country of the Pony Express. There are campgrounds along the trail at distances of from 25 to 50 miles.

Rockhounding

SMOKY HILL RIVER, south of Hays. In gravel pits along the river, rockhounds find moss agate, dendrite opal, and some petrified palm wood. A good place to look is south of Wakeeney at Sieberts Sand and Gravel Site.

Boating

CORPS OF ENGINEER RESERVOIRS. There is boating on the following reservoirs: Marion, Kanopolis, John Redmond, Council Grove, Wilson, Toronto, and Milford. There is also boating on Tuttle Creek Lake and Perry Lake.

Conservation & Wildlife

CHEYENNE BOTTOMS, just north of Great Bend, is a 19,000-acre wildlife refuge. Waterfowl may be seen all year round.

FLINT HILLS, northeast of El Dorado, contain the only remaining substantial segments of native tallgrass prairies, which once extended from Indiana to Texas and north into Canada.

MARAIS DES CYGNES WATERFOWL REFUGE AREA, 5 miles northwest of Pleasanton. Man-made marshes are home to waterfowl.

MAXWELL STATE GAME PRESERVE, 6 miles north of Canton, has one of the state's largest buffalo herds, as well as elk, deer, and beaver.

MONUMENT ROCKS, south of Oakley, are wind-carved and water-eroded 60-foot-high chalk formations, the sedimental remains of marine life. They have been designated a natural landmark by the U.S. Department of Interior.

MICHIGAN

Camping

BEWABIC STATE PARK, 4 miles west of Crystal Falls, has a campground close to Fortune Lake.

BRIGHTON RECREATION AREA, 3 miles southwest of Brighton, has a campground on Bishop Lake with 222 campsites.

BURT LAKE STATE PARK, just south of the village of Indian River, has a shady campground with artesian well water.

THE MIDWEST 139

CHEBOYGAN STATE PARK, 3 miles northeast of Cheboygan, on Duncan Bay, offers rustic camping.

D. H. DAY CAMPGROUND, just west of Glen Arbor, is situated in a wooded area close to the famed Sleeping Bear Sand Dune.

HARRISVILLE STATE PARK, just south of Harrisville on Lake Huron, has a well-developed campground.

HARTWICK PINES STATE PARK, 7 miles northeast of Grayling, offers camping in one of the Lower Peninsula's most beautiful forests.

HIAWATHA NATIONAL FOREST in the Upper Peninsula offers fine camping at a number of Forest Service campgrounds. Brevoort Lake is one of these, a well-developed camp located on the shores of Lake Michigan 15 miles west of the Mackinac Bridge.

HIGGINS LAKE STATE PARK—NORTH, 5 miles west of Roscommon, has well-wooded campgrounds. There are other camping sites at Higgins Lake State Park—South.

HURON NATIONAL FOREST. There are excellent campsites in the forest.

INDIAN LAKE STATE PARK, 4 miles west of Manistique, offers camping in a forest in the middle of the Hiawatha country made famous by Longfellow. The park's west unit is 7 miles west of Manistique, and has a secluded campground.

LAKE GOGEBIC STATE PARK, 12 miles northeast of Marenisco, has a campground on the lake.

MANISTEE NATIONAL FOREST offers fine camping in a number of campsites.

MICHIGAN STATE FORESTS. Michigan is blessed with a number of beautiful state forests, all of which have splendid camping sites. These sites are ideal for campers who want solitude in a wilderness setting.

OTTAWA NATIONAL FOREST. Sylvania campground near Watersmeet is outstanding. Light camping is permitted elsewhere in this magnificent virgin woods.

PINCKNEY RECREATION AREA, southeast of Gregory, has fine campgrounds on Bruin Lake.

PORCUPINE MOUNTAINS STATE PARK, 20 miles west of Ontonagon, offers some of the finest camping in the Midwest. In the Presque Isle River unit there is another superb campground some 16 miles north of Wakefield. It is reached through a virgin forest.

STRAITS STATE PARK, adjoining the city of St. Ignace, has camping with a view of the Mackinac Bridge.

TAHQUAMENON FALLS STATE PARK, near Paradise, has camping in a remnant of what was once a vast wilderness.

Backpacking & Trail Riding

ISLE ROYALE NATIONAL PARK offers some of the best backpacking in mid-America. You should make boat reservation in advance to get to the Midwest's only national park. The 160 miles of trails are ideal for backpacking, but off-trail travel is not easy because of the boggy areas and dense forests of this park. All backpackers must register with the rangers and obtain fire permits. A trip into the Isle Royale backcountry requires careful planning and appropriate equipment. There are fine camping areas situated at strategic intervals, and backpackers may camp anywhere providing they are out of sight of the trail and observe the strictest of good woods manners. It is necessary to boil all drinking water taken from either Lake Superior or any of the inland lakes, because of the presence of liver flukes deposited by the infected moose herd. Chemical treatment of the water is not enough.

OTTAWA NATIONAL FOREST around Watersmeet offers fine backpacking over onetime logging roads, which are reserved for use as trails only.

PORCUPINE MOUNTAINS STATE PARK, near Ontonagon, requires that backpackers register at the park office before entering the interior. They may not take any disposable metal and glass containers into the interior and must observe good woods manners. Adirondack shelters have been erected for backpackers. They are available on a first-come, first-served basis and may not be reserved. Trailside cabins are also available. Accessible only on foot, the cabins must be reserved in advance. Hikers may camp off the trails but not within a quarter of a mile of the shelters. The most popular trail is the Government Peak Trail, but others, such as the Escarpment Trail and the North Mirror Lake Trail, have their adherents.

SHORE–TO–SHORE RIDING AND HIKING TRAIL stretches across the Lower Peninsula from East Tawas to Traverse City, passing near Kalkaska.

WILDERNESS STATE PARK, 8 miles west of Mackinaw City. A truck trail built for the fire patrol encircles the park, but the interior is untrammeled. Trails lead hikers into the huge park. There are overnight cabins on the trails.

Hiking

ALLEGAN STATE GAME AREA, near Allegan, has cross-country trails, including Swan Creek Foot Trail, passing a millpond and through the forest.

MUSKEGON STATE PARK, 4 miles west of North Muskegon. Trails traverse the dunes and lead to crests from where a hiker can see Lake Michigan.

P. H. HOEFT STATE PARK, 5 miles northwest of Rogers City, offers foot trails among fine examples of Huron Dunes.

PORCUPINE MOUNTAINS STATE PARK, 20 miles west of Ontonagon. This backpacker's country is also a fine place for day hikes.

WATERLOO RECREATION AREA, between Jackson and Chelsea. Hikers follow the trails through the rolling hills and climb to the summits for panoramic views.

Biking

MACKINAC ISLAND allows no autos to sully its shores. This makes it a fine place for bikers.

MICHIGAN CROSS-COUNTRY CYCLE TRAIL. Orange triangles posted along back roads lead hikers from new Newaygo on a circle tour to near Sanford. For a map booklet write to the Cycle Conservation Club, P.O. Box 745, East Lansing, Michigan 48823.

Rockhounding

KEWEENAW PENINSULA. Abandoned Upper Peninsula copper mines yield interesting specimens of ore overlooked by the miners. The old mine pits extend from the Porcupine Mountains to the end of the Keweenaw Peninsula.

LAKE MICHIGAN SHORE. From Frankfort north along the shore to the Petoskey area is a rockhounder's delight. To be found are agates, amygdaloids, breccia, jaspilite, conglomerates, quartz, epidote, chert, and some jade. Here too is where the well-known Petoskey stone, now Michigan's state stone, is found. The Petoskey stone is a colorful coral fossil.

Bicycling—Michigan

LAKE SUPERIOR SHORE. The beaches yield a number of fine stones, ranging from pebbles of basalt or lava to native copper and agates.

Canoeing

AU SABLE RIVER, Middle Branch, west of Grayling, is one of the Midwest's most popular canoeing streams. From Grayling to Mio is 75 miles. The takeout point favored by most canoeists is at Oscoda. Campsites are numerous.

BRULE RIVER. Canoes and pick-ups can be arranged for at Iron River or Crystal Falls. There are a few rapids that an intermediate canoeist can essay. The Iron River's reddish waters flow into the Brule Between this point and where the Brule and the Paint join to form the Menominee, there are several takeout points.

ESCANABA RIVER. The main stream offers a canoe trip of from a week to two weeks. Canoeists put-in at Gwinn in the morning to take advantage of the water falling from the Princeton power dam. Takeout point is at the West Gladstone bridge on County 420. It is possible to arrange at a Gwinn garage to be met. The upper river is rocky, but farther downstream the canoeist encounters swampy areas. The West Branch is also a good canoeing stream. Canoeists start at Boney Falls Dam.

FORD RIVER. Put-in point is north of Ralph. There are two portages at a rapids soon after starting and a mile below Broken Back Bridge.

INDIAN RIVER. Canoeists put in at the U.S. Forest Service Widewater Campground in Schoolcraft County and paddle down this flat-water stream. Indian River Campground makes a good camping spot on a trip that usually takes from two to three days. The trip ends at the boat landing on Indian Lake.

ISLE ROYALE NATIONAL PARK. The deep fjordlike bays and offshore islands of the archipelago provide miles of protected waters for canoeists. Canoe portage trails also lead to inland lakes on the main island. One such trip links Tobins Harbor with the north shore bays via a system of short portage trails. Another ties together Lakes Whittlesey, Siskiwit, Intermediate, and Richie. Caution: Rocky shores sometimes make landing difficult, and sudden lake storms can whip up canoe-swamping waves. Canoeists should keep a keen eye on the developing weather and should never attempt to paddle through the open waters of Lake Superior. There are no canoes for rent in the park.

KALAMAZOO RIVER. Canoeists descend the river from Allegan Dam to Saugatuck. It's a four-day trip with stopovers in canoe camps along the river, mostly in the Allegan State Forest.

MANISTEE RIVER. A 200-mile trip of at least 10 days begins at County 612 crossing in Crawford County and runs through the forest to the dock area on the north end of Manistee Lake. There are campsites and supply points along the way.

MENOMINEE RIVER runs along the border between Wisconsin and the Upper Peninsula of Michigan. Canoeists run the river for five days, portaging around dams and shooting the white waters. Some of the rapids should be tried by experts only. Every year beginner canoeists manage to mangle their canoes on the rocks.

MUSKEGON RIVER is said to be a mild-tempered stream with no dangerous rapids. Put in at Houghton Lake to thread the Dead Stream Swamp above Reedsburg Dam. Camping areas are easy to find during a one- to two-week trip along the 227-mile course. Takeout point is at Muskegon.

NET RIVER. Canoeists put in on Park Siding Road Bridge, 12 miles north of Amasa. A dam near the point and Chipmunk Falls, 5 miles downstream, must be portaged. There is another portage at Snake Rapids. Canoe rentals are at Crystal Falls and Amasa. The trip runs through uninhabited wild country, and at least one camp must be made.

ONTONAGON RIVER from Military Bridge on US 45 to Lake Superior is a fine, short canoe stream. It is necessary to portage the rapids. The river's four branches are not suitable for canoeing.

PINE RIVER. Put in at Hoxey for a canoe trip of 70 miles that takes three to four days. The river most definitely is not for novices, since it has a powerful and swift current and some dangerous stretches.

TAHQUAMENON RIVER provides a one- to two-week trip beginning north of McMillan. The first day's trip must be at least 15 miles, for there are no camping sites in the extensive willow marsh through which the canoeist passes. Campsites are numerous below the marsh. Drinking water may be obtained from springs, but the river water cannot be used. There are portages at the upper and lower falls, and most canoeists will also want to portage around the rapids 2 miles above the lower falls. Some may want to line through or use a drag.

THUNDER BAY RIVER from Lake Fifteen, with put-in point southwest of Atlanta, offers 83 miles of challenging canoeing. The first 15 miles are shallow and fast. There is a portage at the Hillman Dam and around two logjams below Hillman. Below Hillman to Long Rapids, the river twists for 22 miles through swamps, farms, and timbers. A half mile below Long Rapids is some difficult white water, and there is another tricky stretch some 5 miles farther down. The last 15 miles of the trip are through backwaters with short portages around Seven Mile Dam and Four Mile Dam. Takeout point is at Alpena.

Boating

GREAT LAKES WATERS. Michigan's Great Lakes ports look out onto some of the

THE MIDWEST 141

nation's finest boating waters. Boating is popular on Lakes Michigan, Huron, and Superior and on such smaller lakes as Lake St. Clair. Mackinac Island is a boater's favorite port of call.

ISLE ROYALE NATIONAL PARK offers ideal boating. Some campgrounds are accessible only by boat. Boaters must register with the rangers when arriving. Since the waters of Lake Superior are frequently rough, boats of 20 feet or less are dangerous to use on a trip to the island. Gasoline may be purchased for a boat at Rock Harbor or Windigo in the park.

Conservation & Wildlife

HARTWICK PINES STATE PARK, 7 miles northeast of Grayling. An Interpretive Center tells through its exhibits the story of the white pine. There are stands of white and red pines and hemlock and a replica of an early logging camp.

INTERLOCHEN STATE PARK, 15 miles southwest of Traverse City, has one of the last stands of virgin pine in the state.

ISLE ROYALE NATIONAL PARK offers a fascinating ecological study, for it is a wilderness park where life continues in the forest as in primeval times. The park has a large herd of moose, and these are preyed upon by a pack of wolves. Other common mammals include the beaver, red fox, and snowshoe hare. More than 200 kinds of birds are found, and evergreens and hardwoods meet on the island in a transition forest. There are self-guiding nature trails, and the rangers offer an interpretive program.

MACKINAW STATE FOREST. A nature drive begins some 9½ miles north of Mancelona. The effects of logging in the river valley, deer overbrowse, and other phenomena can be studied.

OTTAWA NATIONAL FOREST. The Sylvania Visitor Information Station introduces vacationers to the northwoods with its forests and lakes. The exhibits and dioramas show the influence of man on the forest. The bald eagle and heron are found in the forest.

PERE MARQUETTE STATE FOREST. The Lost Lake Nature Trail is not far from Traverse City. A 4½-mile hike leads to an improved fish and waterfowl habitat, shoreline showing the effects of flooding, wood duck nesting areas, a stand of aspen, an area subjected to repeated flooding by beaver dams, and a blueberry marsh.

LAKE SUPERIOR STATE FOREST has a nature tour that starts on County 403, south of Roberts Corner. (Roberts Corner is on Michigan 28, about 3 miles south of Newberry.) Tourists see such things as a mixed red and jack pine plantation, a sharp-tailed grouse management area, a timber improvement stand, and a commercial timber harvest.

MINNESOTA

Camping

CHIPPEWA NATIONAL FOREST contains a complex of camping areas in the Cass Lake area. Among the best of these camping grounds are Pike Bay, named for Zebulon Pike, who explored the area, at the south end of Cass Lake; Norway Beach, a large modern camp; and Star Island on Lake Windigo.

MINNESOTA STATE PARKS CAMPGROUNDS rank among the best in the Midwest. They range from the 32 primitive sites at Banning State Park near Sandstone to the campsites at Zippel Bay State Park, northeast of Williams. Beaver Creek Valley State Park, 3 miles west of Caledonia, for example, has 40 modern and 35 primitive campsites and a pioneer group camping area. Blue Mounds, near Luverne in the western part of the state, is another outstanding camping area. Camping is also permitted overnight in a number of state highway waysides.

MISSISSIPPI RIVER HEADWATER RECREATION AREA. The Corps of Engineers has provided still another system of outstanding camping sites in the Cross Lake area, Leech Lake area, Sand Lake area, Pokegama Lake area, Gull Lake area.

STATE OF MINNESOTA RECREATION AREAS contain excellent campgrounds. The grounds are kept as small as possible and are intended primarily for tents. Trailers and recreational vehicles not over 20 feet in length can usually be accommodated. Within the tenting areas, natural growth is left as a screen between the sites. There are recreational areas in Beltrami Island State Forest near Warroad at Bemis Hill, Blueberry Hill, Faunce; in Big Fork State Forest near Talmoon at Long Lake; in Birch Lakes State Forest near Melrose at Birch Lake; in Bowstring State Forest near Deer River at Cottonwood Lake; in Cloquet Valley State Forest near Brimson at Cedar Bay and Whiteface River; in Crow Wing State Forest near Crosby at Greer Lake and Lougee Lake; in Finland State Forest near Finland at Eckbeck; in General C. C. Andrews State Forest at Willow River; in George Washington State Forest near Nashwauk at Bear Lake, Beatrice Lake, Larson Lake, Lost Lake, Owen Lake, and Thistledew Lake; Huntersville State Forest near Orr at Ash River, Gappa's Landing, King Williams Narrows, Mukooda Lake, Wakemup Bay, Woodenfrog; in Koochiching State Forest near Big Falls at Johnson Landing; in Land O' Lakes State Forest near Outing at Washburn Lake; in Paul Bunyan State Forest near Lake George at Bass Lake, Gulch Lakes, and Mantrap Lake; in Pillsbury State Forest, near Pillager at Rock Lake; in Pine Island State Forest near Big Falls, at Ben Linn Landing and Sturgeon River Landing; in Red Lake State Forest at Waskish; in Sand Dunes State Forest near Elk River at Ann Lake; in Savanna State Forest near Jacobson at Hay Lake; in Two Inlets State Forest near Park Rapids at Hungry Man Lake; and at several dozen other locations.

SUPERIOR NATIONAL FOREST offers outstanding campsites in several dozen places. Some are accessible only by canoe or trail.

Backpacking & Trail Riding

KEKEKABIC TRAIL. The Kekekabic Trail starts a half mile beyond the Tuscarora side road on the Gunflint Trail and leads to the Paulson Mine trail. This cross-country foot trail visits Gunflint and Kekekabic Lookout towers and skirts lakes such as Honker, Thomas, Disappointment, Parent, Snowbank, and Lake One. A hiker should check with the ranger station on the condition of the trail before he starts. Old logging roads in the Arrowhead country offer other possibilities for backpacking.

MINNESOTA VALLEY TRAIL from Fort Snelling south to Le Sueur is not completed, but backpackers are already following its 70-mile route. Trail riders also are pioneering it. The trail system consists of a series of state parks, waysides, and rights-of-way stretching along the Minnesota River.

Hiking

ARROWHEAD COUNTRY near Grand Marais. Hikers follow old logging road trails. From near Croftville, trails lead to Devil Track Canyon and Pincushion Mountain. From near Hovland hikers also follow a trail along the Arrowhead River that runs to the mysterious Devils Kettle.

BAPTISM RIVER STATE PARK, 4½ miles above Silver Bay on the north shore of Lake Superior. A trail leads inland for 1½ miles to the falls. Another leads to the river's mouth.

CARIBOU FALLS STATE PARK, on the north shore of Lake Superior, 11 miles north of Minnesota 1. One of the state's most beautiful trails leads about a mile upstream to the falls.

CASCADE RIVER STATE PARK, 10 miles southwest of Grand Marais on the north shore of Lake Superior. A popular trail traces the Cascade River through narrow chasms.

GRAND PORTAGE NATIONAL MONUMENT. The historic Grand Portage trail is much the same today as it was in voyageur days, and hikers clamber over its lichen-covered rocks, observe its hidden springs with their black waters, and catch an occasional glimpse of a moose. The scenic, 9-mile portage trail leads from the rebuilt stockade across the Canadian border.

GUNFLINT TRAIL is a motor road that leads into the wilds from Grand Marais. Hiking trails lead from the road. The Caribou Rock Hiking Trail takes the Hungry Jack Lake road to a high point overlooking lake and forest. The Magnetic Rock Trail leaves the highway between Tuscarora Junction and Sea Gull Lake and takes a hiker to a 40-foot slab of rock left standing upright by the glaciers. The Northern Light Lake Trail runs 12 miles to Mount Baldy. The Stairway Portage is a trail to beautiful Rose Lake and a waterfall on the Canadian border, and South Lake Hiking Trail runs past three lakes, beginning with Poplar Lake, and is 4 miles long.

ITASCA STATE PARK at the headwaters of the mighty Mississippi. Trails lead through the splendid woods.

JAY COOKE STATE PARK. A foot trail begins at park headquarters and crosses the rushing torrent of the St. Louis River on a swinging bridge.

KODONCE RIVER STATE PARK, on the north shore of Lake Superior, 11 miles east of Grand Marais, has trails leading through the rocky gorge to the waterfalls on the river.

PILLSBURY STATE FOREST, near Pillager. The Pillsbury Riding and Hiking Trail appeals to both hikers and riders.

SCENIC STATE PARK, 6 miles east of Bigfork, has timber trails.

SPLIT ROCK STATE SCENIC WAYSIDE, on the north shore of Lake Superior. The Days Hill Trail begins at the parking lot and climbs to the bald rock dome far above the lake. From the top there is a panoramic view of the famed Split Rock Lighthouse.

Rockhounding

CUYUNA IRON RANGE localities near Ironton produce Binghamite, usually red or yellow and of gem quality. Silkstone is commonly found with Binghamite and can range from yellow to brown to gray-blue or green or a combination of these colors.

COLD-WATER AGATE finds are made along the dry washes of the Zumbro River near Mazeppa. The stones develop in weathered limestone cavities.

FIVE MILE ROCK, east of Grand Marais, is the site of a hillside near Minnesota 61 where rockhounds find thunder egg agates. The agates are hard rock nodules with center portions of red and white banded agate.

GOOD HARBOR BAY and some other localities of the Lake Superior north shore produce prehnite, a pale green silicate found as waterworn pebbles, sometimes flecked with native copper.

GRAND MARAIS BEACH on the Lake Superior north shore produces basanite, a dense, velvet black variety of jaspery quartz. It is found as waterworn pebbles and resembles basalt except for its greater hardness.

GUNFLINT TRAIL near Grand Marais. Amethyst, ranging in color from lavender to purple, has been collected from veins and rock crevices along the trail.

HOPKINS MINE, at Crosby-Ironton, is a place to look for rhodochrosite. The scarce rose red variety may be found in mined veins.

MARY ELLEN MINE, near Biwabik, is a source of Mary Ellen jasper, which is red or pink with red or white swirls. Other jasper is found in glacial drifts. A common variety is flecked or freckled deep red to purple.

MONROE-TENER MINE, near Chisholm, has ramsdellite, radiating clusters of shiny black crystals in a dull gray matrix. The crystals are rare.

NATIVE COPPER, light rose in color, has been found in mines near Pine City.

PARADISE BEACH AGATE is found in the basalt along the north shore of Lake Superior about 13 miles northeast of Grand Marais. The stones are small, well-formed, and generally red-orange with very pronounced white bands.

PORTSMOUTH MINE DUMP, at Ironton, is an ideal place to look for cubes of pyrite, the "fool's gold" of legend.

ROBERTS MINE DUMP, north of the village of Cuyuna, is a good place to look for manganite. This mineral occurs in prismatic-crystal groups, which may be striated.

SAGAMORE PIT, on the Cuyuna Iron Range, produces groutite, wedge-shaped crystals in manganese ores. The crystals have a high luster.

STAUROLITE, an iron silicate best recognized as twinned crystals formed in metamorphic rocks, is found near Royalton. Cruciform twins or X-shaped twins are common, and Minnesotans call them fairy crosses.

TOFTE BEACHES, near Tofte on the Lake Superior north shore, are a prime source for thomsonite. The beaches are in private hands, and a fee is usually charged. Lintonite is often found with thomsonite. It resembles a green or gray-green jelly bean in size and shape.

Canoeing

BIG FORK RIVER CANOE TRAIL, in the Chippewa National Forest, begins at Bowstring Lake near the Indian village of Inger. Canoeists follow the route for 220 miles to its outlet at the Rainy River near International Falls. There are campsites along the trail.

BOUNDARY WATERS CANOE AREA has names like Ogishkemuncie, Gabimichigami, and Saganaga lakes and has 14,000 square miles of wilderness canoeing. Jump-off places at Ely, Grand Marais, and Crane Lake have outfitters. The canoe trails follow the routes of the voyageurs and offer some of the world's most exciting wilderness water adventure. The canoe area includes the northern third of the Superior National Forest, extending for some 200 miles along the Canadian border. The wilderness areas are reserved for canoeists, but it is possible to drive as far as the canoe area by forest roads. Note: In this area a canoe camper's wilderness skills are well tested. A camper must remember that hungry bears covet his supplies, that mosquitoes can be bothersome, and that he must have good maps. There are scores of canoe routes to choose from. Maps can be obtained from the U.S. Forestry Office in Duluth, the Tourist Division of the Minnesota Department of Economic Development, St. Paul, and the U.S. Department of Agriculture, Washington, D.C. The maps show sites of historic interest, campsites, and natural features. Canoe routes are defined. The waters of the area are noted for their purity. A canoeist entering the area must obtain a free travel permit in person from any Superior National Forest office or from most outfitters and resorts located adjacent to the Boundary Waters Canoe Area. Nonburnable, disposable food and beverage containers are not permitted. All empty containers and other refuse that cannot be burned must be packed out. Parties must be limited to no more than 15 people to reduce the impact on the soil. If a canoeist is crossing into the equally fascinating Canadian waters just across the border, he must check with Canadian officials. A visit to the Voyageur Visitor Center at Ely would make a trip into the wilderness a more meaningful experience.

ST. CROIX STATE PARK, Minnesota's largest state park, offers exceptional canoeing on the St. Croix River's channels and inlets with both fast and slow water.

Boating

HIAWATHA VALLEY. Houseboats may be rented at Mississippi River towns such as Wabasha for pleasurable boating weekends or weeks on the upper Mississippi and Lake Pepin. The river's oxbow lakes, side channels, meanders, sloughs, and swamps make a watery maze for a boater to explore.

LAKE SUPERIOR NORTH SHORE is a popular boating region with ports and marinas along the coast from Duluth on north.

RAINY LAKE. This enormous border lake is one of the houseboating paradises in North America. Houseboaters tie up in remote coves and islands to fish and swim or ramble along the shore. There are rentals near International Falls on Rainy Lake and on the Ash River.

Sport Diving

LAKE SUPERIOR NORTH SHORE. Divers favor the clear waters of the lake.

MINNESOTA LAKES. Minnesota divers have been descending in some of the state's 13,000 lakes. The best time to dive, according to William Matthies, Brainerd diving veteran, is in the spring, when underwater visibility averages 30 to 35 feet. Algae building in the summer cuts visibility.

Conservation & Wildlife

BEAR PIT, near Tofte, is a likely place to see bears during afternoons and evenings as they come to feed.

INTERSTATE STATE PARK on the St. Croix River preserves the beautiful dells of the St. Croix, where perpendicular walls rise as high as 200 feet above the narrow river channel. The Glacial Gardens is a fantastic area of potholes created by the swirling waters of the Ice Age river.

ITASCA STATE PARK contains thousands of acres of virgin Norway pine, as well as the headwaters of the Mississippi.

UPPER MISSISSIPPI REFUGE, near Winona, shelters up to 252 species of birds. The refuge bottomlands harbor myriads of marsh and water birds, such as herons, egrets, bitterns, and rails. The bald eagle can be found below the dams or near the mouths of tributaries where crippled waterfowl and fish make good feeding. Muskrat, mink, beaver, otter, raccoon, skunk, weasel, and fox also live in the refuge. There are gray and fox squirrels, cottontails, and whitetailed deer. Visitors may boat into the area and may camp on refuge islands in the river for short stays.

MISSOURI

Camping

BIG OAK TREE STATE PARK, 10 miles southeast of East Prairie, provides camping close to tall oaks.

DANIEL BOONE NATIONAL FOREST. Little Scotia Pond, southeast of Salem, is situated on the site of an old mining town. Other campgrounds in the forest are at Berryman Camp, Brazil Creek, Edward Beecher and Harmon Springs near Berryman, and at Davisville. Lane Spring is near Rolla, and Loggers Lake is close to Bunker. Marble Creek west of Ironton, Markham Spring near Williamsville, Mill Creek southwest of Newburg, Paddy Creek close to Roby, Silver Mines west of Fredericktown, and Sutton Bluff northeast of Centerville are other camping areas. All are small except Davisville, Silver Mines, and Markham Spring.

CORPS OF ENGINEERS LAKES. There are campgrounds on Bull Shoals Lake, Clear-

Lake of the Ozarks, Missouri

water Lake, Norfolk Lake, Stockton Lake, Table Rock Lake, Pomme de Terre Lake, and Lake Wappapello.

CROWDER STATE PARK, 2 miles west of Trenton, provides camping complete with electric hookups and showers.

CUIVRE RIVER STATE PARK, 5 miles northeast of Troy, has camping areas. Four group camps serving nonprofit youth groups are also available.

DANIEL BOONE MEMORIAL FOREST, near Warrenton, has wilderness camping.

DR. EDMUND A. BABLER MEMORIAL STATE PARK, 20 miles west of St. Louis, offers camping.

JOHNSON'S SHUT-INS STATE PARK, 8 miles north of Lesterville, has campgrounds close to the east fork of the Black River.

LAKE OF THE OZARKS STATE PARK, near Osage Beach, has a fine campground. There are also six camps for youth groups.

LAKE WAPPAPELLO, 12 miles north of Poplar Bluff, has excellent camping on the shore.

LEWIS AND CLARK STATE PARK, 20 miles southwest of St. Joseph. Family campers pitch their tents where explorers Lewis and Clark made an overnight stop on their famous expedition.

MARK TWAIN NATIONAL FOREST has fine camping grounds at Big Bay, near Shell Knob; Buffalo Creek, west of Doniphan; Cedar Creek, south of Grandin; Compton, northeast of Briar; Deer Leap and Float Camp, near Doniphan; Gateway, at Winona; Greer Crossing, northeast of Alton; Hawes Memorial, southwest of Van Buren; McCormack Lake, south of Winona; and Shell Knob, at Shell Knob. Sugar Hill and Sycamore are near Willow Springs, and Water Cress Spring is near Van Buren.

MARK TWAIN STATE PARK has several campgrounds, including one for nonprofit youth groups, near the shrine commemorating Mark Twain's birthplace.

MONTAUK STATE PARK, 21 miles southwest of Salem, at the headwaters of the Current River, has a campground near a spring that produces 40 million gallons of water a day.

OZARK NATIONAL SCENIC RIVERWAYS. Campgrounds are on Alley Spring, at Alley Spring; at Big Spring, at Van Buren; and at Owls Bend, Pulltite Spring, and Round Spring, at Round Spring.

ROARING RIVER STATE PARK, 7 miles south of Cassville, offers camping close to the huge spring which is the headwaters of the Roaring River.

TABLE ROCK STATE PARK, 5 miles southwest of Branson, offers camping.

THOUSAND HILLS STATE PARK, near Kirksville, has fine camping areas.

VAN METER STATE PARK, 12 miles northwest of Marshall, has camping close to an important archeological site.

WASHINGTON STATE PARK, 14 miles northeast of Potosi, has camping areas with modern rest rooms and showers. The park contains a concentration of hundreds of petroglyphs.

Backpacking & Trail Riding

MARK TWAIN NATIONAL FOREST. The Berryman horse and hiking trail loops through the Potosi Ranger District. Start at Berryman Camp, 17 miles west of Potosi via Route 8 and one mile north on Forest Road 2206. Big Piney Trail winds through 17 miles of the Paddy Creek area. Start one mile north of Roby on Route 17.

Hiking

BOONE'S LICK STATE PARK, northwest of Columbia. A trail takes hikers past the spring where Daniel Boone's sons, Daniel M. and Nathan, made salt in the early 19th century.

MONTAUK STATE PARK, 21 miles southwest of Salem, is noted for its trails.

OZARK MOUNTAINS. Trails wind through the high country and around the shores of the Lake of the Ozarks. Trails lead through the woods to the Current River and the Jacks Fork in the Ozark National Scenic Riverway system.

THOUSAND HILLS STATE PARK, near Kirksville, has hiking trails.

Canoeing & Rafting

OZARK NATIONAL SCENIC RIVERWAYS. The Current and Jacks Fork rivers provide 140 miles of rushing waters that are ideal for float trips. There are campgrounds at Montauk State Park at the north end of the riverways, and there are private camps along the rivers. Camping is permitted only in designated areas or on gravel bars. In difficult places, where the water is shallow, floaters get out and walk their canoes or johnboats through. There are canoe outfitters along the way. Other Ozark float waterways are the Big Piney, Roubidoux Creek, Bryant Creek, North Fork, Eleven Point, Black, White, Osage, Flat Creek, James, Niangua, Meramec, Huzzah, Gasconade, and Courtoi Creek. Poling a johnboat downstream can be one of the most relaxing of all outdoor vacations.

Boating

LAND OF LAKES. Boaters flourish on the man-made Ozark lakes. The Lake of the Ozarks, Table Rock Lake, and Bull Shoals Lake are ideal for boats. Wappapello and Clearwater lakes are equally popular with boaters, who seek out the lakes' lonely coves for secluded vacations. The Lake of the Ozarks, 40 miles southwest of Jefferson City, is one of the best-known boating lakes in the Midwest.

Sport Diving

TABLE ROCK LAKE's clear waters make it popular with diving enthusiasts.

Conservation & Wildlife

BIG OAK TREE STATE PARK, 10 miles southeast of East Prairie, has the state's largest pin oaks. The largest tree stands 127 feet tall.

BIG SPRING STATE PARK, west of Poplar Bluff, has the largest single-outlet spring in the United States. From it flows 846 million gallons of water daily.

DANIEL BOONE MEMORIAL FOREST, near Warrenton, remembers the celebrated wilderness scout by preserving wild turkey, quail, foxes, squirrels, deer, and raccoons.

ELEPHANT ROCKS STATE PARK, north of Graniteville, possesses outstanding granite formations. The huge granite boulders resembling elephants are as big as 27 feet tall, 35 feet long, and 17 feet wide. They are believed to be about 1.2 million years old, and the largest weighs 680 tons.

OSAGE RIVER, in the Ozarks, is the spawning grounds of the rare paddlefish, which can weigh up to 160 pounds and has existed virtually unchanged since prehistoric times. The fish has a long

Chadron State Park, Nebraska

snout with sensitive sense organs used in feeding on plankton.

OZARK NATIONAL SCENIC RIVERWAYS is home to a variety of wildlife. The Ozark flora is dominated by oak-hickory and oak-pine, and there are also trees and shrubs noted for their flowers and fruit. Wild animals in these uplands include deer, wild turkey, gray and fox squirrels, raccoons, opossum, and skunk. There are bobcats.

TRIMBLE WILDLIFE AREA, near Trimble, is outstanding. Other wildlife areas worth visiting are Brickyard Hill, near Watson; Lake Paho, near Princeton; Honey Creek, near Savannah; Fountain Grove, near Meadville; and Pony Express, near Maysville.

NEBRASKA

Camping

CHADRON STATE PARK, south of Chadron. There is a group camp as well as an area for tent and trailer camping.

HARLAN COUNTY RESERVOIR, near Republican City, has camping facilities.

NEBRASKA NATIONAL FOREST also has campsites.

NEBRASKA STATE RECREATION AREAS. Camping is permitted in most of these areas as well as at a few state wayside areas and at Special-Use areas.

NIOBRARA STATE PARK, Niobrara, contains a camping area.

PONCA STATE PARK, near Ponca. Camping grounds for tents and trailers are available.

Trail Riding

CHADRON STATE PARK, Chadron. Horses are available for trail rides.

MAYWOOD TRAIL RIDE, Maywood. On the last Sunday in April, 1,400 horseback riders gather in Maywood to canter across the plains on this annual trail ride.

Hiking

FORT ROBINSON STATE PARK, near Crawford. A trail leads from the historic fort where Crazy Horse was stabbed to death, to the site of the Red Cloud Agency.

SCOTTS BLUFF NATIONAL MONUMENT. Hikers can follow a portion of the Oregon Trail's original ruts.

Rockhounding

AGATE FOSSIL BED NATIONAL MONUMENT, near Gering, preserves an extraordinary geological area.

AGATES are found in the sandpits in the areas around Fairbury and Steele City. The bright-colored rocks take a nice polish. Petrified wood and moss agate are also found in this area. Jasper can be found in sandpits near Fairbury.

FAIRBURN AGATES are found in Lame Johnny Creek and in the Red Canyon area in northwestern Nebraska.

FORT ROBINSON STATE PARK, near Crawford. Rockhounds look for agates. A lapidary display is in the museum.

FOSSILS are found at Weeping Water in a quarry close to town.

GAGE COUNTY ROAD DEPARTMENT ROCK QUARRY, at Wymore, is a good place to look for geodes, some with blue calcite crystals.

LITTLE BAD LANDS, 20 miles north of Crawford, are the sources of iris agate. Fairburn agate is also found.

PETRIFIED WOOD. Orella vicinity is a good place to look for the colorful samples brought down by the glaciers.

PLATTE RIVER SANDPITS, on both sides of the river near Ashland, are good places to look for agates, petrified wood, and jasper. The pits are private property, so be thoughtful.

QUARTZ-LINED GEODES may be found 5 miles south of Blue Springs on the east bank of the Blue River. White Geodes come from a quarry southwest of Homesville on the west side of the Blue River.

Canoeing

BIG BLUE RIVER. Between Seward and Crete, the river is somnolent and lazy, but at Crete, the stream takes on more life and is worthy of a canoeist's interest. A popular trip is from Hoag Bridge north of Beatrice to Riverside Park in Beatrice.

CALAMUS RIVER is a sedate Sand Hills stream. From Nebraska, about 20 miles south of Ainsworth, to Burwell is a 48-mile trip. There are no portages, and excellent campsites are available with landowners' permission.

DISMAL RIVER is navigable for a 50-mile stretch between Nebraska 97, about 12 miles south of Mullen, to Dunning. There is some fast water near the Hooker-Thomas county line. Portages are not necessary. The stream has a sand and shale bottom. Camping sites are easy to find along the river.

ELKHORN RIVER is a good stream for a four- to five-day trip from West Point to Two Rivers Recreation Area on the Platte River. Canoeing is at its best in the spring when the water is deep.

MISSOURI RIVER between Gavins Point Dam and Ponca offers a 60-mile stretch of river unchanged from voyageur days.

THE MIDWEST

There is fine camping at Gavins Point Dam and Ponca State Park, but overnight camping on the white sand dunes and sandbars along the river is a pleasure. Side trips up tributary streams are also possible.

NIOBRARA RIVER. There are two canoe trips on the historic waters; one is a three-day trip of 34 miles and the other a four-day trip of 56 miles. There is one portage around the Public Power Dam east of Valentine, which divides the two trips. Canoeists have to avoid sandbars, shale areas, and boulders, but the canoeing is easy. Section one begins at Nebraska 97, south of Nenzel, and ends at the dam. Section two starts at the dam and runs to US 183, northwest of Bassett. Permission to camp on private lands should be obtained in advance of the trip.

NORTH PLATTE RIVER offers a variety of canoe trips. From Hershey to Cody Park in North Platte is a short trip among islands and conflicting channels.

PLATTE RIVER is a fine canoeing stream with a sandy bottom. Because of the diversion of water for irrigation purposes, the stream east of Columbus is not a practical one during the summer. For 100 miles from Columbus to the Missouri River is a good canoe trip with camping on sandbars or at state campgrounds.

REPUBLICAN RIVER has sandy banks and bottom. A 70-mile trip begins at McCook and runs to the Harlan County Reservoir.

Boating

NEBRASKA'S LAKES. Boaters explore the man-made lakes of Nebraska, which include Harlan County Reservoir, Lake McConaughy, and Lewis and Clark Lake. The boaters look for hidden coves and places to fish.

Conservation & Wildlife

DESOTO NATIONAL WILDLIFE REFUGE, near Blair, protects migratory wildfowl.

FORT NIOBRARA NATIONAL WILDLIFE REFUGE, near Valentine, shelters a herd of shaggy buffalo as well as a herd of longhorns, the cattle that once roamed the range.

WILDCAT HILLS STATE RECREATION AREA AND GAME REFUGE, near Gering, shelters a herd of buffalo as well as deer and elk.

NORTH DAKOTA

Camping

BEAVER LAKE STATE PARK, 3 miles north of Burnstad, offers fine camping.

BUTTE VIEW CAMPGROUND, 2 miles east of Bowman, is quite new.

FORT BERTHOLD INDIAN RESERVATION, west of Garrison, has camping at the Four Bears Park.

FORT LINCOLN STATE PARK, 4 miles south of Mandan. There is camping close to the fort from which Custer set out on the Black Hills Expedition of 1874.

LAKE METIGOSHE STATE PARK, northeast of Bottineau, offers camping in a developed campground, as well as primitive camping.

LAKE SAKAKAWEA STATE PARK, 1 mile north of Pick City, has both modern and primitive camping.

LITTLE MISSOURI BAY STATE PARK, 18 miles north of Killdeer, has camping in rough backcountry.

THEODORE ROOSEVELT NATIONAL MEMORIAL PARK campgrounds are at Squaw Creek and Cottonwood.

TURTLE RIVER STATE PARK, 22 miles west of Grand Forks, has both modern and primitive camping.

Trail Riding

LITTLE MISSOURI BAY STATE PARK. Guided trail rides head into the Little Missouri badlands near Killdeer. Contact Thorris Sandvick at his ranch north of Killdeer for horses and guide service.

LITTLE MISSOURI TRAIL RIDES, Rhame. Two- to four-day rides into scenic badlands operate throughout the summer. Contact Bill Coutts, Rhame.

SULLY'S CREEK STATE PARK, 2½ miles south of Medora, is an ideal place for riders. There is a primitive campground and a horse corral.

THEODORE ROOSEVELT NATIONAL MEMORIAL PARK. Where the "Rough Rider" president rode, vacationers now ride out from Valley Ranch in the South Unit.

TURTLE RIVER STATE PARK, near Arvilla, offers trail rides.

Hiking

LAKE METIGOSHE STATE PARK, northeast of Bottineau, has 8 miles of hiking trails.

THEODORE ROOSEVELT NATIONAL MEMORIAL PARK has hiking trails. These include the Squaw Creek Trail, Caprock Coulee Trail, Jones Creek Trail, and the 12-mile Petrified Forest Trail.

Rockhounding

CENTRAL DRIFT PRAIRIES are covered with boulders of all sizes and shapes carried down to this area by continental glaciers from the Hudson Bay region.

LIGNITE OPEN COAL MINES, Beulah. Vacationers watch lignite being open-pit mined.

NORTH DAKOTA BADLANDS. Near Sentinel Butte, the fossilized bones of the three-horned dinosaur, triceratops, and extinct rhinoceroses, camels, and turtles can be found.

THEODORE ROOSEVELT NATIONAL MEMORIAL PARK contains petrified wood. The beautiful silicified trunks of ancient cedar, redwood, and sequoia may be photographed, but pieces of petrified wood must not be collected.

Boating

LAKE SAKAKAWEA, backed up by Garrison Dam near Riverdale to Williston. There is boating. Boats may be launched at the Four Bears Park on the Fort Berthold Indian Reservation.

Conservation & Wildlife

J. CLARK SALYER II NATIONAL WILDLIFE REFUGE protects thousands of migrating waterfowl during the spring and fall months. It is located northwest of Tower.

ICELANDIC STATE PARK, 4 miles west of Cavalier, has a 3½-mile self-guided trail through the Gunlogson Arboretum.

OHIO

Camping

MUSKINGUM WATERSHED CONSERVANCY DISTRICT, in the area around

New Philadelphia, provides extraordinary camping. There are over 3,000 camping sites on the lakes.

OHIO STATE PARKS. All 47 of the Ohio state parks that allow camping welcome campers both winter and summer. There are Class A sites, which have approved water under pressure, drinking fountains, wastewater drains, flush toilets, laundry and shower facilities, numbered lots, picnic tables, and fire rings or outdoor grills. The Class B sites have approved well or hydrant water, vault-type latrines, wastewater drains, either marked or unmarked lots, picnic tables, and fire ring or outdoor grills. Primitive types have only pit-type latrines and waste containers. There is no charge for primitive sites. Hueston Woods State Park, 5 miles from Oxford, is a good example of this progressive state's campgrounds. Campsites are near Acton Lake. There are also camping areas in a nearby wooded hollow. Tar Hollow State Park, 22 miles southeast of Circleville, has walk-in primitive sites.

Backpacking & Trail Riding

BUCKEYE TRAIL offers 600 miles of backpacking, through a wide variety of Ohio scenes. The trail crosses reclaimed strip-mined lands, passes lakes, wildlife refuges, and follows canal towpaths and old Indian routes, country roads and, if necessary, highways. There are still not enough camping places along the trail, but the Buckeye Trail Association is continuing to open up more. In state parks, forests, and wildlife areas, backpackers are permitted to camp only in designated primitive campsites. Section A of the trail is from Cincinnati to Toledo. The trail continues on across the state to its terminus in Lake County at Headlands Beach State Park, northeast of Cleveland. Maps and guidebooks may be obtained from the Buckeye Trail Association, P.O. Box 254, Worthington, Ohio 43085.

STATE FOREST BRIDLE TRAILS include: Blue Rock, 14 miles southeast of Zanesville; Fernwood, at Bloomingdale; Dean, 15 miles north of Ironton; Hocking, near Conkles Hollow Park, southwest of Logan; Maumee, 13 miles west of Toledo; Mohican, 4 miles southwest of Loudonville; Pike, 6 miles south of Bainbridge; Scioto Trail, between Chillicothe and Waverly; Shade River, at Reedsville; Tar Hollow, 22 miles southeast of Circleville; Zaleski, in Zaleski. There are campgrounds especially for horsemen at Beaver Creek State Park, 8 miles northwest of East Liverpool; Hueston Woods State Park, near Oxford; Lake Hope State Park,

148 THE MIDWEST

northeast of Zaleski; Tar Hollow State Park, 22 miles southeast of Circleville and a 15-minute ride from the cross-state Buckeye Trail. The Shawnee State Forest, west of Portsmouth on the Ohio River, has a 43-mile main loop with side trails that are worth exploring.

ZALESKI STATE FOREST. A 22-mile overnight trail runs through parts of Vinton and Athens counties.

WAYNE NATIONAL FOREST. The Lake Vesuvius Trail has been extended to 30 miles.

Hiking

GLEN HELEN, Yellow Springs, is a forest preserve with good trails.

HOCKING HILLS, near Logan, appeal to adventurous hikers who enjoy exploring the cave country.

NELSON-KENNEDY LEDGES are located near Garrettsville. There are interesting geological formations to visit here. Hiking is rough.

PAINT CREEK VALLEY, around Bainbridge, has rugged terrain for hikers.

TAR HOLLOW STATE PARK AND FOREST contains the excellent 16-mile loop Chief Logan Trail as well as a section of the Buckeye Trail.

ZALESKI STATE FOREST. There is a 10-mile day trail that winds through the forest.

Biking

AMISH BIKEWAY begins at Punderson State Park and runs through Geauga County.

COVERED BRIDGE BIKEWAY rambles from Rising Park in Lancaster through an area that is famous for its 19th century bridges.

LITTLE MIAMI RIVER SCENIC BIKEWAY follows the river valley from Yellow Springs to Cincinnati.

MILAN CANAL BIKEWAY is a 27-mile trip between Milan and Huron.

OLD MILL BIKEWAY starts near Yellow Springs at John Bryan State Park and passes the 1869 Clifton Mill.

TOP OF OHIO BIKEWAY begins in Bellefontaine.

Rockhounding

FLINT RIDGE is on Licking County 668 north of Brownsville, halfway between Newark and Zanesville. Flint collecting is permitted in the vicinity, but not within the park itself.

HUESTON WOODS STATE PARK. College Corner has such an abundance of Ordovician fossils that collectors may take them for personal collections. No commercial collecting is allowed.

Canoeing

CUYAHOGA RIVER canoe trips begin at Ohio 168 south of Burton. The rapids near Hiram are the first obstacle. A portage is necessary if the water is too rough. Canoeists must leave the river where Ohio 303 bridges the stream and put in at the first bridge below Lake Rockwell, which is the city of Akron water supply. No boating is permitted in this stretch. A dam at Munroe Falls requires another portage. Canoeists leave the river again at Cuyahoga Falls Water Works Park. The falls, a dam, and the gorge make canoeing impossible.

MAUMEE RIVER. Put-in point on the Maumee River is at Pontiac Park on Route 424 in Defiance. At Independence Dam and State Park, a canoeist can inspect the restored Miami and Erie Canal lock and dam. Old Canal bypasses the dam and then reenters the river one mile below Florida. Beware of logs and of the dam at the end of the canal. There are camping grounds some 20 miles east of Napoleon at Providence Park on the north shore of Grand Rapids Dam. By taking the canal around the south side of the dam, canoeists bypass the rapids. Four miles downstream are the Ostego Rapids. Take the south bank around the rapids, continue paddling for 2 miles to more rapids, and then leave the river at Missionary Island.

MIAMI RIVER. There are almost 140 miles of streams available to the canoeist beginning at a point a few miles below Indian Lake. The put-in place is at Ohio 274. There are access sites every few miles all the way down the river. The last possible takeout place is at the Corps of Engineers site 3½ miles short of the Ohio River. There are dams to be considered but no dangerous rapids. Supplies are available at towns along the way.

MOHICAN RIVER, around Loudonville, is one of Ohio's favorite canoeing streams. There are canoe liveries in the area. Launchings may be made on the Clear Fork Branch at Hemlock Grove Camp in the Mohican State Forest. Year-round camping is allowed in the tree-shaded ravine. Downstream 3.7 miles from the put-in place, the Clear Fork joins the Black Fork to form the Mohican River.

MUSKINGUM WATERSHED CONSERVANCY DISTRICT, near New Philadelphia, offers excellent canoe waters on its man-made lakes.

Boating

LAKE ERIE. Boaters put out on the waters of this great lake.

MUSKINGUM WATERSHED CONSERVANCY DISTRICT. There is a marina on each of the 10 lakes.

OHIO RIVER. Houseboat the river from Cincinnati. The Ohio is equally popular with other boaters.

Sport Diving

OHIO STATE PARKS permit scuba and skin diving in 28 parks. Acton Lake in Hueston Woods, Tar Hollow at Laurelville, and Stonelick at Edenton are worth considering.

Conservation & Wildlife

CEDAR SWAMPS STATE MEMORIAL, south of Urbana, is administered by the Ohio Historical Society's Division of Natural History. Admission to the swamps is by appointment only because of the need to protect the delicate balance of life. Rare and unusual plants live in the swamps, which were formed as the last glacier melted away to the north.

HUESTON WOODS STATE PARK, 5 miles from Oxford, contains virgin beech-maple woods.

MALABAR FARM, near Lucas, is the ecological triumph of the late Ohio author, Louis Bromfield. A visit to Malabar Farm gives a vacationer insight into methods of conservation. Farm wagons take visitors on tours of the farm. Guests also hike the Malabar Nature Trails and enjoy the beauty of Doris Duke Woods.

RECLAIMED STRIP LANDS. The Hanna Coal Company has created Sallie Buffalo Park, a half mile south of Cadiz on stripped lands. Four lakes and campsites are provided to the public without charge. Four miles north of Cadiz is the Harrison State Forest, which was created by the Ohio Division of Forestry and Reclamation. There are campsites there too. Six miles east of Cadiz is the Fernwood State Forest. This land, also owned by the Ohio Division of Parks and Recreation, provides campsites and hiking and riding trails. Several other notable examples of strip mines that were once eyesores but that have been transformed into verdant parks and forests are: Friendship Park, 12 miles east of Cadiz, and Sugar Creek Community Park in Sugar Creek. The Muskingum Valley Scout Reservation, 3 miles southeast of Coshocton, is the happy result of conservation collaboration between the Peabody Coal Company and the Scouts. Still another notable conservation project has been carried out by the Ohio Power Company and the Ohio Division of Wildlife in the Ohio Power Recreation Area southeast of Zanesville. The process of land reclamation is an encouraging one.

SOUTH DAKOTA

Camping

BADLANDS NATIONAL MONUMENT maintains two camping areas, with 140 campsites at Cedar Pass and 6 sites at Sage Creek.

BLACK HILLS NATIONAL FOREST, in the Black Hills, has 30 camping areas, with about 700 sites. "We are staying away from the one-night 'motel' camps and are concentrating on destination camps in the Hills," explains Charlie Hathaway, spokesman for the forest. The forest camps preserve the forest setting and do not provide sewer, water, or electric hookups for campers. The Forest Service does provide vault toilets, drinking water, and fire grates.

CUSTER STATE PARK, in the Black Hills, near Custer, has campsites with modern facilities throughout the park. They are small enough to give each family privacy. There are 10 major campgrounds. Camps are located at Game Lodge Resort, at Sylvan Lake Resort beside Sylvan Lake, at Stockade Lake Resort beneath the ponderosa pine, and near Blue Bell.

MISSOURI RIVER'S GREAT LAKES. There are 1,200 campsites along the lakes, maintained by the Corps of Engineers. There are commodious campgrounds at Big Bend Dam's Lake Sharpe and three campgrounds at Lake Oahe. The State Game, Fish, and Parks Department maintains 346 campsites at eight recreational areas along the Missouri. Only Chamberlain, Yankton, and Fort Randall Dam campgrounds are sometimes congested.

WIND CAVE NATIONAL PARK has the 100-unit Elk Mountain campground near park headquarters. The park does not permit overflow camping.

Backpacking & Trail Riding

BLACK HILLS TRAIL RIDE, six days in the saddle over mountains, through canyons,

Badlands National Monument, South Dakota

THE MIDWEST 149

along cliffs, and through gushing streams. Every year a couple of hundred people take the ride. They start at such places as Custer State Park and end up where the trail boss leads them.

CUSTER STATE PARK. Backpackers challenge the French Creek Gorge Wilderness Area. They hike downstream among the granite boulders from the land of yellow-bark pines to the domain of the scrub oak. The trek is only 12.1 miles, but the gorge is both wild and rough.

SAGE CREEK WILDERNESS BASIN in the Badlands has hiking trails through the 40,000-acre preserve.

SILVER ARROW TRAIL, mapped by the Boy Scouts, begins from Camp Old Broadaxe near Nemo and passes Pactola and Sheridan lakes. The trail then loops over Harney Peak to Mount Rushmore for a total of 55 miles.

Hiking

BADLANDS NATIONAL MONUMENT. The Door Trail near the eastern entrance to the monument leads to a notch in the Badlands wall, known locally as the "door." From the notch there is a panorama of the Badlands.

BEAR BUTTE TRAIL, Bear Butte State Park. A trail begins near Sturgis and leads to the summit of the butte. What begins as an amble up a switchback through jack pines ends as a scramble up loose talus slopes past Indian ceremonial rings.

CUSTER STATE PARK. The trail to Sunday Gulch begins near Sylvan Lake and leads into the Needles. A natural stone corridor followed by the trail is called Sunday Gulch. Another trail leads to the summit of Harney Peak, the highest mountain east of the Rockies. One path to the 7,242-foot level begins at Sylvan Lake while a second begins at Palmer Gulch.

HARTFORD BEACH STATE PARK on Big Stone Lake has three hiking trails developed by the State Game, Fish, and Parks Department. The Wilcox Lake loop passes an Indian ford and glacial moraine. The Aspen Hiking Trail leads to an abandoned fur trapper's dugout. The Observation Point and Military Trenches Hiking Trail runs to the site where a U.S. Cavalry expedition of 4,000 men and 225 mule-drawn wagons once camped.

PINE RIDGE RESERVATION. The Sioux Indians invite visitors to hike the trail through Crazy Horse Canyon.

PRESIDENTS TRAILS, all are 10 miles long and all converge on Mount Rushmore. Take your pick.

SIECHE HOLLOW STATE PARK, near Sisseton, has a favorite trail for weekend hikers. It leads through a hardwood hollow said to be haunted because of the moaning made by the creeks and the glowing swamp gas viewed at night. Hikers cross rustic bridges and view plants and herbs used by the Indians to make medicines.

Rockhounding

BADLANDS NATIONAL MONUMENT. Fossil Exhibit Trail, about halfway through the monument, reveals the fossilized bones of horses, tiny camels, and saber-toothed tigers lying exactly as they fell to the earth millions of years ago. There are marked trails, but no collecting is allowed in the monument.

BIG BADLANDS, from Kadoka to Wall, is one of the largest graveyards of animals that existed 20 to 30 million years ago. The area south of the Badlands National Monument between the towns of Interior and Scenic is also a prime collecting area for gemstones. Some of the stones found in western South Dakota gravels are: multicolored agates; blue, gray, and white chalcedony; red or orange carnelian; black and white onyx; red, yellow, and mottled jasper; brown, golden, pink, crimson, and white petrified wood; ivory or peach-colored agatized coral; apricot-colored moonstone feldspar; rose, smoky or milky quartz; and puddingstone. There are fossils along the Cheyenne River, golden barite crystals along Elk Creek, and rattle-rocks full of quartz crystals in the hills of Imlay.

GRANITE QUARRIES, near Milbank in the northeastern section of the state, yield beautiful rose and purple-colored stone.

GRAVEL PIT, near Wasta, is a prime place to look for gems and fossils.

INTERIOR. Off South Dakota 40 between the towns of Interior and Scenic (south of Badlands National Monument) are excellent rockhounding areas. Highway and railroad right-of-ways are good places to look. Among the semiprecious stones found in the area are multicolored agates; blue, gray, and white chalcedony; red or orange carnelian; black and white onyx; red, yellow, and mottled jasper; brown, golden, pink, and white petrified wood; peach-colored agatized coral; moonstone feldspar; smoky or milky quartz; and puddingstone.

MINE DUMPS. Rockhounds comb the old mine dumps in the Black Hills near Rapid City, Hill City, Rochford, Keystone, Pringle, Deerfield, Lead, and Deadwood. They pan for gold and turn up garnets, tourmaline, and beryl.

PLACER STREAMS, Black Hills. The tragic floods of June 1973 had one good effect: they scoured out the canyon streams so that gold seekers are finding placer gold in the gravels churned up by the raging waters. Some canyons were cut as much as eight feet deeper, revealing large pockets of crystals, fossils, and boxwork.

Canoeing

LITTLE WHITE RIVER, on the Sioux reservation, is a good place to canoe Indian-style. The Sioux welcome visitors.

MISSOURI RIVER. Two hundred Boy Scouts pioneered the new 53-mile Lewis and Clark Historical Canoe Trail. The 70 canoes stretched nearly a mile as they made their way from Pickstown to Springfield on a part of the river that is much as it was when Lewis and Clark came this way in 1804. Takeout point was at Sioux City. There was camping in a primitive area on the Curt Snodon Ranch, west of Niobrara on the Nebraska shore.

Boating

BLACK HILLS LAKES. Boat camping is popular on lakes Pactola, Sheridan, and Angostura. All three have marinas.

MISSOURI RIVER'S GREAT LAKES are ideal for boating and boat camping.

Sport Diving

MISSOURI RIVER'S GREAT LAKES offer possibilities for scuba divers.

Conservation & Wildlife

BADLANDS NATIONAL MONUMENT offers three nature walks. They are "touch-me" type walks so that a hiker can sift through his fingers the sands, from which so many significant finds have been made.

CUSTER STATE PARK. One of the world's largest buffalo herds roams the park's range. Sometimes motorists encounter the herd making its leisurely way across the highway. Jeep trips also take visitors to see the buffalo. Other wildlife in the park are deer, elk, antelope, turkeys, mountain goats, bighorn sheep, and the ubiquitous prairie dog, whose villages with their sentinels watching camera-clicking tourists are located on the meadows. The buffalo can be dangerous. Motorists are urged to stay in their cars when they are nearby, and nobody should ever come between a mother buffalo and her calf. Panhandling burros encountered by visitors along the roads are diverting citizens of the park.

WIND CAVE NATIONAL PARK also has a fine buffalo herd, pronghorn antelope, deer, and villages of prairie dogs.

WISCONSIN

Camping

AMERICAN LEGION STATE FOREST has both established campgrounds and campgrounds in the wilderness.

APOSTLE ISLANDS. There's wilderness camping on Stockton Island, which is included in the Apostle Islands State Forest. Campsites are at Presque Isle Point and Quarry Bay.

BIG BAY STATE PARK RECREATION AREA is on Madeline Island in Lake Superior, near Bayfield. There is camping. Car ferries operate to the island for eight months; the remainder of the year a motorist can drive across the ice from Bayfield and camp at no charge.

BIG FOOT BEACH STATE PARK on Lake Geneva has camping grounds near the water.

BRUNET ISLAND STATE PARK, 1 mile north of Cornell, has two campgrounds.

CHEQUAMEGON NATIONAL FOREST near Park Falls has excellent camping.

COPPER FALLS STATE PARK, northeast from Mellen, has fine campgrounds.

DEVILS LAKE STATE PARK. The family campgrounds are close to the lake and its beaches.

DOOR COUNTY. There is camping at three state parks: Peninsula State Park, between Fish Creek and Ephraim; Potawatomi State Park, just west of Sturgeon Bay; and Rock Island State Park, off the coast of Washington Island, accessible by boat only.

GOVERNOR DODGE STATE PARK, between Spring Green and Dodgeville, offers ample camping in the state's largest state park.

KETTLE MORAINE STATE FOREST, near Greenbush, has fine campsites at Mauthe and Long lakes and at Greenbush.

LAKE WISSOTA STATE PARK, 7 miles northeast of Chippewa Falls, has family campgrounds in a wooded area overlooking the lake. The campgrounds were planned with the privacy of each group in mind.

LUCIUS WOODS STATE PARK, Solon Springs. The campgrounds are close to the old voyageurs route through St. Croix Lake.

NICOLET NATIONAL FOREST has splendid campgrounds in a beautiful forest that was once a logged-over wasteland. The headquarters of the forest are at Rhinelander.

NORTHERN HIGHLAND STATE FOREST has family and wilderness campsites in its 130,000 acres.

PERROT STATE PARK, north of the village of Trempealeau. The campgrounds are in a woods.

POINT BEACH STATE FOREST, near Two Rivers, offers idyllic camping where summer heat is seldom felt.

RED CLIFF INDIAN RESERVATION, near Cornucopia. The Indians charge a fee to camp in a pleasant campground.

TERRY ANDRAE STATE PARK, near Sheboygan, has camping on the shores of Lake Michigan.

Backpacking & Trail Riding

CHEQUAMEGON NATIONAL FOREST. A well-marked foot path leads through the Rainbow Lake Wilderness Area.

ELROY-SPARTA TRAIL. This hiking and biking trail leads among wooded hills, streams, and farms, through several small towns, and plunges through tunnels. It follows the old Chicago and North Western Railroad line.

KETTLE MORAINE STATE FOREST, near Greenbush. The Glacial Trail leads through the up-and-down drumlins, eskers, kettles, and kames, and it is a good workout for a weekend. The trail meanders through a pine forest mixed with stands of oak, shagbark hickory, and ironwood and then climbs over steep hills and dips into deep kettles. Backpackers sleep overnight in shelters. The trail emerges from the forest at a point near Kewaskum. There is also a bridle trail and a campground especially for horsemen. The Horseman's Recreation Area in the southern unit of the forest is on County NN just south of Palmyra. There is a fenced corral, parking space for horse-hauling rigs. New Prospect Horseman's Campground is off County SS in the northern unit of the forest.

NICOLET NATIONAL FOREST offers trail riding along the Forest Service's roads.

OLD LOGGING TRAILS near St. Germain are suitable for hiking through the area. The trails crisscross the region.

PARK FALLS TO TUSCOBIA TRAIL runs along another abandoned right-of-way for 72 miles near Rice Lake. Unbridged creek and river crossings make this trail an adventure.

Hiking

AMERICAN LEGION STATE FOREST has two fine hiking trails.

COPPER FALLS STATE PARK, northeast of Mellen. A network of trails follows the Bad River Gorge. They lead to vistas as much as 150 feet above the river.

DEVILS LAKE STATE PARK. One of the Midwest's most scenic and challenging trails loops around the lake. It climbs high up the rocky cliffs, where mountaineers test their gear and skills.

INTERSTATE STATE PARK, near St. Croix Falls. There are eight marked trails. Some rim the river bluffs; others cut deep into the woods.

KETTLE MORAINE STATE FOREST. Day hikers follow the many trails or hike along a segment of the Glacial Trail.

LIZARD MOUND STATE PARK, northeast of West Bend, has a trail through the mound area.

MISSISSIPPI BLUFFS. Hikers explore the bluffs bordering the river. Much of this land is state owned but some is privately owned and the permission of the land owner should be obtained.

PENINSULA STATE PARK, between Fish Creek and Ephraim, features excellent hiking trails.

PERROT STATE PARK, north of the village of Trempealeau, has hilly hiking trails.

POINT BEACH STATE PARK, near Two Rivers. Hikers stroll the 6 miles of beach. Interesting trails are found on each ridge.

ST. GERMAIN LIONS CLUB TRAILS near St. Germain. The club has laid out several well-marked hiking trails from 1 to 3 miles long.

Biking

GREEN COUNTY TRAILS. The Green County Publicity Committee publishes a pamphlet for bikers listing nine major trails totaling 110 miles. A bike path from New Glarus to Brodhead follows a 23-mile stretch of abandoned railroad bed.

WAUKESHA COUNTY BICYCLE ROUTE tours the county near Waukesha from Frame Park beside the Fox River to such points as North Prairie, where men dug for oil in 1866, past dairy farms and Oconomowoc Lake.

WISCONSIN BICENTENNIAL NORTH-SOUTH BIKEWAY. The new bikeway stretches 325 miles from LaCrosse to Bayfield.

WISCONSIN BIKEWAY stretches 297 miles from Kenosha to LaCrosse. It is one of the longest bike trails in the United States. The trail passes country stores where supplies can be replenished, camping places, wildlife areas, and bathing beaches. The Elroy-Sparta Trail is part of the bikeway. Bikers ride along a level path covered with limestone screening to provide a smooth riding surface. Bridges are covered with planks, and some are guarded with railings. The trail runs through tunnels originally cut for the railroad. Primitive campsites, shelter houses, and other facilities are along the way. Some of the locations are: 3 miles south of Sparta off Wisconsin 71; Sparta City Park; Norwalk Village Park; Wilton Village Park; Kendall Village Park; Elroy City Park; Wildcat Mountain State Park; McMullen Park; and Tomah City Park.

Rockhounding

GRAVEL QUARRIES, in the vicinity of Prairie du Chien. Rockhounds look for agates.

KETTLE MORAINE STATE FOREST, near Greenbush. In this geological wonderland hikers sometimes find copper ore brought by the glaciers from copper-bearing formations farther north. Diamonds also were brought south by the glaciers from some mysterious Canadian source. Not many of these gems have been found, but one man discovered a diamond weighing 15⅜ carats.

MINERAL POINT. The historic Cornish mining town is at the heart of the lead mining district. The Historical Society Museum has a rock collection, which should give rockhounds an idea of the collecting possibilities in this rugged area.

Canoeing & Rafting

BARK RIVER, near Rome. Canoeists paddle through the tall marsh grasses to get a glimpse of the green herons and sandhill cranes. The canoe trail ends near the millpond dam in Rome.

FLAMBEAU RIVER WATER TRAIL begins at Turtle Dam and contains some exciting rapids. A good access place is at Park Falls Country Club. From Park Falls to Ladysmith the Flambeau comes into its own as one of the best white-water canoe trips in the Midwest. Its roaring rapids test a canoeist's skill and determination. Portages are necessary around dams at Park Falls, Pixley, and Crowley, at Big Falls Dam and at Cedar Rapids and Beaver Dam Rapids. The river completes its course into Ladysmith through virgin forest. The lower stretches of the Flambeau from Ladysmith to the Chippewa River offer fast-flowing water with only two dams at Port Arthur and at Thornapple that require portages. The South Fork of the Flambeau is also an exciting canoeing stream from Round Lake to its confluence with the North Fork. There are three short portages around small dams.

MANITOWISH RIVER WATER TRAIL, near Boulder Junction. Put-in place is the north end of High Lake where it touches State Forest Road B. There are only two portages: an old logging dam about 2 miles east of the State Forest Road M bridge, and another old dam and rapids just above the Highway K bridge, west of Boulder Junction. By water from High Lake to the Rest Lake outlet dam, where US 51 crosses the river, is about 30 miles. This distance can be covered in a couple of days or the trip can be extended to a week. There are campsites along the way on state land. This is a flat-water trip. From Rest Lake to the Flambeau Flowage is another easy trip with no portages in normal water stages.

ST. CROIX RIVER WATER TRAIL, from Solon Springs, is a splendid river trip with rapids and flat water. The rapids are exciting but not dangerous. The sandy banks below the initial swampy stretch provide good campsites. Below Wisconsin 70, islands in the stream divide the river and provide false channels to make canoeing more interesting. Access points are no problem clear down to the Mississippi.

WAUPACA RIVER WATER TRAIL. The Crystal and Waupaca rivers make an easy trip, which begins at Rural and ends at Weyawega. There are some entertaining rapids near Parfreville, and rounding a bend it is always possible for a canoeist to find himself bearing down on a herd of Wisconsin dairy cattle placidly moseying across the stream.

WISCONSIN RIVER WATER TRAIL starts at the river's source, Lac Vieux Desert, near Land O' Lakes, and runs downstream. At Watersmeet, the Eagle River, another good canoeing stream, and the Wisconsin come together at the Eagle River Dam. A portage is necessary. Otter Rapids, a mile farther along, is a test of a canoeist's steering skills. In Rainbow Lake a canoeist must watch out for submerged stumps and portage around the dam. Rainbow Rapids is thunderous and exciting. Whirlpool Rapids should be portaged. Bradley Park in Tomahawk is a good campsite. From Merrill to Nekoosa the river is deep and slow. There are plenty of camping places and also dams that have to be portaged. From Nekoosa to the Mississippi River, the canoeist paddles through the Petenwell Flowage. Portages include one around a dam at the Wisconsin Dells and at the Prairie du Sac Dam where the power company provides assistance during working hours and at other times by appointment. There are many islands that can be used as campsites. Beneath Prairie du Sac it is important to camp on a sandbar that is well above water level. The river may rise or fall from two to five feet within 48 hours by the opening and closing of the dam gates at Prairie du Sac. Tower Hill State Park, near Spring Green, has a fine campground.

WOLF RIVER WATER TRAIL. Considered by many midwestern canoeists as the most dangerous and exciting river in their part of the country, the Wolf is indeed rugged. Inexperienced canoeists should avoid it. There are tough carries, frequent tip overs, and long rocky stretches as well as some rapids that are really rough. The best stretch of wild water is in the Menominee Indian Reservation. The tribal council charges $2.50 per person to canoe the stream. There are unimproved campsites along the route. Beneath Shawano to Lake Winnebago the Wolf becomes an easygoing stream without dams or rapids, a good place to practice for a later trip on the upper Wolf. There are campsites by the river. Floating the Wolf River on inflatable rubber rafts is also a popular sport here. Rafts may be rented at White Lake.

Boating

APOSTLE ISLANDS, in Lake Superior near Bayfield. There are almost 1,000 square miles of enticing blue-water sailing and cruising among the islands famed for their beauty. The islands offer shelter from storms. Bayfield boat basin is also a harbor or refuge.

DOOR COUNTY. The ports of Door County are popular with Great Lakes boaters, who frequent both the Lake Michigan and Green Bay shores. Rock Island is a state park beyond Washington Island. There is a boat dock and a campground.

GREEN LAKE. Marinas on the lake and launching spots make this a popular boating lake.

ISLAND CAMPING. Wisconsin has hundreds of navigable lakes. In them there are 617 charted islands given to the state by Congress in 1912. Half of these islands are open either to overnight or extended boat camping. To locate a vacation island, a boater should get in touch with the Department of Natural Resources representative in Spooner, Rhinelander, Green Bay, or Eau Claire.

MISSISSIPPI RIVER. Houseboating is popular, with picnicking on sandbars, swimming and fishing, and camping at established sites on the shore away from it all. Houseboats may be rented at Alma, La Crosse, and other river ports. Marinas are available the length of the Mississippi, and boating is going strong. Wooded islands and sandbars offer boaters overnight camping. If camping on a sandbar for any length of time, a boater should check with the local conservation manager. There is sailboating on Lake Pepin.

Sport Diving

APOSTLE ISLANDS. Divers find exceptionally clear water and beautiful underwater rock formations. There are a number of wrecks in the vicinity, but these have not been accurately located.

DEVILS LAKE STATE PARK. The water of the lake is clear, and divers come upon large fish.

Wolf River, Wisconsin

DOOR COUNTY PENINSULA. In waters offshore there are more than 200 charted shipwrecks. Divers find the wrecks to be underwater challenges. Possibilities include the 400-foot sailing ship *Louisiana*, which lies in 30 feet of water north of Washington Island.

GREEN LAKE, near the town of Green Lake, has clear water and unusual depths. Scuba divers find lesson plans all the way up to certification, scuba diving equipment rentals, and boat rentals.

ST. GERMAIN LAKES. Scuba diving is popular in the lakes near St. Germain.

Conservation & Wildlife

BEECH WALK at Two Creeks reveals the remains of a prehistoric forest 10,000 years old.

CHEQUAMEGON NATIONAL FOREST. Black bear, white-tailed deer, raccoon, snowshoe rabbit, squirrel, and ruffed grouse are all to be seen in the woods. To see deer, travel early in the morning or at dusk and choose little-traveled roads and drive slowly.

FIVE LAKES EXPERIMENTAL PROJECT. Scientists are studying Lakes Escanaba, Palette, Nebish, Mystery, and Spruce to determine the effects of open fishing seasons on fish populations.

GREEN MEADOWS FARM, Waterford. Guides take junior and senior high school students on ecology tours of the farm to point out soil types, planting patterns, erosion, flooding, rocks native to the area, and glacial formations.

HORICON MARSH, near Mayville, is home to thousands of geese and other waterfowl. During the summer months boat trips can be taken through the nature area. The southern portion of the marsh is maintained by the state as the Horicon Marsh Wildlife Area; the northern portion is in the Horicon National Wildlife Area.

ICE AGE NATIONAL SCIENTIFIC RESERVE includes 32,500 acres in Devils Lake State Park, the Sheboygan Marsh, the north unit of the Kettle Moraine State Forest, the Two Creeks Buried Forest, the Campbellsport Drumlins, Cross Plains, Mill Bluff Park, and Interstate Park.

JACKSON HARBOR DUNE LAKE PARK on Washington Island contains a variety of rare plants, some unique to the island. The dunes are impressive.

KAKAGON AND BAD RIVER SLOUGHS, near Ashland, are two great unspoiled marshlands that are full of birdlife and large and small mammals. Small fee boat landings at and near Odanah provide access to the sloughs.

LAKE WISSOTA STATE PARK, 7 miles northeast of Chippewa Falls, contains the lake's sandy shores and woodland, prairie- and forest-marsh areas. Walking quietly through the park, a nature lover may see white-tailed deer, fox, ruffed grouse, and other animals, and enjoy the sight and sound of many songbirds.

NICOLET NATIONAL FOREST. Tours take visitors to the Alvin Creek Deer Yards. Sheltering the deer are 74,000 acres of evergreens. On the Oconto River forest tour, a motorist can stop at 12 places on

THE MIDWEST 153

the 20-mile route to learn about wildlife management as it is practiced in the forest. A beaver dam may be seen on the Peshtigo River tour. There is an osprey nest. The Catwillow Wildlife Management Area is near Laona. The walking trails take hikers to a man-made waterhole frequented by deer and to an aspen regeneration area.

POWELL MARSH WILDLIFE AREA, of the Northern Highland State Forest, is a 13,000-acre marsh used by ducks and geese. In the fall it is a very busy place.

THE RIDGES SANCTUARY, Baileys Harbor, is a natural garden containing the largest number of rare plants to be seen in Wisconsin. They include 25 species of orchids and subarctic species deposited during the glacial period.

TREES FOR TOMORROW CENTER at Eagle River offers a self-guided tour. demonstrating the methods of conservation.

WILD RICE HARVESTING around Eagle River is done today much as it was by the Indians centuries ago. Harvesters knock the ripe grain into a canoe, with a birch stick. The Vilas County agent at Eagle River can tell a vacationer where the harvesting is being done.

MANITOBA

Camping

BIRDS HILL PROVINCIAL PARK, 14 miles north of Winnipeg. There is a large trailer and tent campground on the south side of the park's lake.

CLEARWATER PROVINCIAL PARK, north of The Pas, has well-equipped campgrounds at three locations.

GRAND BEACH PROVINCIAL PARK on Lake Winnipeg, 57 miles north of Winnipeg. The campground has easy access to the beach. Elk Island may be used for wilderness-type camping.

GRASS RIVER PROVINCIAL PARK, about 40 miles southeast of Flin Flon, is almost roadless, a true wilderness campground.

NORTHWEST ANGLE PROVINCIAL FOREST has campsites in the Moose Lake Recreational Area. The Trans-Canada Highway runs 35 miles north of here.

PORCUPINE PROVINCIAL FOREST, farther north, past Swan River, offers wilderness camping.

RIDING MOUNTAIN NATIONAL PARK has camping at five grounds, the largest being at Wasagaming and Lake Katherine. Camping outside established campgrounds is not permitted, although hikers on overnight trail trips may bivouac en route, providing they register with a park warden before and after their trip.

WHITESHELL PROVINCIAL PARK. There are 15 camping areas, with excellent sites for tenting and trailering. Facilities range from fully serviced sites to primitive sites in the wilderness, that can be reached only by foot or boat.

Backpacking

GRASS RIVER PROVINCIAL PARK, about 40 miles northeast of Flin Flon. A skilled backpacker with a yen for wilderness hiking and camping will find his yen satisfied in this rugged park with its 565,000 acres of Precambrian shield country.

RIDING MOUNTAIN NATIONAL PARK. Backpackers who register with a park warden before and after a trip may get permission to bivouac outside established campgrounds while on the trail.

Hiking

BIRDS HILL PROVINCIAL PARK, 14 miles north of Winnipeg, has hiking trails.

RIDING MOUNTAIN NATIONAL PARK. Day hiking or riding can be made over 30 miles of trails in the Wasagaming district. The Lake Katherine and Clear Lake districts have trails as well.

WHITESHELL PROVINCIAL PARK. The McGillivray Trails lead to the falls.

Rockhounding

HIGHWAY 2, near Souris, is the place to look for jasper, agate, petrified wood, and epidote found as pebbles and fragments in gravel pits.

WHITESHELL PROVINCIAL PARK. There are tourmaline crystals to be found near West Hawk Lake in a pegmatite dike. Between Barren and West Hawk Lake, scheelite occurs in two types of deposits. One is associated with quartz, garnet, amphibole, and calcite; crystals of molybdenite are found in quartz veins at the western end of Barren Lake, north of Falcon Lake.

WINNIPEG RIVER. Along the river, rockhounds find gray zinnwaldite, purple lepidolite, lilac-colored curvilameller, lithia mica, crystals of spessartite and platy columbite, white-pink and greenish beryl, and rose quartz.

Canoeing

KAUTINIGAN ROUTE. Put in at Wallace Lake off Highway 304 to the Berens River Settlement on Lake Winnipeg via Aikens Lake, Gammon River, Sasaginnigak Lake, Family Lake, and the Berens River. This is a 300-mile trip penetrating the rugged Indian country.

MISTIK CREEK CANOE ROUTE. It begins at Mistik Creek Wayside and ends at Bakers Narrows Provincial Recreation Area, both being on Highway 10, between Cranberry Portage and Flin Flon.

RIVIERE AUX RATS CANOE ROUTE. Beginning at "La Montagne de Cypres," about 4 miles southeast of the highway bridge across the Riviere Aux Rats (Rat River), the canoeist follows the river to its confluence with the Red River and then down the Red to St. Boniface. It is a 140-mile voyage that traces a historic voyageur trail.

SASAGINNIGAK CANOE COUNTRY. Canoeists put in at Wallace Lake but take an alternate route through the Bloodvein, Leyond, and Dogskin rivers.

WHITEMOUTH RIVER CANOE ROUTE. Put in at Whitemouth Lake in southeast Manitoba. Canoeists paddle for 125 miles along the Whitemouth River to its meeting with the Winnipeg River at Seven Sisters Falls. The first part of the trip is in the wilderness and the second is through a pastoral countryside.

Conservation & Wildlife

CLEARWATER PROVINCIAL PARK. This far north park contains a large herd of moose, northern birds, and waterfowl.

CONSERVATION TRAINING MUSEUM, Hadashville. Conservation classes are held in the museum for school groups. The museum is open to the public at these times.

DUCK MOUNTAIN PROVINCIAL PARK, northwest of Dauphin, contains a major elk herd as well as moose and bear.

RIDING MOUNTAIN NATIONAL PARK. The wapiti and moose are the largest members of the deer family and are numerous in the park. The wapiti may usually be seen in the open forest, and the moose near lakes and beaver ponds. Bison also are in the park. The timber wolf and the Canada lynx, black bear, and coyote are present.

SPRUCE WOODS PROVINCIAL PARK. Naturalists take pleasure in following the trails of Ernest Thompson Seton, the naturalist-author who hiked the area often.

WHITESHELL PROVINCIAL PARK. The Assinika Nature Trail follows the turbulent Whiteshell River.

ONTARIO

Camping

ALGONQUIN PROVINCIAL PARK. There are a number of campgrounds accessible from the highway. Campers who wish to camp overnight in the interior of the park must obtain an interior camping permit at Canoe Lake, Lake Opeongo, Rock Lake, or at most access points around the park perimeter.

BLACKSAND PROVINCIAL PARK, 40 miles north of Nipigon. This park on Lake Nipigon has wooded campsites.

CROWN LANDS. In the northern Ontario wilderness, campers are setting up their camps on crown lands. Good camping manners cannot be stressed enough.

ESKER LAKE PROVINCIAL PARK, 22 miles northeast of Kirkland Lake, has a well-equipped campground in a natural environment park.

GEORGIAN BAY ISLANDS NATIONAL PARK. Beausoleil Island has 12 primitive campgrounds, and there is one each on several of the islands in the eastern sector. The serviced Cedar Spring campground is in the headquarters area. Primitive campgrounds are open all year. Recognized groups may use the Beausoleil Point group camp on Beausoleil Island that has been set aside for their use.

KAP-KIG-IWAN PROVINCIAL PARK, on the Englehart River 1½ miles south of Englehart, offers camping in a wilderness natural environment park.

LAKE SUPERIOR PROVINCIAL PARK, on Lake Superior's northeast shore, has excellent campsites.

NEYS PROVINCIAL PARK, west of Marathon, provides camping beside Lake Superior.

QUETICO PROVINCIAL PARK. Dawson Trail Campground on French Lake is a fine place to camp, 30 miles east of Atikokan. It offers 135 developed campsites.

RAINBOW FALLS PROVINCIAL PARK, just east of Rossport, has secluded campsites.

ST. LAWRENCE ISLANDS NATIONAL PARK. A small developed campground is at Mallorytown Landing, with another on Grenadier Island. Camping is allowed on many park islands. Camping fees are collected at Mallorytown Landing and at the developed camp on Grenadier Island.

SIDNEY BAY RESERVATION, Cape Croker, near Wiarton. The Indians have developed an unusual tent and trailer camp.

French River, Ontario

The nine camping areas are situated imaginatively. There are both well-marked campsites and rough camping areas. Water is drawn from bubbling springs. Tent campers predominate. The Ojibway Indian camp staff is outstanding.

Backpacking

ALGONQUIN PROVINCIAL PARK. The Highland Hiking Trail leads to Head, Harness, and Mosquito lakes and is 17 miles long. Camping along the way, hikers cover the jaunt in two or three days.

BRUCE TRAIL. This 430-mile trail along the Niagara Escarpment from Tobermory to Niagara Falls is one of the continent's

Bancroft, Ontario

outstanding backpack routes. The Bruce Trail Association is endeavoring to set up three-sided shelters along the trail, but the shelter chain is far from complete. Hikers camp. The trail is marked, but sections of it may be overgrown by brush during the summer. Most of the trail is on private land.

GANARASKA TRAIL from Port Hope to Omemee offers 35 miles of cross-country hiking. Two camping areas are available for hikers, at the Garden Hill Conservation Area, and at the upper chalet of the Peterborough Ski Club near Bethany.

OPEONGO LINE. The trail starts at Farrell's Landing on the Ottawa River and runs northwesterly to Lake Opeongo, within the park. The old colonization and logging road still has original stretches of cobblestone and corduroy roadway. The trail is about 100 miles long. Hikers meet the sturdy descendants of the first Irish, Scottish, German, Polish, and French immigrants, who still live on the Opeongo Line. The trail makes use of county roads, bush trails, half-forgotten roads, and passes downtown streets and through rugged wilderness.

RIDEAU TRAIL links Canada's capital of Ottawa with Kingston, where the St. Lawrence flows out of Lake Ontario. The trail represents 180 miles of hiking through country rich with lakes, forests, streams, and intriguing rock formations.

Hiking

ALGONQUIN PROVINCIAL PARK. Novice hikers may make a comfortable one-day hike by taking a shortcut trail around Provoking Lake, instead of hiking the entire Highland Hiking Trail. Another route leads to the viewpoint south of Faya Lake and is 6 miles long. Several other hiking trails leave Highway 60.

GEORGIAN BAY ISLANDS NATIONAL PARK. There are over 20 miles of hiking trails on Beausoleil Island. The trails lead to all parts of the island.

GREEN BELT, around Ottawa, has well-kept trails winding through natural bushland and timber stands.

POINT PELEE NATIONAL PARK offers hiking on the Woodland Trail and the Boardwalk Trail, which leads into a marsh with an observation tower.

Rockhounding

ALLANITE crystals of rare beauty are found in Olden Township, Frontenac County.

BANCROFT. Home of the annual five-day Gemboree, Bancroft is the heart of a mineral kingdom.

CANADA TALC MINE, Madoc. Small brown crystals of tourmaline are found in the schist.

FARADAY URANIUM MINE, near Bancroft, is the source of some of the world's finest specimens of uranophane. Small gypsum crystals are sometimes found in the sedimentary rocks. Tourmaline is also discovered in the mine.

FORKS OF THE CREDIT RIVER are a good place to look for celestite of a bright orange variety.

ILMENITE is found in Faraday Township.

MAC DONALD MINE, near Hybla. Now abandoned, the mine has produced many rare minerals including a number of radioactive species. The mine dumps are easy to search.

MARMORATON IRON MINE, near Marmora, is the source of pyritohedrons.

MC INTYRE MINE SCHUMACHER, in the Porcupine District, is a good place to look for gold ore specimens.

PRINCESS QUARRY, in Hastings County, is a source of sodalite, which is mined for use as an ornamental mineral.

SPAIN MINE, Griffith Township in Renfrew County, yields molybdenite.

STONE QUARRY, near Dundas, is the source of white to blue celestite.

THUNDER BAY is in the heart of amethyst discoveries.

TRIBAG MINE, 17 miles from Batchawana. Pyrite crystal cubes are found here.

URANINITE, found in Cardiff Township of Haliburton County, is located by collectors equipped with Geiger counters.

WALKER QUARRY, near Thorold. Dolomite crystals are found at the quarry.

YORK RIVER. Corundum and sodalite are found in the Bancroft area. Both ruby and sapphire specimens are also discovered here.

Canoeing

ALGONQUIN PROVINCIAL PARK. There are 15 canoe routes listed for the park as well as many more less-used courses and side trips that more experienced trippers may wish to take. This is ideal country for a canoeist to lay out his own course, but this sort of canoeing is not for the novice who is unfamiliar with the wilderness. All provisions and equipment must be carried, for this is a true wilderness. Once a canoeist has put in, he is entirely on his own. The canoeist is required to keep the wilderness clean, and each campsite must be treated with respect. Remember your canoe and wilderness training. There are patrol planes over the area during fire weather in the summer season, and they'll respond to SOS signals or calls.

ATIKAKI WILDERNESS AREA of northwestern Ontario has six major rivers. The wildlife is fascinating.

MATTAWA PROVINCIAL PARK preserves the Mattawa as a wild river. An interesting canoe camping trip can be made along the river. Put-in point is on the west end of Trout Lake. Camping spots are available throughout the trip along the shores of the river and lakes. The Mattawa was the water route for Alexander MacKenzie in 1794, and he too ran the white water.

QUETICO PROVINCIAL PARK has superlative canoe routes matching those on the Superior National Forest side of the Boundary Waters Canoe Area. The 1,750-square-mile wilderness park is available only to canoeists, who follow ancient Indian routes. There are some 900 miles of dashing streams, rivers, and lakes encompassed in the trails. Atikokan is the headquarters for a number of canoe outfitters. They not only can supply gear, canoes, and provisions but also maps, expert advice, and detailed suggestions for planning your trip, right down to circuit, rivers, portages, and camping places.

Boating

LAKE HURON AND GEORGIAN BAY. The sparkling waters of Lake Huron are bordered by marinas in key ports. The Bruce Peninsula between the lake and the bay is set amid outstanding boating waters. Big Tub and Little Tub at Tobermory are natural protected harbors, and Tobermory is a town popular with boaters. In the Georgian Bay Islands National Park there are fine islands that can be reached by boats via routes of the Great Lakes or the Trent-Severn waterways. Well-marked channels help the boater among the islands. There are campsites on Beausoleil Island and on Bone Island.

LAKE ONTARIO. Toronto has created a new harbor accommodating 350 boats in an offshore development. Lake Ontario provides fine cruising waters.

LAKE SUPERIOR. The world's largest body of fresh water has dramatic bays and 31,000 square miles for cruising.

THOUSAND ISLANDS. The St. Lawrence Seaway between Canada and the United States is ideal for boating. Marinas on both sides of the river make boating convenient. The islands in the St. Lawrence Islands National Park all have docks in sheltered coves, and some have anchor buoys in deep water for the use of bigger boats or for use when the docks are crowded. There are developed campgrounds at Mallorytown Landing and on Grenadier Island. Camping is allowed on all park islands. There is a launching area in the park at Mallorytown Landing for small boats. Maps are available at a nominal fee from the Canadian Hydrographic Service, Department of Energy, Mines and Resources, 615 Booth Street, Ottawa, or at many marinas and hardware stores on the river.

TRENT-SEVERN WATERWAY SYSTEM. The waterway leads north for 240 miles through a chain of lakes and rivers. There are 43 locks and a marine railway. Boaters must carry a copy of the canal regulations on board.

Sport Diving

FATHOM FIVE PARK, in the waters off the Bruce Peninsula near Tobermory, features an interpretive center and marine museum. Sport divers explore some 20 sunken wrecks in the waters off Tobermory. Sublimnos, Canada's first habitable underwater observatory, lies in 25 feet of water in Dunks Bay, just south of Tobermory, on the Bruce Peninsula. Hundreds of divers from Canada and the United States have descended to Sublimnos to study the freshwater flora and fauna of the bay. Under the direction of Dr. Joe Mac Innis, one of North America's leading divers and underwater researchers, Sublimnos is undertaking a "scientific study of physical, chemical, meteorological and biological conditions in fresh water."

Conservation & Wildlife

ALGONQUIN PROVINCIAL PARK. Rangers invite visitors to wolf-howling nights. With recorded calls, they call to the wolves, who howl back. Besides the timber wolf, the park is home to deer, bear, moose, beaver, otter, and many species of fish.

GEORGIAN BAY ISLANDS NATIONAL PARK. The islands, a legacy of the Ice Age, are covered by a mixed-wood forest of long-needled pines, hemlock, and cedar growing among deciduous trees such as maple, oak, beech, and birch. There are white-tailed deer on Beausoleil Island and several kinds of shrew. Vole and mouse are found as well as weasel and red fox. Water mammals include muskrat, beaver, mink, and otter. There are species of amphibians. Beausoleil Island is one of the last haunts of the swamp rattler. Although this shy reptile is poisonous, it is protected because it is becoming extinct.

KLOTZ LAKE PROVINCIAL PARK, 30 miles east of Longlac, has Oak Ridge Trail, a nature trail that leads to a fish hatchery. At the hatchery, an unusual fish blind has been constructed at the end of a 100-foot boardwalk that runs out in the pond. A visitor may sit in the blind and view trout, stickleback, minnows, and turtles in their own environment.

LAKE OF THE WOODS, set into the Canadian Shield on the Manitoba-Ontario-U.S. border, has a variety of birdlife. A nature lover may see a flight of double-crested cormorants, a nesting osprey, great blue herons, and a pair of bald eagles on a two-day trip. The rare white pelican nests in these waters.

POINT PELEE NATIONAL PARK. The southernmost tip of the Canadian mainland contains mink and muskrat in the marsh, and deer, coyote, raccoon, skunk, gray squirrel, and cottontail rabbit in the woodland.

PUKASKWA NATIONAL PARK, on the north shore of Lake Superior, is a wilderness, with abundant wildlife including caribou, deer, moose, mink, otter, marten, beaver, lynx, bobcat, wolf, and fox.

QUETICO PROVINCIAL PARK. There are 29 types of mammals, ranging from the mouse to the moose. Black bear can be a nuisance if you don't keep your camp clean. Nesting in the park are 61 species of birds.

ST. LAWRENCE ISLANDS NATIONAL PARK. The deciduous forests are home to small mammals and a variety of birds. Ring-billed and herring gulls, blue herons, black-crowned night herons, and black ducks are numerous. Spotted sandpipers and kingfishers are found near the water.

THE SOUTHWEST

The first Anglo-Americans came to the Southwest in caravans of wagons filled with trade goods. They trekked over the Santa Fe Trail, sleeping under the stars. Today this great highway of commerce can be followed by trail riders or backpackers for hundreds of miles across the range country of New Mexico. The trail cuts through a corner of Philmont, the vast ranch in northeastern New Mexico where senior Boy Scouts and Explorers find adventure in the mountains and high plateaus. In this land that Kit Carson knew so well, not only today's young people but adults as well are rediscovering the deep satisfactions of outdoor living.

Arizona, New Mexico, Oklahoma, and Texas—these are the states of the sunny Southwest. Not all the region is sunbaked and arid. Texas is a huge part of the Southwest, and Texas is just as much the damp bayou country of its southeast as it is the dry, high plains of the panhandle. The Big Thicket of East Texas is a marvelous wilderness ardently defended against timber interests by people who love the outdoors. It is a sanctuary for threatened species, and to a canoeist or a hiker, it is a place of haunting beauty. It deserves to be made a national park to save for the future an area as meaningful in its own way as is Big Bend National Park in the southwestern part of the state.

The southwestern outdoors is a kaleidoscope of beauty. There are the red and caramel cliffs crowding about Red Rock Crossing in Arizona's Oak Creek Canyon. Trail riders splashing their horses through the stream ride where the Hollywood cavalry has long galloped to make several generations of Western movies. There are the White Mountains of Arizona too, a high country inhabited by the Apache Indians. The Apache invite vacationers to camp and hike among brawling trout streams in the nation's largest stand of ponderosa pine. Until recent years the Indians were bitterly resentful of white visitors, but now their expression is, "be my guest." They still expect whites to have the same love of the outdoors and appreciation for the land that they have.

Rainless months and hot sun make not only Arizona but New Mexico a desert region, where an outdoorsman must not push beyond the limitations imposed by his need for water. But this is also the region of azure skies, of mesas and mountains, of the alpine Sangre de Cristo Mountains. In the high country it is the land of ponderosa, fir, and spruce; the mesas are crowned with juniper and piñon. There is no aroma more satisfying than the scent of piñon in a campfire.

The Southwest may be dry, but it also has hundreds of man-made lakes, including Arizona's huge Lake Mead and Lake Texoma on the border between Texas and Oklahoma, the largest body of water between the Great Lakes and the Gulf of Mexico. Oklahoma alone has more than 200 lakes, offering outdoor recreation ranging from boating to camping on the beach.

There are national parks, monuments, and recreation areas in the Southwest that defy comparison. After all, there is only one Grand Canyon, which took the Colorado River seven million years to cut into the lofty plateau of Arizona for 217 unsurpassed miles of staggering depth, a panorama of weird, eroded rock forms and brilliant hues. Hikers and riders on muleback take the trails down into the canyon for an unforgettable experience.

New Mexico also has a notable national park in Carlsbad Caverns. Carved into the limestone by ground waters, the caverns are so vast that one room alone contains a 1¼-mile underground trail that loops around its stony circumference. The room is appropriately called the "Big Room." At dusk, bats fly out of the Bat Cave to feed and provide visitors with a squeaking, chittering cloud of winged acrobats.

The rolling hills of Oklahoma also have their beauty. The Chickasaw National Recreation Area contains both hills and mineral springs as well as a herd of buffalo ranging free. Oklahoma also has spurs of the Ouachita Mountains, which are ideal for backpacking.

The Southwest is a varied land that contains the sandy beaches of the Padre Island National Seashore of Texas; the subtropical ambiance of the lower Rio Grande, where palm trees hold up their crowned heads; and the North Rim of the Grand Canyon, where in the winter blizzards blow.

Petrified Forest National Park, Arizona

ARIZONA

Camping

CAVE CREEK RECREATION AREA, north of Douglas, offers prime camping at Idlewild Forest Camp, Stewart Forest Camp, and Sunny Flat Forest Camp.

FORT APACHE RESERVATION. The Apaches make no charge for camping in public camping areas but limit a stay to 10 days at any one campground and restrict campers to posted areas. After 10 days tent and trailer campers are charged a small fee. Indians even leave cut wood at campsites in this hospitable area where the Apaches say, "*Hondah*," or "Be my guest."

GLEN CANYON NATIONAL RECREATION AREA. At Wahweap Campgrounds, 4½ miles north of Glen Canyon Dam, there are campsites.

GRAND CANYON NATIONAL PARK has campgrounds at Grand Canyon Village and Desert View on the South Rim, and at Bright Angel Point near the North Rim Inn on the North Rim. The Roaring Springs campground is at the end of the North Kaibab Trail on the canyon's floor.

KAIBAB NATIONAL FOREST. Campers pitch their tents at Ten X and DeMotte.

LAKE MEAD NATIONAL RECREATION AREA. There are campgrounds at Temple Bar on Lake Mead and undeveloped facilities at Greggs Hideout, Pierce Ferry, Bonelli Landing, and Kingman Wash.

LAKE MOHAVE. Campers find a campground at Katherine Landing and Willow Beach.

MADERA CANYON RECREATION AREA, southeast of Tucson, offers camping at Bog Springs.

MOUNT GRAHAM RECREATION AREA, southwest of Safford, offers camping at Arcadia, Shannon, Hospital Flat, Soldier Creek, and Riggs Flat.

MOUNT LEMON RECREATION AREA provides campgrounds at Molino Basin, Rose Canyon, Bear Wallow, Spencer Canyon, and Peppersauce. The area is northeast of Tucson.

NAVAJO RESERVATION. Tribal campsites are numerous, and family campers are welcome. Among the finest campsites are those in the Navajo tribal parks at Monument Valley, Lake Powell, and on the Little Colorado River Gorge.

OAK CREEK CANYON. Beautiful campsites are situated along the creek close to Red Rock Crossing, where the steep walls of the canyon have given dramatic effect to many Hollywood movies. Campsites are in the Coconino National Forest.

ORGAN PIPE NATIONAL MONUMENT. The campground is in a desert garden.

PAPAGO INDIAN RESERVATION offers a campground near the foot of Baboquiviri Mountain, southwest of Tucson.

PENA BLANCA RECREATION AREA, northwest of Nogales, has camping at Calabasas Canyon, White Rock, and Pena Blanca. The area is northwest of Nogales.

PRESCOTT NATIONAL FOREST. There are excellent campgrounds at Mingus Mountain, Granite Basin, White Spar, and in the Indian Creek Recreation Area.

RUCKER CANYON RECREATION AREA provides camping at Rucker Lake, Cypress Park, Bathtub, and Rucker. The area is north of Douglas.

TUCSON MOUNTAIN PARK. Palo Verde campgrounds is west of Tucson.

Backpacking & Trail Riding

CHIRICAHUA NATIONAL MONUMENT. Exciting backpacking trips and trail rides may be made over the horseback and foot trails that reach into the wilderness where Cochise and his braves once holed up.

FORT APACHE RESERVATION. The vast forested reaches of the White Mountains offer excellent backpacking and packing possibilities.

GRAND CANYON NATIONAL PARK. A one-day mule trip takes visitors to the canyon floor over the twisting Bright Angel Trail. The two-day trip enables travelers to stop over at the ranch beside Bright Angel Creek and to return the next day on the Kaibab Trail. Hikers also take the trails to the canyon floor. Permits are required, and hikers must carry water for the trip. The trip down is easy, but the climb from the floor back to the rim is punishing. There is a trail to the rim at Yaki Point called the South Kaibab Trail, and there is the North Kaibab Trail that runs to the North Rim, 14 miles away. Four campgrounds are along the trail. There are also muleback trips into the canyon from the North Rim.

SUPERSTITION MOUNTAINS. Trail Riders of the Wilderness undertakes a spring trail ride through this rugged desert and mountain area in the Tonto National Forest. Riders trek to Frazier Canyon, Angel Springs, oases of mountain laurel, and to Night Hawk Springs—one of Geronimo's refuges.

Hiking

CORONADO NATIONAL MEMORIAL. A foot trail ascends Coronado Peak, from which there is a view of the San Pedro Valley and the land explored by Coronado's expedition of 1540. A 3-mile trail follows Smugglers' Ridge.

MONTEZUMA NATIONAL MONUMENT. A self-guiding trail leads to the 20-room cliff dwelling. Once the Pueblo Indians made meal of the pods and soap from the gray thorn berries of the prickly catclaw shrubs that still grow along the Sycamore Trail.

SUNSET CRATER NATIONAL MONUMENT. Trails lead over the lava flow, but the crater rim is closed.

SUPERSTITION MOUNTAINS. Every year the Phoenix Dons Club puts on the Lost Gold Trek—a search for the Lost Dutchman Mine—in the Superstition Mountains. From the Dons' base camp at the foot of the mountains, guides take hikers, in groups of about 50, to the points mentioned in the story of the "Lost Dutchman."

TONTO NATIONAL MONUMENT. A rugged trail climbs to the 14th century Pueblo dwelling.

WALNUT CANYON NATIONAL MONUMENT. A foot trail leads to 25 of the cliff dwellings in the monument.

Rockhounding

LYNX CREEK, near Prescott, is a popular place for panning gold. Most rockhounds count themselves lucky to find a tiny speck, but some find small nuggets.

PETRIFIED FOREST NATIONAL PARK contains the most remarkable collection of petrified wood in the world. Some petrified logs reproduce the smallest details of the wood. The wind has polished the stone. No collecting is allowed, of course.

TORTILLA FLAT, on the Apache Trail northeast of Phoenix, is a good place to look for semiprecious stones.

SOUTHWESTERN STATES

Rafting

COLORADO RIVER. A favorite put-in place for rafts is Lee's Ferry, southwest of Page. Neoprene rubber rafts hurtle through the rapids of the river as it makes its way through the canyon. The dramatic descent of the river takes "river rats" through the Grand Canyon National Park. Takeout point is usually at Temple Bar. There are commercial operators who provide the entire wherewithal for a Colorado River raft trip. The National Wildlife Federation also offers a Grand Canyon Safari.

Boating & Boat Camping

GLEN CANYON NATIONAL RECREATION AREA. The 1,960-mile shoreline of Lake Powell offers extraordinary boat camping. Wahweap Marina is a logical departure place. Boaters can explore narrow canyons and also travel to half-drowned caves.

LAKE MEAD NATIONAL RECREATION AREA. Boating and boat camping on this wide expanse of water in the desert are popular.

Sport Diving

LAKE MEAD NATIONAL RECREATION AREA. Skin diving is permitted away from activity areas.

Conservation & Wildlife

ARIZONA-SONORA DESERT MUSEUM, in Tucson Mountain Park west of the city, is a living museum of the desert where visitors may meet desert fauna close up. Among the exceptional features of the museum are the Orientation Room, the beaver-otter-sheep complex, the underground tunnel, the watershed exposition, the canyon habitat for small cats, and the nature trails and botanical gardens.

DESERT BOTANICAL GARDEN, in Papago Park on the east side of Phoenix, contains 10,000 species of desert plants from all over the world.

GRAND CANYON NATIONAL PARK. A ranger-naturalist leads hikers over the Transept Trail on the North Rim. The geological wonder of the canyon that awes every visitor is one of the great open books of nature in the world.

HOUSE ROCK VALLEY, near Jacob Lake, protects a herd of buffalo.

JOSHUA TREE FOREST. The best stand of Joshua in the state is found along US 93 close to Kingman.

KOFA GAME RANGE, south of Quartzsite, protects desert bighorn sheep and other wildlife.

LAKE HAVASU NATIONAL WILDLIFE REFUGE is on a main north-south flyway and has a large variety of waterfowl.

LAKE MEAD NATIONAL RECREATION AREA contains some 60 species of animals ranging from desert bighorn, coyote, cougar, and bobcat to tiny rats.

ORGAN PIPE CACTUS NATIONAL MONUMENT contains 516 square miles of desert. The organ-pipe cactus is particularly notable, but there are also fine ocotillo, saguaro, cholla, and other flora. Gambel's quail, whitewing and mourning doves, the cactus wren, and other birds are seen.

SABINO CANYON, Tucson. The Sabino Canyon Nature Trail climbs a deep cut in the foothills of the Santa Catalina Mountains.

SAGUARO NATIONAL MONUMENT. The monument protects a forest of the giant cactus, which may live to be over 200 years old and reach heights of 35 feet. There are nature trails.

SOUTHWESTERN ARBORETUM, on US 60 near Superior, is outstanding. Drive east of the arboretum up Queen's Creek and Devil's Canyons on US 60, where you will find ever-changing views of magnificent yucca and rocky pinnacles.

SUPERSTITION MOUNTAINS AREA, off US 80 east of Phoenix, contains a spectacular desert at the foot of the mountains. Take the dirt desert byways for a look at the trees, cacti, and desert blooms.

NEW MEXICO

Camping

APACHE SUMMIT CAMPGROUND is high in a pass in the Sacramento Mountains. It is in the Mescalero Apache Reservation. There is also camping on the reservation at Eagle Lake.

BANDELIER NATIONAL MONUMENT, south of Los Alamos, offers camping in Frijoles Canyon near monument headquarters.

BLUEWATER LAKE STATE PARK, near Prewitt, has camping sites.

CAPULIN MOUNTAIN NATIONAL MONUMENT offers camping close to the extinct volcanic crater.

CARSON NATIONAL FOREST. Wooded campsites are available in the Red River Valley close to purling trout streams. In the Wheeler Peak Wild Area, primitive camping is adventurous.

CHACO CANYON, 54 miles south of Bloomfield, on New Mexico 4, offers camping near the ruins of prehistoric pueblos.

EL MORRO NATIONAL MONUMENT. There is camping close to celebrated Inscription Rock.

HYDE MEMORIAL STATE PARK, in the Sangre de Cristo Mountains, 8 miles northeast of Santa Fe, is a popular camping site.

JICARILLA RESERVATION. The Indians permit camping at Dulce Lake, La Jara Lake, and Stone Lake.

LAGUNA LARGA. This is a Forest Service campground 32 miles northwest of Tres Piedras on Forest Road 78. The elevation is 9,000 feet. Other nearby camp areas in the mountains are provided by the Forest Service at Upper Lagunitas, 40 miles northwest of Tres Piedras on Forest Road 87, and Lower Lagunitas, 32 miles northwest of Tres Piedras.

NATIONAL RECREATION AREAS. The Bureau of Land Management provides free campsites in 6 areas: Aguirre Springs, 22 miles east northeast of Las Cruces, on US 70; Angel Peak, 19 miles south southeast of Bloomfield, on US 44; Datil Well, 63 miles west of Socorro, on US 60; Rio Grande Gorge, 35 miles north of Taos, on New Mexico 3; Santa Cruz Lake, 14 miles east of Espanola, on New Mexico 76; and Three Rivers Petroglyph Site, 36 miles southwest of Carrizozo, on US 54.

NAVAJO LAKE STATE PARK, east of Farmington, is an important recreational area with good camping.

NAVAJO RESERVATION. Campgrounds are at Haystack, ½ mile south of Window Rock, Arizona, on the Arizona-New Mexico border, and also near Shiprock.

SANTA CLARA PUEBLO. The Indians permit camping at the campgrounds in the recreation area, about 11 miles west of Espanola on New Mexico 30.

Great Salt Plains National Wildlife Refuge, Oklahoma

VALLEY OF FIRES STATE PARK, 3 miles west of Carrizozo. The camping units are close to the lava formations.

Backpacking & Trail Riding

BANDELIER NATIONAL MONUMENT. The backcountry is wild and rugged.

GILA NATIONAL FOREST. The sprawling wilderness area is closed to motor vehicles, but backpackers and horseback riders are more than welcome.

PECOS WILDERNESS AND CARSON NATIONAL FOREST, in the Sangre de Cristo Mountains, is high country at its best. The Engerbretsons, outfitters in Mora, provide gear and also Great Pyrenees dogs if desired. The dogs carry packs and are trained in survival operations. Backpackers and trail riders entering this wilderness are urged to let forest rangers know their plans. Every year people not accustomed to this trackless region have to be located by the rangers and brought out. Trails lead through the mighty Sangre de Cristos to the Pecos River headwaters.

RED RIVER VALLEY. Both backpackers and horseback riders find the Wheeler Peak Wild Area a challenge.

RIO GRANDE GORGE STATE PARK, 5 miles north of Questa and then 5 miles west on an improved road, extends about 70 miles northward to the Colorado state line. Foot and horse trails lead from the La Junta and Chiflo sites to shelters at the bottom of the gorge.

Hiking

BANDELIER NATIONAL MONUMENT. Hikers strike out over the rugged wilderness trails or stroll over easy trails to see the Indian ruins.

CAPULIN MOUNTAIN NATIONAL MONUMENT. Trails lead around the rim and into the crater formed by volcanic action 7,000 years ago.

FORT UNION NATIONAL MONUMENT. A self-guiding trail leads through the ruins of this fort, built as a bastion on the Santa Fe Trail. A hiker can follow the actual ruts of the Santa Fe Trail nearby for scores of miles.

HYDE MEMORIAL STATE PARK, 8 miles northeast of Santa Fe, has well-marked hiking trails leading through the lofty Sangre de Cristo Mountains.

Rockhounding

BOTTOMLESS LAKES STATE PARK, 16 miles southeast of Roswell, is closed to rockhounds, but nearby hills often yield Pecos "diamonds," small quartz crystals.

ROCK HOUND STATE PARK, 12 miles southeast of Deming, is a happy hunting ground for rockhounds, who search in the volcanic rocks for varieties of agate.

Conservation & Wildlife

CARLSBAD CAVERNS NATIONAL PARK. Every evening from late May through October, the bats fly out of the cave to feed on insects. Just before the flight begins, a park naturalist explains what is going to happen, but this still does not prepare the usual visitor for the exodus of some 5,000 bats a minute.

THE SOUTHWEST 163

CITY OF ROCKS STATE PARK, 22 miles northwest of Deming, has an outstanding cactus garden.

GILA CLIFF DWELLINGS, north of Silver City. From Scorpion Campground a "Trail into the Past" explains how the desert plants were used by the ancient Cliff Dwellers.

WHITE SANDS NATIONAL MONUMENT. Tourists hike among the 275 square miles of gypsum dunes. Foxes and coyotes live in the area, but the only animals that most tourists are likely to see are the white lizards and the white pocket mice.

ZOOLOGICAL - BOTANICAL GARDENS STATE PARK OF THE SOUTHWEST, at Carlsbad, has an extensive cactus collection. Both the flora and the fauna of the region may be seen.

OKLAHOMA

Camping

ARKANSAS - VERDIGRIS NAVIGATION SYSTEM. There are campgrounds along this remarkable new water highway.

BLACK MESA STATE PARK, 30 miles northwest of Boise City, offers camping in the rugged hills.

BOILING SPRINGS STATE PARK, 8 miles northeast of Woodward, is a shady forest on the plains. There are campgrounds.

CHICKASAW NATIONAL RECREATION AREA, near Sulphur, has six all-year campgrounds.

OKLAHOMA LAKES. Camping on the shores of Oklahoma's many man-made lakes is popular in a state that only a generation ago had no substantial bodies of water. The lakes and reservoirs include: Carl Etling, Fort Supply, Ellsworth, Lawtonka, Great Salt Plains, Murray, Thunderbird, Hulah, Atoka, Oologah, Greenleaf, Hudson, Webber Falls, Spavinaw, Eucha, Robert S. Kerr, Foss, Altus, Texoma, Canton, Fort Cobb, Grand, Eufaula, Wister, Keystone, Tenkiller, Broken Bow, and Fort Gibson.

OUACHITA NATIONAL FOREST has camping at the Billy Creek Recreation Area, Lenox Vista, Winding Stair, and Emerald Vista.

WICHITA MOUNTAINS WILDLIFE REFUGE, near Cache, has many campsites.

Hiking

ALABASTER CAVERNS STATE PARK, 6 miles south of Freedom. A trail leads down into Cedar Canyon and up to and over the Natural Bridge.

CHICKASAW NATIONAL RECREATION AREA, near Sulphur, has hiking in woodlands and on mountain slopes.

RED ROCK CANYON STATE PARK, ½ mile south of Hinton. A trail leads into the canyon, carved in the red rock.

Rockhounding

CALLIXYLON PETRIFIED WOOD is found in the vicinity of Ada. It dates from the Devonian period, 350 to 400 million years ago, and is some of the oldest petrified wood to be found in the world.

GYPSUM COUNTRY, around Waynoka, yields a specimen known as the rattlesnake egg. It is a rounded rock with black and white designs.

NOBLE AREA, east of Norman, is a likely place to look for barite rose rocks.

SALT PLAINS SELENITE CRYSTAL AREA is in the Great Salt Plains National Wildlife Refuge. Collecting of the crystals is allowed from 8 A.M.–5 P.M. on weekends and holidays from April 1 to October 15.

Canoeing & Rafting

GLOVER RIVER, in southeastern Oklahoma, is for experienced canoeists only, since it has many tricky rapids.

ILLINOIS RIVER. There is a boat access and campsite at the Watts Public Access Area, near Watts. Downstream floaters glide along in either johnboats or canoes, with or without guides. There are campgrounds along the riverbank. Take-out point is at Carter's Landing, 70 miles from the start of the float. This is at the headwaters of Lake Tenkiller. The Illinois is an easygoing stream with mild rapids. Operators who can supply equipment and guides are found at Sparrow Hawk Camp, Peyton's Place, Eagle Bluff Camp, Hanging Rock Camp, and at Cherokee Floats, Inc.

Boating

ARKANSAS RIVER NAVIGATION SYSTEM. Boaters ascend this system that makes the port of Catoosa, near Tulsa, head of navigation.

OKLAHOMA LAKES provide boaters with a variety of boating waters. There are campsites on the lakeshores.

Sport Diving

LAKE TENKILLER. Scuba divers believe that the lake's clear waters are among the best for diving in the Southwest.

Conservation & Wildlife

ALABASTER CAVERNS STATE PARK. Eight species of bats are found in the area. Six species live in the cave and the other two are occasionally seen in the park's trees.

GREAT SALT PLAINS NATIONAL WILDLIFE REFUGE is a unit in a chain of refuges reaching from Canada to Mexico. More than 250 species of waterfowl make it a stopping-off place. Hikers follow the Eagle Roost Nature Trail to study the various wildlife habitats. Beaver and white-tailed deer, wild turkeys, egrets, and herons as well as eagles are seen along the trail, which begins near the refuge office. The refuge is situated on the Great Salt Plains Reservoir, about 8 miles northeast of Jet.

MC CURTAIN COUNTY WILDERNESS AREA, near Broken Bow, consists of a series of narrow wooded ridges supporting a rich community of plants and animals. Visitors walk the primitive westside ridges and slopes with a wilderness guide and cross a narrow channel of Broken Bow Lake to the rugged east side. The area has been set aside to preserve its complex ecology.

WICHITA MOUNTAINS WILDLIFE REFUGE, near Cache, is renowned for its authentic herd of 300 longhorns and its herd of buffalo ranging free. There are also deer, elk, raccoon, armadillo, beaver, coyote, fox, prairie dogs, and over 200 species of birds.

WOOLAROC MUSEUM, near Bartlesville. Visitors drive through a wildlife preserve. Buffaloes and longhorns roam free.

TEXAS

Camping

ABILENE STATE PARK. There is fine camping on Lake Abilene. Campsites are in a grove of pecans that once sheltered Comanches.

ANGELINA NATIONAL FOREST. There are excellent campsites at the following recreational areas in the forest: Boykin Springs, southeast of Zavalla; Letney, southeast of Zavalla; Townsend, north of Broaddus on the eastern shore of Sam Rayburn Reservoir; Harvey Creek, east of Broaddus; Caney Creek, southeast of Zavalla; Sandy Creek, east of Zavalla; Bouton Lake, southeast of Zavalla; and Banister, northeast of Broaddus.

BIG BEND NATIONAL PARK. Camping is at The Basin, at Cottonwood near Castolon, and at Rio Grande Village. There are steep grades on the road leading to The Basin, and campers towing a trailer should consult with a ranger before making the trip.

DAVY CROCKETT NATIONAL FOREST contains camping areas at: Ratcliff Lake, between Kennard and Ratcliff; Neches Bluff, southwest of Alto; and Holly Bluff, northeast of Apple Springs.

GUADALUPE MOUNTAINS NATIONAL PARK. There is a drive-in campground near the mouth of Pine Springs Canyon, and there are other designated backcountry primitive camping areas.

PADRE ISLAND NATIONAL SEASHORE. There is camping at established campsites or on the beach itself in this longest expanse of pristine beach in the United States.

Big Bend National Park, Texas

PALO DURO CANYON STATE PARK. There is fine camping in this magnificent abyss that slices through the panhandle plains.

SABINE NATIONAL FOREST offers camping at these recreational areas: Red Hills Lake, north of Milam; Indian Mounds, southeast of Hemphill; Willow Oak, 15 miles southeast of Hemphill; Ragtown and Lakeview, both on Toledo Bend Reservoir.

SAM HOUSTON NATIONAL FOREST has camping in these areas: Double Lake, southwest of Coldspring; Stubblefield Lake, west of New Waverly.

Backpacking & Trail Riding

BIG BEND NATIONAL PARK. Hiking "off the beaten path" is adventurous, but a backpacker must be aware of the dangers of desert backpacking. Water is a serious problem for all hikers. Some of the most remote and least known country in the park lies in the Deadhorse Mountains. Trails in this area can be followed only by hikers skilled at reading old maps. Snakebite kits are recommended. Among these backpack trails that will test even the most ardent backpacker are: Ore Terminal Trail, Marufa Vega Trail, Strawhouse Trail, and Telephone Canyon Trail. There are other trails in the Sierra Quemada, at Apache Canyon, Burro Mesa Pouroff, Mariscal Mountain, and Mesa de Anguila. Horse trails lead to scenic viewpoints, such as the Window and the South Rim.

GUADALUPE MOUNTAINS NATIONAL PARK. There are 55 miles of primitive trails for hikers to follow leading to such places as McKittrick Canyon, the relict forest in the "Bowl," Pine Springs Canyon, and Dog Canyon. Steep and rugged trails also lead to the top of Guadalupe Peak and Bush Mountains. Trail riding is also possible.

SALT GRASS TRAIL RIDE. Once a year, in late February, riders come together at Brenham to take a 4-day trail ride on an old cattle trail to Houston and to attend that city's annual livestock show and rodeo.

Hiking

BIG BEND NATIONAL PARK. The park contains a number of outstanding day-hike trails. A strenuous trail to the South Rim is not for novices, but there are other shorter trails in the Basin. The Lost Mine Trail takes a hiker to an overlook at the head of Juniper Canyon, from where he can look for miles into Mexico. Lost Mine Ridge is at the top of the trail, and down below a hiker can see all of the wild Big Bend country spread out beneath him.

BIG THICKET NATIONAL PRESERVE. The woods roads and trails of this deep tangled woods north of Beaumont should be hiked only with a local guide. Hikes can be taken from the Alabama-Coushatta Indian Reservation near Woodville.

GARNER STATE PARK. Hikers climb the towering hills.

OIL SPRINGS TRAIL, near Woden. The Texas Forestry Association maintains the 10-mile trail along the long-abandoned right-of-way of the old Nacogdoches and Southeastern Railroad. If you believe in ghosts, don't take the trail after dark, for it is reputed to be haunted by the ghost of a railroad brakeman who goes along the right-of-way swinging his lantern, looking for his head which was cut off long ago in an accident.

PADRE ISLAND NATIONAL SEASHORE. A hike along the beach allows a person to look for driftwood or even Spanish coins that sometimes wash up from sunken galleons off the shore.

SAM HOUSTON NATIONAL FOREST features foot trails through the big timber and along the secluded streams near the Big Thicket National Preserve.

Rockhounding

APACHE MOUNTAINS. Once the mountains were ocean reefs and floors, and today marine fossils can be found in their limestone and sandstone sides.

SIERRA DIABLO MOUNTAINS, north of Van Horn. Abandoned copper mines scar the mile-high peaks. Rockhounds with a yen for adventure find the old mine rubble worth searching, but proper wilderness precautions must be taken. Water is a serious problem.

WHITE POINT, across Nueces Bay from Corpus Christi, is a favorite place for collectors of selenite crystals.

WOODWARD RANCH, Alpine. Frank Woodward, a geologist, welcomes rockhounds to his ranch, where for a small fee they may search for fire opals, carnelians, agates, and many other stones.

Canoeing & Rafting

BIG BEND NATIONAL PARK. Rubber rafts take adventurous floaters through Mariscal Canyon. There are exciting rapids on the Rio Grande capped by the Slot, where the river foams through a narrow gate in the rocks.

DEVILS RIVER. At high water, floaters put in at the Dolan Creek Ranch to glide down the river, a tributary of the Rio Grande.

VILLAGE CREEK in the Big Thicket offers an extraordinary canoe trip through one of the nation's richest wildlife areas. At dusk a canoeist may be hurried to his destination by the howl of a wolf, echoing over the stream.

Boating

GULF COAST. Saltwater boating is outstanding along the coast. The network of passes and inlets and other sheltered waters and the nearness of hospitable ports make boating easygoing.

TEXAS LAKES. The man-made lakes of Texas provide happy places for southwestern boaters.

Sport Diving

GULF. When diving in the gulf, divers use a boat out of Brazosport. The *Aqua Safari*, skippered by Lewis Shafer, specializes in taking out divers. Another popular skin-diving area is off Port Aransas. Divers dive at the offshore rigs off Mustang and Padre islands.

TEXAS LAKES. Texas divers prefer to use the following lakes because of their clear waters: Travis, Possum Kingdom, Amistad, and Buchanan.

Conservation & Wildlife

ARANSAS NATIONAL WILDLIFE REFUGE, near Rockport, the winter home for the whooping cranes, is still fighting for the survival of the species. The refuge is also home to 500 species of waterfowl and songbirds.

BIG BEND NATIONAL PARK. Life on the Great Chihuahuan Desert is varied. Mesquite, strawberry cactus, sotol, yucca, ocotilla, and cholla are just a few of the cacti. The foothills are forested with piñon and juniper, and ponderosa pine and Douglas fir grow in the ravines and canyons in the mountains. In the Chisos there are flagtail deer, mountain lion, and black bear. Mule deer, antelope, and javalina are found in the foothills and on the plain. The park is also home to such birds as the Inca dove, white-necked raven, and golden eagle.

BIG THICKET NATIONAL PRESERVE, north of Beaumont, is part woods and part marsh, home to an enormous variety of plants and animals. Of the world's eight known kinds of flesh-eating plants, seven may be found in the Big Thicket. The thicket is home to rare birds, to wolves, and to Mexican cats. Virgin stands of pines and hardwoods make up the thicket, but there are also magnolia trees, dogwood, redbuds, wild azaleas, and orchids. This magnificent forest is under study for a possible national park, but at the same time its destruction is threatened by timber interests. Conservationists who have studied the preserve have found it to be one of the most fascinating places in the Southwest.

BLACK GAP WILDLIFE MANAGEMENT AREA, near Marathon. Wildlife managers here are studying various ways to protect bobcats, cougars, mule deer and pronghorn antelopes in this 100,000 acres of brushy mountains. White-winged dove and quail are also inhabitants of this area.

MAC KENZIE STATE PARK, at Lubbock. Prairie dogs live in Prairie Dog Town as they have since before settlers entered the region.

MOUNT FRANKLIN, El Paso. The southern tip of the Rockies is 7,192-foot-high Mount Franklin, overlooking the city of El Paso. The mountain is rich in both flora and desert fauna.

MULESHOE NATIONAL WILDLIFE REFUGE, west of Littlefield. Migratory waterfowl flying over the south Texas high plains set down in this protected wildlife area.

PADRE ISLAND NATIONAL SEASHORE. The seashore is under one of the greatest flyways in North America, and there are tremendous numbers of migratory birds as well as resident birds, such as white and brown pelicans, American and snowy egrets, little blue and great herons, and the laughing gull.

PALMETTO STATE PARK, near Luling, is a sylvan retreat full of exotic plants.

SEA RIM STATE PARK, near Sabine Pass, is a 2.5-mile beach and marsh area, home of several rare and endangered species of wildlife.

WELDER WILDLIFE REFUGE, 7½ miles north of Sinton, is the largest privately endowed refuge in the world. There are more than 1,000 deer, wild turkey, and a variety of birds. Thursday tours begin at the laboratories and classrooms and go through the refuge.

THE ROCKIES

The craggy Rocky Mountains appalled the westering pioneers because they had to get over the high passes before the fall storms broke or risk being trapped in the snow. Today much of the Rocky Mountains is still a wilderness, where bear, mountain lion, sheep, and antelope still roam. In Grand Teton National Park, in Wyoming, moose graze undisturbed in lush wilderness pastures, and at South Pass, through which the wagon trains once rumbled, deer and antelope still play.

Prospectors entered the West to chisel and chip at rocks in search of gold and silver. Today's rockhounds still seek out precious ores but also look for gems and curious rock formations. They search in the tailings of old mines and look for mines of their own.

Outdoor vacationers in the Rocky Mountains hike through snowfields in Glacier National Park, saddle up for a pack excursion into the backcountry of Yellowstone National Park, or go rafting through the rapids of the Mad River Canyon of the Snake in Wyoming. It has long been possible to drive an auto to the jump-off point for a wilderness experience in the Rockies, but now vacationers are finding that if they travel light they can take a bus or train to their jump-off point. After all, a backpack takes less room in a bus baggage compartment or train baggage rack than does a suitcase.

The Rocky Mountains are the rooftop of the nation, through which the continental divide zigzags its way. Across Colorado the divide runs high above tree line in the alpine tundra. It meanders across Wyoming's lofty plateaus in such an undramatic way that it is hard for a vacationer to discover where it lies. Yet east of it, streams run to the rivers that run to the Gulf of Mexico, and west of it, streams run to the rivers that run to the Pacific Ocean. Everything east of the divide is called eastern slope, and everything west of it is called western slope, and friends have been known to fall out over which slope affords the best recreation in the outdoors.

The roll call of the Rocky Mountain states: Colorado, Idaho, Montana, Nevada, Utah, and Wyoming. Add to this impressive list the Canadian provinces of Alberta and Saskatchewan, and there emerges one of the most magnificent outdoor recreation areas in the world. The Colorado Rockies alone contain 1,500 peaks taller than 10,000 feet, and 54 summits higher than 14,000 feet. Yet these mountains, as well as others in the U.S. West and many in Canada, are accessible by trail so that on foot or on horseback a vacationer can explore them. Certainly inexperienced hikers and people in poor physical shape should be careful, because of the effects of high altitudes and the rough terrain. There is a golden rule that can cover a few hours' hike as sensibly as it covers a week's backpack: the trail back to the jump-off point always seems longer than the trail going out.

On a Western trail ride a vacationer eats plain grub served up from a chuck wagon and sleeps beneath skies where the stars gleam big and bright. He finds that he is in a land of superlatives where it is easy to believe a claim made by Jim Bridger, one of the greatest of the scouts and mountain men. "Out thar in Yellowstone," he used to opine, "thar's a river that flows so fast it gets hot on the bottom." He claimed that a man could catch a trout in the stream and cook it in a spring of boiling water. Everybody back east thought the old scout was making it all up, but today in Yellowstone National Park, you could do it without a hitch if the rangers didn't object to your dangling your catch into one of the scalding basins.

Utah and Nevada stand in contrast to the other states and provinces, for they have not only forested mountains but vast alkali flats and jumbled badlands. Utah has some of the most face-of-the-moon landscapes in the world, mostly encompassed in national parks and monuments, and Nevada too is remarkable for its extraordinary landscapes. The great basin lying between the westernmost slopes of the Rockies and the towering peaks of the Sierra Nevadas holds not only alkali wastes and sagebrush flats but hills and lesser mountains and the Great Salt Lake, a remnant of a vast inland sea of another time in the world's history.

"Bring me men to match my mountains," wrote the poet Walter Foss, who loved the unbroken wilderness that was in his time the primeval West. In the American and Canadian West vacationers seek each in his own way to match the mountains, and they return to their workaday lives better men and women, boys and girls, for it. Whether their experience has been floating the Colorado or the Snake on a raft, hiking into the Canadian Rockies from Banff, or rockhounding in an abandoned mine in Nevada, they have come to share in the natural heritage of the West.

Bighorn National Forest, Wyoming

COLORADO

Camping

BLACK CANYON OF THE GUNNISON NATIONAL MONUMENT. There are campgrounds on both rims.

BONNY RESERVOIR, north of Burlington, has two campgrounds on its 14-mile shoreline.

CURECANTI NATIONAL RECREATION AREA contains a campground at Elk Creek, in the heart of the Colorado western slope adjoining the Black Canyon of the Gunnison.

DINOSAUR NATIONAL MONUMENT contains campgrounds at Split Mountain Gorge and Echo Park.

GRAND MESA, east of Grand Junction, is an enormous flat-topped mountain, 10,500 feet high. There are outstanding camping areas on the mesa.

GREAT SAND DUNES NATIONAL MONUMENT has a campground close to the striking sand dunes.

LATHROP STATE PARK, west of Walsenburg, contains idyllic camping spots.

ROCKY MOUNTAIN NATIONAL PARK. The park contains over 1,000 camping sites in such places as Glacier Basin, Aspenglen, and Moraine Park. Other camping sites are at Timber Creek Campground on the western slope, Wild Basin at the beginning of the Wild Basin trail network, Longs Peak at the foot of the mountain, and Endovalley.

ROOSEVELT NATIONAL FOREST has excellent campgrounds close to Estes Park.

SHADOW MOUNTAIN NATIONAL RECREATION AREA, southwest of Rocky Mountain National Park, has some fine campsites.

SOUTHERN UTE TOURIST CENTER. Camping facilities are available at Lake Capote, near Ignacio. The tourist center, owned by the Southern Ute tribe, offers up-to-date vacationing the Indian way.

WHITE RIVER NATIONAL FOREST, in northwestern Colorado, contains excellent campgrounds.

Backpacking & Trail Riding

DINOSAUR NATIONAL MONUMENT. Horseback trips into the backcountry are popular. Trips along the Canyon Rim Trail and into Anderson Hole to the Yampa River and to the Gates of Ladore are offered by Petersen Pack Trips, in Maybell. Other horseback trips can be arranged.

EAGLE NEST PRIMITIVE AREA, in the vicinity of Dillon, can be reached only on horseback.

GUNNISON NATIONAL FOREST has 27 peaks over 12,000 feet, and it is prime country for pack trail trips into the backcountry. The 88,000-acre West Elk Wild Area is accessible to backpackers and horse trailers.

ROCKY MOUNTAIN NATIONAL PARK contains some of the finest high country backpacking possibilities in North America. There are about two hundred worthwhile trails of varying lengths and difficulty. Among the favorite longer trails are the Bear Lake-Grand Lake Trails, the trail from Wild Basin to Grand Lake, and the trail over the Mummy Range to Lost Lake. Backpackers here must accustom themselves to the high altitudes. The trail over the Mummy Range reaches 13,000 feet, and all the trails are to be undertaken after proper preparation and conditioning.

SAN JUAN BASIN, northeast of Durango, is favored by pack trippers. Saddle horses for trail rides and for pack trips are available at a riding stable at Vallecito.

SAN JUAN NATIONAL FOREST is outstanding country for pack trips. Wilderness outfitters and guides are located at Durango. All a rider has to bring is his sleeping bag.

UNCOMPAHGRE WILDERNESS. The Wilderness Society sponsors a backpack into the wild mountains of the Uncompahgre country. The outfitter is situated in Montrose.

WEMINUCHE WILDERNESS, combining the Upper Rio Grande and San Juan primitive areas, is a half-million-acre wilderness limited to backpackers and trail riders. The Wilderness Society offers a trail ride into the wilderness from Wagon Wheel Gap. Another Wilderness Society trip, this one a backpack, is possible from Wagon Wheel Gap into the La Garita Wilderness, a magnificent upland region of high peaks and flowered meadows.

WHITE RIVER NATIONAL FOREST, in northwestern Colorado, is noted for its primitive areas, which are accessible only to backpackers and trail riders. There are hundreds of miles of trails to explore in this rugged high country west of the Continental Divide.

Hiking

COLORADO NATIONAL MONUMENT. There are hiking trails leading among the sheer-walled canyons, monoliths, and fluted columns of this fantastically eroded country.

CORONA PASS AND BYERS PEAK, near Winter Park, have several good hiking trails.

GREAT SAND DUNES NATIONAL MONUMENT. The Monteville Trail provides an enjoyable stroll through a small valley.

LATHROP STATE PARK, 2 miles west of Walsenburg. Hiking trails ascend Lathrop Peak. The trails lead among rock outcroppings, piñon pine, and juniper.

MESA VERDE NATIONAL PARK. Hikers must register with rangers before taking the trails that lead to the ruins. The Pictograph Point Trail runs from the museum around the cliff base along the east side of Spruce Tree and Navajo canyons. There are other trails in the Morfield Canyon area of the park.

ROCKY MOUNTAIN NATIONAL PARK. There are over 300 miles of trail in the park, and a hiker can take anything from a short stroll over a trail off Trail Ridge Road or hike to the top of Longs Peak. A hiker should not take to a trail alone and should advise the nearest ranger station if he is attempting a dangerous or precipitous trail. This is high country, and there always can be sudden storms to discomfit a party on the trail.

WHITE RIVER NATIONAL FOREST. From Trappers Lake a trail leads to the Devil's Causeway, a narrow basalt ridge over 1,000 feet high.

Rockhounding

GOLD MINES. At such old gold mining towns as Gold Hill, Cripple Creek, Central City, Idaho Springs, Georgetown, or Breckenridge, gold panners still take gold from streams. There are some commercial operations where a visitor pays for the privilege of panning. Other places a property owner may let him pan free or for a share in the profits.

ROCKY MOUNTAINS. There are outstanding exposures of crystalline rocks and rare and beautiful minerals in the

THE ROCKIES

mountains. No specimens may be collected in national parks and monuments.

SILVER MINES. Amateur miners look for native silver as well as silver salts around old mining towns such as Leadville, Aspen, Silverton, and Lake City.

Canoeing & Rafting

COLORADO RIVER. Rafters meet Adventure Bound guides at the Ramada Inn in Grand Junction no later than 8:30 A.M. on the day they have reserved to make a trip through Westwater Canyon. The rafts run through Horsethief and Ruby canyons as well. It is a restful two days.

DINOSAUR NATIONAL MONUMENT. The churning rapids on the Green and the Yampa rivers afford some of the nation's most exciting rafting. Experienced river rats take vacationers on three- to five-day journeys down the rivers in neoprene pontoon boats. Such rapids as the Whirlpool and Split Mountain are household words to rafters all over the West.

GREEN RIVER. Canoeists paddle from the Swinging Bridge in Browns Park for 17 miles to the Ladore Canyon Ranger Station in Dinosaur National Monument. There are extremely dangerous rapids within the monument, and canoeing through them is prohibited.

RIO GRANDE RIVER. Canoeists put in at Wagon Wheel Gap and paddle 25 miles downstream to Del Norte.

YAMPA RIVER, from Lily Park downstream for 18 miles to the boundary of Dinosaur National Monument, is a good canoeing stream.

Conservation & Wildlife

DINOSAUR NATIONAL MONUMENT. At the Dinosaur Quarry Visitor Center, vacationers watch workmen use jackhammer, chisel, and pick to cut away barren rock to reveal fossil bones of dinosaurs. There are also interesting self-guiding nature trails and campfire programs that interpret the scientific features of the monument.

GREAT SAND DUNES NATIONAL MONUMENT. A nature trail starts in the lush forest, runs past tumbling streams and through quiet glens, and ends up in a barren desert, where dunes tower to 1,000 feet.

PAWNEE BUTTES, west of Sterling. Prairie birds nest in the cliffs where fossilized remains of prehistoric horse and camel have been excavated.

ROCKY MOUNTAIN BIOLOGICAL LABORATORY, in the old mining camp of Gothic, 8 miles north of Crested Butte. Students spend the summer studying wild plant and animal life.

ROCKY MOUNTAIN NATIONAL PARK. Among the nature trails in this great nature preserve is the Moraine Park Trail. A self-guiding walk around Bear Lake is also a popular way to meet some of the small mammals and birds of the park and study at firsthand the work of glaciers.

WHITE RIVER NATIONAL FOREST, near Aspen, has a nature trail for blind people. They listen, feel, and smell the beautiful wilderness around them.

IDAHO

Camping

ALBENI COVE is a Corps of Engineers camp just west of Priest River on US 2.

BITTERROOT NATIONAL FOREST. Paradise Campground is 15 miles north of the Magruder Ranger Station on a dirt road. Trailers and other recreational vehicles should not attempt the road. Indian Creek, 8 miles north of the Magruder Ranger Station, is just as beautiful but also not suitable for trailer camping.

BOISE NATIONAL FOREST offers camping at a large number of sites at such places as French Creek on the Cascade Reservoir, and on the North Fork of the Payette River, where there are units at Swinging Bridge, Big Eddy, Cold Springs, and Canyon.

BUREAU OF LAND MANAGEMENT CAMPGROUNDS are located at Mirror Lake, Tingley Spring, Killarney Lake, and Pack River Viewpoint.

CACHE NATIONAL FOREST provides camping at nine places. Cold Spring is 11 miles south of Soda Springs, and Emigration is 18 miles northwest of Paris.

CARIBOU NATIONAL FOREST contains campsites at a large number of places. Some of the best are at Hoffman, 5 miles south of Alpine, and Scout Mountain, 17 miles southeast of Pocatello.

CHALLIS NATIONAL FOREST. There are fine campgrounds at Bighorn, 11 miles east of Featherville; Basin Creek, 9 miles northeast of Stanley; and Blind Creek, 22 miles northwest of Clayton. These are only a few of the many fine camping areas in the forest.

CLEARWATER NATIONAL FOREST offers camping at Wendover Camp on the Lewis & Clark Highway; Aquarius, adjacent to Canyon Ranger Station; and Three Devils, 20 miles east of Kooskia on US 12. There are more than a dozen other fine camping areas.

COEUR D'ALENE NATIONAL FOREST offers camping at Bell Bay, 3 miles north of Harrison on Lake Coeur d'Alene; Mokins Bay, on the east side of Chatcolet Lake; and at Devil's Elbow and Avery Creek on the Coeur d'Alene River.

FARRAGUT STATE PARK, 4 miles east of Athol, is where the Scouts held their World Jamboree. Family campers find that camping by Lake Pend Oreille is a pleasure.

HEYBURN STATE PARK, between Plummer and St. Maries, is the oldest of the state's parks. Campsites are well developed.

IDAHO POWER COMPANY CAMPGROUNDS are located along the reservoirs created by the company's Brownlee, Oxbow, and Hells Canyon dams. There are four campgrounds along the 100-mile stretch of the Snake.

INDIAN CREEK STATE PARK, 35 miles north of Priest River, has camping on beautiful Priest Lake.

KANIKSU NATIONAL FOREST. There are a number of camping areas. Among the most beautiful are those at West Luby Bay on the west shore of Priest Lake and at Meadow Creek on the Moyle River, 15 miles northeast of Bonners Ferry. Three Pines and Bartoo are island campgrounds in Priest Lake.

LEWIS & CLARK HIGHWAY. The historic route taken by the explorers Lewis and Clark in 1805–06 traverses the Bitterroots. There are campsites along the 133-mile way from Lolo to Kooskia so that auto tent campers and RV campers can set up for the night along the road. Camping areas are at Wild Goose, Apgar Creek, Glade, Green Flats, Powell, White Sands, Whitehouse, Colt Creek, Wendover Bar, Hoodoo Lake, and Lee Creek.

NEZ PERCE NATIONAL FOREST offers camping in 18 areas, including the celebrated Selway-Bitterroot Area, where there are campsites at Big Fog Saddle, Race Creek, and Indian Hill Ridge. The

170 THE ROCKIES

ROCKY MOUNTAIN STATES

Snowmass Mountain, Colorado

campgrounds at Selway Falls, 22 miles east of Lowell by a good gravel road, are handy to hiking in the Selway-Bitterroot Wilderness.

PAYETTE NATIONAL FOREST contains many camping areas. Some of the favorites are at Black Lake, 44 miles northwest of Council by forest road; Huckleberry, 30 miles northwest of Council by forest road; and Hazard Lake, 27 miles northwest of McCall on Idaho 55.

PONDEROSA STATE PARK offers superb camping on a peninsula jutting into Payette Lake near McCall.

POTLACH FORESTS provides campgrounds at Beauty Bay, 13 miles southeast of Coeur d'Alene; Vanderpoel, on US 95 near the junction with Idaho 3; E. C. Rettig, 2 miles south of headquarters on Idaho 11; and Campbell's Pond, 6 miles north of Pierce.

REGISTER AND MASSACRE ROCKS STATE PARKS offer camping 20 miles southwest of American Falls, where emigrants to Oregon carved their names on Register Rock.

ST. JOE NATIONAL FOREST. Some of the fine campgrounds are at Tin Can Flat, Turner Flat, and Mammouth Springs.

SALMON NATIONAL FOREST has outstanding campgrounds. Middle Fork Peak grounds, 22 miles southwest of Cobalt, is at a bracing 8,800 feet, and Twin Creeks, 5 miles northwest of Gibbonsville, is handy to a patch of huckleberries.

SAWTOOTH NATIONAL FOREST campgrounds range from Father & Sons, 19 miles west of Oakley, to Alturas Lake, 36 miles north of Ketchum. There is a wide variety of campsites at other points.

SAWTOOTH NATIONAL RECREATION AREA AND WILDERNESS. There is camping in over 40 recreation sites, ranging from Lola Creek to the North Fork. Wilderness camping is popular too.

TARGHEE NATIONAL FOREST offers camping in such places as Upper Coffee Pot on Henry's Fork above the Island Park Reservoir and at Mike Harris, 4 miles southeast of Victor on Idaho 31.

THREE ISLAND CROSSING STATE PARK. Campers pitch their tents close to where pioneers taking the Oregon Trail pitched theirs. Portions of the Oregon Trail may still be seen close to the campground.

Backpacking & Trail Riding

HELLS CANYON-SEVEN DEVILS SCENIC AREA extends over 130,000 acres in three national forests located in both Idaho and Oregon. Backpackers and trail riders follow the trails once known to Indians, trappers, and prospectors.

SAWTOOTH NATIONAL RECREATION AREA AND WILDERNESS. In this land of snow-clad mountains, rushing streams, glacial basins, timbered slopes, and upland meadows is some of the finest of the state's backpacking and trail riding. Most of the lakes and scenic spots can be reached only on foot or in the saddle. There are hot fishing spots, abandoned mining camps, and outdoor adventure to be found.

SELWAY-BITTERROOT WILDERNESS, near the Idaho-Montana border north of the Salmon River, is the nation's largest official wilderness. Its 1,239,840 acres are home to the world's biggest elk herd. Only horseback and foot trails lead into the wilds.

Hiking

CRATERS OF THE MOON NATIONAL MONUMENT. There is a trail good for a two-hour hike to Great Owl Cavern. Veteran hikers who check in with the ranger may also explore the lava wilderness in the southern part of the monument.

NATIONAL FOREST TRAILS. All of the national forests in Idaho contain excellent trails for hiking. These may be picked up at most campgrounds and picnic areas. If a hiker does not have a map of the forest, he would be well advised to pay strictest attention to his orientation, for too many hikers get lost in the Idaho forests every year. Day hikes may also be taken into the wilderness areas described for backpackers.

Rockhounding

ADAMS COUNTY. Rubies and pink garnets are found at Rock Flat near New Meadows. Diamonds have also been discovered in the same area as have sapphires and corundum crystals.

CUSTER COUNTY. Rare zeolite is found near Challis. There is also a forest of petrified wood in the vicinity. Cryptocrystalline quartz may be found in a blood-red sandstone near the East Fork of the Salmon River.

EMERALD CREEK in the St. Joe National Forest, 6 miles north of Clarkia, then 6 miles on gravel-and-dirt Palouse River Road. There are garnets to be found.

GEM COUNTY. Fire opals are found in the lava beds of Squaw Butte near Emmett. They are salmon-pink or cherry-red in color and have great brilliance. Agates of light blue color are found in the vicinity. Agatized and opalized wood also is found along Willow Creek.

OWYHEE COUNTY. Succor Creek on the western edge of the county is a place to look for red and green agates in a two-tone combination and "thunder eggs," in which the center may be filled with fluids or crystals.

WASHINGTON COUNTY. Petrified wood is found along Mann Creek, northwest of Weiser. The grain of the wood is very prominent and the color is yellow. Beacon Hill nodules are found in the Beacon area west of Weiser.

Canoeing & Rafting

HELLS CANYON. Adventurous floaters run through Hells Canyon of the Snake. Guides or a licensed outfitter are advised, and a forest ranger should know when and where you are going before you enter the canyon. The most difficult portion of the stream is below Hells Canyon Dam to Sheep Creek. There are dangerous falls and rapids to trap the amateur, and there is no way to beach a boat. Wild Sheep Rapids and Granite Creek Rapids are particularly redoubtable. There are campsites along the Snake.

MAIN FORK OF THE SALMON RIVER is called the "River of No Return," for once a rafter launches out on its turbulent flow he has no choice but to continue down the canyon to its end. Canyon walls rise as much as a mile over the rushing current as the 22-foot rubber rafts pitch among Gun Barrel Rapids, Dry Meat Rapids, and Devil's Teeth Rapids. The first known attempt of explorers to run the Salmon ended in disaster. In 1832 four Hudson's Bay Company trappers tried to float down the river in a boat made of hides. Two drowned, and the others finally reached Fort Nez Percé 30 days later virtually naked. Today, with the improved equipment and rafts, descending the Salmon River is even safe for families.

SELWAY RIVER. Still more adventurous floaters attempt this smaller and far less known river in the north.

Conservation & Wildlife

CRATERS OF THE MOON NATIONAL MONUMENT. Starting at the Visitor Center, visitors take trails that lead to the fascinating volcanic formations. There is a nature trail through the formation named the Devil's Orchard. The trail leads to eerie cinder fields and crater-wall fragments.

DE VOTO MEMORIAL GROVE, along the Lochsa River on US 12, is an area of giant cedars dedicated to the memory of Bernard De Voto, the writer and conservationist.

SAWTOOTH NATIONAL FOREST. The Redfish Lake Visitor Center tells the human and natural history of the Sawtooth Primitive Area, a wilderness domain of 200,000 acres. Fishhook Creek Nature Trail begins near the center. At the nearby Salmon River, naturalists explain the life cycle of the Chinook salmon and how it makes its 800-mile journey from salt water to the headwaters of the river to spawn.

MONTANA

Camping

FLATHEAD NATIONAL FOREST. There are fine campgrounds along the North Fork of the Flathead River.

GLACIER NATIONAL PARK. Campgrounds range in size from 6 to 200 campsites, and some offer trailer spaces. The most important campgrounds are at Lake McDonald, Swiftcurrent, Rising Sun, Two Medicine, and St. Mary Lake. Hikers find that Kintla Lake Campground, in the North Fork Valley close to the Canadian border, is well worth the effort to reach.

LEWIS AND CLARK NATIONAL FOREST also has outstanding campgrounds.

MONTANA STATE PARKS. The state's 43 state parks have facilities for camping.

NATIONAL FOREST CAMPGROUNDS. The remaining nine national forests in Montana are also justly appreciated for their fine camping. A vacationer in the state finds excellent campgrounds at almost every quarter.

ROCKY BOY INDIAN RESERVATION AND RECREATION AREA has new facilities for camping. The reservation is at Rocky Boy.

WHITE CLIFFS OF THE MISSOURI RIVER. There are camping sites along the river traversed by Lewis and Clark.

Backpacking & Trail Riding

ABSAROKA PRIMITIVE AREA is in the Gallatin National Forest, just north of Yellowstone National Park. Trails lead into the area from Yellowstone National Park and from nearby towns. Moose are abundant in the area.

THE ANACONDA-PINTLAR WILDERNESS. Backpackers and trail riders penetrate rugged mountains atop the Continental Divide. The wilderness is in the Deerlodge, Beaverhead, and Bitterroot national forests southwest of Anaconda. The Hiline Trail along the top of the range is the most important of dozens of trails.

BEARTOOTH PRIMITIVE AREA in south-central Montana, southwest of Billings, is in the Custer and Gallatin national forests. Backpackers and riders follow trails up the Stillwater River, the East and West Rosebud Creeks, Red Lodge Creek, Rock Creek, and from Cooke City into the interior. This is a wilderness where few people go There are peaks to climb and glaciers to explore.

BOB MARSHALL WILDERNESS contains 950,000 acres of wild country within a triangle formed by the towns of Missoula, Kalispell, and Great Falls and is in the Flathead and Lewis and Clark national forests. On foot or on horseback vacationers travel along the trails that lead into the heart of the mountains. Guides and outfitters are available.

CABINET MOUNTAINS WILDERNESS. A line of tall peaks rises above the timbered valleys and ridges in northwest Montana in the Kootenai and Kanisku national forests. Trails take riders and backpackers into the interior of the wilderness. It is a land of awesome snow-clad peaks and glacial lakes, rushing cascades, big-game animals, and red cedar and white pine.

GATES OF THE MOUNTAINS WILDERNESS, on the Missouri River near Helena, is named for the mountains that Lewis and Clark first found opposing them. The wilderness area is in the Helena National Forest. Horseback and backpacking trips take vacationers to limestone cliffs. Trails pass through narrow gorges. There are elk, deer, bear, and mountain goats in the wilderness area.

GLACIER NATIONAL PARK. With almost 1,000 miles of trails, Glacier is foremost in backpacking and trail riding among the national parks. The Waterton Valley, the Belly River, and the Bowman and Kintla valleys are a few of the splendid isolated parts of the park that can be reached on overnight trail trips. Outfitters at the park can arrange guided pack trips of a week or more or provide hiking parties with a packer, a pack horse, and a cook if so desired.

MISSION RANGE PRIMITIVE AREA is a spectacular wilderness in the Flathead National Forest between Missoula and Kalispell. Horse trails penetrate part of the area, but riders must pack in their feed. Much of the area has no trails, and backpackers who are skilled in traveling cross-country find it a challenge. Others should remember that getting lost can be very easy indeed.

SALMON RIVER BREAKS PRIMITIVE AREA contains 40 miles of trackless area along the Salmon River. Access to this wild river area is by trail. Some of the trails lead to the canyon of the river, others to the abandoned cabins and orchards of old-timers who lived off the forest and the river.

SELWAY-BITTERROOT WILDERNESS. This is the largest wilderness in the United States, located on both sides of the Bitterroot Range, and it includes territory in both Idaho and Montana. Hikers and riders alike find this magnificent country to explore.

SPANISH PEAKS PRIMITIVE AREA is in the Gallatin National Forest 20 miles southwest of Bozeman. Trails can be followed on foot or on horseback.

Hiking

BIGHORN CANYON NATIONAL RECREATION AREA. Hiking trails are being opened in the heart of the Crow Indian Reservation. Cross-country hikers must check in with rangers.

GLACIER NATIONAL PARK. Many of the park's 1,000 miles of trails are appropriate for day hikes. Among these is the Avalanche Lake Trail, an easy hike that leads to unsurpassed beauty. It starts at the Avalanche Campground just off the Going-to-the-Sun Highway. The hiker need not be laden down with overnight gear when taking the trail to Sperry Chalets, since he can stay overnight in the chalet. A hiker comes off the trail and sits down to a good meal at the chalet.

NATIONAL FORESTS. Trails lead into all of the national forests in Montana. Day hikes may be carried out also in the wilderness and primitive areas.

ROSS CREEK SCENIC AREA, south of Troy on Montana 202. A trail leads among the giant cedars. The centuries-old trees tower over the hiker. The scenic area is administered by the U.S. Forest Service as part of the Kootenai National Forest.

Trail Riding—Idaho

Rockhounding

ELDORADO BAR SAPPHIRE MINE, near York. Gold miners noticed "curious blue glasslike stones" during the 1860s. These turned out to be sapphires, and now sapphire miners screen the gravels to look for the precious stones. They also take their turn at panning for gold. There are camping facilities, and during the summer lapidarists in York will cut your finds.

FORT PECK RESERVOIR. One of the outstanding areas for fossils is in eroded terrain along the lakeshore east of the Hell Creek Recreation Area. Permission to look for fossils must be obtained from public or private landowners.

YELLOWSTONE RIVER. The Montana moss agate is found in large quantities along the river from Yellowstone Park to Glendive.

YOGO SAPPHIRES. The heart of the yogo sapphire country from which a large share of the nation's sapphires has come is Lewistown.

Canoeing & Rafting

BEAVERHEAD RIVER from Clark Canyon Dam downstream to Pipe Organ highway bridge is suitable for smaller boats and rubber rafts. Unfortunately, other parts of the Beaverhead suffer from cross fences and rock diversions at irrigation headgates.

BIG HOLE RIVER from Divide Dam to the bridge crossings below Glen or near Twin Bridges is another popular floating stream.

JEFFERSON RIVER. Floaters can enter from either the Big Hole or Beaverhead rivers and continue on down into the Missouri to Toston Dam.

MADISON RIVER. Floaters enter the river at Varney Bridge about 13 miles above Ennis and descend to Three Forks. The floating is easy from the bridge to Ennis Lake. Below Ennis the river breaks out into several channels, but the floating remains easy. Through Beartrap Canyon the floating becomes highly hazardous because there are lots of boulders and the water is fast. The river is in a canyon and is relatively hard to reach, so injuries can be very serious. The section should be attempted only by experts. Below Beartrap Canyon the river flows through a broad valley. Below the Norris-Bozeman Bridge the river meanders and is easy to navigate.

MISSOURI RIVER. The Upper Missouri is a popular float stream. Floaters put their rafts into the river near Trident or enter the river by putting into the Jefferson or Madison rivers near Three Forks. The Toston Dam interrupts the trip. Another enjoyable trip is from the old highway bridge at Toston to Townsend. Takeout point is at the Fish and Game access site near the Townsend Bridge or at the Canyon Ferry Reservoir where there are access sites at one of the marinas. Canoeists also find the river interesting. Boaters also put into the Missouri River at the highway bridge below Holter Dam. From Fort Benton to Fred Robinson Bridge, some 160 miles downstream, is the last of the wild Missouri. It remains much as Lewis and Clark first saw it. It makes up part of the state's Recreational Waterway System. Missouri River Cruises, an outfitter at Fort Benton, offers trips down the Missouri from Fort Benton. Trippers camp on the riverbanks. The outfitter can also provide canoeist and a canoe return service.

YELLOWSTONE RIVER. The river is being floated in its entirety from the boundary of Yellowstone Park to Pompey's Pillar below Billings. It is one of the state's Recreational Waterways. The part from the park through Yankee Jim Canyon, above Livingston, is the most hazardous, and only experienced floaters should attempt it. Below Livingston there are few serious hazards, but below Billings there are a number of dangerous structures.

Conservation & Wildlife

BOWDOIN NATIONAL WILDLIFE REFUGE, east of Malta, shelters waterfowl, upland game birds, deer, and elk.

CHARLES M. RUSSELL NATIONAL WILDLIFE RANGE, at Slippery Ann in the Missouri River Breaks terrain, contains a scenic loop wildlife drive.

GLACIER NATIONAL PARK. The naturalist program is one of the most extensive in the national park system. There are fine nature trails and overnight trips to Sperry Glacier, Granite Park, and Garden Wall.

HUNGRY HORSE VISITOR CENTER in the Flathead National Forest. From the Visitor Center a vacationer can see the mighty reservoir and face of the dam. Exhibits tell about water management.

MADISON RIVER EARTHQUAKE VISITOR CENTER, in the Gallatin National Forest, reveals the terrible force of the August 17, 1959, earthquake, which struck 20 minutes before midnight. At stops along US 287 travelers can see the fault scarps, battered roads and buildings. The center is built upon the debris of the quake.

NATIONAL BISON RANGE protects one of the most important remaining herds of bison. The range also holds white-tailed and mule deer, elk, bighorn sheep, and pronghorns. There are a few Rocky Mountain goats. A self-guiding drive-through tour is possible during the summer from June 1 through September 30. The auto trip is 19 miles in length and begins and ends at range headquarters.

NEVADA

Camping

BEAVER DAM STATE PARK provides camping in a setting of pine forests and lofty cliffs. It is 35 miles southeast of Caliente.

BUREAU OF LAND MANAGEMENT CAMPGROUNDS. These include Tamarack Point on Walker Lake, 17 miles north of Hawthorne, and Wild Horse Reservoir Camp, 74 miles north of Elko.

HUMBOLDT NATIONAL FOREST. There are campsites 3 miles from Lehman Caves. Other campgrounds are at Lye Creek, 55 miles northeast of Winnemucca; Jack Creek, 63 miles northwest of Elko; Gold Creek, 77 miles north of Elko; and Currant Creek, 50 miles southwest of Ely. There are a number of other campgrounds in the forest.

ICHTHYOSAUR MONUMENT STATE PARK offers camping close to the remains of the prehistoric sea reptiles. The park is 23 miles from Gabbs.

KERSHAW-RYAN STATE PARK, 3 miles south of Caliente, is another popular camping park.

LAKE MEAD NATIONAL RECREATION AREA. There are campsites on the Nevada shore of the lake. They include Boulder Beach, Las Vegas Bay, Echo Bay, and Cottonwood Cove.

LAKE MOHAVE CAMPGROUNDS are at Willow Beach, 27 miles from Boulder City, and Cottonwood Cove, 14 miles east of Searchlight.

TOIYABE NATIONAL FOREST. Campgrounds range from the one at Big Creek, 15 miles south of Austin, to Nevada Beach, on Lake Tahoe, 25 miles west of Carson City.

VALLEY OF FIRE STATE PARK has campsites at Mouse's Tank and Atlatl Rock.

WARD CHARCOAL OVENS STATE PARK, 15 miles south of Ely, has primitive camping sites.

Hiking

BEAVER DAM STATE PARK is high in the mountains, where hiking through the pine forests is a pleasure.

VALLEY OF FIRE STATE PARK. Hikers stroll among weird rock formations to such favorites as Elephant Rock, the Beehives, Donald Duck, and the White Domes. Marked trails lead to the most fascinating spots.

Rockhounding

PERSHING COUNTY is a rockhound's paradise since it is one of the most highly mineralized parts of the state. Among the minerals to be found are: tungsten, gypsum, mercury, diatomaceous earth, iron, perlite, gold, silver, antimony, sulfur, and fluorspar. It is arid country, and rockhounds must be sure they bring along plenty of water. If they are going to venture away from the main roads, good orienteering skills are necessary.

THE ROCKIES

VIRGIN VALLEY DISTRICT of Humboldt County is renowned for fire opals of exceptional quality. Color ranges from deep black to almost transparent. The field is in a lonely desert 25 miles south of Denio. A flawless black opal weighing 17 troy ounces was found here in 1919.

Boating & Boat Camping

LAKE MEAD NATIONAL RECREATION AREA. Boating on Lake Mead is a family sport. Boats and motors can be rented or chartered. Houseboats are popular. Boat camping on the shoreline is a good way to get close to the desert, which borders the water.

Sport Diving

LAKE MEAD NATIONAL RECREATION AREA. Scuba diving is permitted on Lakes Mead and Mohave except in or near boat harbors or within 500 feet of swimming beaches or where otherwise posted. Diving increases in popularity yearly.

Conservation & Wildlife

HUMBOLDT NATIONAL FOREST. The Wheeler Peak Scenic Area contains five vegetative life zones ranging from the desert to the arctic-alpine. Forest naturalists present campfire programs near the Visitor Center to tell about the ecology of the area. A drive starts at the center and runs through the desert, among glacial lakes and cirques, and climbs to 10,000 feet at Wheeler Peak.

LEHMAN CAVES NATIONAL MONUMENT. The area around the caves is wild and beautiful. Mule deer may be seen feeding in the meadows or escaping through the forests. An occasional mountain lion may be seen. Owls, bluebirds, and water ouzels are found along nearby streams.

PYRAMID LAKE. This remnant of ancient Lake Lahontan is at the center of a fascinating wildlife area. Pelicans nest on Anaho Island as they have since before white men came. The white pelicans have a wingspread of at least eight feet.

UTAH

Camping

ASHLEY NATIONAL FOREST has a score of campgrounds. Spirit Lake is 22 miles southwest of Manila, and Wandin is 15 miles north of Neola.

BUREAU OF LAND MANAGEMENT CAMPGROUNDS in Utah include those at Calf Creek, Hatch Point, Windwhistle, Lonesome Beaver, McMillan Spring, Price Canyon, San Rafael Bridge, Simpson's Spring, Starr Springs, and Red Cliffs.

BRYCE CANYON NATIONAL PARK has two campgrounds near the Visitor Center.

CACHE NATIONAL FOREST. There are excellent camping areas spotted throughout the forest.

CANYONLANDS NATIONAL PARK has campgrounds at Squaw Flat. In the Island in the Sky area and in the backcountry, primitive camping is permitted at designated locations.

CAPITOL REEF NATIONAL PARK. There is a campground near the park headquarters.

CEDAR BREAKS NATIONAL MONUMENT offers camping.

DIXIE NATIONAL FOREST. There are campgrounds in the forest. They are designed to fit into the terrain and do not have all the conveniences that some campers desire. There is camping at Pine Lake, 12 miles southeast of Widstoe, and at Red Canyon, midway between Bryce Canyon and Panguitch.

FISHLAKE NATIONAL FOREST, MANTI LA SAL NATIONAL FOREST, UINTA NATIONAL FOREST, and WASATCH NATIONAL FOREST all have campgrounds well worth staying in.

NATURAL BRIDGES NATIONAL MONUMENT has a camping area near the Visitor Center.

STATE PARK CAMPGROUNDS are at Bear Lake, Big Sand Lake, Coral Pink Sand Dunes, Dead Horse Point, Green River, Hyrum Lake, Minersville Lake, East Canyon Lake, Great Salt Lake, Otter Creek Lake, Rockport Lake, Scofield Lake, Snow Canyon, Steinaker Lake, Utah Lake, Wasatch Mountain, Willard Bay, Yuba Lake, Goosenecks, Gunlock Lake, Huntington Lake, Indian Creek, Kodachrome Basin, Palisade Lake, Piute Lake, Escalante Petrified Forest, Golbin Valley, Newspaper Rock, Deer Creek Lake, Lost Creek Lake, and Millsite Lake.

ZION NATIONAL PARK. South campground is near the inn, and the Watchman Campground is just inside the south entrance.

Backpacking & Trail Riding

CANYONLANDS NATIONAL PARK. Backpackers like to take the trail down Salt Creek to Angel Arch. Outfitters can make arrangements for both hikers and riders to enter the Canyonlands backcountry.

CAPITOL REEF NATIONAL PARK. Backpackers hike through Muley Twist Canyon in the Waterpocket Fold.

DIXIE NATIONAL FOREST. A backpacking trail leads from Deep Creek to Zion National Park.

HIGH UINTAS PRIMITIVE AREA north of Altamont is a roadless area preserved as it was thousands of years ago with the exception of pack and hiking trails.

ZION NATIONAL PARK has many interesting backcountry trails. The West Rim Trail and the Kolob Trail are both popular with hikers and riders. The Narrows Trail is another excellent trail.

Hiking

ARCHES NATIONAL PARK. Foot trails lead to the celebrated arches, windows, pinnacles, and pedestals carved by erosion and the winds into the red rock.

BRYCE CANYON NATIONAL PARK. The most popular hike is over the Navajo Loop among the beautiful formations. Although the Under-the-Rim Trail is 35 miles long, sections of it are near the park road and make good short hikes.

CAPITOL REEF NATIONAL PARK. A self-guiding trail leads to Natural Bridge, and another to a onetime Mormon refuge.

LOGAN CANYON near Logan has some fine hiking trails.

MIRROR LAKE is located east of Kamas. There are hiking trails beside its pellucid waters.

ZION NATIONAL PARK. The Narrows Trail is popular with hikers who want to follow the steep-walled canyon of the Virgin River for a few hours. Trails to Angels Landing and to Lady Mountain are rough but short enough to make easy half-day hikes.

Rockhounding

CLEVELAND-LLOYD DINOSAUR QUARRY AND VISITOR CENTER, east of Huntington, contains one of the richest known deposits of dinosaur fossils.

DINOSAUR NATIONAL MONUMENT. At the Visitor Center of this monument, which ranges across the border into Colorado, the staff may be watched as they continue to uncover fossils.

SHEEP CREEK CANYON GEOLOGICAL AREA, south of Manila, has formations dating back 2½ billion years.

VERNAL FIELD HOUSE OF NATURAL HISTORY, at Vernal, has extraordinary displays of dinosaur fossils and minerals.

Canoeing & Rafting

CANYONLANDS NATIONAL PARK. Floaters begin at the highway bridge in the town of Green River and head downstream on the Green to the confluence with the Colorado. After that there are 40 tumultuous miles of rough waters in Cataract Canyon. The float trip ends up in the calm waters of Lake Powell. Outfitters in Moab take parties through the canyon's maelstrom.

GREEN RIVER. Floaters float 130 miles on the river through the Castle country. They camp on the idyllic riverbanks. There are also over 60 rapids to lend excitement. Floaters rendezvous at Vernal.

Sport Diving

BEAR LAKE near Garden City attracts skin divers.

Conservation & Wildlife

ASHLEY NATIONAL FOREST. At the Flaming Gorge Visitor Center, visitors learn about water conservation and the purposes of the 502-foot-high dam on the Green River. The impounded waters create a lake 94 miles long that extends into Wyoming.

BEAR RIVER BAY NATIONAL WATERFOWL MANAGEMENT AREA. Living in the 65,000 acres are 200 different bird species. This area is one of the largest bird shelters in the world. This and other refuges on the Great Salt Lake are home to some 2 million migrating birds each year. Nesting colonies of great blue herons, great white pelicans, Caspian terns, and California sea gulls are on islands.

CEDAR BREAKS NATIONAL MONUMENT. The colors of the amphitheater rim change with the angle of the light falling on them. Deer may be seen grazing on the meadows at the beginning and end of the day.

OGDEN BAY STATE WATERFOWL REFUGE AREA, close to Layton, shelters geese, ducks, and marsh birds.

TIMPIE SPRINGS STATE WATERFOWL MANAGEMENT AREA is a fine place for bird-watching. It is west of Grantsville.

ZION NATIONAL PARK. All of Utah's magnificent national parks have nature walks well worth anybody's interest, but Zion perhaps has the best. The Weeping Rock Trail and the Canyon Overlook Trail are self-guiding nature trails of both beauty and significance.

WYOMING

Camping

BIGHORN CANYON NATIONAL RECREATION AREA. At Horseshoe Bend, 17 miles from Lovell, 125 camping sites are available.

BIGHORN NATIONAL FOREST contains over 50 camping areas.

BOYSEN STATE PARK, near Shoshoni, has fine campgrounds, located below Boysen

Grand Teton National Park, Wyoming

Dam in the mouth of the dramatic Wind River Canyon.

DEVILS TOWER NATIONAL MONUMENT has a campground close to the foot of the towering rock formation that became America's first national monument.

KEYHOLE STATE PARK, is 8 miles from I-90, between Sundance and Moorcroft at the end of an improved gravel road. Campers have no difficulty in finding sites close to the Keyhole Reservoir, which is ideal for water sports.

MEDICINE BOW NATIONAL FOREST. Sites in this forest were originally designed for tent camping only, but some campsites have been enlarged to accommodate small tent trailers and pickup campers. There are also newer campgrounds for travel trailers, but trailers over 18 feet long are not easily accommodated at these sites.

SHOSHONE NATIONAL FOREST. There are excellent campsites in the forest at Beartooth Lake, Dead Indian, and Wapiti. Good campgrounds are found in the Wapiti Valley on the Cody Road to Yellowstone.

YELLOWSTONE NATIONAL PARK has some of the most overcrowded campgrounds in the West, but they continue to attract campers because of their proximity to the wonders of the park.

Backpacking & Trail Riding

BRIDGER WILDERNESS, along the face of the Wind River Range is in the Bridger National Forest. There are more than 500 miles of trails that reach up into the 10,000-foot level of the mountains. Wild flowers and a variety of wild game, including moose and bighorn sheep, become part of the hiker's mountain world. Entrance stations are at: Lower Green River Lake, New Fork Lake, Elkhart Park, Boulder Lake, and Big Sandy.

CLOUD PEAK PRIMITIVE AREA, in the Bighorn National Forest, contains wild and rugged cirques awaiting the intrepid backpacker and rider.

GRAND TETON NATIONAL PARK. There are 150 miles of trails for backpackers and riders to follow. The trails afford splendid views of the Grand Tetons, penetrate into deep canyons, follow streams, and cross alpine meadows. Those seeking rugged experiences can try the Glacier, Cascade Canyon, Lakes, and Indian Paintbrush trails. The variety of wildlife along the trails is remarkable.

TETON WILDERNESS of the Teton National Forest is a 563,000-acre wild country that borders Yellowstone. It is in turn bordered on the east by the South Absaroka Wilderness, making it possible for a backpacker or rider to travel for more than 80 miles without leaving the wilderness. The wilderness is home to part of the world's largest elk herd, moose, bighorn sheep, deer, and black and grizzly bear. The trail along Thoroughfare Creek was a favorite route of the Shoshoni and Blackfoot Indians. The North Absaroka Wilderness lies east of Yellowstone National Park and contains another remarkable backpacking area among such creeks as Hoodoo, Sunlight, and Dead Indian.

WAGONS WEST. Five covered wagons take vacationers on a trip through the wilderness of the Teton National Forest along the Buffalo River. Outfitter L. D. Frome's wagons follow forest fire and logging roads and pioneer trails. Frome is headquartered in Afton.

YELLOWSTONE NATIONAL PARK. Away from the traffic jams of the Grand Loop Road, Yellowstone has almost two million acres of well-marked trails. Backpackers and trail riders find the Howard Eaton Trail encircles the park.

Hiking

CURT GOWDY STATE PARK is in the foothills of the mountain range separating Cheyenne and Laramie. Hills that are around Granite and Crystal lakes are appealing to hikers.

DEVILS TOWER NATIONAL MONUMENT. A foot trail encircles the tower.

GRAND TETON NATIONAL PARK. The trails cover a variety of terrain and are of varying lengths and difficulty. Trails at Jenny Lake and Colter Bay are ideal for short hikes.

SINKS CANYON STATE PARK, 10 miles southwest of Lander, is noted for its variety of hiking trails.

YELLOWSTONE NATIONAL PARK. Trails lead from the roads to the principal features of this renowned park. A foot trail, for example, leads across the Firehole River at Midway Geyser Basin, and at Biscuit Basin another footpath leads to boiling Sapphire Pool.

Rockhounding

ARROWHEAD FLINT can be obtained near Lusk.

EDEN VALLEY WOOD, a petrified wood that seems to be made of living fiber, is found near Green River.

RAINBOW AGATES may be found in the vicinity of Riverton.

TURRITELLA AGATES are in good supply south of Wamsutter.

VEDAUWOOD, in the Pole Mountain District of the Medicine Bow National Forest, is a strange rock formation popular with rockhounds.

WIGGINS FORK, near Dubois, is an important source of petrified wood.

YELLOWSTONE NATIONAL PARK. Although collecting in Yellowstone is forbidden by law, rockhounds nonetheless find the petrified forests in the park exceptionally beautiful.

Canoeing & Rafting

BIGHORN RIVER can be navigated by both rubber rafts and canoes as it courses through Bighorn basins and through monumental Bighorn Canyon.

GREEN RIVER. Modern-day explorers float the Green either privately or commercially. The best floating is from the Warren Bridge through Daniel to the junction of the New Fork east of Big Piney.

NORTH FORK OF THE SHOSHONE is the site of a 5-mile commercial float.

NORTH PLATTE RIVER. The best floating is in the spring when the water is higher. After all, the early-day river navigators said the Platte was "a thousand miles long and six inches deep."

SNAKE RIVER. Rising in the Teton Wilderness below Yellowstone National Park, the river courses through some 100 miles of mountains. Commercial operators offer floats in rubber rafts. The float through the wilds brings vacationers face to face with wildlife. The river is also popular with canoeists. Beyond the entrance of the Gros Ventre River, the Snake becomes a larger and faster stream. Mad River Canyon brought early explorers to grief, but it only adds thrills to a floater's experience on the Snake. Parklands Expeditions in Jackson Hole offers five-day float adventures, depending upon water conditions.

Conservation & Wildlife

DEVILS TOWER NATIONAL MONUMENT.

A prairie dog colony is near the monument entrance.

GRAND TETON NATIONAL PARK. The valleys and mountains, the forests and wild flowers and the wildlife all have their fascination. The deer family in the park is represented by elk, moose, and mule deer. There are both black and grizzly bear. Bighorn sheep, beaver, weasel, coyote, and a host of birds all reside in the park.

YELLOWSTONE NATIONAL PARK is one of the world's most fascinating geological and scenic areas. It is also a remarkable wildlife preserve, featuring its famous bears. There are splendid nature trails.

ALBERTA

Camping

ALBERTA FOREST SERVICE provides rustic campsites in remote areas.

ALBERTA PROVINCIAL PARKS. There are 53 parks; most offer camping.

ALBERTA TRANSPORTATION has created 250 rustic campsites with cooking shelters, stoves, picnic tables, chopped wood, and dry toilets.

BANFF NATIONAL PARK. The park's 11 campgrounds include those at Lake Louise, Tunnel Mountain, Two Jack Lake, and Johnston Canyon.

ELK ISLAND NATIONAL PARK. There are camping facilities at Sandy Beach.

JASPER NATIONAL PARK has a number of campgrounds, the largest being Whistlers.

ROCKY MOUNTAIN HOUSE DISTRICT. There is splendid wilderness camping in the 7,500 square miles west of Rocky Mountain House. There are campgrounds for both tents and trailers located along the David Thompson Highway, most of them close to streams.

WATERTON LAKES NATIONAL PARK. There are fine campgrounds in this onetime Blackfoot stronghold. Close-to-nature camps are found at Snowshoe and Alderson lakes.

WOOD BUFFALO NATIONAL PARK. There is one developed campground at Pine Lake. Elsewhere in the park, camping must be done under natural conditions.

Bighorn Sheep—Wyoming

Backpacking & Trail Riding

BANFF NATIONAL PARK. There are 700 miles of trails leading into remote spots suitable for backpacks. People on overnight trail trips may bivouac en route, but they must register before and after the hike.

ELK ISLAND NATIONAL PARK has miles of trails. Visitors on overnight trail trips may camp outside the established campgrounds, but they must register with a park warden before and after their hike.

HIGH HORIZONS. This Banff organization is well staffed with trained mountain guides. They take boys, ages 14 to 18, on wilderness backpacking trips, starting near the Saskatchewan River Crossing on the Icefields Parkway and up the Siffleur River to Pipestone Pass and beyond. Another trip begins on the Trans-Canada Highway, 15 miles west of Banff, and heads up Redearth Creek to the Shadow and Egypt lakes area.

JASPER NATIONAL PARK has over 600 miles of trails. If on overnight trail trips, a backpacker may camp in wilderness areas, but he must register before and after each trip with a park warden.

ROCKY MOUNTAIN HOUSE DISTRICT. The mountainous wilderness west of Rocky Mountain House is ideal for trail rides and backpacks.

WATERTON LAKES NATIONAL PARK. The 110 miles of trails lead to interesting areas. Many of the trails have primitive campgrounds. If a hiker is planning to travel off the trails or bivouac overnight, he must register with a park warden before and after his trip. Hikers on the higher trails near timberline and the alpine meadows are likely to see bighorn sheep.

WOOD BUFFALO NATIONAL PARK. There are no well-marked trails, and backpackers find this an extraordinary place for wilderness adventure. The Salt Plains, the escarpment, sinkholes, sinkhole lakes, and plateaus are fascinating. Fire permits must be obtained from a park warden for backcountry camping.

Hiking

BANFF NATIONAL PARK. Day hiking is particularly popular on the trails in the Lake Louise and Moraine Lake districts.

ELK ISLAND NATIONAL PARK. A hiker can obtain a map of all the hiking trails in the park at the information center.

ICEFIELDS PARKWAY connects Banff and Jasper national parks. There are several trails leading from the parkway to such points as the Valley of Five and Parker Ridge Viewpoint.

JASPER NATIONAL PARK. Some of the most popular hiking trails are at Pyramid Lake, Mount Edith Cavell, Lake Annette, Lake Edith, and Maligne Canyon areas. Other trails begin at Jasper townsite.

WATERTON LAKES NATIONAL PARK contains ideal trails for day hikes to intriguing points.

THE ROCKIES

WOOD BUFFALO NATIONAL PARK. Although there are no formal hiking trails, a veteran hiker can explore the territory to suit himself.

Bike Hiking & Camping

ROCKY MOUNTAIN CYCLE TOURS, Banff, offers guided bike tours of Banff, Yoho, Jasper, and Kootenay national parks. On 2- to 5-day tours, bikers camp at night in the mountains. Traveling cooks prepare hearty meals. Daily bike clinics are held.

Rockhounding

DINOSAUR TRAIL. Motorists follow the 30-mile trail through the Valley of the Dinosaurs, near Drumheller. The Graveyard of the Dinosaurs is a remarkable find of fossils. The Dinosaur and Fossil Museum in Drumheller is engrossing.

DONALDA is a village 25 miles north of Stettler. Rockhounds range the area in search of petrified wood, quartz crystals, and dinosaur fossils.

Conservation & Wildlife

BANFF NATIONAL PARK. The wildlife and plants range through prairie, forest, and arctic forms. Cougar and wolf, elk, deer, sheep, moose, coyote, lynx, mountain goats, and rodents all live in the park. Grizzly roam the high country. Visitors must not feed the animals.

ELK ISLAND NATIONAL PARK. The Parkland and Lakeview trails are self-guiding nature trails leading through several different vegetation zones. There are some 30 species of mammals protected in the park.

ICEFIELDS PARKWAY. This spectacular route is among the great nature roads of the world as it passes among the Canadian Rockies. The road passes within a mile of Athabasca Glacier, and an access road takes visitors right to it. A snowmobile tour of the ice mass is offered.

JASPER NATIONAL PARK. Dominated by ice-capped mountains, Jasper is a nature preserve of unexcelled magnificence. The habitats and habits of such animals as the black and grizzly bear share interest with those of the shy Columbian and golden-mantled ground squirrel.

WATERTON LAKES NATIONAL PARK. The higher reaches of the park near timberline are home to bighorn sheep and Rocky Mountain goat. Ptarmigan, marmot, and ground squirrel become familiar friends to visitors. When threatened by cougar or coyote, the deer, elk, and sheep escape over the rock outcrops.

WOOD BUFFALO NATIONAL PARK protects the rare wood bison, a larger, darker northern relative of the plains bison. There are also plains buffalo, and the intermingled herds total over 10,000. Moose, woodland caribou, and black bear may also be seen in this park.

SASKATCHEWAN

Camping

PRINCE ALBERT NATIONAL PARK has campgrounds located at Beaver Glen, Namekus Lake, Hiaikeh Lake, Waskesiu, and at The Narrows. There are also small primitive campgrounds at Crean, Kingsmere, and Trapper's lakes.

PROVINCIAL PARKS. Campsites in the parks may be rustic wilderness or have well-developed facilities. The three wilderness parks are Lac La Ronge, Nipawin, and Meadow Lake. There are also 73 regional parks offering camping.

Backpacking

PRINCE ALBERT NATIONAL PARK. There are 150 miles of trails leading through this boreal park. Overnight hikers must register with a park warden and obtain a fire permit.

Hiking

BUFFALO POUND PROVINCIAL PARK, at Buffalo Pound Lake, has interesting trails.

PIKE LAKE PROVINCIAL PARK, 19 miles southwest of Saskatoon, has hiking trails.

PRINCE ALBERT NATIONAL PARK. There are many fine hiking trails. A colorful trail leads to Grey Owl's cabin.

Rockhounding

CYPRESS HILLS, south of Maple Creek. Rockhounds find selenite crystals in the shales exposed in the valley of Frenchman River and also along Swift Current Creek.

NARROW OF MACKINTOSH BAY. Red garnet crystals are found in biotite schist on a hill just north of the narrows, a few miles east of Goldfields on the north shore of Lake Athabasca.

WHITESAND RIVER DISTRICT. Gravel pits near Yorkton yield carnelian, a native agate that may be yellow, red, or orange.

Canoeing

CHURCHILL RIVER WATERSHED offers some extraordinary canoe trips of from 5 to 18 days duration. One route from Lac Ile-a-la-Crosse to Otter Lake extends for 240 miles. The Otter Lake, Stanley Lake, Ishwatikan Lake, Thomas Lake, Hunter Bay, Lac La Ronge, La Ronge trip is 90 miles long. There are also challenging canoe routes along the Sturgion-weir and Saskatchewan rivers.

WILDERNESS PROVINCIAL PARKS. There are canoe routes through the three wilderness parks: Lac La Ronge, Nipawin, and Meadow Lake.

Conservation & Wildlife

CONDIE NATURE REFUGE, 10 miles northwest of Regina, offers guided tours over nature trails in the summer.

CYPRESS HILLS, south of Maple Creek near the town of Cypress Hills. The plant and animal life in the craggy hills is unique to the province.

INDIAN HEAD TREE NURSERY, Indian Head. Demonstration plantings interest visitors to the farm, which produces and distributes trees for farm shelterbelts on the Canadian prairies.

LAST MOUNTAIN LAKE, about 75 miles north of Regina, is the main viewing area for sandhill cranes. Anywhere from 3,000 to 4,000 birds may drop in on a single day between mid-August and early September.

PRAIRIE DOG TOWN, south and east of Val Marie. There are six colonies, with over 1,000 prairie dogs. Sage grouse, rattlesnakes, and burrowing owls are also common.

PRINCE ALBERT NATIONAL PARK. The interpretive center is at Waskesiu townsite. There are self-guiding nature trails. The plants and animals are those to be found in prairie, aspen park, and boreal forest. The badger lives in the prairie for the most part, elk in the parkland, and the gray wolf in the forest. White-tailed and mule deer, moose, black bear, and woodland caribou also live in the park.

Yoho National Park, British Columbia

THE PACIFIC COAST 181

THE PACIFIC COAST

The sunset end of the continent is marked with cliffs besieged by the sea, with chaparral-clad mountains, and streams that tumble down steep valleys to surge into the rolling surf. The same waters that lave the beaches of California, Oregon, and Washington also wash against the beaches of Alaska and Hawaii as well as the westernmost Canadian province of British Columbia, for all of these states and the Canadian province are tied together by the blue Pacific. Robert Louis Stevenson called the Monterey coast of California "the most magnificent meeting place of land and water in existence." He might just as well have been speaking of the Sunshine Coast of British Columbia or the fabled upthrust of Diamond Head on Oahu's beach at Waikiki.

An outdoor vacationer can stroll on the beach at ebb tide near Anacortes, Washington, to watch sea urchins, orange sea cucumbers, and crimson sea plumes emerge from the retreating waters. He can hike up a timber trail into the mountains of British Columbia or trek through the dry interior of California to an oasis in the desert. Where only a century and a quarter ago the Donner party almost starved to death in the desolation of blizzard-gripped Donner Pass in the High Sierras, families hiking on a summer day stop for a picnic lunch.

Wildlife can be a grizzly encountered on a twist in the trail in Alaska, a whale sounding near the shores of southern California, or sea lions basking on the rocks. Mountain sheep, wolves, elk, caribou, moose, all the other mammals, great and small, of the north can be found in the mountain fastnesses of southeast Alaska, a region Alaskans call the "Banana Belt," because its climate is so much milder than the frigid regions of the interior and far north.

The Pacific Coast is a mountain hiker's paradise. The 90-mile Wonderland Trail completely encircles the snowy summit of Mount Rainier in Washington's Mount Rainier National Park. Side trails cross the ageless ice of the glaciers. In Lassen Volcanic National Park in California there are hundreds of miles of trails, some leading to infernos of hot bubbling mud and others to secluded mountain glens. There are splendid trails at Crater Lake National Park, in Oregon; leading into the volcanic craters on the Big Island of Hawaii; and in Olympic National Park, in Washington, where whole families explore the flowered meadows of Hurricane Ridge or the rank growths of the rain forest that sweeps up the Pacific side of the Olympic Mountains.

The famous John Muir Trail reaches 200 miles through the high country from Happy Isles in Yosemite National Park to the foot of gigantic Mount Whitney. It meanders through parts of Sequoia and Kings Canyon and Yosemite national parks and the Sierra and Inyo national forests. Hikers fish, search for rock specimens, snap pictures, observe wildlife, and at the end of the day's journey stretch out their sleeping bags beneath open skies. Yet the John Muir Trail is only a part of the Pacific Crest Trail that runs from the Canadian border clear to the border with Mexico, one of the world's most challenging backpacking trails.

The Pacific Coast is as spectacular for its giant trees in Humboldt Redwoods State Park, north of San Francisco, as it is for Mount McKinley in Alaska—the highest peak on the North American continent. California possesses beaches and sunny coves on the Azure Coast and placer streams tumbling over gold-bearing gravel, where weekend skin divers have discovered that they can take out a good day's pay in the yellow metal; and Oregon has not only snow-mantled Mount Hood but the mighty Columbia River. Half of Oregon is in timber, and conservation has become a way of life in a state where the legislature has enacted forward-looking laws to combat the littering that has plagued all the American states.

Paul Bunyan's realm also includes Washington, British Columbia, and Alaska. Thick stands of fir, ponderosa, hemlock, and sugar pine are masses of green even in the wintertime. It is not surprising that Washington is called the "Evergreen State."

Hawaii and Alaska are the nation's newest states. Both have fiery volcanic furnaces beneath their surfaces. Both are subject to massive natural convulsions—sometimes a quake shakes the Alaska coast, or the volcano of Mauna Loa spews molten lava down onto the fertile fields of Hawaii.

Hawaii and Alaska are for the most part studies in contrast. Hawaii is an ocean paradise of eight great islands and 20 small coral isles, while Alaska is an immensity of land. Alaska's southeast is swept by rains and mists from the sea, rolling in to cloak the rugged mountains, deep fjords, and the blue-green glaciers. The vast interior and frigid north are what was called "Seward's Ice Box" and "Seward's Folly" after Secretary of State Seward purchased Alaska from Russia. Beyond the forests of Alaska is the tundra of the arctic, and finally there is the chain of the Aleutians, islands of fog and mists and of giant bears who have no fear of man, reaching westward into the Pacific toward Asia.

PACIFIC COAST STATES
Barren Areas Above Timber
Evergreen Trees
Mixed Evergreen and Deciduous Trees
Deciduous Trees
Shrub
Grass
Barren Arid Areas
Below Sea Level No Vegetation Shown
Capitals
Cities
1 inch = 127 Statute Miles
Miles 0 25 50 75 100 125
Lambert Conformal Conic Projection
CANADA
UNITED STATES
WASHINGTON
OREGON
CALIFORNIA
NEVADA
IDAHO
MONTANA
UTAH
ARIZONA
WYOMING
MEXICO
U.S.
Pacific Ocean
Vancouver
Victoria
Bellingham
Strait of Juan de Fuca
CAPE FLATTERY
OLYMPIC NAT'L PARK
OLYMPIC MTS.
Seattle
Tacoma
OLYMPIA
Aberdeen
Spokane
Wenatchee
Yakima
Walla Walla
Lewiston
Coeur d'Alene
Longview
CAPE DISAPPOINTMENT
COLUMBIA BASIN
MT. RAINIER NAT'L PARK
MT. RAINIER 14,410 FT.
Portland
The Dalles
Pendleton
Baker
SALEM
Eugene
Bend
MT. HOOD 11,235 FT.
BLUE MOUNTAINS
Roseburg
CAPE BLANCO
Medford
Klamath Falls
CRATER LAKE NAT'L PARK
KLAMATH MTS.
GREAT BASIN
Goose Lake
Upper Klamath Lake
Harney Lake
Malheur Lake
Summer Lake
Lake Abert
Boise
SALMON RIVER MTS.
Snake River
Columbia River
Great Falls
WATERTON GLACIER INTERNATIONAL PEACE PARK
YELLOWSTONE NAT'L PARK
GRAND TETON NAT'L PARK
Great Salt Lake
GREAT SALT LAKE DESERT
Ogden
Salt Lake City
Provo
Utah L.
REDWOOD NAT'L PARK
LAVA BEDS NAT'L MON.
Eureka
CAPE MENDOCINO
LASSEN VOLCANIC NAT'L PARK
Shasta Lake
Winnemucca
Elko
Humboldt River
Pyramid L.
Reno
Lake Tahoe
Carson City
Walker Lake
SHOSHONE MTS.
Ely
Tonopah
Sevier Lake
Cedar City
ZION NAT'L PARK
BRYCE CANYON NAT'L PARK
PT. ARENA
Clear Lake
SACRAMENTO
Oroville Res.
San Francisco
San Jose
Stockton
YOSEMITE NAT'L PARK
Mono Lake
BOUNDARY PK. 13,140 FT.
KINGS CANYON NAT'L PARK
Fresno
MT. WHITNEY 14,495 FT.
SEQUOIA NAT'L PARK
DEATH VALLEY
DEATH VALLEY NAT'L MON.
282 FT. BELOW SEA LEVEL
Las Vegas
Lake Mead
LAKE MEAD NAT'L REC. AREA
GRAND CANYON NAT'L MON.
GRAND CANYON NAT'L PARK
COLORADO PLATEAU
COCONINO PLATEAU
HUMPHREYS PK. 12,633 FT.
Flagstaff
Monterey Bay
PT. PINOS
PT. SUR
PT. BUCHON
PT. CONCEPTION
Santa Barbara
MOJAVE DESERT
Buena Vista Lake
San Bernardino
JOSHUA TREE NAT'L MON.
Los Angeles
Long Beach
Gulf of Santa Catalina
San Diego
Salton Sea
Colorado River
Havasu Lake
Phoenix
Gila River
Yuma
CM TERRAIN PACIFIC COAST STATES
COPYRIGHT BY
RAND MC NALLY & COMPANY
MADE IN U.S.A.
Longitude West of Greenwich

ALASKA

Camping

CHUGACH NATIONAL FOREST. There are many camping areas. Trail River Campground is near berrying, and all the others have their attractions. The largest grounds are at Russian River, Hidden Lake, Trail River, and Williwaw.

GLACIER BAY NATIONAL MONUMENT. There are no established campgrounds, but the shoreline and islands of the bay offer unlimited camping possibilities.

KATMAI NATIONAL MONUMENT. The campground is near the outlet of the Brooks River into Naknek Lake. If you don't bring your own gear, Wien Air Alaska will rent equipment to you at reasonable rates at the airline's Brooks River Lodge.

MOUNT MC KINLEY NATIONAL PARK. Campsites at Riley Creek and Savage River are on a first-come basis, but those beyond Savage River must be reserved. These include campgrounds at Sanctuary River, Teklanika River, Igloo Creek, and Wonder Lake. A camper going beyond Savage River may use his private vehicle for access only. Transportation beyond his campsite is by shuttle bus.

NORTH TONGASS NATIONAL FOREST. There are outstanding camping grounds on the west shore of Mendenhall Lake close to Mendenhall Glacier and at other spots, such as Auke Village, Starrigavan, and Sawmill Creek, near Sitka; and at Ohmer Creek, near Petersburg. Signal Creek camping ground is in the Ketchikan area.

Backpacking

CHILKOOT TRAIL. The trail used by the Klondike gold rushers of 1898 is a formidable hiking trail beginning at Dyea, near Skagway, and climbing through Chilkoot Pass to Lake Lindeman, where the gold rushers took to boats. There backpackers can cut overland from Lake Lindeman to the White Pass and Yukon Railroad and ride the narrow-gauge cars back to the coast. Or backpackers can continue on to Lake Bennett on the new extension to the trail, have the "gold miners'" lunch, served at the railroad station, and then take the train to the coast. There are shelters at some points on the trail below the pass and one above the pass. Since the trail crosses into Canadian territory, authorities in Skagway must be informed of backpackers' plans. The Canadian government has added the 80-square-mile corridor along the trail from the U.S. border to Lake Bennett as a Canadian section of a new Klondike Goldrush International Historic Park.

MOUNT MC KINLEY NATIONAL PARK. There is a dearth of hiking trails in the park (only 20 miles in the almost two million acres), and the heavy brush, tundra, and rushing streams make cross-country hiking extremely difficult. All backpackers should be extremely capable and check in with rangers before attempting a hike. At Camp Denali, tundra treks are organized to show physically fit persons the fine art of backpacking over trailless terrain.

NORTH TONGASS NATIONAL FOREST. Backpackers are urged to stay on roads and trails in the forest unless they are adept at cross-country hiking. Hikers are told by rangers to travel with others and carry a 30-06 or larger rifle when in brown bear country.

WHITE MOUNTAINS TRAIL starts at Milepost 42 on the Steese Highway and runs north for 15 miles along an old tractor road that leads to Nome Creek. It runs northerly across Beaver Creek, then climbs to a high ridge outcrop. Going north along Dog Sled Ridge, the trail turns west, crosses four minor creeks and their dividing ridges, and then passes south of Cache Mountain. It follows the ridgeline east of the White Mountains to Beaver Creek. The hiker crosses a large bog to reach the tractor trail that leads south on the last 15 miles to Milepost 25 of the Elliott Highway. Hikers must know how to recognize landmarks and follow maps. BLM trail markers and rock cairns are located along the 80-mile trail.

Hiking

KATMAI NATIONAL MONUMENT. Among the hiking trails are the Old Rex Beach Trail and the trail that leads to Brooks River Falls, where salmon leap. A tough trail leads to the top of 2,520-foot Dumpling Mountain.

MOUNT MC KINLEY NATIONAL PARK. The park's 20 miles of trails include the McKinley Bar Trail, which leads from Wonder Lake campground to the bar of the McKinley River. The trail crosses tundra and spruce bogs.

NORTH TONGASS NATIONAL FOREST. Trails lead from the Visitor Center and Mendenhall Campground to Mendenhall Glacier and other points.

Rockhounding

CHUGACH GEM & MINERAL SOCIETY, in Anchorage, operates field trips for rockhounds to various Alaska points.

CHUGACH NATIONAL FOREST. Gold panners find pay dirt, yellow dust, and golden nuggets in the bedrock of forest streams.

NOME BEACH. Gold panners can still pan gold on the beach where fortunes were made in the gold rush.

Canoeing

BIRCH CREEK. The access is at North Fork Bridge, Milepost 94 of the Steese Highway. If the North Fork proves shallow, it is necessary to portage ¼ mile to the creek itself. Some rapids are classed as very difficult. Takeout point is at Milepost 147 at the bridge on the Steese Highway, for a total trip of 140 miles.

CHENA RIVER. Put in at the end of Chena Hot Springs Road and continue down a river of only moderate difficulty to end of the canoe trail at Fairbanks. Total trip is 70 miles.

FORTYMILE RIVER. The put-in point is close to the bridge at Milepost 49 on the Taylor Highway. The end of the trail is at Eagle, also on the Taylor Highway. There are rapids ranging from easy to exceedingly difficult, which are seldom attempted even by the very experienced.

YUKON RIVER. The last highway access to the river is 160 river miles north of Eagle at Circle. There are no rapids, but there are cross currents that can be troublesome. This is a fast-moving, silt-laden, and deep stream.

Conservation & Wildlife

CHUGACH NATIONAL FOREST. Naturalists at Portage Glacier Recreation Area show visitors the wonders of nature, ranging from icebergs to lichens. Wildlife in the Chugach is varied. The Kenai moose, Dall sheep, brown and black bear, mountain goat, and elk are all here.

GLACIER BAY NATIONAL MONUMENT. A naturalist finds the transition from the world of ice to the climax forest of the glacial regions to be fascinating. A boat sets out every morning from Bartlett Cove dock for a visit to the 200-foot-tall face of Muir Glacier, as well as to 15 active tidewater glaciers. Seals, porpoises, sea lions, killer and humpback whales sport in the bay. Sometimes boat passengers spot brown, black, and glacier bears; Sitka blacktail deer; wolves; coyotes; lynx; and wolverine on the shore.

KATMAI NATIONAL MONUMENT. The monument is famed for bear, moose, birdlife, and the Valley of Ten Thousand Smokes, although only a few of the smokes remain. Pumice rock, thrown up by the great volcanic eruption of 1912 in the valley, floats.

MENDENHALL GLACIER, in the North Tongass National Forest, is an ideal place to study a glacier's secrets. Scientists carry on their research on the Juneau ice field.

MOUNT MCKINLEY NATIONAL PARK. Unless a visitor is a skilled outdoorsman with a penchant for the backcountry, the best way to see the park's famed wildlife is to ride the shuttlebus roundtrip on the 90-mile park road, stopping off at the various viewing points. The park features Mount McKinley, at 20,320 feet, the highest point in North America.

CALIFORNIA

Camping

BRANNAN ISLAND AND FRANKS TRACT STATE RECREATION AREAS have campsites primarily intended for tent campers.

CASTLE CRAGS STATE PARK, near Castella, has spacious campgrounds.

DEATH VALLEY NATIONAL MONUMENT. Camping is popular during the fall, winter, and spring.

DEVILS POSTPILE NATIONAL MONUMENT. Campgrounds are at the northern end of the monument.

DONNER MEMORIAL STATE PARK. Campers set up their tents close to where most of the Donner party starved to death in Donner Pass.

GROVER HOT SPRINGS STATE PARK, near Markleeville. Camping is popular at Quaking Aspen and Toiyabe.

HUMBOLDT REDWOODS STATE PARK. At Burlington unit near park headquarters there is a camping area. A larger area is at Hidden Springs, and there is additional camping at Albee Creek.

JOSHUA TREE NATIONAL MONUMENT. There is a campground.

Sequoia National Park, California

THE PACIFIC COAST 185

LASSEN VOLCANIC NATIONAL PARK. Campgrounds are at Manzanita Lake, Kings Creek, Butte Lake, Horseshoe Lake, Juniper Lake, and Warner Valley.

MALAKOFF DIGGINS STATE HISTORIC PARK, near Nevada City, has primitive campsites.

MCARTHUR-BURNEY FALLS MEMORIAL STATE PARK, near Burney. Campsites are scattered through the woods.

PRAIRIE CREEK REDWOODS STATE PARK, near Orick. Family campgrounds are at Elk Prairie and Golf Bluffs Beach.

SAMUEL P. TAYLOR STATE PARK, near Lagunitas. Campgrounds are in redwood groves.

SAN DIEGO COAST STATE BEACHES. Campgrounds at South Carlsbad and San Elijo are on bluffs overlooking the ocean. Stairs lead from the campgrounds to the beaches.

SEQUOIA AND KINGS CANYON NATIONAL PARKS. Campgrounds are at Giant Forest, Lodgepole, Dorst Creek, General Grant Grove, and Cedar Grove.

SEQUOIA NATIONAL FOREST has excellent camping areas.

YOSEMITE NATIONAL PARK. Tuolumne Meadows is an idyllic camping place and is the only camp on the high country trails that can be reached by car. Campgrounds in the valley are almost always filled in the summer, but there are other campgrounds at Bridalveil Creek, Crane Flat, Wawona, Hodgdon Meadow, and White Wolf. More secluded tent campgrounds are at Yosemite Creek, Porcupine Flat, and Tenaya Lake.

Backpacking & Trail Riding

HEART BAR STATE PARK contains a section of the California Riding and Hiking Trail. There is a campground restricted to horsemen.

JOHN MUIR TRAIL is one of the great backpacking trails of the continent. A trip from Happy Isles to Mount Whitney is possible during a season, but most backpackers and trail riders content themselves with sections of the trail. Among the outstanding outfitters leading groups over this trail is Joe Wampler, of Berkeley.

LASSEN VOLCANIC NATIONAL PARK. Saddle and pack trips into the wilderness eastern portion of the park are popular.

MARBLE MOUNTAINS, in northwestern California, provide excellent hiking for backpackers who are accustomed to using USGS topo maps.

SAMUEL P. TAYLOR STATE PARK has a campground for horsemen riding the California Riding and Hiking Trail.

SEQUOIA AND KINGS CANYON NATIONAL PARKS. The backcountry is accessible over a thousand miles of trails. The beautiful High Sierra Trail joins the John Muir Trail at Wallace Creek. Backpack and pack trips are popular into the wilderness. Talk with a park ranger before starting off into the backcountry, and don't overextend yourself.

YOSEMITE NATIONAL PARK. The John Muir Trail begins at Happy Isles and crosses Tuolumne on its way along the Sierra Crest. There are more than 700 miles of trails in the park. Saddle trips by mule are popular to such beautiful spots as Glen Aulin and Merced Lake.

Hiking

CASTLE CRAGS STATE PARK. Hikers follow the trails through the park and into the wilderness beyond.

DEVILS POSTPILE NATIONAL MONUMENT. Trails lead to the top of the postpiles and to the Rainbow Fall on the Middle Fork of the San Joaquin River.

HENRY COWELL REDWOODS STATE PARK. Trails run through the semiwilderness area south and west of the campground. Easier hikes can be made over the North Powder Mill Trail and the Pine Trail.

LASSEN VOLCANIC NATIONAL PARK. Trails lead to Lassen Peak, from Kings Creek Meadows to the falls, and to Bumpass Hell. Another trail runs to the Sulphur Works. There are many other trails worthy of a hiker's attention.

LAVA BEDS NATIONAL MONUMENT. Trails lead among the great cinder cones, chasms, and 200 caves left by the volcanic disturbances in the area. Skull Cave contains a river of solid ice, and Fern Cave is carpeted with ferns and mosses.

MOUNT SAN JACINTO WILDERNESS STATE PARK has trails leading to Deer Springs and to the Devil's Slide.

SEQUOIA AND KINGS CANYON NATIONAL PARKS have fine trails. A 2-mile hike runs to Moro Rock. Another trail leads to Beetle Rock and still another to Crystal Cave. These are just a few of the scores of trails in the parks.

YOSEMITE NATIONAL PARK offers excellent hiking. Trails begin at most campsites and lead to places that will inspire the hiker.

Rafting

STANISLAUS RIVER. Tough inflated rafts manned by experts bring adventurous vacationers down the current on two-day float trips.

TUOLUMNE RIVER. Floaters try the raging waters as they come down out of the Sierra Nevada.

Boating & Boat Camping

CALIFORNIA COAST. The coast is alive with boaters who enjoy the Pacific's waters. From San Diego to the forested headlands of the northern tip of the state there are friendly harbors and bays.

LAKE OROVILLE STATE RECREATION AREA features boat-in camps at Craig Saddle, Foreman Point, Goat Ranch, Bloomer Primitive Area, and South Bloomer.

SACRAMENTO DELTA is popular with houseboaters who explore the 1,000-plus miles of waterways and tie up at the banks at the end of the day. There are campsites for boaters as well.

Sport Diving

LA JOLLA COVE, at San Diego. A submarine canyon begins in the shallows only 700 feet from shore and reaches out to sea for 17 miles. At the mouth of the canyon, divers have found a prehistoric submerged Indian village. It may be surveyed only under the direction of archaeologists.

PFEIFFER-BIG SUR STATE PARK has underwater preserves that can be explored only by experienced divers.

Conservation & Wildlife

ANZA-BORREGO DESERT STATE PARK. Some 700 miles of vehicle trails take visitors through this unusual desert preserve.

CABRILLO NATIONAL MONUMENT. Visitors watch the gray whales migrating past the point from mid-December to mid-February.

Haleakala, Maui

DEATH VALLEY NATIONAL MONUMENT. More than 650 different kinds of flora live in the valley. Desert bighorn sheep may also be seen. The valley is one of the driest and hottest places in the United States.

ELDORADO NATIONAL FOREST. The Stream Profile Chamber shows the underwater world of a living stream in action.

INYO NATIONAL FOREST. The Mammoth Visitor Center explains the phenomena of the area: the earthquake fault; the volcanic craters; and the bristlecone pines, the world's oldest living things, which have been growing here for more than 4,000 years. There are guided walks to Indian caves and geysers.

JOSHUA TREE NATIONAL MONUMENT. The Joshua tree, found only in the desert of the southwest, varies from 10 to 40 feet and may best be seen from March through May, when it is in bloom.

LASSEN VOLCANIC NATIONAL PARK. Of the many evidences of the power of nature in the park, the most remarkable are the areas devastated by the mammoth river of mud. Naturalists conduct tours to the many fascinating places in the park.

POINT REYES NATIONAL SEASHORE is ideal for bird-watching. Limantour Estero is famous for the shorebirds, and Abbott's Lagoon is equally renowned for waterfowl.

REDWOOD NATIONAL PARK protects the magnificent coastal redwood. Visitors come to see the world's tallest living trees, with trunks as much as 25 feet in diameter.

SEQUOIA AND KINGS CANYON NATIONAL PARKS preserve the giant sequoia. Mount Whitney, the highest peak in the conterminous United States, is in the Sequoia National Park.

YOSEMITE NATIONAL PARK. The grandeur of the Sierras, the variety of the area's wildlife and plants make Yosemite one of the outstanding places in North America for naturalists to study and explore.

HAWAII

Camping

HALEAKALA NATIONAL PARK. Campgrounds are at Hosmer Grove near the park entrance.

HAPUNA BEACH STATE RECREATION AREA, on Hawaii, has tent camping and facilities for trailers and campers.

HAWAII VOLCANOES NATIONAL PARK has campgrounds at Namakani Paio and Kipuka Nene. There are also camper cabins available at Namakani Paio Campground.

KALOPA STATE RECREATION AREA, on Hawaii, offers tent camping only in a forested area.

KOKEE STATE PARK, on Kauai, allows tent camping and trailers and campers near spectacular Waimea Canyon.

LYDGATE STATE PARK, on Kauai, allows tent camping only in the beach area.

MACKENZIE STATE RECREATION AREA, Puna District of Hawaii, the "Big Island," has camping in an ironwood grove.

PALAAU STATE PARK, on Molokai, allows tent camping only in a forested mountain area.

POLI POLI SPRINGS RECREATIONAL AREA, on Maui, is accessible only by four-wheel drive vehicles and allows tent camping only.

WAIANAPANAPA CAVE STATE PARK, on Maui, allows tent camping only above the rocky coastline.

Backpacking & Trail Riding

HALEAKALA NATIONAL PARK. Backpack camping in Haleakala Crater is allowed in designated areas by permit only. To reserve one of the three cabins in the crater, write or telephone the park superintendent. Thirty miles of well-marked trails lead into the crater. Horseback trips are also possible into the crater. If you bring your own horse, you may make the trip without a guide, but if you rent the horses, you must have a guide. Fenced horse pastures are located near the cabins in the crater.

HAWAII VOLCANOES NATIONAL PARK. The trail to the summit of Mauna Loa is arduous, and it takes three days. There are overnight resthouses at the 10,000- and 13,680-foot levels. Hikers should get permission at park headquarters to use the resthouses.

Hiking

HALEAKALA NATIONAL PARK. A hiker in a hurry can make the trip into the crater in one day. The Halemauu Trail leads to Holua Cabin and back. Sliding Sands Trail may also be taken with the return made over Halemauu Trail. Short hikes may also be made along Halemauu Trail to the crater rim or to the top of White Hill.

KEAIWA HEIAU STATE RECREATION AREA, on Oahu. The Aiea Loop begins at

THE PACIFIC COAST 187

the picnic grounds above Aiea and follows the ridge for a long swing out and back. This is a fine family hike.

NA LAAU TRAIL, on Oahu, begins at Makalei Place off Diamond Head Road just beyond Kapiolani Park at a marker indicating the trail through Na Laau Arboretum. A side trail leads up to the high rim of Diamond Head. This is steep, and a hiker must be wearing shoes that grip or he'll soon be in serious trouble.

RAIN-GAUGE READING HIKE. Once a month a rain-gauge reading party takes a rough climb up Honokohau valley to Puu Kukui on Maui. This rugged eight-hour ramble takes place on the last Saturday of each month.

Bike Hiking & Camping

HAWAII BICYCLE TOUR. Bikers cycle along the magnificent east coast, with cliffside views of the ocean and the cane fields of the Hamakua Coast. The bikers stay in state parks along the way and encircle the island.

OAHU BIKE TOUR. A three-day bike trip encircles the island with stopovers at Laie and Makaha Inn.

Rockhounding

KOOLAU RIDGES behind Kaneohe, on Oahu, have red and yellow jasper in the basalt.

OLOMANA PEAK, Oahu, is the place to look for Hawaiian moonstones, which are banded agate and chalcedony. Moonstones can also be found in the crater of West Molokai.

PUU IO SLOPE, on Mauna Kea, is a good place to find crystals of augite and olivine. The slopes of Paapaa and Puu Pa are also likely places to search.

Boating

CATAMARAN SAILING is popular. The modern catamaran, descendant of the double canoes of old, sails the coasts.

Sport Diving

HONOLULU. The boat *Scuba Duba* works out of Honolulu and takes divers out for snorkeling or scuba diving in the clear waters around Oahu. There are other groups offering diving from the Ala Wai Yacht Harbor and from Lahaina on Maui.

KONA waters are ideal for scuba diving. Water temperatures are around 80 degrees, and underwater visibility is always over 150 feet. Travel packages include hotel, boat, and all equipment.

Conservation & Wildlife

AKAKA FALLS STATE PARK, on the island of Hawaii. A remarkable variety of ferns grows around the falls, which drop 420 feet.

EWA FOREST RESERVE, on Oahu. Exotic fruit and flowers may be seen in this lush tropical forest.

HALEAKALA NATIONAL PARK is primarily fascinating for its geology, but it also is a good place to see the apapane, iiwi, and amakihi, birds native only to Hawaii. The Silversword Loop Trail shows fine groups of the beautiful silverswords.

HAWAII VOLCANOES NATIONAL PARK. With the exception of the native bat, all mammals now wild in the park were introduced. Naturalists find the park a good place to study how life came to Hawaii, youngest island of the chain.

OREGON

Camping

BARLOW ROAD. Tent campers can drive along this pioneer road, which survives as a Forest Service fire access road. Camps can be set up at sites along the trail.

CAPE LOOKOUT STATE PARK, 12 miles southwest of Tillamook. Campsites overlook the beach.

CRATER LAKE NATIONAL PARK. There are four campgrounds within the park: Rim Campground, near Rim Village; Cold Springs, 7 miles inside the south entrance; Annie Spring, near the junction of the south and west entrance roads; and Lost Creek, 3½ miles inside the east boundary.

SILVER FALLS STATE PARK, 26 miles east of Salem, has camping facilities.

SIUSLAW NATIONAL FOREST. There are campgrounds handy to the beach in the Oregon Dunes Recreation Area.

WILLAMETTE NATIONAL FOREST. In the Waldo Lake Recreation Area there are 226 camping sites in three modern campgrounds along the edge of the lake.

Backpacking & Trail Riding

EAGLE CAP WILDERNESS of the Wallowa-Whitman National Forest. Backpacking and packing in with horses and mules are the ways to enjoy this wild country. There are commercial packers and outfitters available. An exceptionally interesting variety of trails reach into the wilderness.

FOREST TRAILS OF THE COLUMBIA GORGE in the Mount Hood National Forest offer exciting backpacking. The Eagle Roadless Area on the slopes of the gorge is also a paradise for trail hiking.

HELLS CANYON, on the Snake, is the destination of the Snake River pack trips, based in Joseph.

PACIFIC CREST TRAIL. The celebrated backpacking trail passes through five national forests on its way across Oregon. The Oregon section begins at the Columbia River near Bonneville Dam. The trail climbs out of the Columbia River gorge to follow the high ridge of the Cascades for almost 400 miles. Winding southward on the flanks of Mount Hood, it passes Mount Jefferson, Three Fingered Jack, and the three Sisters—North, Middle, and South. The trail enters the beautiful lake region and runs through Crater Lake National Park along the uppermost crest to Four Mile Lake on the side of Mount McLaughlin. Near the southern end of the Cascade Range it passes Lake of the Woods and crosses Oregon 66 before continuing on into California.

ROGUE RIVER TRAIL is usually backpacked in two sections—from Grave Creek to Battle Bar and from Battle Bar to Illahe. The two sections together total about 40 miles.

WALDO LAKE RECREATION AREA, in the Willamette National Forest. A loop trail around the lake makes a good backpacking route.

Hiking

CRATER LAKE NATIONAL PARK has fine hiking trails leading to such places as the crater of Wizard Island, Garfield Peak, The Watchman, Mount Scott, and the Pinnacles. There are also shorter hikes over the Discovery Point Trail on the rim and through Castle Crest Wildflower Garden.

FOREST TRAILS OF THE COLUMBIA GORGE in the Mount Hood National Forest. Among the popular foot trails are Angels Rest, Wahkeena, Perdition, Larch

Mountain, and Multnomah Creek Way. There are also loop trips beginning and ending at the following points: Wahkeena, Eagle Creek, Herman, Horsetail, Larch, and Gorton.

WALDO LAKE RECREATION AREA in the Willamette National Forest. Waldo Lake Trail 3590 makes a 20-mile loop around the lake.

Rockhounding

CLARNO FORMATION, north and west of US 26, yields thunder eggs.

HAYSTACK CANYON, near Spray, yields fossil turtles and land tortoises.

PRINEVILLE, CROOK COUNTY, area has 1,000 acres of claims open to the public. Authorities do not permit use of power equipment or explosives. Agate, sagenite, jasper, and limb casts are found.

Canoeing & Rafting

DESCHUTES RIVER of central Oregon. Descents of the foaming waters are made in inflatable canoes.

ROGUE RIVER. Flat-bottomed, high-bowed McKenzie-type drift boats and rubber rafts are usually employed for floating the river. Canoes and kayaks are counted unsafe in rapids below Grave Creek. From Grants Pass to Grave Creek the river is exciting, but from Grave Creek to Mule Creek Canyon the river is difficult, with long rapids, powerful and irregular waves, dangerous rocks, and boiling eddies. At Rainie Falls there is a vertical drop of about 10 feet, and boats must be portaged or lined around the falls. The boats continue on down the river, although the going is rough, with difficult rapids, particularly between Blossom Bar and Brushy Bar, to Lobster Creek.

Boating & Boat Camping

WALDO LAKE RECREATION AREA, in Willamette National Forest, offers enjoyable boating and boat camping.

WILLAMETTE RIVER. Launching ramps help make this a popular boating river.

Conservation & Wildlife

CAPE LOOKOUT STATE PARK, 12 miles southwest of Tillamook. Bird-watchers can find over 150 kinds of birds. A trail leads from the ridge down to the cape, and from the trail birds may be seen flying to and from nesting and resting places on the headland walls.

CAPE PERPETUA VISITOR CENTER, Siuslaw National Forest. The visitor center shows the powerful forces at work where the mountains meet the sea. An auto tour begins at Devils Churn and winds through 22 miles of forests, hills, and valleys. The tide pools are fascinating at low tide, when they contain hermit crabs, sea urchins, and sea anemones.

CRATER LAKE NATIONAL PARK. There are some 60 kinds of mammals, ranging from the ubiquitous golden-mantled ground squirrels to the black bears. The American bald eagle, drastically reduced in numbers by a reckless use of some pesticides, is making an important stand in this remote area. The park is also home to Clark's nutcracker, named for William Clark of the Lewis and Clark Expedition, who discovered it. The bird pecks at bark like a woodpecker but is undeniably a crow.

EAGLE CAP WILDERNESS, northeast of Baker. The Wallowa gray-crowned rosy finches are found only in the high country of Eagle Cap Mountain, where they nest close to snowfields, on rocks, and in meadows.

SEA LION CAVES, Florence. An elevator takes visitors to the caves where sea lions live.

WASHINGTON

Camping

BAY VIEW RECREATION AREA, 7 miles west of Mount Vernon, has 100 tent campsites as well as trailer hookups.

BELFAIR RECREATION AREA, 3 miles west of Belfair on the Olympic Peninsula, has fine campsites.

MOUNT RAINIER NATIONAL PARK. The principal campgrounds are at Longmire, Paradise, Cougar Rock, Ohanapecosh, Sunrise, and White River. There are smaller and more secluded campgrounds at Tahoma Creek, Sunshine Point, Mowich Lake, and Ipsut Creek.

OLYMPIC NATIONAL PARK. The entrance roads bring visitors to campgrounds. Camping near the Pacific beaches, with the mountains rising behind, is a pleasurable experience.

OREGON STATE PARKS also have fine camping sites.

TWIN HARBORS RECREATION AREA, 3 miles south of Westport, has a large number of camping sites in several camping areas.

Backpacking & Trail Riding

MOUNT RAINIER NATIONAL PARK. The Wonderland Trail encircles the mountain, a distance of 90 miles. Shelter cabins are a day's hike, 8 to 12 miles, apart. The Northern Loop Trail is a branch of the Wonderland Trail.

NATIONAL FORESTS. The nine national forests in the state have 6,600 miles of riding and hiking trails. Of these trails, 2,900 miles are easy to follow, but the remaining 3,700 miles require woodswise backpackers and riders. The most outstanding of the trails is the Cascade Crest Trail, which follows the crest of the mountains from the Canadian border into Oregon.

NORTH CASCADES NATIONAL PARK. Rough climbs may discourage all but the best-trained mountaineers, but there are also 345 miles of trails that are much easier to hike or to follow on horseback.

OLYMPIC NATIONAL PARK has over 600 miles of hiking trails. The backcountry has trailside shelters at many places.

Hiking

MOUNT RAINIER NATIONAL PARK. Parts of the Wonderland Trail can be enjoyed as day hikes because the trail is accessible through spur trails to the park road. There are more than 300 miles of trails in the park.

OLYMPIC NATIONAL PARK. Many of the more than 600 miles of trails in the park are ideal for day hikes. Obstruction Point is the beginning of fine trails.

Rockhounding

AGATE BAY, on Strait of Juan de Fuca just west of Crescent Bay. Agates are found in the gravel beaches. The stones weathered out of glacial drift and the basalt.

GINKGO PETRIFIED FOREST, near Vantage. The forest should be viewed but not touched. Outside its boundaries rockhounds can look for petrified wood with a limit of 25 pounds per person.

THE PACIFIC COAST 189

QUILLAYUTE RIVER. Near the mouth of this Olympic Peninsula river are sources of spherulitic jasper. The stones are found in the gravels at the mouth of the river and up and down the coast in the vicinity.

WIND RIVER, about 17 miles north of Carson. Opals occur as amygdules in lava buttes.

Boating & Boat Camping

COULEE DAM NATIONAL RECREATION AREA. The impounded Columbia appeals to boaters. There are boat-launching ramps and docks. Camping sites are handy to the beaches.

PUGET SOUND is a boating paradise unrivaled in the world. The beauty of the waters, the freedom from dangerous shoals, the protection of islands, and sheltered inlets make it ideal. The Puget Sound region extends from Olympia at the lower tip north past Tacoma and Seattle to the Canadian border. There are 3,000 miles of shoreline, hundreds of islands and bays, harbors and headlands. Many of the islands are delightful to land on.

Sport Diving

PUGET SOUND. Sport divers explore the waters for old wrecks and resort to wrestling octopus for entertainment.

Conservation & Wildlife

MOUNT BAKER NATIONAL FOREST. There are 81 square miles of glaciers in the forest and in the adjacent North Cascades National Park.

MOUNT RAINIER NATIONAL PARK. The Trail of the Shadows is a beautiful nature trail. A 2½-mile guided trip goes to the Paradise Glacier Ice Caves.

NORTH CASCADES NATIONAL PARK. A boat trip on Lake Chelan provides a magnificent approach to the mountains.

OLYMPIC NATIONAL FOREST. Elk and other wildlife are common sights in the Soleduck Valley.

OLYMPIC NATIONAL PARK. Trails and roads take nature lovers into the fastnesses of this marvelous park with its several lush rain forests. From the 50 different species of mammals on the land to the sea lions and whales and 5 species of seals offshore, the park beguiles visitors.

WIND RIVER TREE NURSERY in the Gifford Pinchot National Forest. Millions of seedlings are grown for reforestation purposes.

BRITISH COLUMBIA

Camping

ALICE LAKE PROVINCIAL PARK, near Brackendale, has a developed campground with 86 sites.

Wallowa Mountains, Oregon

GLACIER NATIONAL PARK. The largest campground is at Mountain Creek. Two other campgrounds are at Illecillewaet and Loop Creek, both just west of Rogers Pass.

GOLDEN EARS PROVINCIAL PARK, has a campground near Alouette Lake.

KOKANEE GLACIER PROVINCIAL PARK, north of Nelson, has no developed campgrounds. Wilderness camping is not restricted to certain sites, but favorite places are at the outlets of Kaslo and Kokanee lakes and near the north end of Tanal Lake.

KOOTENAY NATIONAL PARK provides campsites at Redstreak, McLeod Meadows, and Marble Canyon.

PACIFIC RIM NATIONAL PARK has camping at Green Point, a rocky bluff cutting Long Beach in two.

STRATHCONA PROVINCIAL PARK, on Vancouver Island, offers camping at Buttle Lake and at Ralph River.

WELLS GRAY PROVINCIAL PARK, northeast of Vancouver in the Cariboo Mountains, offers camping in a primitive wilderness. There are three developed campgrounds at Clearwater Lake, Dawson Falls, and Mahood Lake. Wilderness camping is on the shores of Clearwater, Azure, and Mahood lakes.

YOHO NATIONAL PARK includes Kicking Horse, Hoodoo Creek, and Chancellor Peak campgrounds for tents and RV's. Tent campgrounds are at Takakkaw Falls and Lake O'Hara.

Backpacking & Trail Riding

KOKANEE GLACIER PROVINCIAL PARK. This virtually undeveloped park appeals to those who like their country wild.

KOOTENAY NATIONAL PARK. Hikers on overnight trips must register with the warden. Trails lead throughout the park.

MONASHEE PROVINCIAL PARK. There is a fine hiking trail leading to the far end of Peters Lake, where there is a good place to camp.

PACIFIC RIM NATIONAL PARK. The 45-mile West Coast Trail follows the coastline from Pachena Bay to Port Renfrew. A few primitive campsites dot the trail for overnight stops.

YOHO NATIONAL PARK. Backpackers come into their element in the wilderness of this beautiful park. Lake O'Hara campground may be reached only by walking or horseback riding.

Hiking

CAMERON LAKE PROVINCIAL PARK. A trail up Mount Arrowsmith starts near the picnic grounds in this park on Vancouver Island.

GLACIER NATIONAL PARK. Hiking trails lead to the Illecillewaet and Asulkan glaciers and to the ridge of Mount Abbott. A mile east of Rogers Pass a trail leads toward Mount Tupper and the Rogers group of peaks. There are also trails up Connaught and Cougar creeks to Cougar Valley and the Nakimu Caves.

LIONS DAY HIKE. Vancouver hikers hike up the trail over Unnecessary Mountain to the peaks of the Lions. There are some difficult points in the trail on the climb to the summit cairn.

STAMP FALLS PROVINCIAL PARK. Trails lead to the falls.

YOHO NATIONAL PARK. Fine hiking trails lead through the park.

Rockhounding

FRASER RIVER BARS. Gems brought down by the current and deposited at the bars include agate, garnet, jasper, jade, and serpentine. Some bars are Agassiz, Ruby Creek, Flood, Hope, Yale, and Spuzzum.

KAMLOOPS AREA. Agate, hyalite, jasper, and petrified wood are found in the Kamloops region. Agate is located on the banks of the creeks that flow into the eastern end of Kamloops Lake near Tranquille.

SHAW SPRINGS RESORT, halfway between Lytton and Spences Bridge on the South Thompson River. Blue-gray agate can be found on the south bank of the river opposite some railway tunnels on the north side.

Canoeing & Rafting

BOWRON LAKE PROVINCIAL PARK, in the Cariboo Mountains, 90 miles southeast of Prince George, features the Circuit, a canoe route some 73 miles in length. Campsites are along the six large lakes, the smaller lakes, and the streams.

CHILCOTIN RIVER. This wilderness river also offers exciting white-water rafting. After passing through the Goose Necks of the Chilcotin, boaters enter Big Creek Rapids, in which everyone is guaranteed a soaking. Big John Canyon is the most tumultuous part of the voyage.

FRASER RIVER. Canadian River Expeditions takes guests on inflated raft trips through the tempestuous rapids of Moran Canyon on the Fraser. Bridge River rapids just below the Canyon defies even rubber rafts except at favorable water stages.

Boating & Boat Camping

BRITISH COLUMBIA PROVINCIAL MARINE PARKS. The British Columbia coastline, with its flotillas of islands, coves, fjords, anchorages, and both sheltered and open waters, is remarkable cruising water. British Columbia has established marine parks with docks and mooring buoys, beaches and camps. Among these are: Newcastle Island, Princess Margaret, Smuggler Cove, Prideaux Haven, Disney Spit, Pirates Cove, and Rebecca Spit.

Sport Diving

STRAIT OF GEORGIA. Some of the greatest sport diving in the world is in these clear and cold waters. Divers observe a rich variety of sea life, including exquisite coral, which grows at 100-foot depths. Divers find jade in Pindar Cove.

Conservation & Wildlife

MOUNT REVELSTOKE NATIONAL PARK. The park is a study in climatic contrasts between the lower slopes and valleys and the high mountains and plateaus.

PACIFIC RIM NATIONAL PARK. The edge of the sea has tide pools in rocky shores, shaded caves, and surf-washed rocks, which all support fascinating marine life. Colonies of seabirds and sea lions also intrigue naturalists.

SHUSWAP LAKE PROVINCIAL PARK, 12 miles from Squilax, is a good place to watch Pacific sockeye salmon spawn in the gravel beds of the Adams River.

VASEUX LAKE, in the Okanagan Valley, is the site of an effort to save the remaining California bighorn sheep in British Columbia.

YOHO NATIONAL PARK. Alpine and subalpine fauna and flora are fascinating to study. Moose, white-tailed and mule deer, and wapiti share interest with the grizzly, coyote, and marten.

Index

A

Abram S. Hewitt Forest, 99
Acadia National Park, 73
Adirondack Mountains, 99
Aleutians, 182
Algonquin Provincial Park, 73
Allegan State Game Area, 74
American Forestry Association, 61
American Youth Hostels, 46, 50, 58
Appalachia, 106
Appalachian Trail, 16, 80, 99
Aransas National Wildlife Refuge, 76
Arkansas River, 55
Azure Coast, 182

B

backpacking, 14–25
 climbing, 22
 conditioning, 19–20
 drinking water, 21, 23, 25
 equipment, clothing, food, 17–19
 meals, 22–23
 on the trail, 21–25
 planning, 15–17
 safety, 21, 22, 23–25
backpacking, *directory of:*
 Alaska, 184; Alberta, 179; Arizona, 160; Arkansas, 111; British Columbia, 191; California, 186; Colorado, 169; Connecticut, 82; Florida, 113; Georgia, 116; Hawaii, 187; Idaho, 172; Illinois, 134; Iowa, 138; Kentucky, 118; Maine, 85; Manitoba, 154; Maryland, 122; Massachusetts, 87; Michigan, 140; Minnesota, 142; Missouri, 145; New Brunswick, 93; Newfoundland and Labrador, 94; New Hampshire, 87, 89; New Jersey, 100; New Mexico, 163; New York, 102; North Carolina, 125; Nova Scotia, 95; Ohio, 148; Ontario, 155–156; Oregon, 188; Pennsylvania, 104; Saskatchewan, 180; South Dakota, 149–150; Tennessee, 127; Texas, 165; Utah, 176; Vermont, 91; Virginia, 129; Washington, 189; West Virginia, 130; Wisconsin, 151; Wyoming, 178
Badlands, 133
Baffin Island National Park, 17
Banff National Park, 26
bicycles, 49
Big Bend National Park, 15, 26, 60, 158
Big Thicket, The (Texas), 55, 158
bike hiking, 45–50
 equipment, clothing, 48–49
 pace, 49–50
 planning, 46–47
 safety, 47, 49
 transportation arrangements, 50
bike hiking, *directory of:*
 Alabama, 108; Alberta, 180; Florida, 113–114; Georgia, 116; Hawaii, 188; Illinois, 134; Indiana, 137; Iowa, 138; Kansas, 139; Kentucky, 119; Louisiana, 120; Maine, 85; Maryland, 122; Massachusetts, 87; Michigan, 140; Mississippi, 124; New Brunswick, 93; New Hampshire, 89; New York, 102; Nova Scotia, 95; Ohio, 148; Pennsylvania, 104; Rhode Island, 90; Vermont, 91; Virginia, 129; Wisconsin, 152
Black Hills, 26, 52, 133
boating, 63–67
 equipment, 67
 etiquette, 67
 operating know-how, 65–67
 rules, 66
 safety, 67
 types of houseboats, 66
boating, *directory of:*
 Alabama, 108, 110; Arizona, 162; Arkansas, 111–112; British Columbia, 191; California, 186; Connecticut, 84; Florida, 115; Georgia, 117; Hawaii, 188; Illinois, 136; Iowa, 138; Kansas, 139; Kentucky, 119; Louisiana, 121; Maine, 86; Maryland, 122; Massachusetts, 87; Michigan, 141–142; Minnesota, 144; Mississippi, 124; Missouri, 145; Nebraska, 147; Nevada, 176; New Brunswick, 94; Newfoundland and Labrador, 94; New Hampshire, 89–90; New Jersey, 100; New York, 102; North Carolina, 125; Nova Scotia, 96; Ohio, 149; Oklahoma, 164; Ontario, 157; Oregon, 189; Pennsylvania, 105; Prince Edward Island, 96; Puerto Rico, 131; Quebec, 97; Rhode Island, 90; South Carolina, 127; South Dakota, 150; Tennessee, 127; Texas, 166; Vermont, 92; Virginia, 129; Virgin Islands, 131; Washington, 190; West Virginia, 130; Wisconsin, 152–153
Bob Marshall Wilderness, 26
Boston Mountains, 106
Bottle Hollow, 73
Boundary Waters Canoe Area, 55
Bowron Lake Provincial Park, 55
Brown County, Indiana, 133
Bruce Peninsula of Ontario, 69
Brule River, 57
Bureau of Land Management, vi
Butterfield Overland Stage, 48

C

Cajun country, Louisiana, 106
Callaway Gardens, 73
camping, 1–13
 campfires, 9
 children, 6
 cooking and cleanup, 11
 drinking water, 9
 equipment, clothing, 6–7
 etiquette, 3, 13
 pitching a tent, 8
 planning and packing, 3–8
 safety, 11–13
 sanitation, 9
camping, *directory of:*
 Alabama, 108; Alaska, 184; Alberta, 179; Arizona, 160; Arkansas, 110; British Columbia, 190–191; California, 185–186; Colorado, 169; Connecticut, 82; Delaware, 112; Florida, 113; Georgia, 115; Hawaii, 187; Idaho, 170; Illinois, 134; Indiana, 137; Iowa, 138; Kansas, 139; Kentucky, 117; Louisiana, 120; Maine, 84–85; Manitoba, 154; Maryland, 122; Massachusetts, 87; Michigan, 139–140; Minnesota, 142; Mississippi, 123; Missouri, 144–145; Montana, 173; Nebraska, 146; Nevada, 175; New Brunswick, 92–93; Newfoundland and Labrador, 94; New Hampshire, 87; New Jersey, 100; New Mexico, 162–163; New York, 100, 102; North Carolina, 124; North Dakota, 147; Nova Scotia, 94–95; Ohio, 147–148; Oklahoma, 164; Ontario, 155; Oregon, 188; Pennsylvania, 103–104; Prince Edward Island, 96; Quebec, 96; Rhode Island, 90; Saskatchewan, 180; South Carolina, 126; South Dakota, 149; Tennessee, 127; Texas, 164–165; Utah, 176; Vermont, 90–91; Virginia, 128; Virgin Islands, 131; Washington, 189; West Virginia, 130; Wisconsin, 151; Wyoming, 177–178
Canada, crown lands, 3, 5
Canadian national parks, 4–5
Canadian provincial parks, 4
Canadian Rockies, 167
canoeing, 54–59
 campsites, 59
 equipment, clothing, food, 57
 manners, 59
 outfitters, 58
 safety, 58–59
 skills, 54–55
canoeing, *directory of:*
 Alabama, 108; Alaska, 184; Arkansas, 111; British Columbia, 191; Colorado, 170; Connecticut, 84; Florida, 114; Georgia, 116–117; Idaho, 173; Illinois, 136; Indiana, 137–138; Iowa, 138; Kentucky, 119; Louisiana, 120–121; Maine, 86; Manitoba, 154; Maryland, 122; Michigan, 141; Minnesota, 143–144; Missouri, 145; Montana, 175; Nebraska, 146–147; New Brunswick, 93–94; Newfoundland and Labrador, 94; New Hampshire, 89; New Jersey, 100; New York, 102; Nova Scotia, 95–96; Ohio, 148–149; Ontario, 156–157; Oregon, 189; Pennsylvania, 104; Quebec, 97; Rhode Island, 90; Saskatchewan, 180; South Carolina, 126–127; South Dakota, 150; Tennessee, 127; Texas, 166; Utah, 177; Vermont, 92; Virginia, 129; West Virginia, 130; Wisconsin, 152–153; Wyoming, 178
Canyonlands National Park, 62
Cape Cod National Seashore, 42, 47
Carlsbad Caverns National Park, 158
Catskill Mountains, 99
Cheaha State Park, 37–38
Chesapeake and Ohio Canal Tow Path, 47
Chicago, forest preserves, 133
Chilkoot Trail, 14–15, 17
Clark Historical Canoe Trail, 57
Colorado River, 62, 167
conservation and wildlife, 72–76
conservation and wildlife, *directory of:*
 Alabama, 110; Alaska, 184–185; Alberta, 180; Arizona, 162; Arkansas, 112; British Columbia, 191; California, 186–187; Colorado, 170; Connecticut, 84; Delaware, 113; Florida, 115; Georgia, 117; Hawaii, 188; Idaho, 173; Illinois, 136; Indiana, 138; Iowa, 139; Kansas, 139; Kentucky, 119–120; Louisiana,

121–122; Maine, 86–87; Manitoba, 154–155; Maryland, 122–123; Massachusetts, 87; Michigan, 142; Minnesota, 144; Mississippi, 124; Missouri, 145–146; Montana, 175; Nebraska, 147; Nevada, 176; New Brunswick, 94; Newfoundland and Labrador, 94; New Hampshire, 90; New Jersey, 100; New Mexico, 163–164; New York, 102–103; North Carolina, 125; North Dakota, 147; Nova Scotia, 96; Ohio, 149; Oklahoma, 164; Ontario, 157; Oregon, 189; Pennsylvania, 105; Prince Edward Island, 96; Puerto Rico, 131; Quebec, 97; Rhode Island, 90; Saskatchewan, 180; South Carolina, 127; South Dakota, 150–151; Tennessee, 127–128; Texas, 166; Utah, 177; Vermont, 92; Virginia, 129–130; Washington, 190; West Virginia, 131; Wisconsin, 153–154; Wyoming, 178–179
Conservation Education Center, 73, 99
Corner Brook, 52
Corundum Hill, 52
Cousteau, Jacques, 69
Cowee Valley, 52
Crater of Diamonds, 51–52
Crater Lake National Park, 182
Craters of the Moon National Monument, 37
Cumberland Gap, Wilderness Trail in, 106
Custer National Forest, vi

D

Dakota Formation, 52
Delaware River, 57
Destin Bridge, 71
Dinosaur National Monument, 62
Dismal Swamp of Virginia, 72
Donner Pass, 182
Douglas, Supreme Court Justice William O., 73

E

Eldorado Bar Sapphire Mine, 52

F

Fallows, James, 46
Fayette State Park, 5
Finger Lakes, 99
Florida Keys, 68, 106
Florida Wilderness Trail, 16
forest lands of Ohio, renewal of, 72

G

Gaspé Peninsula, 80
Gem State (Idaho), 52
Gila Wilderness, 16
Glacier National Park, 42
Goose Lake Prairie, 74
Grand Canyon, 158
Grand Teton National Park, 42, 52
Great Salt Lake, 167
Great Sand Dunes National Monument, 37
Great Smoky Mountains, 106
green turtle, 75
Greers Ferry Lake, 42
grizzly bear, 3, 11–12, 23–24, 56, 75
Guadalupe Mountains National Park, 15
Gulf Islands, 68

H

Haleakala National Park, 37
Harney Peak, 133
Hawk Mountain, 99
Hiawatha Valley, 63
Highlands Hammock State Park, 42, 47
hiking, 36–42
  conditioning, 39–40
  equipment and clothing, 37, 39
  organized hikes, 41
  pace, 40
  safety, 39–40
  trails for handicapped, 37
hiking, directory of:
  Alabama, 108; Alaska, 184; Alberta, 179–180; Arizona, 160; Arkansas, 111; British Columbia, 191; California, 186; Colorado, 169; Connecticut, 82; Delaware, 112; Florida, 113; Georgia, 116; Hawaii, 187–188; Idaho, 172–173; Illinois, 134; Indiana, 137; Iowa, 138; Kentucky, 118; Louisiana, 120; Maine, 85; Manitoba, 154; Maryland, 122; Massachusetts, 87; Michigan, 140; Minnesota, 142–143; Mississippi, 124; Missouri, 145; Montana, 174; Nebraska, 146; Nevada, 175; New Brunswick, 93; Newfoundland and Labrador, 94; New Hampshire, 89; New Jersey, 100; New Mexico, 163; New York, 102; North Carolina, 125; North Dakota, 147; Nova Scotia, 95; Ohio, 148; Oklahoma, 164; Ontario, 156; Oregon, 188–189; Pennsylvania, 104; Prince Edward Island, 96; Puerto Rico, 131; Quebec, 96–97; Rhode Island, 90; Saskatchewan, 180; South Carolina, 126; South Dakota, 150; Tennessee, 127; Texas, 165–166; Utah, 176; Vermont, 91; Virginia, 129; Washington, 189; West Virginia, 130; Wisconsin, 151–152; Wyoming, 178
Hot Springs National Park, 106
houseboating. See boating
Hudson River, 99
Humboldt Redwoods State Park, 182

I

Idaho's Panhandle, 76
Illinois and Michigan Canal, 41
Indiana Dunes National Lakeshore, 76
Intracoastal Waterway, 65
Inyo National Forest, 42
Isle Royale, 16, 23, 73, 133

J

Jennings Blazing Star Prairie, 99
John Muir Trail, 16, 182
John Pennekamp Coral Reef State Park, 69
Jones, Turk, 74

K

Katahdin Falls, 80
Kauai, 48
Kealakekua Bay, 70
Kent Falls State Park, 80
kettle moraines, 52
Kettle Moraine State Forest, 26–27, 133
Key Biscayne, 37
Key West, 71

Kisatchie National Forest, 73
Kittatinny Mountains, 99
Kluane National Park, 17

L

Labrador shore, 52
La Jolla Cove, 70
Lake Mead, 158
Lake Texoma, 158
Land Between the Lakes, 3, 73, 106
Lassen Volcanic National Park, 182
Laurentides Provincial Park, 73
La Verendrye Provincial Park, 57
limestone canyons, 60

M

Mac Innis, Dr. Joe, 69–70
Maine, coast of, 80
Marina Del Rey, 64
Martha's Vineyard, 80
Matthies, William, 70
Minnesota Valley Trail, 27
Mississippi River, 64, 65, 133
Mount Katahdin, 16, 80
Mount McKinley, 182
Mount Rainier National Park, Wonderland Trail, 182
Mullan Military Road, 5

N

Nahanni National Park, 17
Natchez Trace, 48, 106
National Audubon Society, 75
national monuments, 4
national parks, 4
National Park Service, 4–5
National Wildlife Federation, 61
  Conservation Travel Safaris, 74–75
Natural Bridge Caverns, 99
New River, 61
New York State canal system, 65
Nova Scotia Museum in Halifax, 70

O

Oak Creek Canyon, 158
Ocala National Forest, 37
Oil Springs Trail, 39
Okefenokee National Wildlife Refuge, 73
Okefenokee Swamp, 56, 106
Old Mill Bikeway, Ohio, 47
Olympic National Park, 42, 182
Oregon Trail, 5
orienteering, 43–44
  topographical maps, 43
  offset technique, 43
  pace in orienteering, 43
  beelines in orienteering, 43–44
  compass course, 43–44
  collecting features, 44
  checkpoint, 43, 44
Ouachita Mountains (Arkansas), 15, 21, 106, 158
Owyhee County, 52
Ozark-Shawnee Trail, 16

P

Pacific Crest Trail, 16, 182
Padre Island National Seashore, 47, 158
Pecos Wilderness, 16

Pfeiffer-Big Sur State Park, 70
Pine Creek Gorge, 99
Pocono Mountains, 99
prairie dog village, 75
Presque Isle, 73, 99
Pymatuning Reservoir, 99

R

rafting, 60–62
  equipment and clothing, 61, 62
rafting, *directory of:*
  Arizona, 162; Arkansas, 111; British Columbia, 191; California, 186; Colorado, 170; Florida, 114–115; Georgia, 116; Idaho, 173; Mississippi, 124; Missouri, 145; Montana, 174–175; New York, 102; Oklahoma, 164; Oregon, 189; Pennsylvania, 104–105; Texas, 166; Utah, 177; Virginia, 129; West Virginia, 130; Wyoming, 178
Rainy Lake, 64
Red Rock Lakes National Wildlife Refuge, 76
Rio Grande, 60, 61, 158
rockhounding, 51–53
rockhounding, *directory of:*
  Alaska, 184; Alberta, 180; Arizona, 160, 162; Arkansas, 111; British Columbia, 191; Colorado, 169–170; Georgia, 116; Hawaii, 188; Idaho, 173; Illinois, 134, 136; Indiana, 137; Iowa, 138; Kansas, 139; Maine, 85; Manitoba, 154; Michigan, 140–141; Minnesota, 143; Montana, 174; Nebraska, 146; Nevada, 175–176; New Brunswick, 93; Newfoundland and Labrador, 94; New Hampshire, 89; New Mexico, 163; North Carolina, 125; North Dakota, 147; Nova Scotia, 95–96; Ohio, 148; Oklahoma, 164; Ontario, 156; Oregon, 189; Prince Edward Island, 96; Quebec, 97; **Rhode Island**, 90; Saskatchewan, 180; **South Dakota**, 150; Texas, 166; Utah, 176–177; Vermont, 91–92; Washington, 189–190; Wisconsin, 152; Wyoming, 178
Rocky Mountains, 36, 167

S

Saguenay River, 80
St. Andrews State Park, 71
Sangre de Cristo Mountains, 158
Santa Fe Trail, 158
Satilla River, 57
Scripps Institute of Oceanography, 73
Shaler, Nathaniel S., 80
Shenandoah National Park, 42
Sierra Club, 27, 58, 61, 75
Sierra Nevada Mountains, 167
Sinnissippi Forest, 37
Skidaway Island, 76
Snake River, 167
sport diving, 68–71
  exploring wrecks, 70
  scuba diving, 69
  snorkeling, 69
  underwater photography, 70
sport diving, *directory of:*
  Alabama, 110; Arizona, 162; Arkansas, 112; British Columbia, 191; California, 186; Florida, 115; Hawaii, 188; Louisiana, 121; Minnesota, 144; Missouri, 145; Nevada, 176; New Brunswick, 94; New York, 99; Nova Scotia, 96; Ohio, 149; Oklahoma, 164; Ontario, 157; Puerto Rico, 131; South Dakota, 150; Tennessee, 127; Texas, 166; Utah, 177; Virgin Islands, 131; Washington, 190; Wisconsin, 153
Sunshine Coast (British Columbia), 15
Susquehanna River, 57
Suwannee River Canoe Trail, 56–57

T

Thoreau, Henry David, vi, 80
Thousand Islands, 99
Tobique River, 57
Torrey Pines State Reserve, 70
trail maps, sources for, 15
Trail Riders of the Wilderness, 27
trail riding, 26–27
  equipment and clothing, 27
  outfitters, 26
trail riding, *directory of:*
  Alberta, 179; Arizona, 160; British Columbia, 191; California, 186; Colorado, 169; Hawaii, 187; Idaho, 172; Illinois, 134; Kansas, 139; Maryland, 122; Michigan, 140; Minnesota, 142; Missouri, 145; Montana, 173–174; Nebraska, 146; Newfoundland and Labrador, 94; New Mexico, 163; New York, 102; North Dakota, 147; Ohio, 148; Oregon, 188; South Dakota, 149–150; Texas, 165; Utah, 176; Washington, 189; West Virginia, 130; Wisconsin, 151; Wyoming, 178
Tuxachanie Trail, 38

U

Udall, Stewart, 75
U.S. Army Corps of Engineers, 4
U.S. Forest Service, 4, 37

V

Virgin Islands National Park, 70

W

Wampler, Joe, 20, 27
weather
  backpacking, 17, 21, 24
  camping, 13
  hiking in the desert, 39
  sleeping, 18
White Mountains of Arizona, 158
White, Paul Dudley, 41, 46
White Water Derby, 99
Wilderness Society, 20–21, 27, 58, 74
wildlife, vi, 3, 11–12, 15, 16, 21, 23–24, 37, 38, 41, 42, 45, 55, 56, 62, 65, 68–69, 73, 74, 75, 76
Wisconsin Bikeway, 45, 47
Wood Buffalo National Park, 74

Y

Yellowstone National Park, 26, 167

About the Author

Richard Dunlop has been a hiker since boyhood, when he used to escape into the forest preserve areas in and around Chicago and follow trails along the rivers. Backpacking, trail riding, biking, and canoeing have all been favorite activities that he has shared with his wife, Joan, and their four children. For some 14 years he has been extremely active in Scouting, training many groups of boys and girls to get the most out of hiking and backpacking.

A prolific writer, with a half-dozen books and more than a thousand magazine and newspaper articles to his credit, Mr. Dunlop's major interests are travel, outdoor activities, conservation, archeology, and Americana. His concern for the environment and his interest in ancient artifacts are not limited to this country, however—he has traveled in and written about places on every continent (and has hiked extensively on three).

Mr. Dunlop is a past president of the American Society of Travel Writers, a professional group in which he has been active since its inception 20 years ago. His affiliations also include the Authors League of America and the Society of Midland Authors. For two years he was winner of the Mark Twain Award for outstanding travel articles.

A graduate of Northwestern University, he now lives with his photographer wife, Joan, in a Chicago suburb.

Made in the USA
Middletown, DE
29 March 2020

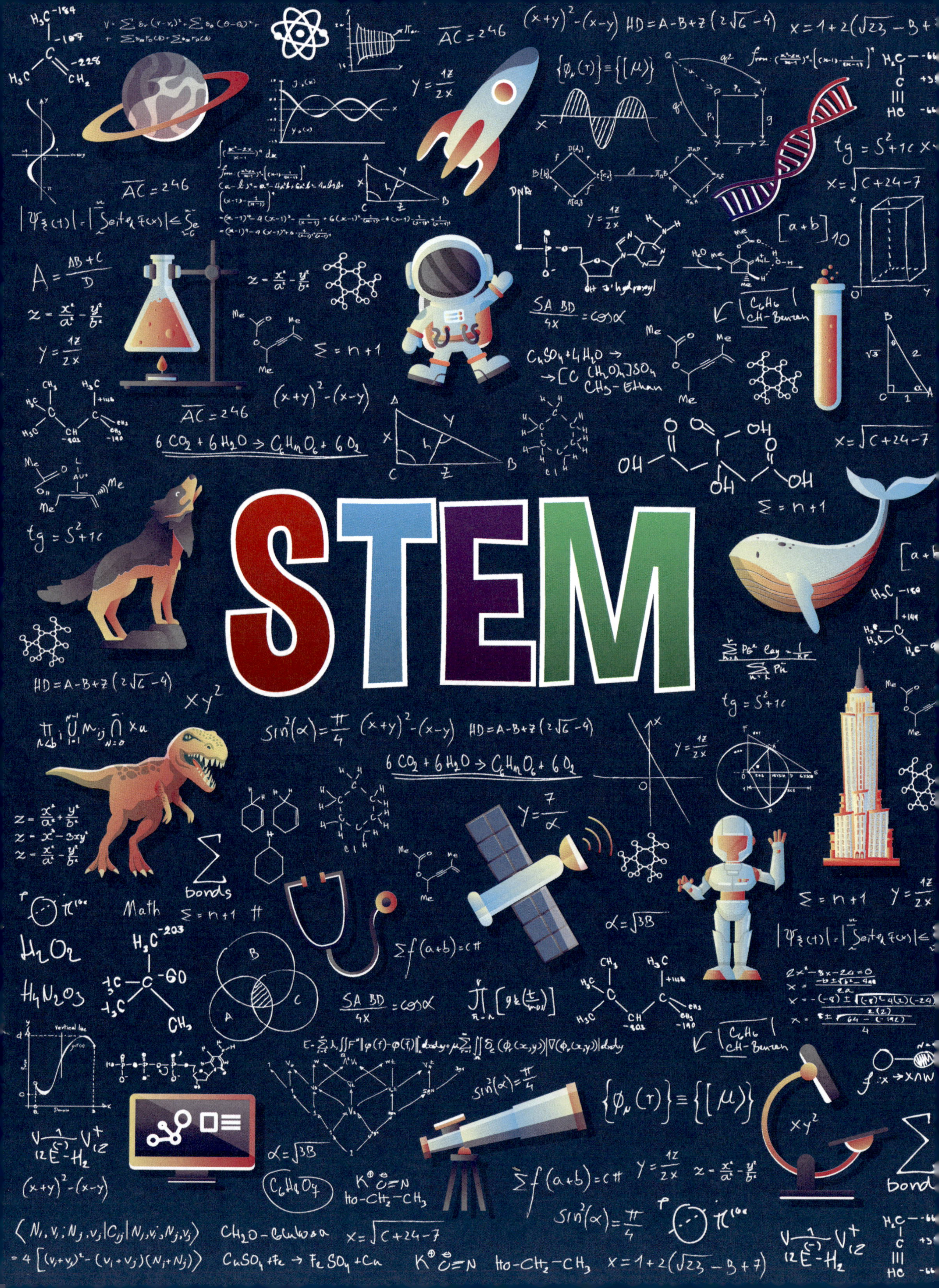

STEM

101 BLACK WOMEN IN SCIENCE, TECHNOLOGY, ENGINEERING and MATHEMATICS

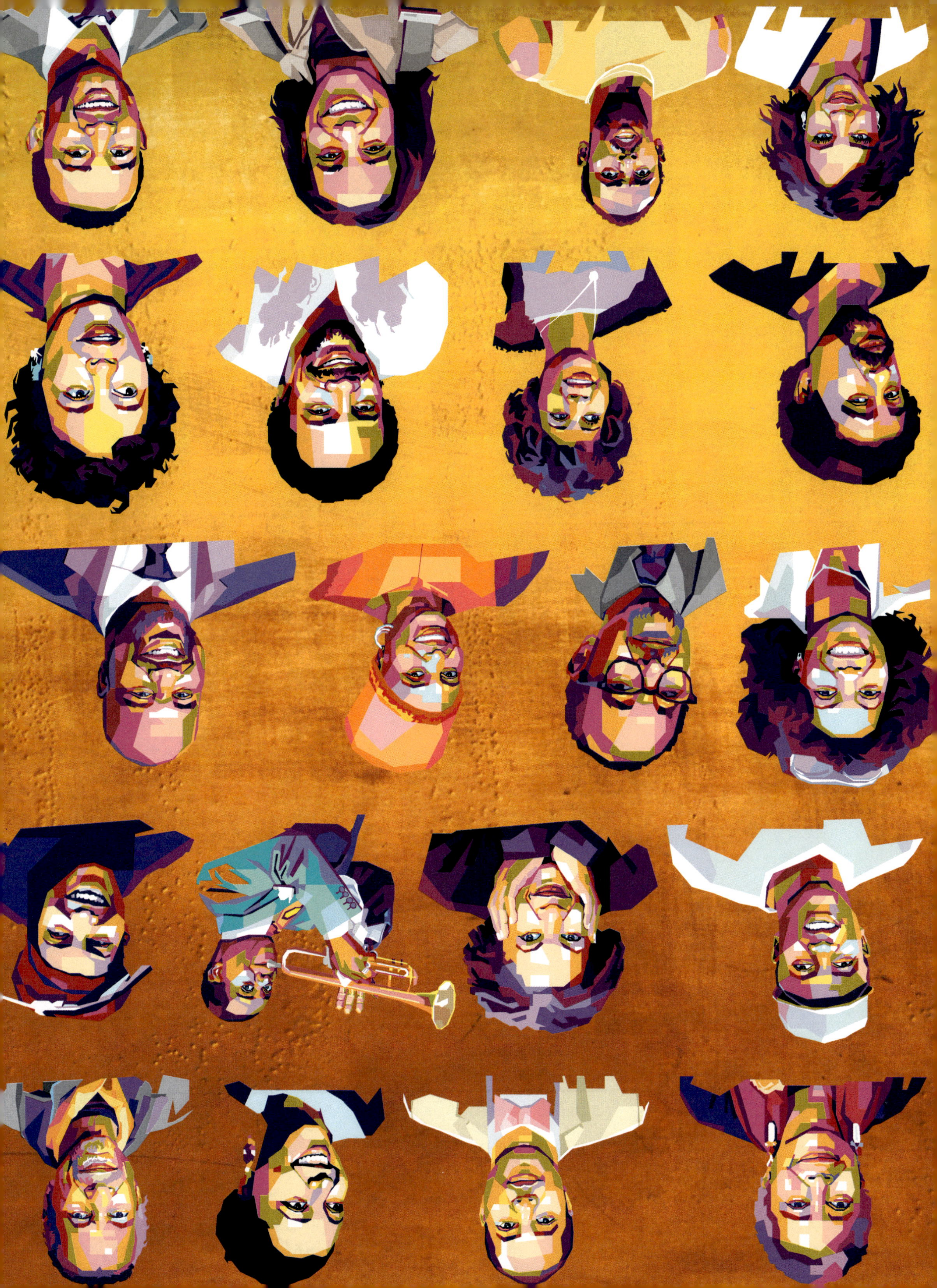

Bedtime

INSPIRATIONAL

Stories

50 Black Leaders Who Made History

Other books by L.A. Amber

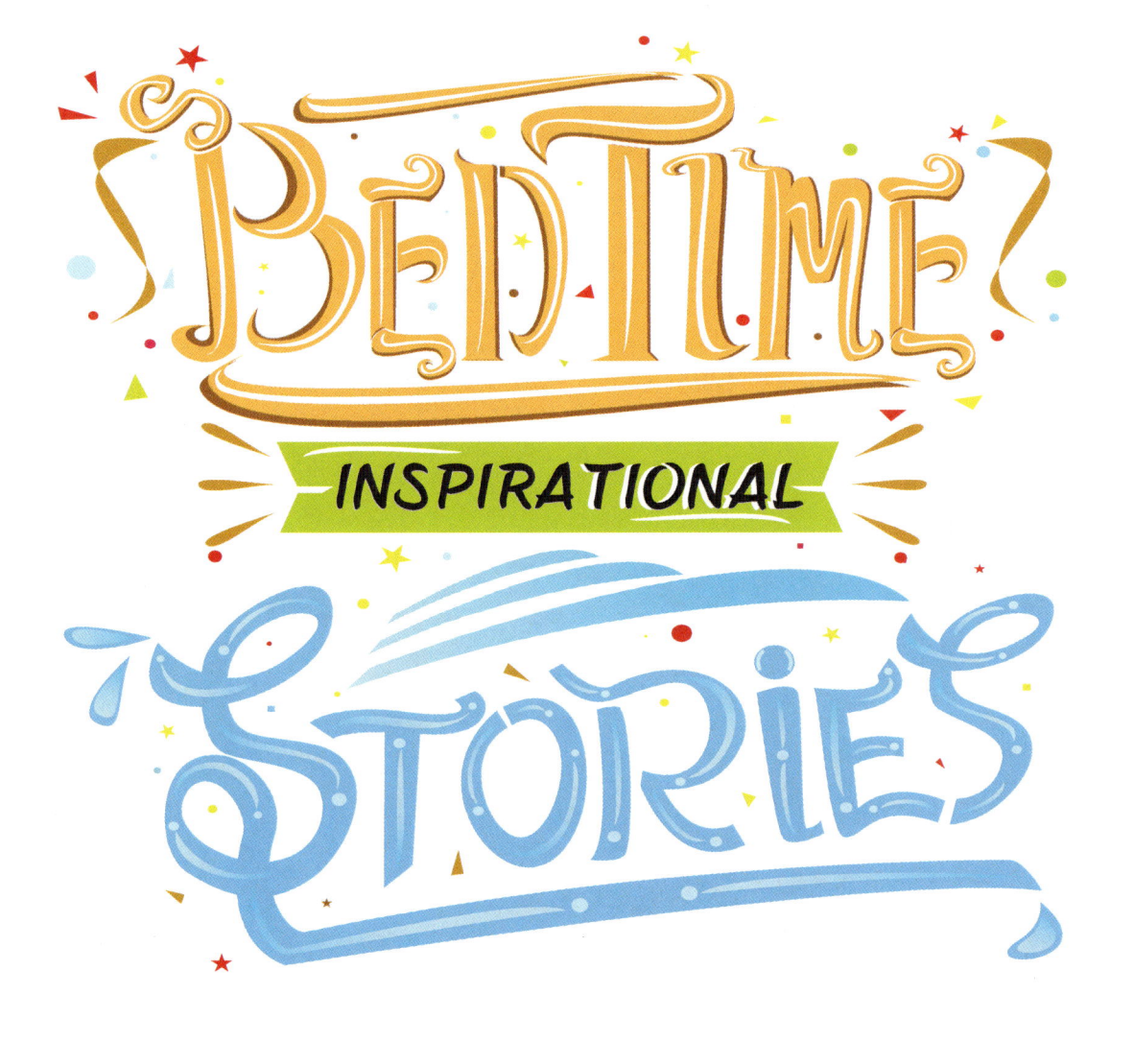

BEDTIME
INSPIRATIONAL
Stories

- I CHOOSE TO BE HAPPY
- I ENJOY TESTING NEW IDEAS
- I LOVE GOING TO SCHOOL BECAUSE LEARNING IS FUN
- I HAVE FEARS, BUT I HAVE THE COURAGE TO FACE THEM
- I BELIEVE I CAN BE WHATEVER I WANT TO BE

I LISTEN TO
MY PARENTS AND RESPECT THEM

I AM GENEROUS

I AM COURAGEOUS

I AM HELPFUL

I AM POLITE AND COURTEOUS, EVEN IN THE FACE OF RUDENESS

TRYING MY HARDEST
I AM PROUD OF MYSELF FOR

HEALTHY
I KEEP MY BODY

OVERCOME CHALLENGES
I ALWAYS FIND WAYS TO

WHO LOVE ME
I HAVE LOTS OF FRIENDS

I LOVE MYSELF
EVEN THOUGH I SOMETIMES FAIL

I COMPLETE MY SCHOOL WORK ON TIME EVERY DAY

I AM GRATEFUL

I DRAW INSPIRATION FROM LIFE AND MY ROLE MODELS

MY PARENTS ARE PROUD OF ME

I GET BETTER AND BETTER EVERY DAY

I AM BOLD AND OUTGOING

MY PERSONALITY EXUDES CONFIDENCE

BEING CALM AND RELAXED ENERGIZES MY WHOLE BEING

I AM IN CHARGE OF MY OWN LIFE

MY SIBLINGS AND I HAVE FUN AND FIND NEW WAYS TO ENJOY OUR TIME TOGETHER

I BELIEVE IN MYSELF

- I FOCUS ON SOLUTIONS AND ALWAYS FIND THE BEST ONE
- I HAVE HAPPY THOUGHTS
- I AM A PROBLEM SOLVER
- I TAKE CARE OF MY RESPONSIBILITIES
- I PLAY WELL WITH OTHERS
- I PAY ATTENTION AND LISTEN TO WHAT MY BODY NEEDS TO BE HEALTHY

I AM HELPFUL

I EXPRESS MY IDEAS EASILY

I ENJOY DISCOVERING NEW THINGS

I HAVE AN ACTIVE SENSE OF HUMOR AND LOVE TO SHARE LAUGHTER WITH OTHERS

I AM STEADFAST IN WHAT I BELIEVE

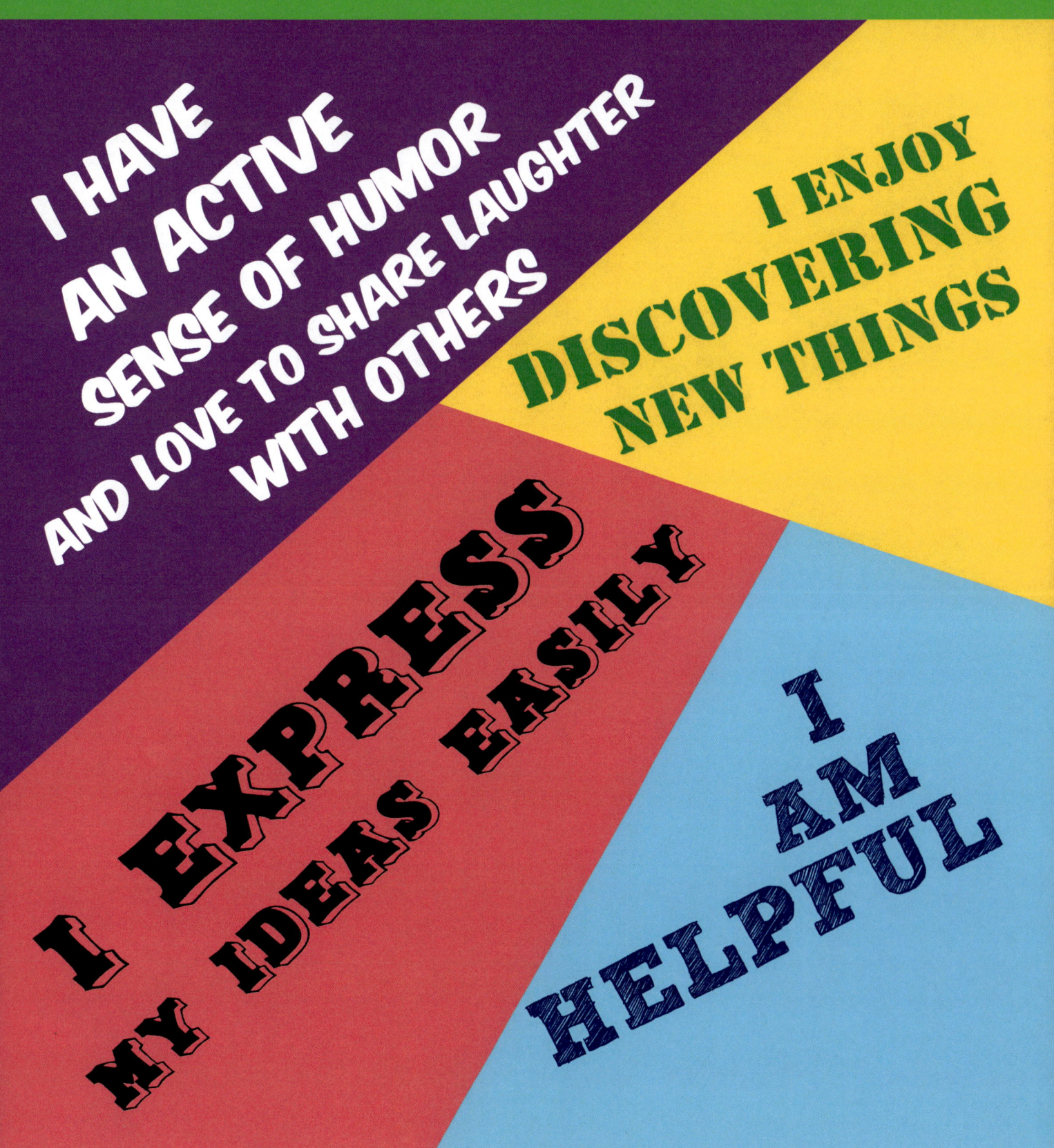

I TURN CHALLENGES INTO OPPORTUNITIES FOR SUCCESS

I SUPPORT OTHERS WITH LOVE AND KINDNESS

BY ALLOWING MYSELF TO BE HAPPY, I INSPIRE OTHERS TO BE HAPPY AS WELL

MY DREAMS ARE COMING TRUE

I AM SPECIAL

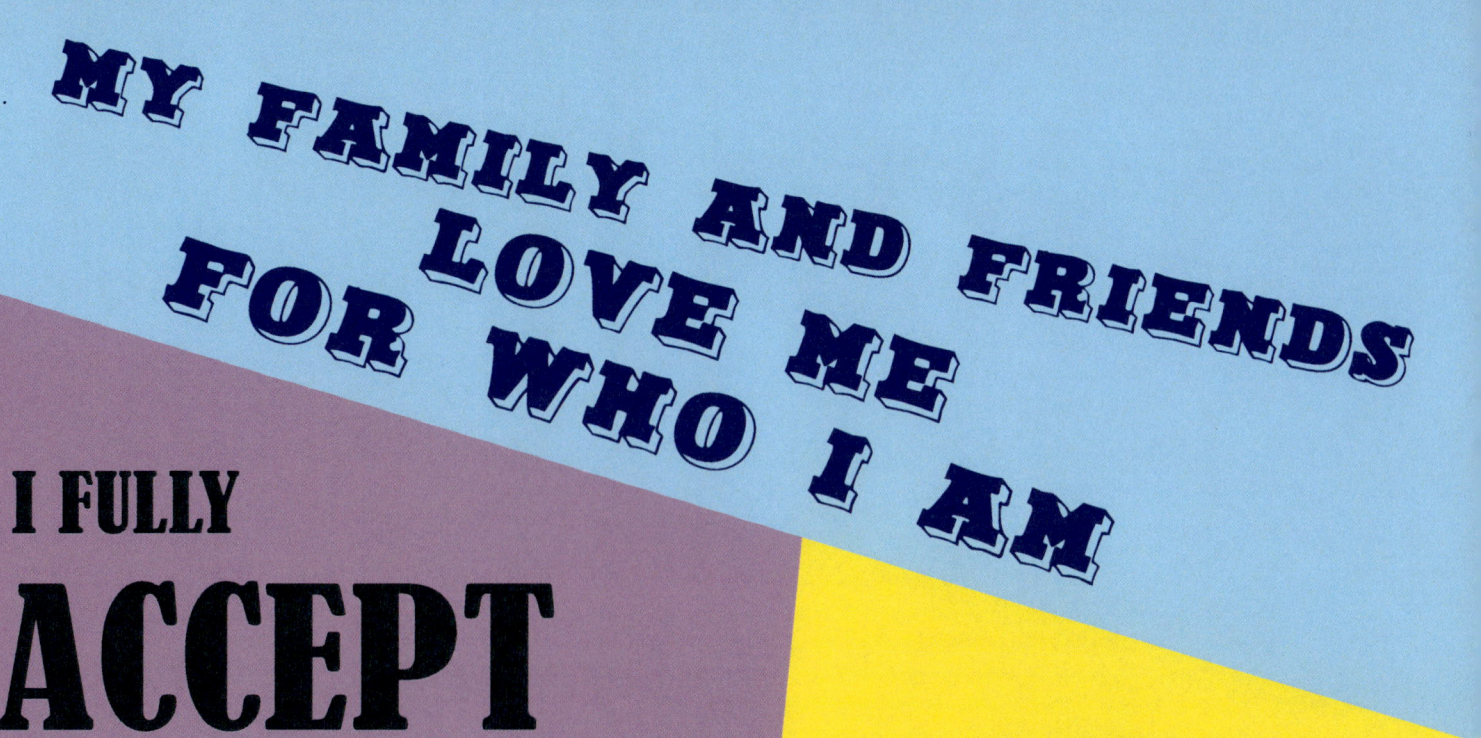

I LEARN FROM MY MISTAKES

I AM KIND

I FULLY ACCEPT MYSELF AND KNOW THAT I AM WORTHY OF GREAT THINGS IN LIFE

I AM PATIENT

MY FAMILY AND FRIENDS LOVE ME FOR WHO I AM

WHATEVER I DO, I GIVE MY BEST

I APPROVE OF MYSELF

I TALK ABOUT MY FEELINGS

ADVERSITIES ARE CHALLENGES I CAN LEARN FROM

I AM MAKING A DIFFERENCE IN PEOPLE'S LIVES

POSITIVE AFFIRMATIONS

SAY THEM ALOUD

BONUS MATERIAL

BEDTIME
INSPIRATIONAL
STORIES

"TURN your wounds *into* WISDOM."

Leanna Archer
New York City, New York, United States (1995 –)
Founder and CEO of Leanna's Inc.

LEANNA ARCHER

Most business owners are in their thirties and forties. However, a girl named Leanna was much younger than that when she started her own hair care business. She was only eleven! Leanna started her business by using her grandmother's recipes for hair care products—recipes she'd brought with her when her family emigrated from Haiti. Her grandmother had used traditional Haitian recipes for her own hair care products her entire life. They worked well too, and Leanna enjoyed making and using them.

The products contain only natural ingredients. This means that they don't contain chemicals that can harm your health. People like using natural products.

Leanna started out by selling her products to friends and neighbors. They said that her

Did you know that at sixteen years old, Leanna Archer was the youngest CEO to ring the NASDAQ stock market bell?

products were so amazing that Leanna should start a real business. Leanna's hair care products are very popular even now, and her business makes a lot of money. Leanna's business is called Leanna's Inc. She is the CEO of her business, meaning that she is the boss. Are you an entrepreneur? Would you like to be your own boss?

Leanna uses money from her business to help other people. She has a charitable foundation called the Leanna Archer Education Foundation. This foundation helps to provide food, shelter, and education to children in need.

Leanna has been interviewed by newspapers and magazines about her success. This has helped let other people know about her hair care products too. People all around the world use Leanna's wonderful products now. She is famous and very respected.

Life Lesson

Do you have a business idea?

The world is full of great business ideas, but success only comes through action. You will never regret failure, but you will regret not trying. Believe that you can succeed, and you will find a way to do so. No one succeeds immediately, and everyone was once a beginner. Just do something you truly believe in. I support you all the way!

P.K. Subban

Toronto, Ontario, Canada (1989 -)
Professional Ice Hockey Player and Philanthropist.

"GROWING UP, it was tough to BALANCE but looking back I APPRECIATE MY PARENTS' efforts to make sure I was WELL-ROUNDED."

P. K. SUBBAN

Once upon a time, a young boy moved with his family from the Caribbean to Toronto, Canada. Hockey is a very popular sport in Canada, and it wasn't long before P. K. Subban was playing hockey every chance he got. P. K. played hard to become the best player he could be.

His talents and potential were obvious to the talent scouts early on. Unfortunately, there weren't many black kids in hockey at that time, and P. K. had to deal with racist attitudes from others. He didn't let other people discourage him, though, or keep him from following his dream.

P. K. was first drafted to the Montreal Canadians. He played for Montreal for many years. Later, he was traded to a team in Nashville in the United States. P. K. also played for Team Canada in the 2014 Olympics. The team won the gold medal!

Did you know that the first hockey puck was made in the 1800s out of cow dung?

There have only been eighty-seven black hockey players in the NHL so far. P. K. was among the fi rst to successfully break through barriers when he established his hockey career. His dream was to be a professional hockey player, and he would not let other people's prejudices stop him. You should never let other people's thoughts and words get in the way of your dreams!

P. K. Subban is known for his dedication and talent. In order to be a great player, he knew that he needed to train very hard and take care of his body.

Life Lesson

Why should you take care of your body?

You only have one body, so you need to look after it. Our bodies are built like machines. To keep our machines running smoothly, we need to exercise, eat nutritious food, and sleep well.

Alicia Keys

Manhattan, New York, United States (1981 -)
Musician, Singer, and Songwriter

"Failure isn't AN OPTION. I've erased THE WORD 'fear' from my VOCABULARY, and I think when you erase fear, you can't fail."

ALICIA KEYS

When she was a little girl, Alicia Keys was faced with adversity and harassment every single day. Living in a dangerous area of New York City, she found threats on every corner. Because of that, Alicia decided to wear gender-neutral clothes and hairstyles so that she could be easily mistaken for a boy.

But music got Alicia through her tough childhood, and she knew how to play the piano effortlessly by the age of twelve. Alicia started writing songs and poured all her thoughts and feelings into them. And that hard life would prepare her for what was to come.

When she first stepped into the music world, she saw that there were wolves in the music industry just like the ones she

Did you know that Alicia Keys's real name is Alicia Augello-Cook?

saw in the street; these were just wolves in sheep's clothing. They wanted Alicia to dress and act a certain way and sing songs the way they wanted her to sing them. The music executives wanted to completely change her and make her a star based on who she was not.

But Alicia knew better. She got out of her big contract and signed with another, smaller record label. And once she could be herself, there was no stopping her. In the early 2000s, she started releasing albums just how she wanted them and found overwhelming success. She became one of the bestselling artists of all time and earned fifteen Grammy Awards, seventeen NAACP Awards, and many others.

And after all these successes, Alicia Keys still felt like she was what people wanted her to be. She felt like the eyes of the world were on her and she had to be perfect at all times. But after seeing how women were judged and expected to wear makeup to make themselves something they're not, Alicia decided to stop wearing it altogether. She started making red carpet appearances sporting her fresh, natural look and stopped caring about what other people might think.

Life Lesson

Do you love yourself just the way you are?

When Alicia Keys decided to embrace herself and how she naturally looked, she became much happier and even better-looking. She gave up on trying to look how everyone expected her to and let her music speak for itself.

Serena Williams

Saginaw, Michigan, United States (1981 -)
Professional Tennis Player.

"I really think a **CHAMPION** is **DEFINED** not by their wins but by **HOW THEY CAN RECOVER** when they fall."

SERENA WILLIAMS

Not too long ago, a three-year-old girl named Serena Williams picked up a tennis racket to play her own version of tennis. She worked many hours as she got older to become a great tennis player. Her hard work paid off in a big way!

At nine years old, Serena went to a special school for young tennis players. She was one of the best, but her father eventually took her out of the school in order to coach her himself.

Her sister Venus is a tennis player too. Serena and Venus made a great doubles team—two tennis players working as a team against two other players. They worked well together and won often, making history as a tennis team of sisters.

Did you know that tennis originated in France? When players first played the game, they hit the ball with the palm of their hand. Rackets came into use at a much later date.

Serena and Venus also played against each other. Competing with her older sister wasn't easy for Serena, though. Do you ever feel like you have to compete against your siblings?

Serena is a great example to follow because she can compete against her sister and work with her too. She doesn't let the competition ruin their relationship, and you don't have to let competition turn you against your siblings either. Competing with each other made Serena and Venus better players *and* better sisters.

Serena is still a great tennis player, but she is also known for her generosity now. She gives money and time to organizations that help people in need. She worked hard to become the best player she could be.

Life Lesson

Do you get along with your siblings?

Friends might come and go, but a brother or sister will always be there for you. This relationship can be one of the strongest you have in life. You and your siblings are very lucky to have each other.

Beyoncé Knowles

Houston, Texas, United States (1981 -)
Singer, Songwriter, Dancer and Actress.

"If everything was **PERFECT,** *you would never* **LEARN** *and you would never* **GROW"**

BEYONCÉ

Not all that long ago, a shy girl named Beyoncé Knowles was growing up in Houston, Texas. She had very few friends and often felt lonely. Have you ever felt lonely? It can make you feel very sad. That's how Beyoncé felt. She felt like no one would ever like her because she was so shy.

To help her feel better about herself, her mother enrolled her in dance lessons so that she could make friends with other little girls. Beyoncé wanted more than anything to break out of her shyness, so she gave it a try.

Beyoncé loved her class and was very good at dancing. She tried singing too, and along with her dancing, she discovered that she had true talent! Her gifts for singing and dancing made her feel confident and alive.

She entered a few talent shows and won them all. Her parents soon realized that Beyoncé was happiest when she was performing. They supported her dream to become a star. It was her destiny!

Did you know that when Beyoncé was only nine years old, she won a role in a girls' music group that was eventually called Destiny's Child? Destiny's Child was a hit! They released five albums and won three Grammy Awards!

She made Grammy history when she became the first female artist to win six Grammy awards in one evening.

Beyoncé is no longer a shy, lonely little girl. She is a star! She proved that if you face your fears, you can do anything!

Life Lesson

What are your fears?

Everyone has fears. I have them. You have them. The only difference is in one's willingness to work and move through those fears to get where they want to be. Once you learn how to get over your fears, they go away so that you can live your destiny too!

Tegla Loroupe

Kutomwony, Kenya (1973 -)
Long-Distance Track and Road Runner.

"In a country where only men **are** ENCOURAGED, ONE MUST BE ONE'S OWN INSPIRATION."

TEGLA LOROUPE

In the far away country of Kenya, Africa, Tegla Loroupe was born. Tegla was a strong-willed girl and a very fast runner. She loved to run so much that she often ran to school, which was located several miles from her home.

Many people did not believe her talent for running was worth much, but this did not stop Tegla. She ignored what other people said her life should be. People said she could not be a runner because she was small and frail. But Tegla listened to her heart instead of the other people's voices.

Tegla knew she could run fast, but she wasn't sure how she could use her talents to do something great. She finally decided to compete in big, important races. Her decision led her to become the first woman from Africa to win a race in New York City—the New York City Marathon!

Did you know that Tegla traveled all over the world to promote peace? She believes we can all get along when we choose to care about one another.

She added to her fame by contributing to peace efforts around the world. Tegla even started her own peace foundation. She went back home to the villages in Africa to show leaders that there was no need to fight. She showed them that everyone benefited from living peacefully.

People believed in Tegla and trusted her word. She was a voice for her people. Communities that did not always agree came together to watch Tegla run and celebrate her victories. Tegla Loroupe became a champion for peace. She believes in encouraging people to be exactly who they want to be.

Life Lesson

Are you being your best self?

Don't compromise on who you are. Follow your heart. Listen to your inner voice. Don't worry about what other people think. Don't ever let anybody tell you that you can't be who you are!

Derartu Tulu

Bekoji, Ethiopia (1972 -)
Long-Distance Runner and Gold Medalist.

"He who is not **COURAGEOUS** enough to take **RISKS** will accomplish nothing in **LIFE.**"

DERARTU TULU

Not too long ago, a woman named Derartu Tulu wanted to show that women from her country could accomplish anything. She was the first woman from Ethiopia, Africa, to win a gold medal in the Olympics! To the people in Oromo, Ethiopia, Derartu is a symbol of hope. To girls all over the world, Derartu is also a hero.

Do you like to race your friends on the playground at school? Derartu's first win was in a race on the playground of her elementary school. She ran faster than the fastest boy in her school! Because she did so well, her nickname was "Star of the Mile." She was amazing, but not everyone thought she should run. Even her parents thought that running was for boys. Derartu knew she could accomplish great things as a runner. She believed in herself and ran whenever she could.

Did you know that Olympic gold medals must contain a minimum of six grams of gold and are 92.5-percent made of silver?

When Derartu went to the Olympics, she raced against people from all over the world. Derartu ran like a superhero, zooming around the curves of the track faster than any of the people she was running against. Everyone back home clapped and cheered for her. Her parents cheered louder than anyone! She won her first Olympic gold medal because of that race. She also won the admiration and respect of people all around the world.

Everyone learned how talented women runners could be by watching Derartu. She set an example so that others could believe in themselves too.

Life Lesson

Why is it important to be an example?

Well, what better way is there to help others than by being a good example to them? One of the best ways for us to be encouraged is through someone else's good example. You never know who's watching you either, so make sure you always set a good example everywhere you go.

Michael Jordan

Brooklyn, New York, United States (1963 -)
Professional Basketball Player and Businessman.

"I've failed over **and over** **and** OVER AGAIN *in my* LIFE. And that is why I SUCCEED."

MICHAEL JORDAN

A young man named Michael who grew up in Brooklyn, New York, did not care what game he was playing as long as he won. Winning was everything to him. If you asked him who he was competing against, he always said he was competing against himself. He wanted to play better than he had played before—every single time.

You may not realize it, but you know who I am talking about, because he really did win, win, win! His name is Michael Jordan.

Unbelievably, the first time Michael tried out to play on a basketball team, the coach wouldn't let him. That's right! He was not as good as the other kids there, so the coaches wouldn't even let Michael try. He was so upset that he decided he would practice harder and show everyone just how good he really was.

> *Did you know that a PE teacher invented basketball? The idea came to him in 1891 while he was looking for ways to keep his gym class busy indoors on a rainy day.*

After high school, he played college basketball and then went on to the Olympics. After the Olympics, he became a professional player in the NBA. He was so good at tough basketball shots that some people thought he could walk on air. This is where the name for Air Jordan sneakers came from.

It might seem impossible that Michael Jordan could have ever failed at basketball, but he did. He just didn't let that stop him. Failing only made him try harder. Michael's attitude proves that when you work hard enough, you can do anything.

Life Lesson

Are you trying hard enough?

There are people who will always be better than you are at something, but that doesn't mean you shouldn't work to perfect your skill. Set your goals high, and don't stop practicing until you get where you want to go.

Jackie Joyner-Kersee

East St. Louis, Illinois, United States (1962 -)
Track and Field Athlete. Gold Olympic Medalist.

"It's **BETTER** to **LOOK AHEAD** and **PREPARE,** than to look back and regret."

JACKIE JOYNER-KERSEE

A young girl named Jackie loved to play sports, even though she had severe asthma. She wanted to be a professional athlete, but she knew she would have to overcome the asthma to make her dream come true. And she did! Jackie Joyner-Kersee still holds records as one of the fastest runners ever.

Jackie played sports almost every day—track, basketball, or volleyball. As a teen, she was recognized for her ability to power through any challenge. She was not afraid of pushing right past her limits.

Jackie was a member of the US Olympic track team and competed in the Olympic Games three times. She won gold, silver, and bronze medals. *Sports Illustrated* recognized Jackie as the greatest female athlete of all time. She was also honored as one of the top fifteen players in women's basketball at UCLA.

Did you know that Jackie is one of the best female athletes of all time? She overcame challenges and set new records for female athletes.

Competing in track and field events was very important to Jackie. She felt most alive when she was running and jumping!

Jackie stopped competing when she was older so that she could help kids just like you! She believed that every kid could move past challenges to be the best they could be, even when things were hard at home, at school, or in sports. She went back to her community to help others achieve their dreams in sports the way she had. She encouraged them to make a difference in the world by doing what they did best.

Life Lesson

What challenges have you faced?

Life is full of challenges, so you will have to deal with problems throughout your life. It is the way you deal with them that decides whether you are successful or not.

Barack Obama

Honolulu, Hawaii, United States (1961 -)
Politician, President of the United States
from 2009 to 2017.

"THE FUTURE REWARDS
THOSE WHO PRESS ON.

I DON'T HAVE TIME
TO FEEL SORRY FOR MYSELF.

I don't have time to complain."

BARACK OBAMA

Barack Obama was always intelligent and a good speaker—even as a young boy—but he also had problems, just like many children do. He never had the chance to really know his father, who was a senior economist for the government in Kenya.

Barack lived in Hawaii and in Indonesia. Barry—Barack's nickname when he was in school—soon discovered that there weren't very many African Americans in Hawaii. This made him feel alone and out of place at school, and he struggled with low self-esteem.

Barack worked in a Baskin-Robbins ice cream shop to earn money for college, and now he says he hates ice cream because of working with it so much!

Did you know that, in Indonesia, Barack Obama ate foods such as snake, dog meat, and grasshoppers that were roasted on an open fire? He also had his own pet ape named Tata.

As a young man, Barack worked as a community organizer in Chicago, because he wanted to make the city he called home a better place to live. He later became a lawyer and then a politician. We know he accomplished a lot as a politician, because he became the first black president of the United States. But what you might not know is that while growing up, Barack wanted to be an architect.

President Barack Obama accomplished many things during his two terms in office. He focused a lot on trying to make life better for people who are too poor to pay for medical care and for people wanting a good education. One reason he wanted everyone to have good medical care is because his mother died of cancer at a very young age. This was, in part, because she couldn't afford good medical care.

Life Lesson

Why is it important to take care of your health?

Taking care of your health is a big part of growing up. To be as healthy as possible, you have to take good care of your body. You can do this by eating healthy foods, staying active, and letting the doctor help you when you are sick.

Michael Jackson

Gary, Indiana, United States (1958 - 2009)
Singer, Songwriter and Dancer.

"To **GIVE** someone a piece of your **HEART,** is **WORTH** more than all the **WEALTH** in the **WORLD.**"

MICHAEL JACKSON

Michael Jackson was one of eight children, and he grew up in a two-bedroom house. His parents loved singing and decided to make the family a singing group. The abuse Michael suffered from his father, however, caused him to feel alone and depressed. Michael often had nightmares and couldn't sleep because of the stress he felt as a result of his strict rehearsal schedule and fear of his father's temper.

Michael Jackson and his siblings had great musical talent, and people all over the country loved their music. Later, Michael started singing by himself and became the most awarded musician of all time. He was even called "The King of Pop." He received twenty-three Guinness World Records, forty Billboard Awards, thirteen Grammys, and twenty-six American Music Awards.

Did you know that Michael Jackson's "Billie Jean" was the first music video by a black artist to air on MTV?

Being rich and famous did not cause Michael to forget the feelings of loneliness and fear. He also never forgot what it was like to be poor. He wanted to help others who might feel the same way. Michael donated money to organizations and charities all over the world. He held benefit concerts and donated money to organizations that helped injured children and underprivileged families.

Michael encouraged other musicians, actors, and even his fans to do the same. He discovered that he could use fame to influence and help those who were less fortunate than himself.

Life Lesson

Did you know that your friends have an influence on you?

The company you keep says a lot about you. Friends have a big influence over how you feel, think, and behave. If you choose friends who make poor choices, you might end up making poor choices too. But if you choose friends who inspire and challenge you to become better, you will become a better person.

Mark E. Dean

Jefferson City, Tennessee, United States (1957 -)
Inventor and a Computer Engineer.

"A lot of kids growing up today aren't told that YOU CAN BE WHATEVER YOU WANT TO BE. There may be obstacles, but THERE ARE NO LIMITS."

MARK E. DEAN

As a boy, Mark E. Dean sometimes went to work with his father at a nearby dam. Mark thought the dam was fascinating, and he loved the mechanics that made it function. Mark had a brilliant mind, and he also had a love for science and learning how things work.

Understanding how things work is called *mechanical ability*. In school, Mark had a tough time reading and writing, but he loved math and science. He never had a problem in those two subjects.

Mark's interest in math and science grew even stronger when he was in college. After er he graduated from college, he went to work for IBM, which is one of the biggest computer companies in the world.

Did you know that the first electronic computer, ENIAC, weighed more than twenty-seven tons and took up 1,800 square feet?

Mark was full of ideas and was inspired by everything around him. But not everyone would listen to him when he had an idea he wanted to talk about. When someone didn't listen, he said to himself, "I will just tell someone else!" And that's exactly what he did. He kept telling people his ideas until he found someone who would listen. One of the ideas Mark had was for the first PC (personal computer).

"Everyone should have a computer," Mark said one day. Mark found someone who listened to his idea, and he was able to help IBM create the first home computer. Later, he made the idea even better and created the first home computer with a color screen. Mark became famous for his inventions and ideas. He accomplished all of this because he did not give up. He continued talking to people about his ideas until he found someone who would listen.

Life Lesson

Are you afraid of failure?

Some people are afraid to do things because they are afraid that they are not good enough and are afraid they will fail. Don't be afraid of new things. Don't be afraid to fail. Don't depend on the approval of others. Don't be afraid to look for someone who will say, "We can try it your way."

Mae C. Jemison

Decatur, Alabama, United States (1956 -)
Engineer, Physician and NASA Astronaut.

"NEVER LIMIT YOURSELF because of others' limited imagination, NEVER LIMIT OTHERS because of your own limited imagination."

MAE C. JEMISON

There was once a young girl named Mae C. Jemison who worked very hard in grade school. She studied a lot—even when she could have been playing. Mae was very lucky because her parents always encouraged her. This encouragement gave Mae the courage to apply to college. She was accepted and made very good grades while she was there.

In college, Mae studied engineering and space science, and she later became the first African American woman astronaut. When Mae first traveled into space, she was on a ship called the *Endeavour*. She was in the space shuttle for 190 hours (or one week) during the first expedition.

Did you know that the word astronaut comes from the Greek words astro and nautes? It translates to "star sailor."

While she was on the space shuttle, Mae's job was science mission specialist. This meant that she was responsible for overseeing scientific experiments about gravity and weightlessness that were conducted on the space shuttle.

Have you ever seen videos of astronauts in space? Did you notice that they were floating? This is called *weightlessness*, and it happens because there is very little gravity in space. Gravity is a force that causes objects to be pulled toward each other.

Have you ever felt sick because you were in a car or on a plane? This is called motion sickness. Mae did experiments on motion sickness too. Mae is a brilliant woman who has accomplished great things. Mae knew the value of a good education, and she put all her opportunities to excellent use. She is a role model for anyone who wants to make his or her dreams come true.

Life Lesson

Why is education so important?

Education helps open doors to a lot of opportunities. The more you study and learn, the more opportunities you will have.

Whoopi Goldberg

New York City, New York, United States (1955 -)
Actress, Comedian, Author and Television Host.

"*I am where* **I AM** *because* **I BELIEVE IN ALL POSSIBILITIES.**"

WHOOPI GOLDBERG

Over fifty years ago, a girl named Caryn Elaine Johnson was born in New York City. She grew up with only a mother at home. Caryn and her mom found life challenging because they had very little money. Her mother worked long hours, and raising a daughter was difficult without a partner for support.

Caryn decided that one day she would be famous. When she became a teenager, though, Caryn made some bad choices that caused her dreams of being famous to stay hidden for a few years. Eventually, Caryn decided she needed to turn her life around. One of the first things she did to make that happen was change her name to Whoopi Goldberg.

Whoopi wanted to become a comedian and an actress. She had to take different jobs while she tried to find acting work, but slowly the door of opportunity opened for Whoopi. She was selected to appear on comedy shows. She made people laugh. They loved her!

Did you know that Whoopi is one of the few entertainers to have won an Emmy, Grammy, Oscar, and Tony award? Whoopi was only the second black woman in the history of the Academy Awards to win an Oscar for acting.

Eventually, directors wanted Whoopi to be in their movies. Her first big movie was called *The Color Purple*. Everyone saw that Whoopi was an amazing actress in that movie. She became famous!

Whoopi uses her sense of humor to get people to listen to her message to treat everyone fairly and with respect. She knows that making people laugh gives them a better attitude. People with good attitudes make the world a better place to live.

Life Lesson

Why is humor important?

Through humor, you can soften some of the hardest things that happen to you. Do you laugh enough? You should laugh as much as possible.

Oprah Winfrey

Kosciusko, Mississippi, United States (1954 -)
Talk Show Host, Actress, Producer, and Philanthropist.

"BE THANKFUL for what you HAVE, you'll end up HAVING MORE. If you CONCENTRATE on what you don't have, you will never, ever have enough."

OPRAH WINFREY

Life was tough for young Oprah. Living on a farm, there was always work to do that left little time for playing. One of her chores was bringing water in buckets from the well, because there was no running water in the house!

After doing her chores, Oprah always made sure to do her schoolwork and read. She loved to read! Oprah did well in school too. She was the smartest one in her class and graduated from high school with the highest honors.

Oprah also loved to give speeches at school and at church. She won prizes for her speeches and was able to go to college by using her prize money to help pay for it. Her good grades continued in college, but it was a job on TV that really turned her life around. By the time she graduated college, she was already a local TV star. She was not even twenty-one years old!

Did you know that Oprah Winfrey was the first black woman billionaire and is currently one of the richest African American woman in the world?

Before long, she was offered a TV show of her own—*The Oprah Winfrey Show.* The show was a huge success. People around the world knew her name and recognized her face. Oprah has been in several movies now too. She also started her own company that creates monthly magazines and TV shows, and she gives a lot of money to many different charities.

Even though she is famous and successful, Oprah never stopped reading. On her TV show, Oprah often talked about her favorite books and encouraged people to read them. She helped millions of people learn to love reading like she does.

She credits her grandmother for guiding her to success, because it was her grandmother who encouraged her to give her first speech. This gave Oprah confidence at an early age and helped her have high self-esteem.

Life Lesson

Do you like speaking in public or in front of your classmates?

The ability to give a speech is one of the most valuable skills you can have. Speaking with confidence will improve every area of your life.

Christopher Gardner

Milwaukee, Wisconsin, United States (1954 -)
Investor, Motivational Speaker, Author, and Philanthropist.

"DON'T EVER LET someone tell you, you can't DO SOMETHING."

CHRISTOPHER PAUL GARDNER

Christopher Paul Gardner's mother encouraged him constantly. Even during troubled times, his mother managed to stay calm and confident, continuing to encourage her son to do the same. To Christopher, his mother was a role model. Role models are people you look at and think, "I want to be just like them." Christopher says his mom inspired him to be successful. Everybody should have a role model like Christopher did. Do you? Who is your role model?

Christopher's family didn't have a lot of money. So when Christopher wanted to go to college, he worked several jobs to earn the money he needed.

A few years later, he got married and had a son, but his wife left him because she thought they didn't have enough money. This hurt Christopher a lot, but he focused

Did you know that the movie The Pursuit of Happyness is based on Chris Gardner's life? (Yes, they misspelled "happiness" on purpose!)

on taking care of his son. With no money or home to live in, Christopher and his son slept in parks, public bathrooms, and anywhere else they could find. It was a very hard life for both of them.

One day, Christopher met a man driving a shiny red sports car. Christopher asked the man about his work, and he told him that he was a stockbroker. Christopher wanted to become a stockbroker too. It wasn't easy, but he refused to give up on accomplishing this goal. Today, Christopher Paul Gardner is a famous stockbroker and a millionaire who runs his own company.

Christopher overcame hardship and discouragement to achieve his goals. He achieved them by focusing on his education and devoting himself to his dreams.

Life Lesson

Are you a role model?

You can be. Being a role model is important and powerful. When you become a role model, your family and friends look up to you.

Beverly Johnson

Buffalo, New York, United States (1952 -)
Model, Actress, Singer, and Businesswoman.

"There's not
a hair extension or
a makeup artist that can
make me feel
the way I feel when
I give back."

BEVERLY JOHNSON

There once was an athletic girl named Beverly Johnson. She was an excellent swimmer, and she won championships that almost took her to the Olympics.

Beverly was disappointed when she didn't get to go to the Olympics, but she didn't let her disappointment slow her down. She wanted to be successful—even famous—and so she told herself she wouldn't settle for anything less.

Beverly was a great athlete, but she was also very smart. She did so well in high school that she got a full scholarship to go to Northeastern University in New York. A scholarship is money given to students with good grades who show they are serious about going to school. It's like a reward, but it pays for school or items needed to obtain an education.

Did you know that the first fashion magazine was published in Germany over four hundred years ago?

Beverly's scholarship paid for her college classes and books, but she still had to work so that she could have money for food and clothes. Beverly's friends told her they thought she should try to get a job as a fashion model because she was so pretty. Her friends were right. She got the job she applied for, and it turned out to be a magical experience!

Beverly became the first black model to appear on the cover of *Vogue* and *Glamour*, which are two of the most famous magazines in the world! She has now been on the cover of over five hundred magazines. This was a big deal for Beverly and for other black models. Now they were more likely to be featured on magazine covers too.

Beverly Johnson is a hardworking and determined woman with many talents who has achieved many goals in her life.

Life Lesson

Do you like to do several different things?

What things are you good at doing? Don't settle for doing just one thing. Do everything you like to do and give all of it your very best effort.

Ben Carson

Detroit, Michigan, United States (1951 -)
Neurosurgeon, Author, and Politician.

"HAPPINESS
doesn't result from
WHAT WE GET,
but from
WHAT WE GIVE."

BEN CARSON

Ben was eight years old when his father left the family. Ben's mom had dropped out of school after third grade and gotten married when she was only thirteen, and since she had never had the chance to get a proper education, it was hard for her to get a job that paid enough to support herself and her two boys. But that didn't stop Ben from being a positive and happy boy who loved to learn.

Ben's mother gave him a great deal of encouragement in his education. She made sure that he and his brother read books and wrote book reports every week. Ben once said that reading opened up a new world for him. It helped him use his imagination.

Ben was not always treated very nicely by his teachers and some of the other students in school. Sometimes, his teachers made rude remarks to him because he was black.

Did you know that Ben Carson pioneered a lifesaving operation to separate conjoined twins who were connected at the brain?

Luckily, the encouragement he got from his mother and other teachers was enough to keep him on the right track.

Ben studied hard and earned a scholarship to Yale University. After graduating from Yale, he went to the University of Michigan to become a neurosurgeon. A neurosurgeon is a surgeon who operates on the brain.

Ben Carson didn't listen to people who said he would never succeed. Ben listened to his mom instead and became a great doctor and a person who is dedicated to helping others. Do you listen to your parents? Your parents love you and want what is best for you. Always listen to and respect your parents.

Life Lesson

Do you like to read?

When you read, you learn about people, places, and things you wouldn't have known about otherwise. Through reading, you learn new ways to do things and different ways to solve problems. The more you read, the more you will learn.

Shirley A. Jackson

Washington, D.C., United States (1946 -)
Ph.D. In Nuclear Physics.

"We need *to go back* **to the** DISCOVERY, to posing a QUESTION, *and having* KIDS know that they CAN DISCOVER *the* ANSWERS."

SHIRLEY ANN JACKSON

Shirley was very smart in science and math, and she loved to figure out new ways of solving problems. When Shirley was a teenager, she was accepted into the Massachusetts Institute of Technology (MIT). She was one of the first black women to attend the school. Everyone who knew Shirley was very proud of her accomplishments. Sadly, however, not everyone at MIT was nice to her. Some people did not believe she was smart enough to be there.

Shirley knew she was smart, though, and she worked hard to prove it to everyone who doubted her. Sometimes, Shirley felt sad because she wanted to be accepted by others—but even then, she didn't give up.

Shirley's hard work paid off. She was the first black woman to earn a doctorate from MIT, and she became a famous scientist who helped make the world a safer place. The president even honored her with the National Medal of Science.

Did you know that Shirley Ann Jackson invented caller ID? This is the technology used to find out who is calling you before you pick up your phone and say hello! How cool is that?

Shirley Ann Jackson could have decided to quit when people at school treated her badly or told her she was wasting her time, but she didn't. Shirley never doubted herself!

Life Lesson

Do you have doubts about yourself?

How can you overcome those doubts? Don't be afraid to be yourself. Not everyone will like you, but that's okay. Each time you face your doubts, you gain strength, courage, and confidence in yourself. Your family and friends will always love you, no matter what.

Bob Marley

Nine Mile, Saint Ann Parish, Jamaica (1945 - 1981)
Singer, Songwriter, Musician and Guitarist.

"EVERY MAN gotta right to - DECIDE - his own DESTINY"

BOB MARLEY

On the sunny tropical island of Jamaica, there once lived a little boy who had a heart that overflowed with songs. His name was Bob Marley.

Bob lived with his mother on their farm while his father worked away from home. When Bob was only ten years old, his father died, making it necessary for Bob and his mother to leave their farm and move to a poor area called Trench Town. Their new home was nothing like the lovely little farm Bob had always called home. But Bob didn't let any of this scare him or make him angry. Instead, Bob was still the happy, smiling boy he had always been.

Bob and his mother lived with his best friend, Neville, and Neville's father. Together, they were a family. Neville also had songs in

Did you know that reggae was invented partially by accident?

his heart. He and Bob formed a band. They called themselves Bob Marley and the Wailers. They played a type of music that combined reggae (music from Jamaica with a strong beat) and rocksteady (music with a slow tempo) in their compositions. The music made everyone feel happy and want to dance.

Bob enjoyed making people happy with his music, but he wanted to do even more. He wanted to help people who really needed it. One way he did this was by donating money to schools. One time, he gave all the money he made from a concert to a school for blind children!

Bob shared the songs in his heart to spread happiness to everyone, and he shared his money with those in need. You can do the same thing by paying attention to whatever is in your heart.

Life Lesson

Do you feel happy?

You can be happy even if everything is not perfect, because being happy is something you choose to do. You decide to have a great attitude and make the most of whatever situation you're in, even during bad times. Happiness is one of the keys to success in life. Seeing you happy makes me happy.

Patricia Bath

Harlem, New York, United States (1942 -)
Ophthalmologist, Inventor, and Academic.

"Do not allow **YOUR MIND** to be imprisoned by majority **THINKING**. Remember that the limits of **SCIENCE** are not the limits of **YOUR IMAGINATION**."

PATRICIA BATH

Have you ever received a gift that changed your life? Patricia Bath did. She received a microscope! Looking through the microscope, she saw tiny things on glass slides that fascinated her. That microscope helped her see something bigger too: her love for science!

Patricia faced many struggles as a black girl growing up in the 1950s. She wasn't allowed to do many things white girls her age were allowed to do or go where they were allowed to go. Patricia didn't let this stop her from working hard to achieve her goal of becoming a doctor, though.

During her medical training, Patricia saw a lot of people who did not have access to proper eye care. This bothered Patricia, so she decided to become an ophthalmologist. An ophthalmologist is a doctor that takes

Did you know that the most active muscles in your body are your eye muscles?

care of eyes. She even persuaded other eye doctors to perform surgery for free on people who could not afford it. This was the start of a community ophthalmology program that still helps people who don't have the money to get proper eye care anywhere else.

Patricia worked for many years to bring sight to people who had bad vision and even to those who were blind. She invented special tools that are still used around the world today to help people see. Patricia Bath was the first African American to complete a residency in ophthalmology and the first African American female doctor to receive a medical patent.

It wasn't easy for Patricia to become a doctor, but she didn't give up. Her passion for science and her desire to help people see gave her the courage to keep trying to achieve her dreams.

Life Lesson

What are you passionate about?

Passion is the energy that keeps us going. You can use passion as a powerful force in accomplishing anything you set your mind to. If you know what you want and work hard to get it, nothing can stop you either.

Muhammad Ali

Louisville, Kentucky, United States (1942 - 2016)
Professional Boxer and Activist.

"To be a **GREAT CHAMPION** you must **BELIEVE YOU** are the **BEST.** If you're not, **PRETEND YOU ARE.**"

MUHAMMAD ALI

"When I find the kid who stole my bike," said Cassius Clay, Jr., "I'm going to beat him up!"

"Well," said police officer Joe Martin, "don't you think you should know how to fight before you go trying to beat someone up?"

That angry boy decided to listen to the policeman, and so he went to his boxing club that day. No one guessed that the boy who wanted to get even for a stolen bicycle would become one of the most famous boxers in the world.

Cassius Clay, Jr., is better known as Muhammad Ali, and he inspired millions of people around the world with his boxing skills and his confident attitude.

Did you know that the Hollywood Walk of Fame star for Muhammad Ali is the only one that's placed on a wall and not on the ground? This is because Ali "did not want the name of Muhammad to be stepped on."

Cassius Clay, Jr., was a large boy who was also very fast and strong. Four years after he first stepped into the boxing ring, he became a top boxer and a member of the US Olympic team. He even won a gold medal in his sport!

Muhammad Ali loved to box because he loved to fight. But because of his religious beliefs, he said he would not fight in the Army. The boxing association did not like this, so they suspended him from fighting for a few years. He waited patiently for the time to pass, and as soon as he could fight again, he became a champion.

Muhammad Ali won most of his boxing matches. He was a world champion who fought for what he believed in, both in and out of the boxing ring.

Life Lesson

Do you believe in yourself?

If you believe in yourself, you will always be a winner. When you believe in yourself, anything is possible. Believe and achieve!

Jimi Hendrix

Seattle, Washington, United States (1942 - 1970)
Rock Guitarist, Singer, and Songwriter.

"KNOWLEDGE SPEAKS, *but* WISDOM LISTENS".

JIMI HENDRIX

Jimi did not have a very happy childhood, and his family often moved around just to stay safe. Jimi was a very talented musician, though, and he played music every chance he got.

When his father bought him his first guitar, he could not stop playing! With his guitar in his hands, Jimi believed he could do anything.

He was always strumming his guitar to figure out how to make new sounds. He was ahead of his time in music, thinking of songs with sounds no one had ever heard before. Jimi was always creating new ways of playing and listening to the guitar.

Jimi was always creating new music for other people to enjoy too. Jimi could not read or write music, so he had to record his

Did you know that Jimi played his guitar upside-down because he was left-handed?

musical ideas on tape. People loved Jimi's music. It inspired people and made them feel good about themselves. Through his music, Jimi showed people how everyone could feel connected to one another.

Sadly, Jimi's life was a short one, but his legacy lives on. He inspired thousands to play music in a new way. Jimi Hendrix continues to be one of the most popular arti sts in the history of rock music.

Life Lesson

Do you play any musical instruments?

Playing a musical instrument relieves stress, inspires you, and improves your social life. Music helps us feel good about ourselves and others.

Wangari Muta Maathai

Nyeri District, Kenya (1940 - 2011)
Environmental Political Activist. 2004 Nobel Peace Prize.

"It's the little THINGS CITIZENS DO. That's what will MAKE THE DIFFERENCE. My little thing is PLANTING TREES."

WANGARI MUTA MAATHAI

A famous woman by the name of Wangari Muta Maathai lived in Kenya, Africa. She did wonderful things for her country and the world.

Wangari cared about the environment. The *environment* is what we call the air, water, and land where people, animals, and plants live. She wanted to keep the environment clean, so she started something called the Green Belt Movement. The Green Belt Movement encourages people to plant lots of trees so that there will be plenty of oxygen in the air to help things live.

Wangari also cared about human rights. She wanted people to be happy and treated fairly. Wangari worked so hard to help make this happen that she was given many prizes, including the Nobel Peace Prize. The Nobel Peace Prize is given to special people who do amazing things that help make the world a better place.

Did you know that 27,000 trees are chopped down each day just for toilet paper?

Wangari worked very hard. She earned a doctoral degree in science. A doctoral degree is the highest degree you can get at a university, and Wangari was the first woman in her country to earn one. Some people didn't think she could do it, but she never let anyone discourage her from pursuing her dreams. Wangari also became a university professor. She was involved with many social causes and ended up becoming a member of Kenya's Parliament.

Wangari was extraordinary for lots of reasons. She was hardworking and determined, and she cared about other people and the future of our planet.

Life Lesson

Do you think it is important to care about the environment?

Earth is a fragile planet with limited resources. There are a lot of little things you can do every day to help. Always do your best to take care of our environment. Our lives depend on it.

Pele

Três Corações, Minas Gerais, Brazil (1940 -)
Professional Soccer Player

"SUCCESS is no accident. It is HARD WORK, PERSEVERANCE, LEARNING, STUDYING, SACRIFICE, and most of all, LOVE of what you are doing or learning to do."

PELÉ

Do you play soccer? Pelé is known as the greatest soccer player in history, but he didn't start out that way. When Pelé was a little boy growing up in the country of Brazil, he didn't even have a ball. He had to use what he could find, so he played soccer with a sock filled with paper. He worked hard to improve his skills, even though he didn't have something as simple as a ball! Pelé's soccer skills prove that determination and having a goal are more important than having things.

Pelé was only fifteen years old when he started playing soccer professionally. He was a great player, so he didn't let his age keep him from doing what he loved. Your age shouldn't keep you from doing amazing things either.

Did you know that soccer was created in London's famed Newgate Prison in the early 1800s? Prisoners who couldn't use their hands came up with a sport that only required feet.

One thing that really impressed people was that Pelé was just as good with his right foot as his left foot. His opponents never knew which foot he would use or what he might do in a game. He scored more soccer goals than anyone else in history—1,281 in total! He is also the only person ever to have won three World Cup fi nal matches.

Pelé's real name is Edson Arantes Do Nascimento. He is a hero to the Brazilian people because of his soccer skills and because of everything he does to help the poor people of Brazil learn to believe in themselves. Pelé wants them to know that they don't need money or things to be great. Do you like to play sports? Do you know what the best part of the game is? It's not winning—it's having the opportunity to play. Play hard. Play fair. Play nice. Go far.

Life Lesson

Do you ever feel jealous of others because they have things you don't?

You don't need to feel that way, because things don't make people great. Improving your personal qualiti es and treati ng people the way you want to be treated is what makes you great.

George Carruthers

Cincinnati, Ohio, United States (1939 -)
Inventor, Physicist, and Space Scientist.

"You have to START PREPARING EARLY. Take all the SCIENCE and MATH courses. Emphasize the BASICS."

GEORGE CARRUTHERS

Several years ago, a boy from Chicago created something amazing. He discovered a way for scientists to see and learn more about outer space. This young boy loved outer space. Growing up, he learned everything he could about space and science. His name is George Carruthers, and he created the Far Ultraviolet Camera/Spectrograph. It is a telescope and camera that takes pictures of things in the solar system.

Thanks to George's invention, elements in the celestial bodies that were never seen before can now be seen. His camera can take ultraviolet light readings, as well as photographs of the stars and the planets!

The camera weighs fifty pounds and is plated with gold. Different versions of the camera are used to study and take pictures of comets.

Have you learned about pollution and recycling in school? George's invention allows scientists to see pollution on Earth from outer space. Because of everything the camera can show us, scientists have learned

Did you know that there are eight planets in our solar system? In order, from the closest to the Sun to the farthest away, they are Mercury, Venus, Earth, Mars, Jupiter, Saturn, Uranus, and Neptune. Pluto is even farther away and is considered a dwarf planet.

a lot about keeping our planet clean. George has also helped school teachers learn more about science and space so that they can teach students like you.

Because of his invention, George was inducted into the National Inventor's Hall of Fame. This is a very special honor and something George was extremely proud of.

Life Lesson

Do you have any ideas for things you would like to invent?

Your invention could really make a difference and help others, just like George Carruthers's invention did. Don't be afraid to turn your ideas into something real. Who knows what you might end up doing to help the world?

Ellen J. Sirleaf

Monrovia, Liberia (1938 -)
Politician, President of Liberia.

"If your DREAMS do not scare you, they are NOT BIG ENOUGH"

ELLEN JOHNSON SIRLEAF

Have you heard of Liberia? Liberia is a country in Africa that was established by freed black people called Americo-Liberians. Not long ago, a brilliant and confident woman named Ellen Johnson Sirleaf, who lived in Liberia, did something daring to help bring peace to her country. She did it because she wanted the Liberian people to have a bright future.

Years ago, in Liberia, a terrible civil war broke out that lasted for fourteen years. During that time, schools were shut down—meaning many children were not taught to read. It was a very dangerous time, and the people lived in fear for their lives.

Ellen decided to run for public office so that she would have the power to help the people of Liberia. Ellen Johnson Sirleaf

Did you know that immigrants named Liberia? Liberia means "Land of the Free" in Latin.

ended up becoming the president of her country! Once elected president, she pushed for change and a better future.

Do you like going to school? Ellen wanted the children of Liberia to go to school again too. She opened free schools for students at the elementary school level, and she began enforcing laws to protect women and girls.

President Sirleaf was the first female head of state to ever be elected in Africa. She has a lot of support from the people who live there and has won the respect of people all over the world. She has even been awarded the US Presidential Medal of Freedom and the Nobel Peace Prize!

Children in Liberia are learning to read again. Liberians live happy and healthy lives, and the youngest students only know Liberia as a country that is fair and free. Thanks to Ellen Johnson Sirleaf's hard work, the country is now a better place.

Life Lesson

Have you ever wondered how you can make the world a better place?

Little things make a huge difference. Treat others with kindness every day. Help others whenever you can. When you do, you have exactly what it takes to make the world a better place. We are very grateful for you.

Wole Soyinka

Abeokuta, Nigeria (1934 -)
Playwright and Poet. 1986 Nobel Prize in Literature.

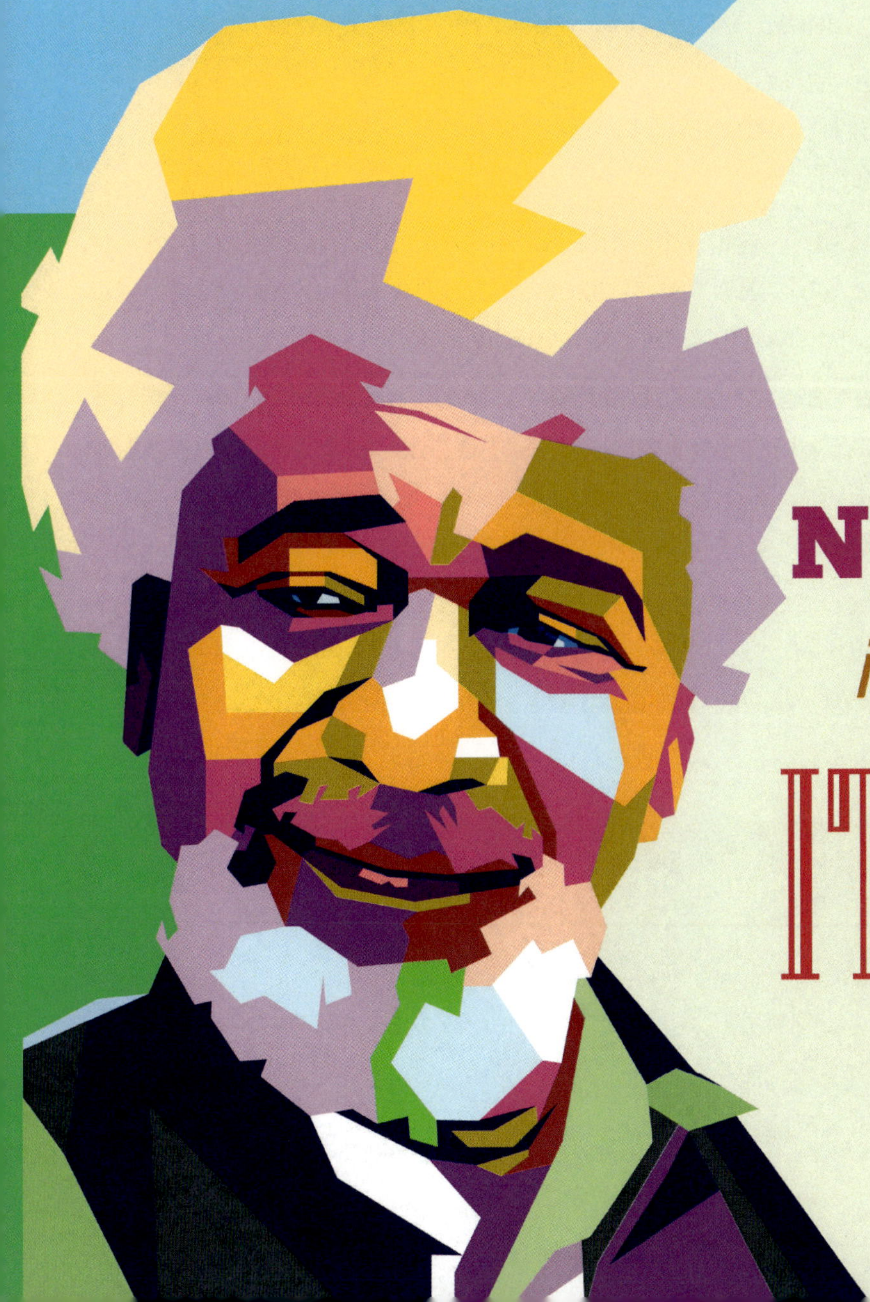

"A TIGER does NOT SHOUT its tigritude, IT ACTS."

WOLE SOYINKA

You're probably too young to have heard of Wole Soyinka. Wole is a famous writer from Nigeria.

Wole's father was an Anglican minister. His mother owned a store, and she was also involved in politics. Wole was educated in Nigeria and in England. While a college student in England, he edited the university magazine.

Do you like plays and poems? What about writing them? Wole is a playwright, poet, and novelist. Wole understands that writing is a great way to express yourself!

Wole is also involved in politics. He cares about the people of his country. He wants to make sure that they are not oppressed, and he tries to prevent powerful people from treating average people unfairly.

Did you know that Wole won the Nobel Prize in Literature? He was the first African to be given this award. The Nobel Prize in Literature is given to the best writer in the world.

Wole is respected all over the world for his abilities and creativity. He is also admired for his political work. He is accomplishing great things with his life because he is good at many different things. He likes to use his talents and abilities to help others.

Wole has always been very smart. He was curious and asked lots of questions when he was a kid. His curiosity made him want to help people who were being treated unfairly.

Life Lesson

Do you like to learn?

When you are curious, you find lots of interesting things to do. Keep learning and moving forward. Don't be afraid to ask questions and try new things. Try to learn something new every day.

Carmen de Lavallade

Los Angeles, California, United States (1931 -)
Actress, Dancer and Choreographer.

"The best way to make your **DREAMS** *come* **TRUE** *is to* **WAKE UP."**

CARMEN DE LAVALLADE

There was once an energetic and graceful young girl named Carmen de Lavallade. She grew up in a vibrant neighborhood with many different kinds of people, who had many different abilities. One of the things Carmen could do well was dance. Janet, Carmen's cousin, became the very first black prima ballerina. Carmen watched this happen and said, "I'll become a ballerina too!"

Some people tried to discourage Carmen. They said, "You can't do that!" But no matter how many times Carmen heard those words, she refused to listen. Carmen believed that everyone has their own talents and that hers was dancing. So she kept dancing. She danced, danced, and danced some more.

Did you know that Carmen still dances today, at the age of eighty-nine?

When people told her that she would never make it as a professional dancer, Carmen just worked harder. She studied ballet and acting. She performed in many musicals, plays, and operas. She believed anyone could do anything they wanted to do if they just put their mind to it.

One day, Carmen met a dancer named Geoffrey. At the time, there were very few men who were ballet dancers, and so things had been difficult for him too. He encouraged her, telling her that if she was persistent, she would succeed. Do you know what *persistence* means? It means never giving up, even when things get difficult.

Geoffrey and Carmen danced together for a while and made a great team. Soon after they combined their talents, Carmen became the prima ballerina at the Metropolitan Opera. This meant that she was the top ballerina—the star of the show! Her persistence had finally paid off, and her dream became a reality!

Life Lesson

How persistent are you?

Persistence and determination are always rewarded. Persistence can help you overcome almost any challenge you face. Persistence conquers all things. You must keep going, no matter what. Remember that your hardest times often lead to the greatest moments of your life. Always take another step forward, and push through your struggles to succeed.

Ray Charles

Albany, Georgia, United States (1930 - 2004)
Singer, Songwriter, Musician, and Composer.

" JUST
because you can't
SEE
ANYTHING,
doesn't mean
you should
shut
YOUR EYES."

RAY CHARLES

Ray Charles was a man who inspired people through his music. By the time he was three years old, Ray was playing the piano. Because of an eye disease, Ray started losing his sight before his fifth birthday. By the time he was seven, he was completely blind.

It would have been easy for Ray to give up and feel sorry for himself, but he didn't. He would not let blindness stop him from doing what he loved most—playing music and singing.

Ray loved blues and jazz music. Normally, choosing one of them would have meant he had to give up the other. Ray didn't want to do that, so he decided to combine them! Ray Charles created the genre of soul music by combining rhythm, blues, jazz, and gospel. No one had ever done this before. He wrote all his own music and had many popular songs.

Did you know that playing chess was a favorite pastime of Ray Charles? He used a special board with raised squares and holes for the pieces.

Ray knew from the time he was a little boy that he had to work harder than other people to reach his goals. He played music every day and truly loved what he did. Against all odds, he chose to see the world in a different way. He inspired many people with his music.

Ray was a beloved musician of soul. His legacy lives on because he believed in his ability to make his dreams come true. His music continues to be enjoyed by many generations and brings all different kinds of people together.

Remember, Ray wore sunglasses every day and never spoke or acted as if he was blind. His mother treated him like he was "normal," so he acted that way. Pity was the last thing he wanted.

Life Lesson

Never feel sorry for yourself.

Self-pity is your worst enemy. If you go around feeling sorry for yourself, you will never achieve anything. None of us are perfect. You don't have to be perfect to be great. As long as you do what inspires you and give it your best effort, you will go far.

Chinua Achebe

Ogidi, Nigeria (1930 - 2013)
Novelist, Poet and Professor.

"Nobody can teach me
WHO I AM
and
WHAT I NEED
is something
I have to find out
MYSELF."

CHINUA ACHEBE

Chinualumogu Achebe—who everyone called Chinua for short—grew up in Nigeria, a country in the western part of Africa. Chinua was a famous author who became very important to his country by helping to end a war.

Do you like to hear a good story? As a child, Chinua loved it when his father told stories. He asked to hear them over and over again. He never got tired of hearing them.

Chinua also loved books, and his father always encouraged him, "Read! Read! And when you get tired of reading, read some more!" So Chinua did. He read his books over and over again. He especially enjoyed reading English literature.

Chinua also spent his time watching how people behaved, and he listened closely to what they said. He took what he heard and saw, and then he wrote his own books to teach people about what was going on around them.

Did you know that Chinua Achebe's first novel, Things Fall Apart, was rejected by several publishers? Later it became the most read book in African literature and was translated into more than fifty languages.

One day, war broke out in Nigeria. Chinua wanted the war to end. He found two other authors and organized a trip to the United States in hopes of getting help for his country.

Together, the three writers shared their stories with the American people so that they would know what was going on in Nigeria. It worked! Soon after Chinua and his friends had asked the Americans for help, the war in Nigeria came to an end. Chinua was a warrior who fought with words instead of weapons.

Life Lesson

Do you ever stop and think about what you are saying?

Do you realize how powerful your words are? You have the power to discourage or encourage someone, to wound or heal them, to tear them down or build them up. Use your words wisely and carefully.

Martin Luther King Jr.

Atlanta, Georgia United States (1929 - 1968)
Baptist Minister and Leader in The Civil Rights Movement.

"Darkness can't drive out darkness, ONLY LIGHT CAN DO THAT. Hate can't drive out hate, ONLY LOVE CAN DO THAT."

MARTIN LUTHER KING, JR.

Martin Luther King, Jr., lived in a time when people of different skin colors had different sets of rights. When Martin was growing up, white people sat at the front of the bus, while black people had to sit in the back. If all the seats for white people were taken, black people had to give up their seats for whites. Some stores only served white people too. In many places, white and black children had to attend different schools.

"This is wrong," Martin said. "Everyone should be treated the same way. We need to make a change!"

As an adult, Martin preached that all people were born equal and deserved the same rights and privileges. He led many peaceful marches to encourage equality.

Did you know that Martin Luther King, Jr., was the youngest man to receive the Nobel Peace Prize? He was thirty-five years old at the time.

During one of these marches in Washington, DC, Martin spoke about his hope and dream for all people to be treated equally, with the same rights. He wanted everyone to be offered the same respect and dignity. He spoke of a future where children of different races would learn and play together. Over 250,000 people of all different races and religions marched with Martin and attended his speech.

Martin organized marches to support desegregation, black people's right to vote, and other basic civil rights. Most of these rights were successfully enacted into laws with the passage of the Civil Rights Act of 1964 and the 1965 Voting Rights Act.

Martin Luther King, Jr., inspired people everywhere he went. Change happened because Martin and many others had a dream and followed through on it.

Life Lesson

What do you dream of doing to change the world?

Always keep your dreams alive. Write down your goals and dreams, look at them often, and don't stop until you achieve them.

Maya Angelou

St. Louis, Missouri, United States (1928 - 2014)
Poet, Memoirist, and Civil Rights Activist.

"TRY
to be a
RAINBOW
in
SOMEONE'S
CLOUD."

MAYA ANGELOU

When Maya Angelou was a little girl, she had a traumatic experience that left her unable to talk for several years. During this time, she learned a lot about people. She watched, listened, and observed people and their behavior. She did not understand why black people were treated differently from white people.

Why were some people treated better because of their skin color? She couldn't understand why some people thought it was okay to judge others based on their appearance. She also couldn't understand why people thought they could treat her differently just because she was black and a woman.

When she grew up, Maya had many different jobs, but she never forgot how much she loved to read and write. Maya decided to speak out against being treated

Did you know that Maya Angelou mastered six languages—English, French, Spanish, Italian, Arabic, and the West African language Fanti?

differently and badly because of both her skin color and her gender. She became a champion of civil rights and women's rights. One way she did this was by writing poems that challenge and teach us to be kinder. Her poems are still changing people's lives in a positive way.

Maya's poems are about race, inspiration, and self-love. One poem she wrote is called "Human Family." In this poem, she explains that no matter where we are from or what we look like, we have more in common with each other than we realize. In another poem, "Phenomenal Woman," she expresses love for herself and encourages others to take pride in being a woman.

Life Lesson

What is phenomenal about you?

Love yourself first, and everything else will be great. When you look in the mirror or take a walk, think about what makes you an amazing person. Take pride in who you are.

Malcolm X

Omaha, Nebraska United States (1925 - 1965)
Muslim Minister and Human Rights Activist.

"EDUCATION is the passport to the FUTURE, for TOMORROW BELONGS to those who PREPARE for it TODAY. "

MALCOLM X

When Malcolm was a child, his family was harassed and threatened by racists. The family moved more than once because they were trying to escape threats of violence.

Tragically, his father, Earl, was eventually killed. The police refused to admit the truth that racists had murdered Earl. Malcolm's mother, Louise, was so affected by grief that she became very ill and was unable to take care of Malcolm and his siblings. They all went to live in foster homes.

A short time later, Malcolm was forced to live in a juvenile detention center. Even with these obstacles, he did very well in school. He became discouraged, however, when a teacher told him he could never go to college, so at that point he dropped out of school.

Did you know that Malcom changed his last name from Little to X? He said that the name Little had been forced on his ancestors by white owners as a sign of slavery and that the X symbolized his true, unknown African family name.

After dropping out of school, Malcolm got into trouble with the law and ended up in prison. While in prison, he spent most of his time reading and learning. He also decided to change his life.

After he was released from prison, he went on to become one of the greatest Civil Rights leaders in history. He was a captivating speaker. Malcolm's speeches inspired many people to join with him in fighting for their rights.

Malcolm learned from his mistakes and overcame circumstances to transform his own life and the lives of millions of other black people.

Life Lesson

Do you learn from your mistakes?

The only real mistake is the one you make when you believe there are no lessons to be learned from your experiences. Take chances and make mistakes—that's how you grow. I am proud of you for overcoming so much.

James Baldwin

New York City, New York, United States (1924 - 1987)
Novelist, Essayist, Playwright and Poet.

"Those who say it can't be DONE are usually INTERRUPTED by others DOING IT."

JAMES BALDWIN

James Baldwin was a man who watched the events going on in the world carefully. James loved to write, and he boldly used his words to influence others to treat everyone with kindness and dignity.

James left home at an early age to travel to France. James found he could express himself better when traveling to new places like this. He was able to practice his writing skills and learn a new culture at the same time.

Many of James's books became popular, because he wrote in a way that no one had ever written before. He took on difficult issues such as understanding race and how people could be nicer to one another. He believed in equality for everyone. He wanted everyone to see one another for who they were. People were inspired by his words because they helped individuals understand one another better.

Did you know that James lived most of his life abroad, in France? He believed that by learning a new culture, people could better understand themselves.

James was an important voice for the Civil Rights movement. He was brave about helping others speak up for their rights. He knew that every voice mattered—including yours! James knew that if everyone would speak up for one another, the world could be more beautiful and peaceful. Through his words, James created a better understanding of race and humanity for all.

Life Lesson

What is something you can speak up for?

When you speak up for something you believe in, you must always be careful about how you use your words. Words that don't mean much to you may be ones that influence someone else in a good way or a bad way—and for a lifetime. Once words are said, they can never be forgotten or unsaid, only forgiven. Remember: one kind word can change someone's entire day . . . or life.

Nelson Mandela

Mvezo, South Africa (1918-2013)

Politician, and philanthropist, President of
South Africa from 1994 to 1999

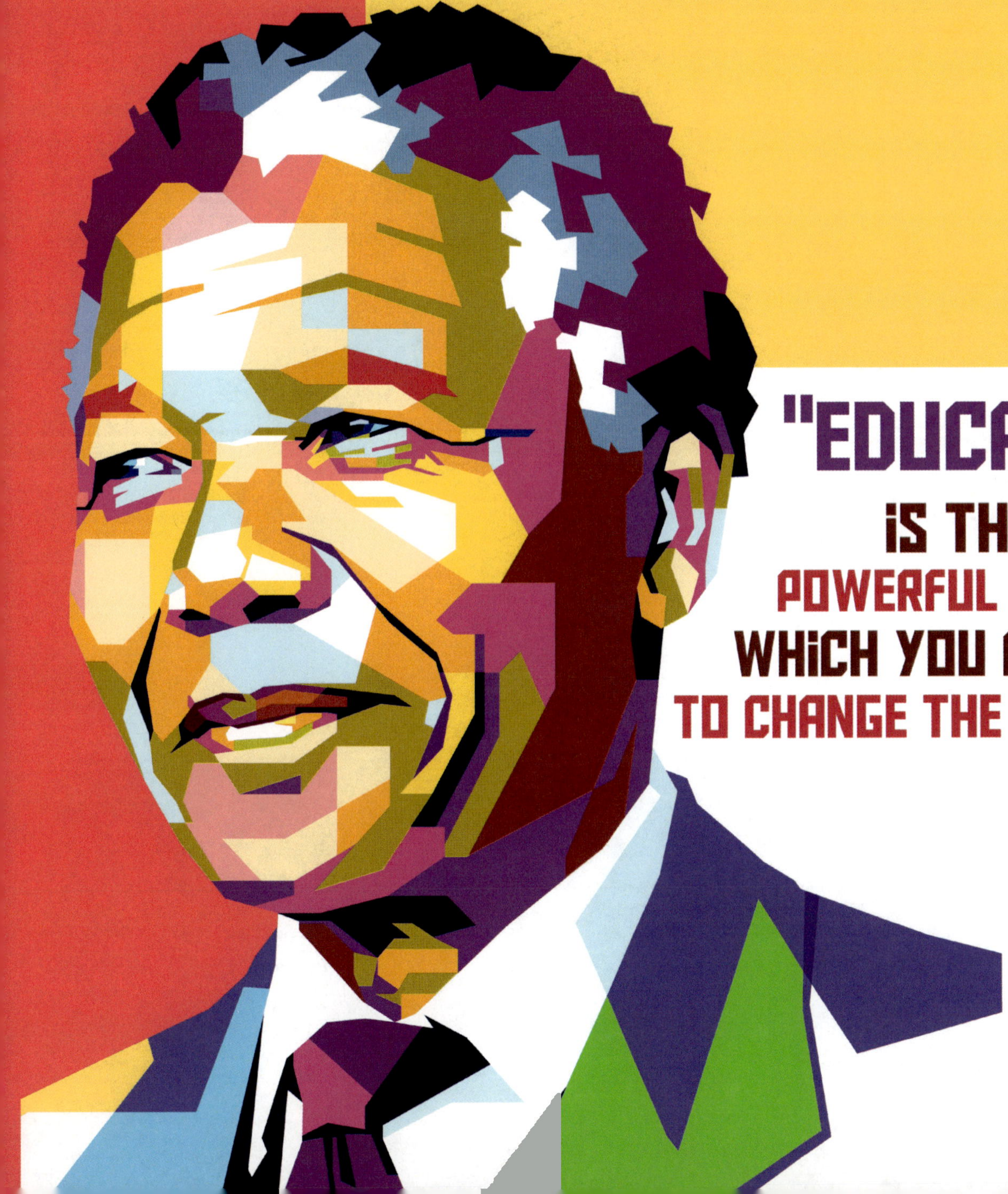

"EDUCATION
IS THE MOST
POWERFUL WEAPON
WHICH YOU CAN USE
TO CHANGE THE WORLD"

NELSON MANDELA

Once, there was a boy born in a place where white and black people had to live separately. That place was South Africa, and the boy's name was Nelson Mandela. Young Nelson loved to read, and he soon learned that white people and black people in other countries did not live like his people did. It was then that he decided to do something about the situation in South Africa. He went to law school, became a lawyer, and fought for civil rights in his country.

He joined the African National Congress (ANC) and used protests and laws to fight for people's rights. The methods he used were not violent, because he did not believe in hurting others to attain a goal. He believed in something that we should all remember: someone else's bad behavior is not an excuse for your own.

Did you know that Nelson's last name on his birth certificate was Rolihlahla? In his Xhosa tribe's language, this name means "pulling the branch of a tree" or "troublemaker."

Sadly, he made some people in South Africa's government angry. They decided he was a troublemaker and put him in jail, where he stayed for twenty-seven years.

Even in jail, though, Nelson didn't give up. He continued to fight for civil rights. The government told him he would be released if he made the statement that black people did not have the same rights as whites, but he refused—and stayed in jail. While there, he wrote books and letters encouraging the black people of South Africa to keep fighting for equal rights.

When he got out of jail, Nelson was so popular and loved that he was elected president of South Africa. He went on to inspire people and change the laws he'd fought against when he was younger.

Life Lesson

How can you inspire others?

You can inspire people in so many ways. Your actions should inspire others to dream more, learn more, do more, and become more. Being your best self inspires others to do the same.

Rosa Parks

Tuskegee, Alabama, United States (1913 - 2005)
Civil Rights Activist.

"YOU *must* NEVER BE FEARFUL *about* what you are DOING *when it is* RIGHT."

◇◇◇◇◇◇◇◇◇

ROSA PARKS
◇◇◇◇◇◇◇◇◇

Have you ever had to stand up to someone who was bullying you? What would you do if your whole town was bullying you? That's the situation Rosa Parks faced. But Rosa confronted her bullies with confidence and self-respect!

Rosa lived in a time when black and white people in the United States believed they should live very separate lives. This practice was known as segregation.

Segregation meant that black people and white people didn't do things together. They couldn't go to the same schools, drink out of the same water fountains, eat in the same restaurants, or even ride together on city buses. You and I know that treating people like this is not fair or right. Rosa knew this too.

Did you know that bus seats were left empty to honor Rosa on the fiftieth anniversary of her arrest?

One day, Rosa Parks decided to remind everyone around her of how unfair segregation was. Her decision made her famous and a hero to people all over the country. What did she do? Rosa refused to give up her bus seat for a white person just because all the seats for white people were full.

Rosa's act of bravery was just one of the things she did to work for civil rights. The term civil rights is used to talk about all of the rights we deserve just because we're people—they are rights we need in order to be treated fairly. Rosa also worked with Dr. Martin Luther King, Jr., for civil rights, earning her the nickname "the First Lady of Civil Rights."

It's not easy to stand up for something you know is right when so many other people are against you. Rosa did it, though, and so can you. Rosa Parks's self-respect inspired many others to stand up against segregation.

Life Lesson

Why is self-respect so important?

When you have self-respect, you love yourself for who you are. You don't just love yourself because you look good or you do something well. When you have self-respect, you know you're valuable. You love yourself just because you are you.

Josephine Baker

St. Louis, Missouri, United States (1906 - 1975)
Entertainer, Activist, and French Resistance Agent.

"You are on the eve of a COMPLETE VICTORY. You can't go wrong. The WORLD is BEHIND YOU."

JOSEPHINE BAKER

Long ago, there lived a beautiful and talented woman named Josephine Baker. She became a famous dancer in Paris, France, in the 1920s. When she was born, she had a different name: Freda Josephine MacDonald. Like many other famous actors, dancers, and musicians, she eventually changed her name. This is called a *stage name*.

Josephine came from a poor family, and people often abused her. By the time Josephine was a teenager, she was homeless. Josephine never gave up, though. She knew she had talent and believed that if she tried hard enough, one day she would be a star. The door to opportunity opened for Josephine one day when someone asked her to move to Paris to be a dancer. They offered her a lot of money to take the job.

Did you know that Josephine Baker was a spy during World War II? She would travel around Europe while touring and carry large quantities of sheet music. What the Customs officials never realized was that much of this music had secret messages written on it in invisible ink.

Josephine didn't hesitate. She went to Paris, and the people there loved her. Everyone wanted to go to her shows and see her dance. Josephine was much happier in Paris than she had ever been in the United States.

Josephine was incredibly smart and a quick learner. In her lifetime, Josephine learned how to speak French, Italian, and Russian. She also starred in several movies made in France!

There were times when Josephine traveled back to the United States to dance and perform. But even though she was loved and famous in France, she was still not treated well in the United States. This didn't matter to Josephine, though. She knew she had talent, and she never gave up on her dream to let everyone know it.

Life Lesson

Do you ever feel like giving up?

Josephine's life reminds us to never give up on our dreams. Always believe in yourself, and never let other people discourage you. I am proud of you for never giving up.

Ralph Bunche

Detroit, Michigan, United States (1904 - 1971)
Political Scientist and Academic 1950 Nobel Peace Prize.

"HEARTS are the STRONGEST when they beat in response to NOBLE IDEALS."

RALPH BUNCHE

Many years ago, there was a man named Ralph Bunche. He was a good student and always embraced the challenges of learning. He faced hard times with his family, but he considered these difficulties just one more challenge to be met. He never let anything stop him from achieving his dreams.

Ralph looked for every possible chance to learn something new. Many of the things he learned from his surroundings helped Ralph understand just how difficult life was for many people. Knowing these difficulties were unfair, he decided to speak up about the things he believed should change.

Ralph stood up for equal rights and was an important figure in the Civil Rights movement. Ralph joined other people who also believed in helping to make the world a better place. It was a lot of work, but he persisted. Though not everyone agreed with him, he stood strong to defend his beliefs. He talked with many leaders and convinced them to work together.

Did you know that Ralph Bunche negotiated the 1949 Armistice Agreements while playing pool with the Israeli and Arab representatives?

Over a period of many months, Ralph spoke to some countries that would not stop fighting. He helped them agree to be nice to one another and live in peace. Ralph was the first African American to receive the Nobel Peace Prize. What an honor it was! Everyone was so proud of him.

Ralph made the world a better place by helping those around him. He was always patient with people who didn't agree with him or with one another. This is called forbearance. Forbearance means to be patient, respectful, and tolerant of others.

Life Lesson

Are you patient with others?

Always remember to treat people with respect, even if you don't like what they are saying. Impatience can cause people to do foolish things, but one moment of patience can stop big problems from happening. To be patient is to be wise, so remember to always be patient. Patience is the companion of wisdom! Thank you for being patient.

Albert Lutuli

Bulawayo, Southern Rhodesia (1898 - 1967)
Teacher, Activist and Politician, 1960 Nobel Peace Prize.

"LEARN from yesterday, LIVE for today, HOPE for tomorrow.

The important thing is not to stop QUESTIONING."

ALBERT JOHN LUTHULI

A brave man by the name of Albert John Luthuli lived long ago in South Africa. At the time, South Africa was a difficult place to live in. Black people were treated unfairly there and were denied the opportunity to live their lives as they wanted to.

Albert was a political leader. He led other black people in fighting for their rights. He was the first African to win the Nobel Peace Prize, a very special award. It is given only to good people who devote their lives to helping others and doing something significant to achieve such goals.

Albert was an extraordinary leader. People listened to him and believed in him. But like many young African boys of his time, Albert had a childhood that did not make it

Did you know that South Africa has eleven official languages?

easy for him to achieve the things he did. When he was only eight years old, his father died. After that, his mother had to work as a washerwoman to support herself and Albert.

But because male members of Albert's family were tribal chiefs, Albert was still given a good education. He eventually became a teacher and did some missionary work. He later had a choice to become the chief of his family's village, but doing so meant that he would have to leave teaching. He loved his job, but he decided to leave teaching because he felt he could do more good for the people as a tribal chief.

In fact, Albert was a wonderful tribal chief. The people of his village knew they could always depend on him. Albert will always be remembered for how he fought to make South Africa a fairer and more just place to live. He is still honored today because he played such an important role in South African history.

Life Lesson

You are also important in this world.

Each of us has a special mission or purpose, just waiting to be discovered. You matter! You are important! Don't ever forget that.

Hattie McDaniel

Wichita, Kansas, United States (1895 - 1952)
Actress, Singer, Songwriter, and Comedian.

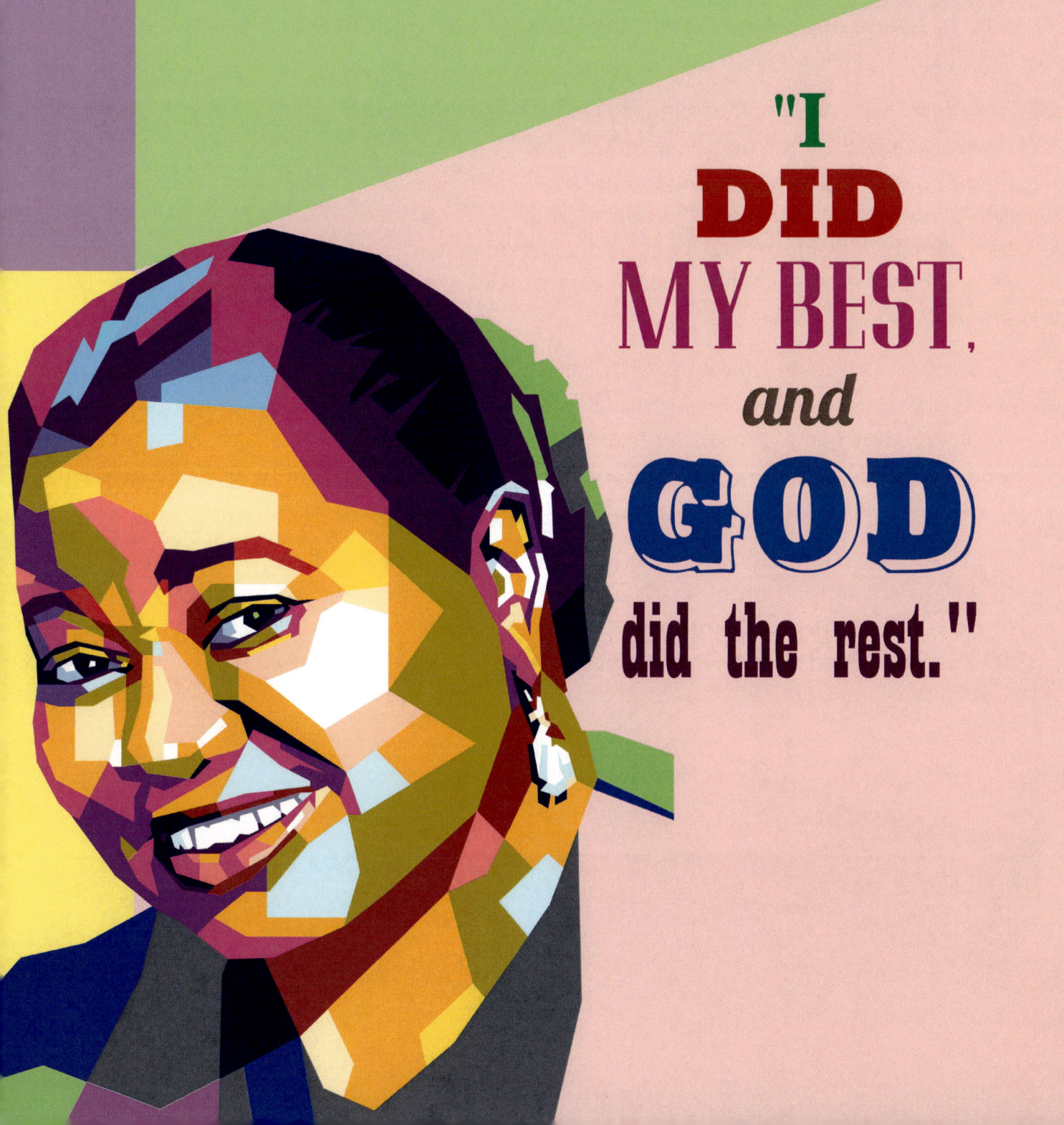

"I **DID** MY BEST, and **GOD** did the rest."

HATTIE MCDANIEL

Hattie McDaniel was born in Wichita, Kansas, in June of 1895. Hattie loved to act and sing. From the time she could talk, you could find her singing her heart out wherever she went!

Hattie's parents and brothers also had a talent for singing and acting. They performed for people all over the Midwest. But Hattie wanted more, so her brothers helped her find her first job in the entertainment world. She toured around the country singing, while also trying to find a job as an actress. Hattie thought she was the luckiest girl in the world when she finally got a job on a radio show.

Did you know that Hattie has two stars on the Hollywood Walk of Fame? Her work paved the way for many other African American actors to succeed!

Do you listen to the radio sometimes? When Hattie was young, the radio was the most popular form of entertainment. People would read stories and plays over the radio. It was like a television or movie with no pictures—just the voices. Hattie was very talented at playing characters on the radio. People loved it!

Hattie continued to work in radio until the day she was hired as an actress in a movie. She was so excited! Throughout her career, Hattie acted in many movies. She is most famous for her part in *Gone with the Wind*, one of the most popular movies ever made. Hattie was also the first African American woman to receive an Academy Award for her acting.

Acting was not always easy for Hattie, though. There were very few acting roles available to African Americans, which made it difficult for her to make a living as an actress. Nonetheless, she never stopped trying. Hattie continued to act, even when people said she could not do it. Hattie made history by believing in herself and trying her very best.

Life Lesson

Do you always try your best?

If you want something badly enough, try, try, try, and keep on trying. In the end, the only people who fail are those who do not try hard enough. You can always be proud of yourself if you try your hardest.

Bessie Coleman

Atlanta, Texas, United States (1892 - 1926)
Civil Aviator

"I decided to open
A FLYING SCHOOL
and
TEACH
other black women
TO FLY"

BESSIE COLEMAN

More than a hundred years ago, there was a little girl named Bessie Coleman. She was the thirteenth child born into a poor family. Bessie and her family often found it difficult to afford food. This made it extra hard for Bessie to focus and learn in school, but she did anyway because she loved learning.

After Bessie graduated from high school, she wanted to go to college, but she couldn't because she had no money to pay for it. Instead, Bessie moved to Chicago and took up jobs to help support her family. She also began reading about airplane pilots and dreamed of becoming one. The more she read, the more her interest grew. She applied to a few flying schools, but she was rejected because she was black and a woman.

Did you know that Bessie Coleman would only perform at shows if the crowd was desegregated and black people were allowed to enter through the same gates as whites?

Being rejected hurt Bessie's feelings, but she didn't let it stop her. She decided to go to France to become a pilot, because her color and gender wouldn't hold her back so much in France. Once she was there, she quickly learned to speak French, and in just seven months, she became the first African American woman in history to get an international pilot's license! Everyone was so proud of her!

Bessie had to work hard for everything she got, and she was treated badly by many because of the color of her skin and her gender.

The world admired Bessie Coleman's flying skills. She was so brave that her stunts became very famous in a short period of time. Even the people who had rejected Bessie learned to respect and admire her.

Life Lesson

Have you ever felt rejected?

There will be times in your life when people reject you or make fun of your dreams. No matter what, you should never let anyone make you believe you should give up. Don't let them make you feel discouraged. Keep dreaming big dreams and work hard, and you will achieve your goals. Allow rejection to give you more energy and determination to push forward.

Mary Mcleod Bethune

Mayesville, South Carolina United States (1875 - 1955)

Educator, Philanthropist, Humanitarian and Civil Rights Activist.

"Without FAITH, nothing is possible. With it, NOTHING IS IMPOSSIBLE."

MARY MCLEOD BETHUNE

Mary McLeod Bethune was the fifteenth of seventeen kids! Mary's parents were former slaves. She and her family lived in a log cabin near the farm where her parents picked cotton for a living.

Mary started working in the cotton fields when she was only five years old. But this didn't stop Mary from going to school—even though the closest school for black children was five miles from her home. She was the only member of her family to go to school, walking the long distance every day.

Mary didn't mind, though. She believed that education was the most important thing and that everyone should have equal rights to a good education. Mary felt so strongly about education that when she got older, she started one of the first colleges for African American women.

Did you know that cotton dates back to 450 BC? Seeds from that period were found in Peru.

Have you ever experienced discrimination? Mary knew what discrimination felt like. That's why Mary became a fighter for both women's rights and civil rights. Mary was called "the First Lady of the Struggle" because she fought so hard for equal rights. She even advised many US presidents, including Franklin D. Roosevelt and Harry S. Truman, on how laws should be made to make sure everyone would be treated fairly and equally.

Mary went from being one of seventeen children living in poverty to advising presidents, educating people, and championing the rights of all citizens of the United States. She went from being a victim of discrimination to fighting it.

Life Lesson

Is there a cause that you feel strongly about?

Stand up for what is right, no matter what. Always work hard for what you believe in, and remember that your life really matters. Always be proud of who you are and stand up for your rights!

Madam C.J. Walker

Delta, Louisiana, United States (1867 - 1919)
Entrepreneur, Philanthropist, and Social Activist.

"Don't sit down and wait for the OPPORTUNITIES to come. GET UP and MAKE THEM."

MADAM C. J. WALKER

Two days after Christmas, a future prominent businesswoman named Madam C. J. Walker was born in Louisiana. When she was born, her name was Sarah Breedlove. Madam C. J. became the first female black millionaire in the United States, but it wasn't easy. Her family didn't have much money when she was growing up, and she had a difficult childhood. As soon as she was old enough to do so, she worked as a laundress—someone who does other people's laundry.

One day, Sarah noticed that she was losing her hair. This bothered her, so she invented her own hair treatment. Other people who had the same problem soon wanted to use Sarah's hair treatment. Sarah recognized that the hair loss she'd had to deal with was something other women suffered from and that making products to help them would be a good business idea. By this time, Sarah was known as Madam C. J. Walker, so she called her treatment the "Walker System."

Did you know that the main ingredients in Madam C. J. Walker's famous shampoo were olive oil, coconut oil, and lye?

Madam C. J. worked very hard, and she toured around the country giving lectures and demonstrations to promote her products. The Walker System of haircare products quickly became extremely popular. Her success earned Madam C. J. a lot of money. She donated much of her money to African American charities and provided money for women's college scholarships. It wasn't long before the business had more than three thousand employees. Many of these employees were door-to-door saleswomen; Madam C. J. provided good job opportunities for black women. Madam C. J. Walker was a brilliant businesswoman who overcame adversity to make her fortune.

Life Lesson

What adversities have you experienced?

Adversity is something we all face from time to time, but you don't have to let it keep you from achieving your goals and being happy. Remember, it's how you overcome these adversities that can make all the difference. Every challenge you conquer will strengthen your ability to face future adversity. You can be proud of yourself when you overcome adversity. It proves you are a good problem-solver.

Ida B. Wells

Holly Springs, Mississippi, United States (1862 - 1931)
Journalist, Newspaper Editor, Suffragist and Sociologist.

"The way to **RIGHT** wrongs is to turn the **LIGHT** of **TRUTH** upon them."

IDA B. WELLS

Ida B. Wells was a girl who grew up to do some truly heroic and amazing things with her life. Ida grew up in a time when things were hard for black people—especially women. Many of her friends were hurt because of other people's acts of hatred. At first, Ida was scared to help. She was not sure what she could do to make a difference. But she knew in her heart that she had to do something.

Ida loved to write, and soon she realized that she could use her writing talents to help others. She traveled to many towns to discover what was really happening, and then she wrote about it.

Not everyone liked her, because she wrote about things that were not pleasant. But she dreamed of peace for everyone, so she kept writing.

Did you know that Ida started the National Association of Colored Women? She created action groups to help other people become brave!

Ida also started groups to help protect the African American community from hatred. She even went straight to the president of the United States to demand rights for them. How brave is that?

Other people's hatred did not stop her from being courageous. She always stood up for what she believed in, even when her life was in danger. She saved many people from danger by taking acti on. Ida was heroic in helping others. She knew that everyone has the power to make a diff erence in someone else's life—they only have to use it.

Life Lesson

How are you making a difference in someone else's life?

We all have a unique set of skills and abilities. With those abilities, we can make extraordinary things happen in the world around us. Making a difference in someone else's life doesn't require you to do something big either. You just need to be there for them in a time of need. Helping others makes you a blessing.

Harriet Tubman

Dorchester County, Maryland, United States (1822 - 1913)
Abolitionist, Humanitarian.

"Always remember,
you have within you
the
STRENGTH,
the
PATIENCE,
and
the
PASSION
to reach for the stars to
CHANGE
THE WORLD."

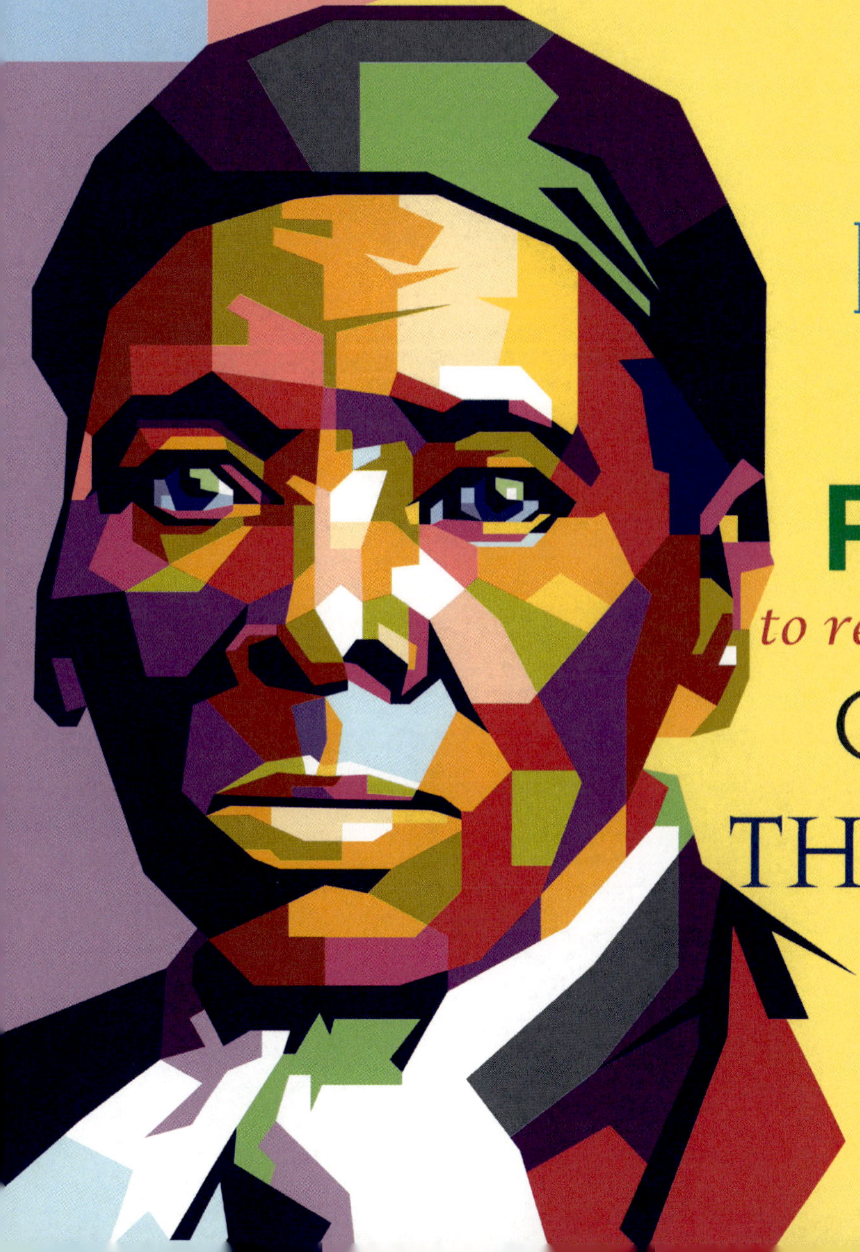

HARRIET TUBMAN

In 1849, a young woman escaped from slavery to become an incredible hero. Her name was Harriet Tubman. Harriet Tubman is still one of the greatest heroes of all time. She was an abolitionist, a spy, an armed military scout, and one of the most successful activists in history!

All heroes have something that makes them special. Harriet's special gifts were intelligence, courage, and fierce determination. She was a nurse, and she could navigate exceptionally well—even at night. She was a real-life superhero, standing up for what was right and never giving up.

People don't talk about it, but Harriet's determination made her an amazing asset to the Union Army during the Civil War. She led the raid at Combahee Ferry, where seven hundred slaves were freed at one time! She even camouflaged herself and tricked men who were looking for her into believing she was someone else.

> *Did you know that Harriet Tubman earned the nickname "Moses" after the prophet Moses in the Bible, who led his people to freedom? She returned to Maryland many times to rescue both family and nonfamily members from the bondage of slavery.*

Do you and your friends have a secret code? Harriet did! She would speak and sing in code so that the slaves she was helping to free would know what to do. She taught slaves where to go and how to get to freedom.

Harriet is one of the most well-known abolitionist heroes of all time. A lot of people look up to her.

Life Lesson

Do you want to be a hero?

A hero is someone who makes great efforts to do the right thing no matter what. Everyone can be a hero if they want to be. You are my hero.

Frederick Douglass

Talbot County, Maryland, United States (1818 - 1895)

Abolitionist, Orator, Writer, and Statesman.

"It is easier to **BUILD STRONG CHILDREN** than to repair broken men."

FREDERICK DOUGLASS

Frederick Douglass was an abolitionist. Abolitionists were the heroes who fought to end slavery. It wasn't easy being an abolitionist. It was something only the bravest and smartest people dared to do.

Frederick Douglass spent most of his life championing the rights of black people and women. He fought hard to abolish slavery in America and to end the unequal treatment of women.

Frederick chose his own name too! Cool, right? He was taught how to read at twelve years old, even though at the time he was still a slave. He then taught other slaves to read until the slave masters stopped the classes. Eventually, Frederick escaped with the help of a freeborn black woman from Baltimore, and Frederick later married her.

Did you know that Frederick Douglass was the first African American to be nominated for vice president of the United States of America?

As an abolitionist, Frederick did everything he could to free black people. He spoke publicly about what slavery was really like, and he educated everyone he came into contact with. Frederick even spoke with Abraham Lincoln! It is amazing to think that he was able to share his thoughts and feelings with the president of the United States.

History shows us that Frederick made a huge difference in the lives of black people. He is a great example of how words—and how speaking up—can really help change things.

Frederick published a few newspapers too. He used his newspapers to teach people about what they could do to stop slavery. Frederick took every opportunity he could to use his education to help others.

Life Lesson

Do you like to share what you know with other people?

When you do, you learn more about the subject. That's because when you explain something to someone else, you understand it better yourself. I love it when you take your time and patience to explain new things.

Sojourner Truth

Rifton, New York, United States (1797 - 1883)
Abolitionist and Women's Rights Activist.

"If we **LAUGH** *and* **SING** *a little it* MAKES IT ALL GO EASIER. *I will not* allow my LIFE'S LIGHT *to be determined* by the darkness AROUND ME."

SOJOURNER TRUTH

A long, long time ago, there was a brave and bold woman named Sojourner Truth. Sojourner was born into slavery. Life was very hard for her, as it was for most slaves. Sojourner did not know what it felt like to be free, but she knew that everyone deserved to be free.

Sojourner wanted to be free so badly that she decided to run away from being a slave. She took her baby daughter with her, hoping to find a better life. Later, Sojourner returned to the place where she had been a slave in order to save her son. She even went to court to gain her son's freedom!

Did you know that Sojourner once met with President Abraham Lincoln and told him the story of her life as a slave?

Amazingly, Sojourner Truth was the first black woman to win a court case against a white man. She won the right for her son to be free and made history all in one day. How incredible!

Sojourner made it her life's mission to stand up for people who were not being treated fairly. She experienced hard times, but it never stopped her from standing up for what was right. She traveled around the country and spoke up for the freedom of women and people of color.

Not everyone agreed with Sojourner's big ideas about how to change the world, but her community always embraced her.

Sojourner knew that every act of courage made this world a better place. She wanted everyone—no matter what color or sex they were—to have a better chance in life. She fought for equal rights until the day she died. By doing so, she paved the way for everyone to be free. That took a lot of courage!

Life Lesson

Are you courageous?

Having courage does not mean that you are not afraid. Being courageous means we face our fears. Courage is being scared but aspiring to do the right thing anyway. You can be courageous too. . . . I know you can!

Thomas L. Jennings

New York City, New York, United States (1791 - 1856)
Innovator, Tradesman and Abolitionist.

"A **MAN** who STANDS for NOTHING WILL FALL for ANYTHING."

THOMAS L. JENNINGS

Over two hundred years ago, an intelligent and talented man named Thomas L. Jennings lived in New York City. Thomas was a famous inventor. He was the first African American ever granted a United States patent, and he got it for inventing a new way to keep clothes clean.

When Thomas was a kid like you, people tried to make him think he could never do anything special. People treated Thomas like they didn't want him around, but Thomas believed in himself and proved everyone wrong.

One day, Thomas became a tailor. He owned a huge store in New York City, where he made beautiful clothes. But back in those days, fancy clothes like the ones Thomas made could not be washed. Washing them in water would ruin them.

Did you know that "dry cleaning" isn't actually dry at all? Water isn't used in the dry-cleaning process, but liquid solvents are.

Have you ever spilled juice on your favorite T-shirt? You don't worry about it, do you? You know your mom or dad can put something on the stain to make it go away. But Thomas's customers did not have anything to take stains out of their clothes.

Thomas wanted to help his customers by inventing a way to remove stains from clothing. So he created an amazing process called *dry scouring*, which was the first form of what we now call dry cleaning. Do you know what dry cleaning is?

Thomas's invention made him rich and famous. But the money and fame did not change who Thomas was on the inside. He donated a lot of his money to causes that helped other African Americans. He never forgot about people who were less fortunate.

Life Lesson

Do you like helping people?

Don't ever pass up the chance to help someone. You might be the only person who takes the time to do so. Make each day count by helping someone different and being kind. Everyone loves it when you put others before yourself.

Toussaint L'Ouverture

Haiti (1743 - 1803)
Leader of The Haitian Revolution.

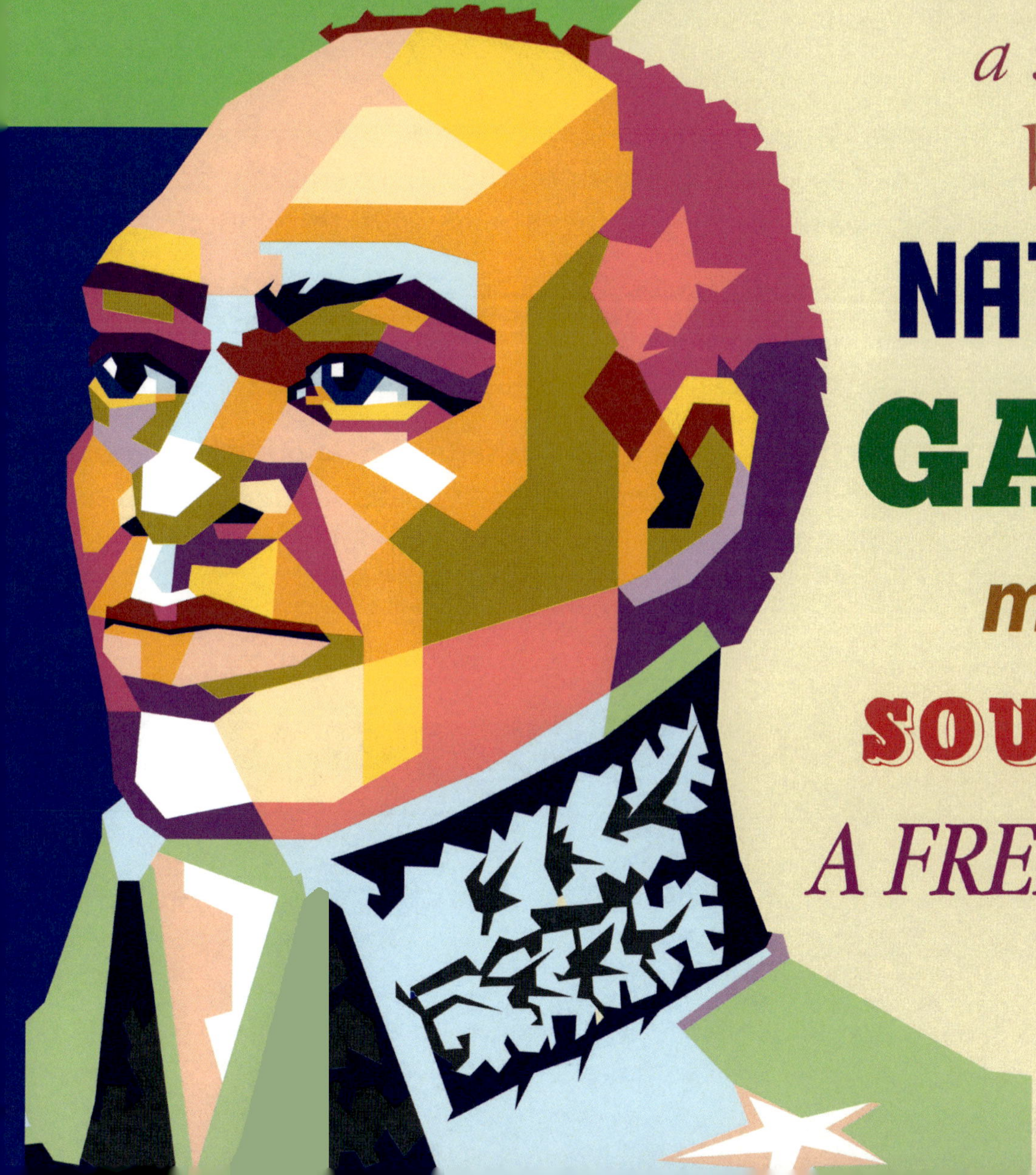

"I was **BORN** a slave, but **NATURE GAVE** me a **SOUL OF A FREE MAN.**"

TOUSSAINT L'OUVERTURE

Have you ever heard of a place called Haiti? Haiti is an island in the Caribbean. In the late 1600s, France took control of Haiti and brought black people from Africa to Haiti to keep as slaves. One of the men they brought to Haiti was an African prince, and he had a son named Toussaint L'Ouverture.

Toussaint was lucky because his master liked and trusted him. He liked him so much that when Toussaint was thirty-three years old, his master gave him his freedom and some land.

Toussaint used his freedom to help others by becoming the leader of an army. He knew slavery was wrong, so Toussaint and his army fought to free the slaves. What they accomplished is now called the Haitian Revolution.

Did you know that when Christopher Columbus first saw Haiti (and the entire Hispaniola Island), he thought he had found India or Asia?

It only took Toussaint and his army a few years to free the slaves. Toussaint's ability to get the job done so quickly made him very famous. His accomplishment was amazing because the black people in Haiti had been slaves for hundreds of years. He was loved and respected by nearly everyone because of his dedication to his people.

Years later, Napoleon Bonaparte, who was the most powerful man in France at the time, captured Toussaint and made black people in Haiti slaves once again. But even then, Toussaint did not let anyone bully him or anyone else. He cared about people who were treated badly and did everything he could to help them.

Toussaint dedicated his life to an important cause, never letting fear get in the way. He became a leader of his people so that everyone would be treated fairly.

Life Lesson

Would you like to be a leader?

Leaders always strive to do the right thing for themselves, their family, and their friends. The challenge of leadership is to be strong yet polite and to always make use of the words "please" and "thank you." I believe you have exactly what it takes to be a leader.

The book also contains fifty positive affirmations, and we encourage saying them aloud daily.

Why positive affirmations? These positive self-statements, when repeated over time, are capable of convincing a child that the statements are true, and by extension, these affirmations will boost their self-esteem.

And why is it important for young kids to know they matter? Children can feel small and insignificant in a busy and complicated world and begin to question their place in life, but such affirmations as this book provides can counteract the effect while allowing them to grow.

As parents and educators, there are three main things that we can give to our children: good memories, good education, and a sense of self-worth.

Our team has created this book to help you to achieve these goals. There are no better memories than the times when we share books with our children, and we hope that the positive messages throughout this book, along with the positive affirmations, will help your child improve his or her self-esteem and quality of self-love. Lastly, we should here acknowledge that each story in this book would merit a book by itself, but hopefully these snippets will inspire you and your child to learn more about each person.

With vivid, compelling art and quotes, this book shows its readers that no matter what obstacles may be put in front of them, they should never give up on their dreams. Simply put, this beautiful book is about the potential within each of us to pursue our dreams and shape our own paths. It is a treasure to cherish with your family forever.

We hope that you find inspiration in these pages, whether you're a girl or a boy, a parent or a teacher! These women and men are black heroes, and they're part of our history and culture.

And no matter who you are, you have a special mission on this planet, and you can make a difference too.

L.A. Amber

$\diamond\diamond\diamond\diamond\diamond\diamond\diamond\diamond$
FOREWORD
$\diamond\diamond\diamond\diamond\diamond\diamond\diamond\diamond$

Books are filled with stories of brave and powerful men and women, but have you ever wondered where the black heroes are?

Bedtime Inspirational Stories celebrates the achievements of the amazing black women and men who have paved the way for future generations.

Unfortunately, in today's world, it can be a challenge to raise positive kids, as they are bombarded with negative messages on a daily basis. More than ever, parents and teachers need to create positive atmospheres for our children in order to help them believe in themselves.

That's why we've proudly created this richly illustrated and inspiring book, ***Bedtime Inspirational Stories: 50 Amazing Black People Who Changed the World***, which highlights the achievements and stories of fifty notable women and men from the eighteenth century to today. Some were born slaves, some grew up in poverty, and some had physical or emotional challenges. Some lived many years ago, and some are still with us. The stories in the book include those of political activists, scientists, artists, musicians, inventors, businesspeople, Nobel prize winners, and more.

Every single one of these individuals overcame adversities and changed the world, building a way for others to live in a better world. Each one worked hard and maintained self-confidence, even when others expressed doubt or said their dreams couldn't be reached.

Children looking for inspiration will surely find it here. This fun and inspiring collection of influential stories provides fifty illustrated examples of strong, independent role models, all of whom impacted the world in some way, shape, or form. Personal aspirations from today's youth are also interspersed throughout the book, so that each story has its own life lesson or principle to be reinforced, alongside a positive message. It's never too soon to start making a difference, and these stories are exhilarating examples of power in action that make for ideal motivation. Help your child develop a strong sense of self by following these stories that can equip children with the powerful mantra: We are masters of our own destiny.

It always seems impossible until it is done

– Pelé – 60

– Wangari Muta Maathai – 62

– Jimi Hendrix – 64

– Muhammad Ali – 66

– Patricia Bath – 68

– Bob Marley – 70

– Shirley Ann Jackson – 72

– Ben Carson – 74

– Beverly Johnson – 76

– Christopher Paul Gardner – 78

– Oprah Winfrey – 80

– Whoopi Goldberg – 82

– Mae C. Jemison – 84

– Mark E. Dean – 86

– Michael Jackson – 88

– Barack Obama – 90

– Jackie Joyner-Kersee – 92

– Michael Jordan – 94

– Derartu Tulu – 96

– Tegla Laroupe – 98

– Beyoncé Knowles– 100

– Serena Williams – 102

– Alicia Keys – 104

– P.K. Subban – 106

– Leanna Archer – 108

– Positive Affirmations – 111

– Other Books by L.A. Amber – 123

– CONTENTS –

– Foreword – 8

– Toussaint L'Ouverture – 10

– Thomas L. Jennings – 12

– Sojourner Truth – 14

– Frederick Douglass – 16

– Harriet Tubman – 18

– Ida B. Wells – 20

– Madam C.J. Walker – 22

– Mary McLeod Bethune – 24

– Bessie Coleman – 26

– Hattie McDaniel – 28

– Albert John Luthuli – 30

– Ralph Bunche – 32

– Josephine Baker – 34

– Rosa Parks – 36

– Nelson Mandela – 38

– James Baldwin – 40

– Malcolm X – 42

– Maya Angelou – 44

– Martin Luther King, Jr. – 46

– Chinua Achebe – 48

– Ray Charles – 50

– Carmen de Lavallade – 52

– Wole Soyinka – 54

– Ellen Johnson Sirleaf – 56

– George Carruthers – 58

You're braver than you believe, and stronger than you seem, and smarter than you think

Bedtime Inspirational Stories is dedicated
to any child who has ever been made to feel unworthy,
to any child who has ever dreamed big but been discouraged,
and to any child who has ever risen up but been silenced.
May it never happen again.

Copyright © 2017, 2020 Mentches Inc.

All rights reserved. This book or any part thereof may not be reproduced or used in any manner without the express written permission of the publisher except for the use of brief quotations in a book review.

This is a creative nonfiction book. It is not a complete biography of the characters' lives. Their life stories are a vehicle to deliver an inspiring and positive message to our children. While every caution has been taken to provide accurate and current information, it is the reader's responsibility to check all information. Neither the author nor publisher can be held accountable for any errors or omissions.

Written by L. A. Amber

Illustrated by T. Z. Nissen

For information or comments, please email us at bedtimeinspirational@gmail.com

Join us on www.facebook.com/bedtimeinspirational/

Visit us at www.bedtimeinspirational.com

Please take a moment to review this amazing book on Amazon

SECOND EDITION: February 2020

Bedtime

INSPIRATIONAL

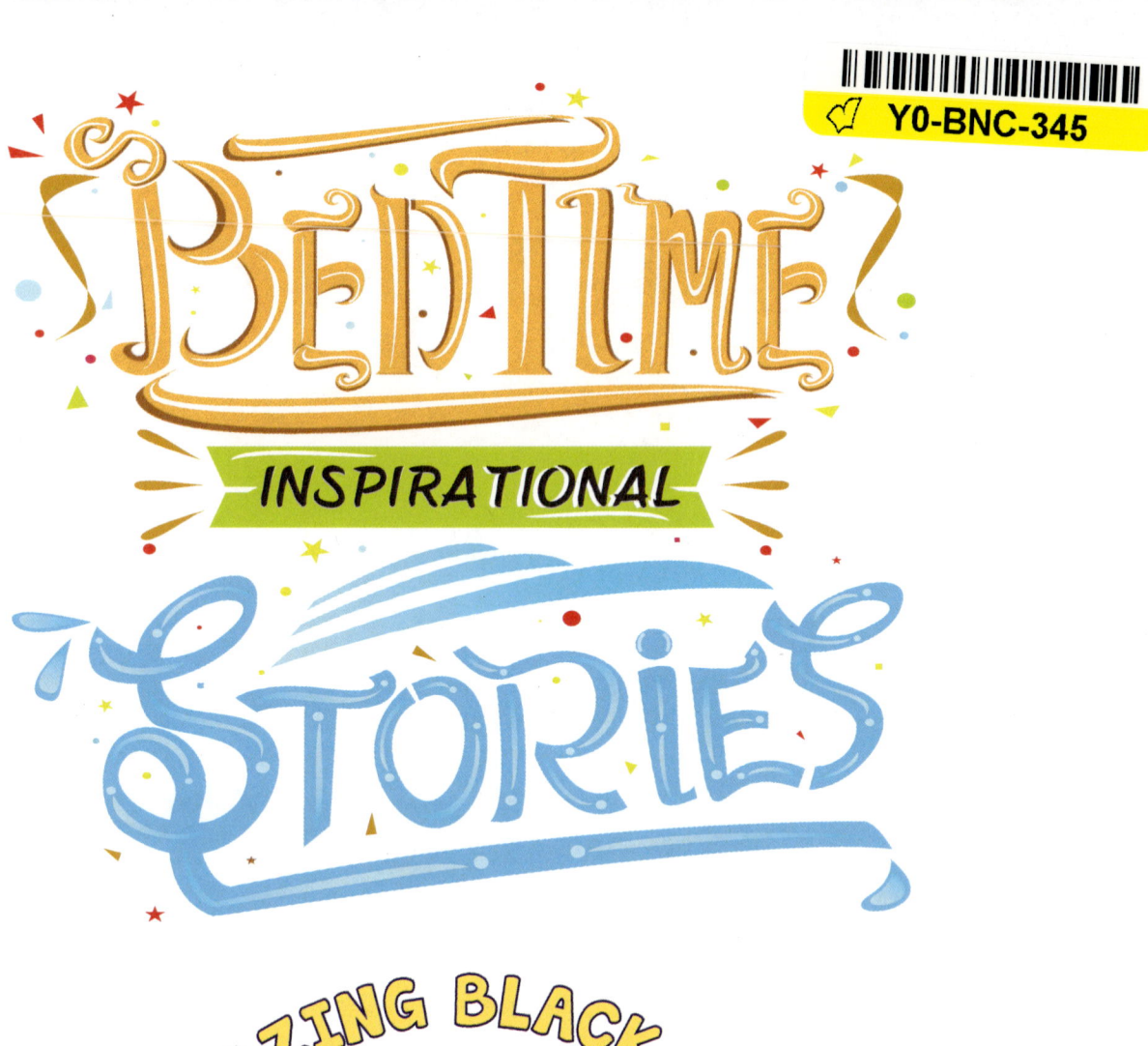

Stories

50 AMAZING BLACK PEOPLE WHO CHANGED THE WORLD

By L. A. Amber